P9-BIZ-199

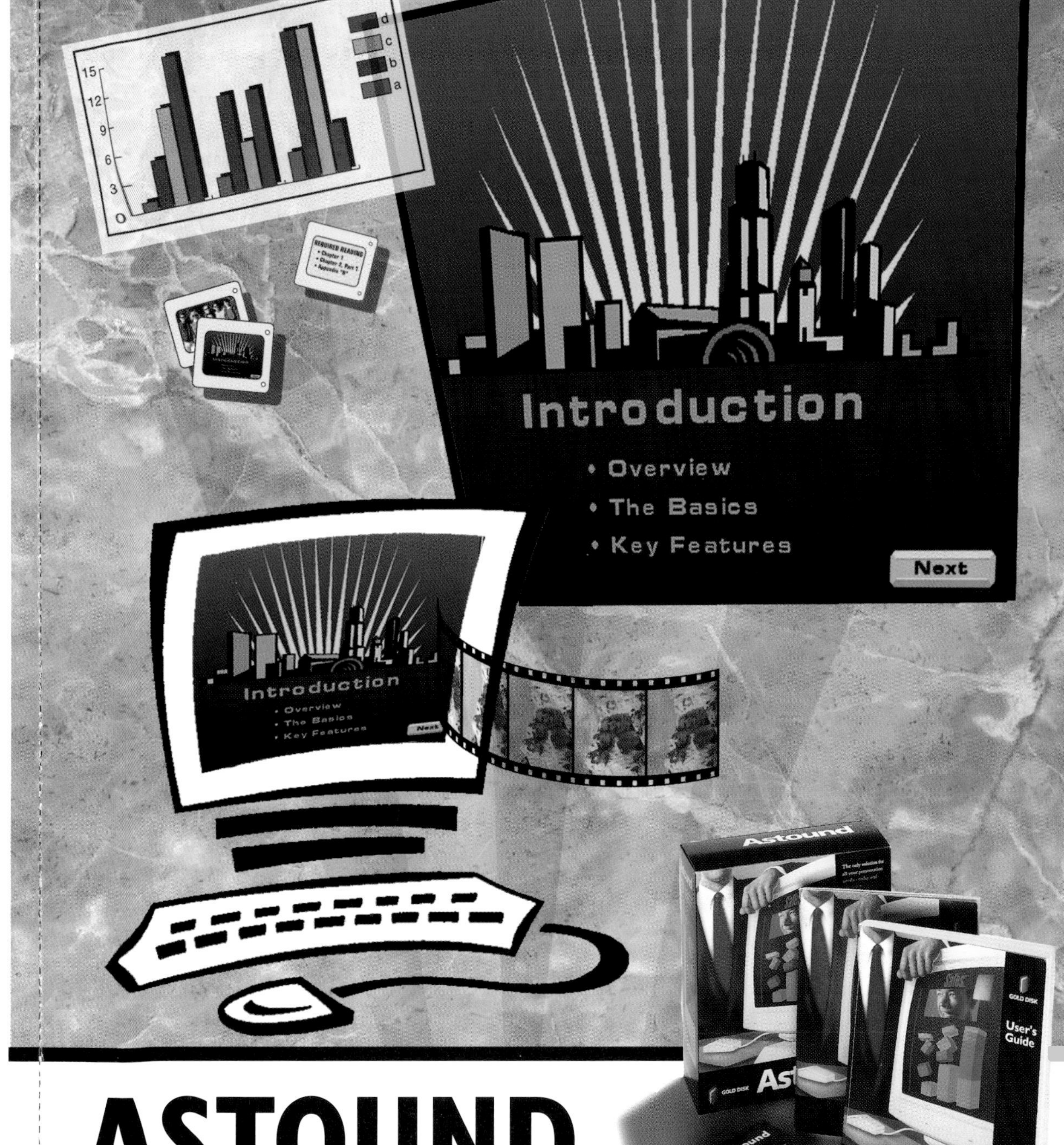

ASTOUND YOUR STUDENTS!

ASTOUND
PRESENTATION SOFTWARE

When you adopt this West title, you will receive the exciting Astound software package.* Astound presentation software by Gold Disk, Inc. makes it easy to add the attention-getting power of multimedia to your lectures.

Visual aids like videos, music, animation, graphics and photos will help focus student attention, illustrate concepts, and guide you through your presentations.

Use Slides Prepared By West
Along with the complete software package, West provides preloaded slides that include charts, graphs, and figures from the text as well as additional problems and visual support for your class. You can simply run these slides or edit them first to fit your presentation.

Or Create Your Own
With Astound, you don't need any special training to become a multimedia whiz. Just open one of the predesigned templates and you're on your way.

A few clicks will let you pick from dozens of animated transitions for your text and graphics. You can also add digital video, animations, sounds, synchronized narration and interaction. And you'll do it all with simple tools and menus.

Graphics and presentations from other presentation programs can be imported into Astound so you can build upon existing work.

When You're Done
You can distribute your lecture to others with the included runtime player, or print your slides and distribute them as handouts.

An Award-Winning Package
Astound has received numerous awards, including the MacUser Eddy Award for Best Presentation Package of 1993; PC Magazine Editors' Choice Award for Best Presentation Package, September 1994; and many others.

Astound is your complete solution for dynamic lectures.

** Ask your West representative for more information and for qualification details.*

Hardware Requirements
For IBM PCs and Compatibles:
- IBM Compatible - 386 Processor or Higher
- Windows 3.1 or Higher
- Minimum 4 MB RAM/ 8 MB Recommended
- VGA Display or Above
- 6 MB of Free Hard Disk Space

For Macintosh Computers:
- MAC Plus or Later/Hard Disk Required
- 68020 or Faster
- Minimum 2 MB RAM/ 4 MB Recommended
- System 6.0.8 or Later/ System 7 Recommended

WEST PUBLISHING

© 1995 West Publishing
9882-4•9-95•MS,ES

FOUNDATIONS
of
CORPORATE FINANCE

FREE COPY

Foundations of Corporate Finance

Kent A. Hickman
Gonzaga University

Hugh O. Hunter
Eastern Washington University

John W. Byrd
Fort Lewis College

West Publishing Company

Minneapolis/St. Paul New York Los Angeles San Francisco

FREE COPY

PRODUCTION CREDITS

COPYEDITOR	Linda Thompson
COVER IMAGE	Original work by Antti A. Nurmesniemi/Studio Nurmesniemi Ky from the exhibition *Mondo Materialis: Materials and Ideas for the Future* created by Steelcase Design Partnership. Photography by Elliott Kaufman. Reprinted with permission.
INTERIOR DESIGN	K. M. Weber
ILLUSTRATION	Patti Isaacs, Parrot Graphics
COMPOSITION	University Graphics
INDEX	Pat Lewis

WEST'S COMMITMENT TO THE ENVIRONMENT

In 1906, West Publishing Company began recycling materials left over from the production of books. This began a tradition of efficient and responsible use of resources. Today, 100% of our legal bound volumes are printed on acid-free, recycled paper consisting of 50% new paper pulp and 50% paper that has undergone a de-inking process. We also use vegetable-based inks to print all of our books. West recycles nearly 22,650,000 pounds of scrap paper annually—the equivalent of 187,500 trees. Since the 1960s, West has devised ways to capture and recycle waste inks, solvents, oils, and vapors created in the printing process. We also recycle plastics of all kinds, wood, glass, corrugated cardboard, and batteries, and have eliminated the use of polystyrene book packaging. We at West are proud of the longevity and the scope of our commitment to the environment.

West pocket parts and advance sheets are printed on recyclable paper and can be collected and recycled with newspapers. Staples do not have to be removed. Bound volumes can be recycled after removing the cover.

Production, printing, and binding by West Publishing Company.

British Library Cataloguing-in-Publication Data. A catalogue record for this book is available from the British Library.

Copyright © 1996 by WEST PUBLISHING COMPANY
610 Opperman Drive
P.O. Box 64526
St. Paul, MN 55164-0526

All rights reserved

Printed in the United States of America

03 02 01 00 99 98 97 96   8 7 6 5 4 3 2 1 0

Library of Congress Cataloging-in-Publication Data

Hickman, Kent A.
Hugh O. Hunter
Foundations of Corporate Finance / Hugh O. Hunter, John W. Byrd.
p. cm.
Includes index.
ISBN 0-314-06477-X (hard : alk. paper)
1. Corporations—Finance. I. Hickman, Kent A. II. Byrd, John W.
III. Title.
HG4026.H82 1996
658.15—dc20   95-38526
CIP

CONTENTS IN BRIEF

FREE COPY

FREE COPY

CONTENTS

FREE COPY

FREE COPY

About the Authors

KENT A. HICKMAN is an associate professor at Gonzaga University. He earned a Ph.D. in finance at Washington State University after completing an M.S. in applied statistics at the University of Northern Colorado. His B.A. in mathematics is from California State University at San Bernardino. Before pursuing a doctorate, Professor Hickman worked for five years as an investment analyst. He also taught high school mathematics and coached basketball for six years. In his spare time, Kent enjoys sports, reading history and fishing with his two daughters.

HUGH O. HUNTER is a professor of finance at Eastern Washington University. Professor Hunter's Ph.D. was earned at the University of Southern California where he majored in finance and business economics. He also holds an M.B.A. from California State University at Long Beach and his bachelors degree in business is from the University of Maryland. Prior to twenty years as a university professor, Dr. Hunter spent four years in the aerospace industry and served in the U.S. Army. An avid reader, Hugh also enjoys sailing and visiting his son and daughter who are in college.

JOHN W. BYRD is a business consultant based in Durango, Colorado, where he also teaches at Ft. Lewis College. A former full-time finance professor and Outward Bound program director, Dr. Byrd has consulting agreements with several NYSE corporations. The past two summers he led treks in the Himalayan Mountains. Dr. Byrd's Ph.D. is from the University of Oregon, his M.P.P.M. is from Yale University, and he earned a B.A. in mathematics from Ft. Lewis College. John and his wife enjoy skiing, biking and mountain climbing during vacations.

Professors Hickman, Hunter and Byrd have over 35 years experience teaching finance. Their research appears in more than 15 journals including the *Journal of Financial Economics*, *Financial Management*, the *Journal of Applied Corporate Finance*, *Financial Practice and Education*, the *Financial Review*, *Accounting Horizons*, the *Journal of Economic Behavior and Organization*, and the *Journal of the Royal Statistical Society*.

A Message to Students

This is a book that we wanted to write. Probably all teachers at one time have said, "If I could write a book, this is how it would be." We approached this book with that thought. Collectively, we have been teaching finance for over 30 years. That is not very remarkable, but it is long enough to form some opinions on how finance should be taught. This book represents a melding of the opinions of the three of us.

In writing this book, we tried hard to avoid the "baby-food syndrome." Some years ago, it was revealed that baby-food manufacturers were putting salt and MSG into baby food so that the taste would appeal to the mother, who was, after all, making the purchasing decision. This is an example of an agency problem, one that we will deal with in the book. In this case, the mother was acting as a purchasing agent for the baby. Similarly, textbooks are meant to be read by students, but professors make the purchasing decision. It is not unreasonable, then, for textbooks to be "flavored" to appeal to professors.

We have tried our best to appeal to students. We have kept the book as short and inexpensive as possible. We have sought to explain the central ideas of finance in plain language. At the same time, we hope to pique your interest in this important, exciting, and challenging field.

You will find the book laced with illustrations and examples. They are there to help you understand and retain the most important ideas. Some are interesting, some are preposterous, and some are just funny. They remind us that humor is present even in a science that deals with that most somber of commodities—money.

Most importantly, we have tried to provide a faithful representation of the field of finance. We have stripped away most of the accounting and statistics and have replaced it with the important ideas of modern finance, most of which are younger than many of your professors.

The following excerpt is from the last chapter and sums up our commitment to this book.

> We sincerely hope that we have provided you with a solid foundation in finance. For many, this will be your only finance course. We would like to hear from you in about 2 years to find out how many of these basic ideas you still retain. If you still remember the most important ones, we will have succeeded. If you don't, we will have to do better. In the preface, we invited your comments. You can help us do better. Let us know how.

You don't have to wait two years to contact us. We welcome all corrections, comments, praise, and criticism. You may write or phone:

Dr. Kent A. Hickman
School of Business Administration
Gonzaga University
Spokane, WA 99258
(509) 328-4220, ext. 3442

A Message to Instructors

Our aim was to write this book for the students. We assume that they come to finance with at least a vague knowledge of accounting, economics, and elementary statistics. We also assume that they have little innate desire to study finance. Therefore, rather than taking an encyclopedic approach, we develop and reinforce the essential ideas of finance. By providing a coherent and logical approach to the subject, we hope to sustain students' interest in finance, build on their background, and appeal to their common sense. The financial balance sheet is a reference point for the discussion of these ideas, and each one is evaluated in terms of its contribution to the creation of firm value.

Not every idea in finance is intuitive, but many are. Therefore, where possible, we appeal to students' common sense to understand the logic underlying the idea. We also include many examples, some fictional and some real. We stress throughout that finance is not an abstraction, but an agglomeration of ideas that have value in the conduct of everyday business and everyday life. We hope that this approach will not only make it easier for your students to learn finance, but will also make it easier for you to teach it. Imagine an introductory finance class in which the students learn the essential ideas with relative ease and approach the class with enthusiasm. Such a class may be as whimsical as a company that maximizes wealth, but we hope that this book at least moves the teaching of finance in that direction, while at the same time maintaining the integrity of the subject matter. We entered this project with the assumption that it was possible to write a book that was both appealing and rigorous. As you guide your students through the book, you will doubtless have ideas that we could share with other instructors and that we can include in subsequent editions. Before these ideas escape, send us a note or an E-mail message. We promise to respond, although that is the only extrinsic reward we can offer.

Telefaxes and E-mail may be sent to Dr. Hugh Hunter.

Fax: (509) 448-0959
Internet: hhunter@ewu.edu
Compuserve: 76330,330
America Online: hughh3

Distinguishing Features of This Text

1. *The theme of value creation is continued and reaffirmed throughout.* In the first chapter, we develop the theme of value creation, and continue that through-

out the text. The ideas developed in each chapter are linked to the firm's central mission of creating value for its shareholders.

2. *The financial balance sheet is used throughout the text.* A central construct, the financial balance sheet, is incorporated throughout the text to provide continuity between the current topic and value creation. The financial balance sheet has several appealing attributes:
   - It is analogous to—and contrasts with—the accounting balance sheet, an already-familiar concept to beginning finance students. This allows the instructor to confront directly one major source of confusion for students: accounting versus financial data and analysis.
   - It is visual and intuitive.
   - It can be used visually to characterize virtually all financial decisions.
3. *The text is conceptual and intuitive.* The key difference between this text and others is its emphasis on the concepts or intuition underlying financial decision making. Many books are a compendium of recipes or formulas into which students plug numbers (or at least students view them as such, and the pervasiveness of hand-held financial calculators has reinforced this point of view). Missing from this approach is an understanding of how profits are earned, prices are set, and contracts are written in real, competitive markets. We believe that students who understand the underlying concepts will not only be better able to apply the tools, but will also know when the tools are not appropriate.

   Examples of this approach include a thorough discussion of where positive net present value projects might be found. Typically, NPV is presented as the output of a black-box formula. We believe that students should think about entry barriers or competitive advantages that will generate positive NPVs. Moreover, students should realize that, unlike many textbook problems, profitable cash flows are unlikely to continue indefinitely. Entry barriers, firms capitalizing on competitive advantages, and the transitory nature of project cash flows are included in the coverage of corporate investing, Chapter 9.

   A second example is the treatment of systematic risk. Students rarely have a strong sense of what types of projects or firms have low or high systematic risk. For instance, our students regularly say that oil exploration has high systematic risk. In fact, finding oil has very little to do with economywide forces although profits from discovery (oil production and refining profits) do. This point is covered in Chapter 8.

   To foster the development of this intuitive understanding of financial decision making, we incorporate the following features:
   - The coherent structure of the text enables the development of topics in a logical fashion and provides linkages between these topics. Students are able to see how finance fits together.
   - Each chapter contains an introduction and summary that link the chapter to those preceeding and following. These features reinforce the structure of the text and impart to students a feel for where they're going and why they're making the journey.
4. *The presentation is streamlined.* Many introductory finance books are filled with sidebars and boxes containing anecdotes on business practices, exam-

ples of points made in the chapter, or, sometimes, explanations of theories. We feel they divert the reader's attention from the important concepts and tools of finance in the body of the text. We have chosen to integrate our discussion of business practices and examples into the body of the text where, we believe, they belong.

5. *The text is accessible to nonfinance majors*. Most business schools require that all students, not just finance majors, take the introductory finance course. Our experience suggests that motivating nonfinance majors is crucial to their learning the material. To this end, we have included material that ties some of the principles of finance to areas such as marketing, production, and accounting. Throughout the text, we endeavor to link financial concepts to students' experiences so that it is more than a course in applied mathematics.
6. *Material is carefully selected.* The text covers all the important topics of corporate finance, some just briefly. We have found that many chapters of lengthy texts are not covered in a one-term introductory course. For example, chapters on bankruptcy, international finance, and small-business management are often ignored. Class time devoted to topics such as cash management, inventory management, and financial ratios is usually much less than text coverage. We have designed a text that comes closer to matching the material we actually teach in our courses. For example, although we include management of working capital (Chapter 14), we do not devote three or four chapters to it.
7. *International finance is integrated.* There is no chapter on international finance. Instead, we have integrated this topic into the text. For example, international capital markets are included in Chapter 7, and international corporate investing is included in Chapter 11. One of the two cases in Chapter 17 deals with international finance. In addition, there are numerous references to international finance throughout. Covering international finance in this manner produces two benefits. First, it ensures that this important topic is covered, at least minimally. Secondly, it sends a signal to students that international finance is not separate from finance itself. It is our belief that one cannot be informed about capital markets without understanding a little of the global markets and that corporate investing must include consideration of foreign product markets and investment opportunities.
8. *There is early emphasis on market value and cash flows.* Dealing with these topics in the early chapters establishes a link between accounting and finance and clarifies these important distinctions. Market versus book value is covered in Chapter 1. Cash flows versus earnings are covered in Chapter 4.
9. *Options are included.* Options are introduced in the text because options contracts are valuable and are integral to many financial decisions. An introduction to options is given in Chapter 3, and their application to corporate investing is covered in Chapter 9.
10. *Capital markets are covered extensively*. In spite of the streamlined approach to finance in this text, substantial space is devoted to the development of capital market theory (Chapter 7 and 8). We have done this for two reasons:

First, capital market theory is a foundation of modern finance; therefore, no financial paradigm can be developed without reasonably thorough coverage. Second, we develop the theory and the evidence in such a way that students will understand the essential logic and importance of this material. As elsewhere in the book, we concentrate on ideas and intuition in developing the theory. Understanding the basic nature and function of capital markets prepares finance students for more thorough coverage in the investments course. Nonmajors will take with them some important and useful ideas.

11. *We take a unique approach to financial analysis.* In addition to ratio analysis, Chapter 15 covers the broader issues of evaluating corporate performance, including the need to search for important performance clues and to temper analysis with judgement.
12. *Capstone chapters are provided.* The chapter on corporate restructuring (Chapter 16) is designed to integrate and reinforce the material, providing a capstone to the course. This allows us to cover a timely, important, and interesting topic that might otherwise be left out of a beginning finance course. The final chapter presents two short comprehensive finance cases. The first is solved; the second ends with a few questions for students to answer.
13. *Pedagogical aids are used.* In addition to those already mentioned, there are numerous other features of the text that are designed to assist the process of learning:
    - Extensive end-of-chapter questions and problems, including solved demonstration problems
    - Key terms highlighted in each chapter and listed at the end of the chapters
    - A glossary of key terms with definitions at the end of the text
    - Solutions to selected end-of-chapter problems in a text appendix
    - Calculator solutions to time value problems presented in the Chapter 5 appendix

SUPPLEMENTS

1. *Instructor's manual.* Although the textbook presentation is linear and streamlined, we acknowledge that instructors may wish to enrich their courses with outside material. Therefore, we have developed an extensive instructor's manual that includes abstracts of articles in the business press and practitioner-oriented journals. The articles are organized by chapter and linked to specific topics. The instructor may use these abstracts to enrich lectures and as a basis for selecting articles for students to read. This structure makes the textbook a tool that the instructor can build on, rather than an all-encompassing package that the instructor is forced to live with.
2. *Solutions to end-of-chapter questions and problems.* These solutions are bound separately, so that instructors can easily make them available to students.
3. *Study guide.* The study guide is written by David Louton of Bryant College. Each chapter of the study guide contains a brief overview of the comparable

text chapter, a restatement of the learning objectives, a rich chapter outline, practice questions and problems with answered solutions, and calculator examples where appropriate.

4. *Test bank.* Donald Sorensen of the University of Wisconsin—Whitewater prepared this ancilliary. The test bank is composed of true-false and multiple-choice questions—70 per chapter—and at least half the problems require analysis and/or computation. The test bank is also available on Westest, a computerized testing program for DOS, Windows, and Macintosh.
5. *Excel templates.* These templates are customized to the end-of-chapter problem sets. They are easy to use but are relatively simple in design. Students are encouraged to use them as models for enhancing their own spreadsheet programming skills. Accompanying the spreadsheets is a small data set containing returns on the stocks of the 20 companies featured in Chapters 7 and 8. Students may use these data to solve capital market problems using spreadsheets.
6. *Transparency acetates.* The transparency set primarily comprises key figures found in the text, but we also developed some additional acetates to enhance lecture material. The Annotated Instructor's Edition provides margin notes for those figures which are available on transparency acetates.

ACKNOWLEDGMENTS

Reviewers are especially crucial for a book that takes a different approach to teaching finance. Our reviewers had, first, to sanction our approach and then force us to deliver on our promises. When we went astray, they let us know. Most of all, they were a wonderfully supportive group, providing us with countless suggestions, exposing our lapses, and telling us when we got it right.

Thomas R. Anderson
Babson College

Michael L. Austin
University of Nevada, Reno

Michael Becker
Valparaiso University

Robert Boldin
Indiana University of Pennsylvania

Michael T. Bond
Cleveland State University

Waldo L. Born
Eastern Illinois University

Robin J. Brenner
The University of Arizona

Barry Doyle
University of San Francisco

John Dunkelberg
Wake Forest University

Stan Eakins
East Carolina University

John W. Ellis
Colorado State University

Suzanne Erickson
Seattle University

Cheri Etling
The Wichita State University

David Fewings
Western Washington University

Manoj Gupta
The Wichita State University

Robert J. Hendershott
Santa Clara University

James D. Keys
Florida International University

David A. Kunz
Southeast Missouri State University

Reinhold P. Lamb
The University of North Carolina at Charlotte

David Louton
Bryant College

Robert A. Lutz
Weber State University

Lee E. McClain, Jr.
Western Washington University

Scott Moore
John Carroll University

James Musumeci
Southern Illinois University at Carbondale

Henry R. Oppenheimer
The University of Rhode Island

R. Daniel Pace
Valparaiso University

Edward L. Prill
Colorado State University

Diane Schooley
Boise State University

J. Allen Seward
Baylor University

Bipin Shah
University of Nebraska at Omaha

Donald E. Sorensen
University of Wisconsin-Whitewater

Joseph V. Stanford
Bridgewater State College

David Y. Suk
Rider University

Y. Elizabeth Sun
San Jose State University

John A. Swiger
Our Lady of the Lake University

Lawrence S. Tai
Loyola Marymount University

Gary Tallman
Northern Arizona University

J. C. Thompson
Eastern Kentucky University

Amjad Waheed
East Tennessee State University

The comments of Mark Schrader and other colleagues were invaluable as were the skills and patience of Jane Cruse in preparing innumerable drafts of the manuscript. We owe special thanks to the following people at West Educational Publishing, who had the difficult task of guiding three rookies through the process of making a book: Stacy Lenzen, who handled production, Sandi Hiller, who coordinated much of the writing, reviewing, and revision, and Stephanie Buss, who handled promotion.

Most of all, we thank Robert Horan, who took on a risky project and stayed with it in good times and bad. We hope that the rewards justify the risk.

The three of us survived this seemingly interminable project with friendships and marriages intact. Our own foibles were more than offset by the character and support of our wives, Gini, Maureen, and Shere. To them, we dedicate this book.

CHAPTER 1

A Financial Model of the Corporation

"I had secured sufficient financial backing, I'd set up fine inventory and cash management systems! I was ready for business, then it hit me . . . I had no product or service!"

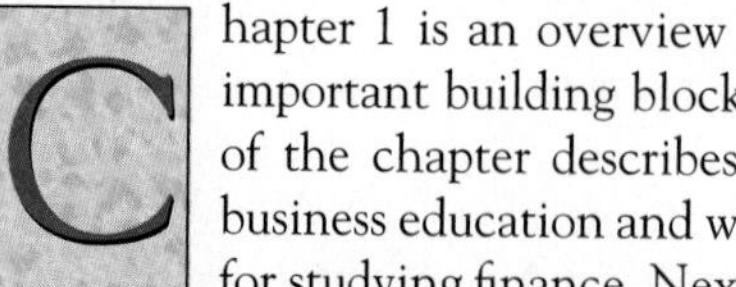

Chapter 1 is an overview of corporate finance and provides you with important building blocks for the rest of the course. The first section of the chapter describes why finance is an important part of your business education and why the corporation was chosen as the vehicle for studying finance. Next, some important features of corporate products, bonds, and stocks are discussed, along with characteristics of the people whose actions affect corporations. A model of the corporation, called the financial balance sheet, is presented in the third section of the chapter. This model is the centerpiece of Chapter 1 and is designed to assist you in visualizing the financial concepts and decisions that you will study throughout this course. The fourth section covers the financial goal of the corporation—shareholder wealth maximization. Some of the problems encountered by corporations in attaining this goal and the effectiveness of corporations as a means of creating wealth are also covered in this section of the chapter. The influences of society, markets, and government on corporations' activities are introduced in the concluding section of the chapter.

More than 47 million individuals own shares of publicly traded corporations in the United States.

WHY CORPORATE FINANCE?

Soon you will be leaving school. You will be deciding whether to rent or buy a home and whether to invest your savings in the stock market or certificates of deposit. You will be choosing what type and how much life insurance coverage you should purchase to protect your family. At work you may find that making a sale depends on your ability to show that your product is a cost-effective investment for your customer. You may be asked to structure a contract that ensures that all parties to the agreement are properly compensated and motivated. Key elements of all these decisions are financial in nature.

The skills and intuition you will develop in this course are critical for making decisions throughout your life. Our aim in this textbook is to enhance your financial reasoning ability. If you are successful in this course, you will find that the cost of tuition will be returned to you manyfold in the future. In short, the time, money, and effort you invest here should reward you with excellent returns.

Ask students which pays the highest rate of interest: a savings account in a bank or a bond issued by Kmart. Point out that the answer Kmart reflects a basic intuitive understanding of the relationship between risk and return, one of the cornerstones of finance.

Much of finance may already be familiar to you. The theories, tools, and concepts covered in this text will simply add a coherent structure to the intuition you have developed through experience. From your day-to-day activities as a consumer, employee, and student forced to deal with a bureaucracy, you possess a large part of the intuition upon which financial theory is based.

Developing financial intuition by understanding the underlying theory gives you a foundation for dealing with many problems. The alternative is learning rules of thumb, which may not prepare you for a rapidly changing financial environment. Fifteen years ago, for example, adjustable-rate mortgages, money market accounts, and universal life insurance did not exist, but all are now pervasive financial products to which you will certainly be exposed. The intuition and underlying theory of finance gives you the flexibility to deal with new, unusual problems as they emerge.

"If you owe $50, you're a delinquent account. If you owe $50,000, you're a small business. If you owe $50 million, you're a corporation. If you owe $50 billion, you're the government," said historian L. T. White, Jr. (1907–1987)

As a vehicle for learning the principles of finance, this course focuses on the corporation. Other choices were available. Examples are public finance, which studies how governments raise and disburse funds, and personal finance, which concentrates on individual financial decisions such as shopping for life insurance and personal investing. Corporate finance was chosen for several reasons. First, many of you will be working for corporations. Understanding key financial considerations in corporate decision making will aid in advancing your career regardless of your major. Second, as an individual you will be making personal investment decisions. Corporate **securities**, such as stocks and bonds, make up a large proportion of the investment opportunities you will have. And last, the same financial approach to problems used in corporate finance is also properly used to make personal, partnership, or public financial decisions. In effect, you are getting the most return for your effort by studying corporate finance.

CORPORATIONS: PRODUCTS, BONDS, STOCKS, AND PEOPLE

This course is about corporations. Corporations are associated with the products they produce and the securities they issue. For example, we know that AT&T provides long-distance service and Boeing manufactures airplanes. The stocks and bonds of these firms are discussed on a daily basis in the media and are closely followed by a large segment of the population.

Some corporations are so linked with their products that the name is part of the language. For example, for many years "a Kodak" was used to mean a camera. Making a copy is often referred to as "Xeroxing." People play "Frisbee."

The goods and services produced by corporations are almost endless in their diversity. Each corporation attempts to match its expertise with consumers' needs in order to produce successful products. Thus, Ralston-Purina processes and sells a variety of agricultural products. General Electric makes and sells refrigerators, radios, and aircraft engines. Yamaha sells motorcycles as well as pianos. Sometimes a corporation's primary products are not what they may first appear to be. McDonald's sells hamburgers, but they also sell uniform quality and service. Why has McDonald's been successful? Is it because their hamburgers are superior or because consumers know what to expect when they enter any McDonald's? McDonald's, we could argue, is successful not because they perceived a need for more hamburgers, but because they satisfy a need for a fast, affordable, uniform hamburger, delivered in a clean environment.

Good product decisions are rewarding. Consumers benefit as their needs and wants are met. Employees are rewarded with continued employment and job security. Communities in which the corporation is located benefit from a strong economic base. Investors who hold corporate securities are also rewarded. Stocks and bonds represent the overwhelming majority of these securities. The money made by corporations is distributed to owners of these securities, the stockholders and bondholders, providing them with returns on their holdings.

"The worst crime against working people is a company which fails to operate at a profit," according to labor leader Samuel Gompers (1850–1924).

Bonds represent loans made by investors to the corporation. Thus, bonds are a form of corporate debt. The firm is obligated to pay its bondholders a fixed series of payments until the bonds mature. These payments, generally made semiannually, are called **coupon payments**. At maturity, the corporation must repay the bondholder the **face amount**, or **par value**, of the bond, usually $1,000. For example, a bond may have a $1,000 face value and a 6% annual coupon rate, make payments semiannually, and mature in 20 years. This bond represents the corporation's promise to pay the bondholder 40 coupon payments (one every 6 months) of $30 each. At the end of the 20-year period, the bond matures and is returned to the issuing corporation. The corporation then repays the $1,000 face value along with the last $30 coupon. The ability of the corporation to meet these obligations hinges on its success in making and selling products or services.

Corporate **common stock** represents an equity or ownership interest in the firm. If a corporation has 100 shares of common stock outstanding, then an owner of 1 share owns 1% of that corporation, and one holding 10 shares of the stock owns 10% of the corporation. Stockholders receive payments from the corporation in the form of **dividends**, usually paid quarterly. Dividends, unlike coupon interest payments on bonds, are not fixed. Dividends may be raised, lowered or not paid at all at the discretion of the corporation. Digital Equipment is a large, well-known corporation that has never paid a dividend. Morrison Knudsen paid dividends for years but suspended its dividend payment in 1995.

As owners, common stockholders elect **a board of directors**. Each share of common stock entitles its holder to vote for directors at the corporation's annual shareholders' meeting. Because most shareholders of large corporations do not attend these annual meetings, most vote through the **proxy** process, similar to the absentee-ballot system used in governmental elections. The board of directors governs the corporation on behalf of the shareholders, determining the dividends to be paid that year, hiring and firing top management, approving corporate strategic decisions, and making compensation decisions.

A readable article describing the rational self-interest model of human behavior is "The Nature of Man" by Michael Jensen and William Meckling in *Journal of Applied Corporate Finance* 7 no. 2, (Summer 1994): 4–19.

Corporate finance is, in large part, the study of the interaction between products, stocks, bonds, and the people who make decisions affecting them. Finance, therefore, includes the study of investors, managers, corporate directors, consumers, and corporate employees. One assumption underlying finance is that people act in their own self-interest, which is considered to be economically rational behavior. It does not pretend to explain the complexity of human behavior, but it does allow us to explain how people are likely to behave when making financial decisions and market transactions. They buy stocks and bonds to increase their wealth. People work to make a living; some people desire power and prestige. People make product purchases to fulfill needs and desires. Some may boycott, strike, vote, or petition because they perceive injustice. In corporate finance, it is important to recognize that the *self-interest* of individuals motivates their actions.

People also act *rationally*. Rationality means that people will, by and large, make the correct decisions, which lead toward fulfilling their self-interest. Departures from rationality are eventually corrected by competition. Competition exists when many individuals are seeking to achieve the same personal goals. We seldom see money lying on the sidewalk, although it is often dropped. The reason is that many individuals are interested in increasing their wealth, and the rational thing to do is to pick up the money!

THE FINANCIAL BALANCE SHEET

The authors of this text have attempted to make this course interesting and useful to you. We have also tried to make your job easier. Whenever possible we illustrate key concepts and theories with easily understood examples. Further, these concepts and theories are put into context throughout the text so you better understand why a topic is important and where it fits into the discipline of corporate finance. To achieve a coherent structure, we have incorporated a visual financial model of the firm, which we call the **financial balance sheet**. This tool will be used to introduce and link topics as we study corporate finance.

You are already familiar with the balance sheet that accountants use to report the status of a firm in its annual report. The financial balance sheet (FBS) is a conceptual counterpart to the accounting balance sheet. The FBS is a model of the corporation that serves several purposes. It is useful for visualizing the financial functions of the firm and their objectives. Theories and concepts can be introduced using the FBS—thereby maintaining a coherent structure throughout the course. Its use helps answer questions such as, Why are we studying this? Also, because it is similar to an accounting balance sheet, accounting and financial decision making can be contrasted and clarified.

The Left-Hand Side of the Financial Balance Sheet

Cash is stressed here, because its classification as an investment is sometimes confusing to students.

Let's begin by describing a simple financial balance sheet and contrasting it with its accounting counterpart. On the left-hand side (LHS) of the financial balance sheet appear the *investments made by the corporation* (as opposed to Assets listed in an accounting balance sheet). It is important to note that LHS accounts are investments—that is, they reflect carefully considered decisions, which, as the investments title implies, should produce some payoff for the corporation. As a simple example, consider the cash account. The level of cash does not happen by accident—the cash is there to help produce more cash. A fast-food restaurant that begins each day with only $10 in the cash register has not made an optimal investment in cash. It will surely lose some customers because the firm cannot make proper change. At the other extreme, if each day begins with $10,000 in the cash register, then the restaurant has overinvested in cash. The excess funds could be better utilized by paying off a loan, thus saving interest expense (or worse, they could be robbed). For the fast-food restaurant, the same logic applies to other investment accounts. An inventory of hamburger buns that is too high results in unused and stale bread, and one that is too low results in lost sales. Too large an investment in furniture and fixtures is wasted money (i.e., too much seating capacity), whereas too low an investment might lead to lost sales (insufficient seating capacity).

The left-hand side of the financial balance sheet includes all the accounts appearing on the accounting statement (cash, inventory, furniture and fixtures, property, plant, etc.), because these are all investments. It is useful, however, to categorize investments into two types: tangible and intangible investments. **Tangible investments** include those things you can touch, or bricks and mortar, as the saying goes. Most of the assets associated with the accounting balance sheet are of this type. **Intangible** assets include patents and copyrights but go well beyond that. This category includes investments that are often just as important to the firm as the more obvious investments in factories and inventory. See Figure 1.1.

One of the most important intangible assets is human resources. Investment in this asset can produce excellent returns. Recruiting and training programs are costly, but the payoffs, in the form of employee productivity, loyalty, and quality service provided customers, may make such investments worthwhile. Other in-

Note that as the economy becomes more service oriented, the assets of many firms become increasingly oriented toward human resources and other intangibles.

FIGURE 1.1

FINANCIAL BALANCE SHEET

The left-hand side of the financial balance sheet includes tangible and intangible assets.

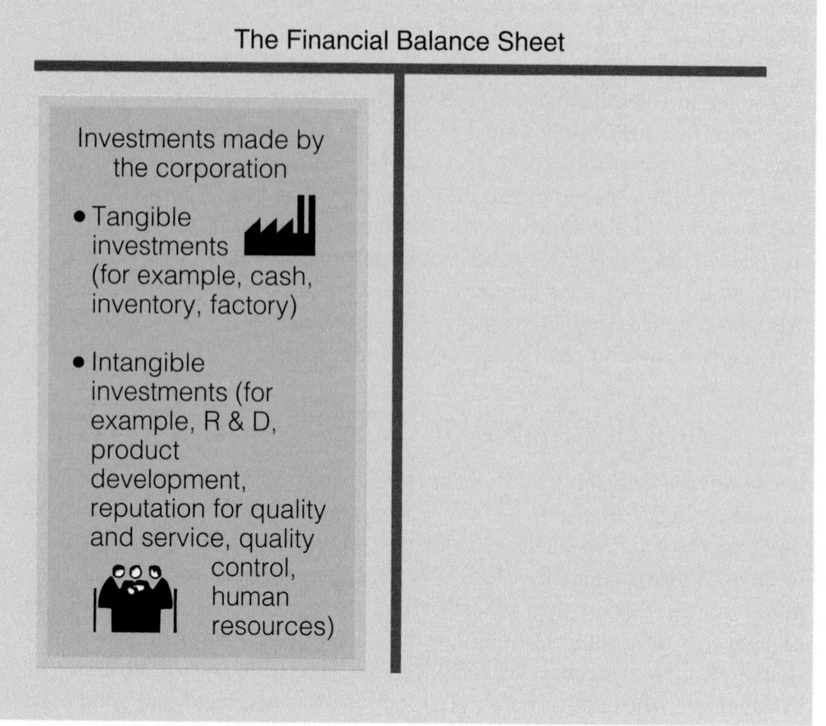

The Financial Balance Sheet
Investments made by the corporation
• Tangible investments (for example, cash, inventory, factory)
• Intangible investments (for example, R & D, product development, reputation for quality and service, quality control, human resources)

Transparency Available

tangibles that create value for the corporation may include establishing the firm's reputation for product quality and customer service, ethical behavior, research and development, and establishing brand recognition.

Both tangible and intangible investments require an outlay of cash that is expected to produce future cash inflows. If the cash outlay is a good financial decision, the cash flows received should have value greater than the initial cost of the investment.

The Right-Hand Side of the Financial Balance Sheet

The right-hand side (RHS) of the financial balance sheet reflects the firm's *sources of financing*. It records the sources of cash that finance the investments reflected on the LHS. The title, Sources of Financing, contrasts with the title Liabilities and Owner's Equity commonly used in the traditional accounting balance sheet. A second difference between the two statements is that the financial balance sheet accounts are divided into two types of claims: residual claims and fixed claims. Each of these types of accounts has a claim on the cash flows generated by the corporation's investments. These cash flows may be generated via the normal cycle of producing and selling products and services. Cash may also be generated through the sale of the entire firm (as might occur in case of a liquidation or a takeover) or through the sale of a division of the corporation. When these cash flows are generated, by whatever means, their distribution is dependent upon the type of claim held by the supplier of financial resources. See Figure 1.2.

Fixed claims receive a contracted, or fixed, amount of cash. If fixed claimants—e.g., bondholders or employees—receive less than this amount, then these classes of claimants have legal recourse to force the firm to meet these fixed obligations. Bank loans and bonds are two examples of fixed claims. They both require contractually specified payments of interest and principal. If these payments are not made in a timely manner, then the bank or bondholder may seek full payment through the legal system. In this case, the corporation that has not met its obligations is in **default** on its payments and may be forced into bankruptcy.

Suppliers of inventory to the corporation may also help finance the firm by not demanding immediate payment for the goods they have delivered. The firm, therefore, has made an investment in inventory, which, for a period of time, is being financed by the supplier. The claim that reflects this financing is an account payable. If the account is not fully paid on time, then the supplier can legally seek repayment. Similarly, workers supply financing to the firm in the form of wages payable. It is no accident, for instance, that some organizations pay their employees on a weekly basis, whereas other firms pay biweekly or monthly. The employees' labor may be invested in finished goods inventory, whereas financing for that labor is being supplied by the workers themselves for a period of a week, two weeks, or a month, depending on the firm's payroll policy. In order not to help finance the firm, employees would need to be paid at the end of each day. Again, if employees are not paid on a timely basis, they may sue the firm for their wages.

Besides legal recourse for payment, a distinguishing characteristic of fixed claims is that, if the firm is extraordinarily profitable in any period, the fixed claimants receive no more than the amount they are owed. For example, when a business has a good year, no bank expects the firm to repay more than the

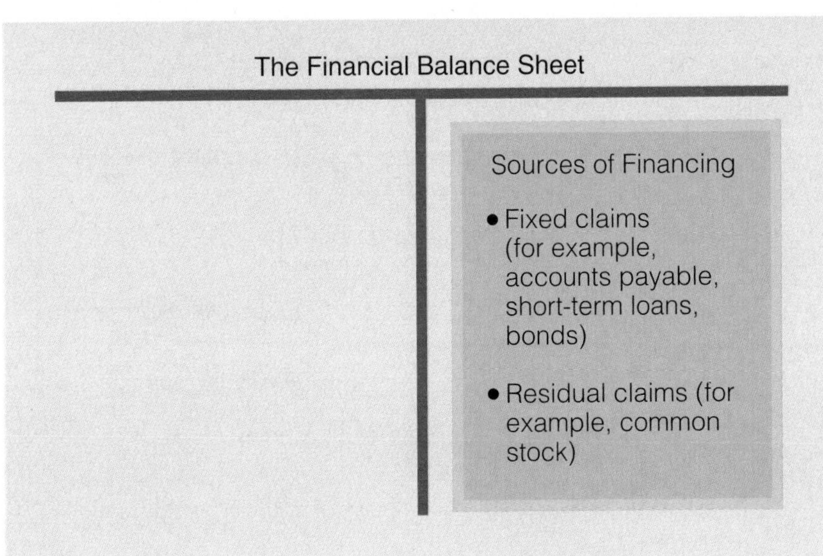

The Financial Balance Sheet
Sources of Financing
• Fixed claims (for example, accounts payable, short-term loans, bonds)
• Residual claims (for example, common stock)

FIGURE 1.2

FINANCIAL BALANCE SHEET

Sources of financing, including fixed and residual claims, are recorded on the right-hand side of the financial balance sheet.

Transparency Available

amount of the loan and accrued interest. Fixed claims, therefore, have legal protection against losses but do not share in profits. The amount of a fixed claim is limited to the amount of the loan or the value of the resources provided to the firm.

Even with legal protection, fixed claimants still are exposed to the risk of loss. There is no guarantee that normal business or even a forced liquidation of a firm will generate enough cash to satisfy all the fixed claims. Fixed-claim investors assess the likelihood of loss when arranging the terms of loans to the corporation.

This brings us to **residual claims**, best represented by common stock. Residual, as the name implies, means that common stockholders have a claim on cash flows that are left over once fixed claims are paid. If, in any year, a corporation generates cash in excess of that required to pay fixed-claim obligations, then that residual cash belongs to the firm's common stockholders—the *residual claimholders*. These cash flows may be distributed in the form of dividends or retained by the company to help it grow and thereby increase the value of the stockholders' ownership stakes. The potential size of these residual cash flows is unlimited.

When a firm's cash flows are just enough to cover its fixed payments, the residual claimants may receive no cash distribution, and they have no legal recourse to force one. Fixed claims, therefore, take *priority* over residual claims when cash flows are distributed. Residual claims, with their greater upside potential returns, must also bear a greater risk of losses because of their lower priority. See Figure 1.3.

At this point, we have modeled the corporation's basic functions. Capital is supplied to the firm, creating claims on the firm's future cash flows. These claims are conceptually recorded on the RHS of the financial balance sheet. This capital is utilized by the corporation to make investments that will generate cash flows in the future. These investments are shown on the LHS of the financial balance sheet, and the cash flows they generate are distributed to claimants who have supplied capital to the corporation or reinvested in the company.

FIGURE 1.3

FINANCIAL BALANCE SHEET

LHS and RHS, showing the flow of cash through the corporation.

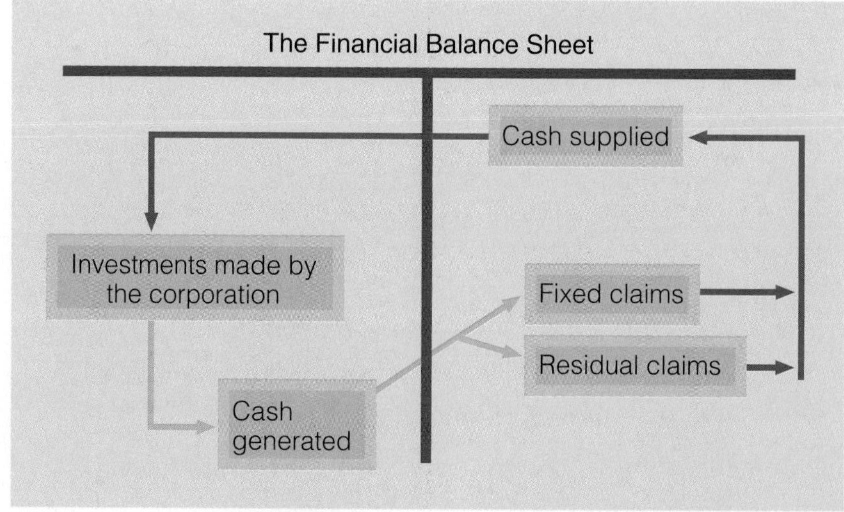

Transparency Available

Three Major Distinctions: The Financial Balance Sheet versus the Accounting Balance Sheet

We must pause to highlight three features of finance that differ from accounting, as shown in Exhibit 1.1. First, finance focuses on **cash flows**, whereas accounting focuses on profit or net income. You should remember that accounting net income includes deductions that involve no outlay of cash—depreciation being the classic example. A corporation, therefore, may have an accounting loss in a year (negative net income), yet the firm may have generated enough cash flow to meet its fixed claims and, perhaps, even make cash distributions to its residual claimants as well. Thus, we focus on cash because ultimately only cash can pay the bills or be invested.

A second distinguishing feature is that accountants record the historical cost of assets on the LHS and the historical amount of capital contributed in the RHS accounts. In finance, we are more concerned with the current value of these accounts. An example illustrates why. Consider a firm that invested in undeveloped real estate in downtown Houston in 1950. If the property cost $10,000 in 1950, it would appear on the LHS of 1992's accounting balance sheet at its original cost of $10,000. The current value, however, might be $1,000,000. Which figure is relevant for decision-making purposes? The opposite sometimes holds true as well: A manufacturer may have an inventory of beta-type VCRs in which it historically invested $1,000,000, but today VHS-type machines dominate the market. What is the current value of these beta machines—more than the original $1,000,000 investment or less? Again, which number is relevant?

A long-running debate at the Financial Accounting Standards Board (FASB) is whether to require greater market disclosure in accounting statements, especially for the banking industry.

The third point we want to make is that an accounting balance sheet is readily available for all to see, whereas the financial balance sheet is a conceptual construct—you won't find it printed in an annual report. Sharp managers and financial analysts, however, have a clear mental picture of the FBS and understand how decisions will affect its accounts. The development of that same mental picture and intuition is one of the objectives of this course.

Acquisition of Capital

Let us return to the financial balance sheet. The cash invested by the corporation, reflected on the LHS of the financial balance sheet, is raised by the firm via three

Transparency Available

EXHIBIT 1.1

KEY DIFFERENCES BETWEEN ACCOUNTING STATEMENTS AND THE FINANCIAL BALANCE SHEET

ACCOUNTING FOCUS	FINANCIAL FOCUS
1. Net income, profits, earnings.	1. Cash flows.
2. Records assets at their historical cost and claims at the historical amount contributed.	2. Records the current values of LHS investments made by the firm and the current value of RHS claims.
3. Reported in audited financial statements.	3. Not observable; its condition is determined by analysis. Accounting statements act as clues, or evidence, of the true financial condition of the corporation.

methods (Figure 1.4). The first method is **spontaneously generated loans** or **credit**, such as payables to suppliers or employees, and taxes payable. The firm has LHS investments, such as inventory, a portion of whose costs are borne for a period by suppliers who do not demand immediate payment. These types of fixed claims held by suppliers are usually short term in nature. They are spontaneous because the firm does not have to formally seek approval for such loans each time the credit is granted.

The second method of raising cash is *issuing and selling securities* to individuals and institutions. Firms are able to attract this capital because LHS investments are expected to yield returns that are as attractive or more attractive than alternative investment opportunities available to these suppliers of capital. Such securities may represent fixed claims on cash flows, such as bonds and bank loans, or common stock, which represents a residual claim. Notes payable are short-term fixed claims, term loans are generally intermediate-term claims, and bonds

Transparency Available

FIGURE 1.4

THREE METHODS OF CAPITAL ACQUISITION

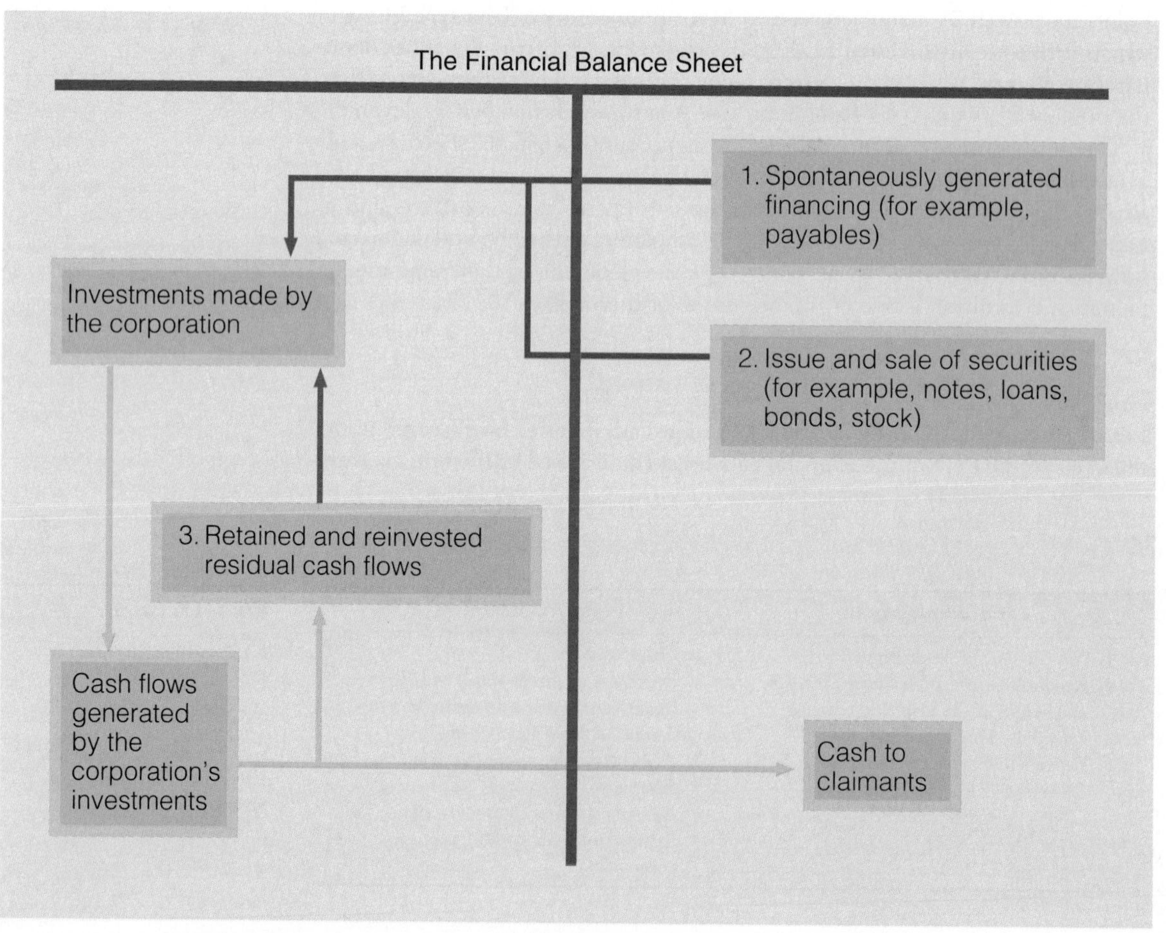

generally are long-term claims. Common stock is a perpetual claim, because it might never be repaid by the corporation.

Once issued and sold, the corporation's outstanding securities, particularly its stock and long-term bonds, are actively traded among individual and institutional investors. Such trading produces changes in the prices of the firm's outstanding securities, reflecting either changes in the attractiveness of competing investments, changes in investors' expectations of the returns the firm's investments will generate, or a combination of both factors. This **secondary trading** of securities produces no additional capital for the firm itself, but it reflects the traders' refined opinions of the firm's value and so acts as a measure of how investors regard the corporation's future prospects.

The final method for acquiring capital is through the *retention of residual cash flows*. These cash flows belong to the stockholders, but the firm may choose not to pay out all this cash as dividends, deciding instead to retain the cash and reinvest it in promising LHS projects.

It is convenient to view the corporation as a conduit that acquires capital from individual and institutional investors and invests this capital in promising projects on behalf of these claimants. Subsequent buying and selling of the corporation's securities produces changes in the prices of these claims.

These price changes produce no capital for the firm but nonetheless play an important role in corporate finances. Price changes reflect claimants' ongoing judgment regarding the attractiveness of the LHS investments, the value of which underlies the prices of the RHS claims. The prices of the firm's securities act as ongoing "report cards" on the effectiveness of the corporation's decision making and management. Increases in the prices of traded claims provide claimants with increases in wealth. *Price appreciation*, along with payments received directly from the corporation (i.e., dividends and interest), provides investors with a return on their investment in corporate securities.

THE FINANCIAL GOAL OF THE CORPORATION

The financial balance sheet models the corporation's financial activities. In the following section, these activities are linked to management's goal. Because managers direct the corporation, they must have a clear understanding of the corporate goal. They must understand for whom they work and what their job is if they are to be effective.

Management's Job

Managers of a corporation make two types of important financial decisions (Figure 1.5). First, managers choose which investments the firm makes *(LHS decisions)*. Second, managers choose the sources of capital used to finance these investments *(RHS decisions)*. What should managers' objectives be as they make these decisions?

To answer this question, recall that a corporation's management team operates the company on behalf of its owners, the stockholders. Stockholders invest their money and accept the risk of being a residual claimant because they hope the value of their investment will grow; that is, shareholders invest to increase their

FIGURE 1.5

Two types of managerial decisions correspond to the LHS and RHS of the financial balance sheet.

Transparency Available

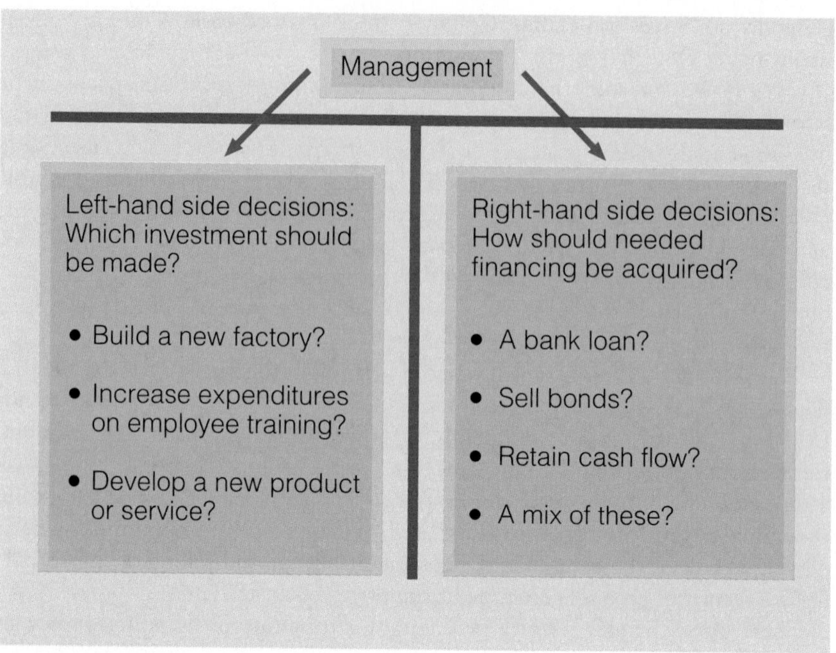

Berkshire Hathaway's 1993 *Annual Report* states, "Our long-term economic goal . . . is to maximize the average annual gain in intrinsic business value on a per-share basis. We do not measure the economic significance or performance of Berkshire by its size; we measure by per-share progress." This quote reinforces the wealth-maximization principle and may also lead into a discussion of the fallacies in the "growth is good" or "bigger is better" misconceptions.

wealth. Therefore, as employees of the stockholders, managers must make decisions that will increase shareholder wealth. See Figure 1.6.

The job of managers, as employees of the stockholders, is to *maximize the wealth of these residual claimants*. For the cash generated by productive LHS investments to be large enough to flow to residual claims, there must also be more than enough cash to satisfy the fixed claims. Therefore, **maximizing shareholder's wealth** will generally be in the interest of fixed claimants as well.

FIGURE 1.6

Corporate governance illustrated using the financial balance sheet.

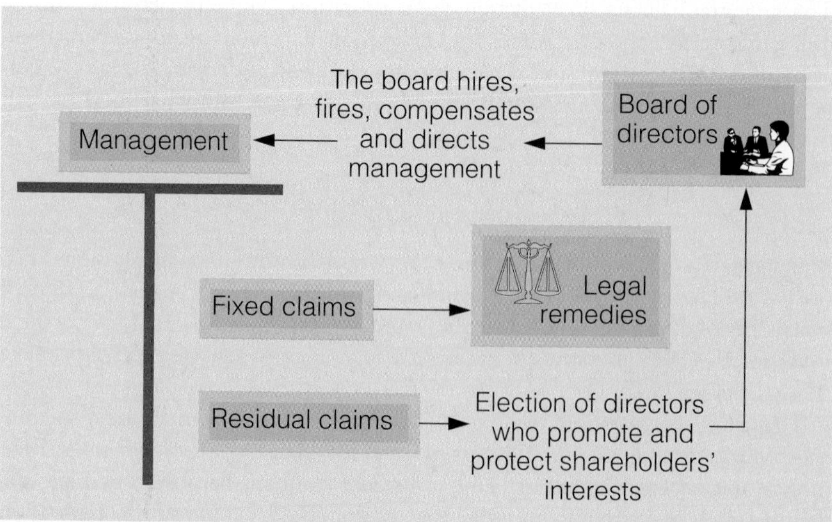

Transparency Available

Creating Wealth

Managers can meet their objective of maximizing shareholder wealth by making investments (on the LHS) whose *value* is greater than the amount of capital utilized (on the RHS) to finance these investments. Therefore, managers must have the ability to assess the value of potential LHS investments and to make the lowest-cost RHS capital-acquisition decision.

Stress the difference between profit and value. Profit can be shortsighted and ignores risk, whereas values does neither.

Let's illustrate wealth creation with a very simple example. Consider a firm that has the opportunity to invest in a single project whose value is greater than its cost. At the end of this project, the firm will be liquidated, and all cash will be distributed to the claimants. Management correctly identifies the attractive project and finds sources of capital to finance the cost of the project. The investment is made and almost instantly generates the expected cash flows. Because the value of the investment is greater than its cost, the cash flows more than cover the amount necessary to repay *all of both* the fixed claims *and* residual claims used to finance the project. Because the project has more value than cost, there are funds left over once all claims are repaid. These additional funds accrue to the residual claimants. These leftover, or residual, cash flows thus increase stockholders' wealth beyond that originally contributed to finance the project. Exhibit 1.2 illustrates the wealth-building process.

If this project's payoff were certain, investors had full access to all information regarding the project, and the payoff were almost immediate, then shareholder wealth would increase as soon as the investment in the project was made—even before the cash flows were distributed. Recall that stock, once issued and sold by the corporation, is traded among individuals. These investors set the price of the stock based on their beliefs regarding the security's attractiveness. If they knew, with certainty, the stock for which they paid \$50 a share would soon distribute \$54 a share, what would be the value of that stock to the investors? Clearly, the price of the stock would immediately increase to very near \$54 per share. Thus, when the company's managers make decisions that maximize the wealth of residual claimants, they also maximize the price of the company's common stock.

EXHIBIT 1.2

A THREE-MINUTE CORPORATION ILLUSTRATING THE WEALTH-BUILDING PROCESS

Minute 0
- A project is identified requiring a \$100 investment by the firm.
- The project will produce \$105 in cash flows 1 minute after the firm makes its investment.

Minute 1
- Sources of capital are identified:
  - A 1-minute loan of \$50 bearing an interest rate of \$1 per minute.
  - Stock can be sold for \$50.

Minute 2
- \$100 of capital is raised from the two sources.
- The \$100 investment in the project is made by the firm.

Minute 3
- The project generates the \$105 cash flow.
- The fixed claim of \$51 is paid in full: \$50 principal repayment and \$1 interest.
- The residual cash flow of \$54 is paid to stockholders, increasing their wealth by \$4.

Transparency Available

This example is greatly simplified, and we will take the rest of the book to develop fully your understanding of wealth creation through corporate decision making. You must learn how the value of an investment project depends not only upon the size of the cash flows that it is expected to generate (as in our preceding example), but also upon the degree of confidence claimants have that those cash flows will be achieved. In other words, value also depends upon the risk associated with the investment. Another factor that must be considered when estimating value is the timing of the cash flows the investment generates. Claimants prefer to receive cash flows earlier rather than later. The longer claimants wait for a given payoff, the less valuable that payoff is to them, all else being the same. Last, the value of a particular investment also depends upon how attractive that investment is vis-à-vis alternative investments.

Managers must, therefore, consider the size of a project's expected cash flows, their timing, the riskiness of these cash flows, and the returns available to shareholders on alternative investments as they assess value in pursuit of stockholder-wealth maximization. See Exhibit 1.3.

Information Asymmetry

One of the difficulties claimants have in assessing how well management is doing in achieving its goal of shareholder-wealth maximization is a lack of information. In large corporations, neither the board of directors nor stockholders can review all management decisions. Thus, managers have much more information than those individuals who are not involved in the day-to-day operations of the firm. This relationship is characterized as an **asymmetry of information** between corporate **insiders** and **outsiders** because the two groups do not have equal (or symmetric) information. Managers, as insiders, have a pretty clear view of both the RHS and the LHS of the financial balance sheet. Claimants who are not also employees of the corporation can observe the RHS sources of capital, because most of these claims are represented by actively traded securities (bonds and stocks), but LHS investments may be viewed only obscurely. Thus, outsiders have less information to use in drawing conclusions about the value of the activities of the corporation than do insiders. See Figure 1.7.

EXHIBIT 1.3

FACTORS DETERMINING AN INVESTMENT'S VALUE

FACTORS AFFECTING VALUE	THEIR EFFECT ON VALUE
1. The expected level of cash flows	1. The higher the expected cash flows, the higher the value of the investment, all else being the same.
2. The riskiness of cash flows	2. The more uncertain are the expected cash flows, the lower the value of the investment, all else being the same.
3. The timing of cash flows	3. The longer it takes to receive the cash flows, the lower the value of the investment, all else being the same.
4. The returns available on alternative, similar investments	4. If other similar investments offer higher returns, the less valuable is the investment, all else being the same.

Transparency Available

The degree of information asymmetry is largely dependent upon the size, complexity, and organizational structure of the corporation. Large corporations with stock **widely held** by millions of investors are characterized by a **separation of ownership** (held by the common stockholders) **and control** (held by managers). Stockholders of such giant companies individually own a very small proportion of the corporation; thus, they have little incentive to closely scrutinize managerial action. Additionally, with such a small stake, individual shareholders have little voting power with which to affect a change if they are dissatisfied with the management and the board. Such shareholders tend simply to sell their shares in the corporation if they are unhappy. Such organizations tend to have a relatively large degree of information asymmetry.

Small, **closely held** corporations often have fewer shareholders, each having a large financial stake in the firm. These claimants have a greater incentive to monitor decision making. The closer scrutiny of outsiders reduces the degree of information asymmetry. In the extreme case, insiders may own a very large stake in the corporation, and information asymmetry is minimized. Many small businesses are organized as corporations. Often there is only one residual claimant, who holds all the common stock and also manages the business. In such a case, there is no information asymmetry between management and the residual claimant, because they are one and the same. Even here, some asymmetry exists because fixed claimants remain corporate outsiders (e.g., suppliers and bankers) and so have less information about the company than the owner/manager.

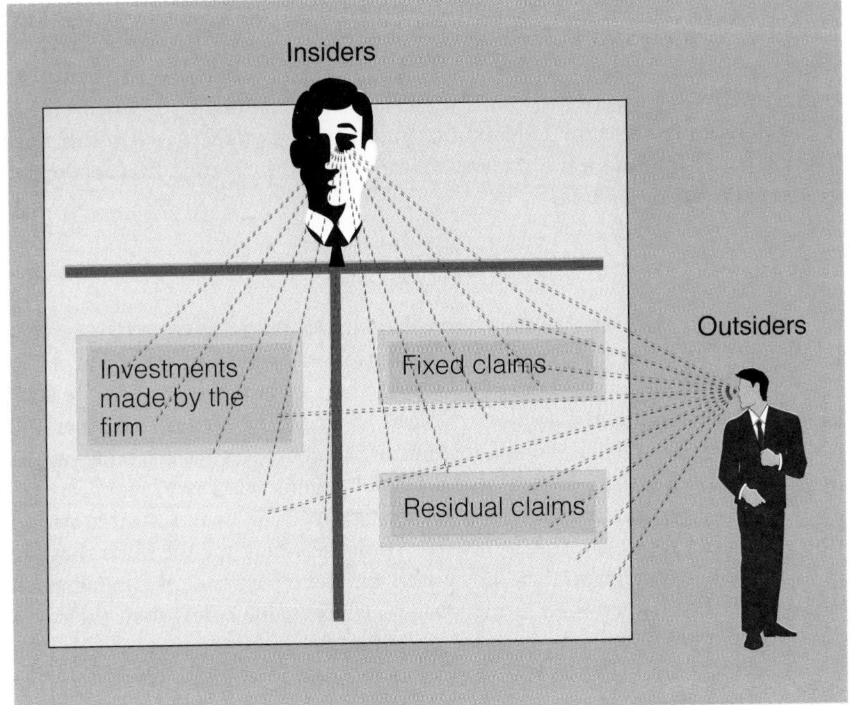

FIGURE 1.7

ASYMMETRY OF INFORMATION BETWEEN CORPORATE INSIDERS AND OUTSIDERS

Transparency Available

There are costs associated with information asymmetry. Corporate insiders, for example, may trade the firm's outstanding securities and reap huge profits based on their superior knowledge of the firm's prospects. The cost associated with **insider trading** would eventually be borne by society. Outsiders would soon lose faith in the fairness of trading the company's securities because of their information disadvantage. The ability of the firm to raise capital would be hampered as potential capital suppliers became reluctant to commit their funds for fear they are paying too much. Lack of financing would leave promising investment projects untouched, leading to a stagnant economy or one in decline. To protect the integrity and fairness of the trading system, society has legislated strict regulations on the trading of corporate securities by insiders. Ivan Boesky, a celebrated securities trader, was sent to prison as a result of his violations of insider trading laws.

Other information asymmetry costs are borne by the corporation. A good example is audited financial statements. Corporations hire reputable accounting firms to examine and, following well-defined standards, attest to the accuracy of information reported by insiders (the firm's management). Banks supplying financing to the corporation generally require that certain conditions be met by the firm throughout the life of the loan. For example, to ensure that these **protective covenants** are being met, banks may require that audited financial statements be regularly provided by the firm. Such statements reduce information asymmetry between the firm and these fixed claimants. Restrictive covenants are also included in bond agreements, and audited financial statements are a reporting requirement for virtually all actively traded corporate securities.

In the 1980s an interesting phenomenon took place with frequency never before seen. Many large, complex and widely held corporations' stocks were purchased in their entirety by relatively small groups of individuals or institutions in a process known as a leveraged buy-out. In essence, widely held firms were transformed into closely held firms. One important rationale for these billion dollar transactions was the reduction of information asymmetry. How can a reduction of this information gap translate into the wealth creation that apparently motivated these megadeals?

Agency Costs

To answer that question, we must more fully understand the costs that accompany information asymmetry and the separation of ownership and control. As we noted earlier, managers control the firm, whereas shareholders own the firm. Managers are acting as the *agents* of the firm's *principals*, or owners. Managers are hired to act on the owners' behalf, maximizing shareholders' wealth and—in the process—satisfying the corporation's fixed obligations. However, managers are also concerned with their own welfare and act in their own self-interests. At times managers, acting to satisfy their own desires, may take actions that are costly to claimants yet produce no wealth for these suppliers of capital. Such actions may be characterized as investments whose value is less than their cost and are, therefore, in direct conflict with the goal of maximizing shareholder wealth. Some corporate expenditures on perquisites may contradict shareholder wealth maximization.

Perquisites (or *perks*) are benefits to employees beyond their compensation packages and are often cost-effective investments. Many executives, for example, are supplied a company-owned car. Shareholders may benefit from such investment—it may be less costly to simply supply the corporate president with a vehicle than to reimburse her for mileage. The company-owned car also assures stockholders that the corporate reputation for being a quality institution is enhanced by having clients met in a clean, comfortable mode of transportation. On the other hand, suppose the president of the firm is supplied with a $200,000 Rolls-Royce rather than a $40,000 Lincoln. Will the decision to supply her with the Rolls produce additional value greater than the cost differential of $160,000? The Rolls seems to be a questionable investment. This is an example of an *excessive perquisite,* an expense that benefits an executive while producing no increase in shareholder wealth. On whose judgment does the authorization of such expenses fall? Ordinarily management makes these decisions. This is an example of an **agency cost**, a cost that arises because of the separation of principals and agents in large corporations (Figure 1.8).

Another source of agency costs is **shirking** by top management. A corporation's top managers are selected and are highly compensated because the board feels they have the talent and will expend the effort to seek out value-creating investment projects. But only the managers know precisely how much effort they are directing to their job. Because managerial effort is difficult to monitor, managers can reduce their efforts (i.e., shirk) and thereby generate costs for shareholders with no offsetting benefits. Such managers may choose to take a 3-hour lunch, for which they are richly compensated but which produces no increase in shareholder wealth. Shirking by top management sets a costly example, because the behavior percolates down through the corporation.

Studies have shown that top executives' pay is positively correlated with the size of the corporation. Some incentive, therefore, exists for chief executive officers (CEOs) to engage in **empire building**. A firm may expand in size (add LHS investments) with less regard for the value of these investments than for the impact that a larger firm has on the CEO's pay, power, and prestige. Empire

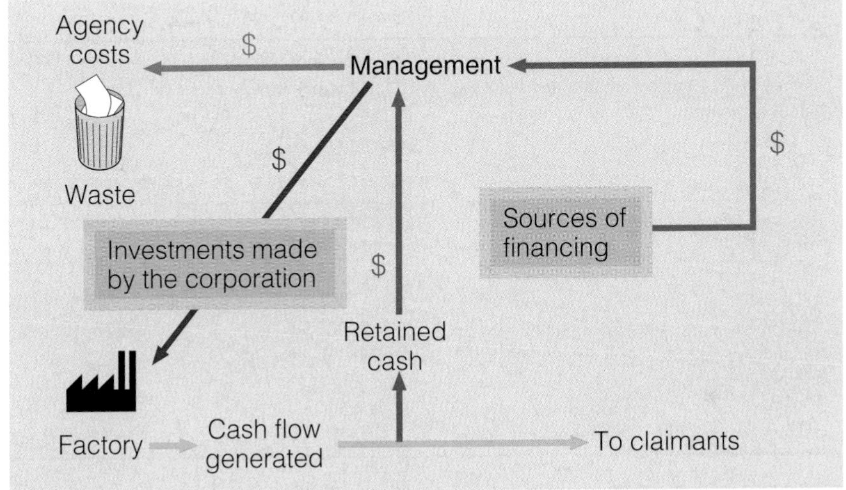

FIGURE 1.8

The agency problem creates costs for the business, wasting corporate resources.

Transparency Available

building has been documented as one of the most damaging agency costs in its impact on shareholder wealth.

An important characteristic of these examples of the agency problem is that they would not exist if information asymmetry did not also exist. The megamergers of the 1980s often were economically linked to the reduction of agency costs. By replacing wasteful management, by increasing the accountability of management to a smaller group of claimants whose stake is high enough to motivate close monitoring of the firm, and by the dismantling of ill-conceived and inefficient empires, wealth gains were achieved as many corporations became closely held through buy-outs in the 1980s.

Competing Organizational Forms

Even with the problems inherent in the widely held corporation—problems such as information asymmetry and agency costs—the modern corporation dominates the economic landscape in several key respects. The bulk of domestic sales (90%) and profits (80%)[1] are generated by the corporate form of business organization.

To be sure, **sole proprietorships** and **partnerships** are also important—they perhaps best embody the entrepreneurial spirit and often are the spawning ground for major corporate entities. Proprietorships and partnerships also have less significant agency problems than do widely held corporations. These organizational forms are also attractive because of their relatively low organizational costs, and their owners may benefit from lower taxes. (See Exhibit 1.4.) Corporate cash flows to residual claimants (dividends) are subject to *double taxation*—once at the corporate level and again at the individual level—but proprietorship and partnership income is taxed only once, as part of the owner's personal tax return.

A good example of a large enterprise is the building of the railroads in the 19th century. The transcontinental railroads were too costly to be financed by an individual or even a small group of people and were too risky for investors unless their liability was limited. Therefore, the railroads depended upon the corporate form of organization in order to secure financing.

But the corporation has attributes that offset the advantages of proprietorships and partnerships. These attributes are particularly important for large firms, requiring large amounts of capital. To raise the huge sums necessary to finance large-scale businesses, entities must accept the difficulties inherent in the separation of ownership and control, because there are few individual investors with sufficient personal wealth, expertise, and willingness to both own and manage a

EXHIBIT 1.4

TAX ADVANTAGE OF PARTNERSHIPS AND PROPRIETORSHIPS

Assuming a corporate tax rate of 20% and a personal tax rate of 25%, it is clear that corporations' owners are at a disadvantage taxwise, because their income is subject to double taxation.

	PARTNERSHIPS AND PROPRIETORSHIPS	CORPORATIONS
Income before business-level taxes	$1000	$1000
Income tax rate at the business level	0%	20%
Income tax payable at the business level	$0	$200
Income to owners before personal income taxes	$1000	$800
Personal income tax rate	25%	25%
Personal income taxes owed	$250	$200
After-tax cash flow to owners	$750	$600

Transparency Available

[1]U.S. Bureau of the Census, *Statistical Abstract of the United States*, 1990, 110th edition, p. 521.

corporate giant. Thus, to finance big businesses it is often necessary to have many owners (stockholders) who are willing to relinquish control to hired managers. Now, let us consider the characteristics of the corporate form of organization that enable it to dominate alternative structures.

First, through the issuance of common stock, a highly transferrable security is used as the medium for exchanging ownership interests in the business. The ability of stockholders to sell their shares easily is important if individuals are to be persuaded to take an ownership interest in a firm over which they have limited control. Such claimants, as mentioned earlier, can "vote with their feet," selling their shares when they wish. Morever, if many stockholders become dissatisfied, then selling pressure, behaving in accordance with the law of supply and demand, will drive down share prices. The supply of such a corporation's stock available for sale on the secondary market will increase, whereas demand for the securities decreases. This decline in the price of the corporation's securities indicates to the board of directors that action needs to be taken. By contrast, partnership and proprietorship ownership interests are less transferrable and marketable. For example, partnerships often require the approval of remaining partners before a dissident partner can sell his or her interest to a third party. In the end, many partners are stuck with their investment and are powerless to change it. Thus, the ease with which stock may be bought and sold (its *marketability*) is a strong advantage of the corporation, aiding its ability to raise capital when compared to alternative business forms.

A second contrasting characteristic is the liability of owners. Sole proprietors and partners (with the exception of **limited partners**—see Exhibit 1.5) not only

Transparency Available

EXHIBIT 1.5

Some key characteristics of the forms of business organization are contrasted for corporations, partnerships, and proprietorships.

	CORPORATIONS[1,2]	PARTNERSHIPS[3]	PROPRIETORSHIPS
Taxation	Twice, once at the business level, once at the individual level	Once at the individual level	Once at the individual level
Liability	Limited to the amount invested	Unlimited	Unlimited
Ownership and control	Separated, majority of stockholders are not usually managers	Partners own and control the enterprise	By definition, ownership and control are in the hands of a single individual
Transferability of ownership	Relatively easy through sale of stock	Potentially difficult	Potentially difficult
Access to capital	Best	Moderate	Most restrictive
Information asymmetry and agency costs	Potentially high	Relatively low if all partners are equal and active	Very little, because there is no separation of ownership and control

[1]S corporations differ in that they are treated much like partnerships. S corporations' business-level income flows to the individual tax returns without business-level taxation.

[2]Closely held corporations are similar to partnerships except in the area of taxation and liability.

[3]Limited partnerships are managed by a *general partner*, and *limited partners* have limited liability. In limited partnerships, there can be high agency costs because the general partner is acting as the limited partners' agent. Thus, limited partners are much like stockholders except in the areas of taxation, transferability, and access to capital.

risk their original investments in a business, but must stand ready to meet any shortfall the enterprise may experience in meeting its fixed obligations from their personal resources. A huge legal judgment against a proprietorship or partnership may lead to the personal bankruptcy of its owners. This is not the case with the corporate form of organization. Stockholders have **limited liability**, meaning that they can lose no more than the amount they have invested in the stock. In a corporation, residual claimants cannot be forced to make up shortfalls in meeting fixed claims once corporate assets have been fully liquidated. Again, this corporate attribute is especially critical in larger firms with diffuse ownership. Few individuals would be willing to expose their resources to risk, without direct control over how those capital contributions are utilized, if their liability is unlimited.

The last advantage of the corporate form is its conceptually unlimited life. Partnerships depend on a team acting as both owners and managers. Like any team, the loss of a key player or players can destroy its effectiveness. In proprietorships this difficulty is exacerbated because the team consists of one player, the loss of whom completely changes the character of the entity. To replace players in partnerships or proprietorships, an individual must be sought with the wealth, expertise, and willingness to be both a manager and an owner. If such an individual cannot be located, the business must be liquidated. Corporations, on the other hand, are faced with less critical problems of this nature. Replacing lost owners is relatively simple because of marketability of the stock, as already discussed. Loss of key management personnel, although potentially difficult, is less of a problem than that encountered in other organizational forms because the replacement need not be willing to also become a major owner, as required by a proprietorship or partnership.

Over the past century advances in technology, more cost-effective means of transportation and distribution, advances in communications, a rising standard of living, and the globalization of markets have provided many investment opportunities for corporations, requiring large amounts of capital to finance their growth. Organizations have sought the most efficient means of meeting these needs. Many would argue that the advantages of corporate organizational forms outweigh the disadvantages as firms become large. Witness their dominance.

CORPORATIONS AND SOCIETY

The relative efficiency of the corporate form of organization has led to its being the structure of choice for firms foreseeing attractive growth opportunities. The efficiency of corporations has led to criticisms as well. Corporations are often portrayed as cold-hearted in their pursuit of economic gains. They are charged with ignoring the communities in which they operate, lacking concern for the welfare of their customers, and even ignoring the planet in their relentless pursuit of profits.

Some critics of corporations charge that the goal of shareholder wealth maximization is too narrow for the good of society. These critics contend that corporations should act in a **socially responsible** manner. Although social responsibility has different meanings to different people, circumstances do indeed exist when the good of society is at odds with the welfare of corporate shareholders.

For example, in its manufacturing endeavors a firm may produce **externalities**, such as air pollution, but the cost of cleaning up this dirty air may be borne not by the corporation but by society. Thus, shareholders receive higher returns as society bears some of the costs of producing the product.

These charges are often true on a case-by-case basis and must be taken seriously by all corporations, even nonoffenders, because corporations as legal entities exist at the pleasure of society. Should society see pervasive abuses, it will surely restrict the freedom of corporations to act.

Businesses—and corporations in particular—are remarkably resilient. Abuses of labor, unethical securities practices, and consumer fraud have led to major legislative initiatives during this century that restricted the freedom of firms. Yet, the competitive drive toward shareholder wealth maximization allowed corporations to meet society's legal mandates and continue to thrive. It is this goal, combined with marketplace competition, that has allowed businesses in our society to produce ever-higher standards of living. Compare our economy with those in which other goals have supplanted shareholder wealth maximization. Alternative goals, such as the former Soviet Union's objectives of universal employment and equal distribution of wealth, have proven to be socially irresponsible in the sense that resources were not put to their best use. Resulting inefficiencies in such societies have not been beneficial to their members. Therefore, the competitive nature of the financial goal, while sometimes producing socially irresponsible corporate behavior, is also responsible for the economic well-being our society enjoys.

The appendix to Chapter 15 discusses ethics from a financial perspective.

SUMMARY

In this chapter several key concepts that underlie finance were introduced. These are the blocks upon which the bulk of the course is built. The main points of the chapter are, therefore, important enough to merit repetition here:

- The financial balance sheet was used to illustrate the firm's capital acquisition and investment activities.
- Residual and fixed claims' characteristics were discussed, including the priority of claims, default and legal recourse, and voting rights.
- The major distinctions between finance and accounting were drawn.
- Shareholder wealth maximization was introduced as the financial goal of the corporation.
- Wealth creation was illustrated as corporate investment in any project whose value is greater than its cost.
- A project's value was discussed as being dependent upon the size of expected cash flows, the riskiness of those cash flows, their timing, and the returns available on alternative investments of similar risk.
- Agency costs and information asymmetry were discussed as impediments to maximizing shareholder wealth.
- Competing forms of business organization were compared to the corporate form.
- Corporations were noted to exist at society's pleasure and must be sensitive to social concerns. Overall, economic efficiency and well-being may be the most important products of corporations competing to serve their shareholders.

Also covered were characteristics of bonds (coupon payments, par value, etc.), characteristics of stock (dividends, etc.), and assumptions about the way people tend to behave (rational self-interest). Taken altogether, the topics of Chapter 1 have provided an introduction to finance by focusing on the corporation. However, we have yet to look at the environment in which the corporation operates. Chapter 2 discusses how markets and the government affect corporations. As you will see, these external factors both challenge corporations and provide corporations with opportunities.

KEY TERMS

securities
bonds
coupon payments
face amount
par value
common stock
dividends
board of directors
proxy
financial balance sheet
tangible and intangible investments
fixed claims
default
residual claims
cash flows
spontaneously generated loans or credit
secondary trading

maximizing shareholder wealth
information asymmetry
insiders
outsiders
widely held corporation
separation of ownership and control
closely held corporations
insider trading
protective covenants
agency costs
perquisites
shirking
empire building
sole proprietorship
partnership
limited partners
limited liability
social responsibility
externalities

QUESTIONS

1. What is the primary goal of financial management?
2. Identify at least three characteristics that differ between fixed claims and residual claims.
3. What are the three major distinctions between accounting and finance?
4. Identify and discuss the three methods firms have available for raising the cash used to fund investment projects.
5. Identify four factors that determine value.
6. Do you think agency cost would tend to increase as information asymmetry increases between corporate insiders and outsiders? Why?
7. Which forms of business organization offer the owners limited liability?
8. McDonald's recently began accepting credit cards as payment for their products. As a result, accounts receivable increased. This increase indicates a decision by management to make a greater investment in these restaurants' receivables. If this decision was a good one given the goal of shareholder wealth maximization, discuss how accepting credit cards leads to the increase of shareholders' wealth.
9. If the Disney corporation began producing X-rated movies, the firm would risk destroying its investment in what intangible asset?
10. Do you think that individuals are more socially responsible than corporations? If they are, should corporations contribute some residual cash flows to charitable causes of the corporation's choice, or should these cash flows be distributed to stockholders who may then make contributions to whom *they* choose, if they desire?
11. An investment seems likely to produce cash flows, after all expenses are paid, equal to twice its cost. Does this necessarily mean it's a good investment? Why not? What other factors should be considered?
12. Here is an old joke about limited partnerships: A limited partnership is where, at the beginning, the limited partners have the money and the general partners have the experience. At the end, the joke goes, the general partners have the money and the limited partners have the experience. Explain this joke in light of the separation of ownership and control, agency costs, and what you know about the characteristics of limited partnerships as a form of business organization.

13. The great majority of stock trades do not involve newly issued stock. This means that investors are buying and selling these shares among themselves and no new capital is raised for the corporation from these trades. Yet, the price at which a stock trades is important to the firm. Why?
14. A factory appears on an accounting balance sheet at its historical cost of $1,000,000 (disregarding depreciation). Why might such a factory actually be worth $10,000,000 or perhaps only $100,000? Make up an example showing why a factory might appear at a higher figure on the financial balance sheet than an accounting statement and one example why one might appear at a lower figure.
15. Why might a self-interested citizen rationally vote for a tax increase to build a new high school, even though this citizen does not have children (and does not intend to have any)?
16. Are all perquisites non–wealth producing? How might you decide if a perk is an agency cost or a cost effective LHS investment?
17. If an automobile manufacturer contributed $1 million to public television but did so anonymously, would this be a socially responsible act? Would it be in the shareholders' best interest?
18. From Question 17, if the automaker made the same contribution and was given publicity for its generosity, then do you think the donation was beneficial to shareholders? How would you decide if the donation and resulting publicity was a good investment decision?
19. Suppose corporations are taxed at an 18% rate and individuals are taxed at a 30% rate. Now, imagine that a business has income before any taxes of $5,000. Compare the after-tax cash flow to the business owner if the enterprise were organized as a proprietorship, a partnership, and as a corporation. Based on after-tax cash flows, which form of organization should the owner choose?
20. Referring to the business in Question 19, suppose the firm's product is fireworks. Would an astute owner choose, perhaps, the corporate form of organization in spite of disadvantage based on tax arguments?
21. Suppose a manager announces that the firm she directs is going to expand by purchasing another company. Why won't this manager state in the announcement that she is making the acquisition as part of her empire-building strategy?
22. In an economically competitive market, we state in the chapter that competition will correct irrational behavior. How does this work? (*Hint*: Suppose that people are competing for resources. If they consistently pay too much for the resource, what will happen? If they try to pay too little for the resource, what will happen?)
23. Describe how a firm might invest in building its reputation. How might that investment pay off, creating wealth for the firm's owners?
24. How might an individual go about building a good reputation? Could it be economically valuable?
25. Calculate the change in shareholders' wealth for the following 3-minute corporation.

    Minute 0: A project costing $500 is identified that will produce cash flows of $510 one minute after the investment is made.

    Minute 1: Sources of capital are identified:

- A 1-minute loan of $300, bearing an interest rate of 1% per minute
- Stock sold for $200

Minute 2: The $500 of capital is raised and the investment in the project is made.

Minute 3: (You complete.)

26. Referring to Question 25, if there was no risk associated with this project, how much would you pay for the stock at minute 2 (just after it was issued)?
27. Corporations often include in their officers' pay large amounts of stock. Can you explain the use of this form of compensation as a method for helping to solve the agnecy problem described in the chapter?
28. How could each of the following areas of business administration contribute to shareholder wealth?
    a. Marketing
    b. Human resource management
    c. Production management
    d. Accounting

CHAPTER 2

The Effect of Markets and Government on the Firm

You tell the governor that if he doesn't come up with some subsidized financing, free land, a tax deferment, a new highway and airport, it's no deal.

While many businesses feel threatened by government regulation and taxes, the government presents firms with opportunities as well. In Chapter 2, we explore the impact of government and of markets on financial decision making.

Liken this to learning the rules of the game. You cannot compete successfully unless you understand the rules of play.

hapter 1 provided an overview of finance and introduced the *financial balance sheet*. The chapter discussed the goal of corporate managers—shareholder wealth maximization—and some reasons that managers may not achieve that objective. Chapter 1 also described the advantages and disadvantages of the corporate form of organization. Chapter 2 completes the development of the financial balance sheet by considering the environment in which corporations operate. Governmental rules and market forces define that environment. The long-term viability of any business depends on how well managers understand the limits and opportunities that these external forces exert on their organization. The key objective (or *bottom line*, in business parlance) of this chapter is describing where managers are likely to find value creating investment opportunities.

Limitations and opportunities for businesses often arise from laws passed by federal, state, and local governments. Many governmental units collect taxes on business income and use taxes to modify business behavior by applying different tax rates to different types of activities. Governmental agencies limit or prohibit some activities through administrative regulation in order to protect consumers and the environment. Truth-in-advertising laws, product-safety laws, and pollution-control regulations are examples of how the government has limited corporate activities to benefit or protect other constituencies. Governments also pass laws that protect corporations. Examples of laws that help firms prosper from their innovation or protect them from unfair competition include patents, copyrights, and predatory pricing prohibitions.

Within the limitations and opportunities provided by this legal framework, corporations compete in markets that operate according to laws of supply and demand. Corporations sell the items they produce in **product markets**. Product markets also provide the raw materials and other inputs that firms use in their production process. To create value for their shareholders, corporate managers must pay careful attention to the product markets as they choose the mix of items to produce and decide how best to produce them. Successful managers have a knack for figuring out what consumers want and providing it at an acceptable price. The left-hand side of the financial balance sheet reflects the product market decisions made by managers as they work toward increasing the wealth of shareholders.

Besides product markets, firms also participate in **financial markets**. A company's financial market activities appear on the right-hand side of the financial balance sheet under long-term liabilities and equity. Financial markets supply the funds that firms use to purchase productive assets, such as factories, machinery, trucks, computers, and offices. Financial markets also provide a mechanism for valuing a firm's securities. Investors buy and sell stocks and bonds in these markets. These transactions determine security prices and, thereby, the value investors place on a firm. You can think of this value as the grade investors have given managers. Corporate managers who produce products consumers want at an acceptable price see the price of their firms' shares rise. This is equivalent to earning an A. Managers who, through laziness, incompetence, or bad luck, continually pursue unprofitable activities see the value of their firms' shares fall. For such managers a grade of F stands for fired.

In both product and financial markets, information availability and ease of entry play important roles in determining whether wealth increasing opportunities exist. In financial markets, prices typically reflect new information very quickly. For example, if a pharmaceutical company announces it has developed a cure for AIDS (acquired immune deficiency syndrome), within minutes its stock price will reflect investors' best guess about the company's profits from the drug. Such markets are referred to as being **informationally efficient**. What informational efficiency implies about making money in financial markets is one of the important lessons in this chapter. Product markets vary in their competitiveness. Markets that firms can easily enter and exit and in which firms produce very similar goods are called **perfectly competitive**, whereas markets where entry is restricted or goods are differentiated are considered **imperfectly competitive**.[1] Your economics class undoubtedly introduced these terms. As you will see, much of corporate finance draws on material from micro- and macroeconomics. Perfect and imperfect competition are particularly important concepts in this course. In fact, we will conclude the chapter by taking a hard look at market imperfections and how corporate managers use them to increase the wealth of a firm's shareholders.

GOVERNMENTS AND CORPORATIONS

Governments exist at the national, state, and local levels and provide citizens a mechanism for making collective choices. Governmental choices are collective in the sense that citizens, or their representatives, agree on a course of action. Markets for goods and services, on the other hand, involve individual choices. Collective decisions are also made by groups other than governments. For example, clubs, charities, and religious groups make collective decisions. Governments, however, can implement or enforce their decisions through their powers to tax, penalize, and imprison. Therefore, the collective choices made by governmental bodies are much more far-reaching than those of other groups.

In making collective choices, governments must respond to a variety of constituents. Environmentalists want clean air and water and protection for wilderness areas, the timber industry wants access to logs, automakers want to be able to compete with Japanese and European manufacturers, and consumers want low prices at the grocery store. These are just a few of the tensions with which legislators at the federal, state, and local levels must deal. In response to these conflicting demands, the U.S. economy is a mix of free markets, heavily regulated industries, and still other areas that have limited entry but are not directly regulated.

There is nearly continuous policy debate in the United States regarding how much competition is enough, what regulation is necessary to ensure competition, the form that regulation should take, and what is the appropriate role for government in the economy. Laws arising from this political activity vary with the ebb and flow of public opinion and political thought. To promote competition in the airline industry and long-distance telephone service, those industries were

Ask students to consider what their phone and utility bills would be if these industries were not regulated.

[1]Generic goods or commodities are products that consumers choose only on the basis of price. Differentiated goods are chosen according to attributes such as price, color, taste, style, manufacturer's reputation, and advertising effectiveness.

largely deregulated in the mid-1970s, followed by banking a few years later.[2] Public utilities commissions (PUCs) continue to regulate rates charged by natural monopolies, such as local gas, electric, and phone companies, but even these companies face competition when they enter unregulated markets. Natural monopolies arise when a single company offers significantly lower costs than those of competing companies sharing the same market. Two competing companies must install duplicate systems of pipes, wires, or cable, for which customers must eventually pay. A single company avoids such costly duplication and thereby offers customers lower rates. Cable television and cellular telephone companies also operate in markets with various degrees of governmental regulation. Consumers support deregulation if increased competition is likely to result in lower prices but favor regulation in areas such as cable TV, where a monopolist could wield great power. Business people typically claim to prefer free markets, yet corporations often lobby governments to limit the import of certain goods, prohibit takeovers, and provide tax incentives.

As the last paragraph suggests, the government plays a number of different roles in the economy. We take no position on what role or roles government should play. Instead, we take the economy as given, a mix of competitive and regulated markets, and proceed from there. Success in business requires understanding how governmental decisions affect the opportunities available to corporations. From our perspective, governments affect business in three ways: by creating incentives for certain types of behavior; by providing support for production and exchange; and, by limiting or prohibiting some activities. Although these categories—incentives, support, and prohibitions—may not include all government effects on business, they provide a useful starting point for examining the interaction between government and business.

Incentives Created by Governments

Nicolas Kristof, a Beijing-based reporter for the *New York Times*, recounts how it was impossible for him to find a nonpirated version of MS DOS software in China.

The federal government encourages innovation through patent or intellectual property laws. These laws protect inventors' efforts by giving them sole rights to the product or technology for a stated period of time. Without such protection there would be little incentive to expend effort or money developing new products. As soon as a new product appeared, imitators would copy it, so the developer would have little chance of recouping his or her investment. Because the government protects inventors from imitators, corporations invest more in research and development activities than they would otherwise. Thus companies produce more new goods and services, which help customers attain a higher quality of life, than they would without patent protection. In early 1995 the value of patent protection was headline news as the United States confronted China about the large-scale pirating of copyrighted goods such as books, computer software, movies, audio tapes, records, and compact disks. The holders of the copyrights estimated lost royalty revenue due to the unauthorized duplication of these items exceeded $1 billion annually. Not only does that situation point out the potential value of copyrights, but it also demonstrates some of the risks associated with global business when not all countries have or enforce similar legal codes.

---

[2]Deregulation does not mean that all economic regulation has disappeared. Banking regulation has been greatly relaxed, but banking remains one of our most regulated industries.

Tax policy can also be used to encourage certain types of business activity. The corporate tax deductibility of interest paid to borrow money, combined with the inability to deduct dividend payments to stockholders, creates an incentive for firms to finance investments with debt. The federal government has used an investment tax credit (ITC) to spur business investment in productive assets. When the ITC is in effect, companies purchasing long-lived assets earn a tax reduction. Typically, the amount of the tax credit varies with the amount invested in capital equipment. For instance, the total tax credit might be 10% of the purchase price of the equipment. This effectively reduces the price of such investment. Such a tax policy stimulates job creation in two ways: as demand for new equipment increases, manufacturers of the equipment hire more employees, and the new equipment may require that additional employees be hired to operate it.

To attract businesses, state and local governments often offer tax reductions to new firms that locate in their region. In some cases, the new firm pays no state or local tax whatsoever for a specified number of years. For example, when BMW, the German automobile manufacturer, began looking for a factory site in North America, the state of South Carolina offered to lease land for the plant to the company at $1 per year, to assess no state taxes for several years, and to provide job training for new employees. States and municipalities sometimes offer direct financial assistance to business firms through low-interest loans, called *industrial development bonds*. The low interest rate reduces the cost of investment and thereby encourages firms to expand. Investors willingly accept the lower interest paid by these bonds because of the tax advantages attached to the bonds.

Incentives are also emerging in environmental areas. The Clean Air Act (as amended in 1990) permits firms that more than meet national air quality standards to sell that excess to polluters. By allowing manufacturers to trade these pollution credits, the government encourages companies that can most efficiently clean up their emissions to exceed air standards, while also allowing firms for which cleanup is more expensive to continue to operate. In this way, the overall air quality standard is attained at the minimum total cost.

Incentives offered by government units can have a significant effect on business decisions. Part of a manager's job is understanding and taking advantage of these governmental policies. At the conclusion of this chapter we discuss how managers incorporate this understanding into the projects they pursue.

Governmental Support for Production and Exchange

Technical innovation and job creation are two business activities that government bodies support. The federal government funds billions of dollars of research at universities and national laboratories each year. Although much of this research does not immediately turn into products for consumers, it does provide much of the fundamental knowledge for product development. By funding research labs, the government increases the likelihood of significant scientific breakthroughs. For example, government-funded research is the basis for medical treatments such as organ transplants as well as consumer products such as personal computers and cordless telephones.

The government plays an important role in all our lives: public schools, most roads, bridges, and airports, safe food, most utilities, and so on.

Every day we use government-provided goods and services. Roads, airports, water and sewer systems, bridges, parks, and schools are just a few examples of items that governments often supply their citizens. This infrastructure supports business activity by providing employees with training, allowing the transportation of goods, employees, and customers and supplying some of the inputs required for production. Moreover, the construction of infrastructure projects generates payrolls that stimulate consumer demand for goods and services.

Is professional certification only for consumers? Ask students how certification might also help professionals.

The government also supports business activity in other, less direct, ways. Regulation of capital and commodity markets helps companies obtain investment funds and raw materials at competitive prices.[3] Insurance for bank deposits encourages individuals to save, which provides funds for banks to lend to individuals and small businesses. Professional certification of doctors, dentists, lawyers, and engineers provides a tacit assurance of quality. This increases consumer confidence and consumer use of these professional services. A well-developed legal system encourages business activity by penalizing firms that engage in unfair trade practices and assuring that contractual commitments will be honored. As we mentioned earlier, in China there is almost no recognition of intellectual property, such as copyrights and patents. In such an environment, businesses have no incentive to invest in the research and development necessary to create new products, because imitators will take away their profits.

Limitations on Business Activity

Regulators carry out cost-benefit analyses of regulations. Almost no rules call for 100% purity or 100% safety. Requiring 100% purity or safety is too expensive.

The government has become increasingly responsible for the well-being of consumers and workers. Product-safety laws establish design, material, and performance standards that products must meet before they are offered to the public. Examples include crash tests and measures of gasoline mileage of cars and trucks, clinical tests of new drugs to determine both the drug's effectiveness and whether injurious side effects exist, and testing food products for contaminants. Occupational safety legislation protects workers by establishing standards for working conditions. Truth-in-advertising laws prohibit manufacturers from making false claims about a product's performance or attributes. Thus, consumers can purchase goods with some assurance about the quality and performance of the item. Environmental-protection laws reflect collective decisions about how community resources such as air and water can be used. Like consumer-protection laws, some environmental rules set standards to protect the health or safety of community members.

Legislation on product quality, worker safety, and environmental protection places a burden on business. Eventually consumers pay for these protective activities, because companies pass through extra costs in the form of higher prices. When considering an increase in the regulatory burden on business, legislators must decide if it is better (in the sense of being cheaper and more effective) for the government to act as a watchdog for all consumers and workers than for individuals to carry out these investigations separately. If regulatory costs become too high, some businesses will fail, because consumers will not pay a price that covers production costs. Besides the lost income of employees and owners of failed companies, consumers lose, because they no longer have as wide a selection of goods to choose from. Determining the appropriate amount of governmental

---

[3] In the next section of this chapter, we discuss how governmental involvement in capital markets creates a level playing field and so increases investor participation.

protection requires weighing benefits against costs. The analysis of social and environmental protection is particularly difficult, because often neither costs nor benefits are easily measurable. Like most economists before us, we have no simple prescription for determining whether or how much governmental intervention is optimal. We leave further discussion of this complex topic to more advanced courses.

Summary: Government and Business

Figure 2.1 shows some of the ways that governments affect business. Government bodies—federal, state, and local—determine the rules of the business game. As in any competitive game, success requires understanding the rules. A thorough understanding of the rules of the game not only reduces the likelihood of inadvertently pursuing illegal or inappropriate actions—and suffering the accompanying penalties—it also enhances the development of successful strategies. For example, safety standards that required airbags in automobiles created a new industry designing and manufacturing airbags for the automotive industry. Responding to concerns about chemical waste, hundreds of new firms have emerged

Transparency Available

FIGURE 2.1

FINANCIAL BALANCE SHEET WITH GOVERNMENT

The government affects the investing and financial decisions of corporations in many ways.

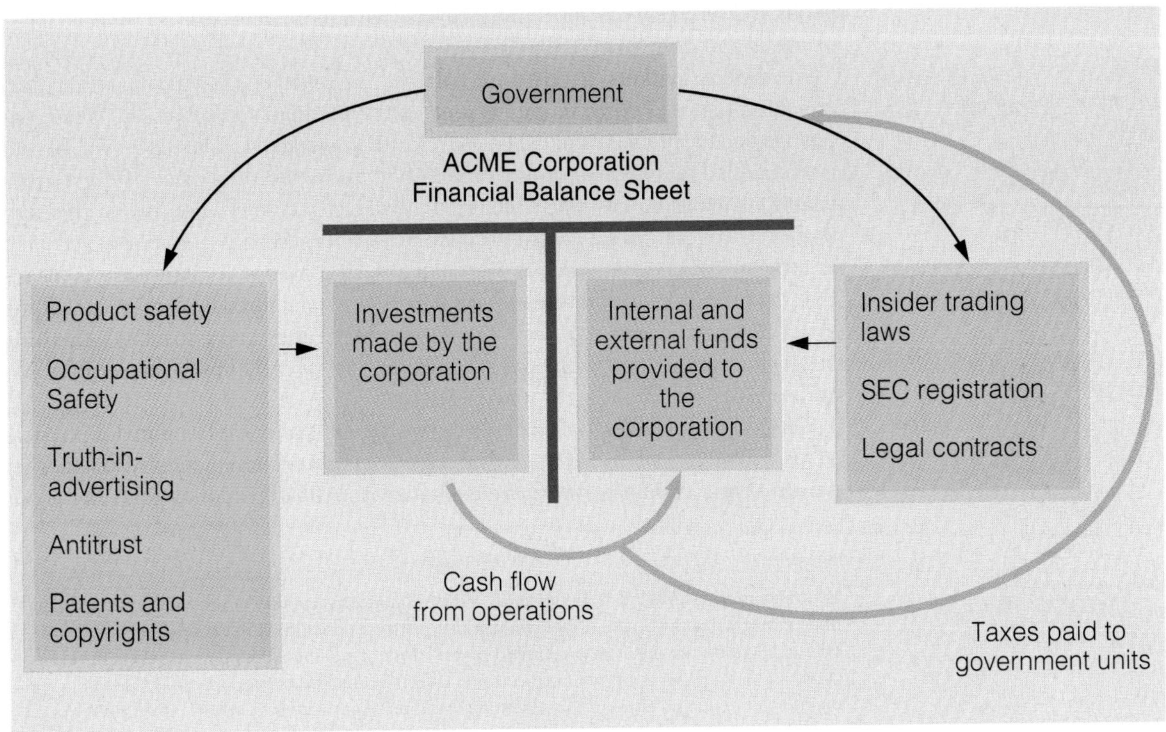

to identify and correct chemical waste problems. Therefore, corporate managers should view governmental involvement in business activities not just as costly intervention, but also as creating opportunities.

MARKETS AND EXCHANGE

Some General Comments About Markets

Before describing the markets in which corporations operate, we want to discuss the role of markets in general. All markets, no matter what their form, have a common purpose; they provide a mechanism for individuals and businesses to exchange goods and services by bringing interested buyers and sellers together. Transactions between willing participants result in both parties being better off. If each trader did not believe that the trade was in his or her interest, they would not make the exchange. Therefore, markets enhance people's well-being.

Markets lower search costs. For example, compare equipping an apartment with a single stop at a large discount store to doing so at a series of garage sales.

Markets are essential to any economic system, and evidence of markets is found in even ancient societies. Markets come in a variety of shapes and sizes. They can be places, such as shopping malls and the floor of the New York Stock Exchange. But exchange no longer requires going to a particular physical location. Modern telecommunications allow markets to be computer networks or television programs. And everyone has experienced the growth of catalog shopping. The importance and desirability of convenient and speedy exchange means that markets undergo constant refinement and change. Immense energy and ingenuity go into developing ways to facilitate exchange. Everyone benefits as exchange becomes easier and cheaper, and more sellers (with a broader range of goods and services) can meet more buyers (with more money and a broader range of needs and desires).

In ancient markets, goods were bartered, or exchanged, without any money changing hands. Today, money is used as the medium of exchange.[4] When exchange occurs, price is established even in *barter markets*. For instance, if a Toyota is exchanged for 30 cases of fine French burgundy, then the price of the Toyota is established as 30 cases of wine, or the price of a case of wine is one-thirtieth that of a Toyota. Money facilitates exchange, because it is commonly accepted as a means of counting and storing value. Using money in transactions means that the French are not limited to driving cars manufactured by companies willing to trade for wine and that Japanese car manufacturers can consume something other than burgundy. Exchange without money severely limits the set of goods and services available to consumers.

Often our view of markets and exchange extends only to shopping for physical items. However, when we buy or hire services, we exchange money for another person's time. When we work we exchange our time for money (and the goods

[4]Not all barter occurred in ancient times. With the nonconvertibility of the ruble, much initial trade with the former Soviet Union was through barter. Pepsico took its profits from soft-drink sales in the form of vodka. In the United States barter or trading clubs allow members to trade goods and services without money. Electronic ledgers keep track of transactions. Of course, some might argue that the tallies in this electronic bank represent a kind of money, albeit not physical cash or coins, but with most of the attributes of a medium of exchange.

and services it can buy). Although exchange often involves the simultaneous payment of money and receipt of a good or service, sometimes one side of the exchange is delayed. This occurs frequently in the field of finance. Investing money today brings no immediate benefits. What is being bought is the expectation of more money in the future. Similarly, a college education requires paying now (in terms of time and money) for future benefits (a better job and broader view of the world). These examples show that markets need not involve the simultaneous exchange of money for goods.

Markets and Information

Markets not only facilitate exchange, they also generate and process information. Information is the lifeblood of markets. Without information, much exchange would not occur and many markets would not exist. The single most valuable type of information created by markets is *price*. Prices established by transactions in relatively free and competitive markets are the most fundamental measure of economic value. The market price of an asset, good, or service provides information about equivalent nontraded items. Using current market prices we can infer the value of many items without having to actually sell them. Prices also help individuals and businesses plan for the future. Prices tell potential buyers and sellers the current value placed on an item. With that information, producers can decide whether to expand or contract their production of particular items, and consumers can adjust their spending and savings patterns.

Reinforce the concept of prices as allocating signals by asking students to consider how they find substitutes when the price of an item rises.

Prices also help allocate raw materials to their highest-valued uses and cause talented workers to migrate to employers willing to pay them the highest wage for their skills. As demand for sought-after goods (and services) pushes prices up, the producers of those goods (and services) can afford to pay more for inputs, so they bid skilled labor and raw materials away from other users. By shifting inputs to their most highly valued use, prices help determine the most efficient allocation of scarce resources within an economy.[5] Indeed, prices are the primary piece of information used to coordinate the incredibly varied activities of a modern economy.

In many societies where haggling occurs, prices depend on the skill and perseverance of the buyer and seller.

There are different kinds of prices. We place much more trust in *market prices* than in other types of prices. If you have ever shopped for a car, a computer, a camera, or a piece of stereo equipment, you know about *list*, or *suggested retail, prices*. Few transactions actually occur at these *asking*, or *list*, prices (if no one has ever mentioned this to you, you should look for a few new friends and start reading ads in big city newspapers before your next purchase). In fact, these listed prices, such as automobile sticker prices, are virtually ignored by consumers.[6] Computer magazines display this disregard for list prices by publishing what they

[5]You probably recognize this as the neoclassical market model of economics. For a very thorough, but readable, discussion, of this model—its benefits and limitations—see Chapter 3 of Paul Milgrom and John Roberts, *Economics, Organization and Management*, (Englewood Cliffs, N.J. 07632: Prentice Hall, 1992).

[6]Interestingly, in late 1992 several auto manufacturers began campaigns to make the *sticker price* the *sales price*. For example, Saturn dealerships advertise that they do not haggle over price; you pay the sticker price.

call *street prices*, the price a consumer with a bit of sophistication pays for an item.

We want to stress the importance of prices being set in markets. In some socialist countries prices were determined by bureaucrats. In the former Soviet Union, immense economic distortions resulted from nonmarket prices: bread once cost less than the grain used in its production! Only with the information provided by prices set in competitive markets can an economy approach an efficient allocation of resources.

The Two Meanings of Efficiency

As you may have learned in an economics course, economic efficiency refers to the allocation of resources across an economy; that is, economists talk about **allocative efficiency**. An efficient allocation implies that no alternative allocation will increase consumer satisfaction. Sometimes economics texts refer to allocative efficiency as a Pareto optimal allocation of resources. **Pareto optimality** requires that there is no alternative allocation that would make one person better off without harming someone else. If such an alternative exists such that one person benefits without harming anyone else, it is a more efficient (or a Pareto superior) allocation of the economy's resources. Thus, in economics *efficiency* usually refers to the allocation of resources to various uses within an economy.

The term efficiency has a specific meaning in finance, where we speak of the efficiency of financial markets. **Efficient financial markets** quickly adjust prices to reflect new information, so we describe this type of efficiency as **informational efficiency**. The degree of efficiency in a market depends on the type of information used to determine prices and the competition to use that information. Informational efficiency is one of the most important concepts in finance, so we will be developing the concept in greater detail later in this chapter. Economists' use of allocative efficiency assumes prices are also informationally efficient. If prices do not reflect all available information, then the signals they send will not result in an efficient allocation of resources. Thus, the two connotations for efficiency actually converge.

CORPORATIONS AND MARKETS

Today's reengineering and flattening of corporations is the latest stage in an ongoing process to make businesses more efficient and responsive to market demand.

One important lesson of modern finance is that corporations are defined in large part by the markets in which they operate. Therefore, in many respects finance is the study of markets. Understanding the markets in which corporations participate is essential to understanding corporations themselves. The financial balance sheet identifies two categories of such markets, product and financial. Corporate assets, such as plant, equipment, and human resources, are shown on the left-hand side of the financial balance sheet and reflect the corporation's activity in product markets. The right-hand side of the financial balance sheet shows how the firm financed those assets; that is, it presents a record of the firm's activities in the financial markets. As Figure 2.2 shows, the corporation acts as a conduit, linking investment funds from the financial markets to goods and services in the product markets. The corporation invests the funds in machinery, factories, raw

FIGURE 2.2

FINANCIAL BALANCE SHEET WITH MARKETS

How the corporation interacts with the product and financial markets.

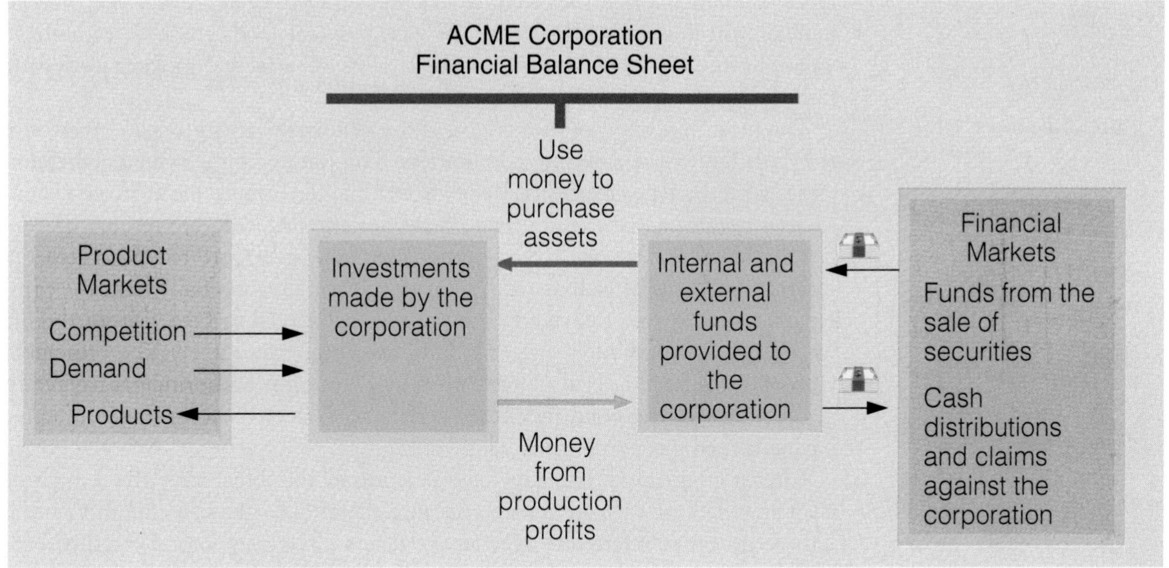

materials, and skilled personnel, which are organized to produce items that consumers want.

Transparency Available

Our discussion of markets begins in the next section, where we describe the financial markets in which firms obtain funds. We also discuss the attributes required for these markets to generate prices that quickly and accurately reflect all the available information about a company and its future prospects. The information contained in this section is important to students whether or not they plan on becoming financial managers. Anyone who invests in stocks, has a retirement plan, uses credit, or thinks he or she may want to start a business someday needs to understand something about financial markets.

FINANCIAL MARKETS

Corporations dominate our economy in part because they have ready access to financial markets. Financial markets provide funds to firms for investment in productive assets. Besides furnishing funds for corporate investment, financial markets also provide investors opportunities to put their savings to work. By coordinating the savings activities of individuals and the investment needs of corporations, financial markets play a key role in the continuing economic development of our country. In this section, we describe the basic attributes of financial markets and continue our discussion of market efficiency.

Financial Securities, Transferability, and Liquidity

As we begin our study of financial markets we focus on stocks and bonds, the most common financial securities issued by corporations. There are many more types of financial securities than stocks and bonds, because every year new financial instruments are introduced. As with physical goods, these securities have value; however their value derives from the rights attached to their ownership rather than their physical attributes.

The most important of these rights is the claim a security gives an investor to the cash flows of the issuing corporation. The nature of these financial claims varies with the type of security. Recall from Chapter 1 that some are fixed claims, such as bonds or loans, and others, such as common stock, are residual claims. Bondholders lend money to the corporation and, in return, receive a series of interest payments as well as repayment of the amount originally lent, the principal amount. Interest payments are typically scheduled twice a year for the life of a bond. At the bond's maturity date, the corporation repays the principal.[7] Corporations have a legal obligation to make interest and principal payments, as scheduled in the **bond indenture contract**.[8] Failure to make the contractual payments can force a company into bankruptcy.

After a company pays all its fixed or contractual obligations, the remaining cash flows belong to shareholders. Because shareholders have a claim to what is leftover, they are referred to as *residual claimants*. The corporation can distribute cash to shareholders in the form of dividends. Alternatively, the company may keep some or all of the residual cash flows to invest in new projects or products; money that shareholders have a claim to but that is kept in the firm is called **retained earnings**. If managers invest these funds wisely, the company's stock price rises to reflect the higher anticipated future cash flows. Shareholders benefit in two ways from their ownership stake in a corporation: they may receive cash dividends and/or they may sell the firm's stock at a price higher than they paid. The sale of a share of stock results in a **capital gain** (or a capital loss) if the sale price is greater (or less) than the purchase price. Both bonds and stocks can create capital gains; however, capital gains are more often associated with common stock. The total return from an investment in common stock includes both the return from dividends and the return from capital gains.

McDonald's did not pay dividends for many years. Instead, the company retained its cash and used the money to finance the construction of new restaurants.

The very important decision about how much cash to retain in the company varies from industry to industry and varies during a company's life cycle. Older, more stable companies often generate more cash than needed to finance their investment opportunities, so they distribute cash as dividends. Many new, high-growth companies pay no dividends, choosing instead to use all residual cash

---

[7]A bondholder may sell a bond prior to maturity, receiving whatever the market price is for the bond at that time. Once a bond is sold, the new owner receives the remaining interest and principal payments.

[8]The borrowing corporation makes a bond indenture contract with a trustee, usually a bank or trust company. The indenture obligates the borrowing company to comply with a set of predetermined conditions that the trustee monitors on behalf of the lenders. The indenture conditions typically include maintaining certain levels of liquidity and limit additional borrowing, the sale of significant assets, and the payment to shareholders of large cash dividends. The objective of these constraints is to help assure that bondholders will receive their promised interest and principal payments in full and on time.

flows to expand the firm. Presumably, if managers and the board of directors decide to retain cash in the firm, that cash will finance investments that will increase the wealth of shareholders by increasing the future cash flows to which shareholders hold a claim. If the company does not have wealth-increasing investment opportunities, it should distribute the money to shareholders, who can then invest it elsewhere. The decision of whether to invest cash on behalf of shareholders or distribute cash to shareholders is an important one in corporate finance. We devote several chapters of the text to discussing methods for determining whether or not investments will increase shareholder wealth.

In addition to the claim to cash flows, attributes such as transferability and liquidity can affect a security's value. With very few exceptions, financial securities are *negotiable*, meaning that they may be sold or transferred to other investors. A distinguishing feature of corporations, compared to other types of business organizations, is the ease with which ownership can be transferred from one investor to another. **Transferability** of ownership contributes to the longevity and growth potential of corporations. Although all securities traded in financial markets are negotiable, the ease with which transfer occurs varies depending upon a security's **liquidity**. Liquidity refers to the ability to sell a security quickly without having to offer a substantial price reduction to attract buyers. Securities that trade infrequently, often called **thinly traded**, are particularly prone to problems of illiquidity.[9] One of the key benefits of well-developed financial markets is the increased liquidity such markets provide. By bringing together more buyers and sellers, liquidity increases and the costs of transferring ownership fall.

Primary and Secondary Markets

Securities trade in financial markets, the best known of which are the stock exchanges in New York, London, and Tokyo. These markets are phenomenally active and competitive. You probably have seen pictures of the trading floor of the New York Stock Exchange, with its frenzied and seemingly chaotic activity. Yet, for all their notoriety, these exchanges do not raise money for corporations; instead, they provide a market for investors to buy and sell existing stocks and bonds. These exchange markets are called **secondary markets**. So dominant are these secondary markets that an investor may spend a lifetime trading stocks and bonds and never directly contribute money to a corporation. However, secondary markets are very important because the price discovery that occurs in these markets determines the market value of corporations and signals investors' beliefs about how companies are expected to perform in the future. Secondary market prices provide a report card on the performance of corporate managers.

Markets that handle the initial issuance of securities, securities that actually raise money for the issuing corporations, are called **primary markets**. Primary markets bring new security issues to life. Two categories of primary market

[9]Illiquidity is not just a theoretical concern. During the 1980s investors placed billions of dollars into a variety of limited partnerships, often in the real estate or energy areas. By the 1990s, with the decline of the real estate and oil and gas markets, the value of these partnership interests had fallen. Compounding the problem was the illiquidity of these securities. Investors who wanted to get out could do so only by accepting pennies on the dollar. In part, their losses were due to the illiquidity of these particular securities.

Most IPOs are oversubscribed. When an average person gets an allocation of shares, it is often seen as a mixed blessing: Getting the shares is good, but the fact that everyone ahead of you in line turned them down is bad.

transactions exist: *seasoned* and *unseasoned.* A **seasoned security issue** occurs when a corporation issues more of an existing security. For example, if AT&T issues additional shares of its common stock, it is a seasoned issue; the stock being issued already trades in the marketplace, so investors know a great deal about its value from secondary trading in the stock. In fact, secondary market transactions will largely determine the price and other terms of trade for new seasoned offerings. If the market price for AT&T stock on the New York Stock Exchange is $60, there would be few buyers for a new issue of the same stock priced at $65 or even $61. **Unseasoned issues** are new securities; the issuing company has no identical security that is currently publicly traded. Unseasoned issues (often called an **initial public offering**, or IPO) have no track record, so they require more effort to value than do seasoned issues. This lack of historical market information about a company results in a systematic underpricing of IPOs. On average, the initial price assigned to a new unseasoned stock issue is about 15% low; that is, the price assigned the stock by underwriters (the investment bankers organizing the stock offerings) is about 15% below the price the stock will trade at immediately after it is issued. Various theories have been suggested for this phenomenon. One theory argues that because so little information is available about the stock, it must be underpriced so that relatively poorly informed investors will buy the shares. A second theory proposed by some knowledgeable investors suggests that underwriters knowingly underprice new issues and then allocate the underpriced shares to favored clients, who earn a significant profit by selling the first day of issue.

FIGURE 2.3
PRIMARY AND SECONDARY CAPITAL MARKETS

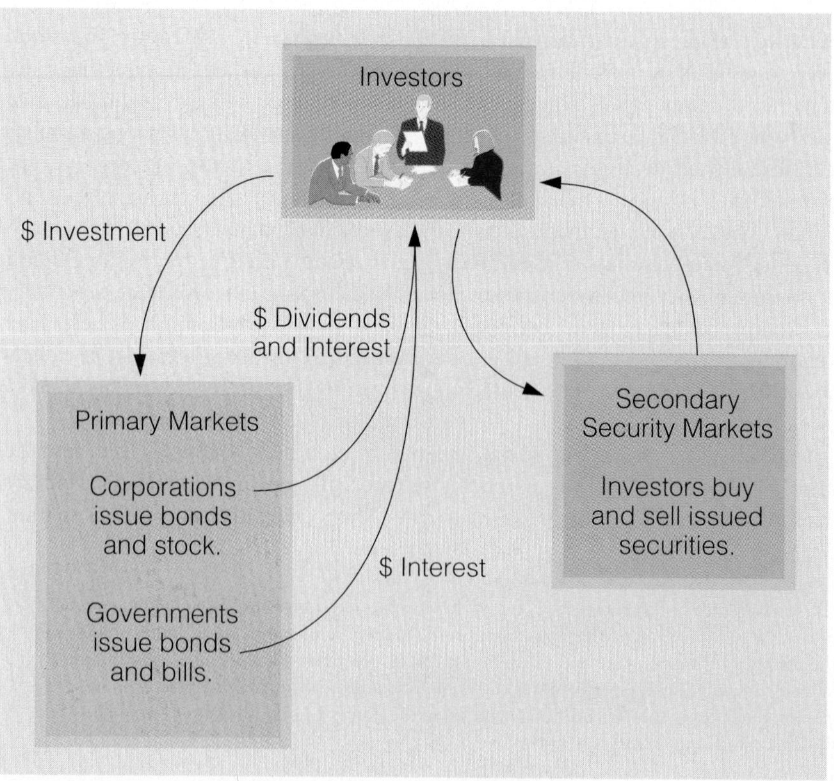

Transparency Available

Money and Capital Markets

Companies access the financial markets to obtain funds for long-term growth as well as for short-term or seasonal needs. Within finance *short-term* has come to mean securities with maturities of 1 year or less. Short-term securities trade in **money markets**. Money market instruments include commercial paper and U.S. Treasury bills. **Commercial paper** is a promissory note (with a maturity of 270 days or less) issued by a company. **U.S. treasury bills**, which are sold weekly, have maturities of 13, 26, or 52 weeks. By convention, *long-term* refers to securities with a life greater than 1 year from the date of their original sale. Economists sometimes make a somewhat finer distinction: *Intermediate-term* securities have maturities of 1 to 10 years. Thus, U.S. Treasury notes fall into this category, as do some corporate debt instruments. Intermediate and long-term securities, such as stocks and bonds, trade in **capital markets**. As with capital markets, there are primary and secondary money markets. Figure 2.4 summarizes the distinctions between money and capital markets and primary and secondary markets.

Short-term corresponds roughly to the concept of *current* in accounting.

Money markets process an enormous volume of transactions, a much higher volume than the capital markets. One of the reasons for this activity is that many money market claims are very short lived, some as short as one day. Imagine renewing a borrowing or lending arrangement every day. Many banks do exactly that. These are the markets in which a large portion (about 30%) of all U.S. government debt is financed and in which the largest national and international banks are particularly active.[10] As interesting as money markets are, we shift our focus to the capital markets, where corporations make long-term financing decisions and where secondary trading establishes prices that reflect the success of managerial decisions and effectiveness of the corporation as a wealth producing entity.

	Money Markets	Capital Markets
Primary	Original issuance of short-term securities Treasury bills Commercial paper	Original issuance of long-term securities Corporate stocks and bonds Treasury bonds
Secondary	Trading among investors in short-term securities	Trading among investors in long-term securities • NYSE • AMEX • NASDAQ

FIGURE 2.4
FINANCIAL MARKET CLASSIFICATION

Transparency Available

[10]For a thorough discussion of money markets, see Marcia Stigum,*The Money Market: Myth, Reality and Practice*, (Homewood, Ill.: Dow Jones-Irwin, 1983).

Secondary capital markets occur in two forms: exchanges and over-the-counter markets. The most familiar capital market is the New York Stock Exchange (**NYSE**). The NYSE is the oldest and largest stock exchange in the United States. Of the exchanges, second in importance to the NYSE is the American Stock Exchange (AMEX). A number of regional stock exchanges compete with the NYSE and AMEX. Boston, Philadelphia, and San Francisco (the Pacific Stock Exchange) all have stock exchanges. Purchasing shares of stock listed on the NYSE (or any other stock exchange) typically requires contacting your local *stockbroker* (sometimes called a commission broker, a retail broker, or an account executive) with your order information. The stockbroker relays your order to the brokerage firm's headquarters, which then transmits the order to the brokerage's *floor broker* positioned on the trading floor of the NYSE. The floor broker takes the order to the trading post for the particular stock you want to buy, say IBM or Xerox. Your floor broker looks for floor brokers representing sellers, and bidding ensues until an acceptable price emerges. If so, an exchange occurs. Note that transactions between floor brokers involve representatives of the seller and buyer setting the transaction price in an auctionlike setting. If the floor broker cannot find a seller at an appropriate price, your order may be filled by the **specialist** in the stock or may be entered in the specialist's order book for later execution if the price moves in the right direction. Each stock has an assigned specialist, who maintains a fair and orderly market in his or her particular stock or stocks. The NYSE expects specialists to use their personal accounts to even out temporary imbalances between sell and buy orders. Thus the New York Stock Exchange can be thought of a specialist-based auction market; the specialist is very much at the center of trading activity on the floor of the New York Stock Exchange, and many trades involve price setting by auction.

To be listed on the NYSE a company must meet certain financial standards and follow the NYSE's information disclosure policy. Initial listing requirements include having at least 2,200 shareholders, a market value of at least $18 million (market value is the number of shares outstanding times the price per share), and pretax profits of at least $2.5 million for the most recent year and $2 million for the preceding two years.[11] In addition to these financial attributes, companies must agree to follow the NYSE's disclosure rules, which require accurate and timely disclosure of any information that will likely affect the value of the companies' securities. Listing requirements for other exchanges are less demanding than those of the NYSE.

The **over-the-counter** (OTC) **market** lists the stocks of far more companies than the NYSE, though the dollar value of NYSE-listed companies exceeds that of the OTC. When companies first make an offering of stock to the public (called *going public*) they most often do so by being traded over the counter. Most trading in corporate bonds occurs in the over-the-counter market. The term over the counter comes from the period in the development of financial markets when banks were the primary dealers in stocks and bonds. Investors completed transactions at bank counters, thereby trading over the counter.

---

[11]Some variations to these requirements are allowed. For instance, companies satisfy the pretax earnings standard by having aggregate earnings over the most recent three years of $6.5 million and earnings of at least $4.5 million in the most recent year. See the annual *NYSE Fact Book* for current listing requirements.

Trading in the largest and most active OTC stocks occurs through the National Association of Securities Dealers Automated Quote System **(NASDAQ),** a nationwide computerized network of dealers. Computer terminals linked to the NASDAQ system give brokerage firms access to all the current quotations for all stocks on the system (no bonds are traded through the NASDAQ system). Price quotations include **ask prices** (what the dealer will sell the security for; the price they are *asking*) and **bid prices** (what they will pay for the security). The ask price always exceeds the bid price, albeit sometimes by only a few cents. Buying a NASDAQ system stock requires the broker (or a trader at a brokerage company's headquarters) to find the lowest asking price and contact the dealer offering that price to confirm the transaction. Trading on the NASDAQ system relies far less on person-to-person communication than trading on the NYSE and so offers fewer opportunities for auctionlike price setting than do transactions on stock exchanges. Evidence suggests that NASDAQ's dealer system results in higher trading costs per dollar of stock price.[12] In the future, stock exchanges may follow the approach taken recently by the Toronto Stock Exchange. Its system combines the speed and accuracy of modern computers with the auction pricing of the specialist system. A specialist maintains an orderly market in each stock. But the specialist's order book has been replaced by an electronic order book that shows all offers to buy and sell. When prices cross, transactions occur. Because the process can be monitored, there is little room for customers to wonder if they paid too much or received too little for their shares.

The relative activity of the New York and American stock exchanges and NASDAQ is shown in Exhibit 2.1. Over the past 10 years, the number of shares traded per day on the NASDAQ has grown to nearly equal the volume traded on the NYSE. However, if volume is measured in dollars, the NYSE far outstrips

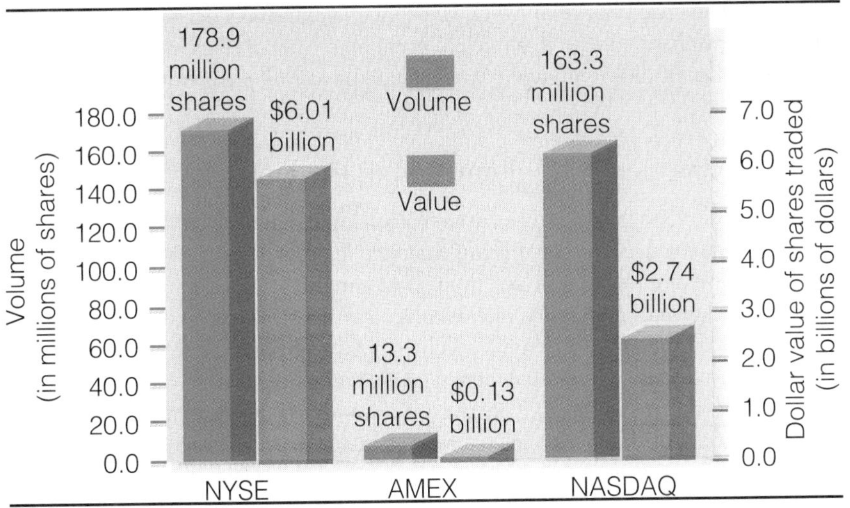

EXHIBIT 2.1

A COMPARISON OF DAILY SHARE VOLUME AND DAILY DOLLAR VOLUME AT THE NEW YORK AND AMERICAN STOCK EXCHANGES AND THE NASDAQ MARKET, 1991

SOURCE: *Securities Industry Yearbook, 1992/1993*, Securities Industry Association, pp. 878–9.

[12]For a very readable discussion of differences in the specialist and dealer-based trading systems, see Gretchen Morgenson, "Fun and Games on Nasdaq," *Forbes* (August 16, 1993): 74–80.

all other U.S. stock markets. By the end of 1992, stock trading volume on the NYSE was averaging over a billion shares a week, with an aggregate value in excess of $8 billion daily.

Whenever you buy or sell securities, whether you trade on the NYSE or NASDAQ system, you pay **transaction costs**. These costs include the commission paid to your broker and the **bid-ask spread**, the difference between the bid price and the asking price. If you buy a share of stock you pay an ask price, and when you sell you receive a bid price. For heavily traded stocks the bid-ask spread is small (less than 1% of the share price), but for infrequently or thinly traded stocks, the spread can be significant (in the range of 3% to 6% of the share price).[13]

Non–U.S. Financial Markets

Since the early 1970s, when fixed foreign currency exchange rates were replaced by market-determined rates, competitive foreign financial markets, called *Euromarkets*, have developed rapidly, driven by modern technology and the imperatives of international trade. Today, investors can buy IBM stock on the Tokyo Stock Exchange or Toyota stock on the New York Stock Exchange. A U.S. company can use the Euromarket to finance a construction project in France by issuing bonds denominated in German deutsche marks. The bonds may be sold, or underwritten, by the London office of a Japanese securities firm. These international markets provide increased investment and financing opportunities for corporate managers. Managers who ignore these markets do so at their own peril.

Stock exchanges are emerging throughout the world. In India, there are more than 3,000 publicly traded stocks, second only to the United States in the number of traded stocks. Active stock markets exist in Russia, Korea, Turkey, Thailand, Zimbabwe, most Latin American countries, and in the People's Republic of China. In fact, the Shanghai Stock Exchange is extremely active, despite being in a noncapitalist country. Exhibit 2.2 compares various stock markets in terms of the number of different stocks traded and the value of the companies listed.

Competition and Information in the Financial Markets

In investing the question is not how good a company is. Even terrible companies can be good investments at the right price.

Although there are many complicated institutional details associated with financial markets, the basic force driving financial market transactions is amazingly simple: People are trying to make money. Companies that issue securities in the primary markets compete with one another for investors' dollars. Investors trading in secondary markets compete to buy stocks and bonds that appear likely to pay large dividends, interest payments, or capital gains, relative to other securities. Competing investors bid up the price of shares of companies with good prospects and bid down the share price of those with declining prospects. In

[13]Very low priced, infrequently traded *penny stocks* often have bid-ask spreads in excess of 25%, meaning an investor must see the price of his or her stock increase by 25% just to break even on the investment.

EXHIBIT 2.2

A Comparison of Stock Markets Around the World According to Number of Stocks Listed and Market Value as of December 1992

ECONOMY	NUMBER OF STOCKS	MARKET VALUE OF STOCKS (IN BILLIONS OF DOLLARS)
Industrial Markets		
Canada	1,119	243.02
France	786	350.86
Germany	665	348.14
Japan	2,118	2,399.00
Switzerland	180	195.29
United Kingdom	1,874	838.58
United States	7,014	4,757.88
Emerging Markets		
Argentina	175	18.63
Brazil	565	45.26
Chile	80	29.64
Colombia	80	5.68
Greece	129	9.49
India	2,781	65.12
Indonesia	155	12.04
Jordan	103	3.37
Korea (South)	688	107.45
Malaysia	366	94.00
Mexico	195	139.06
Nigeria	153	1.22
Pakistan	628	8.03
Philippines	170	13.79
Portugal	191	9.21
Taiwan	256	1,101.12
Thailand	305	58.26
Turkey	145	9.93
Venezuela	66	7.60
Zimbabwe	62	0.63

SOURCE: Adapted from Stijn Claessens, Susmita Dasgupta, and Jack Glen, "Return Behavior in Emerging Stock Markets," *The World Bank Economic Review*, Vol. 9, NO. 1 (January 1995): 131–51.

many ways, securities are seen as substitutes. Investors actively shift their funds to those securities with the brightest prospects. A confirmed Pepsi drinker, who might never consider changing to Coca-Cola or Dr. Pepper, has no compunction at all about selling stock in PepsiCo and buying stock in Coca-Cola. Investing is about money and the prospects of companies, and brand loyalty plays little role. Therefore, one soda pop stock is as good as another, and the best one is the stock that provides the highest expected total return (i.e., dividends and capital gain), no matter whether the investor likes the taste of the product or not.

Stock prices are about the future. The best stock picker has a fairly accurate picture of the future and can envision how a company will prosper in that future.

Investors compete with one another to make better predictions about the future cash flows associated with financial claims. If you correctly predict that a company's prospects have improved before other investors, you can buy shares at a bargain price. Conversely, if you realize that a company's fortunes have fallen before the crowd does, you can profit by selling shares now and repurchasing them at a lower price later.[14] Because all investors are competing for the same goal—to predict a security's future cash flows—the relevant information focuses on how companies will fare in the future. Investors crave information that helps them make better predictions (or form more accurate expectations) about a firm's prospects than other investors. In a sense, investors compete with one another for better information and better methods of processing that information. An immense information industry has evolved to serve the needs of investors. Brokerage houses offer research in exchange for commissions; thousands of professional investors sell advice through newsletters; there are dozens of electronic databases and computer programs for investment analysis; and, every year dozens of books appear with tips on how to *beat the market*.

Every day thousands of investors digest the latest information and make investment decisions based on this information. Competition among investors assures that security prices accurately reflect the consensus opinion or expectation about a security's future cash flows. Thus, security prices are an objective, or unbiased, assessment of a company's value, given the available information. That securities are accurately priced is something like a good-news/bad-news joke. The good news is that securities are fairly priced, so investors will not, on average, get tricked and lose lots of money. The bad news is that securities are fairly priced so investors will not, on average, outsmart the market and make an extraordinary amount of money.

Everyone has heard about someone, an uncle or family friend, who has made a fortune in the stock market. This happens. Sadly, many people have lost their fortunes in the stock market, but you rarely hear about them. Investor competition does not imply that no one ever becomes enormously wealthy trading securities. It does mean that the majority of investors earn just a normal return—not too big, not too small—from investing in stocks and bonds. Some investors do better than others and some do worse, but the average return is just sufficient for investors to continue to invest in the market.[15] Expected returns vary across securities. We will see later in the text that returns are related to risk; that is, investors expect higher returns for investing in riskier securities. Chapters 7 and 8 develop this very important relationship between risk and return.

Informational Efficiency in Financial Markets

As we have just discussed, investors compete with one another for information that will give them an edge in assessing the value of financial securities. This competition means that security prices quickly reflect the information used by investors. Remember that once an investor obtains and analyzes pertinent in-

---

[14]Investors sometimes carry out transactions called short sales, in which they sell a stock they don't own but have borrowed, planning on buying it in the future to even out the transaction. This strategy is especially applicable to situations where investors believe that a stock's price will fall. They sell today at a high price, and buy in the future at a lower price. The purchase allows them to return the borrowed stock, and the difference between the high selling price and lower purchase price is their profit (less transaction costs, of course).

[15]If average or expected returns were too low, then investors would not invest. This would cause security prices to drop, raising returns. If returns were too high, investors would flood the market, bidding up prices. An equilibrium occurs when actual long-run returns match long-run expected returns.

formation, he or she must rush to implement the buy-sell decision before other investors can take advantage of the information. In this race to buy or sell securities, prices respond by rising or falling. Therefore, security prices quickly reflect new information.

Financial markets in which prices reflect all relevant information are called *informationally efficient* markets. There are some questions, however, about the type of information that security prices incorporate and how accurately and quickly prices reflect that information. Because the buying and selling activities of investors drive security price changes, a more precise statement of the issues might be: What type of information do investors use to form expectations about security values, and how accurately and quickly does that information appear in security prices? These questions are of particular interest to investors and corporate managers, because the answers help determine how profitable financial market activities are likely to be. The answers to these questions also provide a method of classifying financial markets according to their degree of efficiency. Financial economists talk about three possible levels of market efficiency: *weak form*, *semistrong form*, and *strong form* efficiency. These classifications differ according to the type of information that is quickly incorporated into security prices.

The **weak form** of the **efficient markets hypothesis** assumes that security prices incorporate only historical price and volume data. If markets are weak-form efficient, then investors cannot earn abnormally high profits using trading rules based on historical price and volume patterns. Weak form efficiency challenges *chartists* or *technical analysts*, who claim that they can identify profitable security investments by examining charts and graphs of historical price and volume data. Compelling evidence exists that securities markets are weak-form efficient. That financial markets are at least weakly efficient makes sense. Suppose there was a pattern of prices that investors could use to predict future prices. For example, suppose stock prices always increase on Wednesdays. Because investors have nearly costless and immediate access to price and volume data, they can quickly identify such a pattern. Smart investors would buy stock on Tuesdays, preparing for the Wednesday rally. Their strategy would be to sell late on Wednesday, after security prices rose, and earn supranormal profits. Still-smarter investors would buy shares on Monday (or the previous Thursday or Friday) to get ready for the Wednesday rally. But in preparing for the Wednesday rally, the buying activities of the smart investors would drive prices up on Mondays and Tuesdays, reducing, if not completely eliminating, the trading profits on Wednesday. Once investors recognize a pricing pattern, they will invest in anticipation of that pattern and thereby eliminate it. Therefore, it is highly unlikely that investors can earn abnormal profits using strategies based solely on historical price and volume information.

Hint: Bring in an example of a stock price that has changed in response to a news release to reinforce the notion that prices respond to public information.

The **semistrong form** of the efficient markets hypothesis assumes that security prices fully reflect all publicly available information, including historical price and volume data. If markets are semistrong form efficient, then investors cannot earn abnormally high returns by trading on publicly available information about the company or its industry, such as corporate annual and quarterly reports, press releases, articles in the *Wall Street Journal* or other business publications, or government statistics. Investment professionals refer to analysis of such data as **fundamental analysis**. Semistrong form efficiency implies that, on average, fundamental analysis will not result in abnormally high profits. It is not necessary that all investors have this information, but enough must that sufficient trading occurs to cause prices to adjust to new information. In general, the economic research finds that our major financial markets are semistrong efficient. There is evidence, however, that the market prices of *neglected stocks* (stocks with a very limited following of analysts and investors) only slowly reflect publicly available information. With few analysts or investors to figure out how new information will affect a company's prospects, it may take some time for a stock's price to adjust to new information about the company, its competitors, or its industry.

We do not want to leave the impression that semistrong form efficiency impounds only recent factual or financial information about a company into security prices. Market participants use all available types of information to form expectations about a company's future; that is, they try to anticipate what a company's value will be or how the company will perform in the future. A few examples might clarify this concept of anticipatory, or forward-looking, pricing. Suppose a company announces that its strategy for the next few years is to acquire firms in several business areas. Its stock price reacts in anticipation to what that implies about the company's future cash flows. When the company announces an actual acquisition it is making, the stock price response reflects how investors feel about this specific acquisition compared to what they anticipated. Thus, the announcement of a potentially profitable acquisition might be met with a reduction in share price, if investors had expected an even more profitable acquisition. Similarly, each quarter when companies announce their earnings, stock prices may fall on earnings increases and rise on earnings decreases if the increases were less than anticipated or the decreases were not as large as anticipated.

Stock prices, on average, increase about 3.5% at the announcement that a company's founder has died suddenly. See the Instructor's Manual for the citation.

In markets that are semistrong form efficient, stock prices vary in response to a wide range of new information. Prices provide a scorecard that shows how investors feel about a company's future prospects given corporate decisions and a changing environment. If management has positioned the company to take advantage of economic trends then prices rise. On the other hand, if management has not foreseen changes in its product markets then investors will reflect that lack of foresight in a lower share price. In some cases managers cannot be expected to move entirely out of an industry that investors do not favor. Even in this case, however, share price acts as a report card on managerial quality. A good management team will foresee problems and prepare for them, so their company's share price will fall less dramatically than competitors'. Thus, share price adjustments, relative to a competitive universe, provide a valuable tool for evaluating the quality of a company's management team.

The third category of market efficiency is **strong-form efficiency**, which assumes that security prices fully incorporate all public information plus all nonpublic information, such as information available only to the managers within a corporation. Strong-form efficiency occurs if trading by corporate insiders, using their privileged information, moves stock prices to accurately reflect that information. There is no doubt that inside information exists. There is doubt, however, about whether the trading of insiders incorporates that information into security prices. We know that when significant news items are released to the public, such as the award or loss of a major contract or a new technological discovery, stock prices change dramatically. This suggests that if insider trading based on the information occurred, it did not occur in sufficient volume for prices to completely reflect the information. There is a growing interest in the buying and selling of corporate executives. Every Wednesday the *Wall Street Journal* publishes the "Inside Track" column, which discusses recent trades by corporate insiders.[16]

Doubt about strong-form efficiency also arises from laws prohibiting insider trading. These laws attempt to create a *level playing field* for outside investors. The problem these laws address is one of asymmetric information. **Asymmetric information** means that one person or group has more information than some other person or group. Asymmetric information is not necessarily bad. In the case of stock market investing, however, it can create serious problems. If outside investors know that insiders can make stock market trades using their privileged information, they will be hesitant to trade. Outsiders know they will undoubtedly lose money in trades with insiders.[17] Therefore, allowing insiders to trade on private information drives other investors out of the market, reducing liquidity and the investment dollars available for corporate growth. Laws prohibiting **insider trading** increase investor trust and, thereby, their willingness to invest.

The used-car market provides a good example of asymmetric information.

The penalties for insider trading are severe. All profits from the illegal trades must be forfeited, fines and prison sentences may be imposed. Furthermore, stockbrokers, bankers, and lawyers can be banned from future involvement in the securities business, if convicted of insider trading. As the insider trading cases of Dennis Levine, Ivan Boesky, and Michael Milken in the late 1980s show, federal prosecutors and the U.S. Securities and Exchange Commission take insider trading crimes very seriously.

Figure 2.5 shows how the various levels of market efficiency compare in terms of their assumptions about the information reflected in security prices. Notice how the various types of market efficiency relate to the information that is included in stock prices. You may also think of efficiency in terms of asymmetric information. Markets are efficient in the weak form because there is no asym-

Increasing information included in stock prices
Weak-form efficiency
Stock prices reflect price and volume information.
Semistrong-form efficiency
Stock prices reflect all publicly available information.
Strong-form efficiency
Stock prices reflect all public and private information.

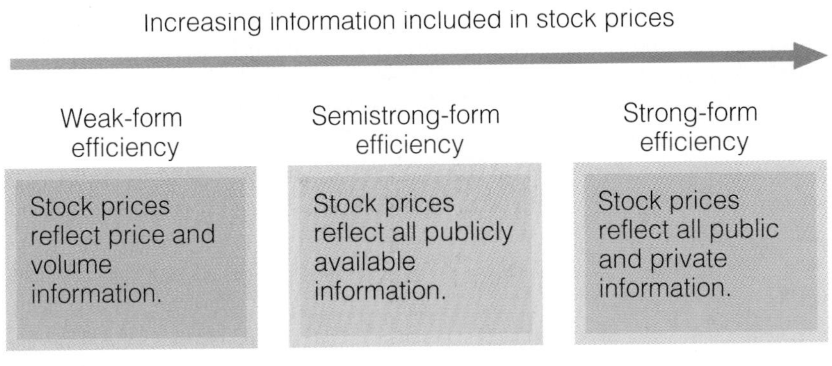

FIGURE 2.5
LEVELS OF FINANCIAL MARKET EFFICIENCY

Transparency Available

[16]For an interesting discussion of the trading profits earned by executives buying and selling shares in their own company, see "Insiders Reap Big Gains From Big Trades" by Alexandra Peers, *Wall Street Journal* (September 23, 1992): C1.

[17]For example, suppose a manager knows that the firm's quarterly earnings will be much lower than investors anticipate. The manager could sell stock before the news is released at a price of $45. After the news release, the price might fall to $40. The noninside investors who bought shares from the manager at $45 find themselves owning shares worth only $40.

metry of information regarding historical price and volume data; that is, everyone has exactly the same information about historical prices and trading volumes. Semistrong-form efficiency holds in many markets, because there are few differences (or asymmetries) among investors in terms of their access to public information. Strong-form efficiency rarely holds because of obvious asymmetries of information. Strong-form efficiency states that stock prices include some private (and therefore unavailable) information, but this requires that insiders trade on that information, which is illegal. Without sufficient numbers of investors trading on private information, that information cannot work its way into stock prices.[18]

Informational Efficiency and Profits From Investing

The lesson of efficient markets is that it is extremely difficult to earn abnormally high returns from investing using publicly available information. Many students find this result discouraging, because it dashes their hopes of making an easy fortune in the stock market. But there is encouraging news as well: At any moment in time actively traded financial securities will be fairly priced, so you may reasonably expect to earn a fair return on your money. In other words, you don't have to be a genius to do quite well with your savings.

Reinforce the idea that to succeed companies must produce goods and services of value to consumers.

Applying the lesson of efficient markets to corporations is straightforward. Corporate managers will rarely enhance the wealth of shareholders (the key decision criterion for managers) through financial market transactions in efficient markets. In many ways this is good news for corporate officers. Efficient markets imply that prices reflect available information, or that prices are fair. When companies issue securities, on average, they receive a fair price for those securities. Therefore, managers can concern themselves primarily with how the funds will be used, not on how the funds were obtained. Efficient markets make the job of financial managers simpler. Moreover, fair and efficient financial markets, such as those with prohibitions against insider trading, encourage investors to participate and thereby increase the pool of available funds. A larger supply of investment dollars translates into a lower price for those dollars, so corporate managers benefit in a second way. In efficient markets, they gain access to fairly priced and relatively inexpensive funds.

If corporate managers cannot profit from transactions in efficient financial markets, they must look elsewhere for profitable investment opportunities. The obvious place to seek profits is in the product markets. As we will see in the next section, if shareholder wealth is to be enhanced, the product markets are the place to do it.

PRODUCT MARKETS

Perfect and Imperfect Competition

Impress on students that economic theory provides a valuable framework for making many types of investment decisions.

In perfectly competitive product markets, no single producer has an advantage in cost, product quality, distribution or any other aspect of the business, and

[18]A single investor can shift prices if other investors believe that person has special knowledge and they learn of trades made by that informed investor.

consumers instantaneously substitute items from one producer for those from another, basing their decisions exclusively on price. From microeconomics, we know that in markets with a high degree of product substitutability and easy entry, competition drives selling price to the minimum average cost of production, and producers earn only a normal profit. Moreover, to remain competitive firms must constantly try to improve their production technology. Therefore, with perfect competition, goods are produced as efficiently as possible and consumers pay the lowest price that allows production to continue.

Competition is valuable for two reasons: It increases productive efficiency (i.e., reduces waste) and creates lower prices (i.e., increases consumer wealth).

Although perfectly competitive markets are rare, highly competitive markets are more common than you might imagine. Markets selling products that are considered commodities, such as gasoline, coal, steel, sugar, and wheat, are extremely competitive, with many consumers using price as their primary purchase criterion. Generic products at supermarkets represent products that are very nearly commodities, because many shoppers look at price alone when buying these items. Competitive markets emerge from two sources. Some products are commodities (and therefore perfect substitutes), so the markets selling those products become highly competitive. For example, one pound of sugar is very similar to any other pound of sugar, assuming minimal standards of product quality, such as cleanliness, are satisfied. Highly competitive markets also emerge when a market allows easy entry. Such a situation occurred in the personal computer market. Even as late as the mid-1980s, IBM and Compaq were able to charge premium prices for their personal computers. As computer technology became more widespread, the high prices charged by U.S. producers attracted entry into the market. Low-cost machines from new companies in the United States (for example, Dell) as well as from established Asian producers quickly cut into IBM's and Compaq's market share. Eventually they were forced to lower prices and devise new methods to market their machines. The ability of competitors to build substitutes for the IBM and Compaq computers dramatically increased the competitiveness of the personal computer market.

Can you see any similarities between perfectly competitive product markets and efficient financial markets? In both markets, participants should expect to earn only a normal profit. Investors, like consumers of commodity goods, shop based on price. When their analysis identifies a promising security, they happily substitute that security for others in their portfolio. Are shares of stock commodities? Not really, but entry is easy. Suppose that a firm issued a security with some features that investors wanted. Investors would bid up the price of the security to obtain those features. Other companies could easily duplicate those features and issue competing securities.[19] The ease of entry allows a sufficient number of such securities to be issued, so investors no longer have to pay a premium. Although successful innovators initially earn large rewards, these rewards are short lived as success attracts imitators and competitors.

Kellogg's spends $32 million each year advertising Frosted Flakes! *Source: Life* (February 1995): 68.

In imperfectly competitive markets, producers use product differentiation and brand loyalty to impede substitution. **Product differentiation** depends on consumers having fairly complex needs or desires. Product differentiation requires identifying specific consumer needs and then producing a product or service

[19]Imitation of security design is not prohibited. It is extremely difficult (close to impossible) to receive a copyright or patent for a financial security. Without such protection, the features of securities can be freely copied.

specially designed to satisfy those needs.[20] This process is amply demonstrated with a product as simple as shampoo. To differentiate their product from generic shampoo, manufacturers produce shampoos for people who dye their hair, have perms, have dry or oily hair, have black, blond, or red hair, have dandruff or other scalp diseases, or shampoo often. Shampoos come with and without conditioners, with vitamins, with recommendations from celebrities, with designer names attached, and in a variety of fragrances and colors. And, there are a number of shampoos designed specifically for children. The goal of this immense effort in shampoo research and promotion is to produce a shampoo that fits consumers' needs so well that they have no incentive to change brands. Once this brand loyalty is established, consumers will pay a premium price for their preferred product rather than substitute for a less desirable brand of shampoo. By slowing the urge to substitute, producers earn higher than normal profits and thereby enhance shareholder wealth (if product development and advertising costs do not exceed the price premium).

The process of differentiation goes on continuously. Innovators must constantly improve existing products and develop new ones, because imitators quickly copy (or nearly copy) successful items. The existence of higher-than-normal profits attracts these entrants. With more producers vying for a particular market segment, price—and, thereby, profit—typically falls. Supranormal profits from product innovation can be very short-lived. Therefore, managers must constantly seek new opportunities and shift their product mix into those emerging markets. The days of making a single product and relaxing as the money rolls in (if there ever were days like that) are over. Competition within the United States, as well as from abroad, means that managers must be extremely vigilant in monitoring market conditions and be prepared to fight for existing products while continuously looking for new products and markets.

Creating Shareholder Wealth in the Product Markets

It is helpful to reinforce the value of the nonfinance business disciplines.

From our discussion of imperfect competition, we can begin to describe the factors required to create wealth for shareholders in the product markets. To earn the supranormal profits that enrich shareholders, most of the following six factors must be satisfied.

1. Consumers must have relatively complex tastes for the product.
2. The perceived needs or desires of a particular consumer group or segment must be able to be identified.
3. Sales price must exceed the cost of developing, producing, and marketing the item.
4. The segment must be large enough to make production worthwhile.
5. The features that make the product especially appropriate for the targeted segment must be able to be communicated.
6. If successful, entry by potential competitors must be able to be impeded.

[20]Innovators on Wall Street have begun using the differentiation concept. Each year new financial instruments debut, with special attributes that make them attractive to a narrow clientele of investors. These instruments may earn their creators a somewhat higher-than-expected return in the short run, but difficulties in copyrighting financial products means that competitors quickly copy good ideas. Entry by imitators reduces the returns to a normal level.

The first factor defines the types of products that can be differentiated. Omitted from this set are commodities, such as steel, oil, flour, sugar, and gasoline. When consumers use only a single or few attributes to choose between substitute products, there is very little room for differentiation and price becomes the prime consideration. The attraction of supranormal profits is so great that we sometimes see companies trying to differentiate their commodity-type products. Oil refiners, such as Texaco, Chevron, Exxon, and Shell, try to differentiate their gasolines by including engine-cleaning or mileage-enhancing additives. The inability of consumers to see the effectiveness of these additives may make such efforts futile. Later in this section we discuss an alternative explanation of consumers preferring brand name gasoline.

The second factor requires identifying some set of attributes of the targeted segment so an appropriate product or service and an effective communication strategy can be developed. The third and fourth factors assure that the product will be profitable. If the targeted group is very unique, then a well-specified product may earn a large price premium. The uniqueness of the segment (and its estimated demand) determines how much investment can be made in research, development, and setup costs. Similarly, a large segment supports more investment than a small segment. Sophisticated market research helps managers make these strategic choices.

The fifth factor addresses advertising. A product that ideally matches a target group's needs is worthless if people do not know about it. Advertising communicates the features of differentiated products. To be worthwhile, investments in advertising must produce increases in sales or keep existing customers from shifting to competitors' products. The *advertising wars* waged by soft-drink manufacturers show how protecting market share can drive advertising decisions.

Business success requires constant vigilance: developing new products, protecting existing markets from entry, and trying to find lower-cost production methods.

From our perspective, the sixth factor may be the most important. Long-term benefits for shareholders require that managers find ways to protect differentiated products from imitators. As we discussed earlier, a successful product invariably attracts imitators, and once an alternative appears, substitution drives prices down. Short-term benefits to innovation exist because it takes time for competitors to determine if the market segment is valuable enough to enter and to develop a competing product. Over a prolonged period, competing products appear and the supranormal profits that benefit shareholders vanish. The longer the company can postpone this erosion of above-normal profits, the better off shareholders will be.

Competing products often enter a market at a lower price than the original product. This approach attracts consumers. If the two products are very similar, then price becomes a determining factor in consumers' buying decisions. The lower price also reflects the lower costs of imitation. The new entrant does not have to do as much research and development as the innovator and so has lower costs. Consumers obviously benefit from entry via imitation. After entry, they purchase items at lower prices. There is, however, a serious problem with imitation. If many firms follow a wait-and-copy strategy, innovative firms have little incentive to develop new products, particularly those that require substantial research and development investment. Investing in new products allows short-term profits to be earned, but competitors quickly reduce those profits through imitation and entry. Imitation reduces innovation. Without the draw of long-term profits, it is often not beneficial to shareholders to make new product investments.

Location also offers protection from imitation. Location cannot be copied. Wal-Mart and McDonald's succeed in part because they are so good at identifying good locations.

The problem of imitation reducing the incentive to invent is so serious that laws have been passed to address it. Patent and copyright protection postpone the direct imitation of new products. Patents allow firms to sustain a competitive advantage. Patents apply to technological innovations, not services or financial instruments. Moreover, patent protection is not complete. A clever competitor can design around a patent by adding or modifying features on the original product.

Legal protection is not the only method used to protect innovation. Some companies protect and prolong their market opportunities because they have some asset that competitors find costly or difficult to duplicate. Examples of such assets are established plants and distribution channels or access to superior technology or information. Competitors may decide that the investment in plant or distribution channels is too high to warrant entry. Some firms may make investments in excess factory space or particularly efficient distribution channels to ward off competitors. Such strategic investments tell potential entrants that the incumbent firm will fight ferociously before giving up market share to a new entrant. Potential entrants may look for other opportunities rather than get involved in a costly battle. Large investments in advertising can provide the same signal to potential competitors. The entrant must invest in advertising equal to or greater than that of the incumbent. Having to make large investments in advertising can discourage entrants. Strategic investment may also involve choosing a good location for a store or manufacturing facility. There are many other clever ways that producers have devised to discourage competitors. A comprehensive list is probably impossible to construct, because managers are constantly trying to design new ways to protect their market niches.

Earlier we discussed how gasoline refiners try to differentiate gasoline, which is very nearly a commodity good. Although consumers have great difficulty determining if gasoline additives provide any benefits, many consumers appear to ignore price differences and buy brand name gasoline. Such behavior may not have anything to do with product differentiation but may represent consumers looking at total cost or minimum quality standards. Name brand gasoline may offer drivers a perceived guarantee of a minimal standard of quality. Many drivers are willing to pay a premium for this assurance.

Franchises, such as McDonald's and Burger King, also offer a known standard of quality. When you travel you may prefer to eat at a well-known restaurant chain, such as McDonald's, Wendy's, or Burger King, rather than try an unknown cafe. The unknown diner might offer much greater value, or it may be quite awful—greasy, dirty, poor-tasting food, limited selection, and so on. The national chains offer a known standard of quality. In many situations, consumers prefer a certain known quality to uncertain quality. This may explain the value of franchises. McDonald's, Wendy's, and Burger King (and motel chains such as Travelodge, Best Western, and La Quinta) offer customers an implicit quality guarantee. If you have a bad experience at one outlet, you can make your feelings known by not using other outlets in the chain. Franchisees understand this spillover effect, so they use peer pressure as well as contracts to assure that all franchise outlets maintain a minimal standard of quality. Independent restaurants, gas stations, or motels have little to lose if your experience is a poor one. The chances of a repeat visit are small, so they forfeit repeat business for immediate profit.

SUMMARY

In this chapter, we have discussed the environment in which businesses operate. Government, in its effort to address the needs and desires of various constituencies, stimulates some types of business behavior while limiting or prohibiting other types of activities. Within the boundaries established by government, businesses participate in two kinds of markets. The financial markets provide funds for expansion and also assign value to the securities of publicly traded companies. The firm's financial market activities are reflected on the right-hand side of the financial balance sheet. The left-hand side shows the firm's involvement with the product markets. Product markets provide raw materials for production and a market for the company's goods and services. Product markets offer almost the only opportunity for earning above-normal returns, and even these opportunities are limited. To earn higher than normal profits, a company must find and protect a market niche (or niches). Moreover, the company must be able to satisfy the consumers in this market segment with goods that the firm can produce profitably. Protecting the niche requires preventing or discouraging competitors from entering. The government provides some protection from competition through patents and copyrights. As you can see, earning high returns for shareholders requires an understanding of marketing, business strategy, and manufacturing operations as well as financial management.

Our discussion of financial markets centered on the efficiency of those markets—that is, how quickly and accurately new information appears in security prices. With abundant information and many participants seeking the same goal—to earn a high return by buying and selling securities—we argued that financial security markets are extremely efficient. The government helps assure the integrity and efficiency of financial security markets by mandating a level playing field for investors.

As future managers, it is important that you understand some of the implications of financial market efficiency. First, changes in the value of a company's prospects will quickly and accurately be reflected in the market prices of the company's securities (its stock and bonds). Thus, the market value of the firm offers an objective, or unbiased, assessment of the quality of management's performance. Second, financial markets offer companies access to capital at fair, competitive rates and so offer individual investors fair and competitive returns on their investments as well. Therefore, although corporate managers should carefully analyze the decisions that affect the right-hand side of the balance sheet, it is unlikely that those decisions will yield the high returns that shareholders dream of.[21]

Unlike financial markets, where everyone is looking for money, in product markets consumers often want an array of attributes in the goods and services

---

[21]Later we will discuss how carefully choosing the mix of debt and equity used to finance the company's assets can affect the value of the firm. Although decisions on the right-hand side of the balance sheet can affect shareholder wealth, the opportunities for increasing shareholder wealth in the financial markets are extremely limited compared with the opportunities available in the product markets.

they buy. For example, people buy cars for transportation, but they also consider comfort, safety, pizzazz, image, and different types of performance. Recall that the objective of the financial manager is to maximize the wealth of the company's shareholders. By far the best way to achieve that objective is by carefully choosing and managing the investments on the left-hand side of the balance sheet in order to establish and protect competitive advantages in the product markets. The intense competition faced by businesspeople today means that managers must be prepared to protect their existing products while constantly looking for new products or markets.

This chapter discussed where managers are likely to find opportunities for enhancing the wealth of their company's shareholders. We concluded that managers must look to the product markets. The key consideration in making such investments, as always, is to choose those left-hand side investments whose value exceeds their cost. How we determine when that criterion is satisfied is the subject of the next six chapters. The next chapter provides an intuitive introduction to value, which is the cornerstone of finance. Chapters 4 through 8 then demonstrate how this intuition is applied to each of the components of value—estimating expected cash flows and considering their timing and riskiness—and then all the pieces are combined into a single method for evaluating proposed investments. This chapter told you where to look for promising products, and the following six chapters show you how to determine whether or not those potential products are actually worth the investment required of the firm.

KEY TERMS

product markets
financial markets
informationally efficient
perfectly competitive
imperfectly competitive
allocative efficiency
pareto optimality
efficient financial markets
informational efficiency
bond indenture contract
retained earnings
capital gain
transferability
liquidity
thinly traded
secondary markets
primary markets
seasoned security issue
unseasoned issues
initial public offering
money markets
commercial paper
U.S. treasury bills
capital markets
NYSE
specialist
over-the-counter market
NASDAQ
ask price
bid price
transaction costs
bid-ask spread
weak-form efficiency
efficient markets hypothesis
semistrong form efficiency
fundamental analysis
strong-form efficiency
asymmetric information
insider trading
product differentiation

QUESTIONS

1. How do dividends and interest payments differ with respect to scheduling and certainty?
2. Are the consequences to the corporation more serious for missing a dividend or missing an interest payment?
3. Owning a share of stock gives a shareholder a claim on what type of cash flows?
4. Answer true or false. (If false, explain why.)
   - **a.** Patents provide products with an eternal protection from imitation.
   - **b.** Economists agree that consumers would benefit if all industries were free of regulatory constraints.
   - **c.** Most trading in securities occurs in the secondary market.
   - **d.** Liquidity means being able to sell a security immediately at your asking price.
   - **e.** The efficient markets hypothesis states that if you efficiently analyze stocks and bonds, it is possible to earn above-average returns over extended periods of time.
   - **f.** In the weak form of market efficiency, security prices reflect historical patterns of prices and trading volumes.
5. Fill in each blank.
   - **a.** Corporate bonds are sold and traded in ______ (money/capital) markets.
   - **b.** Security prices are determined in ______ (primary/secondary) markets.
   - **c.** Stocks and bonds are liquid because of the existence of ______ (primary/secondary) markets.
   - **d.** The ______ (product/financial) markets offer companies the best opportunities for enhancing shareholder wealth.
   - **e.** Perfectly competitive product markets offer the ______ (greatest/least) opportunities for increasing shareholder wealth.
   - **f.** The semistrong form of market efficiency assumes that all ______ (public/private) information is quickly impounded in security prices.
6. Does *liquidity* add to or detract from the value of a security? Explain.
7. Suppose the financial markets are semistrong-form efficient. If Merck, the large pharmaceutical company, announces it has just developed a drug that is effective against the AIDS virus, what will happen to its stock price? What about the stock prices of competitors in the pharmaceutical industry? What would the announcement-date stock price response be if Merck regularly made public the progress of its development efforts?
8. Do companies that sell commodity-type products (i.e., products sold in nearly perfectly competitive markets) advertise? Why or why not?
9. Explain how laws that prohibit insider trading affect the availability of investment funds and trading liquidity.
10. Why do we say that stock prices determined in efficient financial markets provide a scoreboard about corporate executive decision making?
11. Discuss why financial market efficiency is important to corporate managers from two perspectives: (a) as a *report card* of their performance and (b) as they raise capital to finance left-hand side investments.

12. Explain why if a company announces that its earnings are 25% lower than the previous quarter, its stock price may rise. (*Hint*: Remember that stock prices are forward-looking.)
13. Why might a unique location lead to abnormally high profits for a fast-food store?
14. Consider your answer to Question 13. Who would capture most of these profits if the landowner selling the vacant lot to the fast-food chain understood the location's potential and was able to quantify its value? Contrast this to the landowner who does not understand the lot's potential.
15. Consider a franchise, such as McDonald's, which has a reputation for cleanliness, a uniform product, and fast service. Suppose a franchisee has an outlet and can cut costs by hiring fewer employees, cleaning the restrooms less frequently, and putting less meat in the hamburgers. Thus, this franchisee earns abnormally high returns by *cutting corners*. If this behavior is widespread and unabated, what affect will it have on the stock price of the McDonald's Corporation? Why?
16. Referring to Question 15, if you were a corporate manager at McDonald's, what would you do to protect the interests of shareholders? Stated somewhat differently, what left-hand-side investment does McDonald's make to protect its competitive advantage?
17. We classified wheat as a commodity-type good. Users freely substitute between competitors, making their purchase decisions almost entirely on price. If wheat is a commodity-type good, what about bread?
18. Suppose you have an antique oriental rug that has recently been appraised by an expert as being worth $5,000. You also own 100 shares of stock that is traded on the New York Stock Exchange at $45 per share. Now imagine that you must raise as much money as possible in the next 24 hours. Which asset do you think would generate the most cash in this limited period of time? Which asset is the most *liquid* and why?
19. You have a summer job working for a large corporation whose stock trades on the New York Stock Exchange. You are assigned the task of cleaning out an old storage room and you discover a box filled with 200,000 gold coins, worth $1,000 each. The first thing you do is call a stockbroker and buy some of the corporation's stock. The next day the announcement of your discovery is made to the press, and the price of the stock rises. Your action violated insider trading rules (and you could go to jail!). Did it also violate semi-strong-form market efficiency?
20. Rather than breaking the law, as in Question 19, you wait to buy the stock until the day after the public announcement of the discovery. Now, however, the stock price does not do anything dramatic for weeks, and you make no extraordinary return on your investment. What happened? Does this scenario violate semistrong market efficiency?
21. As a divisional manager for a large manufacturer of yard furniture and garden equipment, you make the first analysis of new product ideas before sending them to a companywide committee for funding. One of your employees has just presented a proposal to you. He proposes to add several Velcro strips to both lawn furniture frames and pads to eliminate problems of the pads slipping off of the frames. He claims this will set the company's furniture apart from competitors', and his analysis shows continued sales growth as well as

higher profit margins. Would you send his proposal and analysis, as it stands, to the committee? If not, what would you ask him to reconsider?

22. Name one way that the government enhances and one way it restricts shareholder-wealth maximization in the pharmaceutical industry. If shareholders suffer under some types of government intervention, who wins and how do they win?
23. Tax policy creates behavioral incentives. Explain how corporate behavior would change in each case.
    a. Interest expense on debt was no longer a tax deductible expense.
    b. The government paid all retraining and relocation expenses, plus the first year's wages, for new hires who had previously lost their jobs in the Pacific Northwest's timber industry.
24. Suppose you can see into the future. You look ahead 20 years and identify several firms that have enormous stock price increases between now and then. You immediately go out and buy shares of stock in all of the companies and wait for the price to jump. What must occur before you reap the benefits of your insights?
25. Comment on the following statement by a first-year MBA student:

    The *efficient markets hypothesis* says that all investors earn a normal rate of return for the risk they bear; therefore, if I buy shares in a well-known company, I should expect to receive constant annual returns of about 12% or 13%, year in and year out.

26. Does liquidity affect the efficiency of financial markets? In other words, is the pricing of thinly traded stocks as efficient as the pricing of stocks that are constantly being traded?
27. In markets where there are no brokers or agents, where buyers and sellers deal directly with one another, are transaction costs zero? Explain why or why not.
28. Taxes create incentives for certain types of behavior. Suppose that the U.S. Congress suddenly eliminated all taxes on profits earned buying and selling securities—that is, they eliminated the capital gains tax. How would investors respond and who would benefit?
29. In a market that is weak-form efficient, price movements are said to have no memory. Explain this saying.
30. Consider the following history of product development. First, there was soap. Then came shampoo. Then dandruff shampoo and "no-tears" baby shampoo were created. Shampoo for dyed hair was also created about this time.
    a. Do you think this story is as much an economic story as it is a story about chemistry? Why or why not?
    b. Why do you think there is no shampoo (that the authors know about) that is both no-tears and for dyed hair?
31. A dealer of a NASDAQ-traded stock quotes a *bid price* of $14 a share and an *ask price* of $16. If you buy 100 shares of this stock and sell a month later, what is your profit or loss if the price quotations did not change and no dividends were paid during the 1-month holding period?
32. Do you think that Euromarkets and the emerging stock markets around the globe enhance or detract from the efficiency of U.S. financial markets?

33. Many limited partnership shares (units) were sold in the primary financial markets during the early 1980s. Unfortunately for the purchasers of these investments, there is no active secondary market for most of these limited partnership units.
    - **a.** Do you think these units are highly liquid? Why or why not?
    - **b.** Can you think of other investments with an active primary market but that lack an active secondary market?
    - **c.** What effect do you think the lack of a secondary market has on an investment's primary market? (*Hint*: Consider the baseball card craze. Do you think that baseball card manufacturers have a stake in the active trading of baseball cards among collectors?)

CHAPTER 3

Value: The Cornerstone of Finance

. . . of course I'll be taking a loss.

Value is related to the benefits of owning an asset, along with the risk that those benefits will not actually materialize. Smart Eddie's customers may not realize much benefit from owning this old jalopy even if they buy it below Eddie's cost. We'll take a closer look at the elements that contribute to value in Chapter 3.

Some observers claim that stakeholders other than shareholders need to be considered. In many cases serving shareholders also serves these other groups.

To reduce anxiety, we try to link some of what students already know or have experienced to financial thinking.

hapters 1 and 2 described the corporation and its environment. The corporation creates value for shareholders by modifying a set of inputs into a more highly valued set of outputs. This process can involve changing a raw material such as iron ore into steel or combining planes, trucks, and people so packages arrive anywhere in the world within 24 hours of being sent. To create shareholder wealth, corporate managers must identify and pursue profitable investments and ignore unprofitable ones. This chapter introduces the fundamental concepts used in evaluating investment opportunities.

The chapter begins by showing how some fundamental financial concepts arise from human behavior. From your experience as a student, employee, consumer, and family member, you already have many of the insights about human behavior needed to understand the intuition underlying financial decision making. In this chapter, we help you apply those insights to the valuation of investment opportunities.

The valuation process introduced here and developed in more detail in Chapters 4 through 9 applies equally to corporations choosing products to manufacture, investors studying stocks and bonds, and individuals making investment decisions about houses, cars, or retirement. The same fundamental concepts apply to all types of investments. Making an investment requires that someone decides to commit funds today for greater expected wealth in the future. In committing funds, the investor gives up the use of that money until the investment pays off. Committing money to an investment means postponing some consumption and giving up other investment opportunities. Learning how to evaluate investments means learning when committing funds today is likely to result in more future wealth. It also means learning to compare various types of investments to determine which are likely to be the most beneficial. Evaluating investments is a very valuable skill, whether your investments are limited to family finances—buying a car or house or planning for retirement—or involve multimillion dollar corporate deals. Therefore, even if you don't become a corporate executive or a stock broker, the concepts and tools introduced here will help you make better financial decisions for your family. This chapter is the first step in learning those concepts and tools.

The key elements of the chapter are:

- Six factors that investors consider when evaluating a potential investment
- The *required rate of return* and its importance in valuing investments
- The basic valuation equation used to evaluate investment prospects

If you understand these concepts, you are well on your way to making good financial decisions.

HUMAN BEHAVIOR AND THE EVALUATION OF INVESTMENTS

Corporate finance and financial decision making involve people transacting and making decisions. It should not be surprising, then, that much of what we study in finance classes can be linked to various aspects of human behavior. We discuss several behavioral traits important to economic decisions and from them develop six factors that investors consider when making investment decisions.

We simplify our discussion of the human behavior underlying finance by focusing on corporate financial decision making. This simplifies our task in a number of ways. First, as we discussed in Chapter 1, corporate managers have a clear duty to the shareholders of the corporation. Their job is to maximize the wealth of the shareholders. This provides a clear criterion with which to evaluate potential investments: Does the investment increase shareholders' wealth, and, of the investments available, does it provide the maximum increase? Second, corporate financial transactions typically involve strangers (or at least involve parties that are not close friends or family). Separating financial decisions from personal relationships reduces the types of human behavior that might influence investment decisions.

We identify three primary aspects of human behavior that appear to affect economic decisions. The first is *rational self-interest*: concern over how a decision will affect a person's well-being. The second is *risk aversion*: the preference for less risk. The third factor is the *time preference of money*: the preference for earlier rather than later cash flows.

Rational Self-Interest

This economic concept goes back at least to Adam Smith's *Wealth of Nations*.

Individuals make decisions based on how they think the decision will affect their well-being. Corporate managers make decisions that benefit shareholders not just out of duty, but because such behavior increases the likelihood of promotion, pay raises, and bonuses. If corporate incentive structures are designed properly, managers acting in their self-interest will concurrently make the best decisions for shareholders. The concept of **rational self-interest** often triggers images of companies doing anything to increase profits—polluting, mistreating employees, making poor-quality products, or providing mediocre service. But rational self-interest does not imply such behavior. Managers' self-interest—pay, promotion, bonuses—depends on making decisions that assure the long-term profitability of the firm. Treating employees or customers poorly might increase profits one time but almost assuredly has a detrimental effect over the long term. Similarly, excessive pollution eventually results in fines, an unhealthy community, and a soiled public image. Therefore, rational self-interest, combined with the manager's duty to shareholders, dictates against actions that harm the long-term viability of the corporation.

Risk Aversion

Business degrees are often associated with a higher probability of getting a job after graduation, so such degrees may be an example of risk aversion.

The second behavioral characteristic we identify as important to investment decisions is **risk aversion**. Risk aversion implies that individuals prefer less risk to more risk and that individuals willingly pay to reduce risk. The insurance industry exists for just this purpose. Risk aversion also implies the converse of paying to reduce risk; that is, investors must be paid to accept additional risk. Risky investments must offer special benefits to attract investors. Corporate managers must relate an investment's risk to the premium shareholders require for bearing that level of risk.

Time value, or interest, may be thought of as rent paid for the use of an asset, money.

Time Preference of Money

The third trait we identify as influencing investment decisions is the **time preference of money**. Both individuals and corporations display a preference for receiving investment payouts earlier rather than later. As we discuss later, this time preference arises for several reasons: the cost of giving up other investment opportunities, the increased risk associated with longer investment periods, the greater exposure to unanticipated inflation, and the desire to be compensated for postponing consumption.

From these behavioral tendencies we derive the following six factors that investors consider when evaluating potential investments:

- The investment's expected future cash flows
- The timing of the cash flows
- The expected effect of inflation over the investment period
- The investment's risk (or the variability of the investment's cash flows)
- New options or opportunities created by the investment
- The payoff from alternative investment opportunities

Our objective in this chapter is to provide a rationale for using these six factors in the evaluation of investments and to combine them into a single model of investment valuation.

RATIONALITY AND HAPPINESS

We assume throughout this text that people are rational and clever; that is, we believe that people generally make good decisions, are not easily fooled, and quickly recognize and take advantage of beneficial opportunities. This doesn't imply that individuals can foretell the future or that they always make the correct decision. It does mean that within the limits of the information they have (or can reasonably acquire) and their ability to process that information, they make the best decisions they can.

We also assume that people try to maximize their happiness (an economist would say that people make decisions to maximize their utility). For investors, maximizing utility translates into maximizing their wealth. Wealth measures their potential consumption of goods and services. Most individuals are investors, directly or indirectly. Investing in stocks and bonds, participating in retirement programs, and having savings accounts are all examples of how individuals invest. They willingly postpone current consumption in the hope of consuming more in the future.

It might be useful to mention that people make trade-offs between work (money) and leisure, trading potential income for time, and vice versa.

In terms of wealth, we assume that people prefer having more rather than less; the greater a person's consumption power, the happier they are. How people choose to use their wealth—on themselves, their friends and family, their community, for altruistic purposes, or on a mix of these—is up to them. Even people who devote their lives to charitable activities would prefer to have more, rather than less, to give to those causes. Having more wealth means they can provide more for whomever or whatever purpose they choose.

Combining our assumptions of rationality and wealth maximization produces a model of human behavior based on rational self-interest. When faced with a decision, people will figure out, to the best of their ability, how to maximize their personal gain. As we will see throughout the text, this model of rational self-interest helps explain the way that corporations are designed, contracts are written, and prices are determined. One of the most important lessons you can take away from your finance course is recognizing how rational self-interest affects the transactions in which you are involved.

RATIONAL SELF-INTEREST: EXPECTED CASH FLOW MATTERS

Cash Flows and Market Values Versus Accounting Earnings, Profits, and Book Values

Stress early and often the importance of cash, and distinguish cash from accounting earnings or accounting income.

Rational self-interest implies that investors assess investments based on the future consumption opportunities the investment is expected to provide. Because consumption requires money, an investment's cash flows measure its ability to increase the consumption capability of investors. Individuals need cash to acquire goods and services; corporations need cash to pay employees, to service debt, to distribute as dividends to shareholders, and to buy additional productive assets. Therefore, we argue that cash flows are the appropriate measure of an investment's benefits.

People sometimes use the terms net income, earnings, and profit when they actually are talking about cash flow. This use is incorrect. In finance and accounting these three terms—net income, earnings, and profits—refer to items from a company's income statement, not to actual cash flow. Various accounting rules (such as revenue recognition methods, the matching principle, and noncash charges) cause these income statement measures to differ from cash flow. In Chapter 4, we discuss why these differences arise and describe how to translate accounting profits or earnings into cash flows. At this point, the important thing to remember is that when evaluating investment opportunities, we need to estimate the cash flows from the investment, not the earnings or the accounting profits.

Accounting rules can also make the **book value of assets**, such as machinery, buildings, land, and inventory, differ from the **market value**, or cash value, **of the assets** if the assets were sold. Accountants compute the book value of a firm's assets as the asset's historical cost less accumulated depreciation. However, the book value may not be close to the sales price, or market value, of the asset. For example, a company buys a high-speed lathe for $30,000 in 1988. Over the next 5 years, following standard accounting practices, they depreciate the machine $3,000 per year. By 1993, the book value of the lathe is $15,000 ($30,000 − 5 × $3,000). Suppose that over that same period great technical strides have brought a new generation of lathes to the market. These new lathes have computer-assisted operation, require fewer employees to operate, waste less material, and produce precision metal parts to a finer tolerance than the older designs. In addition, they sell for about $35,000. If the company tries to sell the old lathe, which has a book value of $15,000, they may find the most anyone will pay is $6,000 or $8,000. Thus, the market price is well below $10,000, but the book value is $15,000. The depreciation does not consider the effect of obsolescence on the lathe's value, so it does not reflect the actual selling price or market value. Because we are interested in cash flows, the amount we would receive if we sell the asset (the market value) is more important than the asset's book value. (Note, however, that book values can have important tax consequences and so cannot be totally dismissed).

We suspect that if cash flow was announced, followed by the corresponding earnings news, there would be no stock price response to the earnings announcement, because all the important information was in the cash flow news.

Rational self-interest tells us that cash flows and market values matter to investors. An investment's cash flows and market value provide a gauge of the purchasing or consumption power that an investment will generate. Therefore, we must base an investment analysis on the cash flows or market values associated with the investment. For example, a share of stock generates cash flows in the form of quarterly dividends. Changes in share price (the stock's market value) also affect shareholder's wealth, because share price indicates how much cash the share can be sold for at a given point in time. Rationality suggests that investors care more about a share's dividends and market price than they do about accounting earnings or profits. That is not to say that investors don't pay attention to accounting earnings or profits. If earnings or profits signal how dividends or share price might change, then investors will (and do) react to news about these accounting numbers. Keep in mind, however, that the reaction arises because of the message that earnings and profits carry about cash flows.

Expected Cash Flows

The common formula for the mean assumes equal weights across all observations, but the expected value allows these weights to change and so is more flexible.

When we discuss cash flows from investments, we are talking about *future*, or **expected, cash flows**. Investing today generates payoffs in the future. Therefore, when evaluating investment opportunities, we must try to estimate each investment's expected cash flows. In finance, we say that investors form expectations about these future payoffs. The best estimate of an investment's future payoff is called the **expected value** of the future cash flows. The expected value is similar to a weighted average. Suppose a security analyst (a person who analyzes stocks and then makes recommendations to clients on whether to buy, hold, or sell the stocks) believes that Chevron Oil will pay a dividend next quarter of between 80¢ and $1.00. More precisely, the analyst thinks that there is a 20% chance the dividend will be 80¢, a 50% chance it will be 90¢, and a 30% chance it will be $1.00. The expected value of Chevron's next dividend is the sum of the possible outcomes (80¢, 90¢, and $1.00) times their respective probabilities (20%, 50%, and 30%). Arithmetically, the expected dividend is

$$\begin{aligned}\text{expected dividend} &= 0.20 \times 80¢ + 0.50 \times 90¢ + 0.30 \times \$1.00 \\ &= 16¢ + 45¢ + 30¢ = 91¢\end{aligned}$$

The expected value is slightly more than 90¢ because the analyst assigns a slightly higher probability to the $1.00 outcome than to the 80¢ outcome; that is, the expected value is weighted slightly toward $1.00 and slightly away from 80¢. Notice that the analyst predicts that the dividend will be either 80¢, 90¢, or $1.00. Nowhere does the analyst predict a dividend of 91¢. The actual outcome (80¢, 90¢, or $1.00) will not be the expected value of 91¢. Although we compute an expected value for a given point in time (next quarter's dividend, next year's sales, etc.), expected values are long-run averages. If this set of possible outcomes and probabilities occurred many times, then the average dividend from those multiple occurrences would be 91¢, the expected value.

As this example shows, the *expected value* is a probability weighted average. Each possible outcome is weighted by the likelihood that it will occur and then these weighted outcomes are summed. Mathematically, the expected value is expressed as

$$\textbf{expected value} = \pi_1 CF_1 + \pi_2 CF_2 + \pi_3 CF_3 + \cdots + \pi_n CF_n = \sum_{i=1}^{n} \pi_i CF_i$$

where CF_i represents one of the possible cash flow levels (for instance, in the Chevron example, $CF_1 = 80¢$) and π_i represents the probability of that cash flow level actually occurring (the probability associated with the 80¢ outcome in the Chevron example is $\pi_1 = 20\%$). The probabilities, π_1 through π_n, must sum to 1.0, or 100%. The *sigma* $\sum$, is a summation sign, which means we add all the separate elements created as our counter *i* goes from 1 to *n*. The formula for expected value allows for an unlimited number of possible outcomes, because *n*, the last outcome, can be as large as we want it to be. We will use the equation for expected value in several sections of the text.

Calculating the Expected Return from an Investment in a Share of Stock

A concept we use throughout the remainder of the chapter is **expected return**. The expected return provides a way to compare investments. Before describing expected return, we discuss returns more generally. The return from an investment is the dollar amount you make (or lose) divided by the amount you initially paid to make the investment. In the case of shares of stock, the dollar amount you receive can come in the form of dividend payments and/or capital gains (share price changes). We calculate returns from owning common stock as follows:

$$\text{Return} = \frac{\text{ending price} - \text{starting price} + \text{dividends}}{\text{starting price}}$$
$$= \frac{\text{change in price} + \text{dividends}}{\text{starting price}}$$

For example, suppose that you bought a share of stock for $50, 1 year later it was worth $55, and during the year it paid $2 in cash dividends. Then your return is 14%:

$$\text{return} = \frac{\$55 - \$50 + \$2}{\$50} = \frac{\$5 + \$2}{\$50} = \frac{\$7}{\$50} = 0.14 = 14\%$$

In general, the return on an investment is all cash received from the investment in excess of the initial outlay for the investment, divided by the initial outlay. For shares of stock the cash flows involve dividends and changes in the market price of the stock; for bonds the cash flows include interest payments and, possibly, repayment of principal or changes in the market value of the bond's price; for investments in productive assets such as machinery or factories, the cash flows include all intermediate cash flows generated by the assets and, possibly, the change in the market value of the asset.

Dividend yield is often used when describing some types of stocks, such as utilities.

The returns from owning stock come in two forms: dividends and change in market price. Because investments in shares of stock occur so often, special terms denote these two sources of returns. The return from a change in the share's price is called the **capital gain**, and the return from dividend income is called the **dividend yield**. Thus, an alternative expression for the return from owning stock is

$$\begin{aligned}\textbf{stock return} &= \frac{\textbf{ending price} - \textbf{starting price} + \textbf{dividend income}}{\textbf{starting price}} \\ &= \left(\frac{\textbf{change in price}}{\textbf{starting price}} + \frac{\textbf{dividend income}}{\textbf{starting price}}\right) \\ &= \textbf{capital gain} + \textbf{dividend yield}\end{aligned}$$

In the example we just did, the price change was \$5 and the dividend income was \$2. Because the initial price was \$50, the capital gain is 10% and the dividend yield is 4%, computed as follows:

$$\begin{aligned}\text{return} &= \frac{\$55 - \$50 + \$2}{\$50} \\ &= \frac{\$5}{\$50} + \frac{\$2}{\$50} = 0.10 + 0.04 = 10\% + 4\% = 14\%\end{aligned}$$

The capital gain represents the return from price appreciation, and the dividend yield represents the return from any dividend the firm paid during the period. The return from some stocks comes entirely from price appreciation, because those companies pay no dividends. For other stocks, much of the return is in the form of dividends. Investors may have a personal preference for returns in the form of capital gains or in the form of dividends. For example, during some periods capital gains income and dividend income have been taxed differently, so investors in higher tax brackets will have a stronger preference for the low-taxed form of returns. Therefore, investors select stocks in part based on the type of income the stock produces as well as on the level of the return.

To make investments comparable we usually annualize their returns; that is, we adjust returns to show what the investment would have returned had it been held for exactly 1 year. Without such an adjustment, comparing investments is very difficult. Computing annual returns provides a fairer basis of comparison than examining the returns of investments held for various periods of time. One way to annualize returns is to divide the return by the actual time the investment was held in years. For example, suppose that you buy a share of stock for \$50, 6 months later it is worth \$53, and over that period it paid \$1 in cash dividends. The return over the 6-month holding period (referred to as the **holding period return**) is 8%, and the **annualized return** is 16%:

$$\textbf{holding period return} = \frac{\$53 + \$1 - \$50}{\$50} = \frac{\$3 + \$1}{\$50} = \frac{\$4}{\$50} = 0.08 = 8\%$$

$$\textbf{annualized return} = \frac{\textbf{holding period return}}{\textbf{holding period in years}} = \frac{0.08}{0.5} = 0.16 = 16\%$$

Because the holding period is only one-half year, the annual return must be twice the holding period return. For holding periods longer than one year, the annualized return is less than the holding period return.

Unfortunately, returns are not always positive. Suppose, on a hot tip, you buy 1,000 shares of stock of a brand-new medical technology company for $2.00 per share. The company's promised product never materializes, and 2 years later the stock is selling for 50¢ per share. No dividends were ever paid. You decide to take your loss and sell. You earn a return of −75%. This negative 75% return means that you lost three-quarters of your initial investment, or $1,500 = 0.75 × (1,000 × $2.00). We calculate the return as we did before:

$$\text{return per share} = \frac{\text{change in price}}{\text{initial price}} = \frac{\$0.50 - \$2.00}{\$2.00} = \frac{-\$1.50}{\$2.00}$$
$$= -0.75 = -75\%$$

$$\text{annualized return} = \frac{\text{holding period return}}{\text{holding period in years}} = -\frac{0.75}{2} = -0.375 = -37.5\%$$

The examples just shown calculated returns upon an investment's completion. The actual selling price and dividend distributions from the investment were known. These are called **realized returns,** or **ex post returns** (from the Latin phrase for "done after"). Although we are interested in realized returns, to make investment decisions we need estimates of an investment's future returns—that is, we want to estimate the returns we expect to receive from an investment. The *expected return,* or **ex ante return** ("done before") from an investment is calculated in the same manner as the realized returns, with *expected* future cash flows replacing the known quantities.[1]

$$\textbf{expected return} = \frac{\textbf{expected price} - \textbf{starting price} + \textbf{expected dividends}}{\textbf{starting price}}$$
$$= \frac{\textbf{expected change in price} + \textbf{expected dividends}}{\textbf{starting price}}$$

Suppose a share of stock costs $95 today and we believe there is a 25% chance the stock's price will be $90 one year from now, a 50% chance the price will be $100, and a 25% chance of a price of $115. Then the expected value of the share

[1]Here is an example to help distinguish *ex ante* and *ex post.* Suppose your local TV station announces it is going to have a Star Trek film festival, which will involve showing all the episodes of Star Trek over a single weekend. You and some friends decide to have a Star Trek party. Everyone helps make the food and drink list and agrees to share the cost. Beforehand you think your share of the bill will be between $25 and $35, probably very close to $30. Your ex ante estimate of costs is $30. When the shopping is actually done, you find out that you owe the group $31.45. This is the ex post cost, or realized cost, which is known with certainty.

price one year from today is $101.25.[2] We do not expect any cash dividends to be paid during this period. The expected annual return is

$$\text{expected return} = \frac{\$101.25 - \$95}{\$95} = \frac{\$6.25}{95} = 0.0658 = 6.58\%$$

The expected return from investing in this stock is 6.58%. Whether this return is high enough to attract investors depends on a number of factors, including the investment's risk, the expected return offered by other investments, and investor expectations about inflation. If we look at this stock 1 year from now we can compute the realized return, which will almost certainly differ from our expected return. Before investing, however, the expected return is our best estimate of the stock's future return.

By stating all future cash flows as expected values—the expected value of the future stock price and the expected value of the dividend—we can compute the expected return from owning a share of stock. The components of the expected return are the expected capital gain and the expected dividend yield.

RISK AVERSION AND INVESTORS' REQUIRED RATE OF RETURN FROM AN INVESTMENT

Risk Aversion Defined

Risk aversion does not imply that a person is necessarily a worrier or fearful, but it does imply that he or she wants to be compensated for bearing risk.

Throughout this text, we assume that investors are *risk averse.* Risk aversion means that a person prefers a sure outcome to an otherwise equivalent risky one. To accept additional risk, the investor must be compensated with a higher expected return. For example, suppose that for $95 an individual could make either of two investments: Investment A pays $100 with certainty, but Investment B offers an equal chance of either $80 or $120. Each of Investment B's outcomes has a 50% chance of occurring, so the expected value of the payoff from Investment B is $100, as follows:

$$\text{expected outcome} = 0.50 \times \$80 + 0.50 \times \$120 = \$40 + \$60 = \$100$$

Because both investments have the same initial investment and expected outcome, they have identical expected returns of 5.26%:

$$\text{expected return} = \frac{\text{expected outcome} - \text{investment}}{\text{investment}}$$

$$= \frac{\$100 - \$95}{\$95} = 0.0526 = 5.26\%$$

Although the expected values and expected returns of the two investments are identical, the risk differs. There is no risk associated with Investment A. The investor knows exactly what will be received. With Investment B, however, there is some uncertainty about the actual outcome—the payoff could be $80, a $15 loss, or the payoff could be $120, a $25 gain. Given that the two investments

[2]Expected value of share price = 0.25 × 90 + 0.50 × 100 + 0.25× 115 = $22.50 + $50.00 + $28.75 = $101.25.

have the same expected payoff of \$100, a risk averse investor always chooses Investment A, the \$100 with certainty. For the same expected payoff, a risk averse individual always prefers the more certain alternative.

Now consider Investment C, which offers an equal chance of \$50 or \$150. As in the case of Investments A and B, Investment C costs \$95 and has an expected payoff of \$100.[3] Investment C's possible outcomes are much more dispersed than those of either Investment A or Investment B. Figure 3.1 shows Investments A, B, and C. The vertical axis represents the probability of a particular outcome: the taller the bar, the more likely the particular outcome. There is only one outcome shown for Investment A, \$100, and it has a probability of 100%. An outcome with a probability of 100% is a sure thing; that single outcome will occur with certainty. As the diagram shows, the possible outcomes for Investment

Students often focus on the possibility of receiving the higher payoff. Risk-takers look at uncertainty that way. Risk aversion implies that losses outweigh equivalent gains.

Transparency Available

FIGURE 3.1

THE PROBABILITIES AND DOLLAR OUTCOMES OF INVESTMENTS A, B, AND C

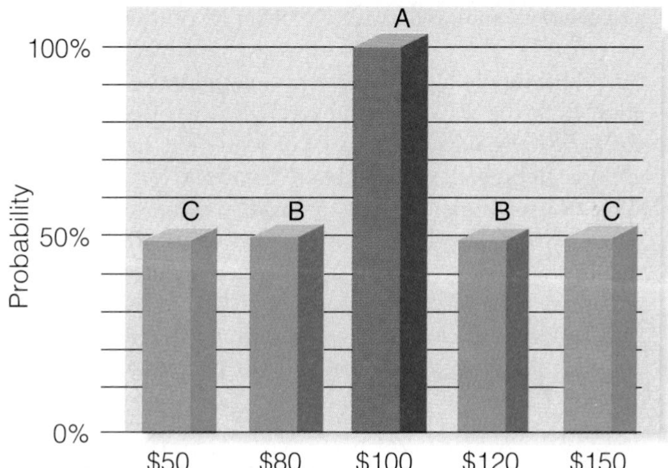

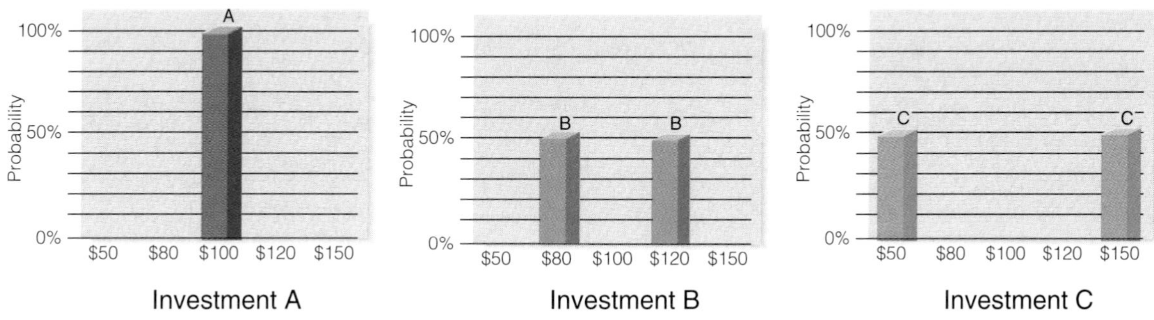

[3]Investment C's expected payoff, or ex ante payoff, is computed as follows:

$$\text{expected outcome} = 0.50 \times \$50 + 0.50 \times \$150 = \$25 + \$75 = \$100$$

C are much more dispersed than those of Investment B. They range from $50 to $150, whereas Investment B's possible outcomes range from only $80 to $120. The greater dispersion or variability of possible outcomes for Investment C makes it a riskier investment. A risk averse investor would be very worried about the possibility of receiving only $50 from Investment C, thereby suffering a $45 loss on the investment. The dispersion of outcomes, particularly low or bad outcomes, concerns risk averse individuals. In fact, a characteristic of risk averse investors is that, starting from the same income level, the pain associated with a financial loss more than offsets the pleasure associated with a gain of the same magnitude. Risk aversion implies an asymmetry in which the dissatisfaction of a $1 loss is greater than the added satisfaction associated with a $1 gain. All else equal, the more dispersed an investment's possible outcomes, the less attractive risk averse investors find the investment.

This variance formula is identical to the standard (equally weighted) variance formula, but equal weighting is no longer assumed. If $\pi = (1/n)$, then the two formulas are identical.

Because risk averse investors dislike variability in outcomes, a natural indicator of risk is the dispersion or variability of an investment's possible outcomes. We have an obvious statistical measure of variability or dispersion: the variance (or its square root, the standard deviation).[4] The variance is the average of each value's squared deviation from the mean. In terms of investments with various possible outcomes, each with a probability of occurrence, we modify the expression slightly. The variance of expected returns is the sum of the following series: the probability of a particular outcome times the square of that outcome's deviation from the investment's expected value. Recall from statistics that as the variance (or standard deviation) increases, the distribution of possible outcomes also increases, both on the high side and the low side. Given identical expected values, larger variances imply a larger spread, or dispersion, among the possible outcomes and, thereby, greater risk. Risk averse investors prefer investments with small variances, or a small variability across outcomes.

Examples: High-technology firms are vulnerable to competitors' innovation; retailers, to changes in disposable income, changing tastes, and changing demographics.

A number of sources can create variability in an investment's expected returns. One approach to estimating the potential variability of a company's returns is to consider the factors that affect the company's ability to sell its products at a

[4]The ex ante, or expected, variance of a set of possible outcomes is computed by subtracting the expected value from each outcome, squaring that difference, multiplying the squared value by the probability of that outcome, and summing all those products. If π stands for probability, CF stands for cash flow (or outcome), EV(CF) stands for the expected value of the cash flows, and there are n possible outcomes, then the variance is computed according to the following equation:

$$\begin{aligned}\text{variance} &= \sum_{i=1}^{n} \pi_i(\text{CF}_i - \text{EV(CF)})^2 \\ &= \pi_1(\text{CF}_1 - \text{EV(CF)})^2 \\ &\quad + \pi_2(\text{CF}_2 - \text{EV(CF)})^2 + \cdots + \pi_n(\text{CF}_n - \text{EV(CF)})^2 \\ \text{standard deviation} &= \sqrt{\text{variance}}\end{aligned}$$

Investment C has two possible, equally likely, outcomes of $50 and $150 and an expected value of $100. The variance of Investment C is computed as follows:

$$\begin{aligned}\text{variance (C)} &= 0.50(\$50 - \$100)^2 + 0.50(\$150 - \$100)^2 \\ &= 0.50(-\$50)^2 + 0.50(\$50)^2 \\ &= 0.50(\$2{,}500) + 0.50(\$2{,}500) = \$2{,}500 \\ \text{standard deviation (C)} &= \sqrt{\$2500} = \$50\end{aligned}$$

Compare this to less risky Investment B's standard deviation of $20 (variance (B) = $400).

profit. Here are examples of some factors that can affect a company's profitability and thereby its cash flow: changes in consumer tastes, competitors introducing superior products, changes in consumer disposable income, changes in interest rates, changes in exchange rates, price increases by suppliers, changes in tax laws, and political events. Depending on how the company does business these factors may have no affect or a great affect. Companies doing lots of international business are subject to different risks than those operating domestically, and some industries seem more vulnerable to certain types of uncertainty than others. An understanding of a company and its industry goes a long way in achieving insight into the uncertainty the company faces.

An Aside on Risk Aversion and Nonfinancial Behavior

Why do people who participate in "dangerous" sports use safety equipment such as helmets?

Risk aversion is not just an economic theory having to do with uncertain investments. Most people's behavior suggests they are somewhat risk averse. In fact, the entire insurance industry exists to reduce the uncertainty in people's lives. You may be suspect of this notion of risk aversion. There are certainly examples of people accepting and even enjoying taking risks. Gamblers know that over the long run the casino will win, but they gamble anyway. Some people enjoy risky sports or hobbies—sky diving, mountaineering, car racing, and so on—which seems to dispute the claim that people are generally risk averse. We are quite willing to admit that some people enjoy the thrill of risk taking, but we remain convinced that most *investors* are risk averse.

There are several distinctions that can be drawn between the risk-loving behavior we sometimes see and the risk aversion that exemplifies investor behavior. Gamblers typically take a relatively small sum of money (compared to their total wealth) to Las Vegas or Atlantic City.[5] The activity of gambling has a minor effect on their wealth but is an enjoyable form of recreation for them. Accepting small losses during a vacation in a gambling center differs little from paying to go to a movie or a concert. The same people that gamble for recreation may be very cautious investors. The difference is that their investment decisions involve a larger portion of their wealth, and that wealth is designated for a purpose, such as retirement or their children's college educations. Therefore, we continue to believe that most people make investment decisions in a fairly conservative fashion; that is, regarding their investments, most people behave as though they are risk averse.

Risk Aversion and Risky Investments

It might be worthwhile to help students see where the discussion is heading: Investors need higher expected returns to bear higher risk.

Being risk averse does not imply that investors always choose the investment with the lowest risk. In fact, one of the most important topics in finance involves the study of how people decide to make risky investments. In this chapter we

[5]Some individuals do not gamble by risking relatively small amounts as a form of recreation but instead risk, and lose, large amounts of money, money that they need to pay their bills. Compulsive gamblers may be risk seekers; they are addicted to risk and soon find themselves in financial difficulty. Gamblers Anonymous is an organization designed to help such people control their risk-seeking behavior. That risk-seeking may require therapy further attests to the normality of risk aversion.

introduce the intuition underlying these decisions about risky investments. In Chapters 7 and 8 we deal with this topic in much greater detail. We begin with an example. Consider the safe investment, Investment A, and a new investment that also costs $95, Investment D. Investment A still pays $100 with certainty, but Investment D offers an equal chance of $85 or $125. The expected value of Investment D's payoff is $105, its expected return is 10.53%, and its return standard deviation is $20.

$$\text{expected value (D)} = 0.50 \times \$85 + 0.50 \times \$125 = \$42.50 + \$62.50 = \$105$$

$$\text{expected return (D)} = \frac{\$105 - \$95}{\$95} = 0.1053 = 10.53\%$$

$$\text{variance (D)} = 0.50 \times (\$85 - \$105)^2 + 0.50 \times (\$125 - \$105)^2 = \$400$$

$$\text{standard deviation (D)} = \sqrt{\$400} = \$20$$

Recall that Investment A, which also requires a $95 investment, has an expected payoff of $100, an expected return of 5.26%, and, being certain, a standard deviation of returns of 0. Depending on how risk averse a person is, they may choose Investment D rather than the certain, but less profitable, Investment A. Risk averse individuals will make risky investments if the investment promises a high-enough expected return. The expected return on the risky investment must be sufficiently high to offset investors' aversion to the investment's risk.

Consider a third possible investment, Investment E. Investment E costs $95 and has an equal chance of paying investors $90 and $130, so it has an expected value of $110 and an expected return of 15.79%. We have constructed Investment E to have the same standard deviation as Investment D, $20. Investment E has the same risk as—but a higher return than—Investment D.

$$\text{expected value (E)} = 0.50 \times \$90 + 0.50 \times \$130 = \$45 + \$65 = \$110$$

$$\text{expected return (E)} = \frac{\$110 - \$95}{\$95} = 0.1579 = 15.79\%$$

$$\text{variance (E)} = 0.50 \times (\$90 - \$110)^2 + 0.50 \times (\$130 - \$110)^2 = \$400$$

$$\text{standard deviation (E)} = \sqrt{\$400} = \$20$$

Some risk averse investors who would not invest in Investment D will invest in E. For these investors, the higher expected return offered by E sufficiently offsets the risk. The expected payoff from Investment D was not high enough to overcome their risk aversion, but Investment E's expected payoff is. The more risk averse an individual is, the higher the expected value of the risky investment must be for them to forego a safer alternative. This higher expected return is often referred to as a **risk premium**. The risk premium is the extent to which the expected return on a risky investment exceeds the return from a safe investment. The risk premium is the extra expected return that an investment must offer to attract risk averse investors. Chapters 7 and 8 describe how the marketplace determines risk premiums.

Final comments on Investments D and E: Suppose you had invested in D. If Investment E became available, would you change to E or remain invested in D? Recall that Investments D and E have the same risk (standard deviation of returns of $20), but E has a higher expected return. For bearing the same amount of risk, Investment E gives you a higher expected return. Therefore, rational investors would all switch from D to E. We say that Investment E *dominates* Investment D. Investment E is dominant because all investors prefer it to Investment D if they have only these two investments to choose from. This example points out an important characteristic of markets: Two investments with the same risk and different returns will not exist simultaneously in the same market. No one will invest in the low-return investment. This is an application of the **law of one price** from economics: Within a single market, the same good cannot sell for two different prices.

This discussion suggests that we may look at Investments D and E according to their prices. Both investments have the same risk and require the same initial investment of $95. For $95 you can buy an expected return of $105 by investing in D or an expected return of $110 by investing in E. Investment E is superior, because for the same price and risk you have a higher expected payoff. The price for D is too high, resulting in a lower expected return. This points out how price and return are related. The higher the price, the lower the return. To raise the expected return, price must fall. Conversely, as an investment's price increases, its return decreases. There is an inverse relationship between price and rate of return. Later, we discuss how investors adjust expected returns to a level appropriate for a security's risk.

The Risk-Return Trade-Off

Stated in terms of good and bad: To accept something bad (i.e., risk) there must be some offsetting good (i.e., higher returns).

Our discussion of the behavior of risk averse investors leads to one of the most important concepts in finance: **the risk-return trade-off**. For investment to take place, higher risk must be accompanied by higher expected returns. As risk increases, a higher expected return must be offered to entice risk averse individuals away from safer investments. As the expected return from a risky investment rises, risk averse investors begin to become indifferent between the safe and the risky investment. At each investor's indifference point, the risky investment's higher expected return just offsets the investment's risk. For expected returns beyond this point, the individual prefers the risky investment; for returns below it, the investor prefers the safe investment. The risk premium at which investors are indifferent between two investments varies across individuals. People who are very risk averse will require a large risk premium to make a risky investment, whereas those more tolerant of risk will require a smaller premium.

Sometimes identical items sell for different prices at two nearby grocery stores. Convenience (doing all the shopping in one stop) may explain this situation.

Within financial markets each investment offers only a single expected return and, therefore, only a single risk premium. This is comparable to saying that each investment sells for only one price; that is, investments, like goods, follow the law of one price. Investments of greater risk offer higher expected returns and correspondingly higher risk premiums, whereas less risky investments are priced to offer relatively lower expected returns and risk premiums. The particular risk premium demanded by investors varies over time, depending on the riskiness of investments available in the marketplace and investors' attitudes toward risk. This second factor—investors' attitudes toward risk—is sometimes referred to as *investor psychology*. During some periods, investors become very tolerant of risk and risk premiums shrink; at other times investors become more risk averse and risk premiums grow.

One professor, who teaches in a first-floor classroom, has a dramatic way to demonstrate this trade-off between risk and expected payoff. He asks students how much he would have to pay them to jump out of the window. The amounts students demand vary, but they average between $5 and $10, depending on how soft the landing looks. He then asks how much they would demand if the classroom were on the second floor. In all cases, students demand a higher payoff to compensate them for the added risk associated with the longer jump. The point at which students are willing to jump out of the window varies from student to student, depending on their levels of risk aversion.

Other reasons include limited product lines, no economies of scale, limited access to capital, little influence over suppliers, and limited managerial experience.

Historical Returns and Risk

Financial economists have found that investors act a lot like these students. Figure 3.2 presents the actual returns and standard deviations for several types of investments. It shows that investors earn a higher return as risk (measured as the standard deviation) increases. As the diagram shows, a nearly linear relationship exists between annual returns and the standard deviation of those returns. The safest investments are U.S. Treasury bills (often referred to as T-bills). These are short-term obligations of the U.S. federal government and are effectively risk free. At the other end of the chart are the stocks of small companies. Small companies are very risky, as shown by the large standard deviation

FIGURE 3.2

ANNUAL RETURNS AND RISK ON A VARIETY OF INVESTMENTS, 1926–1993

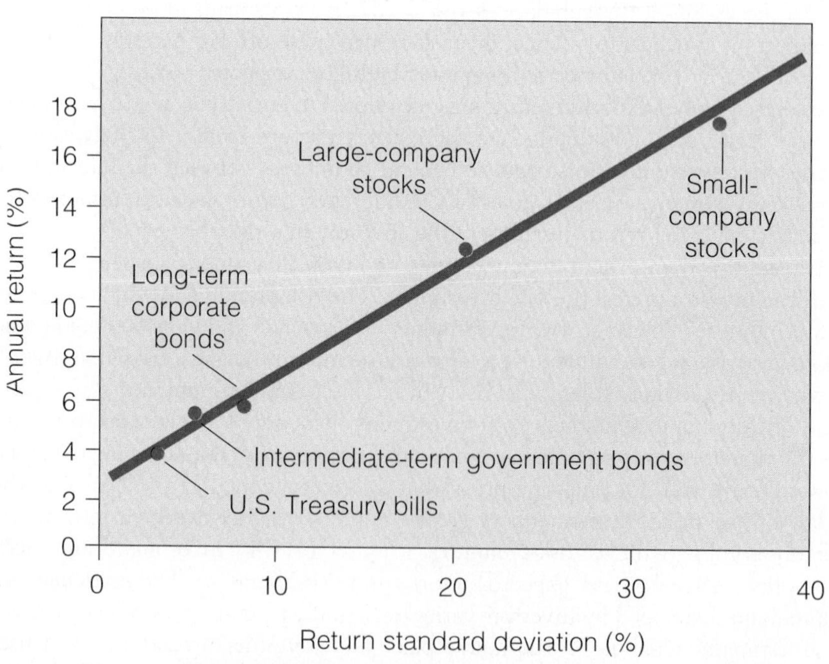

SOURCE: Ibbotson and Sinquefield, *SBBI Yearbook*, (Chicago: Ibottson and Associates, 1994)

Transparency Available

of stock returns. This risk arises, in part, because small firms must compete with larger, more established, companies, so often have trouble gaining sufficient market share to be profitable. Investors understand these risks, so they demand a higher expected return from small-company stocks than from other types of investments. Between these extremes are long-term government and corporate bonds and the common stock of larger firms.

In Figure 3.2 average returns and the variability of returns for each type of investment are computed using data from the 68-year period from 1926 through 1993. Over this very long period we see that investors did indeed earn higher returns by investing in investments with higher risk (higher variability of returns). We must be careful, however, to avoid thinking that investing in common stocks always results in a higher return than investing in government or corporate bonds. Remember that the data plotted in Figure 3.2 are averages computed over a 68-year period. In any particular year, the actual returns might vary dramatically from the average. For example, the average return for large company common stocks over the 68-year period was 12.3%, but that includes 19 years of negative returns. The returns for investments in common stock range from a low of about −43% in 1931 to a high of 54% in 1933. If we eliminate the depression years of the 1930s and begin in 1940, the annual returns to the common stock of large companies still range from −26.5% (in 1974) to 52.6% (in 1954). Therefore, in any given year, an investment might have lost 25% to 30% or made 40% to 50%. Over the long run, these returns average out to be about 12%. To earn this long-run average return, an investor must be patient, suffering some bad years as well as reaping the rewards of some very good years. It is precisely because of this variability in returns that investors demand and receive a higher return from common stocks than from less risky investments such as government bonds.

If the DJIA is at 4600, will it ever reach 6000?

Exhibit 3.1 presents the data used to construct the graph in Figure 3.2. Also shown are the average annual returns for the three decades of the 1960s through 1980s. The pattern shown in the graph in Figure 3.2 generally holds in each of these decades: stocks have higher returns than bonds, and long-maturity bonds have higher returns than short-maturity bonds. There are a few exceptions, such as the 1960s and 1970s, when short-term and intermediate-term Treasury securities outperformed long-term corporate bonds. In the 1970s all bond categories outperformed large-company stocks. This points out the variability in the returns of some of these securities types. Although stocks, on average, pay a higher return, there are good years and bad years, or in this case good decades and bad decades.

The graph in Exhibit 3.1 shows the distribution of annual returns over the period 1926 to 1993 for three different types of securities: small-company stocks, large-company stocks, and intermediate-term government bonds. The more spread out, or dispersed, the returns, the more return variability the security has. Small-company stocks have the most variability, with returns ranging from −58% in 1937 to 142.9% in 1933. As the graph shows, large-company stocks are somewhat less dispersed, with most of the annual returns piled up between −10% and 20%. The distribution of returns to intermediate-term government bonds is tall and lies tightly packed between 0% and 10%. In fact, of the 68 years represented, 76.5% (52 years) of the returns for intermediate-term government bonds are between 0% and 10%. Compare this to large-company stocks for which the central 52 observations lie between −10% and 35% and only 10 of 68 observations (or 15%) lie between 0% and 10%. For small-company stocks the

EXHIBIT 3.1

ANNUAL RETURN SUMMARY STATISTICS AND DISTRIBUTIONS FOR SEVERAL TYPES OF SECURITIES USING DATA FROM 1926 TO 1993

SECURITY TYPE	AVERAGE ANNUAL RETURNS 1926–93	RETURN STANDARD DEVIATION 1926–93	AVERAGE ANNUAL RETURNS 1960s	AVERAGE ANNUAL RETURNS 1970s	AVERAGE ANNUAL RETURNS 1980s
Small Company Stock	17.6%	34.8%	15.5%	11.5%	15.8%
Large Company Stock	12.3%	20.5%	7.8%	5.9%	17.5%
Long-term Corporate Bonds	5.9%	8.4%	1.7%	6.2%	13.0%
Intermediate-term Govt. Bonds	5.4%	5.6%	3.5%	7.0%	11.9%
U.S. Treasury Bills	3.7%	3.3%	3.9%	6.3%	8.9%

SOURCE: Ibbotson and Sinquefield, *SBBI Yearbook*, (Chicago: Ibottson and Associates, 1994)

DISTRIBUTION OF ANNUAL RETURNS BY SECURITY TYPE

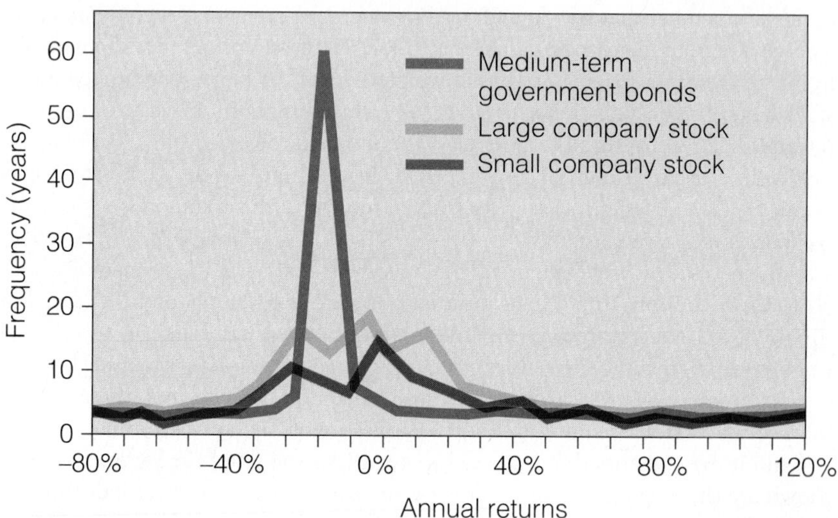

Transparency Available

middle 52 observations lie between −20% and 50%, and only 8 annual returns of the 68 (or 12%) are between 0% and 10%. These numbers imply that for medium-term government bonds, about three-quarters of the time (or a 76.5% probability) investors will earn between 0% and 10%. Most of the time investors have a pretty good idea of what the return will be. For both small and large company stocks, however, the range of annual returns is much broader. Therefore, from year to year investors face much more uncertainty about the returns they will earn from their investments in common stocks. For that uncertainty, they demand a higher expected rate of return.

How Investors Adjust Returns

Demanding a higher expected return is one thing, but making it happen is another. The manner in which investors change the expected return on an investment is surprisingly simple: they bid up or down the price they are willing to pay for the investment. Here is our formula for the expected return for investing in a share of stock:

$$\text{expected return} = \frac{\text{expected price} - \text{initial price} + \text{dividend}}{\text{initial price}}$$
$$= \frac{\text{expected change in price} + \text{dividend}}{\text{initial price}}$$

Suppose that the best estimate of the expected price of the stock 1 year from now is \$100 and analysts expect the dividend to be \$2. If the stock currently sells for \$90,

$$\text{expected return} = \frac{\$100 - \$90 + \$2}{\$90} = \frac{\$12}{\$90} = 0.1333 = 13.33\%.$$

If the consensus among investors is that this return is too low given the riskiness of the stock, they will not pay \$90. People who own the stock see \$90 as a high price, so they want to sell before the price falls too far. With owners wanting to sell but other investors being reluctant to buy at \$90, the price begins to be bid down. As the price falls, the expected return rises, attracting some buyers. For example, suppose the price falls to \$88. Then the expected return increases to 15.91%:

$$\text{expected return} = \frac{\$100 - \$88 + 2}{\$88} = \frac{\$14}{\$88} = 0.1591 = 15.91\%$$

If this return still does not compensate investors for the riskiness of the stock, the price will fall further. As the initial price falls, the expected return rises. Figure 3.3 shows this inverse, or negative, relationship between prices and returns. As the price goes down, the return goes up. By adjusting price through the

Transparency Available

FIGURE 3.3

EXPECTED RETURN AND INITIAL PRICE

The relationship between initial price and expected return for an investment expected to pay a \$2 dividend and be worth \$100 one year from today.

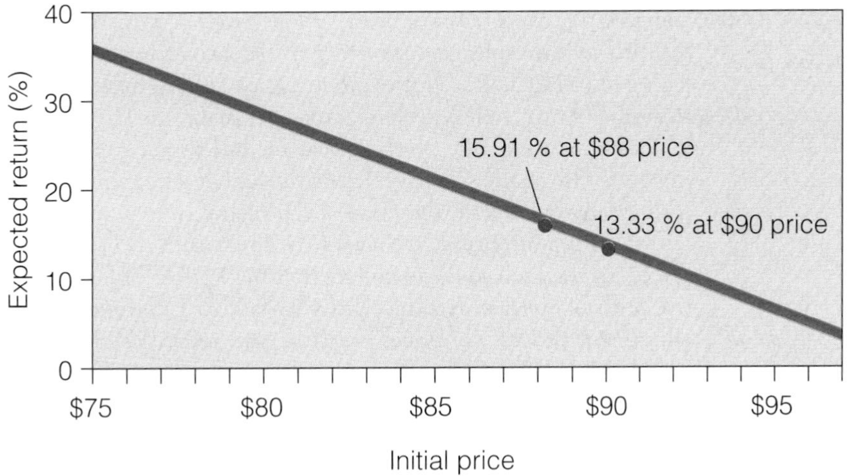

bidding process, investors can adjust a security's expected return to a level appropriate for the security's risk.

Of course, the return-adjustment process also works in the other direction. If a return of 13.33% was seen as very high, given the risk of the stock, then many investors want to buy the stock to earn that high return. In the process, the price would be bid up until the expected return is appropriate for the risk of the stock. No one would bid the price up further, because doing so would mean buying a stock with an expected return too low for the investment's level of risk.

Individual investors cannot bid prices up or down to get any return they want. The adjustment process reflects the consensus opinion of active investors (those who trade securities frequently and, often, in large volumes). Investor opinions about a particular security's future or expected payoff will vary: some will be optimistic (sometimes called **bulls** in Wall Street jargon), and others will be pessimistic (known as **bears** on Wall Street). During the adjustment process, bulls buy and bears sell until demand and supply reach equilibrium. At that point buyers will buy only at a slightly lower price and sellers will offer shares only at a slightly higher price, so no further transactions occur. In time, possibly only minutes or hours after this adjustment occurs, new information can cause a slight change in expectations, stimulating more transactions. The process is ongoing. As new information arrives about companies, industries, and the national and global economy, analysts and investors modify their perceptions of the future cash flows and the riskiness of stocks and bonds. They then buy and sell securities until prices and anticipated future cash flows result in the desired expected returns. This process takes place continuously, and prices are constantly being adjusted to reflect new information.

ALTERNATIVE INVESTMENTS: RATIONALITY AND COMPETITION

Figure 3.2 and the table in Exhibit 3.1 show the historical returns for various types of investments. In our discussion of the risk-return trade-off, we pointed out that investors compare the expected return on a risky investment to the expected return they can earn on other investments. In fact, investors constantly compare the expected returns of various types of investments—and individual securities within those groups—to try to identify bargains. This process of comparing returns across securities produces two results. First, investments of similar risk will offer the same expected return. As mentioned before, this is an example of the economists' rule of one price. In the case of similar securities, rational investors rush to the security offering the higher return and ignore the low-return security. By bidding up the price of the high-return security, investors lower its return. In the meantime, owners of the low-return security recognize it is overpriced, so they sell to try to collect that high price. Their selling activity causes the price of the low-return security to fall, and its return begins to rise. The adjustment process continues until the two securities offer the same expected return. Competition among rational investors assures that investments of similar risk offer similar returns.

The second result relates directly to the graph in Figure 3.2, which shows a nearly linear relationship between historical returns and the variability (measured by standard deviation) of those returns. The points fall along a line. If the expected return offered by a particular type of security is out of line with other returns, then investors buy and sell until those returns once again fall on the line.

In Figure 3.4 returns for large-company stocks fall above the line. Given their riskiness, large-company stocks offer a higher-than-necessary return; that is, large-company stocks are mispriced relative to other investments. Faced with such a situation, would you buy or sell large company stocks? The high return implies a low price (remember the inverse relationship between returns and prices shown in Figure 3.3), so you would buy large-company stocks. One approach to paying for your purchases would be to sell other types of securities, such as government bonds or small-company stocks. If many investors pursue this strategy, the return on large-company stocks will fall as the price rises. This causes the risk-return point representing large company stocks to move down toward the line, as indicated by the arrow. At the same time, selling other types of securities causes their prices to fall and their returns to rise. Eventually, all the risk-return points will again lie on a line.

Economists talk about **equilibrium conditions**—the conditions that exist when a market is in balance so there is neither excess buying nor selling. In our example, equilibrium requires that all the risk-return points be plotted along a line. A risk-return point that lies off the line, as is the case for large-company stocks, means that the capital markets are not in equilibrium. To put the market

Transparency Available

FIGURE 3.4

AN EXAMPLE OF A MISPRICED SECURITY

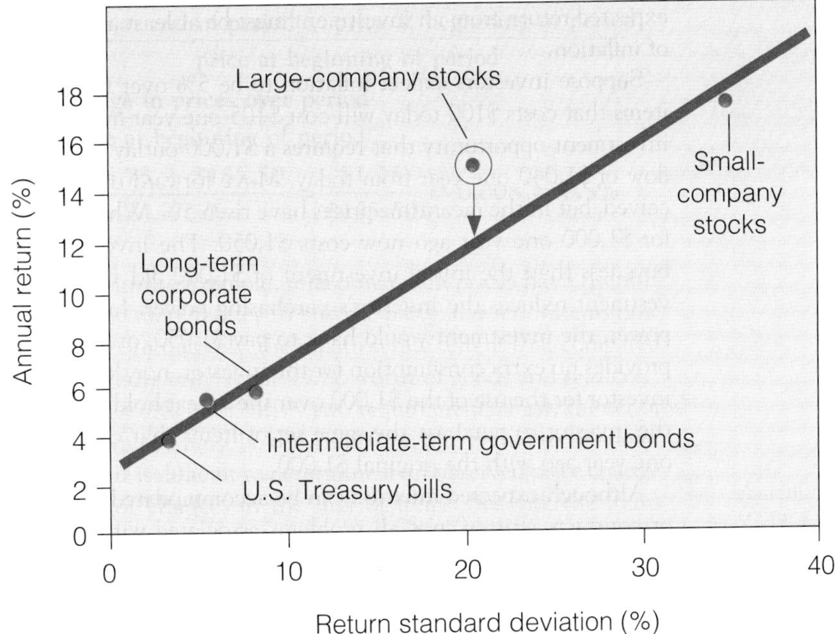

Foregone Opportunities

Investing precludes taking advantage of some other opportunities. It requires making an outlay of money today, so that amount is no longer available to spend or to invest elsewhere. The longer you give up the use of your money, the greater the expected future wealth from the investment must be. It is like rent. The longer someone rents the money, the more rent they pay. Let's pursue the rent example a bit further. If someone has the use of your house for 2 years rather than just 1 year, you would expect to collect more rent. The monthly rent might not change, but the total collected would increase. Money is the same. The longer someone has use of your money, the more you expect to be paid.

When you make an investment, you give up the opportunity to use that money for other purposes. One of the opportunities you give up is the earning of interest on the money. Therefore, when you make an investment you must at least be compensated for the interest you could have earned. Giving up interest income is an **opportunity cost** associated with investing. Investors must be paid for the opportunity costs they bear. The longer an investor must wait to receive the cash flows from an investment, the greater are the opportunity costs (the more interest that could have been earned).

Investors adjust expected returns by changing the price they are willing to pay for an investment. By paying a lower price, the return goes up. This implies that investors will pay more for an investment that promises to pay $1,000 one year from today than for an investment of similar risk that promises a single $1,000 payment 2 years from today. We can generalize this result: Investors pay more for an investment promising an early cash flow than for an investment promising the same cash flow later in time.

The preference for receiving cash flows earlier rather than later applies to corporations as well as individuals. When the managers of a company make investment decisions on behalf of shareholders, they are making a decision between distributing cash to shareholders today or investing that cash with the prospect of having more cash to distribute in the future. As with individuals, the projected future cash flows must be large enough to justify postponing the receipt of the cash. What is returned to shareholders in the future (the *return* they earn on the investment) must compensate them for giving up alternative uses of their money today.

Risk Aversion and the Preference for Earlier Cash Flows

Risk averse investors prefer certainty to uncertainty. Postponing cash flows increases an investment's risk: the longer the wait, the more chance of something going wrong so the cash will not be paid or its consumption value will be unexpectedly diminished. An old adage is appropriate here: A bird in the hand is worth two in the bush. That bit of folk wisdom points out the traditional preference for something today (in the hand) rather than a future payoff, even a greater future payoff, that has yet to be captured.

The increased risk associated with longer delays in receiving an investment's cash flows implies that investors will demand a higher rate of return on investments with longer payoff horizons. For example, next time you go into your bank look at the interest rates offered on certificates of deposit. **Certificates of deposit**

(CDs) come with various **maturity dates,** from a few months to several years. The maturity date tells how long your money will be unavailable to you. Rates on short-term CDs are generally lower than the rates on longer-term CDs. In mid-February 1995 the rates on certificates of deposit varied, as shown in Figure 3.5. These rates in the top chart are for CDs with small opening balances. The rates are higher for *jumbo* CDs, those with initial deposits of $95,000 to $100,000, than for the small-balance CDs, as shown in the bottom chart in Figure 3.5. APY stands for **annual percentage yield**; that is, the rates have been annualized, as described in an earlier section of this chapter. Using annualized rates allows us more easily to compare the returns on the various certificates of deposit.[8]

Because the FDIC, the Federal Deposit Insurance Corporation, insures deposits up to $100,000 in CDs, the risk of not being paid when the CD matures is

FIGURE 3.5

CD RATES

Certificate-of-deposit rates for small-minimum-balance opening deposits ($500 to $25,000) at different maturities as of February 21, 1995.

	Highest Rate in Nation	Average Rate in Nation
Maturity	Rate (APY)	Rate (APY)
6 months	6.65%	5.02%
1 year	7.15%	5.81%
2 years	7.48%	6.32%
5 years	7.79%	6.75%

Certificate-of-deposit rates for jumbo CDs: minimum-balance opening deposits ($95,000 to $100,000) at different maturities as of February 21, 1995.

	Highest Rate in Nation	Average Rate in Nation	Difference between National Average for small and jumbo CDs
Maturity	Rate (APY)	Rate (APY)	Rate (APY)
6 months	6.86%	5.46%	0.44%
1 year	7.30%	6.13%	0.32%
2 years	7.55%	6.70%	0.38%
5 years	7.84%	7.09%	0.34%

Transparency Available

[8]In Chapter 6 we will see that to compare investments such as CDs, we must also consider how often the interest is computed and added to our investment. This is called compounding and affects a security's actual yield.

The *Wall Street Journal* usually has the current yield curve in the Marketplace section under Credit Markets.

minimal. The variation in interest rates arises largely from banks responding to investors' demand for higher returns if their money is tied up for longer periods.

In most time periods we see the pattern just described: higher rates for longer maturities. We can compare the rates at different maturities by looking at the **yield curve**. The name *yield curve* comes from calling the return from investing in bonds the **yield-to-maturity**. Thus, the yield curve plots the yield-to-maturity against maturity. To eliminate default risk (the chance of the interest and/or principal not being paid in full and on time), yield curves are based on U.S. Treasury bills, notes, and bonds. Figure 3.6 shows yield curves from November 1992 and February 1995. These two yield curves display the slightly upward slope typical of most yield curves. Occasionally rates for shorter-maturity instruments exceed the rates paid on longer-term investments, resulting in an inverted, or downward-sloping, yield curve. An inverted yield curve (higher short-term than long-term rates) can occur if investors expect inflation to be high in the short term, but to fall over the long term. Such a situation arose in the late 1970s and early 1980s in the United States, and the yield curve sloped down. If yields are highest for medium-term securities, the yield curve will be slightly humped. Figure 3.7 shows several of the different shapes that can occur.

Theories about Yield Curves

Several theories have been developed to explain the shape of yield curves. The three most accepted theories are liquidity preference, unbiased expectations, and market segmentation.

- The **liquidity preference** theory is based on the conjecture that investors generally prefer to invest in shorter-maturity securities. For example, an investor who wants to invest $10,000 for 2 years would prefer, all else equal, to make a series of 1-year investments. This provides cash after 1-year in case

FIGURE 3.6
EXAMPLES OF YIELD CURVES

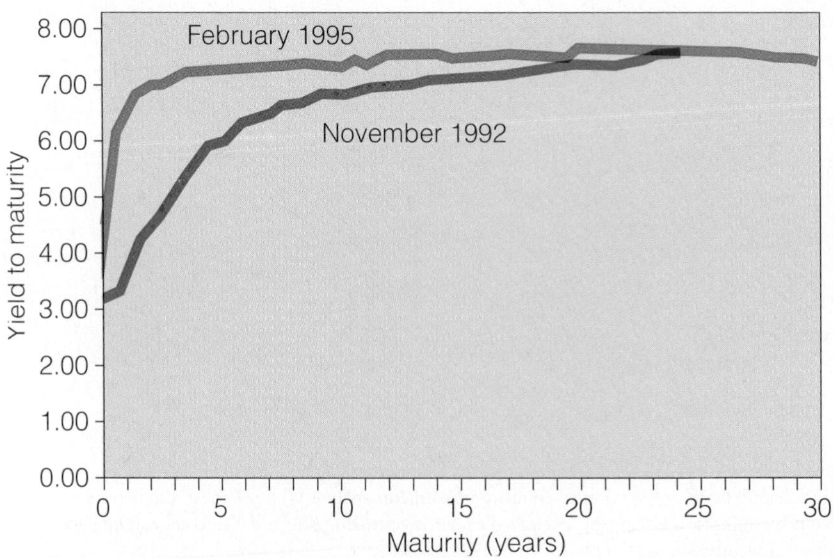

Transparency Available

FIGURE 3.7

OTHER SHAPES OF THE YIELD CURVE

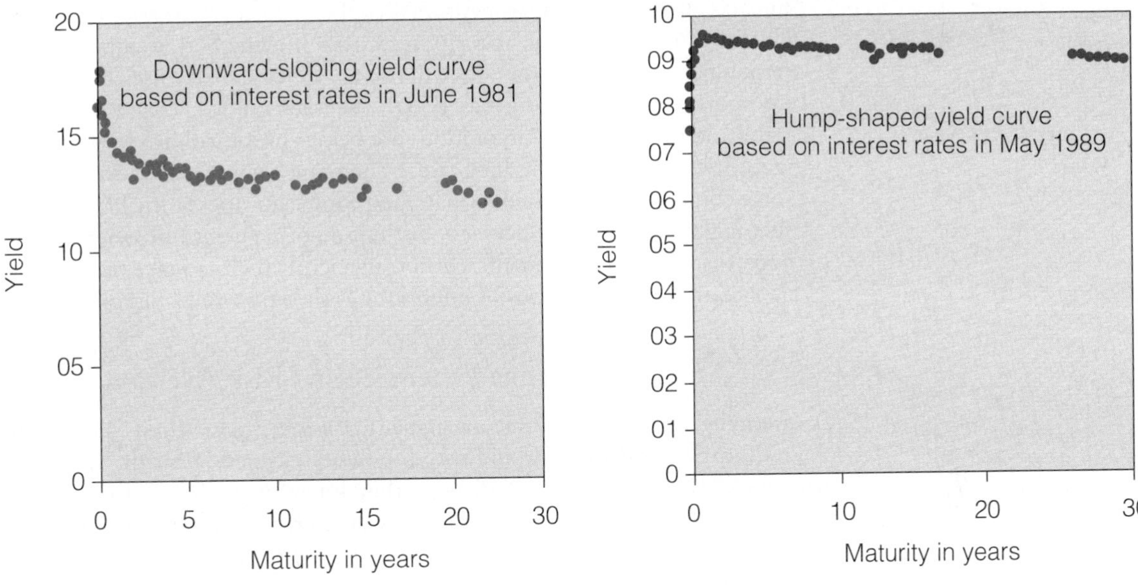

Transparency Available

the investor needs that liquidity for some reason. Alternatively, the investor could use a security with a 2-year maturity and sell the security after 1 year if cash were needed. However, the sales price might be less than $10,000, depending on market conditions at that time. Rather than bear the risk of having to sell at a low price (recall that risk aversion is asymmetric, so the pain of a loss is greater than the offsetting pleasure of a comparable gain), the investor prefers to make the two 1-year investments.

Companies, on the other hand, prefer to borrow money for longer periods, so they prefer to issue longer-maturity securities. According to the liquidity preference theory, investors demand and companies willingly pay an interest rate premium on longer maturity securities. Thus, yield curves generally slope upward to reflect this premium. If interest rates (or inflation) are expected to fall in the future, this can offset the liquidity preference of investors, resulting in an inverted yield curve.

- The **unbiased expectations** theory contends that yield curves show the consensus attitude or expectation about future interest rates, particularly about future rates of inflation. If inflation is expected to increase, then the yield curve slopes up. If inflation is expected to fall, then the yield curve is downward sloping, and if no change is expected, the yield curve is flat. This theory seems to imply that each of the various yield curve shapes should occur with equal frequency. However, most of the time, yield curves are slightly upward sloping (as predicted by the liquidity preference theory). Thus, expectations may be supplementing liquidity preference in determining the shape of the yield curve.

- The **market segmentation** theory argues that there are fairly distinct markets for short-term, intermediate-term, and long-term securities. The shape of the yield curve is determined by the interest rates that equate supply and demand in each of these market segments. Thus, the yield curve shows the market-clearing rates of different maturity securities. If many borrowers want long-term funds, then long-term rates will rise to attract lenders. Similarly, if most investors prefer short maturities, then those rates will fall. This theory seems to rely on investors and corporations not being able or willing to shift among maturities to look for the best rates. There are some legal constraints and some corporate rules of thumb (matching bond maturities to the life of assets) that might create impediments to shifting among segments. In general, economists feel those impediments are not sufficiently high to make this the best explanation of the patterns of interest rates shown in yield curves.

An Aside on Time Preference and Risk Aversion

Occasionally, you will hear someone argue that if they were offered $1000 today or $1000 in 9 months they would take the future payment. Usually their argument goes something like this: Because they know they will need the money more in 9 months than they do now, they would prefer to receive it then. Such examples do not negate our assumption about the time preference people have about receiving cash flows, because such examples are usually about willpower or self-discipline, not the time value of money. A person who needs money in 9 months could take the $1000 today and put it in the bank, where it would earn interest for 9 months. They would have more than $1000 at the end of 9 months. Wanting to receive the $1000 in 9 months probably means the person knows that he will spend it between now and then, and he wants to assure that this will not happen. Do you have more than the necessary amount of federal income taxes taken from your paycheck in order to get a tax refund? That is much the same type of thinking. We aren't saying it is incorrect. In fact, if you know your habits and need a little help saving money, it is a very smart strategy. Such examples, however, are not about people's preference for having cash flows arrive later rather than sooner. Rather, they are about people's self-discipline regarding saving money. In terms of the concepts we have been discussing, this type of behavior may be a case of risk aversion outweighing the time preference for money. Some individuals may realize that their propensity to spend puts their savings at risk. They are willing to give up some interest income in order to protect their savings.

OPTIONS HAVE VALUE: THEY CAN OPEN DOORS AND REDUCE RISK

An Example of an Investment Creating an Opportunity

Introducing options helps prepare students to think more broadly about what an investment brings to the firm. Chapter 9 extends this discussion of options.

When evaluating an investment, investors also consider the opportunities and **options** that open up if the investment is made. An example will illustrate this idea. Suppose you are considering buying a car. There is a wide range of vehicles to choose from: cars, trucks, or vans. As a college student you need to work in the summer to help pay tuition in the fall. Finding summer jobs is difficult, so you need to plan ahead. If you found a car, a truck, and a van that were mechanically in the same condition, had equivalent accessories and operating costs, and so on, how would you choose among them? One consideration might be the opportunities the vehicles opened up to you. For example, the truck might let you start a summer yard-care business, thereby solving your summer job problem. You might decide to pay a bit more for the truck in order to have the option of starting a summer business. The premium you are willing to pay shows how much you value the option attached to the vehicle.

Reducing Risk with Options

Options are not just opportunities to start new ventures. Sometimes an option's primary function is reducing risk (remember, people are risk averse, so they try to reduce or limit risk). Just as people pay for insurance to reduce risk, investors buy options to reduce financial risk.

Here is an example. Suppose you decide to use your truck to start a lawn-care business. After buying the truck you have very little money left to purchase the mowers, trimmers, edgers, and so on, that you need for the business. A possible solution is to rent or lease the equipment. The rental company offers two different plans: leasing for the entire summer or monthly rental. For the entire summer, the monthly rental is slightly more expensive, but you can return the equipment at the end of any month. Because you don't know how many customers, if any, you will actually attract (that is, there is uncertainty regarding your need for the equipment), you might pay the higher monthly rent in order to have the *option* of returning the equipment after one month if you cannot attract enough clients. Having the option to shut down the business costlessly allows you to reduce some of the financial risk associated with uncertainty about attracting clients.

Options often allow investors to postpone a decision until more information is available. A real estate developer might choose to buy an option to purchase a tract of land rather than simply buying the land. The option contract gives the developer the right to buy the land at a set price within a specified period of time—e.g., within 6 months of signing the contract the developer can buy the land for $250,000. After 6 months the option expires, and if the developer wants the land, a new price must be negotiated with the seller. The option allows the developer to have access to the land while having time to better analyze the market, compute development costs, and determine if all the regulatory agencies will approve the development. Buying the land outright would have tied up a lot of money and subjected the developer to the risk of a loss if further analysis showed that the project was not feasible.

Options can reduce risk and enhance the value of an investment. In the future, options and optionlike financial instruments will play an increasing role in corporate finance and possibly in personal financial decisions as well.[9] In Chapter

[9]In late 1994 *derivatives*, or *financial derivatives*, which include options and other optionlike financial instruments, made the financial news regularly. A number of mutual funds, corporations, and government units posted large losses because of large investments in derivatives. Most notable was the Orange County (California) government's loss of more than $1 billion dollars. The impact was sufficient to cause several regulatory agencies to begin examining whether the use of these optionlike financial instruments needed to be controlled.

9 we discuss options again, particularly the way in which options can affect the value of an investment in productive assets such as machinery or factory space.

THE VALUE OF AN INVESTMENT

Now we combine the factors we introduced earlier into a single valuation model. This model relies on two types of information: (1) the amount and timing of the expected cash flows; and (2) the rate of return investors require to make an investment of the sort being analyzed. With this information, the valuation model provides the investment's value in dollars. We begin by discussing the *required rate of return.*

The Required Rate of Return

Some students may be familiar with the concept of reservation price. That concept can be useful in discussing the required rate of return.

In several places in this chapter we have mentioned the **required rate of return**. In our discussion of risk aversion, we concluded that investors require a higher rate of return as the investment's perceived risk increases. That conclusion led to our discussion of the risk-return trade-off—one of the most important concepts in finance—and the *risk premium.* The risk premium is the return in excess of the return on a safe investment that investors require to make a risky investment. To determine an investment's required rate of return, investors add a risk premium to the safe rate of interest. We estimate the yield, or return, on a risk-free, or safe, investment using the yields on U.S. government securities. These securities, Treasury bills, notes, and bonds, are considered to have no default risk because they are backed by the full faith and credit of the U.S. government.

required rate of return = return on U.S. Treasury security + risk premium

There are many possible U.S. Treasury securities from which to choose. The appropriate one will have the same maturity as the investment being examined. The return on a U.S. Treasury security is a nominal interest rate. It has two components: the real interest rate and expected inflation. Therefore, we can rewrite our expression for the required rate of return as

required rate of return = real rate + inflation expectation + risk premium

The expression shows how investors are trying to protect purchasing power and be compensated for bearing risk.

The three components in this expression are very different. The real rate of interest is fairly stable. Historically, it has varied between 2% and 4%. Inflation expectations, on the other hand, have varied dramatically during the past 15 to 20 years. During the 1980s, annual changes in the consumer price index ranged from just above 3% to nearly 14%. Expectations about inflation arise largely from macroeconomic effects—changes in the money supply and the growth rate of the economy and incomes. Predicting inflation is incredibly complicated. Fortunately for investors, nominal interest rates like those on U.S. Treasury bonds include the market's consensus estimate of expected inflation. In general, such market estimates provide better forecasts than elaborate models.

The risk premium that investors require from a particular investment depends on the riskiness of the investment and the current **price of risk** in the capital markets. The riskiness of the investment is determined by the variability of the investment's cash flows.[10] The price of risk depends on investors' attitudes toward risk. At times, investors become more concerned about risk, so risk premiums rise. At other times, investors seem willing to invest in just about anything, with little regard for risk. As investor psychology changes, the risk premium rises or falls. The risk premium widens as market participants become more risk averse and narrows as they become bolder.

The risk premium, along with the real rate of interest and expectations about inflation, determines an investment's required rate of return. We now combine the required rate of return with an investment's expected cash flow to develop a model of investment value.

The Value of an Investment

In finance we are interested in markets and market values. Thus, an asset's value is the price someone is willing to pay for it. When an investor determines an investment's value, the investor is actually determining the price she is willing to pay for the investment. The price is set so that the investment's expected future cash flows meet or exceed the investor's required rate of return for the investment. This is another way of saying that to be attractive to investors, an investment must pay investors at least their required rate of return. From our discussion of how investors adjust returns, we know that in competitive markets, investments that offer an expected return higher than the required return quickly have their prices bid up. This bidding process lowers the expected return, and this process continues until the expected return just equals investors' required rate of return. Therefore, assets traded in competitive markets are priced so investors expect to earn exactly their required rate of return. The general expression used to compute an investment's value is:

$$\text{Value of an investment} = \frac{\text{Expected future cash flows}}{\text{Required rate of return adjusted for time}}$$

The next six chapters will very carefully explain how to estimate expected future cash flows and required rates of return, and how to adjust value for the timing of those cash flows. Valuing assets—stocks, bonds, machines, land, and so on—is one of the most important skills taught in finance courses. The next series of chapters will help you develop this skill.

[10]We see in Chapters 7 and 8 that variability is not as important as *covaribility*. In those chapters we will use covariance, rather than standard deviation or variance, as a measure of an investment's risk. For the time being, however, we will continue to speak in terms of *variability*.

SUMMARY

In this chapter we examined how some general traits of human behavior apply to the evaluation of investments. People want to consume and, being rational, are concerned with cash flows that can be transformed into consumption. They are risk averse, so they must be paid a higher return if an investment is risky. Before investing, they examine the alternative investments available to them. Comparable investments must promise comparable benefits or returns. Moreover, the promised returns must be sufficiently high to offset any loss of purchasing power caused by inflation. The longer they must delay their consumption, the higher the future consumption must be. Finally, people are willing to pay a premium for investments that provide extra opportunities and options.

We combined several of these factors in developing the *required rate of return* for an investment. The required rate of return is the sum of the real interest rate, inflationary expectations, and a risk premium specific to the investment being examined. Investment occurs only if investors expect to earn at least their required rate of return. Although investors gladly accept returns higher than the required rate, competition among rational investors quickly adjusts excess returns to their required level.

Most of the topics introduced in this chapter are covered in more detail in the next five chapters. Chapter 4 examines in more detail the estimation of investment project cash flows. In Chapters 5 and 6 we demonstrate how to treat the timing of cash flows by using discounting techniques to compute present values. How to estimate risk premiums and required rates of return are the subjects of Chapters 7 and 8. Then we put these pieces together into a single procedure for evaluating investments. This investment analysis technique—net present value analysis or discounted cash flow analysis—is one of the primary tools that investors use when deciding which securities to buy and sell and that company managers use when deciding which products to make and which strategies to pursue.

KEY TERMS

rational self-interest
risk aversion
time preference of money
book value of an asset
market value of an asset
expected cash flows
expected value
expected return
capital gain
dividend yield
holding period return
annualized return
realized return
ex post return
ex ante return
risk premium
law of one price
the risk-return trade-off
bulls
bears
equilibrium conditions
inflation
cost-of-living adjustments (COLAs)
consumer price index (CPI)
producer price index (PPI)
nominal rate
real rate
Fisher equation

opportunity cost
certificates of deposit (CDs)
maturity date
annual percentage yield
yield curve
yield-to-maturity
liquidity preference
unbiased expectations
market segmentation
options
required rate of return
price of risk

KEY FORMULAS

$$\text{expected value} = \pi_1 CF_1 + \pi_2 CF_2 + \pi_3 CF_3 + \cdots + \pi_n CF_n = \sum_{i=1}^{n} \pi_i CF_i$$

where π_i is the probability of state i occurring and CF_i is the cash flow if state i occurs.

$$\text{expected return} = \frac{\text{expected price} - \text{starting price} + \text{dividends}}{\text{starting price}}$$

$$\begin{aligned}\text{return on a share of stock} &= \frac{\text{change in price}}{\text{starting price}} + \frac{\text{dividend income}}{\text{starting price}}\\ &= \text{capital gain} + \text{dividend yield}\end{aligned}$$

$$\text{rate of inflation} = \frac{\text{price at end of period} - \text{price at beginning of period}}{\text{price at beginning of period}}$$

$$\text{annualized return} = \frac{\text{holding period return}}{\text{holding period in years}}$$

$$\begin{aligned}\text{nominal rate} &= \text{real rate} + \text{expected inflation}\\ &\quad + (\text{real rate} \times \text{expected inflation}).\end{aligned}$$

$$\text{required rate of return} = \text{real rate} + \text{inflation expectation} + \text{risk premium}.$$

QUESTIONS

1. In this chapter we discussed rationality and its role in valuing investment opportunities. Apply our discussion to the phenomenon of baseball card collecting. As you probably know, baseball cards skyrocketed in price during the 1980s, despite having almost no intrinsic value (the value of the components—ink and cardboard) or practical usefulness. How can you justify the values people place on these cards?
2. The law of one price says that the same item cannot sell for two prices in the same market. Within a community identical items are often priced differently at two different stores. For example, a 24-ounce box of Grape Nuts cereal might cost $2.85 at one store and $2.99 at another grocery store just a few blocks or few miles away. Does this example show that the law of one price does not hold? How can this pricing situation exist while the law of one price holds?

3. Two stocks have the same risk. Consolidated Inc. is priced to return 18%, whereas Diversified returns just 14%. In an efficient capital market, what will happen to the relative prices of these two securities? Comment on the returns the two stocks pay when prices once again reach an equilibrium. Can you say anything about the prices of the two stocks? Will the prices be identical?
4. Many states have lotteries. When the lottery prize becomes quite large, say $10 million or more, many people who almost never buy lottery tickets suddenly decide to try to win the jackpot. Is this behavior rational? (*Hint*: Try to use expected values in your answer.)
5. The table shows hourly wages and accident rates for several occupations. Do these wage rates appear to follow the risk-return pattern of financial securities? Why might wages diverge from the risk-return trade-off pattern seen in efficient and competitive capital markets?

OCCUPATION	AVERAGE HOURLY WAGE	PROBABILITY OF SERIOUS ACCIDENT/DEATH PER YEAR
Carpenter	$12.35	1%
Big-three autoworker	$22.75	1%
Steelworker on skyscrapers	$26.75	4%
Lumberjack	$20.50	6%
Alaskan crab fisher	$22.65	9%

6. In 1994 Orange County, California, lost more than a billion dollars of its pension fund investment. The fund's managers lost the money while attempting to enhance the fund's returns by investing in some very sophisticated and risky securities. You probably could have saved the county's taxpayers millions of dollars by pointing out the lesson illustrated in Figure 3.2. What is that lesson?
7. Can you explain why people go whitewater kayaking but wear a life vest while they are going through the rapids? Are such people risk lovers, risk avoiders, or inconsistent about their feelings toward risk, or is there some other factor involved in their actions?
8. The yield curve relates what two variables? What is the typical shape of the yield curve?
9. Is the expected value the same as the most likely value? Consider a bet with two equally likely payoffs. Is the expected value one of the possible actual payoffs?
10. Does rational self-interest imply that business managers always look for the quickest profit? Explain.
11. Some economists argue that risk aversion depends on wealth and the size of the risk. Do gambling vacations to Las Vegas or Atlantic City appear to confirm or refute this argument?
12. Figure 3.2 and Exhibit 3.1 both show that small company common stocks have more risk (measured as standard deviation of returns) and commensurate higher returns than the common stock of large companies. Can you explain why smaller companies are riskier?
13. Why are investors more interested in cash flow than accounting profits or net income?

14. Retirees often have pensions with cost-of-living adjustments (COLAs). Does having COLAs imply that inflation has no affect whatsoever on their consumption patterns? Do you think COLAs must be made before or after inflation has occurred? How does this timing affect your answer?
15. If an investment offers a higher than required return, is the price too low or too high?
16. Why does Merrill Lynch use a bull as its mascot? Would an investment firm that thought a bear represented its investment philosophy be likely to earn big profits?

DEMONSTRATION PROBLEMS

1. ***Expected Value and Expected Return***

A stock sells today for \$80. Analysts expect the company to pay a \$3 dividend during the next year. Furthermore, they believe that the stock's market price 1 year from today will range from \$75 to \$100 with the following probabilities.

STATE OF THE WORLD	PRICE IN 1 YEAR	PROBABILITY OF STATE OCCURRING
Severe Recession	\$75	0.20
Mild Recession	\$85	0.30
Slow Growth	\$95	0.30
High Growth	\$100	0.20

Use this information to compute (a) the expected price one year from today and (b) the expected return from investing in this stock.

SOLUTION

a. Recall that the expected value formula is

$$\text{expected value} = \pi_1 CF_1 + \pi_2 CF_2 + \pi_3 CF_3 + \cdots + \pi_n CF_n = \sum_{i=1}^{n} \pi_i CF_i$$

where π_i is the probability of state i occurring and CF_i is the cash flow if state i occurs. Applying this formula to the data, we find that the expected price is

$$\begin{aligned}\text{expected price} &= 0.20 \times \$75 + 0.30 \times \$85 \\ &\quad + 0.30 \times \$95 + 0.20 \times \$100 \\ &= \$15.00 + \$25.50 + \$28.50 + \$20.00 \\ &= \$89\end{aligned}$$

b. Recall that the formula for the expected return from investing in stock is

$$\text{expected return} = \frac{\text{expected price} - \text{starting price} + \text{dividends}}{\text{starting price}}.$$

We substitute in the appropriate values (starting price = \$80, expected price = \$89, dividends = \$3) and calculate the expected return as follows:

$$\text{expected return} = \frac{\$89 - \$80 + \$3}{\$80} = \frac{\$9 + \$3}{\$80} = \frac{\$12}{\$80} = 0.15 = 15\%$$

2. ***Annualized Returns***

Suppose someone offers to pay you \$165 in 6 months if you lend them \$150 today. What will your annual rate of return be?

SOLUTION

Your return over 6 months is $\frac{\$165 - \$150}{\$150} = 0.10 = 10\%$. The 6-month holding period is equivalent to 0.5 years, so your annualized return is

$$\text{annualized return} = \frac{\text{holding period return}}{\text{holding period in years}} = \frac{10\%}{0.50} = 20\%$$

3. ***Capital Gains and Dividend Yield***

Last year ACME Inc. stock paid a \$1.00 dividend. The stock started the year with a price of \$13 and ended the year at \$15.50. Compute the total return for the year as well as the capital gain and dividend yield.

SOLUTION

$$\begin{aligned}\text{total return} &= \frac{\text{ending price} - \text{starting price} + \text{dividends}}{\text{starting price}}\\ &= \frac{\$15.50 - \$13.00 + \$1.00}{\$13.00} = \frac{\$2.50 + \$1.00}{\$13.00}\\ &= \frac{\$3.50}{\$13.00} = 0.269 = 26.9\%\end{aligned}$$

$$\begin{aligned}\text{capital gain} &= \frac{\text{ending price} - \text{starting price}}{\text{starting price}} = \frac{\$2.50}{\$13.00}\\ &= 0.192 = 19.2\%\end{aligned}$$

$$\text{dividend yield} = \frac{\text{dividends}}{\text{starting price}} = \frac{\$1.00}{\$13.00} = 0.0769 = 7.7\%$$

4. ***Price and Return***

A share of ZetaTech stock sells for \$30, and analysts believe it will earn a return of 8% over the next year. Investors require a return of at least 12% from share of this risk. How much will ZetaTech's share have to drop to be attractive to investors?

SOLUTION

We use the return formula to find the payoff one year from today. The known factors are today's price and the expected return, and the unknown factor is the future expected payoff. Therefore,

$$0.08\% = \frac{\text{expected payoff} - \text{today's price}}{\text{today's price}}$$

$$= \frac{\text{expected payoff} - \$30}{\$30}$$

$$\text{so expected payoff} - \$30 = 0.08 \times \$30$$

$$= \$30 + 0.08 \times \$30 = \$32.40$$

Now we need to find the price today that equates the payoff to the required return of 12%:

$$12\% = 0.12 = \frac{\text{expected payoff} - \text{today's price}}{\text{today's price}} = \frac{\$32.40 - x}{x}$$

$$0.12x = \$32.40 - x$$

$$1.12x = \$32.40$$

$$x = \frac{\$32.40}{1.12} = \$28.93$$

Therefore, the price must drop to $28.93 for ZetaTech stock to pay the required rate of 12%.

PROBLEMS

1. What would you expect XYZ's stock to sell for one year from now if there is a 20% chance it will sell for $25, a 50% chance it will sell for $30, and a 30% chance it will sell for $35?

   Expected Value
   1. $30.50

2. In Problem 1 what is the expected 1-year return for owning XYZ stock if its price is $28.00 and no dividend is expected?

   Expected Return
   2. 8.93%

3. What is the total return for a stock that was held for one year, during which it paid a $2.00 dividend, if you paid $45.00 for it one year ago and can sell it today for $52.00? What is the capital gain? What is the dividend yield?

   Return, Capital Gain, Dividend Yield
   3. Total return = 20%; capital gain = 15.56%; dividend yield = 4.44%

4. Consider two gambles. A is the flip of a fair coin and pays $100 if a head appears and zero otherwise. B is the roll of a fair six-sided die and pays $300 if a 6 is rolled and zero otherwise.
   a. What are the expected payoffs for the two gambles?
   b. Which gamble is riskier?
   c. If individuals are willing to pay $40 to play gamble A, what is its expected return?
   d. If individuals are risk averse, what can be said about the return on B vis-à-vis A?
   e. Given your answer to d, comment on the amount a person would pay for gamble 'B?'

   Expected Value and Risk Aversion
   4. a. EV(coin) = $50; EV(dice) = $50
   b. Dice bet is riskier (Var(coin) = 2,500; Var(dice) = 12,500).
   c. Expected return(coin) = 25%
   d. Expected return(dice) > expected return(coin)
   e. Pay less than $40 for dice bet.

Inflation
5. 10%

5. If prices for the same combination of goods rise from $100 one year ago to $110 today, what is the rate of inflation over this period?

Inflation
6. Purchasing power decreased by 2%

6. Suppose an investment's nominal interest rate includes an expectation for inflation of 5% for the next year. If inflation over this period is actually 7%, what has happened to investors' purchasing power? Is it expected or unexpected inflation that hurts people on fixed incomes?

Inflation
7. No

7. The CPI (consumer price index) is the most commonly used index for inflation or cost-of-living adjustments. If the market basket on which the CPI is based includes the cost of housing, entertainment, clothing, and a variety of other items and services, will cost-of-living adjustments based on the CPI always perfectly adjust wages for losses in purchasing power?

Annualized Returns
8. Annualized returns: A = 14%; B = 12%

8. Investment A returns 7% over a 6-month holding period, whereas Investment B returns 18% over an 18-month holding period. Which investment would you choose, and why?

Time Value
9. No, less than $1 million

9. Many states now have lotteries. The grand prize in these lotteries is often $1 million, payable over 10 years in $100,000 installments (less state and federal taxes). Is the value of the prize really $1 million?

Risk Aversion
10. State of Washington

10. In Problem 9, suppose the lottery described is sponsored by the state of Washington. Now, imagine that a lottery with identical payoffs is sponsored by the Dogwood Civic Theater Group, Dogwood, Washington. If you could win either lottery, which would you choose and why?

Risk Aversion
11. EV = 0, so would not accept

11. Consider the following bet: You give me $100 and roll two dice. If the sum of the two dice is odd, I give you back $120. If the sum of the spots on the dice is even, I give you only $80 back. Explain why a risk averse person would or would not accept this bet.

Expected Value
12. $2.285

12. Stock analysts regularly make dividend and earnings estimates for one year, two years, and 5 years in the future. Suppose that 20 analysts follow a major retailer, Joe's Club. Of these, 4 (or 20%) estimate that Joe's dividend next year will be $2.00, 5 (or 25%) estimate it will be $2.20, 8 (or 40%) estimate $2.40, and 3 (or 15%) think the dividend will be $2.50. What is the consensus estimate for Joe's Club dividend next year?

Risk and Return
13. EVs are long-run averages.

13. Comment on the following statement: We know that stocks are more risky than bonds. But in 1993 long-term corporate bonds had an average return of 13.19%, whereas large company stocks returned only 9.99%. This evidence shows that the theory about risk and return is hogwash.

Risk and Return disk icon

14. The following table presents 30 years of annual return data for several types of securities. Use a computer spreadsheet to graph the data so you can com-

YEAR	LARGE CO. STOCKS	SMALL CO. STOCKS	LONG-TERM CORP. BONDS	U.S. TREASURY BILLS
1964	16.48	23.52	4.77	3.12
1965	12.45	41.75	−0.46	3.54
1966	−10.06	−7.01	0.20	3.93
1967	23.98	83.57	−4.95	4.76
1968	11.06	35.97	2.57	4.21
1969	−8.50	−25.05	−8.09	5.21
1970	4.01	−17.43	18.37	6.58
1971	14.31	16.50	11.01	4.39
1972	18.98	4.43	7.26	3.84
1973	−14.66	−30.90	1.14	6.93
1974	−26.47	−19.95	−3.06	8.00
1975	37.20	52.82	14.64	5.80
1976	23.84	57.38	18.65	5.08
1977	−7.18	25.38	1.71	5.12
1978	6.56	23.46	−0.07	7.18
1979	18.44	43.46	−4.18	10.38
1980	32.42	39.88	−2.76	11.24
1981	−4.91	13.88	−1.24	14.71
1982	21.41	28.01	42.56	10.54
1983	22.51	39.67	6.26	8.80
1984	6.27	−6.67	16.86	9.85
1985	32.16	24.66	30.09	7.72
1986	18.47	6.85	19.85	6.16
1987	5.23	−9.30	−0.27	5.47
1988	16.81	22.87	10.70	6.35
1989	31.49	10.18	16.23	8.37
1990	−3.17	−21.56	3.78	7.81
1991	30.55	44.63	19.89	5.60
1992	7.67	23.35	9.39	3.51
1993	9.99	20.98	13.19	2.90

Annual returns from Ibbotson and Sinquefield, *SBBI Yearbook*, (Chicago: Ibottson and Associates, 1994)

ANNUAL RETURNS DATA FOR STOCKS, BONDS, AND T-BILLS 1964–93

ment both on trends over time and the distribution of the data. Compute means and standard deviations for each type of security to determine whether the data support the concept that higher risk (i.e. more variable) securities pay a higher rate of return?

15. Using the data in the table, when do you think the United States experienced a period of high inflation? Explain your answer by referring to a data series presented in the table.

14. See Instructor's Manual.
Large co.
11.6% (Ave. Return)
15.6% (Stan Dev.)
Yes, higher risk corresponds to higher returns.

Inflation

15. High inflation during the 1978–86 period

CHAPTER 4

Estimating Cash Flows

The good news is: This baby brought in $250,507,894.15 during the first quarter . . .

In Chapter 4 we will explore a lesson that Acme Coin in just discovering: It is not revenues, or even profits, that matter . . . it's cash flow.

This chapter begins our detailed examination of the specific components that make up the valuation formula introduced in Chapter 3. In this chapter we discuss how cash flows are estimated. Chapters 5 and 6 introduce present value and discounting techniques that help us compute the value today of cash flows to be received in the future. Chapters 7 and 8 show how risk is accommodated in the investment valuation process. Chapter 9 puts together these pieces and demonstrates how investment opportunities are evaluated.

THE IMPORTANCE OF CASH FLOW

Understanding the importance of cash flow, as opposed to accounting profits, is especially important to students thinking about starting their own businesses.

Cash—dollars and cents—is the lifeblood of every business. Companies distribute cash to shareholders in the form of dividends, use cash to pay employees and suppliers and to repay loans, and cash is all that the IRS (Internal Revenue Service) will accept as payment for taxes. For a business to stay healthy, it is cash, not accounting profits, that matter. This may sound like a contradiction, but many profitable, fast-growing small companies have gone out of business because they lacked sufficient cash to pay their bills. Regardless of its profitability, a firm without enough cash to pay its bills risks going bankrupt. Profitability is not identical to having cash. One of the key objectives of this chapter is explaining why accounting profits and cash differ. This difference hinges on several of the rules included in the accounting profession's generally accepted accounting principles (GAAP), so we will present a brief review of some basic accounting concepts.

Cash flow estimation and pro forma analysis are important in many business fields. Stress to students that these tools are widely applicable.

Once we understand how accounting profits and cash flows differ, we describe two methods for translating accounting profits to cash flows. We also demonstrate how to estimate the future cash flows of a brand-new project or investment. Once you have mastered these two techniques—translating accounting data to cash flows and estimating cash flows for a new project—you have achieved the primary objectives of this chapter. You have also gained a sound introduction to tools that are used daily by business people in a variety of fields. For example, before a banker makes a loan, she tries to determine the borrower's ability to pay (in cash) the anticipated loan payments. Investors make buy and sell decisions based on a stock's ability to generate cash dividends or share price appreciation (capital gains). Analysts in the marketing field regularly look at prospective cash flows from new products to decide which products to introduce. Much marketing research is designed to estimate how sales (and thereby cash flow) will be affected by changes in advertising, packaging, and product attributes. In the management area, human resource professionals examine the cash consequences of employee compensation and benefits programs. On the shop floor, manufacturing managers are concerned with saving money through more efficient operations; for instance, will a cash outlay for a new machine result in sufficient future cash savings to justify the purchase? And, the billion dollar megamerger deals of the 1980s depended heavily on estimates of the future cash flows of the merged companies. If the expected cash flows were not there, deals were called off.

THE CASH CYCLE OF A TYPICAL FIRM

We begin this chapter by describing how cash travels through a typical business enterprise. Understanding the **cash cycle** will help show why the profits reported on accounting statements differ from the actual cash generated by the firm's activities.

A Simple Cash Cycle

Students may need help understanding how cash flows through businesses in terms of credit sales, collections, and paying for labor and materials.

The operations of a typical firm are, in order: (1) goods are produced or purchased for resale; (2) sales are made; and (3) cash from the sales is collected. Only at stage 3 does cash flow into the firm, although accounting revenues and expenses may have been recorded at the earlier stages. The cash collected at stage 3 fuels another cycle of production, sales, and collections. Figure 4.1 shows such a cash cycle.

In Figure 4.1, the firm buys materials on credit and generates an account payable (A/P). During the manufacturing process the firm generates additional costs. Production costs include employee wages and benefits, utility expenses, and rent. Another cost of production is the wear and tear on, or depreciation of, equipment. The firm eventually sells the finished products and recognizes revenues and—it hopes—profits. If a credit sale is made, the firm receives no cash at the time of the sale. Instead, the sale creates an account receivable (A/R), and the firm must wait for the customer to pay the bill before any cash arrives. Profits

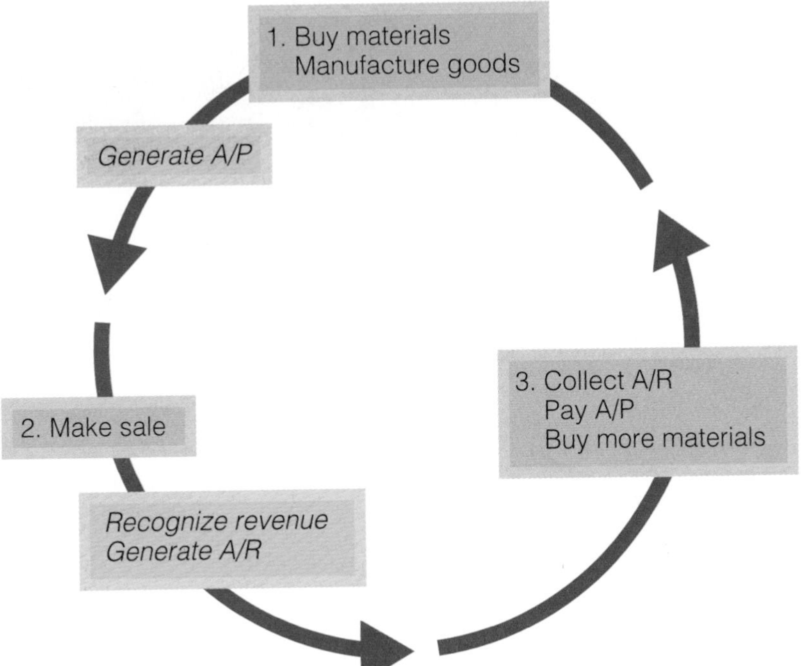

FIGURE 4.1
THE CASH CYCLE

Transparency Available

We have drawn the cash cycle as if it occurs once. In fact, it is a continuous process, and an actual company does each of these steps almost every day.

may be recognized at stage 2, before any cash is actually collected. Thus, accounting profits (or net income) may not represent cash flow.

Figure 4.1 shows a somewhat simplistic cash cycle. It ignores a number of important factors, such as taxes, dividends, cash infusions from the capital markets, maintaining an inventory to avoid stock-outs, and the purchase and sale of productive assets. These are added to the cash cycle diagram presented in Figure 4.2 to give a more complete picture of how cash moves into, out of, and through the firm. As Figure 4.2 shows, taxes and dividends represent cash flowing out of the firm. The company acquires additional cash from the capital markets by selling shares of stock, issuing bonds, or borrowing from financial institutions.

FIGURE 4.2
THE COMPLETE CASH CYCLE

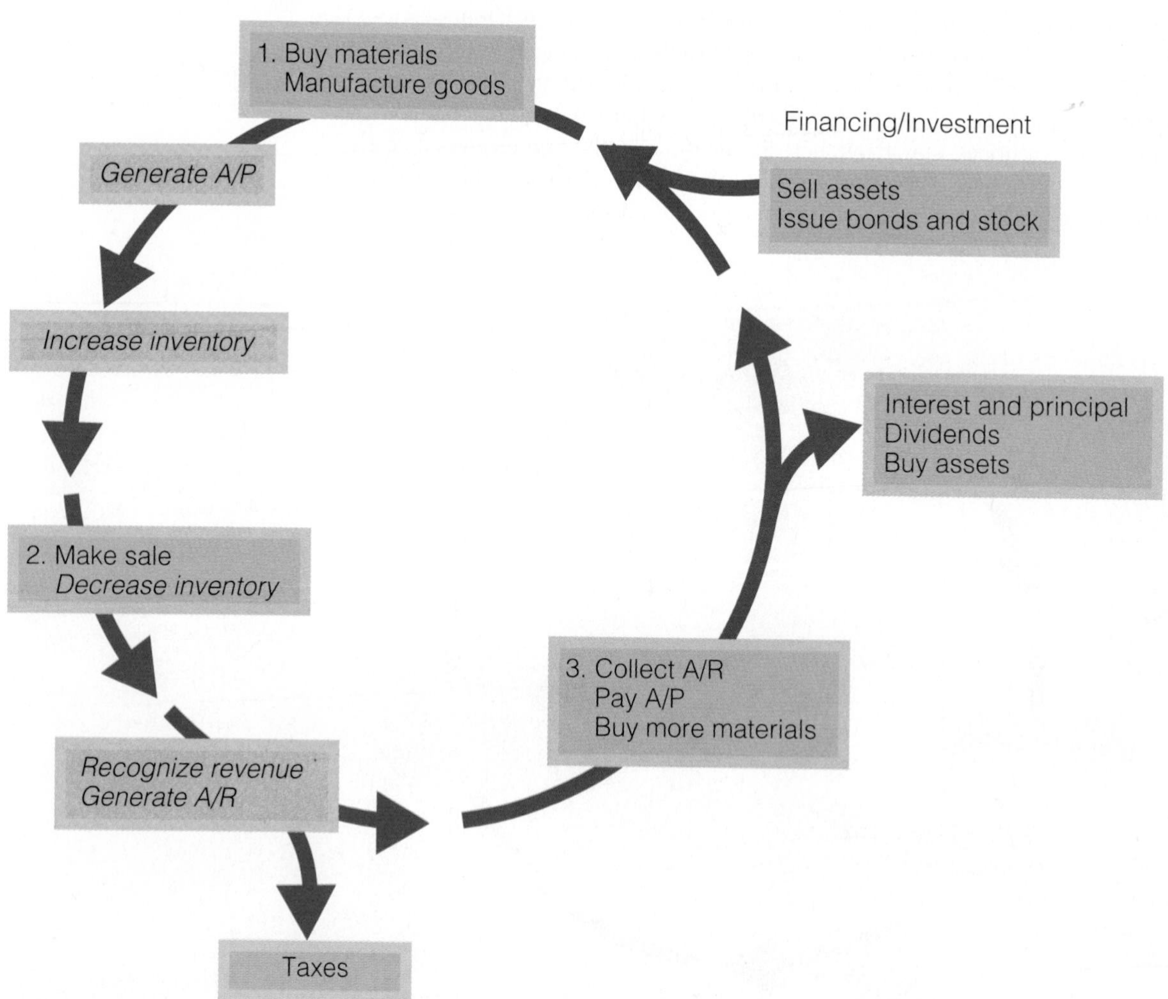

Because the company must pay its lenders interest and repay the amount borrowed, another cash outflow is debt service payments (interest and principal). Two arrows represent the sale and purchase of productive assets, such as machinery, vehicles, and factories. To remain competitive, companies upgrade their manufacturing methods with new equipment, selling the machines that no longer fit their production processes.

In both Figures 4.1 and 4.2, the company waits until it collects cash from its accounts receivable (A/R) to pay its bills and other expenses (A/P and other payables). If a company is able to delay paying its bills until it receives its cash, then, the company is self-financing. It generates sufficient cash, sufficiently quickly, to meet its obligations. In fact, this is usually not the case, although there are some notable exceptions to this rule. Large discount stores, such as Sam's Club and Price Costco, sometimes receive terms from suppliers that create a cash cycle in which they collect cash from customers before having to pay suppliers. This cash cycle allows them to invest and earn interest on the surplus cash until it is needed to pay suppliers. On occasion, discounters will show more income from interest than from actual retailing operations.

For example, interest income for Price Club was $27 million in 1991.

Suppliers of raw materials cannot give customers an unlimited period of time to pay their bills. Like the customer, the supplier has bills to pay and needs cash to pay them. Therefore, suppliers establish credit terms, called **supplier's credit terms**. For instance, a supplier might allow a customer 30 days from the time of shipment to pay for its order. Sometimes paying early, such as within the first 10 days, earns the buyer a *cash discount*. Examples of supplier credit terms are 2% 10/net 30 and 1% 15/net 45. The first set of terms, 2% 10/net 30, tells us that if the purchaser pays the bill within 10 days, he may reduce it by 2%, but the full amount is due within 30 days. The second set of terms says that a 1% discount is available if the bill is paid within the 15-day discount period, but the full amount is due within 45 days.

Calculate the annual cost of forgoing the discount.

Not paying within the 30-day credit period puts the account in arrears. Having a poor payment history can cause serious problems. Companies with poor credit histories may discover that suppliers will no longer sell to them on credit, demanding cash on delivery (C.O.D.). In addition, the supplier will be reluctant to make special efforts to accommodate the needs of a customer with a poor payment record. Special treatment might mean rush delivery, special size or quality of materials, or changing advanced orders. When supplies of materials are limited, poor payers are the first customers to be cut off. As you can see, paying within the prescribed time period is important to maintain good relations with key suppliers.

The trend toward just-in-time (JIT) manufacturing means that companies must have excellent relationships with suppliers.

Suppose a manufacturing firm has 30 days to pay one of its key suppliers. It is quite possible that the manufacturing process plus the time it takes to sell the manufactured item and collect the cash exceeds 30 days. If so, the company must pay its supplier before it receives the cash for the finished item. This **financing gap**—the time between having to pay for materials (and labor, utilities, taxes, etc.) and receiving the cash from sales—must be financed by the firm. The company needs a pool of cash or access to enough credit to cover this gap. Without access to cash, when the bill from the supplier comes due the company will not be able to pay it. Despite having made a profitable sale, the company could find itself in court for having unpaid debts.

Having a financing gap is not bad. It is a normal part of doing business, but the company must be prepared financially.

The Days Model (The Cash Conversion Cycle Model)

A neat way to look at the financing gap is the **days model**, or cash conversion cycle model. The days model requires computing three financial measures, or ratios:

1. The number of **receivables days** is the average number of days that a company has to wait to collect credit sales—that is, how long customers take to pay for their credit purchases. This value is computed as follows:

$$\textbf{receivables days} = \frac{\textbf{average accounts receivable}}{\textbf{annual credit sales}} \times 365$$

   If annual credit sales are not available, we use sales. Also, if the company is growing, it is more accurate to average 2 years of accounts receivable rather than using the most recent number, because accounts receivable reflects sales rates at the very end of the company's fiscal year.
2. The number of **inventory turnover days** is the average number of days stock is in inventory—that is, the average length of time between manufacturing an item (or purchasing an item for resale) and selling it. The number of inventory turnover days is computed as follows:

$$\textbf{inventory turnover days} = \frac{\textbf{average inventory}}{\textbf{cost of goods sold}} \times 365$$

   Again, we average two years of inventory data, particularly if the company is growing and inventory is increasing in a corresponding fashion.
3. The number of **accounts payable days** is the average number of days the company takes to pay its suppliers—that is, the time between purchasing materials and paying for them. This period will depend on the terms given the company by suppliers and whether there are incentives for early payment. Supplier credit is one of the most used forms of credit for businesses. The number of accounts payable days is computed as follows:

$$\textbf{accounts payable days} = \frac{\textbf{average accounts payable}}{\textbf{cost of goods sold}} \times 365$$

Stress that this model gives at best a rough guide to financing need, but it is useful in understanding how current account management affects the company.

Once the three activity ratios are calculated, we combine them in this way:

$$\text{days financing gap} = \text{receivables days} + \text{inventory turnover days} - \text{accounts payable days}$$

We multiply by the average cost of goods sold per day for the company, because the company is interested in its out-of-pocket costs.

The days model compares the length of time the company must wait for cash after purchasing materials to the spontaneous credit provided by suppliers. The net difference between these time periods is the length of the financing gap in days. To turn this into a dollar amount, we multiply by the average cost of goods sold per day for the company. This provides a rough estimate of a company's financing need.

Exhibit 4.1 shows the income statement and balance sheet for Carlson's Floor Coverings, a small company specializing in tile, marble, and synthetic floor coverings. We use the data in Exhibit 4.1 to compute the three activity ratios for the days model, and to estimate Carlson's financing need. First, because many of the accounts are increasing, we compute the average of the receivables, inventory, and payables accounts for 1994 and 1995. If we did not compute these averages, it would distort the activity ratios. These ratios would look too big, because we would be combining balance sheet data from the last instant of 1995, which reflects growth throughout the year, with income statement data for the entire year from January through December.

Using the average of two balance sheet values is very important for growing companies. Without this adjustment, activity ratios will be in error.

EXHIBIT 4.1

FINANCIAL STATEMENTS FOR DAYS MODEL EXAMPLE

CARLSON'S FLOOR COVERINGS
INCOME STATEMENTS FOR 1994–5

	Year Ended 12/31/1994	*Year Ended 12/31/1995*
Sales	217,143	244,655
Cost of goods sold	146,701	164,603
Gross margin	70,442	80,052
GA&S expense	47,328	51,648
Depreciation	6,588	7,256
Interest	2,535	2,638
Taxable income	13,991	18,510
Taxes	3,498	4,628
Net Income	10,493	13,883

CARLSON'S FLOOR COVERINGS
BALANCE SHEETS FOR 1994–5

ASSETS	*As of 12/31/1994*	*As of 12/31/1995*
CURRENT ASSETS		
Cash	8,025	13,245
Accounts Receivable	19,632	23,460
Inventory	29,742	36,077
Total Current Assets	57,399	72,782
Plant, Property & Equipment	67,895	73,895
Less: Accumulated Depreciation	21,356	28,612
Net Plant, Property, and Equipment	46,539	45,283
Total Assets	103,938	118,065
LIABILITIES AND EQUITY		
CURRENT LIABILITIES		
Accounts payable	8,842	9,921
Notes payable—bank	4,472	4,760
Other current liabilities	3,298	3,175
Total Current Liabilities	16,612	17,857
Long-term debt	24,560	23,560
SHAREHOLDERS' EQUITY		
Common stock at par	12,000	12,000
Additional paid-in capital	18,000	18,000
Retained earnings	32,766	46,649
Total Liabilities and Equity	103,938	118,065

Transparency Available

$$\text{average accounts receivable} = \frac{19{,}632 + 23{,}460}{2} = 21{,}546$$

$$\text{average inventory} = \frac{29{,}742 + 36{,}077}{2} = 32{,}910$$

$$\text{average accounts payable} = \frac{8{,}842 + 9{,}921}{2} = 9{,}382$$

Next we compute the activity ratios using 1995 sales and cost-of-goods-sold data. We use 1995 income statement data because it corresponds to the period between the construction of the 1994 and 1995 balance sheets.

$$\text{receivables days} = \frac{\text{average accounts receivable}}{\text{annual credit sales}} \times 365 \text{ days}$$

$$= \frac{21{,}546}{244{,}655} \times 365 = 32.1 \text{ days}$$

$$\text{inventory turnover days} = \frac{\text{average inventory}}{\text{cost of goods sold}} \times 365 \text{ days}$$

$$= \frac{32{,}910}{164{,}603} \times 365 = 73 \text{ days}$$

$$\text{accounts payable days} = \frac{\text{average accounts payable}}{\text{cost of goods sold}} \times 365 \text{ days}$$

$$= \frac{9{,}382}{164{,}603} \times 365 = 20.8 \text{ days}$$

We combine these activity ratios into the days model as follows:

$$\text{financing gap in days} = \text{receivables days} + \text{inventory turnover days} - \text{accounts payable days}$$

$$\text{financing gap in days} = 32.1 + 73.0 - 20.8 = 84.3 \text{ days}$$

It is possible for the financing gap to be negative. You might ask students what a negative financing gap implies about a company's cash needs.

The company must fund 84.3 days of business. That is, the company must finance 84.3 days of sales at their cost of sales per day, which is cost of goods sold divided by 365. Therefore, the financing gap in dollars is

$$\text{financing gap (\$)} = \text{financing gap in days} \times \frac{\text{cost of goods sold}}{365}$$

$$= 84.3 \times \frac{164{,}603}{365} = \$38{,}016$$

The company needs about $38,000 to see it through its cash conversion cycle. This money allows the company to continue to purchase inventory and make credit sales while it waits to collect cash from earlier credit sales. This estimate of financing need is very rough. Later in the text we will show a much more accurate method for estimating financing need in terms of amount and the timing of the need.

WHY ACCOUNTING PROFITS AND CASH FLOWS DIFFER

Generally accepted accounting principles (GAAP) prescribe how accountants record business transactions and construct financial statements. These accounting rules were designed to provide an objective portrayal of a company's business activities and how those activities affect the company's financial position. Three accounting principles are particularly important in understanding why accounting profits often differ from cash flows. These principles deal with the recognition of revenue, how expenses and revenues are matched, and rules regarding how the depreciation of long-lived equipment (i.e., how the wear and tear of equipment) is shown on the income statement. These principles, especially the matching principle, mean that corporate financial accounting is an accrual accounting system, not a cash accounting system. As we discuss these accounting principles, you will see how accrual accounting differs from cash accounting.[1]

Revenue Recognition

The rules of **revenue recognition** state that revenues are recorded when a transaction has occurred. There are several definitions of *transaction.* It may be when the title or ownership of an item changes from the seller to the buyer. It may be at the time of delivery or pickup. Or, in some cases, a transaction might occur when an order is placed. The actual point at which a sale is considered to have been completed varies, depending on the nature of the contract or agreement between the buyer and the seller, the rights of the buyer to renege on the deal, and so on.[2] One thing to notice about the definitions: None define a transaction as occurring when money changes hands.

There is a very good reason for this omission. Many sales are made on credit; that is, the buyer delays paying for several weeks or months or spreads the payments out over time. If sales were recorded only as the cash arrived, the sales figure for a particular period would reflect the cash collected, not the actual sales activities during the period. The objective of the GAAP principles is to provide an accurate picture of a company's activities, the primary one of which is selling products, not collecting cash. Therefore, the accounting rules are designed to focus more on sales and revenue generation than on cash collection.

---

[1]Cash accounting is the system you use in your checkbook. At any moment in time (except for checks that have been written but haven't yet been cashed), the balance shows the cash you have available.

[2]A few companies have used the vagary in the definition of when a sale takes place to inflate their revenues. For example, in the late 1960s and early 1970s several companies selling franchises recorded as current revenue all franchise fees to be received in the next 5 years, even though the franchisees might go bankrupt or could cancel the agreement. By recognizing revenues in this way, these companies had enormous sales growth and lured many unsuspecting investors into buying their stock. When the truth about the companies' accounting practices finally emerged, their stock prices fell like a rock. The Accounting Standards Board responded by tightening the method for recognizing revenue from franchisees.

The Matching Principle

The rules of accounting require that the expenses recorded on the income statement be those associated with the sales recognized during that period. That is, expenses refer to the cost of producing the items sold, not the actual cash outlays for labor, materials, etc., made during the period. For example, suppose a company manufactures 175 air conditioners during the month of April but sells only 100 units. The expenses for April are based on the cost of producing the 100 units that the company actually sold.[3] Even if the company paid cash for raw materials and labor to produce 175 units, the cost of goods sold (COGS) on the income statement reflects the expense of producing only 100 units. The cost of producing the other 75 units will appear on future income statements when those units are sold. If the company has paid cash to its employees and suppliers of raw materials for the 175 units produced, then the expense shown on the income statement understates the cash outlays the firm has made. Correspondingly, net income overstates how much cash the firm has generated during the period.

Students sometimes argue for using a cash basis for financial reporting, but this creates difficulties in assessing performance.

The **matching principle** may also cause net income to understate cash flow. For example, suppose the firm sold 100 units in April but paid for the raw materials used to manufacture those units in May. Then the expense shown for raw materials on the income statement would be greater than the actual cash outlays made in April for materials.

The matching principle is designed to give users of financial statements an idea of the firm's activities during a specific period of time. More specifically, the matching principle is designed to show a firm's profitability. By focusing on revenues or sales and then matching expenses to that sales level, the income statement presents information on the profitability of the company's operations.

Depreciation

When business people use the term **depreciation** they are referring to the allocation of the cost of a long-lived asset to several accounting periods. A machine, vehicle, computer, or building will usually last for more than 1 year. When a company invests in an asset that will be used for several years, it allocates the cost (or spreads out the cost) of the asset over those several periods. The idea is to match the use (or the consumption or wearing out) of the asset to the accounting period in which that use occurs. By reporting depreciation expense on the income statement as the asset is used, accountants attempt to present the total costs of doing business during that particular accounting period.

In terms of estimating cash flows, the allocation of depreciation means that net income is different than the cash generated during the period. This is most easily shown with an example. Suppose Acme Metal Fabricating Company purchases a computer-aided lathe in January of 1995 for $100,000. The lathe is expected to last for 5 years, at which time the company plans on trading it in for a newer model. In 1995, Acme writes a check for $100,000. The entire cash outlay for the lathe is made in 1995. In the years 1996 through 1999, there are

[3]The cost of the unsold 75 units is reflected in the inventory account on the balance sheet. In accrual accounting, any outlays, activities, or income that don't appear on the income statement appear as an asset or liability on the balance sheet.

no cash outlays associated with the lathe, but the company uses the lathe extensively each of those years. To allocate the cost of the lathe over its estimated useful life, the company's accountant adds a depreciation expense of $20,000 to the company's expenses for each of the 5 years from 1995 through 1999 ($5 \times \$20,000 = \$100,000$, the lathe's purchase price).[4] In years 1996 through 1999, the depreciation expense has no corresponding cash outlay. Because of this, depreciation is often called a *noncash expense* or *noncash charge*. The noncash expense lowers net income without affecting the firm's cash position. Of course, in 1995, when the machine was purchased, there was a cash outlay of $100,000, but an expense for use of the machine of only $20,000 was reported. Therefore, in 1995 the net income overstates the cash flows of the firm, whereas in the following 4 years, it understates the cash flows. Later in this chapter, we return to the topic of depreciation and describe in more detail how to compute depreciation expense and how firms benefit from depreciation tax deductions.

Exhibit 4.2 shows an **income statement** for Acme Metal Fabricating Company. The income statement provides a record of the company's activities during a period of time, typically for a 12-month *fiscal* year. In Exhibit 4.2, we identify the income statement accounts that cause net income and cash flow to differ. The sales account may not equal the cash collections for the accounting period because of revenue recognition rules. The matching principle implies that the actual cash flowing into or out of the firm may differ from the amount reported as cost of goods sold and GA&S expense for that period. GA&S expense stands for general, administrative, and sales expense and reflects costs necessary to operate the business that are not directly tied to the production of products. Depreciation expense, as we discussed before, is a noncash charge that allocates the cost of long-lived assets—for example, machines, vehicles, buildings—to the accounting periods during which the asset is used. Therefore, the income statement amount does not reflect an actual cash outlay. In many cases, depreciation is the major factor that causes accounting profits and cash flow to differ.

Although a detailed discussion is beyond the scope of this text, the amount of taxes reported on company income statements often differs from the actual

EXHIBIT 4.2

THE GAAP THAT CAN CAUSE PROFITS AND CASH FLOW TO DIFFER

Acme Metal Fabricating Co.
Income Statement
for the year ended December 31, 1995
($ in 000s)

Sales, net of discounts	$257,000	← Revenue recognition
COGS	176,545	← Matching principle
Gross margin	80,455	
GA&S expense	22,158	← Matching principle
Depreciation	34,780	← Cost allocation
Earnings before taxes	23,517	
Taxes	7,525	
Net Profit or Net Income	15,992	

Transparency Available

[4]Recall from your accounting course that when the company buys the lathe, it records an increase in fixed assets of $100,000. Each year when it records its depreciation expense, it reduces the value of the asset by the amount of the depreciation.

cash payment made to the Internal Revenue Service and/or state taxing agencies. Usually, if you see an account titled "Deferred Taxes" on a firm's balance sheet, there have been some differences between the tax expense on the firm's income statements and the taxes paid in cash.

TRANSLATING ACCOUNTING PROFITS INTO CASH FLOWS

Almost every income statement category can have a recorded amount that differs from the actual cash inflows or outflows for that category. You may ask why accountants don't simply keep track of cash, instead of using the accrual accounting system. In fact, in response to a growing interest in cash flow information, accounting statements now include a statement of cash flows. The **statement of cash flows** is a more detailed, cash-oriented version of the earlier "Sources and Uses Statement" and "Changes in Financial Position" that were standard elements of financial reports for many years. Later in this section we present an example of a statement of cash flows for Acme Metal Fabricating. But even without this statement, we can estimate a company's cash flows fairly easily.

We will describe two methods for transforming data from a company's income statement into an estimate of cash flow: a "quick and dirty" method and a more accurate, albeit longer, method. The quick method, which provides a rough estimate of the cash that the company generated from operations during the accounting period, requires just one step: Add the depreciation expense for the period to net income. That's it!

cash flow from operations = net income + depreciation

Why does this simple computation change net income into cash flow? If depreciation is the only noncash charge in a firm's income statement, then all other expenses are associated with cash outlays. Net income is equal to cash collections less all expenses for which cash outlays were made plus depreciation [net income = cash collections − (cash expenses + depreciation)]. Therefore, by adding depreciation to net income, we have changed the equation to reflect only cash collections and cash outlays [net income + depreciation = cash collections − cash expenses].

A simple way to remember these rules is *assets absorb, liabilities provide.*

For many uses the simple formula shown here is sufficient. If you need to be more precise, you must also consider changes in asset and liability accounts. Examples of such **balance sheet** effects include changes in A/R from credit sales, changes in A/P from the delayed (or early) payment for supplies, changes in debt and equity accounts caused by new funds the firm obtained from (or repaid to) banks or investors, and changes to the plant, property, and equipment account caused by expenditures for (or proceeds from the sale of) long-lived assets. The effects on cash flows due to changes in assets and liabilities are as follows:

The cash account is sometimes confusing. Distinguish between cash available for use and having a cash balance.

- Increases in asset accounts reduce cash: For example, an increase in the accounts receivable account, from the beginning to the end of the accounting period, means less cash was collected than indicated by sales, and an increase in the plant, property, and equipment account means that cash was used to purchase assets.

- Decreases in asset accounts increase cash: For example, selling a machine decreases the equipment account but generates cash.
- Increases in liability and equity accounts increase cash: For example, an increase in the accounts payable account, from the beginning to the end of the accounting period, means less cash was actually paid for supplies than indicated in the expense portion of the income statement. Similarly, an increase in the long-term debt or preferred stock accounts means that additional funds were supplied to the firm by investors.
- Decreases in liability and equity accounts use cash: For example, if a loan to the bank is repaid during the accounting period, the notes payable decrease and cash is used.

Following these rules, the simple cash flow formula is expanded as follows.

cash flow = net income + depreciation − (change in assets)
+ (change in liabilities and equity)

This formula is applied in the **statement of cash flows**. The statement of cash flows usually includes three broad categories of cash flows: cash from operations, cash from investing activities, and cash from financing activities. Cash flows from operations begin with net income and make adjustments for depreciation and changes in receivables, payables, and inventories. Cash flows from investing activities arise from the purchase and sale of marketable securities and productive assets such as machinery. Cash from financing activities include the repayment of debt (a use of cash), the payment of dividends (another use of cash), and the issuance of new securities (a source of additional cash).

Exhibit 4.3 shows Acme's balance sheets for 1994 and 1995, and Exhibit 4.4 shows the statement of cash flows for Acme Metal Fabricating for 1994 and 1995. The statement of cash flows adjusts net income for all the changes in asset and liability accounts that occurred during the accounting period. We construct the statement of cash flows by comparing two consecutive balance sheets, noting any changes. The increase in accounts receivable (Exhibit 4.3) from $17,434 in 1994 to $21,761 in 1995 appears on the statement of cash flows as a decrease or a use of cash of $4,327 ($4,327 = $21,761 − $17,434). The decrease in inventories (an asset account) from $28,442 in 1994 to $26,140 in 1995 appears as an increase in cash flow. Decreasing an asset account releases cash, so cash flow increases. Conversely, decreasing a liability account, such as payment of notes payable, requires cash and thus reduces cash flow. An additional loan or any increase in a liability or equity account provides additional cash, so it enhances a company's cash position. The statement of cash flows reflects all changes between the two balance sheets. Balance sheet items that do not change do not appear on the statement of cash flows in Exhibit 4.4.

The statement of cash flows gives a much more accurate measure of cash flows than the simple formula cash flow = net income + depreciation. In some situations the simple formula will suffice, but for any important analyses the more precise formula should be used.

EXHIBIT 4.3

ACME METAL FABRICATING INC. CONSOLIDATED BALANCE SHEETS FOR 1994 AND 1995

	1995	1994
Assets		
Current Assets		
Cash	2,342	5,221
Marketable securities	2,185	2,108
Accounts receivable	21,761	17,434
Inventories	26,140	28,442
Total Current Assets	52,428	53,205
Plant, property, and equipment	562,457	499,305
Less: Accumulated depreciation	247,128	212,348
Net plant, property and equipment	315,329	286,957
Total Assets	367,757	340,162
Liabilities and Shareholders' Equity		
Current Liabilities		
Accounts payable	14,972	9,102
Notes payable—bank	25,845	28,612
Other current liabilities	8,250	8,250
Total Current Liabilities	49,067	45,964
Bonds (6.5%)	42,500	42,500
Bonds (7.75%)	32,500	32,500
Bonds (9.5%)	14,500	—
Total Long-Term Liabilities	89,500	75,000
Shareholders' Equity		
Common stock, $1 par value, 20,000 shares issued	20,000	20,000
Additional paid-in capital	65,000	65,000
Retained earnings	144,190	134,198
Total Shareholders' Equity	229,190	219,198
Total Liabilities and Shareholders' Equity	367,757	340,162

Transparency Available

EXHIBIT 4.4

ACME METAL FABRICATING INC. STATEMENT OF CASH FLOWS

	1995	1994
Cash Flows from Operating Activities		
Net income	15,992	11,547
Adjustments to net income		
Depreciation and amortization	34,780	26,856
Changes in current assets and liabilities		
Receivables	(4,327)	(2,375)
Inventories	2,302	(3,655)
Accounts payable	5,870	3,455
Net Cash Provided by Operating Activities	54,617	39,483
Cash Flows from Investing Activities		
Purchases of marketable securities	(1,065)	(896)
Sales of marketable securities	988	902
Purchases of property and equipment	(63,152)	(28,334)
Net Cash Used by Investing Activities	(63,229)	(28,328)
Cash Flows from Financing Activities		
Prepayment of notes payable	(2,767)	(2,457)
Proceeds from issuance of bonds	14,500	—
Dividends paid	(6,000)	(4,800)
Net Cash from Financing Activities	5,733	(6,257)
Net Increase (Decrease) in Cash	(2,879)	4,898
Cash at the Beginning of the Year	5,221	323
Cash at the End of the Year	2,342	5,221

Transparency Available

ESTIMATING CASH FLOWS FOR A NEW PROJECT

An Initial Estimate

The value of any investment (a new project, product, stock, bond, or entire business) depends directly on the cash flows that the investment generates. Therefore, before we can analyze an investment opportunity, we must estimate its cash flows. Estimating cash flows for some financial investments is fairly easy, because they involve promises (explicit or implicit) to make cash payments to investors. For example, a corporate bond has a stated coupon rate that defines the semiannual interest payments the bondholder will receive. Similarly, most preferred stock issues have a fixed cash payout, in the form of dividends, that stockholders will receive. For corporate investments, such as starting a new business or buying the machinery to produce a new product, it is much more difficult to estimate the investment's cash flows. Nonetheless, such estimates must be made to determine whether the investment should be made.

In this section, we describe how a financial analyst within a company might estimate the cash flows of a new project. The process is as follows: (1) estimate sales price and quantities; (2) estimate production costs; (3) estimate other costs, including depreciation; (4) construct **pro forma (or projected) income statements**, (5) transform the income statement data into cash flows using the method described in the previous section. As we discuss each of these steps, we will point out where a financial analyst might acquire the necessary information. It will quickly become apparent that financial analysis depends on the skills of people from departments throughout the company—marketing, production, accounting. Finance does not stand alone as a functional area but relies on and supports the activities of the entire business enterprise.

1. *Estimate sales price and quantities*. Once sales price and quantities are estimated, total revenue can be calculated. This stage relies heavily on marketing research. Marketing researchers are particularly skilled at estimating sales using consumer surveys, demographic information, and data from the introduction of similar products. As you can see, successful analysis of a new product requires a team of people with a variety of skills. It is not solely a finance function.

   Sales estimates are made for the length of the project's life. For fad items, such as toys tied to a children's movie, this might be a single season. For consumer goods the product life might be many years. Sales patterns for products entering new markets follow the product life cycle curve. Sales initially grow fairly quickly with initial market penetration and limited competition. Growth eventually slows as the product attains its mature market share. With the entry of improved products or more competitors, either sales quantity or sales price falls, implying a reduction in total revenue. Depending on the situation, the product may be forced entirely out of the marketplace by superior alternatives or, if competitors' products are similar, may generate a fairly constant, low-profit revenue stream for an extended period of time. Sales and revenue estimates that ignore the product life cycle concept will probably not provide the quality of estimation needed to complete a careful analysis. For products entering established markets, penetration and market share growth may be much more difficult. For products entering either new or established

A project's life is sometimes difficult to estimate. Erring by a few years on the life of a long-lived project usually will not have too large an impact on the outcome of the analysis.

markets, the quality of cash flow estimates will depend on the quality of the market research supporting those estimates.

Is a long series of high cash flows likely if entry barriers are low? If not this pattern, then what pattern would be appropriate?

The actual revenue pattern depends on how much protection the product has from its competitors. Protection may occur in the form of patents, copyrights, investment in brand name recognition, and high start-up costs. The higher these barriers to entry, the longer the product's life cycle and the higher are the profits that the product can generate. Besides entry barriers, we need to look at exit barriers. For example, competitors are more inclined to enter a market if leaving is cheap. Exit is costly if production requires machines that are so specialized that they cannot readily be sold once production has ended. When reviewing sales forecasts, we must think about what competitors might be willing to do. This process requires a careful analysis of entry and exit barriers.

Production cost can vary over time due to economies of scale, learning effects, and other efficiencies that the company might capture.

2. *Estimate production costs.* At this stage, the financial analyst teams up with individuals from the operations and manufacturing areas. Engineers and manufacturing managers have some training in this type of cost estimation. Production costs are often categorized as direct or indirect and as variable or fixed. Direct variable costs vary with the number of units being produced and are associated directly with production; these costs include materials and wages for production-line workers. Indirect variable costs also vary with the quantity produced but are not directly involved with production; these costs include wages for machine-maintenance personnel or supply handlers. Usually, we combine these two costs into a single *variable cost*, or *cost per unit* estimate.

We use the "with and without" rule to decide which costs to include. Envision the firm with and without the project and include only those costs that change because of accepting the project.

3. *Estimate other costs, including depreciation.* Other costs of production, often called *overhead*, or fixed costs, can also be categorized as either direct or indirect. Direct fixed costs might include rent for a piece of equipment. The rental cost is set (or fixed) in advance and does not vary with production levels, but the machinery is used directly in the production process. Indirect fixed costs are items such as factory rent, managerial salaries, insurance, and depreciation. Overhead estimates are most often computed by accountants or the company's controller. These individuals have access to the company or plantwide expense information required to estimate these costs. Deciding which fixed costs to include in a project's costs can be tricky. In Chapter 9 we discuss how to identify a project's relevant costs. The general rule of thumb is to exclude costs that are truly fixed (often referred to as *sunk costs*)—that is, costs that will not change whether or not the new product is introduced.

   A cost that needs to be considered is the purchase price of equipment needed to produce the new product. The purchase price and depreciable life of the equipment will determine the periodic depreciation expense associated with the asset's use. It is important to consider depreciation expense, because it reduces taxable income and, thereby, tax payments.

Students tell us that learning how to construct pro formas is one of the important skills they learned in the course.

4. *Construct pro forma (or projected) income statements.* Using the data from steps 1 through 3, we construct the project's income statements for each year (or other accounting period if more appropriate) of the project's life. The income statements will vary over time as sales levels and prices change. Over long periods of time, even fixed costs may change. For example, if the business grows beyond a certain size, an additional manager, with a fixed salary and benefits, may be needed to help supervise the growing business.

The procedure for constructing the *pro forma* income statement is roughly as follows.

a. Obtain sales estimates.
b. Compute cost of goods sold as a percent of sales based on historical data from similar projects, or, if information is available, the costs can be estimated directly.
c. Compute gross margin = sales − cost of goods sold.
d. Determine general, administrative, and sales expense, depreciation expense, and other expenses based on cost estimates, planning projections, or historical patterns from similar projects.
e. Compute taxable income by subtracting the expenses in (d) from the gross margin.
f. Compute taxes using the companywide rate or rates from tax tables; then subtract taxes from taxable income to arrive at net income.

In Appendix 4, we demonstrate how to construct *pro forma* balance sheets. While *pro forma* income statements are sufficient for rough estimates of cash flow, more precise projections require balance sheet information. Moreover, other types of financial decision making rely on having data from future balance sheets.

5. *Transform net income into cash flows*. We showed two methods for transforming net income into cash flow. The simple method just adds depreciation back into net income. This gives a quick estimate of cash flow. Some new product analyses ignore the delay of A/R collections or the postponement of paying A/Ps, so the only step necessary to calculate cash flow is to add depreciation expense to net income. A much more accurate method of cash flow estimation considers changes in net working capital (changes in current assets less changes in current liabilities). In many cases, sales of a new product will be on credit. Recall from our discussion of the cash cycle that accounts receivable generated from credit sales must be financed by the company. This requires additional cash. To build up and maintain inventories also absorbs cash. In part, accounts receivable and inventories may be financed spontaneously by supplier credit in the form of accounts payable. Considerable cash may be needed to support these changes in net working capital, so ignoring these required cash outlays may create a significant understatement of the total cash needed to initiate a project.

   Not all investments in net working capital occur when a project is begun. As sales grow, additional investment in A/Rs and inventories will be required. If competition increases, existing customers may be kept and new customers attracted by more liberal credit terms, which effectively lower the price of the product or service. More generous credit terms generally slow receipt of receivables, so they may further increase working capital needs. Unlike other costs, investments in working capital are released or returned at a project's completion. As the last A/Rs are received and inventories are reduced, the cash tied up in net working capital is released.

Sometimes the entire working capital investment cannot be recovered—e.g., if inventory is damaged or consumers no longer want the items.

These five steps provide a method for estimating the cash flows associated with a proposed project. The estimation process draws on the skills of people from throughout the company—marketing, manufacturing, accounting. The financial analyst rarely makes decisions without conferring with other functional areas. Since collaboration and teamwork is commonplace in most organizations, finance experts need an understanding of nonfinance areas and marketing professionals (or people from other functional areas) will find an understanding of finance to be very helpful.

Example: Estimating Cash Flows for the Steaming Bean Coffee Cart

Coffee drinking is becoming an art form. In Seattle, Washington, coffee drinkers have a special language for ordering their favorite lattes, espressos, or mochas from the hundreds of corner coffee carts that are an institution in that city. Small towns are catching the coffee fever, too. The owners of the Smalltown Bakery and Coffee Shop want to know if a coffee cart would be a profitable investment for them. They would pull the cart to a busy corner near the local college. This particular corner is across the campus from the union building, the only place on campus where students can get a quick cup of coffee. The cart costs $18,000 and will require about $500 of maintenance per year.

Step 1 Estimating Sales Revenue

A little investigation shows that the snack bar at the college union sells a large cup of generic coffee to go for 85¢ and that nearby restaurants and cafes charge between 50¢ and 75¢ for a small cup of coffee with refills. A price premium can be charged for *good* coffee that a person can get quickly and carry with them to class or work. Some people will buy more expensive types of coffee—espresso or cappuccino—so we estimate that the average sales price will be $1.15 per cup.

The college is in session for two 15-week semesters and an 8-week summer session. Weekends are very quiet around the campus, so the cart will only be used on weekdays. Thus, the coffee cart has about 205 possible sales days (2 semesters of 15 × 5 days each plus 8 × 5 days in the summer plus 2 × 5 days for finals and 1 more week for fall registration). A few hours spent on the street corner where the cart will sit as well as wandering around the nearby cafes gives us an idea of the demand for coffee to go. Our sales estimates range from 60 to 90 cups of coffee a day, so we decide to begin our analysis by using an average sales level of 75 cups a day. The manufacturer of the coffee carts has told us that over time sales tend to grow as more people develop a taste for good coffee. Therefore, we estimate daily sales of 85 and 95 cups per day for the second and third years of the project. If we are successful, competitors will emerge. The cafes may offer high-quality coffee to go or the college might start an annex. To reflect the effect of competition, we estimate sales falling to 85 and 70 cups per day in years 4 and 5 of the project. Later we can examine whether we will still make money at more conservative estimates that reduce sales by 15 cups per day, i.e., 60 cups per day in year one rather than 75, and so on. The manufacturer tells us that after 5 years the cart needs a complete overhaul, so we won't project revenues beyond this date.

Combining the price and quantity estimates, we estimate our revenues to be about $17,681 the first year, climbing to nearly $22,400 in year 3. Exhibit 4.5 shows these revenue estimates. The accuracy of these revenue estimates depends on whether the quantity and mix of items sold occurs as projected. We could improve the estimate by spending more time and money on market research.

YEAR	1	2	3	4	5
Sales price	$1.15	$1.15	$1.15	$1.15	$1.15
Selling days	205	205	205	205	205
Sales per day	75	85	95	85	70
Revenue	$17,681	$20,039	$22,396	$20,039	$16,503

EXHIBIT 4.5

SALES REVENUE ESTIMATES FOR THE STEAMING BEAN COFFEE CART

Transparency Available

Have students compute revenues from the Steaming Bean example due to a change in demand.

The appropriate amount of market research varies from project to project. For example, an investment in specialized machinery, for which no secondary market exists, requires more preliminary research than buying assets with active secondary markets. In the first case, if the project fails to meet expectations, the machinery will almost certainly be sold at a deep discount or loss. In the second situation, there are alternative uses for the machines, so they can be sold easily with little or no price discount.

Step 2 Estimating Production Costs

The direct costs of sales include the cups and lids, coffee, sugar, cream, and labor. From our experience at the Smalltown Bakery, we have a very good estimate of what a cup of coffee costs to make. With a cup and lid, the average cost per cup is 18¢. The cart will be at the corner from 7:00 A.M. through 1:00 P.M., and 1 hour is needed to move it to and from its storage area. At $6 per hour for 7 hours per day, the annual labor cost will be approximately $8,610. The cost of transporting the cart to its corner will cost about $3 per day in gas and wear and tear on the truck used to haul the cart. We do not include any storage cost for the cart, because it will be stored in a small space behind the bakery which has no other uses.[5]

Step 3 Estimating Other Costs

The cart will be depreciated over 5 years using the straight-line method. After 5 years the cart will have to be completely overhauled, so it will have no value. The maintenance will be expensed. City business licenses will cost $100 per year. Exhibit 4.6 shows all the costs associated with running the coffee cart.

YEAR	1	2	3	4	5
Coffee costs 18¢	$ 2,768	$ 3,137	$ 3,506	$ 3,137	$ 2,583
Labor (7 hours at $6.00)	$ 8,610	$ 8,610	$ 8,610	$ 8,610	$ 8,610
Transport (at $3/day)	$ 615	$ 615	$ 615	$ 615	$ 615
Business license	$ 100	$ 100	$ 100	$ 100	$ 100
Depreciation	$ 3,600	$ 3,600	$ 3,600	$ 3,600	$ 3,600
Maintenance	$ 500	$ 500	$ 500	$ 500	$ 500
Total Annual Costs	$16,193	$16,562	$16,931	$16,562	$16,008

EXHIBIT 4.6

COSTS FOR OPERATING THE STEAMING BEAN COFFEE CART

Transparency Available

[5]If the storage space had other uses—e.g., if it could be rented—we would have to consider the earnings given up by not pursuing the next best use of the space. We discuss these *opportunity costs* in Chapter 9.

Step 4 Constructing Pro Forma Income Statements

The income statement shows revenues, expenses, taxes, and net income. By combining the data from Exhibits 4.5 and 4.6, we can compute taxable income. We expect that the income tax rate (combined federal and state taxes) will be about 22%. We calculate the tax liability for the year by applying this 22% tax rate to the taxable income. These calculations are shown in Exhibit 4.7.

Step 5 Transforming Net Income Into Cash Flow

In the case of the Steaming Bean Coffee Cart, we have no receivables or payables, so we can use the simple formula for changing net income into cash flow: cash flow = net income plus depreciation. The cash flow estimates are shown in the bottom row of Exhibit 4.7. Cash flow from the coffee cart varies from just under $4,000 in year 5 to $7,863 in year 3. Had there been inventory, receivables, and/or payables, we would have included the year-to-year changes in those accounts in our cash flow estimate.

Notice that the net income amounts severely understate the cash flow the coffee cart generates. Had we stopped our analysis without adjusting net income into cash flow, this investment might not have appeared to be very worthwhile. The cash flow data make it seem much more attractive. Whether or not the investment should be made is a topic for Chapter 9.

Even in this simple application of cash flow estimation, we drew on marketing skills (to estimate the sales price and quantity), economic theory (to reflect the effect of competitive entry), production (to estimate the cost of producing the coffee), and accounting (to construct the pro forma income statements). Financial decision making combines information from throughout the firm into a single analysis. Financial analysis involves putting together various pieces of business and economic information into a single comprehensive, and comprehensible, analysis.

Sensitivity Analysis

Stress that spreadsheet software makes sensitivity analyses simple. Being adept at this type of analysis is almost required for getting an entry-level job in finance.

In the Steaming Bean Coffee Cart example, we used our best estimates of price, quantity, and costs to arrive at an estimate of annual cash flow. **Sensitivity analysis** goes a step beyond our best estimate and examines how changes in revenues or costs affect the cash flow estimates. For example, suppose that the Smalltown City Council decided to raise the fee for business licenses from $100 to $150.

EXHIBIT 4.7

PRO FORMA INCOME STATEMENT AND CASH FLOW ESTIMATES FOR THE STEAMING BEAN COFFEE CART

Transparency Available

YEAR	1	2	3	4	5
Revenue	$17,681	$20,039	$22,396	$20,039	$16,503
Total expenses	$16,193	$16,562	$16,931	$16,562	$16,008
Taxable income	$ 1,489	$ 3,477	$ 5,466	$ 3,477	$ 495
Tax (at 22%)	$ 328	$ 765	$ 1,202	$ 765	$ 109
Net income	$ 1,161	$ 2,712	$ 4,263	$ 2,712	$ 386
Add Back Depreciation	$ 3,600	$ 3,600	$ 3,600	$ 3,600	$ 3,600
Cash flow	$ 4,761	$ 6,312	$ 7,863	$ 6,312	$ 3,986

Does that have a significant effect on our cash flow estimates? What if labor costs increase or the price of coffee beans increases? Examining different scenarios provides insights into the *sensitivity* of the cash flow estimates to changes in various inputs. Identifying the most important cost or revenue variables helps determine where extra research effort might be expended. Sensitivity analysis, or *what-if analysis*, is perfectly suited for computer spreadsheet software. In fact, the more popular spreadsheet programs often include sophisticated what-if analysis modules.

Sensitivity analysis is like elasticities in economics.

Let's look at an increase in the fee for business licenses from \$100 to \$150. It does not change our cash flow estimates very much. As Exhibit 4.8 shows, the cash flow estimates decrease by \$39. This is a reduction of less than 1%, so it cannot be considered very important. Suppose that bad weather reduces the coffee bean crop and prices rise accordingly. Let's say the increase in coffee bean prices raises our production costs per cup from 18¢ to 27¢, a 50% increase. Exhibit 4.8 shows the results for recalculating cash flows based on the higher coffee bean costs. In this case the change is much more dramatic—cash flow falls by more than \$1,000 in most years and by nearly \$1,400 in year 3. Thus, a 50% increase in the cost of making coffee has a much more severe effect than a 50% increase in the cost of the business license.

Sensitivity analysis helps determine a project's risk and where to devote more time on information gathering and analysis.

In most cases, cash flow estimates are most sensitive to the cost items that comprise the largest portion of total costs.[6] In the case of Steaming Bean, labor

Transparency Available

EXHIBIT 4.8

SENSITIVITY ANALYSIS RESULTS FOR THE STEAMING BEAN COFFEE CART

CHANGE IN MODEL PARAMETERS	CASH FLOW YEAR 1	CASH FLOW YEAR 2	CASH FLOW YEAR 3	CASH FLOW YEAR 4	CASH FLOW YEAR 5
Original cash flow estimate at 18¢/cup production costs, labor at \$6.00/hour, and license = \$100	\$4,761	\$6,312	\$7,863	\$6,312	\$3,986
Revised cash flow at 18¢/cup production costs, labor at \$6.00/hour, and license = \$150	\$4,722	\$6,273	\$7,824	\$6,273	\$3,947
Revised cash flow at 27¢/cup production costs, labor at \$6.00/hour, and license = \$100	\$3,682	\$5,089	\$6,496	\$5,089	\$2,978
Revised cash flow at 18¢/cup, license = \$100, and labor at \$6.60/hour	\$4,090	\$5,641	\$7,192	\$5,641	\$3,314

[6]Sensitivity analysis is similar to the concept of *elasticity* in economics. Elasticity measures the percent of change in one variable (such as cash flow) for a 1% change in another variable (such as the price of coffee). A large elasticity implies that one variable has great sensitivity to changes in the other variable.

is the single largest cost item, so we would suspect that even a small change in the hourly wage would have a large effect on our cash flow estimates. Suppose the wage rate shifts from $6 per hour to $6.60 per hour, a 10% increase. The bottom row of Exhibit 4.8 shows the impact of this change: Annual cash flows decrease by nearly $700 from the original estimate. A relatively small change in labor costs, 10%, has a large effect on cash flow; that is, our cash flow estimates are very *sensitive* to slight changes in labor costs. In fact, wage rates just above $7 per hour, about a 17% increase, have about the same impact as a 50% increase in coffee prices. Knowing this, we would want to invest extra effort in determining our future labor costs. Effort expended on more accurately forecasting labor costs will have the greatest effect on improving our cash flow forecasts.

Before-tax and After-tax Cash Flows

Students have a difficult time with the idea of after-tax costs, so we devote a few minutes to explaining the calculation for both costs and increases in taxable income.

after-tax cost = cost(1 − tax rate)

after-tax income change = (change in taxable income)(1 − tax rate)

In Exhibit 4.8, a $50 increase in the cost of a business license reduced cash flow by only $39. The reason that the $50 fee increase did not reduce cash flow by $50, is because the fee increase is a **before-tax expense**. The higher fee increased total costs by $50, which, in turn, reduced taxable income by $50. As taxable income goes down, so does the amount of tax a company must pay. In this case, the company pays $50 × 22%, or $11, less in taxes. This $11 tax savings reduces the effect of the $50 fee increase. The final cost of the fee increase is $39, $50 less the $11 tax savings. So the $50 fee increase is not as bad as it first appeared. This fee is an example of a tax-deductible expense. The **after-tax cost of a tax-deductible expense** is given by the following equation, where tax rate refers to a business's **marginal tax rate**.[7]

$$\textbf{after-tax cost} = \textbf{cost} \times (1 - \textbf{tax rate})$$
$$\$39 = \$50 \times (1 - 0.22)$$

This concept works in reverse for revenues. Suppose coffee sales rise so that taxable income increases by $50. In this case, the company owes taxes on the additional $50. The tax is 22% of $50 = $11. Therefore, the net effect of increasing taxable income by $50 is a $39 increase in cash flow. Note that a $50 increase in sales would contribute even less than an additional $39 to cash flow, because the costs of production must be considered. An extra $50 of sales is about 45 cups of coffee. At a cost per cup of 18¢, it costs $8.10 to produce the extra coffee, so the change in taxable income for a $50 increase in sales is about $42. Considering taxes, this results in a $32.68 increase in cash flow:

$$(\$50 - 45 \times 18¢) \times (1 - 0.22) = \$41.90 \times (0.78) = \$32.68$$

Because taxes are a cash outflow, we must consider the tax consequences of business decisions. To be useful, cash flows must be computed on an after-tax basis; that is, we need to estimate how much cash will remain after taxes are paid. As we study how businesses decide which products to produce or projects

[7] As in economics, the *marginal tax rate* refers to the rate applied to the next dollar of revenue or expense. Contrast the marginal tax rate with the average tax rate, which is the total tax liability divided by taxable income.

to invest in, we will always base such decisions on the after-tax cash flows associated with the product or project. For many businesses the marginal combined federal, state, and local tax rate can be 40% to 50%, so taxes can have a significant impact on business decisions.

MORE ON THE CASH CYCLE: THE EFFECT OF GROWTH

In this section, we return briefly to the cash cycle of the firm. Many small, successful businesses fail each year because the owners do not understand the company's cash cycle. As we discussed before, many businesses pay their bills before they receive cash from their customers. This gap between having to disburse cash to suppliers and receiving cash from customers is called the *financing gap*. For fast-growing businesses, in particular, managers must understand the company's cash cycle and have sufficient cash reserves to cover the anticipated financing gap. As a firm grows, it constantly buys more materials and hires more labor to increase its production levels. Every time around the cash cycle, the firm accrues a larger bill for materials and other production expenses but receives cash from customers for the earlier, lower production level. Therefore, the cash receipts may not be sufficient to cover the growing bills for materials and labor. Many profitable and growing firms have gone bankrupt because they did not have large-enough cash reserves (or access to funds) to finance their cash cycle.

It is worthwhile to warn students about the downside of growth—business failure due to cash shortages.

An example will show how high rates of growth can cause even a highly profitable company to fail if it does not have sufficient cash reserves. Brady's Banners, a sole-proprietorship company, manufactures canvas and nylon banners with holiday themes and by special order. The banners decorate city streets during special holidays, Halloween, and community celebrations. Coverage of the company's products on national television generated enormous demand for the banners. As shown in Exhibit 4.9, the company is profitable in terms of accounting profits; total costs (including taxes) are 82.5% of sales, leaving a net profit margin of 17.5% on sales.

Exhibit 4.9 shows sales, costs, and cash flow over Brady's high-growth period. Banners sell for $100, on the average. The company pays for labor and materials

Suggest that students compute the initial cash needed for Brady's Banner to survive through month 7.

EXHIBIT 4.9

BRADY'S BANNER CASH FLOW DURING HIGH-GROWTH PERIOD

	MONTH 1	MONTH 2	MONTH 3	MONTH 4	MONTH 5	MONTH 6	MONTH 7
Sales (units)	100	150	225	330	440	570	710
Revenues	$10,000	$15,000	$22,500	$33,000	$44,000	$57,000	$71,000
Cost of Goods	$ 8,250	$12,375	$18,563	$27,225	$36,300	$47,025	$58,575
Net profit	$ 1,750	$ 2,625	$ 3,938	$ 5,775	$ 7,700	$ 9,975	$12,425
Cash collections		$10,000	$15,000	$22,500	$33,000	$44,000	$57,000
Cash disbursements	$ 8,250	$12,375	$18,563	$27,225	$36,300	$47,025	$58,575
Net cash flow	($ 8,250)	($ 2,375)	($ 3,563)	($ 4,725)	($ 3,300)	($ 3,025)	($ 1,575)
Starting cash	$10,000	$ 1,750	($ 625)	($ 4,188)	($ 8,913)	($12,213)	($15,238)

If the contract had specified that Acme would pay Mega £450,000 pounds, Mega would have suffered no loss. However, at the new exchange rate Acme would have paid $782,609 to buy the £450,000 to send to Mega. Acme would have found the drill press to be more expensive than it had planned: £450,000 at 0.575£/$ is equivalent to

$$\frac{\text{£}450000}{0.575\text{£}/\$} = \$782{,}609$$

Not surprisingly, a number of methods exist to lock in exchange rates in transactions such as that between Mega and Acme. Using forward and futures contracts, companies can determine the exchange rate that will apply to currency translations to be made in the future. Such contracts provide a low-cost means of avoiding, or *hedging away*, the risk faced by Mega and Acme in our example.

SUMMARY

This chapter discussed cash flow. Cash is the lifeblood of the business enterprise. Despite having accounting profits, without cash a business is doomed. Without cash the company cannot pay its employees, its suppliers, its tax bill, or its bankers. Our discussion of cash flow focused on understanding how cash flows into, out of, and through the company. The cash cycle is a valuable tool for thinking about the day-to-day operations of any business. The days model is a very simple quantitative model of the cash cycle and gives a rough estimate of a company's financing gap. The majority of the chapter discussed how to estimate cash flows from income statement and balance sheet information and how to estimate the cash flows for a new investment project using pro forma income statements (or projected income statements). In addition to estimating cash flows, we introduced the technique of sensitivity analysis, which allows some uncertainty about cash flow estimates to be included in the analysis. This powerful tool can be applied fairly easily using electronic spreadsheets. We also introduced the basics of translating foreign currency into dollars and vice versa. If you have a good understanding of cash flow—its importance and how to estimate it—and have mastered some of the analytic tools introduced in this chapter, you have taken a significant first step in learning how to manage a financially healthy business.

KEY TERMS

cash cycle
suppliers' credit terms
financing gap
the days model
receivables days
inventory turnover days
accounts payable days
generally accepted accounting principles (GAAP)
revenue recognition
the matching principle
depreciation
income statement
statement of cash flows
balance sheet
pro forma (or projected) income statements
sensitivity analysis
before-tax expense
after-tax cost of a tax-deductible expense
marginal tax rate
negative cash flow
exchange rates

KEY FORMULAS

$$\text{receivables days} = \frac{\text{average accounts receivable}}{\text{annual credit sales}} \times 365 \text{ days}$$

$$\text{inventory turnover days} = \frac{\text{average inventory}}{\text{cost of goods sold}} \times 365 \text{ days}$$

$$\text{accounts payable days} = \frac{\text{average accounts payable}}{\text{cost of goods sold}} \times 365 \text{ days}$$

$$\text{cash flow} = \text{net income} + \text{depreciation}$$

$$\text{cash flow} = \text{net income} + \text{depreciation} - (\text{change in assets}) + (\text{change in liabilities and equity})$$

$$\text{after-tax cost} = \text{cost} \times (1 - \text{tax rate})$$

QUESTIONS

1. Explain why accounting profits do not necessarily equal cash flow. Discuss at least two GAAPs (generally accepted accounting principles) in your answer.
2. Most people pay for their groceries with either a check or cash. If a grocery store chain has 30 days to pay its suppliers and the average length of time food items stay on the shelf before being bought is 10 days, what can you say about this company's cash cycle and financing gap?
3. Why do we add depreciation expense to net income to get an estimate of cash flow? What is so special about depreciation expense?
4. Explain why a decrease in an asset account increases a company's cash flow.
5. Liabilities are often considered to be bad. If so, why does an increase in a liability account increase a company's cash flow?
6. If a project analysis shows accounting losses (negative net income), does that assure that the project should not be pursued?
7. Suppose two new companies are identical in all ways except that one uses an accelerated depreciation method and the other uses the straight-line method. Initially, which company will have the higher profits? Which will have the higher cash flow? Explain your answers.
8. In the Steaming Bean Coffee Cart example, sales rose and then fell as competitors entered the good coffee-to-go business. Can you think of ways that the Steaming Bean could have protected its sales; in other words, how could competitive entry been slowed?
9. During the 1980s large banks in the United States had huge loans outstanding to many less developed countries such as Mexico and Brazil. Interest on this debt continued to be recognized as revenue as it was owed, yet many analysts worried that the interest would never actually be paid.
   a. If the interest was recognized as revenue yet never collected, would profits overstate or understate cash flow?
   b. Was this issue centered around the matching principle, revenue recognition, or depreciation?
10. You manage a division of a large manufacturing concern. A new member of the finance staff brings you an analysis of a new product in which units sold per year increase indefinitely. How would you recommend the analyst revise these projections?
11. What does the learning curve imply about production-cost estimates over time? Consider how efficient you are at a new task compared to after you have done it many times.
12. More people take vacations to Europe when the U.S. dollar is strong against European currencies—i.e., when a dollar buys more of the foreign currency—than during periods when the dollar is weak. Explain this phenomenon. If airline ticket prices are set in an airline's home currency, during

periods of strong U.S. currency, would you prefer to fly on United Airlines or Air France (or some other European airline), given that the air carriers had similar departure times, safety records, etc.?

13. If cash flow is the most important measure of a company's viability, why do stock prices respond to announcements about accounting earnings and net income?
14. Define sensitivity analysis and explain what the objective of sensitivity analysis is.
15. One of the authors received an analysis from an MBA student that said the following:

Because there was concern about lower-than-anticipated demand, we reduced both the volume sold and the sales price of the product. Because reduced demand could also affect the cost of materials, we increased the production cost estimate to [the maximum of the estimated range].

a. Does it make sense that when unit demand falls, sales price should also fall? Explain.
b. Does it make sense that when demand falls, production costs (e.g., raw material costs) should increase? Explain.

DEMONSTRATION PROBLEMS

1. ***The Days Model***

During 1995 Taylor Enterprises had sales of \$358,920 and associated cost of goods sold of \$241,481. The average accounts receivable balance for 1995 was \$27,534, and the average inventory balance was \$43,003. Accounts payable averaged \$15,127 during 1995. Use these data to compute Taylor Enterprises financing gap in days and in dollars.

SOLUTION

First compute the following three activity ratios.

$$\text{receivables days} = \frac{\text{average accounts receivable}}{\text{annual credit sales}} \times 365 \text{ days}$$

$$= \frac{27{,}534}{358{,}920} \times 365 = 28 \text{ days}$$

$$\text{inventory turnover days} = \frac{\text{average inventory}}{\text{cost of goods sold}} \times 365 \text{ days}$$

$$= \frac{43{,}003}{241{,}481} \times 365 = 65 \text{ days}$$

$$\text{accounts payable days} = \frac{\text{average accounts payable}}{\text{cost of goods sold}} \times 365 \text{ days}$$

$$= \frac{15{,}217}{241{,}481} \times 365 = 23 \text{ days}$$

We combine these activity ratios into the days model as follows:

$$\begin{aligned} \text{financing gap in days} &= \text{receivables days} + \text{inventory turnover days} \\ &\quad - \text{accounts payable days} \\ &= 28 + 65 - 23 = 70 \text{ days} \end{aligned}$$

We transform days into dollars by multiplying the financing gap in days by the cost of goods sold per day. This gives us a rough estimate of how much money is required to see the company through until it begins collecting cash from customers.

$$\begin{aligned} \text{financing gap in dollars} &= \text{financing gap in days} \\ &\quad \times \text{cost of goods sold per day} \\ &= 70 \text{ days} \times \frac{\text{COGS}}{365 \text{ days}} = 70 \text{ days} \times \frac{241{,}481}{365} \\ &= \$46{,}311 \end{aligned}$$

Thus, a cash buffer of approximately $46,311 is needed by the firm to support its activities until cash arrives from the collection of accounts receivable.

2. ***Cash Flow Estimation 1***

Lincoln Composite Materials produces aerospace parts from fiberglass, Kevlar(TM), and other plastics. Last year Lincoln had net income of $2,746,347 on sales of $68 million. The depreciation expense was $710,558 and taxes were $976,994. Use this information to provide a rough estimate of Lincoln's cash flow.

SOLUTION

$$\begin{aligned} \text{cash flow} &= \text{net income} + \text{depreciation} \\ &= \$2{,}746{,}347 + \$710{,}558 = 3{,}456{,}905 \end{aligned}$$

3. ***Cash Flow Estimation***

Several entrepreneurial recent college graduates, including yourself, are considering organizing a series of Bluegrass music festivals. You have found a group of bands and musicians who will commit to performing over a 3-day period each July for the next 5 years. You have found an old outdoor amphitheater, but it requires some remodeling and new equipment before it can be used. Before you commit to this series of five Bluegrass Festivals, use the following information to estimate the cash flow from the festivals.

1. The musicians, as a group, want a guarantee of $25,000 per year plus $1 per ticket sold. In addition, the musicians need housing. The total housing expense will be $4,500 annually.
2. Refurbishing and equipping the pavilion will generate depreciation expense of $6,500 per year for 5 years.
3. Insurance, security, equipment rental, lighting, and audio services will total about $11,000 per year. Costs for printing, advertising, telephone, postage, etc., related to the festival are estimated to be $9,500 per year.
4. With effective advertising, a member of your group, who is a marketing professional, believes the festival will draw people from throughout the region. Tentatively, an average ticket price of $10 is being considered. Based on similar events elsewhere, she estimates total ticket sales over the

3 days will be about 6,500 the first year, growing to 8,000 in years 2 and 3 and 9,000 in years 4 and 5.

5. The appropriate tax rate for this project is 28%.

SOLUTION

REVENUES					
YEAR	1	2	3	4	5
Tickets	6,500	8,000	8,000	9,000	9,000
Revenue at $10/ticket	65,000	80,000	80,000	90,000	90,000

EXPENSES					
YEAR	1	2	3	4	5
Musicians' fee	25,000	25,000	25,000	25,000	25,000
Musicians' gate receipts	6,500	8,000	8,000	9,000	9,000
Musicians' housing	4,500	4,500	4,500	4,500	4,500
Depreciation	6,500	6,500	6,500	6,500	6,500
Insurance, etc.	20,500	20,500	20,500	20,500	20,500
Total expenses	63,000	64,500	64,500	65,500	65,500

TAXES, PROFITS, AND CASH FLOW					
YEAR	1	2	3	4	5
Profit	2,000	15,500	15,500	24,500	24,500
Tax	560	4,340	4,340	6,860	6,860
Net Profit	1,440	11,160	11,160	17,640	17,640
Cash Flow	7,940	17,660	17,660	24,140	24,140

4. ***Sensitivity Analysis***

Using Demonstration Problem 3, carry out a sensitivity analysis that examines the effect on cash flows if ticket sales are 5% lower than anticipated.

SOLUTION

Ticket sales are 5% below estimates (*Note*: We ignore tax carry forward in this example).

YEAR	1	2	3	4	5
Tickets	6,175	7,600	7,600	8,550	8,550
Revenue	61,750	76,000	76,000	85,500	85,500
Guarantee	25,000	25,000	25,000	25,000	25,000
Gate	6,175	7,600	7,600	8,550	8,550
Housing	4,500	4,500	4,500	4,500	4,500
Depreciation	6,500	6,500	6,500	6,500	6,500
Other expenses	20,500	20,500	20,500	20,500	20,500
Total expenses	62,675	64,100	64,100	65,050	65,050
Profit	(925)	11,900	11,900	20,450	20,450
Tax	0	3,332	3,332	5,726	5,726
Net Profit	(925)	8,568	8,568	14,724	14,724
Cash flow	5,575	15,068	15,068	21,224	21,224

5. ***Foreign Exchange***

Your company has just sold a computer-operated lathe to an automotive manufacturer in Sweden. The sales price of the lathe in U.S. dollars is

$770,000.00. If on the sales date the dollar/krona exchange rate is 0.1370 (each krona costs $0.1370), how many krona will your company receive for the machine? Payment occurs in about 2 months, when the machine is actually delivered and installed in the Swedish plant. If between now and then the dollar/krona exchange rate changes to 0.1411, has your company gained or lost due to the foreign exchange rate fluctuation?

SOLUTION

Each Swedish krona costs $0.1370; therefore, each dollars buys $\frac{1}{0.1370}$ krona, or there are 7.3 krona per dollar. Therefore, the total number of krona your company will receive is

$$\$770{,}000 \times 7.3 = 5{,}621{,}000 \text{ krona}$$

If your company receives 5,621,000 krona 2 months from now when the exchange rate is $0.1411/krona, then the company will be able to exchange those 5.6 million krona into

$$5{,}621{,}000 \text{ krona} \times \frac{\$0.1411}{\text{Krona}} = \$793{,}123.10$$

The company gained because each krona now buys more dollars. Notice that the krona in the denominator of the exchange rate cancels out the krona associated with the number 5,621,000, resulting in a final number of dollars.

PROBLEMS

Cash Flow Estimation
1. $335,000

1. A firm has sales of $2,500,000, cost of goods sold of $1,700,000, GA&S expense of $350,000, depreciation expense of $220,000, and net income of $115,000. Give a rough estimate of the company's cash flow.

Cash Flow Estimation
2. 1994: $47,889; 1995: $50,407

2. Estimate Wilken's Transport Company's cash flow for 1994 and 1995 using the information in the income statements shown below.

WILKEN'S TRANSPORT INCOME STATEMENTS
FOR THE CALENDAR YEARS 1994 AND 1995

	1994	1995
Sales	$454,237	$497,389
COGS	302,203	337,990
Gross margin	152,034	159,399
GA&S	85,795	89,454
Depreciation	22,416	24,156
Interest expense	8,543	9,431
Taxable income	35,280	36,358
Taxes	9,807	10,107
Net Income	25,473	26,251

3. Revise your estimate of Wilken's Transport Company's cash flow for 1995 in the answer to Problem 2 based on the following additional information.
   a. In 1995 plant, property, and equipment increased by $28,975.
   b. In 1995 total current assets increased by $12,942.
   c. In 1995 total current liabilities increased by $7,823.
   d. In 1995 long-term liabilities fell by $8,450 when a loan was repaid.
   e. The company paid no cash dividends in either 1994 or 1995.

Cash Flow Estimation
3. 1995 (revised): $7,863

4. A company's marginal tax rate is 30%. What is the after-tax cost of a $1,000 tax-deductible expense?

After-Tax Cost
4. $700

5. Contributions to recognized charities are tax-deductible. If a person has a marginal tax rate of 22%, what is the after-tax cost of a $600 tax-deductible contribution?

After-Tax Cost
5. $468

6. In terms of the final effect on cash flow, would you prefer a $1 increase in sales or a $1 decrease in costs? Explain. A pro forma income statement might be helpful.

Cash Flow
6. $1 decrease in costs

7. As a venture capitalist you provide funds for start-up companies. Recently you received a financing proposal that included the following two tables and attached commentary. How would you respond to this proposal, if you know that this industry is fairly competitive and that the entire size of the market being served is unlikely to grow more than 1% or 2% per year over the next 10 years?

Sales and Cost Projections
7. Unrealistic projections

In the first table we present sales estimates for years 1 through 10 of operation. Note that we expect sales to grow at an annual rate of 15%, generating increases in market share from 3% of the total market in year 1 to 18% of the market in year 10.

UNNAMED HITECH COMPANY: SALES PROJECTIONS
(IN MILLIONS OF DOLLARS)

YEAR	1	2	3	4	5	6	7	8	9	10
Sales	1.00	1.15	1.32	1.52	1.75	2.01	2.31	2.66	3.06	3.52

In the second table we present cost estimates for years 1 through 10 of operation. Note that we expect costs to grow in absolute amount but decrease as a percent of sales over this 10-year period. We feel that as we climb the learning curve, various production costs will fall and that increased sales will allow us to capture economies of scale. These estimated cost savings will result in steadily increasing profit margins, which, when combined with our projected sales growth, will generate ever-larger profits from year 1 through year 10.

UNNAMED HITECH COMPANY: COST PROJECTIONS (IN MILLIONS OF DOLLARS)

YEAR	1	2	3	4	5	6	7	8	9	10
Costs	0.72	0.82	0.94	1.07	1.22	1.38	1.56	1.77	2.00	2.30
Cost as % of Sales	72.0%	71.5%	71.0%	70.3%	69.5%	68.6%	67.6%	66.6%	65.5%	65.5%

Cash Flow Estimation:
8. Month 1: $770
Month 2: $990
Month 3: $1,130
Month 4: $1,270
Month 5: $1,270
Month 6: $1,270

8. A business student is considering starting her own lawn-care business. She has been doing such work for another company for several years and is ready to be her own boss. She has completed a table that shows her estimates of the number of clients she will have, revenues at $80 per client per month, and costs. She believes she can handle up to 25 yards herself and then will have to hire a helper. Use the table data to estimate monthly cash flows for the business.

	MONTH 1	MONTH 2	MONTH 3	MONTH 4	MONTH 5	MONTH 6
CLIENTS	20	25	30	35	35	35
Revenues (at $80/client)	$1,600	$2,000	$2,400	$2,800	$2,800	$2,800
Costs: Fuel	$300	$375	$450	$525	$525	$525
Fertilizer	$100	$125	$150	$175	$175	$175
Helper's wages	$0	$0	$100	$200	$200	$200
Miscellaneous	$300	$325	$350	$375	$375	$375
Depreciation	$250	$250	$250	$250	$250	$250
Pretax profit	$650	$925	$1,100	$1,275	$1,275	$1,275
Tax (at 20%)	$130	$185	$220	$255	$255	$255
Net Income						
Cash Flow						

Sensitivity Analysis
9. See Instructor's Manual.
Month 1
674 866 962

9. In Problem 8 the financing plan assumes that the number of clients is known with some degree of certainty. Actually, the number of clients could vary from these estimates. How will the cash flow estimates vary if the number of clients was 10% lower or 10% higher than the numbers used in the initial analysis? How about if the number of clients varied by 20% up or down?

Sensitivity Analysis
10. Change in clients more important

10. In Problem 8 do you think that the cash flow estimates are more sensitive to a 10% change in the number of clients or a 10% change in fuel costs? Explain your answer and provide support if possible.

11. You are a new financial analyst at Southwest Surgical Technology (SST) Inc., a large medical technology company located in Dallas, Texas. The company has just developed and completed the FDA testing for a new surgical staple tool that replaces, in many situations, sewn stitches. The marketing, production, and accounting departments have sent you the following memos and data. Use the data to compute cash flow estimates for the new product for the next 10 years.

Cash Flow Estimation: Pro Forma Statements

11. Year	Cash flow
1	−5.0
2	123.3
3	269.5
4	374.0
5	258.0
6	258.0
7	258.0
8	88.6
9	33.0
10	−54.0

Assumes losses in years 1 and 10 can be used against other income.

From: SST Marketing Research
Marketing surveys completed over the last 2 months indicate that initial interest in Product X-126, Nylon Extendible Surgical Stapler, is very high. Based on confirmed adoption rates among survey participants and proposed marketing plans for the product's introduction, estimated sales units and sales dollars are shown in the following table. The table also reflects introductory pricing and sales and price erosion due to competition.

YEAR	1	2	3	4	5	6	7	8	9	10
Units	350	580	900	1,100	1,250	1,250	1,250	1,000	700	300
Price	1,020	1,200	1,200	1,200	1,000	1,000	1,000	850	850	720
Sales ($000s)	357	696	1,080	1,320	1,250	1,250	1,250	850	595	216

From: SST Production/Manufacturing
Re: Product X-126 Production Costs

Preliminary engineering reports estimate X-126 per unit production costs—including all materials, labor, and absorbed indirect costs—to be

QUANTITY	PER-UNIT COST
Fewer than 500 units/year	$665
500 to 1,000 units/year	$632
More than 1,000 units/year	$610

In years 1 and 2 we recommend increasing per unit costs by 10% to accommodate time and material loss as a tooling and manufacturing procedure is established.

From: SST Accounting Department
Re: X-126 Direct Marketing and Management Expenses

1. This product requires a 0.75-time product manager (75% of full-time). Current annual full-time product manager salary and benefits average $79,882. Prorate accordingly.
2. Sales staff expenses include $5,000 per product plus the standard 2½% commission on gross sales less returns and less 88% of uncollected accounts.
3. Advertising is budgeted at $35,000/year for 3 years and then $18,000 for years 4–10.
4. Depreciation expense applicable for this project is $16,000/year for years 1–4 and $9,500 for years 5–7. No depreciation expense is anticipated beyond year 7.
5. The marginal tax rate used in new project analysis is 28%.
6. Other incremental cash expenses are estimated to be 1½% of gross revenues.

Sensitivity Analysis

12. Year	Cash flow
1	−53.2
2	29.9
3	124.9
4	179.9
5	89.6
6	81.4
7	81.4
8	−43.9
9	−48.6
10	−80.8

Assumes losses in years 1 and 8–10 can be used against other income.

12. Additional information about the new surgical staple tool (see Problem 11) has arrived from the marketing and production departments. Use this information to complete a sensitivity analysis of the new surgical staple tool's projected cash flows. Summarize your result in a short memo (1 page) in which you highlight the low end of the estimates; that is, prepare a memo that will alert your superiors to the worst possible scenario that might arise from the production and marketing of this product.

ABRIDGED MEMO
From: SST Marketing Research
Re: Competition for SST Product X-126

Prime Surgical has just announced the successful development of a product similar to our Product X-126, Nylon Extendible Surgical Stapler. Initial evaluation suggests that their product, which will probably be priced about 40% higher than ours, will take away some of our top-end customers. The good news is that Prime has alerted many customers to the need for this type of product. Therefore, it is not certain how this will affect our preliminary sales and price estimates. We recommend that as you complete your analysis, you consider scenarios with 10% reductions in both sales units and sales price to accommodate this unexpected competition. In addition, growing market awareness will almost certainly attract additional competitors earlier than originally anticipated, so we recommend reducing unit sales by 15% in years 6 and 7 and 20% in years 8–10.

Summary: Growing uncertainty suggests that the original sales volume and price estimates may vary up to 10%. In addition, new marketing information suggests that unit sales for years 6 through 10 should be adjusted down.

URGENT MEMO
From: SST Production/Manufacturing
Re: Revision of Product X-126 Production Costs

A design modification in SST Product X-126 calls for the use of a more expensive, but more easily extruded, Boron-based polymer instead of the original heat-flow-ejected resin-based material for the staple housing extension tube (part 17). Due to historic price fluctuations in Boron-based polymers and limited on-site extrusion cost experience with this material, we recommend adding a 12% error (plus or minus) to the original engineering cost estimates. See attached table for revised cost estimates per design change.

QUANTITY	PER-UNIT COST
Fewer than 500 units/year	\$665 ± \$80 = \$585 to \$744
500 to 1,000 units/year	\$632 ± \$75 = \$557 to \$707
More than 1,000 units/year	\$610 ± \$73 = \$537 to \$683

We continue to recommend increasing per-unit costs by 10% in years 1 and 2 to accommodate time and material loss as a tooling and manufacturing procedure is established.

Cash Flow Estimation

13. In 1995 Holdren Drilling Company, a water-well-drilling business, had net income of \$167,000, depreciation of \$94,500 and paid cash dividends of

$60,000. Use this information and the two balance sheets presented below to calculate Holdren's 1995 cash flow. Do these cash flows correspond to the change in the cash account?

ASSETS	1994	1995	LIABILITIES AND SHAREHOLDERS' EQUITY	1994	1995
Cash	21,153	18,451	A/P	65,785	75,236
A/R	125,685	163,578	N/P Bank	135,782	125,782
Inventories	354,986	378,552	Other CL	5,675	12,564
Total Current	501,824	560,581	Total Current	207,242	213,582
PP&E	1,102,658	1,251,741	Long-term Debt	385,000	385,000
less: Acc. Depreciation	325,684	420,184	Common Stock (par and excess)	150,000	150,000
Net PP&E	776,974	831,557	Retained Earnings	536,556	643,556
Total Assets	1,278,798	1,392,138	Total Liab. and Equity	1,278,798	1,392,138

13. 1995 cash flow from operations: $216,381
1995 cash flow from investing: −149,083
1995 cash flow from financing: −70,000
Change in cash position: −2,702

14. Use the balance sheet information for Holdren Drilling Company given in Problem 13 and the following sales and cost-of-goods-sold data to compute Holdren's financing gap in days. Given the ratios you computed, should Holdren's managers be concerned about any particular aspect of its working capital management?

Financing Gap
14. Financing gap = 72 days; A/R seem to be increasing.

SALES AND COGS FOR HOLDREN DRILLING CO.

	1994	1995
Sales	$1,146,876	$1,194,119
COGS	800,384	980,755

15. Fawcett Plumbing Supply buys plumbing supplies directly from manufacturers and then resells them to building contractors throughout western Montana. The company's suppliers give Fawcett terms of net 30; that is, Fawcett has 30 days to pay after ordering items. The nature of the construction business is such that Fawcett's customers take, on the average, 55 days to pay their bills. The company has found that inventory remains in its warehouse an average of 23 days before being sold. The company has cost of goods sold of about $670,000 per year. Compute Fawcett's financing gap in days as well as the approximate amount of working capital the company needs.

Financing Gap
15. Financing gap = 48 days or $88,110

16. L. K. Faucet, Inc., manufactures a range of kitchen and bathroom plumbing supplies. Currently they produce to maintain an inventory of approximately 40 days of sales; that is, their inventory is sufficiently large that they have enough of each item to supply 40 days of demand for the item without having to produce any more of the item. The company has stable sales and total annual cost of goods sold is about $1.3 million.

Financing Gap: Just-in-Time
16. Reduction of $89,041

The company is beginning to adopt some methods from the TQM (total quality management) model, one of which is *just-in-time manufacturing*. With just-in-time manufacturing the company reorganizes manufacturing so it can quickly change production processes between items. This means much lower inventories can be held, so much less of the company's working capital is tied up in the inventory. If L. K. Faucet can trim its inventory days from 40 days to 15 days, how will this affect the amount of working capital invested in inventory? Assume the change to just-in-time affects only inventories.

Financing Gap
17. Earns an extra 0.445% of interest income on every sales dollar.

17. Food Club is a discount grocery chain famous for its low prices and sometimes limited selection. The company buys massive amounts of some items at very low prices then passes the low prices on to customers. This strategy results in a very low profit margin, but nonetheless Food Club has been extremely profitable and its stock price has climbed. Use the following information to comment on how Food Club earns its profits despite having such a low profit margin.
    1. All sales are for cash at the time of sale.
    2. Purchase terms from suppliers are net 30, so Food Club has 30 days from the date the goods are received to pay the bill.
    3. On the average, items are on the shelves in a Food Club store for only 5 days.
    4. Food Club earns 6.5% on its invested funds and pays 9% interest when it borrows.

Foreign Exchange
18. $618.23

18. A friend who is an avid bicyclist found the perfect bicycle on a trip in Italy. She was taken aback and almost decided not to buy the bike when told that the price was 1,000,000 lira. If, at the time, a U.S. dollar bought 1,617.53 lira, how much was the price of the bicycle in U.S. dollars?

Foreign Exchange
19. Thailand $100.20
Japan $205.89
Canada $124.88

19. In Bangkok, Thailand, a very nice hotel costs about 2,500 baht per night, whereas a similar room in Tokyo would cost nearly 20,000 yen and in Toronto, about $175 Canadian. Which is the more expensive city? Use the exchange rates in the table to compare the prices. These rates were reported in the *Wall Street Journal* on February 21, 1995.

COUNTRY (CURRENCY)	U.S. DOLLAR EQUIVALENTS	CURRENCY PER U.S. DOLLAR
Thailand (baht)	$0.04008/Baht	24.95 baht
Japan (yen)	$0.010295/Yen	97.14 yen
Canada (dollar, $C)	$0.7136C	1.4014 $C

Foreign Exchange
20. On arrival, £14.07 more.

20. Suppose you are traveling in Great Britain. Upon arrival the exchange rate is $1.57/£; i.e., each British pound costs $1.57. You change $200 at this rate. A few days later you change money again. This time you change $400 at an rate of $1.63/£; i.e., each British pound costs $1.63. Should you have changed more or less money upon arrival? If you could have exchanged the entire $600 at one time or the other, rather than carrying out two transac-

tions at different exchange rates, how many more pounds would you have had?

21. The following "tombstone" ad is from the *Financial Times*, June 7, 1993. It describes bonds being issued by HSBC Holdings. On the same day the *Financial Times* listed the price of pounds in dollars as \$1.518 per pound. Use this exchange rate to answer the following questions.
   a. How much money is HSBC borrowing in pounds (£) and dollars (\$)?
   b. At the $9\frac{7}{8}$% coupon rate, how much interest will HSBC pay each year in pounds (£) and dollars (\$)?
   c. On June 7, the *Financial Times* also reported that the exchange rate between French francs and British pounds was 8.31 francs per pound, and the rate between German marks and British pounds was 2.47 marks per pound. Recompute both (a) and (b) for French francs and German marks.

Foreign Exchange
21. See Instructor's Manual.
Pounds 250,000 24,688

This announcement appears as a matter of record only

HSBC Holdings plc

(Registered and incorporated in England: Number 617387)

£250,000,000

$9^7/_8$ percent
Subordinated Bonds due 2018

Samuel Montagu & Co. Limited

Cazenove & Co. **Solomon Brothers International Limited**

MIDLAND

Constructing a Pro Forma Balance Sheet

Pro forma or projected balance sheets are often necessary when analyzing the effect of corporate decisions on the company's financial condition. For example, some loans require that the borrower maintain financial ratios at or above a certain level. Therefore, before managers of a company subject to such a loan arrangement initiate changes that could affect the company's balance sheet, they would want to construct pro forma balance sheets to assure that the loan restrictions are satisfied.

Constructing a simple pro forma balance sheet usually requires four steps. More complex balance sheets will require more steps. The construction of the balance sheet depends on having already completed the appropriate pro forma income statement, so the steps given below assumes that the income statement is available.

Step 1

Fill in all of the values that are known or that change in a definite manner. These include many loans and the common stock accounts.

Step 2

Fill in all values that change according to income statement values. These include depreciation and retained earnings.

Step 3

Fill in all values that are projected according to company policy or represent target policy values. These include inventory, accounts receivable, accounts payable, and plant, property and equipment.

Step 4

Balance the assets and liabilities by adjusting a plug figure, usually cash on the asset side and bank loans or notes payable on the liabilities side.

Example: The most recent actual income statement and balance sheet for Texas-Carib Gas Company are shown below. Use these financial statements and the following information to construct *pro forma* financial statements for the firm. Of particular interest to the company is whether the Notes Payable amount can be reduced and whether there will be sufficient cash to continue paying a cash dividend to shareholders.

1. The company expects sales to increase 10% from 1995 sales.
2. In 1995, COGS rose from 65% of sales to 66% of sales. In 1996 the company plans to hold costs to the 1994 rate of 65%.
3. Due to organizational restructuring, GA&S in 1996 will be $470,000, the same as 1995.
4. Due to lower Notes Payable, Interest Expense will fall to $56,000 in 1996.
5. Depreciation Expense in 1996 will be $91,000 and the company will add $170,000 of new assets and dispose of assets with book values of $30,000 during the year.
6. For the purposes of projections the company assumes a flat tax rate of 40%.
7. The company paid out $50,000 in cash dividends in 1994 and 1995, and plans to do so in 1996 if sufficient cash is available.
8. The company tries to maintain a minimum cash balance of $100, and uses Notes Payable to make up short-term cash deficiencies.
9. As part of its restructuring plan, the company plans on Accounts Receivable being reduced to 35-days of Sales by the end of the 1996 fiscal year. Inventory management improvements will reduce inventories to 55-days of COGS. Accounts Payable will remain at 30-days of COGS. The company uses a 360-day year in all its financial calculations.
10. Other liabilities are estimated to be about 1% of sales in 1996.
11. No principal will be repaid on the bonds outstanding in 1996, but interest will be due. The interest on the bonds is included in the estimated Interest Expense of $56,000.

INCOME STATEMENTS FOR THE YEARS ENDED DEC 31, 1994 & DEC 31, 1995
AMOUNTS IN THOUSANDS

	1994	1995
Sales	2000	2200
COGS	1300	1452
Gross Profit	700	748
GA&S	420	470
Interest	55	60
Depreciation	80	83
Taxable Income	145	135
Taxes	58	54
Net Income	87	81

BALANCE SHEET AS OF DEC. 31, 1995 AMOUNTS IN THOUSANDS			
ASSETS		LIABILITIES & EQUITY	
Cash	100	A/P	121
A/R	275	Notes Payable (10%)	100
Inventory	242	Other CL	22
Total Current	617	Total Current	243
Gross PP&E	1200	Bonds (8%)	625
Acc. Depreciation	525	Common Stock	120
Net PP&E	675	Retained Earnings	304
Total Assets	1292	Total Liab & Equity	1292

Before we construct the pro forma balance sheet we must develop the income statement for 1996. The pro forma income statement is shown with explanations for each entry. Numbers in parenthesis refer to the information on page 144.

	ACTUAL INCOME STATEMENTS 1994 & 1995 AMOUNTS IN THOUSANDS		PRO FORMA FOR 1996	
	1994	1995	1996	EXPLANATION
Sales	2000	2200	2420	10% increase (1)
COGS	1300	1452	1573	65% of Sales (2)
Gross Profit	700	748	847	Subtraction
GA&S	420	470	470	Amount given (3)
Interest Expense	55	60	56	Amount given (4)
Depreciation	80	83	91	Amount given (5)
Taxable Income	145	135	230	Subtraction
Taxes	58	54	92	Rate given (6)
Net Income	87	81	138	Subtraction
Cash Dividends	50	50	50	Amount given (7)
to Retained Earnings	37	31	88	Subtraction

Step 1

Fill in all of the values that are known or that change in a definite manner. These amounts include the $625,000 for the 8% bonds and the $120,000 common stock account.

Step 2

Fill in all values that change according to income statement values. These amounts include accumulated depreciation, which increases by $91,000 to $616,000 according to note (5), and retained earnings, which increase by $88,000 to $392,000 if dividends of $50,000 are paid as mentioned in note (7).

Step 3

Fill in all values that are projected according to company policy or represent target policy values. These items include accounts receivable, inventory, accounts payable, and plant, property and equipment. According to note (9), Accounts Receivable will be 35 days of sales or $\frac{\$2{,}420 \times 35}{360} = \$235$; Inventory falls to 55 days of COGS or $\frac{\$1{,}573 \times 55}{360} = \$240$; and Accounts Payable remains at 30 days of COGS so is $\frac{\$1{,}573 \times 30}{360} = \$131$. Note 5 tells us that the company plans to buy \$170,000 and sell \$30,000 of PP&E, so Gross PP&E will increase by \$140,000.

Step 4

Balance the assets and liabilities by setting cash to its desired minimum of \$100,000. We put these values into the pro forma balance sheet in the column titled First Version. Initially we set cash to \$100,000 and the Notes Payable account to zero. The Assets do not balance with the Liabilities and Equity, so in the column titled Second Version, we add \$7,000 to the Notes Payable account to make the two sides of the balance sheet balance. Had the Notes Payable account been negative in the First Version, we would have made it zero and added to the Cash account so the assets and the liabilities and equity would balance.

	ACTUAL BALANCE SHEET AS OF DEC. 31, 1995 IN THOUSANDS	PRO FORMA BALANCE SHEET AS OF DEC. 31, 1996 IN THOUSANDS FIRST VERSION	SECOND VERSION
	ASSETS	ASSETS	
Cash	100	100	
A/R	275	235	
Inventory	242	240	
Total Current	617	575	
Gross PP&E	1200	1340	
Acc. Depreciation	525	616	
Net PP&E	675	724	
Total Assets	1292	1299	
	LIABILITIES & EQUITY	LIABILITIES & EQUITY	LIABILITIES & EQUITY
A/P	121	131	131
Notes Payable (10%)	100	0	7
Other CL	22	24	24
Total Current	243	155	162
Bonds (8%)	625	625	625
Common Stock	120	120	120
Retained Earnings	304	392	392
Total Liab & Equity	1292	1292	1299

Problems

1. Assume that everything in the Texas-Carib Gas Company example is as stated except that GA&S Expense and Accounts Receivable cannot be controlled as planned. Instead of $470,000, GA&S Expense in 1996 will grow to $510,000 and Accounts Receivable will remain at 45-days of Sales. Derive the 1996 pro forma financial statements and determine how these changes affect the company's need for Notes Payable.

2. Assume that everything in the Texas-Carib Gas Company example is as stated (A/R = 35 days; Inventory = 55 days; GA&S = $470,000) but the company buys $250,000 of new equipment instead of the stated $170,000. Derive the 1996 pro forma balance sheet to determine how this change affects the company's need for Notes Payable.

CHAPTER 5

Time is Money

Einstein discovers that time is actually money.

he saying "time is money" could not be more true than it is in finance. People rationally prefer to collect money earlier than later. By delaying the receipt of cash, individuals forgo the opportunity to purchase desired goods or invest the funds to increase their wealth. The foregone interest which could be earned if cash were received immediately is called the **opportunity cost** of delaying its receipt. Individuals require compensation to reimburse them for the opportunity cost of not having the funds available for immediate investment purposes. This chapter describes how such opportunity costs are calculated. Because many business activities require computing a value today for a series of future cash flows, the techniques presented in this chapter apply not just to finance but also to marketing, manufacturing, and management. Here are examples of questions that the tools introduced in this chapter can help answer:

- How much should we spend on an advertising campaign today if it will increase sales by 5% in the future?
- Is it worth buying a new computerized lathe for $120,000 if it reduces material waste by 15%?
- Which strategy should we employ given their respective costs and estimated contributions to future earnings?
- What types of health insurance and retirement plans are best for our employees, given the amount of money we have available?

Being able to give a value to cash received in the future, whether dividends from a share of stock, interest from a bond, or profits from a new product, is one of the primary skills needed to run a successful business. The material in this chapter provides an introduction to that skill.

Stress the use of a time line to help in setting up each problem.

THE TIME VALUE OF MONEY

Suppose a friend owes you $100, and the payment is due today. You receive a phone call from this friend, who says she would like to delay paying you for one year. You may reasonably demand a higher future payment, but how much more should you receive? The situation is illustrated here using a **time line**.

In this diagram "now," the present time, is assigned $t = 0$, or time zero. One year from now is assigned $t = 1$. The **present value** of the cash payment is $100 and is denoted by PV_0. Its **future value** at $t = 1$ is denoted by FV_1. To find the amount that you could demand for deferring receipt of the money by one year, you must solve for FV_1, the future value of $100 one year from now.

The FV_1 value will depend on the opportunity cost of forgoing immediate receipt of $100. You know, for instance, that if you had the money today you could deposit the $100 in a bank account earning 5% interest annually. However, you know from Chapter 3 that value depends on risk. In your judgment, your friend is less likely to pay you next year than is the bank. Therefore, you will increase the rate of interest to reflect the additional risk that you think is inherent in the loan to your friend.

Suppose that you decide that a 10% annual rate of interest is appropriate.[1] The amount of the future payment, FV_1, will be the original **principal** plus the **interest** that could be earned at the 10% annual rate. Algebraically, you can solve for FV_1, being careful always to convert percentages to decimals when doing arithmetic calculations,

$$FV_1 = \$100 + (\$100)(0.10) \tag{5.1}$$

Factoring $100 from the right-hand side of Equation (5.1)

$$FV_1 = \$100(1 + 0.10) \tag{5.2}$$

$$FV_1 = \$100(1.10) \tag{5.2}$$

$$FV_1 = \$110 \tag{5.4}$$

You may demand a $110 payment at $t = 1$ in lieu of an immediate $100 payment because these two amounts have equivalent *value*.

Now, let's say that your friend agrees to this interest rate but asks to delay payment for 2 years.

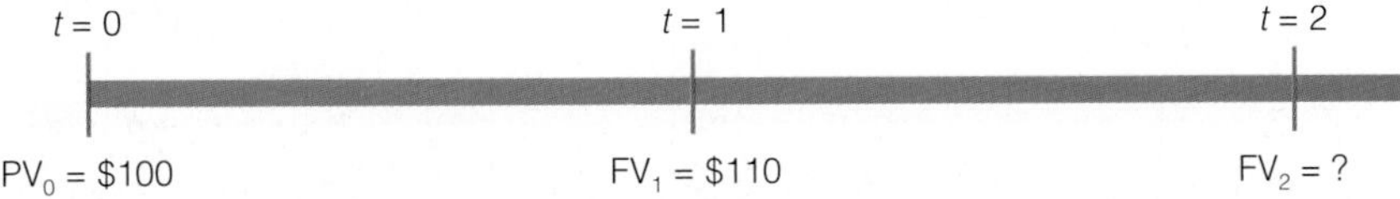

Now we must find FV_2, the future value of the payment 2 years from today. Because we know $FV_1 = \$110$ and we know the interest rate is 10%, we can solve for FV_2 by recognizing that FV_2 will equal FV_1 plus the interest that could be earned on FV_1 during the second year.

$$FV_2 = FV_1 + FV_1(0.10) \tag{5.5}$$

$$FV_2 = \$110 + (\$110)(0.10) \tag{5.6}$$

$$FV_2 = \$110(1 + 0.10) \tag{5.7}$$

$$FV_2 = \$110(1.10) \tag{5.8}$$

$$FV_2 = \$121 \tag{5.9}$$

[1]Chapters 7 and 8 are devoted to assessing risk and finding interest rates that reflect investors' required returns given the riskiness of investments. Hereafter, this chapter will treat interest rates as known, ignoring risk.

You may demand a \$121 payment at $t = 2$ because its time value is equivalent to either \$110 at $t = 1$ or \$100 at $t = 0$, given the 10% interest rate.

The **time value of money** and the mathematics associated with it provide important tools for comparing the relative values of cash flows received at different times. For example, recall from Chapter 1 that to increase shareholder wealth, managers must make investments that have value greater than their costs. Often, such investments require an immediate cash outlay, such as when buying a new delivery truck. The investment (the truck) then produces cash flows for the corporation in the future (delivery fee income, increased sales, lower delivery costs, etc.). To determine if the future cash flows have greater value than the initial cost of the truck, managers must be able to calculate the present value of the future stream of cash flows produced by this investment.

Compounding can be demonstrated by reminding students of Peter Minuit's "good deal" when he bought Manhattan Island for \$24 in 1624. In 1996 that \$24 investment would be worth \$1,787,347,000,000 had it compounded at 7% annually.

COMPOUND AND SIMPLE INTEREST

The preceding section showed that, at a 10% annual interest rate, \$100 today is equivalent to \$110 a year from now and \$121 in 2 years.

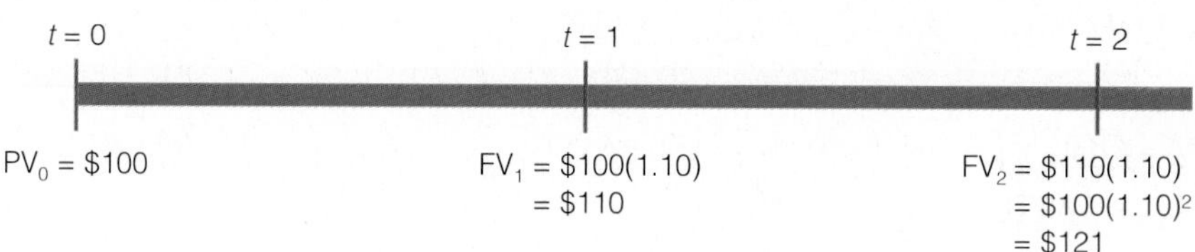

This result can be generalized using the following formulas,

$$FV_1 = PV_0(1 + r) \quad (5.10)$$

$$FV_2 = PV_0(1 + r)^2 \quad (5.11)$$

where r is the interest rate.

Now, let's expand Equation (5.11):

$$FV_2 = PV_0(1 + r)(1 + r) \quad (5.12)$$

$$FV_2 = PV_0(1 + 2r + r^2) \quad (5.13)$$

$$FV_2 = PV_0(1 + 2r) + PV_0(r^2) \quad (5.14)$$

Equation (5.14) is broken down in a special way. The first term on the right side of the equal sign, $PV_0(1 + 2r)$, would yield \$120 given the information we have used in our example. The second term, $PV_0(r^2)$, yields \$1. The value \$120 equals the original principle (\$100) plus the amount of interest earned (\$20) if your friend paid **simple interest**. For example, if you withdraw interest earned during each year at the end of that year, you would earn simple interest. In that case, you would receive \$10 interest payments at the end of years 1 and 2, totalling \$20. If, on the other hand, your friend credited (but did not pay) interest to you every year, then you would earn interest during year 2 on the interest credited to you at the end of year 1. Earning interest on previously earned interest is known as **compounding**. Thus, you would earn an extra dollar, a total of \$121, over the 2-year period with interest *compounded annually*. The example assumed annual compounding because nearly all transactions are now based on compound rather than simple interest. Not all compounding is done on an annual basis, however. Sometimes interest is added to an account every 6 months (semiannual compounding). Other contracts call for quarterly, monthly, or daily compounding. As you will see, the frequency of compounding can make a big difference when calculating the time value of money.

THE TIME VALUE OF A SINGLE CASH FLOW

Continuing our example, let us suppose that your friend who wishes to delay paying you agrees to a 10% annual rate of interest over the 2-year period and will allow you to compound interest semiannually. What will you be paid in 2 years given this agreement? Semiannual compounding means that interest will be credited to you every 6 months, based on half of the annual rate. In effect you will be earning a 5% semiannual rate of interest over four 6-month periods. In other words, the **periodic interest rate** will be half the annual rate because you are using semiannual compounding *and* you will be earning interest for four *time periods* (n = 1 through 4), each period being one-half year long. The new situation is illustrated next.

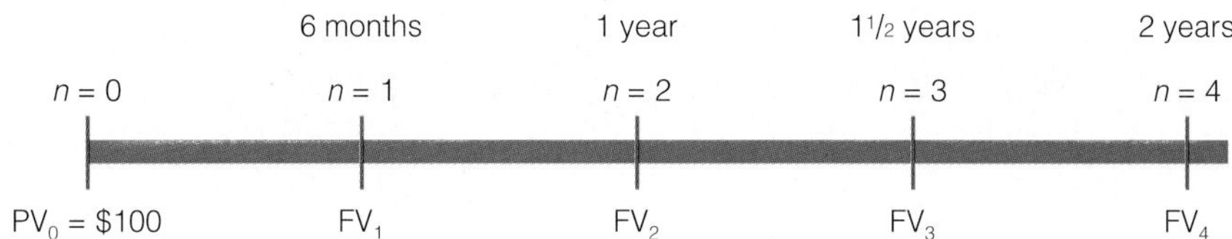

Here, FV_1 is the future value of the \$100 at the end of period 1 (the first 6 months). As before, FV_1 equals the \$100 beginning principal plus interest earned over the 6 months at the 5% semiannual interest rate.

$$FV_1 = \$100 + \$100(0.05) \quad \textbf{(5.15)}$$

$$FV_1 = \$100(1.05) \quad \textbf{(5.16)}$$

$$FV_1 = \$105 \quad \textbf{(5.17)}$$

Therefore, at the end of period one (at $n = 1$) the principal balance you are owed will be \$105. FV_2 will be equal to the principal at the beginning of period 2 plus interest earned during period 2.

$$FV_2 = \$105 + \$105(0.05) \quad \textbf{(5.18)}$$

$$FV_2 = \$105(1.05) \quad \textbf{(5.19)}$$

$$FV_2 = \$110.25 \quad \textbf{(5.20)}$$

Note that we could substitute [\$100(1.05)] for \$105 in Equation (5.19). Doing so, FV_2 could be reexpressed as follows:

$$FV_2 = \$105(1.05) \quad \textbf{(5.19)}$$

$$FV_2 = [\$100(1.05)](1.05) \quad \textbf{(5.21)}$$

$$FV_2 = \$100(1.05)^2 \quad \textbf{(5.22)}$$

Following this pattern, finding FV_3 and FV_4 is straightforward.

$$FV_3 = \$100(1.05)^3 \quad \textbf{(5.23)}$$

$$FV_3 = \$115.76 \quad \textbf{(5.24)}$$

$$FV_4 = \$100(1.05)^4 = \$121.55 \quad \textbf{(5.25)}$$

Equation (5.25) gives the answer we seek. The future value at the end of four 6-month periods is \$121.55. Changing from annual compounding to semiannual compounding has increased the future value of your friend's obligation to you by 55¢. The additional interest earned from semiannual compounding, 55¢, doesn't seem like much, but imagine a firm borrowing \$100 million; then the compounding period—annual, semiannual, quarterly—can turn into tens of thousands of dollars.

The Future Value of a Single Cash Flow

The pattern established here may be generalized into the formula for the *future value of a single cash flow using compound interest.* See Exhibit 5.1.

$$FV_n = PV_0(1 + r)^n \quad \textbf{(5.26)}$$

where

FV_n = the future value at the end of n time periods
PV_0 = the present value of the cash flow
r = *the periodic interest rate*

Transparency Available

EXHIBIT 5.1

THE FUTURE VALUE OF \$100 AFTER 6 YEARS USING 18% INTEREST PER YEAR WITH DIFFERENT COMPOUNDING PERIODS

COMPOUNDING ASSUMPTION	N	R	FV_N
Compounded annually	6	0.18	\$269.96
Compounded semiannually	12	0.09	\$281.27
Compounded quarterly	24	0.045	\$287.60
Compounded monthly	72	0.015	\$292.12
Compounded weekly	312	0.00346	\$293.92
Compounded daily (365 days)	2,190	0.000493	\$294.39

TIME VALUE TABLE 5.1

Equation (5.26), $FV_n = PV_0 (1 + r)^n$, is sometimes written

$$FV_n = PV_0(FVIF_{n,r})$$

In this form, $(1 + r)^n$ is replaced by $FVIF_{n,r}$ which is an acronym standing for *future value interest factor* for *n* periods at a periodic rate of *r*. Values for commonly encountered interest rates and periods have been calculated for FVIF and are given in Table A.1. A portion of Table A.1 is reproduced here.

N	1%	2%	3%	4%	5%
1	1.010	1.020	1.030	1.040	1.050
2	1.020	1.040	1.061	1.082	1.103
3	1.030	1.061	1.093	1.125	1.158
4	1.041	1.082	**1.126**	1.170	1.216
5	1.051	1.104	1.159	1.217	1.276

Suppose you wanted to find the future value of an $800 deposit in a bank that pays 12% annual interest, compounded quarterly, when the money will be left in the account 1 year; then PV = $800, r = 3% per quarter, and $n = 4$. Note that $FVIF_{4,3\%}$ is highlighted in the table and equals 1.126. Thus,

$$FV_4 = \$800(1.126) = \$900.80.$$

The use of tables such as Table A.1 for solving time value problems was very popular prior to the availability of inexpensive calculators. Such tables are limited, however, in their accuracy and because it is impossible to tabulate all possible rates of interest and all possible periods.

which equals the annual *nominal* rate divided by the number of compounding periods per year,

$$r = \frac{\text{annual nominal rate}}{\text{number of periods per year}}$$

$$n = \text{the number of corresponding periods until maturity, or}$$

$$n = (\text{number of years until maturity})(\text{compounding periods per year})$$

It is critical when using this formula to be certain that r and n agree with each other. If, for example, you are finding the future value of $100 after 6 years and the annual rate is 18%, compounded monthly, then the appropriate r is 1.5% per month (18% ÷ 12 = 1.5%), and n is 72 months (6 years times 12 months per year = 72 months). Students often adjust the interest rate and then forget to adjust the number of periods (or vice versa). The answer to this problem is

A useful tool for getting an estimated answer is the rule of 72, which states that an amount will double if the rate times the number of periods equals 72. Thus, $500 deposited in an account that pays 12% annually will be worth about $1,000 in 6 y.

$$FV_{6\times12} = \$100\left(1 + \frac{0.18}{12}\right)^{6\times12}$$

$$FV_{72} = \$100(1.015)^{72} = \$292.12$$

For simple interest, without compounding, the future value is simply equal to the annual interest earned times the number of years, plus the original principal. The formula for the *future value of a single cash flow using simple interest* is

$$FV_n^s = PV_0 + (n)(PV_0)(r) = PV_0(1 + nr) \tag{5.27}$$

where

FV_n^s = the future value at the end of n periods using simple interest,
n = the number of periods until maturity (Generally n simply equals the number of years because there is no adjustment for compounding periods.)
r = the periodic rate (which also usually equals the annual rate because there is no adjustment for compounding periods)

For the previous example, the future value of $100 invested for 6 years in an account paying 18% per year using simple interest is

$$FV_6^s = \$100[1 + (6)(0.18)] = \$208.00$$

Even simple interest can have a significant impact on wealth. Large corporations may have millions of dollars on hand that should be invested at all times. A $50,000,000 check not deposited in time to be credited to today's business costs the company, at 8% annual interest, ($50,000,000)(0.08/365) = $10,959.

Thus, monthly compounding yielded a future value after 6 years of $292.12, or $84.12 more than simple interest in this example. Exhibit 5.1 illustrates the future value of $100, bearing 18% annual interest, with different compounding assumptions. Be sure that you can replicate the solutions illustrated here using your calculator.[2] Simple interest calculations are abandoned at this point because they are so uncommon.

The Present Value of a Single Cash Flow

We have solved for the future value of a current cash flow. Often, we must solve for the *present value of a future cash flow*, solving for PV rather than FV. Suppose, for example, you are going to receive a bonus of $1000 in one year. You could really use some cash today and are able to borrow from a bank that would charge you an annual interest rate of 12%, compounded monthly. You decide to borrow as much as you can now such that you will still be able to pay off the loan in one year using the $1,000 bonus. In essence, you wish to solve for the present value of a $1,000 future value, knowing the interest rate (12% per year, compounded monthly) and the term of the loan (1 year, or 12 monthly compounding periods). Following is a time line illustrating the problem.

[2]To do these problems, you must master the y^x key (or similar key) on your calculator. In this case, y corresponds to $(1 + r)$ in the formula and x corresponds to n in the formula. Be sure your n and r agree, and always be sure you express percentages in their decimal forms before doing any calculations. You should practice with your calculator until your answers match those given in Table 5.1.

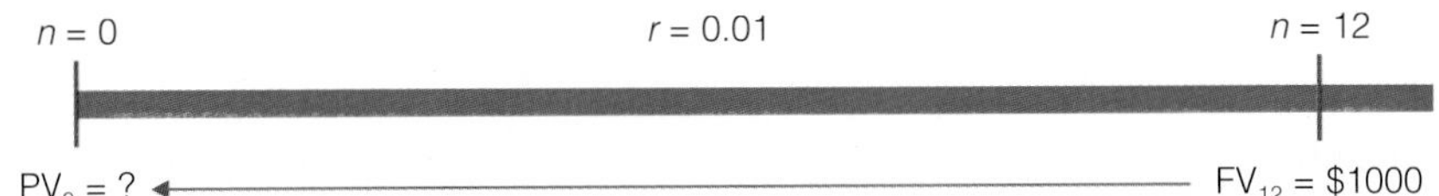

In this case $n = 12$, $r = 1\%$, and FV_{12} is known, whereas PV_0 is unknown. We still use Equation (5.26), substituting in the known quantities and using some algebra.

$$FV_n = PV_0(1 + r)^n \tag{5.26}$$

$$\$1000 = PV_0(1.01)^{12} \tag{5.28}$$

$$PV_0 = \$1000(1.01)^{-12} = \$1000 \frac{1}{1.01^{12}} \tag{5.29}$$

$$PV_0 = \$887.45 \tag{5.30}$$

You could borrow $887.45 today and fully pay off the loan, given the bank's terms, in one year using your $1,000 bonus. Equation (5.29) may be generalized into the *formula for the present value of a single cash flow with compound interest.* Solving for the present value of a future cash flow is also known as **discounting**. This formula is also called the *discounting formula for a single future cash flow*. See Exhibit 5.2.

$$PV_0 = FV_n(1 + r)^{-n} = FV_n \frac{1}{(1 + r)^n} \tag{5.31}$$

The variables PV_0, FV_n, n, and r are defined exactly as they are in the future value formula because both formulas are basically the same, just solved for different unknowns.

Exhibit 5.2 solves for the present, or discounted, value of a $1,000 cash flow to be received in 1 year at a 12% per year **discount rate** using different compounding periods. You should be able to replicate these solutions on your calculator.[3]

Transparency Available

COMPOUNDING ASSUMPTION	N	R	PV_0
Compounded annually	1	0.12	$892.86
Compounded semiannually	2	0.06	$890.00
Compounded quarterly	4	0.03	$888.49
Compounded monthly	12	0.01	$887.45
Compounded weekly	52	0.00231	$887.04
Compounded daily	365	0.000329	$886.94

EXHIBIT 5.2

PRESENT VALUE OF $1,000 TO BE RECEIVED IN 1 YEAR, DISCOUNTED AT A 12% ANNUAL RATE WITH DIFFERENT COMPOUNDING PERIODS

[3]To find present values on your calculator, you may use the y^x key with a *negative exponent* or the $\frac{1}{x}$ key, recalling that a negative exponent means finding the reciprocal, or 1 over the quantity.

TIME VALUE TABLE 5.2

Equation (5.31), $PV_0 = FV_n(1 + r)^{-n}$, is sometimes written:

$$PV_0 = FV_n[PVIF_{n,r}]$$

Here $PVIF_{n,r}$ stands for the *present value interest factor* for n periods at a periodic rate of r. For many common rates of interest and periods, PVIF is tabulated in Table A.2. A part of Table A.2 is reproduced here.

N	1%	2%	3%	4%	5%	6%
1	.990	.980	.971	.962	.952	.943
2	.980	.961	.943	.925	**.907**	.890
3	.971	.942	.915	.889	.864	.840
4	.961	.924	.888	.855	.823	.792
5	.951	.906	.863	.822	.784	.747

$PVIF_{n,r}$ is nothing more than another way of writing $(1 + r)^{-n}$, and Table A.2 simply tabulates these values.

Suppose you wish to know the present value of $2,000, which will be received in 2 years if the discount rate is 5% per year, compounded annually. FV_2 is equal to $2,000 and $PVIF_{n=2,r=5\%}$, highlighted above, equals 0.907.

$$PV_0 = FV_2(PVIF_{n,r}) = \$2{,}000(0.907) = \$1{,}814$$

Present and future value formulas are very useful because they can be used to solve a variety of problems. Suppose you make a $500 deposit in a bank today and you want to know how long it will take your account to double in value, assuming that the bank pays 8% interest per year, compounded annually. Here, you are solving for the number of time periods. You may substitute the known quantities $PV_0 = \$500$, $FV_n = \$1{,}000$, $r = 0.08$ into either formula and solve for n:

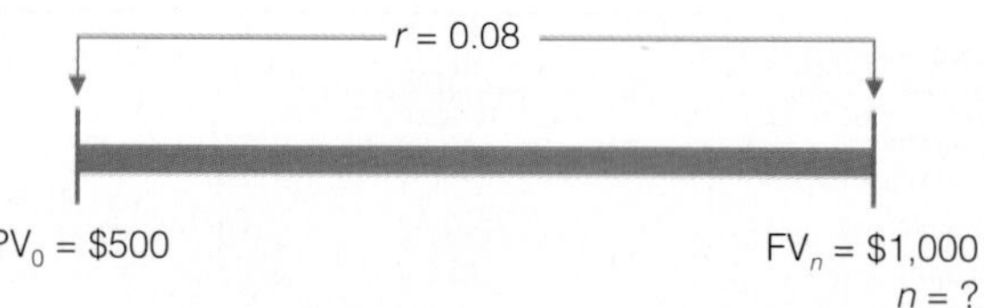

$$PV_0 = FV_n(1 + r)^{-n} \quad \textbf{(5.31)}$$

$$\$500 = \$1{,}000(1.08)^{-n} \quad \textbf{(5.32)}$$

$$(1.08)^n = \frac{\$1{,}000}{\$500} \quad \textbf{(5.33)}$$

$$(1.08)^n = 2 \quad \textbf{(5.34)}$$

At this point, without using logarithms[4] you must use trial and error to solve for n. Suppose you try $n = 10$ as your first guess for n:

$$(1.08)^{10} = 2.1589$$

This value yields a number higher than our objective of 2. Therefore, try $n = 9$, because a lower value of n will yield a lower answer:

$$(1.08)^{9} = 1.999$$

which is close enough. In 9 years the balance in your account will double.

Suppose the account earned 8% per year compounded monthly. To find the time until the account's balance doubled, you would convert the interest rate to reflect monthly compounding ($r = \frac{0.08}{12} = 0.00667$) and solve for the number of compounding periods.

$$PV_0 = FV_n(1 + r)^{-n} \tag{5.31}$$

$$\$500 = \$1{,}000(1.00667)^{-n} \tag{5.35}$$

$$(1.00667)^{n} = 2 \tag{5.36}$$

Using trial and error, the answer turns out to be $n = 105$. This should be interpreted as 105 months because you are dealing with monthly compounding periods. Thus, in 8.75 years the account will double in value when using monthly rather than annual compounding.

This example illustrates an important lesson. It takes less time to achieve a desired amount of wealth with more frequent compounding at a given nominal interest rate. It is no surprise that borrowers prefer less frequent compounding, whereas savers (or lenders) prefer compounding as frequently as possible.

Another type of problem is solving for the interest rate. This time let's suppose that an investment costing \$200 will make a single payment of \$275 in 5 years. What is the interest rate such an investment will yield? Substitute $PV_0 = \$200$, $FV_5 = \$275$, and $n = 5$ into the formula and solve for r.

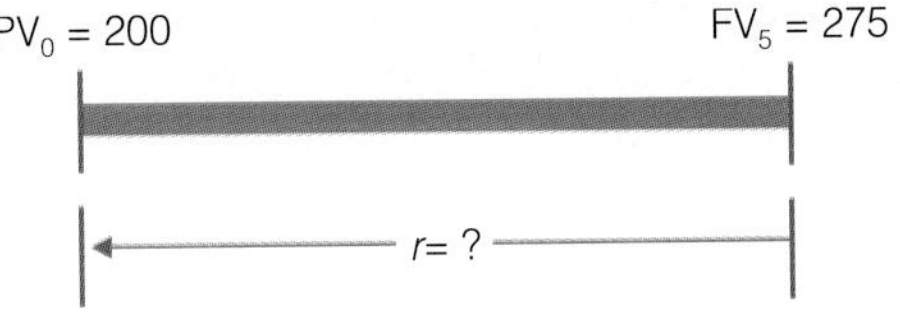

$$PV_0 = FV_n(1 + r)^{-n} \tag{5.31}$$

$$\$200 = \$275(1 + r)^{-5} \tag{5.37}$$

$$(1 + r)^{5} = \frac{\$275}{\$200} \tag{5.38}$$

[4]To solve using logarithms, use the natural log key on your calculator [LN] and the following formula:

$$n = \frac{\ln[FV/PV]}{\ln[1 + r]}$$

$$(1 + r)^5 = 1.375 \tag{5.39}$$

$$1 + r = (1.375)^{1/5} \tag{5.40}$$

$$1 + r = (1.375)^{0.20} \tag{5.41}$$

$$r = (1.375)^{0.20} - 1 \tag{5.42}$$

$$r = 0.06576 \tag{5.43}$$

The answer, $r = 0.06576$, is based on an annual compound rate, because we assumed $n = 5$ years. It is also expressed as a decimal and can be reexpressed as a percentage, 6.576% per year compounded annually.

Effective Annual Percentage Rate

As you have seen, the frequency of compounding is important. Truth-in-lending laws now require that financial institutions reveal the **effective annual percentage rate (EAR)** to customers so that the true cost of borrowing is explicitly stated. Before this legislation, banks could quote annual interest rates without revealing the compounding period. Such a lack of disclosure can be costly to borrowers. For example, borrowing at a 12% yearly rate from bank A may be more costly than borrowing from bank B, which charges 12.1% yearly, if A compounds interest daily and B compounds semiannually. Both 12% and 12.1% are **nominal rates**—they reveal the rate "in name only" but not in terms of the true economic cost. To find the effective annual rate, the **nominal annual percentage rate (APR)** must be divided by the number of compounding periods per year and added to 1. This sum is then raised to an exponent equal to the number of compounding periods per year. Finally, 1 is then subtracted from this result.

$$\text{EAR} = \left(1 + \frac{\text{APR}}{\text{CP}}\right)^{cp} - 1 \tag{5.44}$$

For our example,

$$\text{EAR}_A = \left(1 + \frac{0.12}{365}\right)^{365} - 1 = 0.1275 = 12.75\% \tag{5.45}$$

$$\text{EAR}_B = \left(1 + \frac{0.121}{2}\right)^{2} - 1 = 0.1247 = 12.47\% \tag{5.46}$$

Thus, if you are a borrower, you would prefer to borrow from bank B despite its higher APR. The lower EAR translates into a lower cost over the life of the loan. The disclosure of EARs makes comparison shopping for rates much easier.

Continuous Compounding

Suppose you were lucky enough to find an investment that yielded 100% interest annually. Without compounding, you would double your money in 1 year. Keep in mind that, expressed as a decimal, 100% interest is 1.00, so $r = 1.00$ and the 1-year future value would be $FV_1 = \$1(1 + 1.00)^1 = \$1(2) = \$2$. Now, assume you found a bank that offered 100% nominal annual interest with your choice of compounding periods. Exhibit 5.3 shows the 1-year future value of $1 deposited in such accounts with various compounding frequencies.

Notice that, as expected, the future value of the deposit increases as the frequency of compounding increases until it appears to level off at daily compounding. The same phenomenon appears in Exhibit 5.1. There appears to be a limit to the benefit of increasing the frequency of compounding. In fact, there is such a limit; it is known as **continuous compounding**, meaning that interest is credited to the depositor's account constantly (every microsecond, so to speak). The future value and present value formulas for continuous compounding are

$$FV_n = PV_0(e^{rn}) \tag{5.47}$$

$$PV_0 = FV_n(e^{-rn}) \tag{5.48}$$

The letter ***e*** is one of those special numbers in mathematics that is assigned its own name. (Another one is π, which you may remember is approximately equal to 3.14). The number e is approximately equal to 2.72 (more precisely,[5] it is approximately equal to 2.71828183). That value is the same number that seemed to be the limit of compounding benefit in Exhibit 5.3. Go back to Exhibit 5.1 and find the future value in year 6 of $100 deposited at 18%, compounded daily. That answer is $294.39. Now, find FV_6 if $100 is deposited at 18%, compounded continuously.

$$FV_6 = (\$100)[e^{(0.18)(6)}] = (\$100)(2.71828^{1.08}) = \$294.47 \tag{5.49}$$

When using the continuous compounding formulas, r is always equal to the annual rate of interest and n is always equal to the number of years. Thus, to find the present value of $1,000 to be received in 18 months, discounted at 16% per year, compounded continuously, you would use $r = 0.16$ and $n = 1.5$ years:

$$PV_0 = FV_{1.5}e^{-(0.16)(1.5)} \tag{5.50}$$

$$PV_0 = \$1000(2.71828^{-0.24}) \tag{5.51}$$

$$PV_0 = \$786.63 \tag{5.52}$$

EXHIBIT 5.3

FV_1 OF $1 DEPOSITED IN AN ACCOUNT FOR 1 YEAR BEARING A 100% NOMINAL ANNUAL RATE OF INTEREST AT VARIOUS COMPOUNDING FREQUENCIES

COMPOUNDING FREQUENCY	FORMULA	FV_1
Annual	$FV_1 = \$1(2)^1$	$2.00
Semiannual	$FV_1 = \$1(1.5)^2$	$2.25
Quarterly	$FV_1 = \$1(1.25)^4$	$2.44
Monthly	$FV_1 = \$1(1.0833)^{12}$	$2.61
Weekly	$FV_1 = \$1(1.01923)^{52}$	$2.69
Daily	$FV_1 = \$1(1.00274)^{365}$	$2.7146
Every hour	$FV_1 = \$1(1.000114)^{8,760}$	$2.7181

[5] e is the base of the natural log and is defined as

$$e = \lim_{x\to\infty}\left(1 + \frac{1}{x}\right)^x$$

VALUING MULTIPLE CASH FLOWS

Many problems in finance involve finding the time value of multiple cash flows. Consider the following problem. A charity has the opportunity to purchase a used, mobile hot dog stand being sold at an auction. The charity would use the hot dog stand to raise money at special events held in the summer of each year (at the county fair and at baseball and soccer games). The hot dog stand will only last 2 years and then will be worthless. The charity estimates that, after all operating expenses, the stand will produce cash flows of $1,000 in both June and July in each of the next 2 years and cash flows of $1500 in each of the next two months of August. The auction takes place January 1, and the charity requires that its fundraising projects return 12% on their invested funds. How much should the charity bid for the hot dog stand? The strategy for solving this problem is shown in Exhibit 5.4.

The present value of the stream of cash flows the stand is expected to produce is found by applying Equation (5.31) to each of the six future cash flows. Note that 1% is used as the periodic rate (12% per year ÷ 12 months) because cash flows are spaced in monthly intervals. The charity should bid a maximum of $6,153.07 for the hot dog stand. Given the level of expected cash flows, paying more than this amount would result in the charity earning a lower return than its 12% objective.

The hot dog stand example illustrates the *general formula for finding the present value of any cash flow stream,*

$$PV_0 = \frac{CF_1}{(1+r)^1} + \frac{CF_2}{(1+r)^2} + \cdots + \frac{CF_N}{(1+r)^N} = \sum_{n=1}^{N} \frac{CF_n}{(1+r)^n} \qquad (5.53)$$

where

n = the number of compounding periods from time 0
CF_n = the cash flow to be received exactly n compounding periods from time 0
(e.g., CF_1 is the cash flow received at the end of period 1, etc.)
r = the periodic interest rate
N = the number of periods until the last cash flow

EXHIBIT 5.4

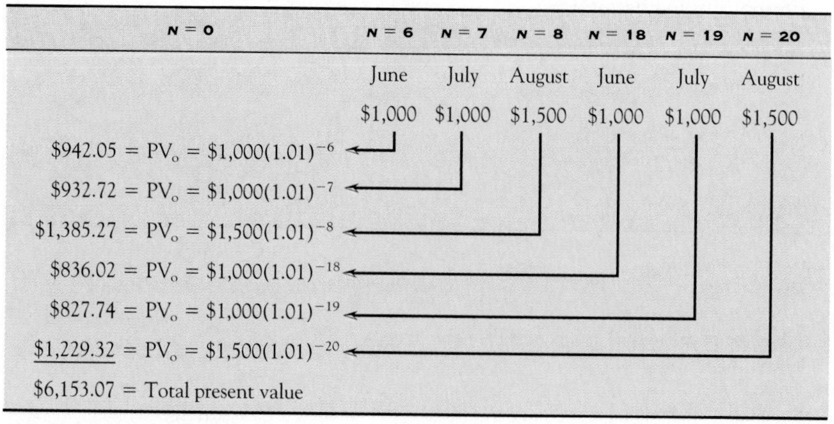

N = 0	N = 6	N = 7	N = 8	N = 18	N = 19	N = 20
	June	July	August	June	July	August
	$1,000	$1,000	$1,500	$1,000	$1,000	$1,500
$942.05 = PV_o = $1,000$(1.01)^{-6}$ ←	↑					
$932.72 = PV_o = $1,000$(1.01)^{-7}$ ←		↑				
$1,385.27 = PV_o = $1,500$(1.01)^{-8}$ ←			↑			
$836.02 = PV_o = $1,000$(1.01)^{-18}$ ←				↑		
$827.74 = PV_o = $1,000$(1.01)^{-19}$ ←					↑	
$1,229.32 = PV_o = $1,500$(1.01)^{-20}$ ←						↑
$6,153.07 = Total present value						

Transparency Available

The *future value formula for a cash flow stream* is also found by finding the future value of each individual cash flow and summing. Terms in the formula are defined as in the present value formula.

$$FV_N = CF_1(1 + r)^{N-1} + CF_2(1 + r)^{N-2} + \cdots + CF_N \quad \textbf{(5.54)}$$

You may question why in Equation (5.54) the first term is raised to the exponent $N - 1$ and why the last term is not multiplied by an interest factor. This situation can be clarified by using a time line. The last cash flow (CF_N) occurs at the end of the last time period and therefore earns no interest.

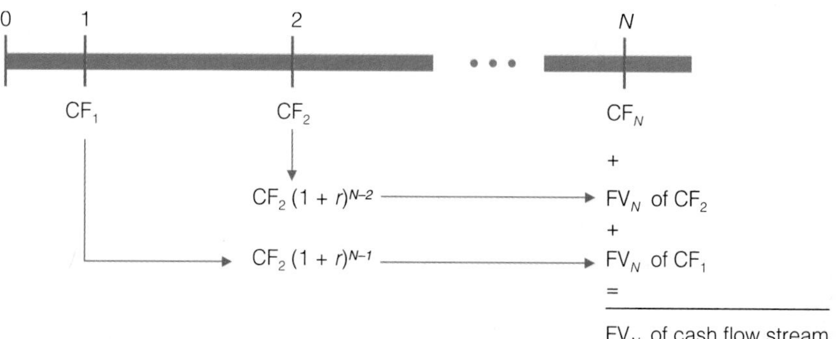

As the time line shows, CF_1 earns interest for $N - 1$ periods, but CF_N earns no interest and is simply added to the other sums to find the total future value. By convention, we assume that the cash flows from investments do not start immediately but are deferred until the end of the first period. This is not always the case, however. Practitioners must carefully analyze any problem to be certain exactly when cash flows will occur. A time line is a useful aide in modeling when the cash flows from a project will occur.

Perpetuities

Some special patterns of cash flows are frequently encountered in finance. Furthermore, the nature of these patterns allows the general formulas to be simplified to a more concise form. The first special case is that of **perpetuities**, which are cash flow streams where equal cash flow amounts are uniformly spaced in time (every year, or every month, etc.). Perpetuity means that these payments continue forever. To illustrate, suppose an investment is expected to pay $50 every year forever. Investors require a return of 10% on this investment. What should be its current price? Recognizing that today's price should equal the present value of the investment's future cash flows, we illustrate the problem using a time line.

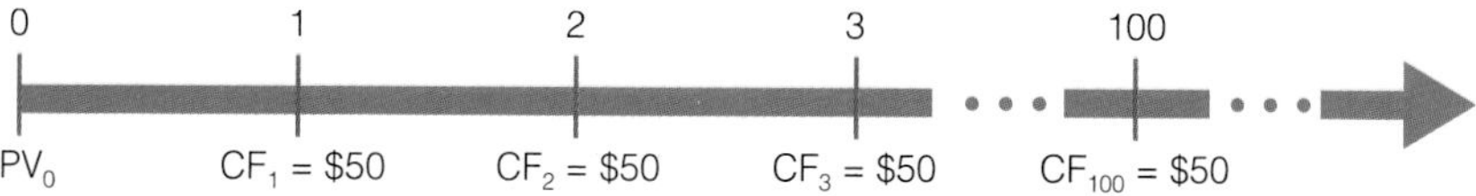

The arrow indicates that these cash flows continue into the future indefinitely. This poses a problem: If there is an infinite number of cash flows, then how can we find all their present values? Let's consider the algebraic expression of this problem.

$$PV_0 = \frac{\$50}{(1.10)^1} + \frac{\$50}{(1.10)^2} + \cdots + \frac{\$50}{(1.10)^{100}} + \cdots \qquad (5.55)$$

$$PV_0 = \$50\left[\frac{1}{(1.10)^1} + \frac{1}{(1.10)^2} + \cdots \frac{1}{(1.10)^{100}} + \cdots\right] \qquad (5.56)$$

The expression in brackets in Equation (5.56) is known as the sum of a **geometric series.**[6] Fortunately, there is a technique for summing such series. The appendix to this chapter shows how to sum a geometric series and then derives the following formula for the *present value of a perpetuity*:

$$PV_0 = \frac{CF}{r} \qquad (5.57)$$

Note that there is no subscript attached to CF, because all the cash flows are the same. Therefore, there is no need to distinguish CF_1 from CF_2, etc. Let's apply the formula to the example. CF = \$50, $r = 0.10$, and

$$PV_0 = \frac{\$50}{0.10} = \$500 \qquad (5.58)$$

Annuities

Retirement payments, bond interest payments, mortgage and automobile loan payments, and lottery jackpot winnings are all examples of annuities.

Of all the special patterns of cash flow streams, *annuities* are the most common. As we shall see, millions of fixed-rate home mortgages are annuities. Automobile loans often fit the annuity pattern, as do many leases.

An **annuity** is a stream of equally sized cash flows, equally spaced in time, which end after a fixed number of payments. Thus, annuities are like perpetuities, except they do not go on forever. The present value of an annuity can be found by summing the present values of all the individual cash flows.

$$PV_0 = \sum_{n=1}^{N} \frac{CF}{(1+r)^n} = \frac{CF}{(1+r)^1} + \frac{CF}{(1+r)^2} + \cdots + \frac{CF}{(1+r)^N} \qquad (5.59)$$

Here N is the number of cash flows being paid and CF is the uniform amount of each cash flow. Solving for PV_0 using Equation (5.59) would be a time-consuming problem if N were large. However, because the right-hand side of the equation is yet another geometric series, it can be simplified to yield the formula for finding the *present value of an annuity*.

$$PV_0 = (CF)\left(\frac{1 - [1/(1+r)^N]}{r}\right) \qquad (5.60)$$

To convince you that Equations (5.59) and (5.60) are equivalent, let's work an example using both approaches. Suppose you wished to know the present value of a stream of \$50 payments made semiannually over the next 2 years. The first payment is scheduled to begin 6 months from today. The annual rate of interest is 10%. The problem is illustrated with a time line.

---

[6]A *geometric series* is a series where each successive term is a constant factor times the term preceding it. For example, the series 1, $\frac{1}{2}$, $\frac{1}{4}$, $\frac{1}{8}$, $\frac{1}{16}$, . . . , is a geometric series, because each term is multiplied by $\frac{1}{2}$ to arrive at the next term. In Equation (5.56) the factor is $\frac{1}{1.10}$, because multiplying any term times $\frac{1}{1.10}$ will yield the next term in the series.

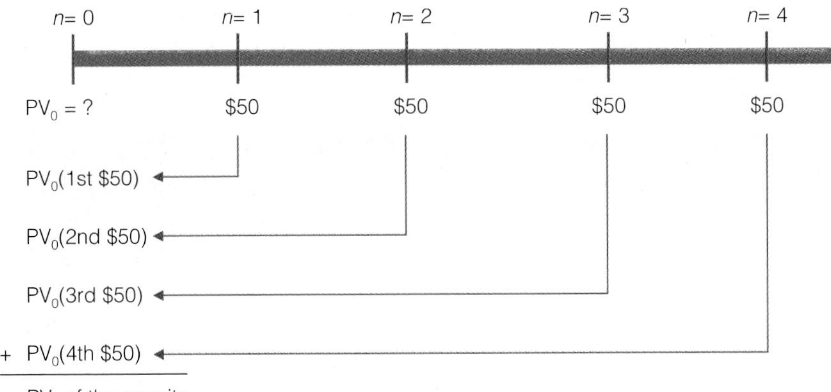

Using Equation (5.59), recognizing that $r = 5\% = 0.05$ semiannually, this problem can be solved as follows:

$$PV_0 = \frac{\$50}{(1.05)^1} + \frac{\$50}{(1.05)^2} + \frac{\$50}{(1.05)^3} + \frac{\$50}{(1.05)^4} \tag{5.61}$$

$$PV_0 = \$47.619 + \$45.351 + \$43.192 + \$41.135 \tag{5.62}$$

$$PV_0 = \$177.30 \tag{5.63}$$

Alternatively, Equation (5.60) can be used to solve the same problem.

$$PV_0 = (CF)\,\frac{(1 - [1/(1 + r)^N])}{r} \tag{5.60}$$

$$PV_0 = (\$50)\,\frac{(1 - [1/(1.05)^4]}{0.05} \tag{5.64}$$

$$PV_0 = (\$50)\,\frac{(1 - [1/(1.21550625)]}{0.05} \tag{5.65}$$

$$PV_0 = \frac{(\$50)(1 - 0.82270247)}{0.05} \tag{5.66}$$

$$PV_0 = \frac{(\$50)(0.17729753)}{0.05} \tag{5.67}$$

$$PV_0 = \frac{\$8.86487626}{0.05} \tag{5.68}$$

$$PV_0 = \$177.30 \tag{5.69}$$

All the steps are shown to aid you in following the calculations. It may appear that using Equation (5.60) is just as time consuming as using Equation (5.59), but consider the work involved had there been 300 payments rather than 4.

The problem just solved is an example of an **ordinary annuity** because cash flows commence at the *end* of the first period. Most loans require interest payments at the end of each period. Rent, on the other hand, is usually payable in advance. Annuities in which cash flows are made at the beginning of each period

TIME VALUE TABLE 5.3

Equation (5.60) can be written

$$PV_0 = (CF)(PVIFA_{N,r})$$

where $PVIFA_{N,r}$ is an acronym for *present value interest factor for an annuity* of N payments at a periodic rate of r%. Table A.3 tabulates values of $PVIFA_{N,r}$ for many common rates of interest and payment periods. A portion of Table A.3 is reproduced here.

N	1%	2%	3%	4%	5%
1	.990	.980	.971	.962	.952
2	1.970	1.942	1.913	1.886	1.859
3	2.941	2.884	2.829	2.775	2.723
4	3.902	3.808	3.717	3.630	**3.546**

The problem in the text, an annuity paying $50 semiannually for 2 years and a 5% semiannual discount rate, can be solved using the table:

$$PV_0 = \$50(PVIFA_{N=4,r=5\%}) = \$50(3.546) = \$177.30$$

are called **annuities due**. Let's change the example we just worked to require that the cash flows be made at the beginning of each period.

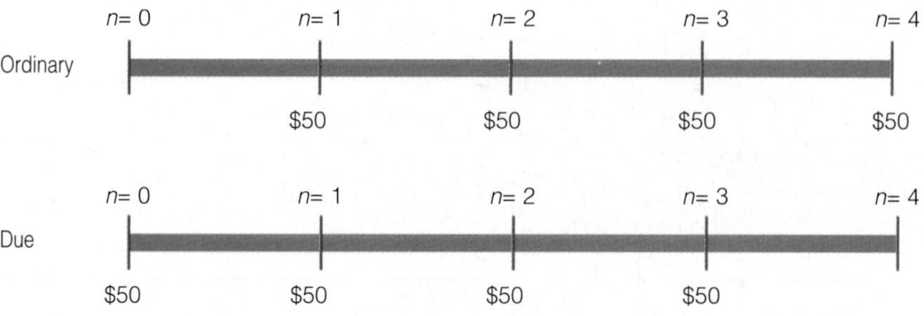

The time line shows that in a four-payment annuity due, each payment occurs one period sooner than in an otherwise similar ordinary annuity. Because of this characteristic, each cash flow is discounted for 1 less period when finding the PV of an annuity due. The formula for finding the *present value of an annuity due*,

$$PV_0^{due} = (CF)\left(\frac{1 - [1/(1 + r)^N]}{r}\right)(1 + r) \qquad \textbf{(5.70)}$$

is simply the formula for an ordinary annuity times $1 + r$, which adjusts for one less discounting period. Thus, it is usually easier to find the PV of an ordinary annuity and multiply times $(1 + r)$ when solving for the PV of an annuity due.

$$PV_0^{due} = PV_0^{ord}(1 + r) \qquad \textbf{(5.71)}$$

Now suppose you save $100 each month for 2 years in an account paying 12% interest annually, compounded monthly. What will be the balance in the account at the end of 2 years if you make your first deposit at the end of this month?

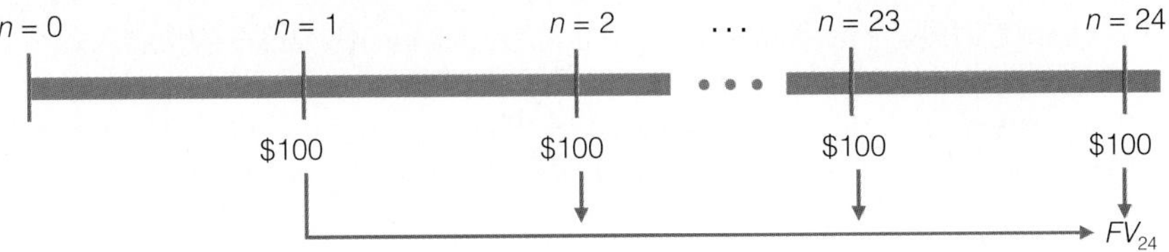

In this case we are trying to solve for the future value of an ordinary annuity.

$$FV_{24} = \$100(1.01)^{23} + \$100(1.01)^{22} + \cdots + \$100 \quad (5.72)$$

Solving our problem in this manner would take considerable time. Fortunately, the future value of an annuity is also a geometric series, which can be simplified. The formula for the *future value of an ordinary annuity* is

$$FV_N = (CF)\,\frac{(1 + r)^N - 1}{r} \quad (5.73)$$

Substituting the values for our example into Equation (5.73) yields the solution.

$$FV_{24} = (\$100)\,\frac{(1.01)^{24} - 1}{0.01} \quad (5.74)$$

$$FV_{24} = \$2{,}697.35 \quad (5.75)$$

If the first deposit were made immediately, our problem would be one of finding the *future value of an annuity due.*

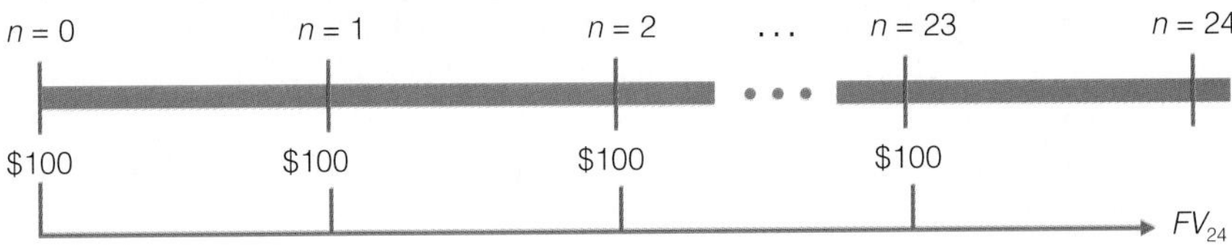

Each cash flow in an annuity due earns one additional period's interest compared to the future value of an ordinary annuity. Thus, the future value of an annuity due is equal to the future value of an ordinary annuity times $1 + r$.

$$FV_N^{due} = FV_N^{ord}(1 + r) \quad (5.76)$$

$$FV_{24}^{due} = (\$2{,}697.35)(1.01) \quad (5.77)$$

$$FV_{24}^{due} = \$2{,}724.32 \quad (5.78)$$

TIME VALUE TABLE 5.4

Equation (5.73) can be written

$$FV_N = (CF)(FVIFA_{N,r}),$$

where $FVIFA_{N,r}$ is an acronym for *future value interest factor for an annuity* of N payments at a periodic rate of r%. Values for common interest rates and payment periods are calculated for FVIFA and given in Table A.4 in the back of the text. A portion of Table A.4 is reproduced here.

N	1%	2%	3%	4%
1	1.000	1.000	1.000	1.000
2	2.010	2.020	2.030	2.040
3	3.031	3.060	3.091	3.122
4	4.060	4.122	**4.184**	4.247

Suppose you planned to deposit \$100 in an account at the end of each of the next 4 years. If the account paid 3% annually, the balance you should have in your account at the end of the 4-year period is determined using a cash flow of \$100 per period, $N = 4$, and $r = 3\%$.

$$FV_4 = \$100(FVIFA_{N=4,r=3\%}) = \$100(4.184) = \$418.40$$

The future value of the deposits would therefore increase to \$2,724.32 if they were made at the beginning of each period. Finally, note that the adjustment from an ordinary annuity to an annuity due is the same whether one is solving for PV or FV [compare Equations (5.76) and (5.71)].

Loan Amortization: An Annuity Application

Many loans, such as home mortgages, require a series of equal payments made to the lender. Each payment is for an amount large enough to cover both the interest owed for the period and some principal. In the early stages of the loan, most of each payment covers interest owed by the borrower, and very little is used to reduce the loan balance. Later in the loan's life, the small principal reductions have added up to a sum that has significantly reduced the amount owed. Thus, as time passes, less of each payment is applied toward interest and increasing amounts are paid on the principal. The final payment just covers both the remaining principal balance and the interest owed on that principal. This type of loan is called an **amortized loan**. An amortized loan is a direct application of the present value of an annuity. The original amount borrowed is the present value of the annuity (PV_0), whereas loan payments are the annuity's cash flows (CFs).

If you borrow \$100,000 to buy a house, what will your monthly payments be on a 30-year mortgage if the interest rate is 9% per year? For this problem the formula for finding the present value of an annuity is used [Equation (5.60)]. The present value is the loan amount ($PV_0 = \$100,000$), there are 360 payments

(N = 360), and the monthly interest rate is 0.75%: 9% ÷ 12 months. The payment amount (CF) is determined as follows:

$$PV_0 = (CF)\,\frac{(1 - [1/(1 + r)^N])}{r} \tag{5.60}$$

$$\$100{,}000 = \frac{(CF)(1 - [1/(1.0075)^{360}])}{0.0075} \tag{5.79}$$

$$\$100{,}000 = \frac{(CF)(1 - 1/14.730576)}{0.0075} \tag{5.80}$$

$$\$100{,}000 = (CF)\,\frac{(0.932114)}{0.0075} \tag{5.81}$$

$$\$100{,}000 = (CF)(124.2819) \tag{5.82}$$

$$CF = \$804.62 \tag{5.83}$$

A stream of 360 monthly payments of $804.62 will cover the interest owed each month and will pay off all the $100,000 loan as well. Of the first payment $750 will be used to pay the interest owed the lender for the use of $100,000 during the first month at the 0.75% monthly rate, and $54.62 will be applied toward the principal. Thus, for the second month of the loan only $99,945.38 is owed. This reduces the amount of interest owed during the second month to $749.59 and increases the second month's principal reduction to $55.03. This pattern continues until the last payment, when only a $798.63 principal balance is remaining. The last month's interest on this balance is $5.99. Therefore, the last $804.62 payment will just pay off the loan and pay the last month's interest too. Figure 5.1 illustrates how the amount of each payment applied toward principal

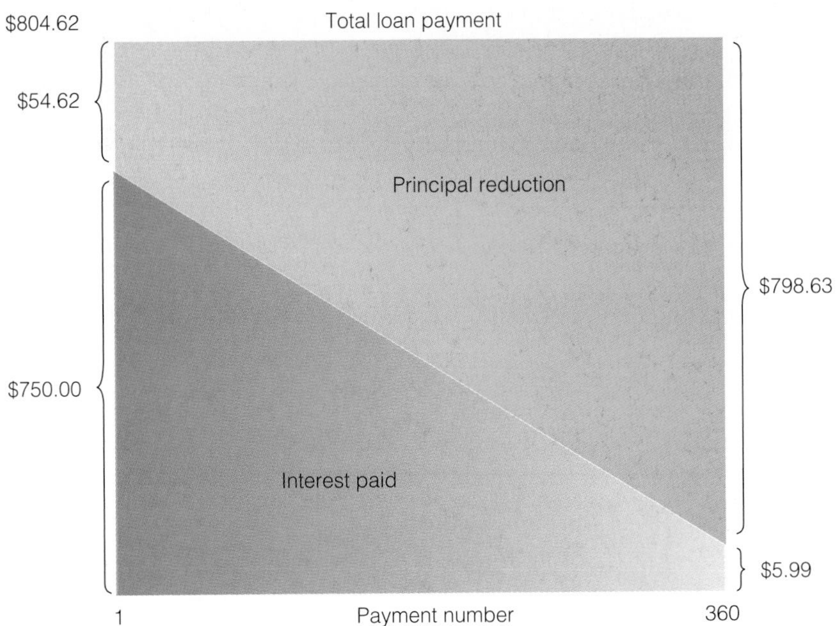

FIGURE 5.1
AMORTIZED LOAN
30-year, monthly payments, $100,000 loan at 9% per year.

Transparency Available

EXHIBIT 5.5

LOAN AMORTIZATION TABLE
$10,000 LOAN, 5-YEAR AMORTIZATION, 10% INTEREST, COMPOUNDED ANNUALLY

Transparency Available

PERIOD	I BEGINNING PRINCIPAL BALANCE	II TOTAL PAYMENT	III INTEREST	IV PRINCIPAL REDUCTION	V ENDING PRINCIPAL BALANCE
1	$10,000[1]	$2,637.97[2]	$1,000[3]	$1,637.97[4]	$8,362.03
2	$ 8,362.03	$2,637.97	$ 836.20	$1,801.77	$6,560.26
3	$ 6,560.26	$2,637.97	$ 656.03	$1,981.94	$4,578.32
4	$ 4,578.32	$2,637.97	$ 457.83	$2,180.14	$2,398.18
5	$ 2,398.18	$2,638.00	$ 239.82	$2,398.18	-0-

[1]Each period's beginning balance equals the prior period's ending balance. The loan balance at the beginning of the first year of this loan is obviously equal to the total loan amount.

[2]This is solved by using equation (5.60).

[3]Interest paid each period equals the rate times the period's beginning principal balance: Column III = (Column I)(r).

[4]Principal reduction each period equals the total payment less the amount applied toward interest: Column IV = (Column II) − (Column III).

[5]Ending principal balance equals the beginning balance minus the period's principal reduction: Column V = (Column I) − (Column IV).

increases over time, with a corresponding decrease in interest expense. Exhibit 5.5 is an *amortization table* showing principal and interest payments on a 5-year, $10,000 loan amortized using a 10% rate compounded annually.

SUMMARY

In Chapter 1 we stated that value depends on the timing of cash flows and in Chapter 3 we discussed why value depends on timing. Chapter 5 developed the tools necessary for quantifying how timing affects value. The chapter covered the formulas used to solve for the present and the future values of both single and multiple cash flows. Perpetuity and annuity formulas were applied to special patterns of multiple cash flows to value these cash flow streams. Also covered were techniques to adjust the interest rate for varying compounding assumptions.

Chapter 5 has covered much of the topic of the time value of money. Next, the concepts and techniques covered here will be applied to finding the value of stocks, bonds, and other securities, Before that, however, it is best to practice the newly acquired skills. The authors cannot overemphasize the importance of mastering time value mathematics. Therefore, as you do your homework, make sure you feel confident in your ability. If not, here's a good place to seek out a quantitatively oriented friend or to investigate your instructor's office hours.

KEY TERMS

opportunity cost
time line
present value
future value
principal
interest
time value of money
simple interest
compounding
periodic interest rate
discounting
discount rate
effective annual percentages rate (EAR)
nominal rate
nominal annual percentage rate (APR)
continuous compounding
e
perpetuity
geometric series
annuities
ordinary annuity
annuity due
amortized loan
annual percentage yield (APY) (see Problem 6)

KEY FORMULAS

future value of a single cash flow

simple interest $FV_n^s = PV_0(1 + nr)$

compound interest $FV_n = PV_0(1 + r)^n$

continuous compounding $FV_n = PV_0(e^{rn})$

present value of a single cash flow

compound interest $PV_0 = FV_n(1 + r)^{-n}$

continuous compounding $PV_0 = FV_n(e^{-rn})$

effective annual interest rate (EAR) $= \left(1 + \frac{\text{Nominal}}{\text{CP}}\right)^{\text{cp}} - 1$

general formula for finding the present value of a cash flow stream

$$PV_0 = \frac{CF_1}{(1 + r)^1} + \frac{CF_2}{(1 + r)^2} + \cdots + \frac{CF_N}{(1 + r)^N}$$

general formula for finding the future value of a cash flow stream

$$FV_N = CF_1(1 + r)^{N-1} + CF_2(1 + r)^{N-2} + \cdots + CF_N$$

present value of a perpetuity

$$PV_0 = \frac{CF}{r}$$

present value of an annuity

ordinary annuity $PV_0^{\text{ord}} = (CF)\left(\frac{1 - [1/(1 + r)^N]}{r}\right)$

annuity due $PV_0^{\text{due}} = PV_0^{\text{ord}}(1 + r)$

future value of an annuity

ordinary annuity $FV_N^{\text{ord}} = (CF)\frac{(1 + r)^N - 1}{r}$

annuity due $FV_N^{\text{due}} = FV_N^{\text{ord}}(1 + r)$

QUESTIONS

1. Suppose you own some land that was purchased by your father 20 years ago for $5,000. You are able to trade this land for a brand new Corvette sports car. What is an example of an economic opportunity you will forego if you proceed with the trade? How would you estimate the opportunity cost of proceeding with the trade?
2. The Corvette dealership from Question 1 is also willing to trade the car for an IOU you own that promises to pay you $2,000 at the end of each year for the next 10 years and $20,000 when it matures at the end of the 10-year period. Investors are currently valuing such IOUs using a 6% discount rate. What is an economic opportunity you will lose if you make the trade? How would you calculate the opportunity cost of the trade?
3. If the market for new automobiles and the real estate and bond markets are all efficient, then what do you think you would discover about the opportunity costs of the trade in Questions 1 and 2?
4. If you won the lottery, would you prefer a $1 million cash settlement or $100,000 a year for 10 years (all else the same, such as taxes)? Why?
5. Would a borrower prefer that interest be compounded annually or semi-annually, all else the same?

6. When interest rates rise, what happens to the present value of a fixed stream of cash flows?
7. Describe the essential differences between the following cash flow stream patterns.

annuity versus perpetuity

annuity due versus ordinary annuity

8. Why have many mortgage companies preferred to make home loans that have adjustable interest rates?
9. If you purchase a home and have the choice of making either an $800 payment each month on the mortgage or $400 payments on the first and fifteenth of every month, which option will allow you to pay off the loan more rapidly, assuming the same APR applies to both options?
10. XYZ, Inc., is signing a 1-year agreement with Acme Health Services to provide XYZ's employees with weekly aerobics classes at the firm's factory. Acme charges a flat fee for their services, with three payment options. XYZ can choose to pay Acme either $12,000 immediately, $1,100 per month for 12 months, or $13,500 at the end of the year. How would you decide which payment option XYZ should choose?
11. Match each cash flow stream described with the time line illustrating the problem. Some of the diagrams do not match any of the cash flows described.
    a. A vacation cabin can be leased to provide its owner with cash flows of $4,000 per year for 5 years. Lease payments will be made at the beginning of each year starting immediately. The cabin's owner requires an 8% annual return on the investment in the cabin. What is the present value of the lease to the owner?
    b. Professor Hickman's daughter is $6\frac{1}{2}$ years old. She is expected to begin college in 12 years. Hickman estimates that college tuition costs will be $20,000 a year for each of the 4 years at that future time. Tuition is paid at the beginning of each year. What should be Hickman's savings goal if he wishes to have a balance in savings when his daughter begins college to fund her tuition expenses? The savings account is expected to earn 6% per year from now until the end of her 4 years at college.
    c. Referring to part b, Hickman plans to invest $200 immediately at the end of each month in a mutual fund that is expected to earn 8% per year compounded monthly. Will he be able to fund his daughter's tuition with this savings plan?
    d. Your rich aunt passed away, leaving you a financial security that pays $500 every 6 months forever. Honest John's Lending Emporium will loan you money with the security as collateral using a 20% annual discount rate, compounded semiannually. How much can you borrow against this financial security from Honest John?
    e. You want to save $30,000 for a down payment on a house. You wish to purchase the home 10 years from now. You can earn 9% per year on your savings and you plan to save an equal amount at the end of each month over this period. How much should you save each month to meet your objective?

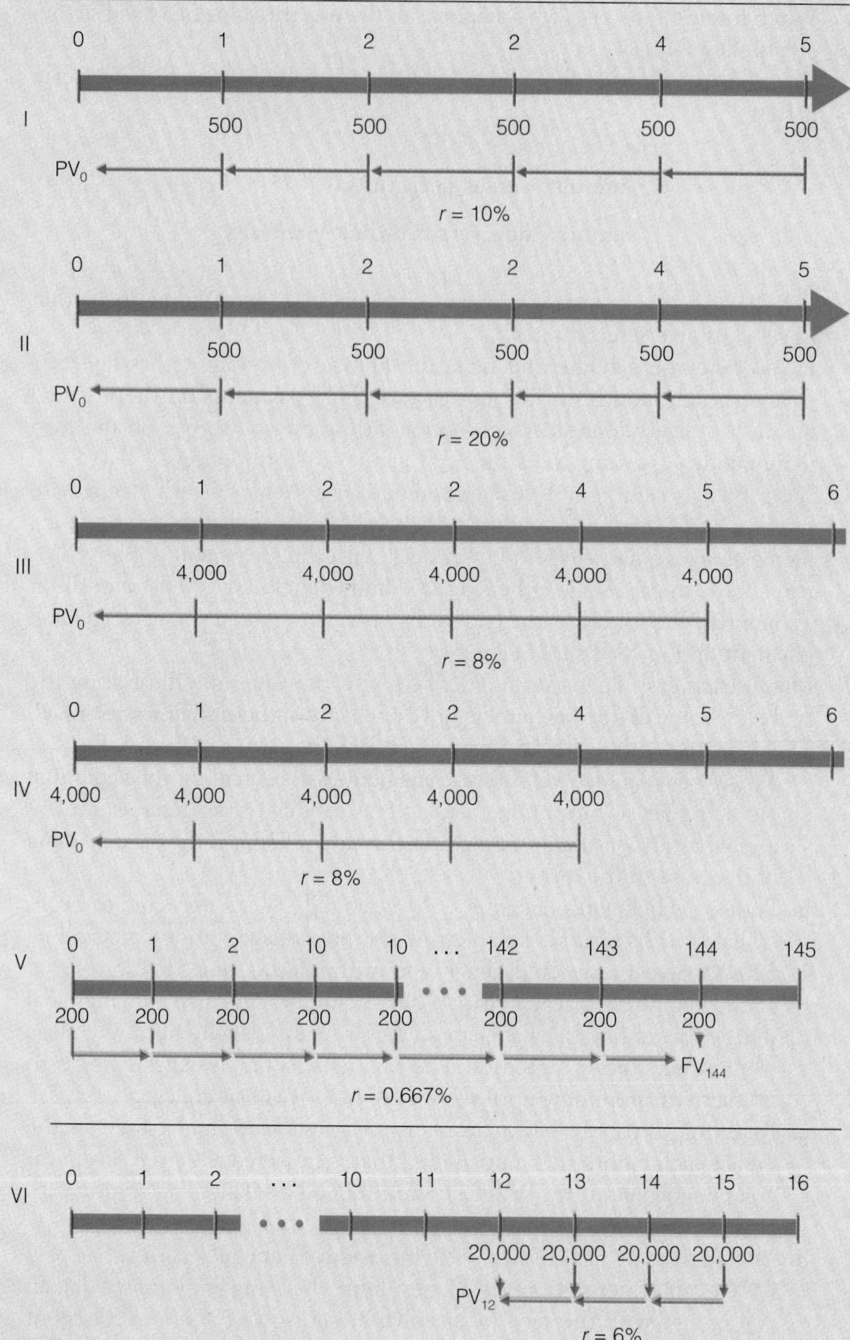

DEMONSTRATION PROBLEMS

1. Suppose \$1,000 is deposited in an account that has an adjustable interest rate. During the first year, the rate is 10%, compounded annually. The second year the rate changes to 8%, compounded quarterly. What is the account's balance after 2 years?

SOLUTION

Illustrate the problem with a time line.

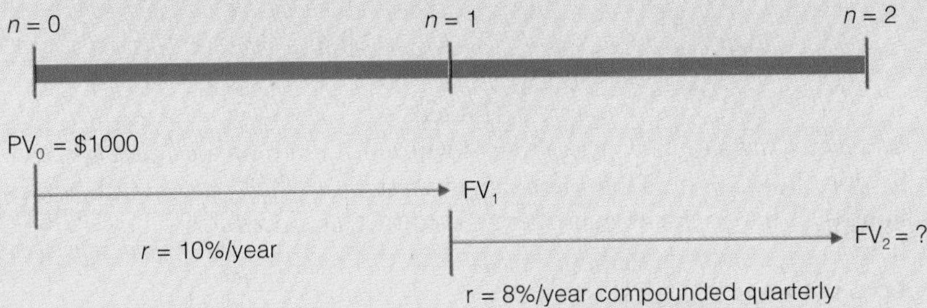

Algebra Solution Set the problem up mathematically and solve:

$$FV_2 = FV_1(1.02)^4$$
$$FV_1 = PV_0(1.10)^1$$

Substituting,

$$\begin{aligned} FV_2 &= PV_0(1.10)(1.02)^4 \\ &= \$1{,}000(1.10)(1.02)^4 \\ &= \$1{,}000(1.10)(1.08243) \\ &= \$1{,}000(1.190675) \\ &= \$1{,}190.68 \end{aligned}$$

Table Solution Solve the problem using the appropriate table:

$$FV_2 = FV_1(FVIF_{\substack{n=4 \\ r=2\%}})$$
$$FV_1 = PV_0(FVIF_{\substack{n=1 \\ r=10\%}})$$

Look up table values and substitute,

$$\begin{aligned} FV_2 &= PV_0(FVIF_{\substack{n=1 \\ r=10\%}})(FVIF_{\substack{n=4 \\ r=2\%}}) \\ &= \$1{,}000(1.10)(1.0824) \\ &= \$1{,}190.68 \end{aligned}$$

Calculator Finding FV_1: Clear registers.

1000	[PV]
0	[PMT]
10	[I%]
1	[N]
[FV]	

Answer: $1,100

Finding FV_2: Clear registers.

1100	[PV]
0	[PMT]
2	[I%]
4	[N]
[FV]	

Answer: $1,190.68

2. An electronics shop advertises that it will sell the top-of-the-line big-screen TV for $2,000. The shop offers an interest rate of 2% per month for 24 months. What payments must be made in this amortized loan?

SOLUTION

Illustrate the problem with a time line.

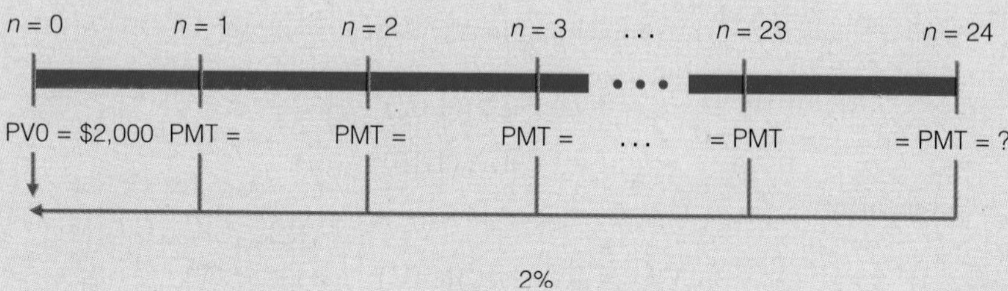

Algebra Solution Set the problem up as the present value of an ordinary annuity.

$$PV_0 = (PMT)\left[\frac{1 - [1/(1 + r)^N]}{r}\right]$$

$$\$2{,}000 = (PMT)\left[\frac{1 - [1/(1.02)^{24}]}{0.02}\right]$$

$$\$2{,}000 = PMT[18.9139]$$

$$\frac{\$2{,}000}{18.9139} = PMT$$

$$\$105.74 = \text{payment}$$

Table Solution

$$PV_0 = (PMT)(PVIFA_{\underset{r=2\%}{0=24}})$$

$$\$2{,}000 = PMT(18.9139)$$

$$\frac{\$2{,}000}{18.9139} = PMT$$

$$\$105.74 = \text{payment}$$

Calculator Clear registers.

2000	[PV]
0	[FV]
2	[I%]
24	[N]
[PMT]	

Answer: $105.74

PROBLEMS

1. Find the present value of $1,000 to be received in 1 year for each of the following annual discount rates.
   a. 10% per year, compounded annually
   b. 10% per year, compounded monthly
   c. 10% per year, compounded continuously

Present Value of a Single Cash Flow
1. a. $909.09
b. $905.21
c. $904.84

2. Find the present value of $2,500 to be received in 2 years for each of the following discount rates.
   a. 12% per year compounded annually
   b. 12% per year compounded semiannually
   c. 12% per year compounded quarterly
   d. 12% per year compounded monthly
   e. 12% per year compounded continuously

Present Value of a Single Cash Flow
2. a. $1,992.98
b. $1,980.23
c. $1,973.52
d. $1,968.92
e. $1,966.57

3. Find the future value of $1,000 deposited for 1 year in each of three banks, which pay the following annual rates of interest.
   a. 12% compounded annually
   b. 12% compounded monthly
   c. 12% compounded continuously

Future Value of a Single Cash Flow
3. a. $1,120.00
b. $1,126.83
c. $1,127.50

4. Find the future value of $2,500 deposited for 3 years in each of three banks, which pay the following annual rates of interest.
   a. 8% compounded annually
   b. 8% compounded semiannually
   c. 8% compounded quarterly
   d. 8% compounded monthly

Future Value of a Single Cash Flow
4. a. $3,149.28
b. $3,163.30
c. $3,170.60
d. $3,175.60

5. In 18 months you will withdraw all your savings in order to purchase an automobile. Your current account balance is $4,000. What will be your balance when you make the withdrawal for each of the following annual interest rates?
   a. 6% (compounded monthly)
   b. 0%
   c. 9% (compounded continuously)

Future Value, The Effect of Different Interest Rates
5. a. $4,375.72
b. $4,000.00
c. $4,578.15

6. EARs (effective annual rates) for savings deposits and certificates of deposits at financial institutions are called **annual percentage yields** (APYs). For each savings accounts, what is the APY?
   a. 12%, compounded annually
   b. 12.2%, compounded semiannually
   c. 12.2%, compounded quarterly

Solving for the Effective Interest Rate
6. a. 12%
b. 12.57%
c. 12.77%
d. 12.68%

d. 12%, compounded monthly
e. As a saver, which account would you choose?

Solving for the Effective Interest Rate
7. a. 9.31%
b. 9.5%
c. 9.2%

7. What are the EARs for the following rates of interest? Where would you borrow given these rates?
a. 9% per year, compounded quarterly
b. 9.5% per year, compounded annually
c. 8.8%, compounded daily (365 days/year)

Solving for the Rate
8. 6%

8. If $200 is deposited in a certificate of deposit (CD) for three years and when the CD that pays $238.20 at maturity, what is the CD's annual rate of interest?

Solving for the Rate
9. 9.05%

9. A bank promises that you can double your money in 8 years by depositing $5,000 in the superior savings plan today. What rate of interest does the superior savings plan pay?

Solving for the Rate
10. 12.246%

10. Suppose you can make an investment that promises to pay you $3,000 in 6 years. The cost of the investment is $1,500. What is the rate of return on this investment?

Solving for the Number of Periods
11. 9.5 y

11. How many years will it take your money to triple in value if it is invested in a mutual fund that is expected to provide a 12% annual nominal return, compounded quarterly?

Solving for the Number of Periods
12. 4.5 y

12. An investment earns 4% quarterly. How long will it take for the investment to double your money?

Solving for the Number of Periods
13. 26 y

13. ABC Enterprises offers its long-time employees a lump sum retirement bonus. At 30 years of service, the bonus equals $50,000. As an incentive to keep well-trained employees in the work force, ABC discounts the bonus at 15% per year for employees who retire early. An employee who is considering early retirement wants to have a $30,000 bonus in order to purchase a motorhome. At how many years of service should the employee consider retirement in order to have the motorhome purchase fully funded? (ABC's policy is to allow retirement only on the anniversary of employment dates; one *cannot* retire at 20.5 years of service, for example).

Present Value of an Annuity Due
14. $351,987.64

14. You hope to be able to withdraw $5,000 at the beginning of each month when you retire. Actuarial tables says that your life expectancy at retirement is 120 months. How much money should you have at retirement to fund these withdrawals if you expect to earn 1% per month on the account's balance?

Present Value of Unequal Future Cash Flows
15. $17,669.72

15. A marina on Lake Michigan is considering purchasing a boat to rent during the summer months to water skiers. The marina requires a 15% annual return on such investments. The boat is expected to generate cash flows of $2,500 a month during the months of July and August and $1,000 a month for June and September. The boat will last 3 years and then be worthless. If the marina plans to purchase the boat on June 1 of this year, what is the present value of the boat investment to the marina? If the cost of the boat is $17,500, do you think the marina should make the investment? (By convention, the cash flows generated by the boat are assumed to occur at the end of each month.)

Future Value of Unequally-Spaced Future Cash Flows
16. $37,553.35

16. What is the future value, at the end of 10 years, of deposits of $5,000 made today, $5,000 made 3 years from today, and $5,000 made 7 years from today into an account bearing a 13% APR, compounded quarterly?

17. If you deposit $1,000 at the end of each year for the first 5 years, $5,000 at the end of each year for the next 3 years, and $10,000 at the end of each of the next 4 years, how much will you have in your bank account at the end of 12 years (r = 12%)?

Future Value of Unequal Future Cash Flows
17. $88,385.82

18. What amount of money will be in an account at the end of 10 years if the account earns 6% annually and the following deposits are made into the account?

Future Value of Cash Flow Stream
18. $39,893.93

BEGINNING OF YEARS	ANNUAL DEPOSIT
1–5	$2,000
6–10	$4,000

19. How much should you deposit today in an account that pays 10% per year if you wish to withdraw the following cash flows in the future?

Present Value of Unequal Future Cash Flows
19. $29,617.83

END OF YEARS	ANNUAL WITHDRAWAL
1–5	$2,000
6–11	$4,000
12–19	$6,000

20. A billboard is expected to increase cash flows by $400 each month for 6 months. What is the billboard's present value if cash flows occur at the end of each month and the firm doing the advertising requires an 18% yearly return on such investments?

Present Value of an Annuity
20. $2,278.87

21. Your parents say they will set aside money in an account bearing 6.5% yearly interest, compounded monthly, to pay for your apartment rent for the next year (they're feeling gratuitous because you made the honor roll last semester). You have found an apartment that rents for $500 per month, payable in advance. Can you help your parents estimate the amount they should deposit to cover the next 12 months' rent?

Present Value of an Annuity Due
21. $5,825.01

22. Solve Question 11, parts b and c.

Present Value of an Annuity Due and Future Value of an Ordinary Annuity
22. b. $73,460
c. $48,960

23. If deposits of $300 made at the end of each month for the next year yield an account balance of $4,000, what annual rate of interest must that account bear?

Solving for the Rate in an Annuity
23. 22.74%

24. Deposits of $500 are made at the end of each year for 8 years. If the account balance at the end of this period is $5,130, what annual rate of interest did the account earn over this time period?

Solving for the Rate in an Annuity
24. 7%

25. A home mortgage has exactly $14\frac{1}{2}$ years remaining until it is paid off. Monthly payments are $380 on this fully amortized loan. The interest rate is 6% per year, compounded monthly. What is the principal balance of the loan?

Solving for a Loan Balance
25. $44,090.58

26. Suppose you are purchasing an automobile. You will borrow $7,000 and make quarterly payments on a 2-year amortized loan. The interest rate is 8% per year.
    a. What is your quarterly payment?
    b. Construct an amortization table for this loan.

Solving for a Payment and a Loan Amortization Schedule
26. a. $955.57/quarter
b. Last interest amount: $18.74

Solving for a Payment and a Loan Amortization Schedule
27. a. $353.05/month
b. Interest paid month 6: $60.82

27. **a.** What will be the monthly payments on a used-car loan of $7,500 if the loan bears 12% interest per year, compounded monthly, and is amortized over 2 years?
b. Construct an amortization table for this loan showing the interest payment, principal reduction and loan balance for each of the first 6 months of the loan.

Present Value of Deferred Annuity
28. $8,225.84

28. How much should you deposit today so that beginning 6 years from now you can withdraw $5,000 annually for the next 3 years (periods 6, 7, and 8)? Assume the interest rate is 9%.

Present Value of Various Cash Flow Patterns
29. a. $9,167.97
b. $8,655.16
c. $12,207.65

29. Given a 15% discount rate, find the present value of each of the following investments.

	INVESTMENT		
END OF YEAR	A	B	C
1	$1,000	$ 0	$ 7,000
2	$2,000	$ 0	$ 0
3	$2,000	$ 0	$ 0
4	$2,000	$ 0	$ 0
5	$2,000	$4,000	$10,000
6	$2,000	$4,000	$ 2,000
7	$2,000	$4,000	$ 0
8	$2,000	$4,000	$ 0
9	$2,000	$4,000	$ 1,000
10	$2,000	$4,000	$ 0

Future Value of Various Cash Flow Patterns
30. a. $37,089.56
b. $35,014.95
c. $49,386.71

30. Find the future value of each cash flow stream in Problem 29 for $r = 15\%$.

Solving for Payments
31. No rebate: $343.71; with rebate $313.38

31. Suppose you are going to purchase an automobile. The car costs $20,000, but you can afford to make an $8,000 down payment. You can borrow the balance of $12,000 from the dealership's finance company at a 2% APR, with monthly payments over 3 years, or you can borrow at an 8% APR, monthly payments over 3 years, and receive a $2,000 rebate on the purchase price. Assume that if you take the rebate option, you will apply it toward the purchase. Which alternative seems best?

Solving for Periods in an Annuity
32. 22 mo

32. You want to vacation in Europe someday. You plan to save $100 a month, beginning today, and estimate you can earn 1% per month on your savings. Your goal is to save $2,400. How long will it take to save this amount?

Inflation Problem
33. $2.06

33. The cost of a loaf of bread is now $1.39. If inflation is expected to be 4% annually, forecast the cost of a loaf of bread 10 years from now.

Inflation Problem
34. 9.25 y

34. How long will it be until bread costs $2.00 a loaf, using data from Problem 33?

Inflation Problem
35. 5.94%

35. If bread costs $1.56 two years from now, then what was the annual rate of inflation over those 2 years? (Assume the cost was $1.39 two years ago).

Retirement: Present Value of an Annuity Solve for Monthly Savings
36. a. $239,037.44
b. $160.26

36. When you retire, you hope to receive $2,000 a month for 20 years. You expect to retire in exactly 30 years.
a. If you believe that you will earn 8% annually on your savings during retirement, how much should you have in your retirement fund at the beginning of the retirement period?
b. Given your answer to part a, how much should you save each month

during your working years to accumulate the necessary retirement fund if you expect to earn 8% per year?

37. Suppose the Bank of Oz will lend you money today but requires no payments for 3 years. However, during this interest-deferral period the loan accumulates interest at a 6% rate, compounded semiannually. The bank amortizes the loan over a 5-year period, requiring semiannual payments and continuing to charge a 6% annual rate of interest, compounded semiannually. What will be the eventual semiannual payment on today's loan of $10,000, keeping in mind that the first payment will be made in exactly 3 years?

Solving for Payment in a Deferred Annuity
37. $1,359.02

38. Imagine that your 5-year-old daughter was given a lottery ticket for her recent birthday. The ticket was the grand prize winner and is supposed to pay $100,000 per year after taxes, for 10 years. The state sued, however, and won the case arguing that it would pay the prize as agreed, but it would not begin payment until your daughter reaches the age of 18 in exactly 13 years. If the appropriate discount rate is 7% annually, what is the present value of your daughter's good fortune?

Present Value of Deferred Annuity
38. $311,855.33

39. Harland Hardcourt is debating whether or not to enter the NBA (National Basketball Association) draft this year or wait one more year. If he enters the draft this year, he believes he will immediately be paid a $2,000,000 signing bonus, followed by a salary of $1,000,000 per year for 15 years. If he waits 1 year he believes that the signing bonus will stay the same, but his salary will increase to $1,200,000 per year. It will cost Harland $25,000 (payable immediately) to remain in school another year while waiting to enter the draft. Assuming that salaries are paid at the end of the year in which they are earned and that savings can earn 6.75% per year, what is today's present value of each of Harland's alternatives? (ignore taxes)

Present Value of Annuity Versus Deferred Annuity
39. Enter draft: $11,253,494; stay in school: $12,250,590

40. (This problem requires you to set it up algebraically and find the sum of a geometric series. It is called a growing annuity.) Suppose you save 10% of your salary each month in a retirement plan. You estimate that the plan will earn 8% per year, compounded monthly. Your current salary is $2,000 per month and you expect it to grow $\frac{1}{2}$% per month. If you make your first deposit at the end of the current month and work for 10 more years, what will be your retirement nest egg (assuming your forecasts are correct)?

Future Value of a Growing Annuity
40. $48,008.18

APPENDIX 5A

Summing a Geometric Series and Derivation of Time Value Formulas

In this chapter several patterns of cash flow streams were expressed as the sum of a geometric series. In a geometric series each successive term is equal to the preceding term times a fixed factor. The series 1, $\frac{1}{2}$, $\frac{1}{4}$, $\frac{1}{8}$, $\frac{1}{16}$, . . . , is an example. Each term is equal to the fixed factor $(\frac{1}{2})$ times its predecessor. Thus, $\frac{1}{2} = (\frac{1}{2})(1)$, $\frac{1}{4} = (\frac{1}{2})(\frac{1}{2})$, $\frac{1}{8} = (\frac{1}{2})(\frac{1}{4})$, $\frac{1}{16} = (\frac{1}{2})(\frac{1}{8})$ and so on. The *sum* of a geometric series refers to a series whose terms are added together, such as $1 + \frac{1}{2} + \frac{1}{4} + \frac{1}{8} + \frac{1}{16} + \cdots$. Expressed as an equation, the value of this sum is

$$S = 1 + \frac{1}{2} + \frac{1}{4} + \frac{1}{8} + \frac{1}{16} + \cdots$$

To solve for the sum of a geometric series we follow four steps.

Step 1

Identify the factor.

Step 2

Multiply both sides of the equation by the fixed factor.

Step 3

Subtract the product in step 2 from the original equation.

Step 4

Solve for S using algebra.

We can use our example,

$$S = 1 + \tfrac{1}{2} + \tfrac{1}{4} + \tfrac{1}{8} + \tfrac{1}{16} + \cdots$$

Step 1

The factor is $\tfrac{1}{2}$.

Step 2

$$\tfrac{1}{2}S = (\tfrac{1}{2})(1) + (\tfrac{1}{2})(\tfrac{1}{2}) + (\tfrac{1}{2})(\tfrac{1}{4}) + (\tfrac{1}{2})(\tfrac{1}{8}) + (\tfrac{1}{2})(\tfrac{1}{16}) + \cdots$$

$$\tfrac{1}{2}S = \tfrac{1}{2} + \tfrac{1}{4} + \tfrac{1}{8} + \tfrac{1}{16} + \tfrac{1}{32} + \cdots$$

Step 3

$$\begin{aligned} S &= 1 + \tfrac{1}{2} + \tfrac{1}{4} + \tfrac{1}{8} + \tfrac{1}{16} + \cdots \\ -\tfrac{1}{2}S &= -\ \ \tfrac{1}{2} - \tfrac{1}{4} - \tfrac{1}{8} - \tfrac{1}{16} - \tfrac{1}{32} - \cdots \\ \hline \tfrac{1}{2}S &= 1 + 0 + 0 + 0 + 0 + 0 \ldots \end{aligned}$$

(Note that all successive terms cancel.)

Step 4

$$\tfrac{1}{2}S = 1$$

$$S = (1)(2)$$

$$S = 2$$

Using these same steps we may solve for the present value of a perpetuity.

$$PV_0 = \frac{CF}{1 + r} + \frac{CF}{(1 + r)^2} + \frac{CF}{(1 + r)^3} + \cdots$$

Step 1

The common factor is $\dfrac{1}{1 + r}$.

Step 2

$$\left(\frac{1}{1 + r}\right)PV_0 = \frac{CF}{(1 + r)}\left(\frac{1}{1 + r}\right) + \frac{CF}{(1 + r)^2}\left(\frac{1}{1 + r}\right) + \cdots$$

$$\left(\frac{1}{1 + r}\right)PV_0 = \frac{CF}{(1 + r)^2} + \frac{CF}{(1 + r)^3} + \cdots$$

Step 3

$$PV_0 = \frac{CF}{1+r} + \frac{CF}{(1+r)^2} + \frac{CF}{(1+r)^3} + \cdots$$

$$-\left(\frac{1}{1+r}\right)PV_0 = -\frac{CF}{(1+r)^2} - \frac{CF}{(1+r)^3} - \cdots$$

$$PV_0 - \left(\frac{1}{1+r}\right)PV_0 = \frac{CF}{1+r} + 0 + 0 + 0 + \cdots$$

Step 4

In this case we solve for PV_0.

$$PV_0\left(1 - \frac{1}{1+r}\right) = \frac{CF}{1+r}$$

$$PV_0\left(\frac{1+r-1}{1+r}\right) = \frac{CF}{1+r}$$

$$PV_0 = \left(\frac{CF}{1+r}\right)\left(\frac{1+r}{r}\right)$$

$$PV_0 = \frac{CF}{r}$$

This is the same formula as Equation 5.57. The future value of an annuity formula was derived using the same approach.

$$FV_n = CF(1+r)^{n-1} + CF(1+r)^{n-2} + \cdots + CF$$

Step 1

The factor is $(1+r)^{-1}$, or $\left(\frac{1}{1+r}\right)$.

Step 2

$$\left(\frac{1}{1+r}\right)FV_n = CF(1+r)^{n-1}\left(\frac{1}{1+r}\right) + CF(1+r)^{n-2}\left(\frac{1}{1+r}\right) + \cdots + CF\left(\frac{1}{1+r}\right)$$

$$\left(\frac{1}{1+r}\right)FV_n = CF(1+r)^{n-2} + CF(1+r)^{n-3} + \cdots + CF(1+r)^{-1}$$

Step 3

$$FV_n = CF(1 + r)^{n-1} + CF(1 + r)^{n-2} + \cdots + CF$$

$$-\left(\frac{1}{1 + r}\right)FV_n = -CF(1 + r)^{n-2} - \cdots - CF - CF(1 + r)^{-1}$$

$$FV_n - \left(\frac{1}{1 + r}\right)FV_n = CF(1 + r)^{n-1} + 0 + 0 + 0 + \cdots + 0 - CF(1 + r)^{-1}$$

Step 4

Here we solve for FV_n.

$$FV_n\left(1 - \frac{1}{1 + r}\right) = CF(1 + r)^{n-1} - CF(1 + r)^{-1}$$

$$FN_n = CF[(1 + r)^{n-1} - (1 + r)^{-1}]\left(\frac{1 + r}{r}\right)$$

$$FV_n = CF\left[\frac{(1 + r)^{n-1}(1 + r) - (1 + r)^{-1}(1 + r)}{r}\right]$$

$$FV_n = CF\left(\frac{(1 + r)^n - 1}{r}\right)$$

This again, is the same formula as given in the chapter [Equation (5.73)]. Solving for the present value of an annuity formula is left as an exercise.

APPENDIX 5B

Solving Time Value of Money Problems with a Financial Calculator

In this appendix we solve several of the examples in Chapter 5 as an illustration of use of a financial calculator. We provide these illustrations with some reservation, however. Many students believe that the most challenging part of time value problems is learning the correct key strokes on their calculators, which couldn't be farther from the truth. The real challenge is modeling the problem—that is, transforming the words into a mathematical expression. Thus, it is most helpful to begin each problem by illustrating it with a time line, whether or not a calculator is used. This appendix is not designed to teach you to use a financial calculator. The manual that came with your calculator serves that purpose. Also, you will become better at using the calculator with practice. Therefore, do not purchase a financial calculator a few days before the test and expect that using it will be any help to you.

The following are some hints for using a financial calculator:

1. Ascertain whether interest key [i] reads data as a percentage or a decimal (e.g., 10% or 0.10).
2. Be sure all memory is cleared.
3. Set your calculator to show more than two decimal places. (It is doubtful that you'll ever be penalized for being too accurate.)
4. Work through your calculator's instruction book.

The following equations from Chapter 5 are solved using a financial calculator.

EQUATION NUMBER	DATA	KEY	ANSWER
25	4	N	
	5	i%	
	100	PV	
		FV	−121.55
29	12	N	
	1	i%	
	1,000	FV	
		PV	−887.45
37	−200	PV	
	275	FV	
	5	N	
		i%	6.5763
61	0	FV	
	5	i%	
	4	N	
	50	PMT	
		PV	−177.30
79	0	FV	
	0.75	i%	
	360	N	
	100,000	PV	
		PMT	−804.62

CHAPTER 6

Time Value Applications: Security Valuation and Expected Returns

Buy 200 shares of Crystal Ball Corp. at 13¼. You can't miss. Trust me.

Chapter 6 applies time value techniques to stock and bond valuation. It is much more accurate and reliable than a crystal ball. Trust us!

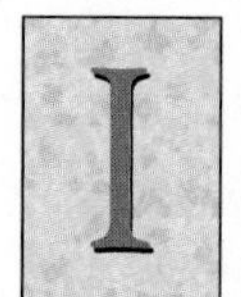

n Chapter 5 we began the study of the time value of money. In this chapter we apply those basics to the valuation of *securities* (stocks and bonds) and to solving for expected returns from investing. Along the way, we present some of the terminology and features of corporate securities.

The ability to solve for the value of a share of common stock is a fundamental skill for a corporate manager to have. Recall from Chapter 1 that it is management's job to maximize shareholders' wealth, an impossible task without knowledge of what factors influence share prices and, therefore, determine the wealth of shareholders. Common and preferred stock valuation as well as bond valuation are also important topics for anyone who may wish to personally invest in such securities. The first part of this chapter introduces security valuation.

Solving for expected returns concludes Chapter 6. When price is known it may be helpful for the manager (or the investor) to estimate the return or yield that can reasonably be expected from a project or investment. Such an expected return can be compared to returns offered by competing projects or investments. For example, an investor would never want to invest in a corporate bond whose expected yield was below that of a less risky government bond.

Before beginning, let's quickly review value. Recall from Chapters 1, 3, and 4 that value is dependent on cash flows to investors, the timing of those cash flows, and their riskiness. The cash flow that a security holder receives is the principal benefit of ownership. Without that benefit, the security would be nearly worthless.[1] Cash flows to stockholders come in the form of *dividends*, and for bondholders the cash received comes in the form of *coupon interest payments*.[2] Chapter 4 discussed cash flows in more detail, whereas Chapters 7 and 8 cover the relationship between risk and the estimation of discount rates. Taken together with the coverage in Chapters 5 and 6, these chapters cover the basic tools necessary for estimating value. Now we apply to securities the time value of money techniques introduced in Chapter 5.

AN APPLICATION OF SINGLE CASH FLOW FORMULAS: ZERO COUPON BONDS

Corporations and the government sometimes issue bonds known as **zero coupon bonds**. These bonds differ from typical bonds in that they make no payments to the bondholders until maturity. Let's consider a bond that matures in 20 years, pays no coupon interest, and has a **par**, or maturity, **value** of $1,000. That is, the investor will receive $1,000 on the bond's maturity date but no other cash payments during the life of the bond. If investors require an 8% annual return

[1]For example, stock certificates of defunct companies sell for almost nothing, deriving their sole worth from the attractiveness of their engraving and not from any direct economic benefit of ownership.

[2]Years ago, bonds actually had small coupons attached to them. When an interest payment was due, the bearer of the bond could go to a bank, clip off the coupon, and exchange the coupon for the interest payment, resulting in the terms *coupon payment* and *coupon rate*.

from this security, based on annual compounding, what should be the selling price of the bond? The problem is illustrated with the following time line:

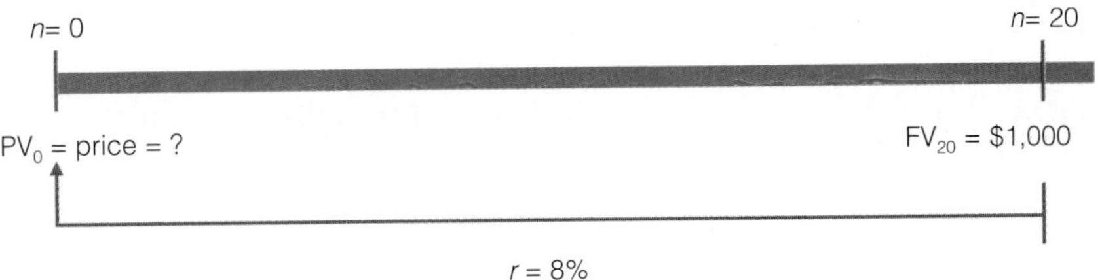

Use Equation (5.31) from Chapter 5 to find the current value:

$$PV_0 = FV_{20}(1 + r)^{-n} \quad (5.31)$$

$$PV_0 = \$1{,}000(1.08)^{-20} = \$1{,}000(0.21455) = \$214.55$$

Many very short term debt securities make no coupon payments and sell at a discount. Thus these instruments, known as *bills*, are a special case of zero coupon bonds.

The secondary market for zero coupon bonds is very active. Suppose one is selling for $425 and matures in 14 years, at which time it will pay $1,000 to its holders. In this case, investors would be interested in the **yield-to-maturity (YTM)**, or return that the bond offers given its current market price and other characteristics.

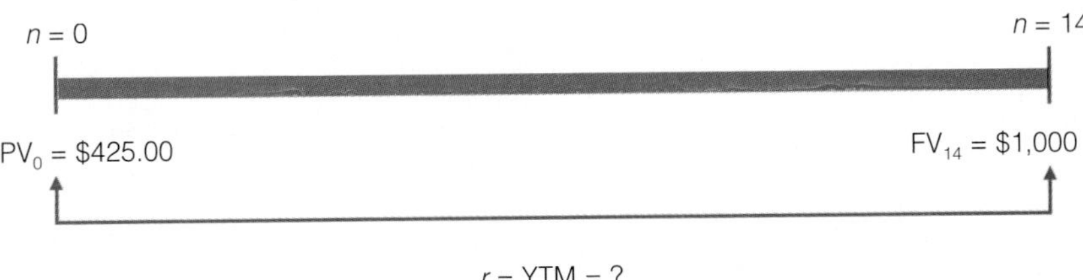

To solve for r, either Equation (5.26) or Equation (5.31) from Chapter 5 can be used.

$$FV_n = PV_0(1 + r)^n \quad (5.26)$$

$$\$1000 = \$425(1 + r)^{14}$$

$$(1 + r)^{14} = \frac{1{,}000}{425}$$

$$(1 + r)^{14} = 2.352941$$

$$1 + r = (2.352941)^{1/14}$$

$$r = (2.352941)^{1/14} - 1$$

$$r = 1.06303 - 1$$

$$r = 0.06303$$

$$YTM = 6.303\%$$

This bond is expected to yield 6.303% if held to maturity.

A PERPETUITY APPLICATION: PREFERRED STOCK

The most common type of perpetuity is **preferred stock**. Preferred stock generally pays a fixed dividend. Thus, eight-dollar preferred refers to a share of preferred stock that promises to pay a dividend of $8 once per year into the foreseeable future. Preferred stock is known as a **hybrid security** in that it combines features of both fixed claims (bonds) and residual claims (stocks). It is *fixed* in the sense that the amount the issuing corporation is obligated to pay does not vary; in this case it is $8 once every year. Preferred stock is *residual* because the dividend need not be paid unless the corporation has cash flows left over once all other fixed claims (such as interest on bonds) have been paid. Preferred claims have a lower priority than do other fixed claims but a higher priority than common stock. Therefore, no dividends can be paid to common stockholders unless preferred dividends have been paid.[3] The present value of a perpetuity formula is used to find the price of a share of eight-dollar preferred. The interest rate equals 16% in the example.

$$\mathrm{PV}_0 = \frac{\mathrm{CF}}{r} \qquad \textbf{(5.57 from Ch.5)}$$

$$P_0 = \frac{D}{r}$$

$$P_0 = \frac{\$8}{0.16}$$

$$P_0 = \$50.00$$

$\mathrm{PV}_0 = \mathrm{CF}/r$ is reexpressed as $P_0 = D/r$ because today's price (P_0) is equal to the present value of future cash flows (PV_0) and preferred's dividend (D) is the cash flow of the perpetuity (CF). The price is $50 per share.

COMMON STOCK: A GROWING PERPETUITY

Common stock, unlike preferred, does not pay dividends that are a constant amount through time. On the other hand, common dividends are equally spaced in time and do continue indefinitely. Common stock therefore satisfies all the perpetuity criteria except for the changing amount of its dividend payment and so is called a **growing perpetuity**.

To find the price of common stock we might use the general formula for the present value of a stream of cash flows. Again, recognizing that $\mathrm{PV}_0 = P_0$ and $\mathrm{CF}_1 = D_1$, $\mathrm{CF}_2 = D_2$, and so on, the formula can be reexpressed in terms of the price (P_0) and dividends ($D_1, D_2, \ldots$) of the common stock:

$$P_0 = \frac{D_1}{(1+r)^1} + \frac{D_2}{(1+r)^2} + \frac{D_3}{(1+r)^3} + \cdots = \sum_{n=1}^{\infty} \frac{D_n}{(1+r)^n} \qquad \textbf{(6.1)}$$

[3]There are many different types of preferred stock: *cumulative* preferred, *participating* preferred, and so on. Any investments text describes the features of these securities.

Clearly, it is impossible to solve this equation explicitly because the cash flows (dividends) go on forever. A number of models have been developed to allow this formula to be solved. The simplest model requires the assumption that successive dividends grow at a constant rate. Let that rate be called g_N, the *long-run normal growth rate of dividends*. The dividends can be expressed as $(1 + g_N)$ times the preceding year's dividend payment:

$$
\begin{aligned}
D_0 &= \text{the current dividend} \\
D_1 &= D_0(1 + g_N) \\
D_2 &= D_1(1 + g_N) = D_0(1 + g_N)^2 \\
D_3 &= D_2(1 + g_N) = D_0(1 + g_N)^3 \\
&\vdots
\end{aligned}
$$

Substituting into Equation (6.1) yields a geometric series,[4]

$$
P_0 = \frac{D_0(1 + g_N)}{(1 + r)} + \frac{D_0(1 + g_N)^2}{(1 + r)^2} + \frac{D_0(1 + g_N)^3}{(1 + r)^3} + \cdots = \sum_{n=1}^{\infty} \frac{D_0(1 + g_N)^n}{(1 + r)^n} \tag{6.2}
$$

which can be simplified by summing the series.

A **constant-growth** stock may be valued using the constant-growth formula,[5]

$$
P_0 = \frac{D_0(1 + g_N)}{r - g_N} = \frac{D_1}{r - g_N} \tag{6.3}
$$

From Equation (6.3) it might appear that we could increase share price by simply increasing the dividend, D_1. However, if we increase the dividend, then we reinvest less cash in the firm. Thus, the dividend-growth rate will decrease, perhaps offsetting the effect of the larger D_1. The interplay between dividends and growth is discussed more thoroughly in Chapter 13.

To illustrate the formula, let's assume a stock has just paid a \$5.00-per-share dividend. We believe that future dividends will grow at a 6% rate forever and investors require a 13% return on their investment in this stock. The stock's price should be

$$
P_0 = \frac{\$5.00(1.06)}{0.13 - 0.06}
$$

$$
P_0 = \frac{\$5.30}{0.07}
$$

$$
P_0 = \$75.71
$$

Common Stock: Nonconstant Growth

The constant-growth valuation model works well for securities whose forecasted financial behavior corresponds to the model's assumption of dividends that grow

[4] Equation (6.2) is a geometric series because each term is equal to $\frac{(1 + g_N)}{(1 + r)}$ times the preceding term.

[5] Because a share of stock cannot have a negative price, Equation 6.3 works only when r is greater than g_N. For another restriction on g_N, see Question 1 at the end of the chapter.

at a constant rate. Some companies, such as electric utilities, compete in mature markets that offer few prospects for rapid growth. Demand for their product is pretty stable, varying little with economic cycles. Such firms may be good candidates for valuation using the constant-growth model.

For many corporations, however, the constant-growth assumption does not hold. Often firms have new products that have competitive advantages over their competitors' products. Patent protection, new technology, low-cost production methods, or brand name recognition may enable a firm to experience rapid growth for a period of time. In the long run, though, this rapid growth is not sustainable, because competitors' technology, manufacturing efficiency, and so on, catch up with the industry leader's, leveling the playing field in the market place. A constant-growth valuation model is clearly inappropriate for firms that experience a period of *nonconstant growth.*

Alternatives to the dividend discount technique for valuation of stock are discussed and tested in "A Comparison of Stock Price Predictions Using Court Accepted Formulas, Dividend Discount, and P/E Models," by Kent Hickman and Glenn Petry, *Financial Management* (Summer 1990): 76–87.

One method for valuing firms in a nonconstant-growth cycle is presented here. Let's assume that we are valuing a stock whose dividends are expected to grow at an 18% rate each of the next 3 years. After this *abnormal growth* period, normal growth will continue at a 5% rate. The company's last annual dividend was $2 per share. The discount rate for the stock is 16%. The following time line illustrates the growth assumptions of this example.

where

$$g_a = \text{abnormal growth rate} = 18\%$$
$$A = \text{length of abnormal growth period} = 3$$
$$g_N = \text{normal or constant growth rate} = 5\%$$

Because today's price should equal the present value of future dividends, the first step is to find the size of these dividends.

$D_0 = \$2.00$ last dividend paid

$D_1 = \$2.00(1.18) = \$2.36$ In year 1 dividends grow at 18%.

$D_2 = \$2.36(1.18) = \$2.78$ In year 2 dividends grow at 18%.

$D_3 = \$2.78(1.18) = \$3.28$ In year 3 dividends grow at 18%.

$D_4 = \$3.28(1.05) = \$3.44$ In year 4 dividends grow at 5%.

It is impossible to solve explicitly for the value of *all* future dividends, and, therefore, it is also impossible to find explicitly the present value of *all* future dividends. However, note that from point A forward, the growth rate is constant. This result means that the assumptions of the constant-growth valuation model are met from period 3 onward. We can, therefore, solve for P_3, the stock's price at time 3, using the constant-growth model. This value, P_3, incorporates the value of all the dividends from time 3 onward. P_3 includes the present value of D_4, D_5, D_6, and so on. Recognizing this gives us a strategy for solving for P_0, the current price.

$$P_0 = \frac{D_1}{(1+r)^1} + \frac{D_2}{(1+r)^2} + \frac{D_3}{(1+r)^3} + \frac{D_4}{(1+r)^4} + \frac{D_5}{(1+r)^5} + \cdots$$

But
$$P_3 = \frac{D_4}{(1+r)^1} + \frac{D_5}{(1+r)^2} + \cdots$$

so
$$P_0 = \frac{D_1}{(1+r)^1} + \frac{D_2}{(1+r)^2} + \frac{D_3}{(1+r)^3} + \frac{P_3}{(1+r)^3} \tag{6.4}$$

Note that P_3 is discounted for three periods, because it is the price as of period 3 on our time line. We already know the values of D_1, D_2, D_3, and r, so these values can be substituted into Equation (6.4)

$$P_0 = \frac{\$2.36}{1.16} + \frac{\$2.78}{(1.16)^2} + \frac{\$3.28}{(1.16)^3} + \frac{P_3}{(1.16)^3}$$

To solve for P_3, recall the constant-growth formula from the prior section:

$$P_0 = \frac{D_1}{r - g_N}$$

It solved for P_0 using D_1 because the constant-growth assumption held from time 0 onward. Now, because constant growth holds from time 3 onward, we can adjust the formula relative to time 3 and solve for P_3.

$$P_3 = \frac{D_4}{r - g_N} \tag{6.5}$$

$$P_3 = \frac{\$3.44}{0.16 - 0.05} = \frac{\$3.44}{0.11} = \$31.27$$

We now have all the values needed to solve for P_0, the current price of the stock.

$$\begin{aligned} P_0 &= \frac{\$2.36}{1.16} + \frac{\$2.78}{(1.16)^2} + \frac{\$3.28}{(1.16)^3} + \frac{\$31.27}{(1.16)^3} \\ &= \$2.03 + \$2.07 + \$2.10 + \$20.04 \\ &= \$26.24 \end{aligned}$$

This price, \$26.24, accounts for the present value of all future dividends. The present values of D_1 through D_3 are solved for explicitly. The present values of D_4, D_5, D_6, and so on, are solved for implicitly by finding the present value of P_3. P_3 is able to incorporate the values of all dividends after time 3 because dividends grow at a constant rate from time 3 onward.

This method is generalized in the following formula.

$$P_0 = \sum_{t=1}^{A} \frac{D_t}{(1+r)^t} + \frac{P_A}{(1+r)^A} \tag{6.6}$$

where

$$P_A = \frac{D_{A+1}}{r - g_N} \tag{6.7}$$

A = the number of years until constant growth begins

$D_{A+1} = D_A(1 + g_N) = D_0(1 + g_a)^A(1 + g_N)$

$D_1, D_2, \ldots, D_A$ = dividends during the nonconstant-growth period

BONDS: AN ANNUITY AND A SINGLE CASH FLOW

Bond investors receive from the corporation both a stream of coupon interest payments over the life of the bond and a payment of par value at maturity. Most bonds make coupon payments semiannually, and corporate bonds generally carry a $1,000 par value. The cash flows for a typical bond are illustrated here:

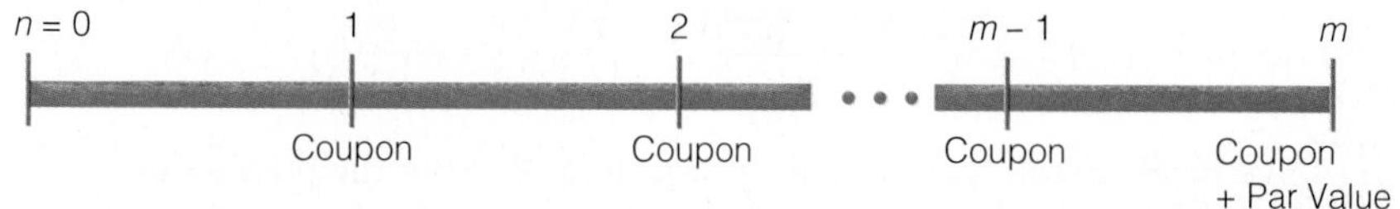

Notes are unsecured bonds whose initial maturities are less than 15 years.

In the diagram, m is the number of coupon payment periods until the bond matures. For bonds paying coupons semiannually, m is twice the number of years until maturity. Every semiannual coupon payment equals one-half the **coupon rate** times the bond's par value. The time line can be used to find the present value (the price) of a bond.

Transparency Available

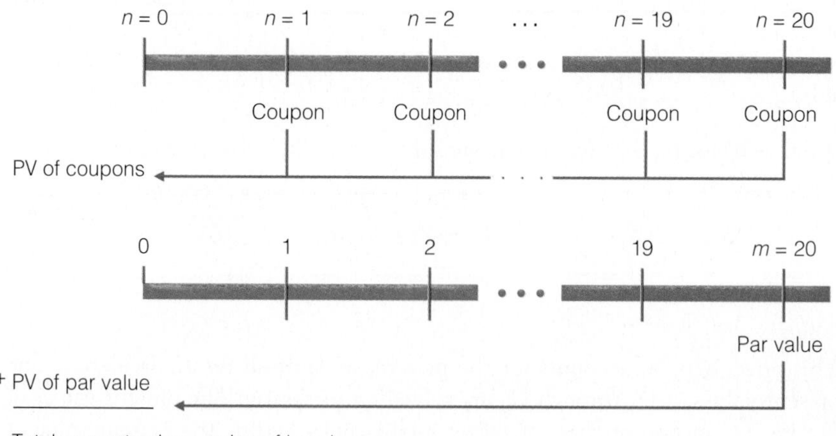

Therefore, the price of a bond is the present value of the coupon stream plus the present value of par value. The coupon stream is an annuity and the repayment of par value is a single cash flow. The formula for solving for a bond's value

is given next, keeping in mind that r is the investors' required return for the bond (the discount rate per payment period).

$$PV_0 = \frac{(\text{coup})(1 - [1/(1 + r)^m])}{r} + \frac{\text{par value}}{(1 + r)^m}$$

A bond that carries an annual coupon rate of 6.5%, makes coupon payments semiannually, has a \$1,000 par value, and matures in 10 years would have a value of \$684.58 if the investors discount its cash flows at a 12% annual rate. Note that the 6.5% annual coupon rate is equal to 3.25% semiannually, yielding the \$32.50 semiannual coupon payment. The 12% annual required return is reexpressed as 6% semiannually to agree with the semiannual payment period, and the number of periods is (10)(2) = 20.

$$PV_0 = \frac{(\$32.50)(1 - [1/(1.06)^{20}])}{0.06} + \frac{\$1,000}{(1.06)^{20}}$$

$$PV_0 = \$372.77 + \$311.80$$

$$PV_0 = \$684.57$$

Note that this bond is selling below its par value (\$684.58 < \$1,000). It is said to be **selling at a discount**. Had the bond been valued at \$1,000 so that price = par value, then the bond would be **selling at par**. A bond whose price is above par is **selling at a premium**. The reason underlying such pricing differences is the relationship between the bond's annual coupon rate and investor's required return for the bond. In our example the annual coupon rate was below the annual required return (6.5% < 12%). If investors paid full par value for the bond, it would only yield the coupon rate—below their requirements for making the investment. Bondholders could not sell this bond for \$1,000 because there would be no demand. In order to market the bond, the bond holder must lower the price until the yield to the buyer equals the required return. Note that when purchasing a bond at a discount, investors will receive not only coupon payments but also a capital gain, because they invest less than \$1,000, yet they receive the full par value when the bond matures. Buying a bond priced at a premium will lower the yield to investors because they will realize a capital loss over the life of the bond, offsetting a portion of their return from the coupon payments. A capital gain or loss becomes part of the bond's return to investors.

A bond would have an annual coupon rate of 6.5% when current interest rates are 12% per year if it was issued several years ago when 6.5% was a competitive interest rate.

Bond Prices and Interest Rates

Bonds are useful for illustrating the relationship between the time value of cash flows and interest rates. Consider a 20-year bond that carries a 10% annual coupon rate, has a \$1,000 par value, and makes coupon payments semiannually. If investors require a 10% return on the date the bond is initially sold to the public, then the bond's price will be \$1,000. It will sell at par. On the following day, let's assume that interest rates rise dramatically and investors now require a 12% annual return on the bond. Those investors who bought the bond on the previous day own a security that pays a series of fixed payments that yield 10% on their \$1,000 outlay. In order to sell the bond, they must lower the price so

FIGURE 6.1

THE INTEREST RATE–BOND PRICE TEETER-TOTTER

Rising interest rates and falling bond prices.

Interest rate risk is a problem only when a bond's coupon is fixed. Many bonds and other securities now offer adjustable rates so that their payments are always at or near the level of current interest rates. Thus, these types of bonds are always priced fairly close to par value, removing much of the interest rate risk depicted in Figure 6.1.

Note that preferred stock is a fixed-payment security with an infinite maturity. Thus, it has substantial interest rate risk, as depicted in the figure.

Transparency Available

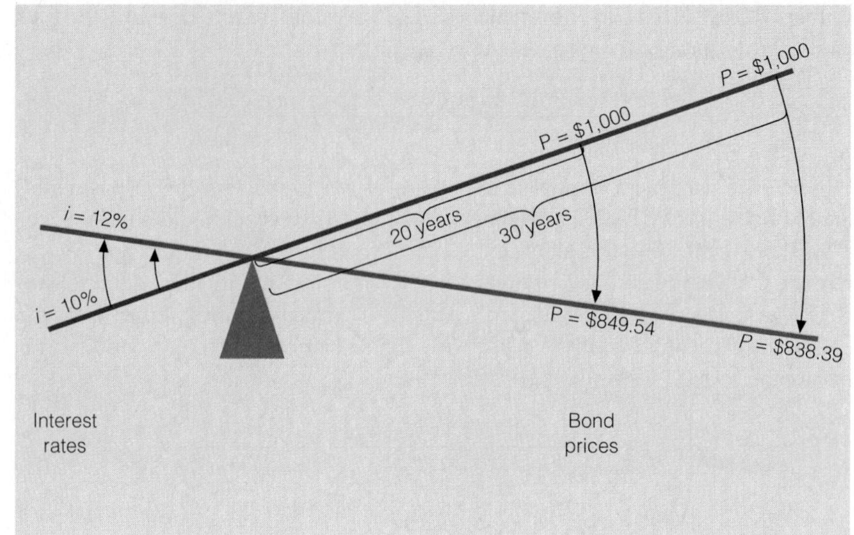

the series of payments will yield a 12% return to the purchaser. Solving for the present value of the bond, given the new 12% annual discount rate, yields a price of $849.54. If rates had dropped to 8%, for example, the bond would sell for $1,197.93. Thus, the price of a bond moves in the opposite direction from interest rates.

Now, let's consider a bond identical to the one just described, except it matures in 30 years rather than 20 years. Again, when the appropriate discount rate is 10%, the bond will sell at par, $1,000. If we solve for the price of the bond using a 12% discount rate and an 8% discount rate, the prices are, respectively, $838.39 and $1,226.23. The longer the maturity of the bond, the more sensitive it is to interest rate changes.

The lessons here are these: Bond prices move in the opposite direction as movements in interest rates, and the longer the maturity of the bond, the greater the change in its price for a given change in rates. This relationship is illustrated in Figure 6.1. Figure 6.1 shows a teeter-totter. When the interest rate side goes down, the price side goes up. The length of the right side of the teeter-totter may be thought of as the time until the bond matures. The longer the right side, the greater the movement in price for a given movement in interest rates. Therefore, the longer the maturity, the more risk there is of a large adverse price change. This risk is called the **interest rate risk**.

SOLVING FOR EXPECTED RETURNS

In the preceding section we solved for the values of preferred stock, common stock, and bonds. Many issues of these securities are actively traded in financial markets. It is often more useful for investors to solve for the returns they might *expect* to realize from an investment in such securities than to solve for their value. After all, prices are generally known in the marketplace, so investors would be more interested in **expected returns** on competing securities instead of prices.

Similarly, corporate managers can compare expected returns from prospective LHS projects when deciding how to allocate the firm's investment dollars among assets. Solving for expected returns is analogous to finding value because the same formulas are used. Instead of knowing the discount rate and solving for price, however, now we know the price and are solving for the rate of return.

Let's consider a preferred stock with a price, as quoted in the *Wall Street Journal*, of \$53.50. We note that this preferred stock pays a \$4.50 dividend annually. Recognizing that this preferred stock is a perpetuity, we substitute the known quantities into the perpetuity formula:

"It is not the return *on* my investment that I am concerned about; it is the return *of* my investment," according to humorist Will Rogers (1875–1935).

$$P_0 = \frac{D}{r}$$

$$\$53.50 = \frac{\$4.50}{r}$$

$$r = \frac{\$4.50}{\$53.50} = 0.0841$$

The return on this preferred is 8.41%. More precisely, 8.41% is the *expected* return because buyers cannot be certain that they will realize the 8.41% return (the firm could go bankrupt).

The expected return for common stock is found using Equation (6.3), if we assume the stock's dividends will grow at a constant rate.

$$P_0 = \frac{D_1}{r - g_N} \qquad \textbf{(6.3)}$$

$$(r - g_N)P_0 = D_1$$

$$r - g_N = \frac{D_1}{P_0}$$

$$r = \frac{D_1}{P_0} + g_N \qquad \textbf{(6.8)}$$

Equation (6.8) is useful for two reasons. First, it can be used to find the expected return on a share of stock. For example, if a share is selling for \$35, next year's dividend is expected to be \$3 per share, and dividends are expected to grow at a 6% rate indefinitely, then the expected return on an investment in the stock is 14.57%:

Reinforce the idea that in efficient markets, price = value and expected returns = required returns.

$$r = \frac{\$3}{\$35} + 0.06$$

$$r = 0.0857 + 0.06$$

$$r = 0.1457 = 14.57\%$$

The second use of Equation (6.8) is to illustrate the sources of the expected return. The first term to the right of the equal sign in (6.8) is the **dividend yield**, D_1/P_0. The second term, g_N, is equal to the **capital gains** rate. For our stock, investors expect an 8.57% return each year from dividends and a 6% return from price appreciation.

Let's now turn to bonds. Because of the complexity of the bond formula, expected returns from bond investments must be solved using either trial and error or a good financial calculator. To illustrate the trial-and-error method, let's solve for the expected return on a bond that sells for \$800, pays coupons semiannually, matures in 10 years, carries a 9% coupon rate, and has a \$1,000 par value.

$$\$800 = \frac{\$45(1 - [1/(1 + r)^{20}])}{r} + \frac{\$1{,}000}{(1 + r)^{20}}$$

Now we must take an educated guess as to what r might be. We do have a clue about r; the bond is selling at a discount. Recall that a bond sells at a discount when its yield is greater than the coupon rate. Therefore, we know that $r > 4.5\%$ (expressing rates on a semiannual basis to conform to the coupon payment period). Suppose our first guess for r is 5.5%:

$$\$800 \stackrel{?}{=} \frac{\$45(1 - [1/(1.055)^{20}])}{0.055} + \frac{\$1{,}000}{(1.055)^{20}}$$

$$\$800 \stackrel{?}{=} \$880$$

Because \$880 is above the actual price, we know we must raise the interest rate, lowering the value of the right side of the equation. This time let's try 6%. Using 6%, the value is \$827.95, still too high but closer. Now let's try 6.25%. This time the answer is \$803.29, close enough using trial and error. The approximate expected return when buying this bond for \$800 is 6.25% semiannually, or 12.5% per year. For a bond, the expected return is also called the bond's *yield-to-maturity* (YTM), as discussed earlier in this chapter.

We will now assume the role of a corporate manager considering an investment in a project. Suppose we are considering buying a delivery truck and estimate the truck will produce cash flows of \$3,000 a year for the next 5 years. At the end of the 5-year period, we expect to sell the truck for \$5,000. The truck costs \$13,500. What is the expected return on the truck investment? First, let's illustrate the cash flows using a time line.

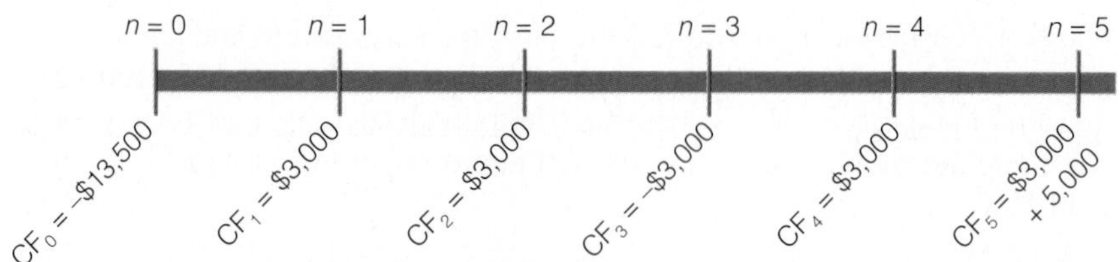

The initial cash flow (CF_0) is −\$13,500, indicating the cost of the truck. Subsequent cash flows are five annual receipts of \$3,000 each and one additional receipt of \$5,000. Cash flow 5 (CF_5) is broken down to show both the \$3,000 cash flow generated by operating the truck during the fifth year and the \$5,000 generated by the sale of the vehicle at the end of year 5. These cash flows represent a 5-year ordinary annuity of \$3,000 per year and a single cash flow of \$5,000.

Therefore, solving for the expected return from the truck investment is similar to finding the YTM on a bond. We must combine the annuity and single cash flow formulas and use trial and error to find the rate that equates the present value of the future cash flows to the truck's cost.

$$\$13{,}500 = \frac{\$3{,}000(1 - [1/(1 + r)^5])}{r} + \frac{\$5{,}000}{(1 + r)^5}$$

Arbitrarily guessing 10% as our initial estimate of r,

$$\$13{,}500 \stackrel{?}{=} \frac{\$3{,}000(1 - [1(1.10)^5])}{0.10} + \frac{\$5{,}000}{(1.10)^5}$$

$$\$13{,}500 \stackrel{?}{=} \$11{,}372 + 3{,}105$$

$$\$13{,}500 \stackrel{?}{=} \$14{,}477$$

It is apparent that 10% is too low a discount rate, because \$14,477 is greater than \$13,500. The correct answer is $r = 12.4\%$. Thus, the expected return on the investment in the truck is 12.4%. The expected return from a project in which a firm is considering investing is also known as the project's **internal rate of return (IRR)**. (Note that computing IRRs is similar to computing YTMs, but convention gives the IRR of a bond the special name, YTM.) In this case the truck's IRR is 12.4%.

If the firm can acquire capital from investors whose required return is less than the project's IRR, then the firm should make the investment. For example, assume the firm could acquire financing at an 11% rate (investors' required return on their investment). If so, the firm should proceed with the investment because its yield (12.4%) is more than the cost of funding the project (11%).

SUMMARY

Chapter 6 has applied the time value skills from Chapter 5 to the valuation of corporate securities. Pricing preferred stock was shown to be an application of the formula for valuing a perpetuity. Common stock, when dividends are expected to grow at a constant rate, was valued using a growing perpetuity formula. Bonds were priced using a combination of the present value of an annuity formula, to value the coupon payments, and the present value of a single cash flow formula, to value the repayment of par value. Variations of these pricing techniques were used to solve for the expected returns of traded securities.

The ability to express equivalent values of cash flows at different points in time is a fundamental skill in finance. As with any skill, practice increases proficiency and understanding in solving time value problems.

We have shown how to estimate cash flows (in Chapter 4) and how these cash flows can be reexpressed as equivalent sums at different times, but we have yet to discuss quantifying the final part of the valuation process: investors' required returns. Chapter 3 discussed the strong linkage between an investment's risk and the return that investors will require from that investment. Quantifying that risk is the subject of Chapter 7, and using that measure of risk to arrive at the appropriate required return is the topic of Chapter 8.

KEY TERMS

zero coupon bonds
par value
yield-to-maturity (YTM)
preferred stock
hybrid security
growing perpetuity
constant growth
coupon rate
selling at par
selling at a discount
selling at a premium
interest rate risk
expected returns
dividend yield
capital gains
internal rate of return (IRR)
current yield

KEY FORMULAS

Price of preferred stock

$$P_0 = \frac{D}{r}$$

Price of common stock, constant dividend growth formula

$$P_0 = \frac{D_0(1 + g_N)}{r - g_N} = \frac{D_1}{r - g_N}$$

Price of common stock, abnormal growth period formula

$$P_0 = \sum_{t=1}^{A} \frac{D_t}{(1 + r)^t} + \frac{P_A}{(1 + r)^A}$$

where

$$P_A = \frac{D_{A+1}}{r - g_N}$$

A = the number of years until constant growth begins.

Price of bonds

$$PV_0 = \frac{(\text{Coup})(1 - [1/(1 + r)^m]}{r} + \frac{\text{PAR VALUE}}{(1 + r)^m}$$

QUESTIONS

1. **a.** Common stock is often modeled as a growing perpetuity in which the growth rate is constant. If the overall economy is expected to grow at 6% per year over the long run, would it be reasonable to expect a firm's stock to grow at an average constant rate of 15% forever? Why or why not? (*Hint*: Imagine the economy as being a pie that gets 6% bigger each year; then imagine the firm as a piece of that pie, where the piece gets 15% bigger every year.)
   b. Can you generalize the result of part (a.) to a rule of thumb regarding the maximum value of g_N that should be used in the constant-growth model?
   c. Negative values for g_N are allowable. Under what circumstances might a firm's growth be foreseen as being negative?
   d. If the constant-growth formula is applied to a stock whose growth rate is zero ($g_N = 0$), then what will the formula resemble? Will D_1 differ from D_0 for a zero-growth stock?
2. If a zero coupon bond drops in price one day, what can you say about the investors' required return for that bond on that day?
3. In efficient markets, the price of an asset equals its value. If the New York Stock Exchange is considered an efficient market and you calculate the expected return for an NYSE stock, how do you think that expected return will compare to investors' required return for the stock?
4. What is the difference between a bond's coupon rate and its yield-to-maturity?
5. Explain the relationship between investors' return requirements and security values.
6. What part of a bond's cash flow stream is an annuity and what part is a single cash flow?
7. Explain why the perpetuity and growing perpetuity valuation formulas do, in fact, incorporate the present values of all these securities' future cash flows.
8. Complete the following table using <, =, >, par, or discount.

YTM > coupon rate	Price ? par	Bond sells at ?
YTM ? coupon rate	Price = par	Bond sells at ?
YTM ? coupon rate	Price ? par	Bond sells at a premium.

9. What is the formula for solving for a perpetuity's expected return?

DEMONSTRATION PROBLEMS

1. A bond sells for $1250, matures in 10 years, and has an annual coupon rate of 14%, payable semiannually. What is the bond's YTM?

SOLUTION

We begin with a time line and by setting up the problem.

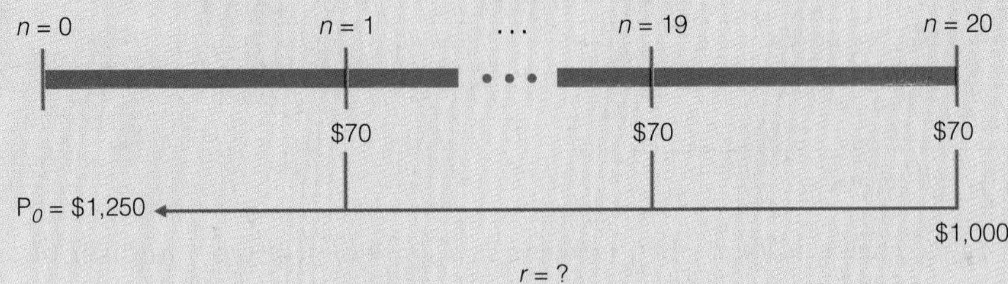

$$\text{bond price} = (\text{PV of annuity}) + (\text{PV single cash flow})$$

$$P_0 = \sum_{n=1}^{M} \frac{\text{coup}}{(1+r)^n} + \frac{\$1{,}000}{(1+r)^M}$$

$$\$1250 = \sum_{n=1}^{20} \frac{\$70}{(1+r)^n} + \frac{\$1000}{(1+r)^{20}}$$

Algebra Solution

$$\text{PV of annuity} = (70)\left[\frac{1 - [1/(1+r)^{20}]}{r}\right]$$

$$\text{PV of par value} = \frac{\$1000}{(1+r)^{20}}$$

Because the bond is selling at a premium, we know $r <$ coupon rate so $r < 7\%$ (semiannually). Try 6%.

$$\$1{,}250 \stackrel{?}{=} (\$70)\left[\frac{1 - [1/(1.06)^{20}]}{0.06}\right] + \frac{\$1{,}000}{(1.06)^{20}}$$

$$\$1{,}250 \stackrel{?}{=} (\$70)[11.470] + \frac{\$1{,}000}{3.2071}$$

$$\$1{,}250 \stackrel{?}{=} \$802.90 + \$311.81$$

$$\$1{,}250 \stackrel{?}{=} \$1{,}114.71$$

Because $1,114.71 is too low, we know the discount rate was too high. Try 5%. Using 5% the present value of the cash flows (the right-hand side of the problem) equals $1,249.24, which is close enough. Because the problem was solved using semiannual coupon payments, the 5% rate is the semiannual yield. The annual yield-to-maturity is twice that, or 10%.

Table Solution

$$\$1{,}250 = \$70(\text{PVIFA}_{\substack{n=20 \\ r=?}}) + \$1{,}000\ (\text{PVIF}_{\substack{n=20 \\ r=?}})$$

Again, trial and error is necessary. If 6% is the initial guess, then

$$\$1{,}250 \overset{?}{=} \$70(\text{PVIFA}_{\substack{n=20\\r=6\%}}) + \$1{,}000(\text{PVIF}_{\substack{n=20\\r=6\%}})$$

$$\$1{,}250 \overset{?}{=} \$70(11.470) + \$1{,}000(0.3118)$$

$$\$1{,}250 \overset{?}{=} \$802.90 + \$311.80$$

$$\$1{,}250 \overset{?}{=} \$1{,}114.70$$

So, 6% is too high. For a second guess of 5%, the two sides are equal and the problem is solved. However, since the problem is set up using semiannual payments, the 5% yield must be doubled to arrive at the annual yield-to-maturity of 10%.

Calculator Solution

Clear registers	
−1250	[PV]
70	[PMT]
1000	[FV]
20	[N]
	[I%]

The answer is given as 4.9948, but because this is based on semiannual coupon periods, the yield must be doubled to obtain an annual yield-to-maturity of 9.9896%.

2. Suppose a stock just paid a dividend of $1.75 per share. Next year the dividend is expected to grow at a 25% rate. After next year, dividends are expected to grow at a normal rate of 6.5%. If investors require a 16% return for this stock, estimate the stock's price.

SOLUTION

First, prepare a time line.

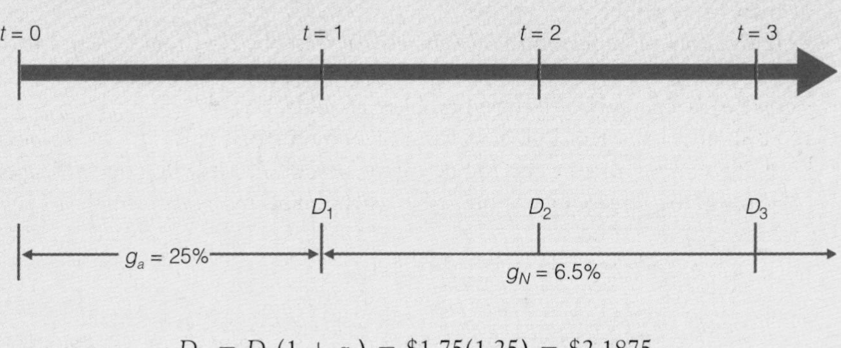

$$D_1 = D_0(1 + g_a) = \$1.75(1.25) = \$2.1875$$

$$D_2 = D_1(1 + g_N) = \$2.1875(1.065) = \$2.329$$

Because growth is normal from $t = 1$ onward, the present value of all future dividends relative to time 1 (D_2, D_3, D_4, etc.) can be found by solving for P_1 using the constant-growth formula.

$$P_1 = \frac{D_2}{r - g_n} = \frac{\$2.329}{0.16 - 0.065} = \frac{\$2.329}{0.095} = \$24.516$$

Now P_0 can be found by solving for the present values of D_1 and P_1.

$$P_0 = PV(D_1) + PV(P_1) = \frac{\$2.1875}{(1.16)^1} + \frac{\$24.516}{(1.16)^1}$$

$$P_0 = \$1.89 + \$21.13 = \$23.02$$

PROBLEMS

Pricing a Zero Coupon Bond
1. $213.80

1. A zero coupon bond has a par value of $2,000 and matures in 16 years. Investors require a 15% annual rate of return on such bonds. For what price is the bond selling?

Solving for the Return on a Zero Coupon Bond
2. 9%

2. A corporation can raise $2,112,000 in capital by issuing 5,000 zero coupon bonds, each having a $1,000 par value. The bonds will mature in 10 years (when the firm must repay $5,000,000). What rate of return are investors requiring on such bonds?

Pricing Preferred Stock
3. $85.71

3. A share of preferred stock pays a dividend of $6 annually. The next dividend payment is expected 1 year from now. Investors require a 7% return on an investment with the same risk as this issue of preferred. What is the preferred's price per share?

Solving for the Return on Preferred Stock
4. 10.17%

4. If the preferred stock described in Problem 3 sold for $59 per share, what would be your estimate of the stock's expected return?

Pricing a Constant Growth Stock
5. $21.00

5. Zeta Enterprises' common stock dividend is expected to grow at a long run rate of 5% per year. The dividend recently paid was $1.40 per share. Investors require a 12% return from Zeta's common stock. What is your estimate of its price?

Pricing a Constant Growth Stock
6. $29.96

6. If Zeta's dividends grow at 7% instead of 5% (as described in Problem 5), then what will be Zeta's price?

Pricing a Constant Growth Stock
7. $21.40

7. If investors' required return on Zeta also increases by 2% (from 12% to 14%), just as its growth rate increased from 5% to 7%, then what will be the impact on Zeta's share price? (refer to problems 6 and 7)

Solving for a Constant Growth Stock's Return
8. 12.97%

8. Assuming a share of Pole Cat Farm's common stock sells for $19, its next dividend is expected to be 75¢ per share, and dividends will grow at 9% per year for the foreseeable future, what is the expected return on Pole Cat's common?

Comprehensive Bond Problem
9. a. X: $864.10; Y: $1,000.00; Z: $802.07
b. X: discount; Y: par; Z: discount
c. X: $750.76; Y: $875.38; Z: $656.82
d. YTM = 4.73%/y

9. Consider the three bonds described here.

	BOND X	BOND Y	BOND Z
Maturity	10 years	10 years	20 years
Annual coupon rate (payable semiannually)	6%	8%	6%
Par value	$1,000	$1,000	$1,000

a. If all three bonds have a required return of 8%, then what will be each bond's price?
b. Which bonds are selling at a discount, a premium, at par?
c. If required returns on these bonds all rise to 10%, what are their new prices?
d. If Bond X were selling for $1,163, then what would be its yield to maturity?

10. To develop a newly discovered gold deposit would cost $10 million (payable immediately). It is estimated that, once developed, the mine would generate cash flows of $150,000 the first year (which are low because most of the year would be spent in developing the mine), followed by cash flows of $12 million and $5 million. These cash flows are assumed to occur at the end of each year. After the third year, the mine would be worthless. What internal rate of return (IRR) would this mine generate?

Finding the IRR
10. 27%

11. An 11-year bond pays interest of $42.50 semiannually and is selling for $862. What are its coupon rate and its yield to maturity?

Solving for YTM, Coupon Rate
11. YTM = 10.66%; coupon = 8.5%/year

12. A bond's **current yield** equals its annual coupon payment divided by the current price of the bond. What is the current yield for the bond described in Problem 11?

Finding the Current Yield
12. 9.86%

13. Acme paid a $2 per share dividend yesterday. Its dividends are expected to grow steadily at 8% per year.
a. What are Acme's dividends expected to be for each of the next 3 years?
b. If the appropriate discount rate for Acme's stock is 12%, then what is your estimate of its current price (P_0)?
c. What is your estimate of the stock's price one year from now (P_1)?
d. If you buy the stock today (and pay P_0 for it) and hold the stock 1 year, selling it for P_1, then what return do you realize?

Constant Growth Stock Value and Demonstrating the Irrelevance of Holding Period on Value
13. a. D_1 = $2.16
D_2 = $2.33
D_3 = $2.52
b. $54.00
c. $58.25
d. 12%

14. Buggy Whip Industries is a company in a declining business. Dividends are expected to decrease at a 10% rate. Last year's dividend was $3.00 per share. The required return for Buggy Whip's stock is 18%. What would you pay for a share of the stock?

Valuing a Negative Growth Stock
14. $9.64

15. If Buggy Whip's stock (described in Problem 14) sold for $13.50, then what return must investors require of the security?

Finding a Negative Growth Stock's Return
15. 10%

16. The Finance Club bought a soft-drink vending machine to place in the lobby of the business school building. The machine cost the club $2,500. The club estimates that the machine will last many decades and produce cash flow of $375 next year and that this cash flow will grow at a 6% rate for the foreseeable future (as soft-drink prices increase with inflation and student enrollments grow). What is the expected return for the club from the soft-drink vending investment (what is its IRR)?

Finding the IRR
16. 21%

17. Beachmaster Suntan Oil's dividend is expected to grow at a 20% rate each of the next 2 years. After that, dividend growth is expected to normalize at about 6.5% annually. Beachmaster just paid a $1.25 annual dividend per share. Investors require a 17% return on Beachmaster's stock.
a. What is the forecasted dividend for each of the next 2 years (D_1 and D_2)?
b. What is the forecasted dividend 3 years from now?

Valuing an Abnormal Growth Stock
17. a. D_1 = $1.50; D_2 = $1.80
b. D_3 = $1.92
c. P_2 = $18.29
d. D_1 = $1.28; D_2 = $1.32; P_2 = $13.36
e. P_0 = $15.96

c. At what price do you foresee Beachmaster's stock selling for 2 years from now (what's your forecasted P_2)?

d. What is the present value of D_1, D_2, and P_2?

e. What's your estimate of today's price?

Valuing an Abnormal Growth Stock
18. $19.34

18. Suppose you revise your estimates for Beachmaster (from Problem 17) and you now expect the 20% dividend growth to last 4 years. If all other assumptions remain the same (g_N = 6.5% and r = 17%), then what is your new estimate of Beachmaster's current stock price?

Valuing a Stock that Currently Pays no Dividend
19. $93.44

19. Delta Computer Graphics, Inc., currently pays no dividend. Its profitability has been phenomenal, however, and investors expect that once a dividend is initiated, it will be large. Investors believe that Delta's first dividend will be $8 per share and will begin being paid 4 years from now. Furthermore, they expect these dividends to grow at an 8.5% annual rate once the firm begins the payments. If investors require a 14% annual return on Delta's stock, what's the current price per share?

Valuing a Stock that Currently Pays no Dividend
20. $71.90

20. If investors revise their expectations for Delta's stock (see Problem 19) and now expect dividends will not begin for 6 years, what will be the revised current price, assuming all other assumptions are unchanged?

Finding Returns for a Firm's Bonds and Stock, Foreshadowing the Weighted Average Cost of Capital
21. YTM = 13%; r = 15%

21. Down the Drain Plumbing Equipment has raised capital by issuing bonds and stock. The bonds have 22 years left until they mature. They pay coupons semiannually at an 8.5% annual coupon rate. These $1,000 par value bonds are currently selling for $675.52. Down the Drain's stock paid a dividend of $2.75 a share last year. Its dividends are supposed to grow at a 14% annual rate for the next 2 years, followed by normal growth of 5% annually. The stock's current market price is $33.78 per share. What is the expected return (YTM) for Down the Drain's bonds and the expected return for Down the Drain's stock?

Valuing an Abnormal Growth Stock
22. $14.56

22. An analyst has made the following explicit estimates of Hee Haw Bridle Company's future dividends.

t	1	2	3	4	5
Div	$1.25	$1.37	$1.40	$1.45	$1.50

After 5 years, Hee Haw is expected to quit growing and pay a constant dividend of $1.50 forever. If investors require a 10% return from a stock with Hee Haw's risk, then what should be the stock's price?

Zero Coupon Bond Pricing, Realized Return
23. a. $182.70
b. $204.62
c. 12%

23. A zero coupon bond matures in 15 years and has a $1,000 par value. The bond's yield to maturity is 12%.

a. What is the bond's current price?

b. What do you expect will be the bond's price 1 year from now?

c. If all happens just as you expect it will, then what return would an investor earn who buys the bond today and sells it in 1 year?

Pricing a Constant Growth Stock, Capital Gains, Dividend Yield
24. a. $18.18
b. $19.45
c. 18%
d. Yield = 11%; gain = 7%

24. A stock is expected to pay a $2 per share dividend next year. Dividends are expected to grow at a steady rate of 7% annually. Investors require an 18% return for investments with the stock's risk.

a. What should be the stock's current price?

b. At what price should the stock sell next year if conditions and forecasts do not change?

c. What would be your total return if you buy the stock today and sell it in 1 year?

d. What would be your return from price appreciation and your dividend yield?

25. In Problem 23, what will the bond's price be in 1 year if, at that time, investors require a 15% yield to maturity for the bond? In this case, what would the investor in part (c) of the problem earn?

Zero Coupon Price Falls as Rates Rise

25. a. $182.70
b. $141.33
c. −22.64%

CHAPTER 7

Risk and Return in the Capital Markets

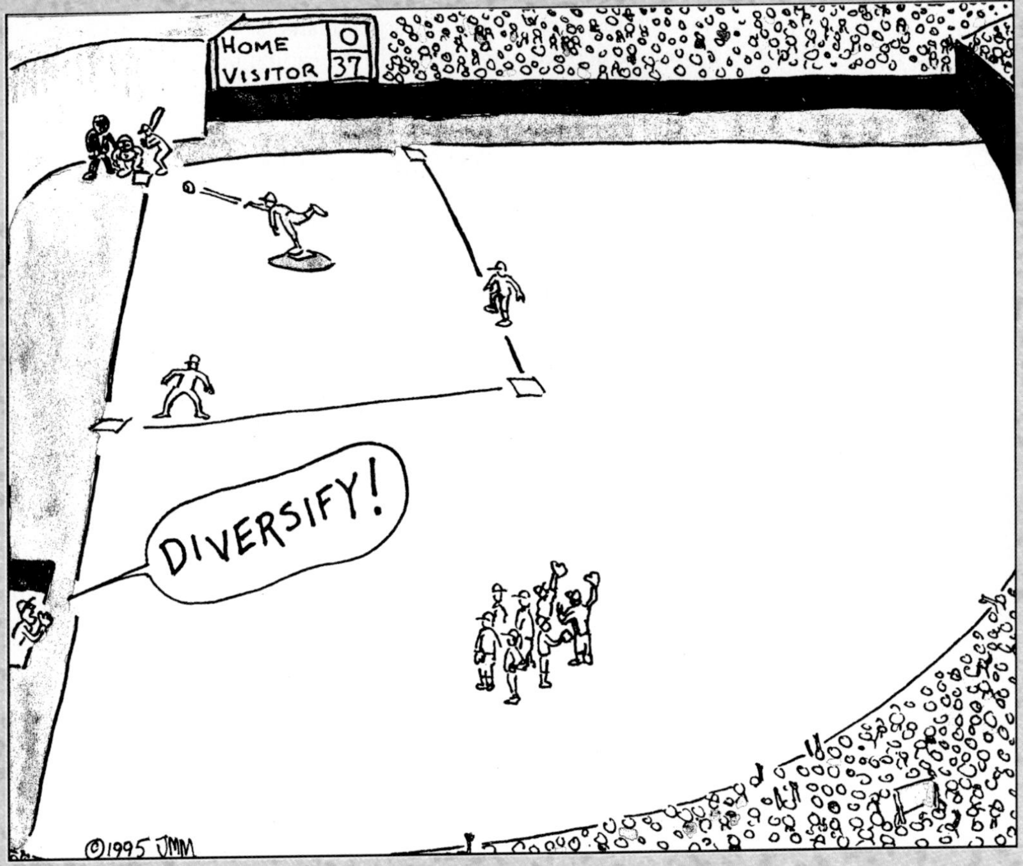

Diversification is not only good advice for baseball players, it is also good advice for investors. In baseball, diversification in the field reduces the risk of allowing a base hit. Chapter 7 demonstrates how diversifying one's investments lowers the risk of losses.

Draw a financial balance sheet, or use the transparency from Chapter 1.

et's look back at what we've covered so far. First, we modeled the corporation as an enterprise that raises funds in the capital markets to finance promising investment projects. These projects produce goods and services to be sold in product markets. The trick for the corporation is to identify promising product market opportunities and then fund those projects that will add value to the corporation.

The principle of valuing assets, whether they be trucks, machines or securities, was introduced in Chapter 3. Value is calculated by discounting expected future cash flows. The discount rate is the investor's risk-adjusted required return.

$$V_0 = \sum_{t=1}^{N} \frac{CF_t}{(1 + R(r))^t} \tag{7.1}$$

Equation (7.1) instructs us to discount each period's cash flows (CF_t) by the required return $R(r)$. Estimating cash flows was covered in Chapter 4. The mathematics of discounting these cash flows were covered in Chapter 5. To this point we have simply provided discount rates, without too much discussion on how they are derived. However, discount rates are important determinants of asset value. In this chapter and the next, we show that most discount rates originate as required rates of return in the capital markets. Therefore, to understand how these rates are derived, we must study the capital markets.

RISK AND RETURN

What We Can Learn from the Capital Markets

We begin our study of capital markets by reviewing two basic ideas introduced in earlier chapters. The first is that risk averse investors expect to receive greater returns as compensation for taking on greater risk. This idea was first introduced in Chapter 3. Evidence of this risk-return relationship is pervasive in the capital markets. For example, investors expect greater returns from common stocks than government bonds. The history of capital markets confirms this expectation. Since 1926, large-company common stocks have produced an average return of more than 10%, whereas long-term government bonds have returned an average of 5%. However, the standard deviation of stock returns is nearly 21%, but that for the bonds is less than 9%, indicating that stocks are considerably more risky.[1]

Review the distinction between expected and required returns.

The second basic idea is that capital markets are generally competitive. In Chapter 3, we saw how investors in a competitive market raise or lower the prices of securities to maintain a basic parity between risk and return. In competitive markets, expected returns are not much different than required returns. If expected returns were much greater, there would be a flood of new investment, driving down returns. If expected returns were much less, disinvestment would raise the expected returns of those who remained in the market by driving down prices.

In corporate finance, we are interested in how investors establish required returns on corporate securities in the capital markets. These investors are cor-

[1]Ibbotson Associates, *Stocks, Bonds, Bills and Inflation*, 1994 Yearbook, p. 31.

porate bondholders and stockholders and, as such, have claims against corporate cash flows and assets. Required returns indicate how investors collectively value the corporation. Recall that, for any investment, required return and the value of the investment are inversely related. This implies that if investors require a greater return on a corporation's securities, perhaps because of increased risk, the value of the corporation is reduced, all else being equal.

Capital markets are an excellent laboratory for studying risk and return. Data on returns for thousands of securities are available. Although the capital markets encompass many types of securities, most attention is focused on the stock market because it is particularly large and active. The stock market is also where corporate ownership claims are traded. Most of this and the next chapter is devoted to discussing risk and return in the stock market. However, the lessons may be applied to all securities and securities markets. We begin with portfolios of securities.

Portfolios

Diversification is intuitive. The assets of most individuals are diversified.

A **portfolio** is a group of securities held by an investor. It may consist of a few securities held by an individual or hundreds held by an institution such as a pension fund or mutual fund. It is rare for an investor to own one or even just a few securities. Most of them understand instinctively that events may overtake any company, threatening the values of its bonds and stocks. Events such as a strike, a natural disaster, a major lawsuit, or the death of a key employee are unpredictable. Even the largest companies are not immune. The death in 1994 of the chief operating officer of Walt Disney left a serious management void at the company. The oil spill from the *Exxon Valdez* in the Gulf of Alaska and the explosion of Union Carbide's chemical plant in India are dramatic examples of events affecting individual companies. Aside from catastrophic events, individual companies may be threatened by shifting technologies and markets. For example, cable TV has reduced the market share of the major networks, and satellite transmission in turn threatens the cable companies. Multinational corporations continually face political risks, ranging from seizure of property to insurrection, in foreign countries. The only way to mitigate the effects of such events is to own securities of a number of companies, preferably in different industries.

Risk that affects primarily one company or industry is called **unique risk**. Unique risk can be mitigated by diversifying your securities portfolio. A diversified portfolio is one that contains securities of enough different companies so that if ill fortune strikes one or a few companies, it will more than likely be offset by the good fortunes of others.

However, there are other risks, which affect many companies in common, that may not be mitigated by diversification. The stock returns of most companies are affected by economic and social events in their countries. For example, few companies would be unaffected by recession, monetary crises, and political turmoil. On the other hand, most would benefit from sustained economic growth and political stability. This common risk is called **market risk**, referring to the stock market. Changes in stock market indices are considered an important benchmark of general economic health.

Although most companies are affected by market risk, not all are affected equally. For instance, rising interest rates are especially harmful to banks and utilities because they are heavy borrowers. Interestingly, the depression of the 1930s, which caused a virtual economic collapse, was a relatively good period for Hollywood because people went to the movies to forget their own troubles.[2]

The distinction between market risk and unique risk is important to investors. Unique risk may be mitigated by holding a diversified portfolio. However, market risk is not so easily dismissed because most companies are affected by general economic and social conditions.[3]

Because common stocks are riskier than bonds, stock investors, in particular, are inclined to maintain diversified portfolios. In fact, most stocks are held by mutual funds and pension funds that are well diversified. For individual portfolios, as well as for mutual and pension funds, overall portfolio performance is more important than performance of the individual stocks. For example, mutual fund investors do not track the performance of each individual stock in the fund. Although individual investors do track each of their stocks, they judge each stock based on its contribution to the risk and return of their overall portfolios. Picking one winning stock is little solace to the investor whose portfolio is losing value or is excessively risky.

Portfolio return and risk are usually gauged relative to those of an *index portfolio.* This index portfolio consists of stocks that are representative of the overall stock market. The best known of these is the **Dow Jones Industrial Average (DJIA)**, which is quoted regularly by the news media. For many, the Dow has become synonymous with the stock market itself.

A Stock Market Index and Sample Stock Portfolio

Explain what stock indices measure and how the DJIA and S&P 500 differ.

We can illustrate how diversification actually reduces portfolio risk by randomly selecting 20 stocks for a hypothetical portfolio and then comparing the risk of the portfolio to the risk of the individual stocks. The 20 stocks are drawn from among 500 stocks in the **Standard & Poor's 500 (S&P 500)** index.[4] Although the S&P 500 is not as widely known as the DJIA, it is considered more representative of the U.S. market because it contains 500 stocks representing all industry segments, as opposed to the DJIA, which contains only 30 industrial stocks.[5] The stocks are listed below, along with a brief description of the company products. In some cases, we shortened the names to those in boldface.

***Black** & Decker* Manufacturer of power tools and home products
Boeing Producer of jet airplanes and missiles
***Brown** & Sharpe Manufacturing* Producer of measuring instruments and machine tools
***Capital** Holding* Insurance holding company
***Cincinnati** Milacron* Manufacturer of machine tools and plastics
Citicorp New York commercial bank
Enron Natural gas pipeline system

---

[2]Actually, many movie studios went out of business, but others, such as MGM prospered.

[3]Unique risk is also called nonsystematic risk, and market risk is called systematic risk.

[4]Each of the 500 stocks was assigned a number, and random numbers corresponding to the stocks were generated by a computer.

[5]For a comparison of the Dow and the S&P 500, see "What To Do About the Dow," *Business Week* (Feb. 22, 1993): 82–83.

***Fleet** Financial Group* New England commercial bank
***Fleming** Companies* Food wholesaler
***Gannett** Co.* Newspapers, television, radio
***Golden** West Financial* Western states savings and loan
***Melville** Corp.* Footwear and apparel manufacturer
Pennzoil Integrated oil and mining
Polaroid Photographic equipment and film
***Quaker** Oats* Manufacturer of packaged foods and toys
***Stone** Container* Paperboard and packaging
Tandy Consumer electronics retailer
***Union** Camp* Paper, packaging, and chemicals
***United** Technologies* Aerospace
***Warner**-Lambert* Drugs, toiletries and food

Although some of the names may not be familiar, these companies are among the largest in the United States. It is important to note that this random selection of stocks has produced a portfolio of remarkable diversity. The portfolio consists of a food processor (Quaker), five diverse manufacturers of consumer goods (Black, Melville, Pennzoil, Polaroid, Warner), a retailer (Tandy), three banks (Citicorp, Fleet, Golden), an insurance company (Capital), six diverse manufacturers of industrial goods (Boeing, Brown, Cincinnati, Stone, Union, United), a publisher (Gannett), a food wholesaler (Fleming), and a gas pipeline company (Enron).

PORTFOLIO RISK AND RETURN

Rates of Return and Standard Deviation

Figure 7.1 plots annual returns for a portfolio containing equal dollar amounts of each of the 20 stocks against returns on the S&P 500. Notice that the portfolio returns closely track those of the S&P 500.

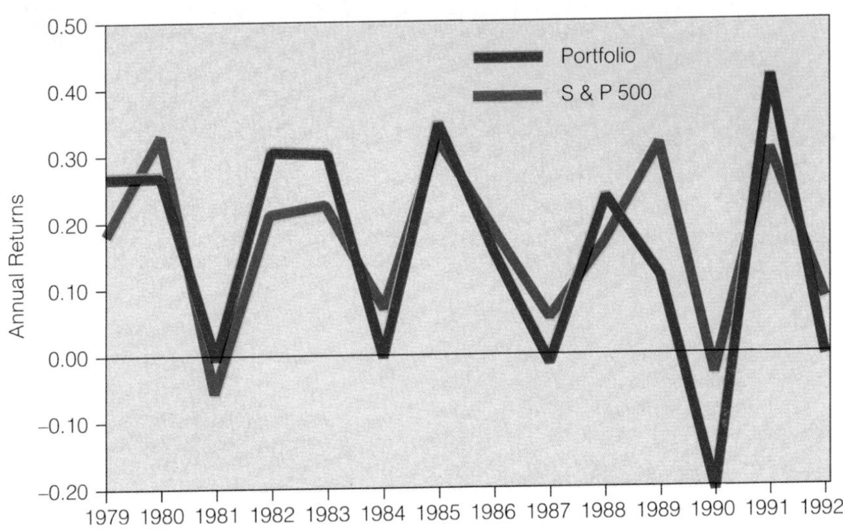

FIGURE 7.1
PORTFOLIO RETURNS

Transparency Available

Figure 7.1 shows how closely returns of the 20 stock portfolio track those of the S&P 500.

The change in shareholder wealth for a given year is the change in stock price plus any dividend paid. To find the rate of return divide this wealth change by the beginning price. The return is calculated using Equation (7.2), where r = the annual rate of return, P_1 = the ending price, P_0 = the beginning price, and D_1 = the annual dividend.

$$r = \frac{P_1 - P_0 + D_1}{P_0} \tag{7.2}$$

Standard deviation and variance (the square of standard deviation) are basic measures of risk. Standard deviation measures the variance of observations from the mean. To calculate the standard deviation (SD) of returns on a stock over a period of N years, we used the following formula, where N = number of observations, r_t = observed r, and $\bar{r}_t$ = mean r.

$$\text{SD} = \sqrt{\frac{\sum_{t=1}^{N} (r_t - \bar{r}_t)^2}{N}} \tag{7.3}$$

Encourage students to use calculators or computers to calculate standard deviation.

Exhibit 7.1 shows the average returns and standard deviations for each of the 20 stocks, and for the portfolio containing equal dollar amounts of each stock. Notice in Exhibit 7.1 that portfolio return is an average of the returns of the individual stocks. By contrast, the standard deviation of returns on the portfolio is much less than the average standard deviation of the stocks. In fact, portfolio standard deviation is lower than that for any single stock. What you see is not

EXHIBIT 7.1

SAMPLE STOCK PORTFOLIO 14-YEAR (1979–1992) RETURNS

	AVERAGE ANNUAL RETURN (%)	STANDARD DEVIATION (%)
Sample Portfolio	12.4	13.4
Union Camp	11.4	17.3
Quaker Oats	21.9	18.5
Gannet Co.	14.7	22.1
Warner-Lambert	13.3	23.0
United Technologies	7.2	23.9
Fleming Companies	13.2	25.7
Capital Holding	17.7	27.2
Enron	16.6	28.7
Pennzoil	10.2	28.7
Citicorp	8.9	30.1
Boeing	13.5	31.0
Black & Decker	3.1	33.5
Cincinnati Milacron	5.8	33.8
Polaroid	3.7	35.1
Melville Corp.	15.7	36.2
Fleet Financial Group	20.6	37.7
Brown & Sharpe Mfg.	0	43.1
Golden West Financial	19.9	43.5
Stone Container	19.2	53.2
Tandy	12.2	60.9

an aberration, but a manifestation of the **portfolio effect**.[6] Simply stated, the portfolio effect is the reduction in risk (standard deviation) that occurs through the blending of stocks into a portfolio. This risk reduction is possible because the portfolio consists of a wide variety of stocks representing many different industries. To learn more about how portfolio risk reduction actually occurs, we must become familiar with the concepts of correlation and covariance.

Correlation and Covariance

An example of negative correlation: "Official dignity tends to increase in inverse ratio to the importance of the country in which the office is held," Aldous Huxley.

Correlation is a familiar concept to anyone who has studied statistics.[7] **Correlation** indicates whether two variables are related and measures the direction and strength of that relationship. Correlation values range from −1 to +1, with a value of 0 indicating no relationship. A +1 correlation indicates that both variables always move in the same direction in constant proportion. For example, we may know that the returns on a particular stock price rise and fall in concordance with returns on the S&P 500 index. If this relationship is consistent, then the correlation of their returns equals +1. A −1 correlation indicates a consistently negative relationship, one in which stock returns always move in the opposite direction from those of the S&P 500. In reality, no relationships in the financial markets are so consistent, meaning that there are no correlations of exactly +1 or −1. This fact is important to remember when we later explain the portfolio effect.

To illustrate correlation among stock returns, we show, in Figure 7.2, the returns of two highly correlated stocks, Fleet Financial and Citicorp. In Figure 7.3, we show the returns for two relatively uncorrelated stocks, Warner-Lambert and Enron. Notice how the returns in Figure 7.2 tend to rise and fall together from one period to the next, whereas those in Figure 7.3 do not.

Covariance measures both degree and magnitude of comovement of two vari-

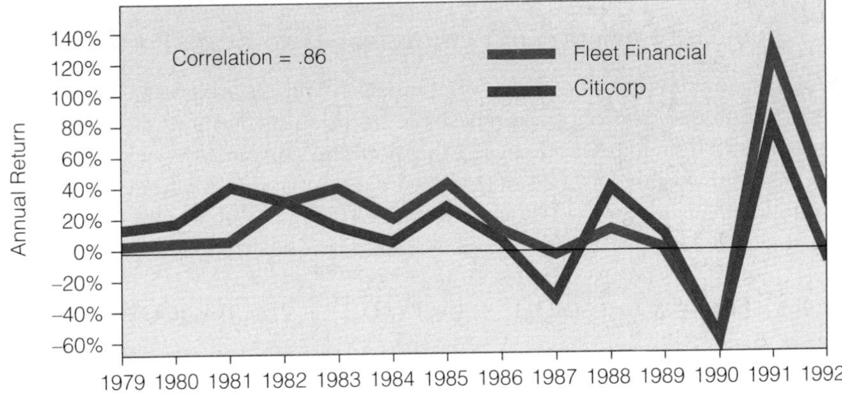

FIGURE 7.2
RETURNS ON TWO HIGHLY CORRELATED STOCKS

Transparency Available

[6]Do not read too much into the returns calculated for these 20 stocks. We have only 14 years of data, and, of course, a calendar year is an arbitrary time period.

[7]Most statistics texts cover the calculation of correlation. Most business calculators and virtually all computer spreadsheets include an algorithm for calculating the correlation coefficient.

FIGURE 7.3

RETURNS ON TWO POORLY CORRELATED STOCKS

Transparency Available

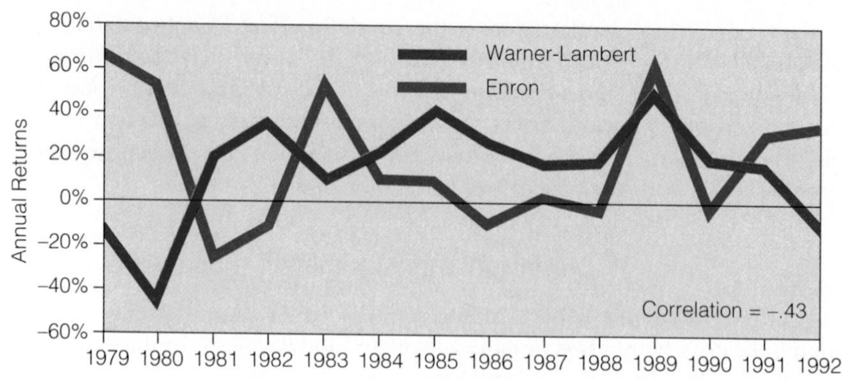

ables, as opposed to correlation, which measures only the degree of comovement. Covariance is the product of the correlation between two variables and their standard deviations.[8] For example, to find the covariance between the returns of Union Camp stock and returns on the S&P 500 index, we start with correlation. The correlation ($CORR_{UC,SP}$) between Union Camp and the S&P is 0.588. This means that the returns tend to rise and fall together (positive correlation), but that this relationship is imperfect (correlation < 1). The standard deviation of Union Camp (SD_{UC}) is 0.173 and the standard deviation for the S&P (SD_{SP}) is 0.124. Multiplying these values produces the covariance, which for Union Camp and the S&P 500 is 0.013.

$$COV_{(UC,SP)} = SD_{UC}SD_{SP}CORR_{(UC,SP)} \tag{7.4}$$

$$COV_{(UC,SP)} = (0.588)(0.173)(0.124) = 0.013$$

RETURN AND RISK OF TWO-STOCK PORTFOLIOS

Standard Deviation of Returns for a Two-Stock Portfolio

We may now use our knowledge of correlation and covariance to further our understanding of portfolio risk. The basic intuition of the portfolio effect and the evidence from Exhibit 7.1 suggest that portfolio standard deviation is actually less than the weighted average of stock standard deviations. Mathematically, the portfolio effect is expressed by covariance. With this in mind, the formula for the standard deviation of a two-stock portfolio is

$$SD_P = \sqrt{(w_B)^2(SD_B)^2 + (w_S)^2(SD_S)^2 + 2(w_B)(w_S)COV_{BS}} \tag{7.5}$$

The weights, w_B and w_S, are the proportions of each stock in the portfolio. SD_B and SD_S are the stocks' standard deviations [Equation (7.3)], and COV_{BS} is covariance [Equation (7.4)]. This is a formidable looking formula; however, it is easily solved using a computer spreadsheet. Yet another way of simplifying the

[8]An alternative method of calculating covariance that does not rely on correlation and standard deviation is presented in Appendix 7A.

calculation is through the use of matrices. The matrix solution is shown in Appendix 7B.

The portfolio effect is illustrated quite well with a portfolio consisting of equal amounts of two stocks, Black & Decker and Stone Container, selected at random from the 20 stocks in Exhibit 7.1. Calculating portfolio standard deviation requires the following information:

Appendix B shows an alternative method, using matrices, for solving for portfolio standard deviation.

$$\begin{aligned} SD_B &= 0.335 \\ SD_S &= 0.532 \\ CORR_{BS} &= 0.832 \\ w_B &= 0.5 \\ w_S &= 0.5 \end{aligned}$$

Covariance is

$$COV_{BS} = (SD_B)(SD_S)(CORR_{BS}) = (0.335)(0.532)(0.832) = 0.148$$

Now, we can solve using Equation (7.5):

$$\begin{aligned} \mathbf{SD_P} &= \sqrt{(w_B)^2(SD_B)^2 + (w_S)^2(SD_S)^2 + 2(w_B)(w_S)COV_{BS}} \qquad (7.5) \\ &= \sqrt{(0.5)^2(0.335)^2 + (0.5)^2(0.532)^2 + 2(0.5)(0.5)(0.148)} \\ &= 0.416 \end{aligned}$$

If we ignored covariance, we could calculate portfolio standard deviation as the weighted average of the standard deviations of the two stocks.

$$\begin{aligned} \text{weighted average SD} &= (w_B)(SD_B) + (w_S)(SD_S) \\ &= 0.5(0.335) + 0.5(0.532) = 0.434 \end{aligned}$$

The weighted average of 0.434 is greater than portfolio standard deviation of 0.416 because weighted average omits a vital piece of information, namely, the covariance between the two stocks. Covariance is vital because it includes correlation. To illustrate the effect of correlation on portfolio standard deviation, assume for a moment that the correlation between the two stocks is 1. In this case, portfolio standard deviation, using Equation (7.5), equals the weighted average.

$$\begin{aligned} COV_{BS} &= (SD_B)(SD_S)(CORR_{BS}) = (0.335)(0.532)(1) = 0.178 \\ SD_P &= \sqrt{(0.5)^2(0.335)^2 + (0.5)^2 + (0.532)^2 + 2(0.5)(0.5)(0.178)} \\ &= 0.434 \end{aligned}$$

When the correlation is 1, portfolio standard deviation equals the weighted average of the stock standard deviations. Similarly, when the correlation is less than 1, the two are not equal.

Notice that the standard deviation of our two-stock portfolio is not very much lower than 0.434 because these two stocks actually have a fairly high correlation of 0.832. Suppose that their correlation were 0. Then

$$\begin{aligned} COV_{BS} &= (0.335)(0.532)(0) = 0 \\ SD_P &= 0.314 \qquad \text{[using Equation (7.5)]} \end{aligned}$$

As you can see, reducing the correlation between returns reduces portfolio standard deviation. Aside from actually measuring correlations of returns, we can rely on common sense to choose stocks for our portfolio. For instance, if we were going to buy just two stocks, we probably would not choose General Motors and Ford because they are in the same industry, and their returns are probably highly correlated. For example, competition from Japanese auto producers affects both companies, as do the demand for automobiles, interest rates, and the price of steel.[9] On the other hand, we should find that returns on General Motors and Microsoft are less correlated because autos and software are less related. Of course, to really lower our correlation, we might consider picking Microsoft and a shoe manufacturer in Malaysia.

Rate of Return for a Two-Stock Portfolio

Despite the emphasis on portfolio risk we cannot forget the importance of expected return. Reducing risk in a portfolio is of little benefit if, at the same time, its expected return is also reduced. The return on this and any portfolio is the weighted average of the returns of the securities (r_B,r_S). The weights (w_B and w_S) are the proportions of total funds invested in each stock. In this case, the weight for each stock is 0.5. The weighted average return on the portfolio consisting of half Black & Decker and half Stone Container is

$$\begin{aligned} r_P &= (w_B)(r_B) + (w_S)(r_S) \qquad (7.6) \\ &= (0.5)(0.031) + (0.5)(0.192) = 0.111 \end{aligned}$$

The Effect of Correlation on Risk for Two-Stock Portfolios

We have already seen that combining Black & Decker and Stone Container stocks into a portfolio results in some risk reduction. This risk reduction is the closest thing to a "free lunch" in economics because you are not asked to give up any return. Portfolio return is the weighted average of individual stock returns, whereas portfolio standard deviation is less than the weighted average of individual stock standard deviations. Because correlations between stocks are always less than 1, this free lunch is always on the menu. Thus, an investor may choose her favorite stocks for her portfolio, as long as these stocks are spread across several industries.

Figure 7.4(a)–(c) shows risk and return plots of portfolios consisting of combinations of two hypothetical stocks. Stock L is the low risk-return stock, with a standard deviation of 0.05 and a return of 0.065, and anchors the lines on the lower end. Stock H has a standard deviation of 0.10 and a return of 0.11 and anchors the upper end. Points along the lines represent different proportions of stocks L and H. In Figure 7.4(a) the midpoint is a portfolio composed of equal proportions of stocks L and H, and portfolios above the midpoint contain more of stock H.

---

[9]The fortunes of competitors in the same industry don't always rise and fall together. In recent years, Ford has successfully taken market share from General Motors. However, General Motors is more diversified and has greater financial strength than Ford, making General Motors more resistant to recessions.

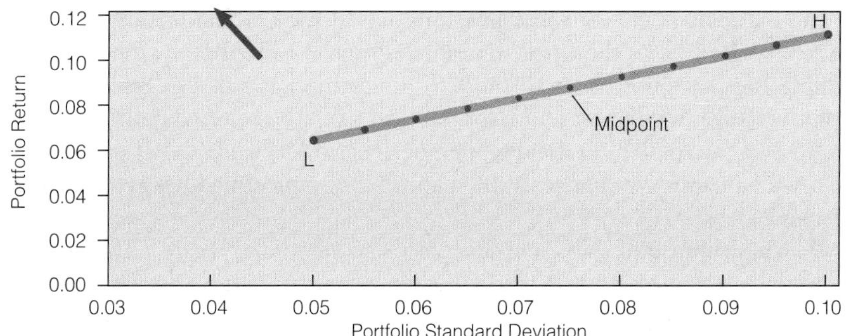

FIGURE 7.4(A)

RISK AND RETURN FOR A TWO-STOCK PORTFOLIO; CORRELATION = 1

Transparency Available

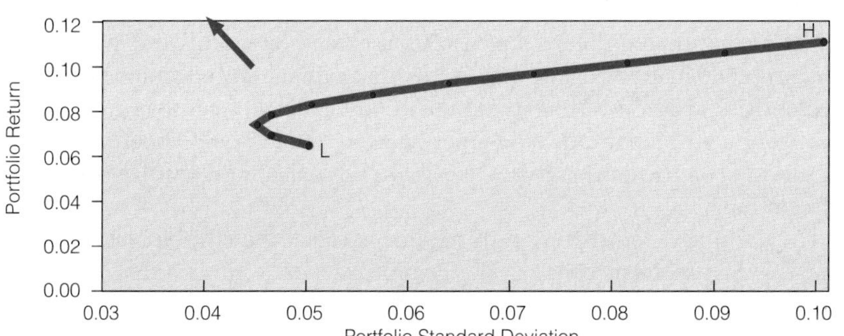

FIGURE 7.4(B)

RISK AND RETURN FOR A TWO-STOCK PORTFOLIO; CORRELATION = 0

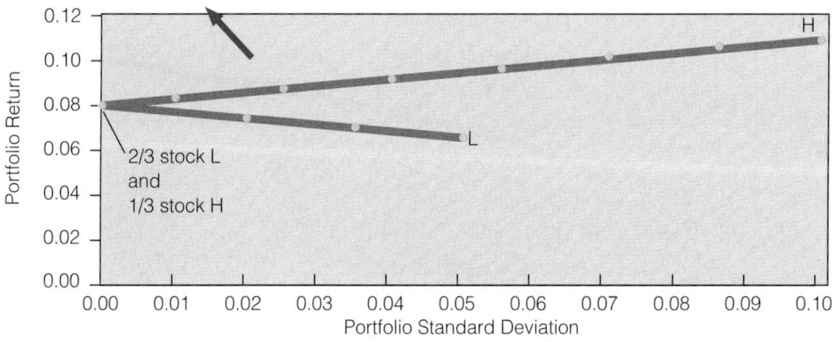

FIGURE 7.4(C)

RISK AND RETURN FOR A TWO-STOCK PORTFOLIO; CORRELATION = −1

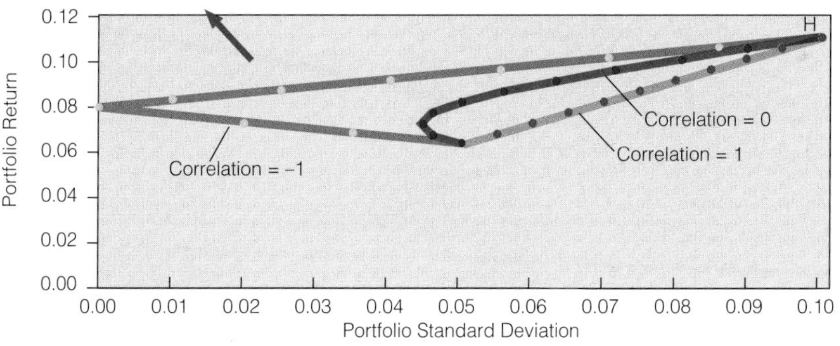

FIGURE 7.4(D)

RISK AND RETURN FOR A TWO-STOCK PORTFOLIO

Investors desire portfolios that appear closest to the upper-left corner of the graph (low risk–high return).

The different shapes of these lines are due to the correlations between the stocks. Notice that as the correlation moves from +1 toward −1, the line connecting the portfolios bends to the left, indicating less risk. Because investors wish to receive the highest return for the least risk, the preferred position on the graphs is at the top left, in the direction of the arrows. Figure 7.4(d) shows more clearly the progressive change in the shape of the connecting lines as correlation changes.

We can demonstrate this same effect using actual stocks. Figure 7.5(a) and (b) shows the same plots for two pairs of stocks taken from the 20-stock portfolio. The two stocks in Figure 7.5(a) are highly correlated. The two in Figure 7.5(b) are not. You can see how the shape of the curve in Figure 7.5(b) gives investors more desirable choices. In Figure 7.5(b) we have marked the portfolio with the lowest standard deviation LR for least risk.

Notice that the portion of the curve that extends below LR in Figure 7.5(b) contains combinations of the two stocks that provide lower return as risk increases. Risk averse investors would not choose portfolios consisting of, in this case, very high proportions of Warner-Lambert. They would choose portfolios that lie only on the portion of the line above LR, reflecting a positive risk-return relationship.

The positively sloped portion of the line is called the **efficient set**, meaning that this line segment contains the complete set of portfolios that a rational

FIGURE 7.5(A)

PORTFOLIO RISK AND RETURN—FLEET FINANCIAL AND CITICORP

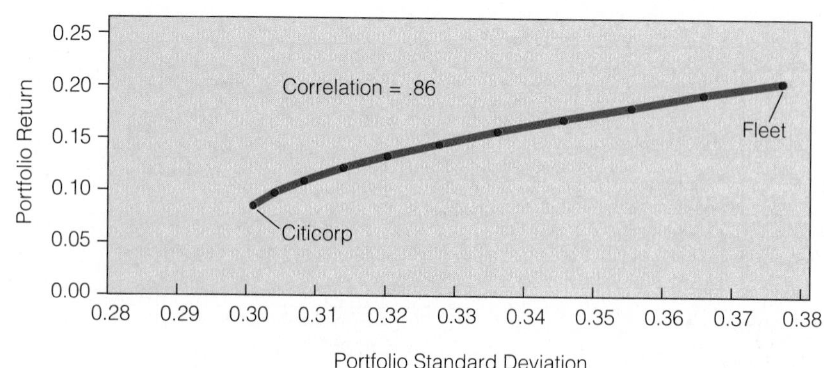

Transparency available

FIGURE 7.5(B)

PORTFOLIO RISK AND RETURN—FLEET FINANCIAL AND WARNER-LAMBERT

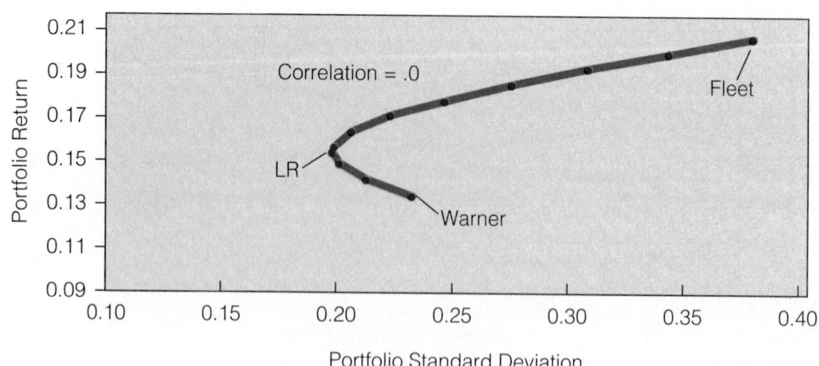

Transparency available

investor would consider. From this efficient set, the investor chooses the portfolio that best matches his risk-return preference.

PORTFOLIOS OF THREE OR MORE STOCKS

Risk and Return of Portfolios of Three or More Stocks

Few investors have just two stocks in their portfolios. Most understand that if two stocks are better than one, then three must be better than two, and so on. This is true, up to a point. Large institutional investors, such as mutual funds, may hold hundreds of stocks, but this is more a result of having a lot of money to invest than a conviction that adding the 200th stock is going to materially lower portfolio risk. We will return to this point. Another factor limiting the number of stocks in a portfolio is the cost of buying, tracking, and selling large numbers of stocks.[10]

As the number of stocks in the portfolio increases, calculating portfolio standard deviation becomes more complex. The complexity increases because we must calculate the correlation and then the covariance for each pair of stocks. For example, adding a third stock requires us to calculate 3 covariances, as opposed to the single covariance for a two-stock portfolio.[11] A fourth stock raises the number of covariance calculations to 6, a hundred stocks raises it to 4950 calculations, and 1000 stocks raises it to 499,500 covariance calculations.

There are many thousands of stocks traded in the United States and many more thousands traded worldwide.[12] Although a single investor will hold a small fraction of those available stocks, she would ideally want to consider the entire population in building her portfolio and pick the best combination, or portfolio, of stocks. This would be quite a task, requiring about 35 million covariance calculations for U.S. stocks alone.

The standard deviation calculation of even a three-stock portfolio is best done on a computer or by using a matrix, as illustrated in Appendix 7B. In Appendix 7B we illustrate the matrix calculation of the standard deviation of a portfolio consisting of equal proportions of Cincinnati Milacron, Black & Decker, and Stone Container.

In contrast to standard deviation, the return for a three-stock portfolio is the weighted average of individual stock returns. For a three-stock portfolio the calculation is

$$r_P = (w_A)(r_A) + (w_B)(r_B) + (w_C)(r_C) \tag{7.7}$$

Adding Stocks to a Portfolio to Reduce Risk

Calculating standard deviation and return for portfolios containing different numbers of stocks reveals important evidence of the portfolio effect. Using the

[10]Brokerage commission fees per share are much lower for transactions of many shares of a single stock than for fewer shares of several stocks.

[11]We must calculate covariances between stocks 1 and 2, 2 and 3, and 1 and 3.

[12]In 1993, 2658 stocks were traded on the New York Stock Exchange, 4758 on NASDAQ, and 974 on the American Stock Exchange.

EXHIBIT 7.2
BUILDING A PORTFOLIO

NO. OF STOCKS	ADD STOCK	PORTFOLIO RETURN	PORTFOLIO STANDARD DEVIATION
1	Black	0.03	0.33
2	Stone	0.11	0.42
3	Cincinnati	0.09	0.34
4	Melville	0.11	0.29
5	Union	0.11	0.25
6	Boeing	0.11	0.22
7	Enron	0.12	0.21
8	Polaroid	0.11	0.20
9	Gannett	0.11	0.18
10	Warner	0.12	0.17
11	Tandy	0.12	0.16
12	Pennzoil	0.12	0.16
13	Fleet	0.12	0.16
14	Citicorp	0.12	0.17
15	Brown	0.11	0.17
16	Golden	0.12	0.18
17	Quaker	0.12	0.18
18	United	0.12	0.18
19	Fleming	0.12	0.17
20	Capital	0.12	0.17

20 stocks from the sample portfolio, Exhibit 7.2 shows the risk and return for portfolios ranging from a single stock to 20 stocks. It is important to note that we are choosing stocks at random to add to the portfolio rather than using some other criteria, such as our favorite companies or the latest hot tip. The portfolio is divided equally among the stocks, so that the weights are 0.2 for each stock in a five-stock portfolio, 0.1 for each stock in a ten-stock portfolio, and so on.

Take a close look at the portfolio standard deviations in Exhibit 7.2. Even though we continue to add risky stocks, portfolio risk shows a reasonably steady decline. This is graphically presented in Figure 7.6. In fact, the only reason why

FIGURE 7.6
REDUCING PORTFOLIO RISK BY ADDING STOCKS

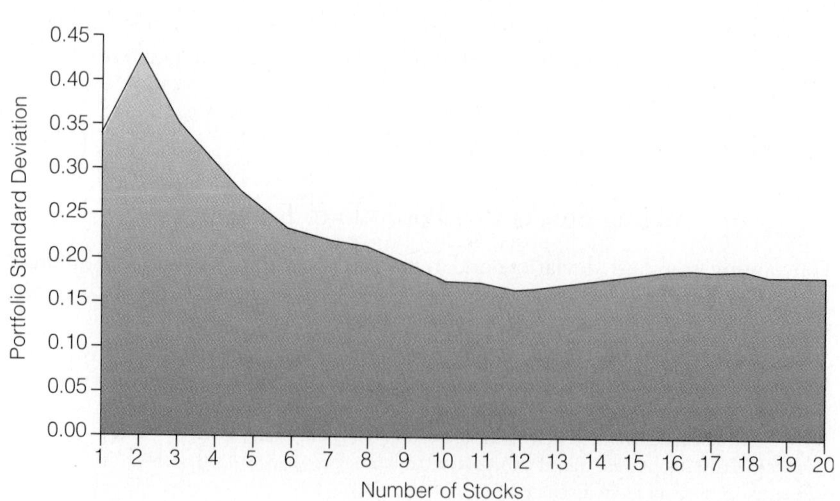

Transparency Available

portfolio standard deviation occasionally rises is because we are adding a particularly risky stock. (Remember that covariance is the product of the correlation and the stocks' standard deviations.) Figure 7.7 shows the decline in portfolio standard deviation for portfolios of stocks of equal variance and covariance.[13] This situation produces a smoother curve. Here we can see clearly the risk reduction that occurs as we add stocks to the portfolio.

Figures 7.6 and 7.7 show that the slope of the curve flattens quickly, meaning that additional stocks contribute less and less to reducing portfolio risk. Figure 7.7 has three curves, each one representing different correlations. Notice that with zero correlation the curve is much steeper, but still little additional risk reduction occurs by the time we add our twentieth stock.

You cannot eliminate portfolio risk.

From this evidence, we are able to draw some important conclusions regarding portfolio risk. They are related in good news–bad news fashion. Fortunately, there is more good news than bad. The bad news is that we cannot eliminate portfolio risk. Each of the curves in Figure 7.7 flattens before risk reaches zero. As a practical matter, most actual correlations will be above zero, so that our 0.2 and 0.7 curves are more realistic.[14] We shortly discuss in more detail why we are not able to reduce risk to zero.

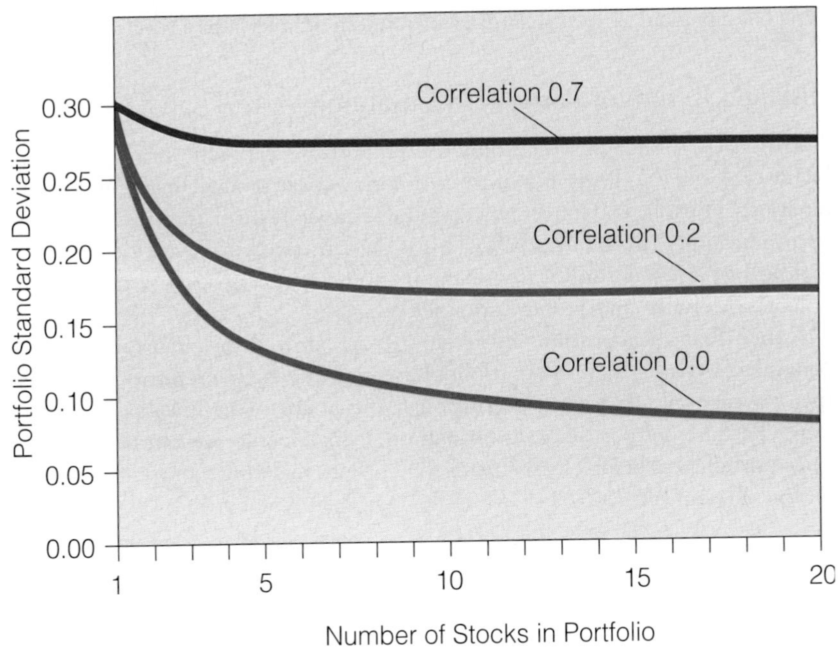

FIGURE 7.7

REDUCING PORTFOLIO RISK

Transparency Available

[13]For stocks with identical variance and covariance, portfolio standard deviation may be calculated as

$$SD_P = \sqrt{\frac{\text{var} + \text{cov}(n - 1)}{n}} \qquad \lim_{n \to \infty} \sqrt{\text{cov}}$$

[14]A 0.7 or higher correlation would indicate that our stocks are related in some way, perhaps in the same or similar industries. You can see in Figure 7.7 why we would want to avoid concentrating our portfolio in just one or a few industries.

It takes only a few stocks to reduce portfolio risk.

The first bit of good news is that it doesn't take many stocks to reduce portfolio risk to the point where the curve flattens. Even modest portfolios of 7 or 8 stocks yield substantial reductions in risk. A portfolio of 8, 10, or 15 stocks is within the reach of many individual investors.[15]

Analyzing stocks' risk, return, and correlations is not necessary to achieve risk reduction.

The second bit of good news relates to our selecting stocks at random. Reducing portfolio risk does not depend on our picking low-risk stocks or searching for low correlations. This fact is important because efficient markets seldom provide "magic" stocks to add to our portfolio. Stocks that are poorly correlated to most other stocks may be in great demand, raising their prices and lowering their returns. The investor then must ask what price, in terms of poor return, he is willing to pay for that low correlation.

Because we can reduce risk by picking stocks at random, however, we don't have to be concerned about trying to outguess an efficient market. We see in Exhibit 7.2 that adding stocks at random to the portfolio reduces risk without sacrificing return. This is evidence of the free lunch enjoyed by investors who hold a diversified stock portfolio.

To extend our good news theme a bit further, reducing portfolio risk requires no special knowledge or special skills at stock picking. A famous metaphor for picking stocks is to hang the stock quotes from the *Wall Street Journal* on the wall and throw darts to select your stocks. You do not even have to exercise yourself greatly: Fifteen or 20 darts is sufficient. This is, in effect, what we did here; but given our skill with darts, using random numbers was a good deal safer.[16]

Risk and Return of Portfolios Containing More Than Two Stocks

Two-stock portfolios in which only the proportions vary fall on a curve, as in Figures 7.4 and 7.5. Portfolios of three or more stocks produce many more combinations. Portfolios no longer plot on a single curve. Instead, they become points in an imaginary risk-return plane. This is demonstrated in Figure 7.8. Here we look at just a few portfolios from combinations of three stocks—United Technologies, Melville, and Stone Container.[17]

With three or more stocks, portfolios are plotted in risk-return space. Most do not lie on the efficient set.

Notice that the portfolios in Figure 7.8 are arrayed in a rough risk-return congruence; that is, high risk portfolios have generally higher returns. To confirm this, try mentally drawing a line through the points. This line has a positive slope. Because our portfolios do not fall on a single curve, we can now identify some portfolios as being clearly better than others, meaning that some do not lie on the efficient set.

---

[15]Of course, many individual investors cannot afford 100 shares apiece of even seven or eight stocks. For small investors, mutual funds offer diversification and professional management, and many can be purchased with an initial investment of as little as $1,000.

[16]In a *Wall Street Journal* contest, dart throwers beat four professional stock pickers for the first 6 months of 1993: "Dart Throwers Come Up Winners Against Pros' Picks," *Wall Street Journal* (July 8, 1993). In another contest, chimpanzees were substituted for human dart throwers, with the same results. None of this implies that random selection is always superior to a more studied approach to stock selection. It does mean that time-consuming and expensive stock analysis may not always justify its cost.

[17]These three stocks were not selected at random. They were chosen because of low correlations and because they represent a wide range of risk and return.

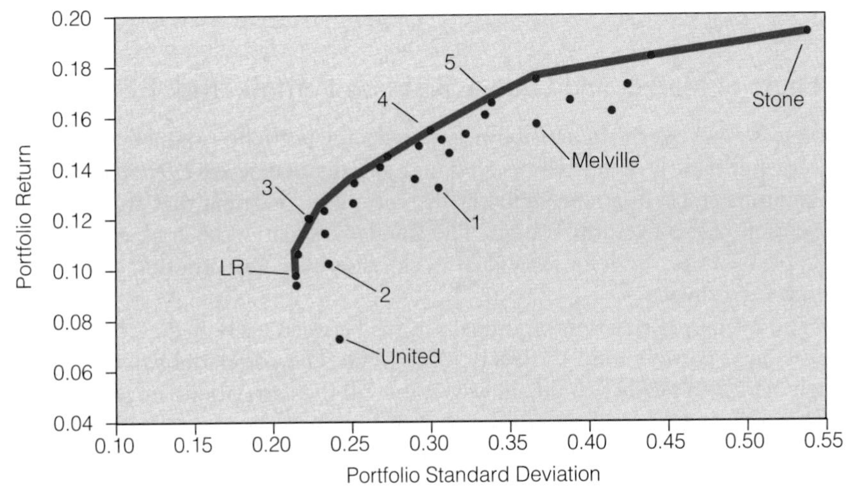

FIGURE 7.8

PORTFOLIO RISK AND RETURN—UNITED TECHNOLOGIES, MELVILLE AND STONE CONTAINER

Transparency Available

In Figure 7.8, we have marked portfolios containing single stocks, the approximate least-risk portfolio, and five others, numbered 1 through 5. We have also drawn line segments connecting the best portfolios, remembering that we seek maximum return for minimum risk. The result only approximates the efficient set because we have plotted just a few of the thousands (infinite) number of possible portfolios. If we had plotted many more portfolios, the points would be so close together that the efficient set would simply be the upper left edge of the nearly continuous array.

Some of the plotted portfolios are in the efficient set, and some are obviously not. Those in the efficient set are LR, 3, 4, 5, and Stone. Those that are not are Melville, 1, 2, and United. Melville is not in the efficient set because 5 is clearly better, having less risk and higher return. In this sense, portfolio 5 dominates Melville. Similarly, 4 dominates 1, 3 dominates 2, and LR dominates United. Any **dominated portfolio** cannot lie on the efficient set. Exhibit 7.3 shows the composition of each portfolio. Notice that even though United and Melville, by themselves, are not in the efficient set, both are well represented in the efficient portfolios, LR, 3, 4, and 5. Again, we see the effect of low correlations between stocks producing efficient portfolios.

PORTFOLIO	PROPORTION: UNITED	PROPORTION: MELVILLE	PROPORTION: STONE
LR	.75	.125	.125
1	.50	0	.50
2	.75	0	.25
3	.50	.333	.16
4	.16	.50	.333
5	0	.75	.25

Correlations: United–Melville, 0.146; United–Stone, 0.093; Melville–Stone, 0.287.

EXHIBIT 7.3

UNITED TECHNOLOGIES, MELVILLE, AND STONE CONTAINER PORTFOLIO COMPOSITION

MARKET AND UNIQUE RISK

Effect of Market and Unique Risks on Portfolio Risk Reduction

So far, we have seen the possibilities for reducing portfolio risk merely by combining imperfectly correlated stocks. This risk reduction occurs even in portfolios containing stocks that are, individually, very risky, meaning that the standard deviation of their returns is high. The standard deviation of stock returns is a reliable measure of risk for individual stocks. However, for portfolios, correlation is the key to risk.

The average correlation of annual returns between each of the 20 stocks in the sample portfolio and the S&P 500 is 0.44. The correlations range from a high of 0.79 to nearly 0. Note, however, that all the correlations are positive, an indication that all stock returns contain at least some market risk. Recall that the market (represented in this case by the S&P 500) exerts an influence on all stocks in the market. This omnipresent risk explains why portfolio risk in Figure 7.7 never drops to 0.

Some companies and stocks are linked by more than the stock market. Stocks from the same industry have higher correlations with each other than with other stocks in the market.[18] Because of their high correlations, investors try to avoid unnecessarily loading their portfolios with stocks that are obviously related. Remember our earlier example of General Motors and Ford. However, our sample portfolio of 20 stocks shows that random choice produces a highly diversified portfolio that greatly reduces portfolio risk. This risk reduction reflects the unique risk present in the returns of every stock. A diversified portfolio ensures, for the most part, that these unique qualities will offset or cancel each other, thus eliminating this form of risk.

Stocks individually contain both market and unique risk. However, in diversified portfolios only market risk remains.

So, although individual stocks contain both market and unique risk, the canceling effect of a diversified portfolio virtually eliminates unique risk from the portfolio. However, no amount of diversification allows investors to escape the

FIGURE 7.9

UNIQUE AND MARKET RISK

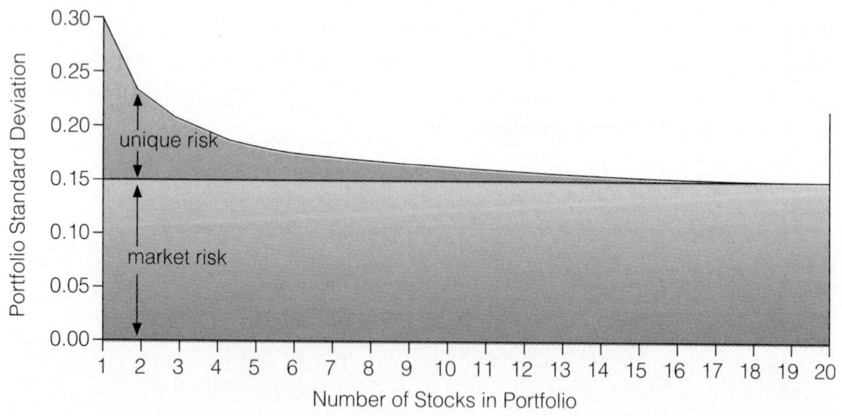

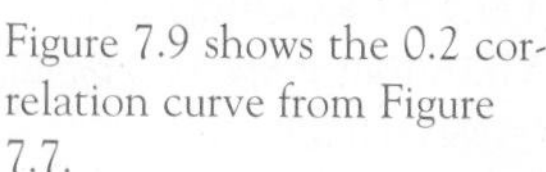
Figure 7.9 shows the 0.2 correlation curve from Figure 7.7.

[18]There can be factors other than industry linking stocks. For example, stocks that are dependent on the same geographic region or are dependent on a common resource, such as cheap electricity or low interest rates, have linkages that are greater than just their ties to the market.

market risk that is common to all stocks. This means that risk can never be eliminated from portfolios of common stocks and that the risk remaining in a diversified portfolio is entirely market risk. In Figure 7.9, the straight line delineates market and unique risk. This graph is the 0.2 correlation curve from Figure 7.7. In this case, eliminating unique risk from the portfolio reduces portfolio standard deviation by about one-half, from 0.30 to 0.15.

How Risk Affects Stock Prices

Investors who understand the principle of diversification and the effect of correlation on portfolio risk may be tempted to use correlation as a basis for selecting stocks for their portfolios. However, because nearly every stock contains market risk, there may be no stocks in the United States that are negatively correlated to the market and to other U.S. stocks.[19] However, if one or two did show up, investors would quickly bid up their prices, lowering their expected rates of return. In this instance, there is no free lunch, because the investor is required to pay for risk reduction by accepting a low return. There is simply no reliable way to remove market risk from a portfolio without sacrificing expected return. Market risk may be like sharing your apartment with a 900-pound gorilla. If you can't get rid of it, you had better learn to coexist. So it is with market risk.

What about investors who take on unique risk by not diversifying their portfolios? These investors are exposed to more risk than those with diversified portfolios and, therefore, would like to receive a higher expected return. However, all investors compete for stocks in an auction market in which stocks are sold to the highest bidders. The highest bidders are those who hold diversified portfolios, containing only market risk, and are therefore willing to accept lower returns. These investors can offer higher prices for the stocks and, in a competitive market, they will simply outbid those who are not diversified.

Undiversified investors wishing to buy the stock must pay the higher price; that is, they must compete with diversified investors. However, this higher price produces a return that compensates the investors for market risk but not unique risk. This arrangement is perfectly acceptable to the diversified investor but not to the undiversified investor. By taking on uncompensated risk, undiversified investors do not have efficient portfolios, meaning that they could do better by diversifying.

In spite of this, not all investors diversify. Inevitably, some try to pick a few winners, willingly—and probably foolishly—taking on unique risk. Others take unique risk because control of a company is more important than diversification. There are families and individuals whose personal fortunes are tied to particular companies. The Bloch family (H&R Block) and Bill Gates (Microsoft) are examples. However, ironically, even they do not control the market prices of their stocks. Prices are set by those who buy and sell, rather than just hold, the stock; and those who buy and sell are generally investors with diversified portfolios.

While investors are fundamentally concerned with portfolio risk, they change

[19]If one finds a negative correlation, he would do well to check his data and calculations. A negative correlation is like the Abominable Snowman: It may be out there, but reported sightings should be treated with skepticism.

the composition of their portfolios by buying and selling individual stocks. Therefore, our coverage of this topic will not be complete until we develop a risk measure for individual stocks that reflects only their contribution to portfolio risk. We will take this important step in the next chapter.

BEYOND PORTFOLIOS OF U.S. COMMON STOCKS

International Diversification

Global investing offers diversification opportunities not available in the United States.

For American investors, diversification has traditionally been limited to U.S. stocks. However, as international financial markets develop, there is less reason to confine portfolios to stocks of a single country.[20] Stock returns are less correlated between countries than they are within a single country. This fact means that investors with single country portfolios may be able to reduce risk by diversifying internationally.[21] Even though risk may be reduced by international diversification, some risk always remains. Although economic, political, and social institutions vary between countries, there are increasing linkages, especially between the developed nations of Europe, Asia, and North America. These linkages allow stocks to be traded across national boundaries, but they also produce dependencies between national economies and markets. For example, a bad day in the Japanese stock market, which trades during the night in the United States, may spell trouble the following morning for the U.S. market. The slowdown in the rate of growth of the Japanese economy in the early 1990s has been attributed in part to slower growth in North America and Europe, Japan's principal trading partners.

However, significant benefits to international diversification are possible. The day may soon come when the failure of an American investor to diversify internationally produces uncompensated risk in her portfolio in the same way that a failure to diversify among domestic industries does today. All that is required is for the flow of information to improve and for trading costs to come down. In fact, these changes are occurring today.

An example of the tilt toward global thinking is the *Business Week* Global 1000 report that ranks companies by the market value of their stocks. The only criterion for inclusion is that foreigners have access to markets on which these stocks are traded. In 1992 firms from 22 nations were included, with four more nations likely to be added.[22] It may not be long before the relevant market index is the Global 1000 rather than the S&P 500.

Figure 7.10 portrays, in a risk-return context, the advantages of global diversification. The general shape of the curve comes from actual data gathered by the Frank Russell Company for the years 1981 through 1989. In Figure 7.10, international diversification increases portfolio return while reducing risk. Initially, international diversification greatly reduces risk; and this continues until

[20]In 1994 there were more than 1,200 foreign stocks trading in the United States. See "The Global Investor," *Business Week* (Sept. 19, 1994): 96–104.

[21]Unfortunately, capital markets of many less developed countries offer the greatest opportunities for diversification by U.S. investors but also present the greatest risks because of political and social instability.

[22]"The Global 1000," *Business Week* (July 13, 1992).

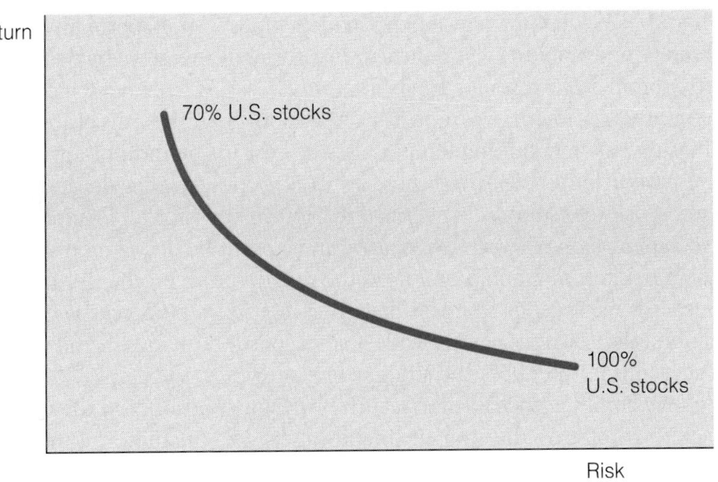

FIGURE 7.10
BENEFITS OF INTERNATIONAL DIVERSIFICATION

the proportion of international stocks approaches 30%. These data suggest that during the 1980s U.S. investors would have benefited by holding some portion of their portfolios in foreign stocks.

The Risk-Free Asset

To this point, we have considered portfolios only of common stocks. We could expand our possibilities to include bonds, precious metals, collectibles and real estate, all of which are partial substitutes for stocks. However, all are difficult to analyze in a portfolio context because the markets in which they trade are quite different. Most investors, perhaps without realizing it, are well diversified through their pension funds, life insurance, home ownership, and perhaps collectibles; although few consider all of these as belonging to a single portfolio.

If we were able to expand our portfolios to include these other investments, new portfolios would appear in our risk-return space, and the efficient set would have to be redrawn. However, we would still be choosing among risky portfolios in the efficient set based on our risk-return preferences. In any case, the importance of correlations, the basic formulas, and the shape of the efficient set would not change.

So far, we have not included riskless securities in our portfolio. Although no security is truly riskless, U.S. Treasury bills come close. Treasury bills are considered risk free because their life span is brief and they are obligations of the treasury, which means that they have little credit risk.[23]

Risk-free securities are an important addition to portfolios. They provide liquidity and a safe haven to investors. Because market risk is present in all stock portfolios, risk-free securities are the only way for investors to reduce their risk below that of the lowest-risk stock portfolio.

Combining treasury bills or money market funds with stock portfolios is a diversification technique followed by most investors.

Most individual investors do not buy Treasury bills but have relatively safe

[23]Credit risk is the risk of default. In this case, it is the risk that the U.S. Treasury will be unable to redeem the Treasury bill 3 months hence.

and liquid bank deposits and money market funds[24] that approximate Treasury bills' safety and liquidity. By contrast, institutional investors buy Treasury bills directly. From 1926 through 1993, 3-month Treasury bills have yielded an average return of 3.7% per year, or just 0.6% more than the rate of inflation,[25] so eliminating risk and gaining liquidity has its cost in the form of lower returns.

The proportion of risk free securities in a portfolio varies depending on the investor's risk aversion and the expected returns on stocks. Figure 7.11 shows how a combination of a risk free security and a portfolio of common stocks would plot on a risk-return graph. Point R_f is the rate of return on the risk-free security. Because it is risk free, its standard deviation is 0 and it plots on the vertical axis. A combination of this security with a stock portfolio lying on the efficient set (the curved line) produces the straight line shown on the graph.[26]

We may combine the risk-free security with any portfolio on the efficient set. However, by rotating the straight line, using R_f as a fulcrum, it is apparent that the greatest slope yields the best possible risk-return combinations. The greatest slope possible is the line that is tangent to the efficient set. That tangency point is M. Portfolios containing both stocks and a risk free security lie along the line segment R_fM. Point A is such a portfolio. Portfolios along the line segment to the right of M, such as portfolio B, contain only stocks. However, these investors

FIGURE 7.11

ADDING THE RISK-FREE ASSET

Transparency Available

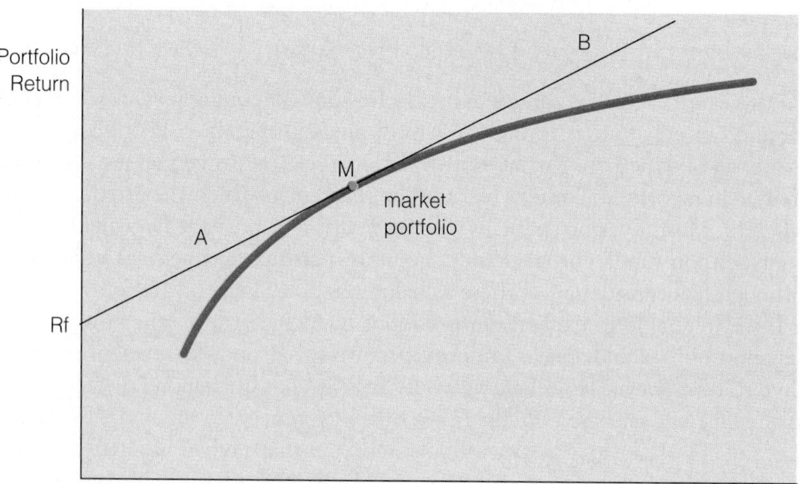

[24]Money market funds invest in safe, short-term securities.

[25]Ibbotson Associates, *Stocks, Bonds* (1994), p. 31.

[26]Both weighted average return and standard deviation are linear, meaning that points representing combinations of the risk-free asset and the stock portfolio plot as a straight line.

$$SD_P = \sqrt{(w_{R_f})^2(SD_{R_f})^2 + (w_M)^2(SD_M)^2 + 2(w_{R_f})(w_M)COV_{R_fM}}$$

reduces to

$$SD_P = \sqrt{w_M^2 SD_M^2} = w_M SD_M$$

because $SD_{R_f} = 0$ and $COV_{R_fM} = 0$.

have achieved greater potential returns, with more risk, by borrowing to buy more of stock portfolio M than their own wealth allows.

The straight line through R_f that is tangent to the efficient set is called the **capital market line**. It is important for two reasons. First, it shows that when we combine a risk free asset with our stock portfolio, we are able to achieve a better risk return position than we could with the stock portfolio alone. Notice that the capital market line dominates the efficient set except (obviously) at the tangent point M. The second benefit of the capital market line is that it now designates one best portfolio on the efficient set. This portfolio is M. Prior to this, we were on our own to pick the one portfolio along the efficient set that best suited our risk-return preference. Portfolio M is called the market portfolio because if all investors have the same portfolio choices—construct the same efficient set—they will all pick portfolio M. Only the stocks in portfolio M will trade. Effectively, then, the stock market consists only of these stocks.

A Reality Check

We are not suggesting that market processes are as pure as suggested by the theory. Our efficient set is built using historical returns and standard deviations; yet decision makers face future returns that are uncertain. Their relevant efficient sets reflect expected, rather than past, portfolio risk and return, and each person has a slightly different notion about what the future will bring. Thus, there are not one but many capital market lines and not one market portfolio but many common stock portfolios chosen.

However, we do not need a literal interpretation of the theory to see the truth of its conclusions. For example, we do not need a single capital market line to know that the availability of Treasury bills and money market funds benefits portfolio managers by providing risk management options and liquidity not otherwise available. Also, although there is no single identifiable market portfolio, there are stocks that are so widely traded and held they appear in most large portfolios. Moreover, by randomly choosing 20 stocks we constructed a portfolio whose returns track closely those of the market index (S&P 500). We would expect the risk and return of most diversified portfolios to be similar. Therefore, we may be able to approximate the characteristics of the market portfolio without ever precisely identifying it simply by holding a diversified stock portfolio.

Summary

This chapter takes the first step in determining required rates of return in the capital markets. In this chapter, we have shown that investors can reduce portfolio risk without sacrificing expected return by diversifying their stock holdings. Diversified portfolios eliminate unique risk. However, there is a limit to the benefits of diversification. Diversified portfolios of about 20 stocks virtually eliminate unique risk, but market risk remains. Market risk is common to all stocks and cannot be eliminated by diversification, regardless of how many stocks the portfolio contains.

The key to risk reduction is finding stocks whose returns are not highly correlated. The lower the correlation, the lower the portfolio risk. However, the presence of market risk places a lower limit on correlation coefficients. Searching for low correlations is unnecessary because selecting stocks at random ensures enough diversification to virtually eliminate unique risk. Conversely, no selection strategy will completely eliminate market risk.

Undiversified investors still face unique risk, but they will not receive a high enough return to compensate for this risk because diversified investors, facing less risk, will accept lower returns by bidding higher prices as they compete for stocks. However, because diversification is easy and inexpensive, there is no reason for investors to face unique risk.

The capital market line combines a stock portfolio on the efficient set with a risk free asset. This combination produces portfolio choices that, in a risk-return context, are better than choices that lie on the efficient set. It has the added advantage of designating only one stock portfolio on the efficient set as the portfolio preferred by every investor. This is the market portfolio.

Chapter 7 shows that stocks are, or should be, held in diversified portfolios. If they are, they are subject to market risk only, the unique risk having been eliminated by diversification. Building on this important conclusion, we turn our attention, in Chapter 8, to the market risk and return of individual stocks. In Chapter 8, we will show that the expected and required returns in the capital markets reflect market risk, and we will construct a risk return model that can be used to calculate required returns.

Key Terms

portfolio
unique risk
market risk
Dow Jones Industrial Average (DJIA)
Standard & Poor's 500 Index (S&P 500)
portfolio effect
correlation
covariance
efficient set
dominated portfolio
capital market line

KEY FORMULAS

Present Value

$$V_0 = \sum_{t=1}^{N} \frac{CF_t}{(1 + R(r))^t}$$

Rate of Return on Common Stock

$$r = \frac{P_1 - P_0 + D_1}{P_0}$$

Covariance

$$COV_{(A,B)} = SD_A SD_B CORR_{(A,B)}$$

Standard Deviation of a Two-stock Portfolio

$$SD_P = \sqrt{(w_B)^2(SD_B)^2 + (w_A)^2(SD_A)^2 + 2(w_B)(w_A)COV_{BA}}$$

Expected Return of a Two-stock Portfolio

$$r_P = (w_B)(r_B) + (w_A)(r_A)$$

QUESTIONS

1. You have a diversified portfolio consisting of equal proportions of 20 stocks. The average standard deviation of your 20 stocks is 10%. Your portfolio standard deviation will probably be (less than, equal to, greater than) 10%.
2. You are a risk averse investor who owns a single stock in a conservative (low-risk) public utility. You are looking for a second stock to buy and are considering either a low-risk public utility stock (not the same one) or a somewhat higher risk auto stock. Which would you buy? Why?
3. Consider two diversified stock portfolios. One contains 500 stocks. The other has 25 stocks. How would you describe the relative risk (standard deviation) of these two portfolios?

   SD_{25} = standard deviation of the 25-stock portfolio

   SD_{500} = standard deviation of the 500-stock portfolio

   SD_{25} is much less than SD_{500}.
   SD_{25} is about equal to SD_{500}.
   SD_{25} is much greater than SD_{500}.
4. Should a particularly risk averse investor ever consider adding a high-risk stock (measured by its standard deviation) to his stock portfolio? Why or why not?
5. The wise investor should minimize the risk of her portfolio. Do you agree or disagree?
6. The primary benefit of common-stock mutual funds is that, by holding hundreds of stocks, they offer much greater risk diversification than an individual investor can achieve with a portfolio of 20 stocks. Do you agree or disagree?

7. Because of our concentration on portfolio risk and the covariance between stocks, is the standard deviation of returns of an individual stock unimportant? Assume that the stock is held in a portfolio.
8. **a.** Explain why, in practice, a portfolio's standard deviation is not the weighted average of the stocks' standard deviations.
   b. Can you think of any instance where portfolio standard deviation equals the average stock standard deviation?
9. All else being equal, the lower the correlation between stocks, the lower the portfolio standard deviation. It seems obvious, therefore, that we should search for stocks with low correlations to add to our portfolio. Do you agree or disagree?
10. What do you think inhibits most investors from routinely calculating portfolio standard deviation and using it to select portfolios? (*Hint*: We can think of two reasons; one is fairly obvious and the other isn't.)
11. If you were trying to convince someone that portfolio diversification is a wise strategy, what arguments would you use? We can think of three strong arguments.
12. What criteria would you use to determine whether a portfolio of U.S. stocks was diversified?
13. Why is international diversification desirable?
14. If you held a portfolio of U.S. stocks, and you wanted to diversify internationally to reduce your portfolio risk, which of the following portfolios would probably achieve the greatest risk reduction?

PORTFOLIO A	PORTFOLIO B
United States	United States
United Kingdom	China
Japan	Argentina
Germany	India

15. Referring to Question 14, are there factors other than risk reduction that might enter into your selection between portfolios A and B?
16. In this chapter, we contend that you don't have to be knowledgeable or very wealthy to benefit from portfolio diversification. Why not?
17. When we are constructing portfolios of more than two stocks, some portfolios do not lie on the efficient set. Those that don't are dominated by those that do. What causes a portfolio to be dominated?
18. In your own words, define market and unique risk.
19. You own stock in a U.S. manufacturing company. All stocks are correlated with the market, but this correlation may vary depending on how we define the market. Rank, from highest to lowest, the correlation our manufacturing stock would have with these three markets:
    1. U.S. stock market
    2. Global stock market
    3. U.S manufacturers' stock market
20. Single stock portfolios contain unique risk. Investors in such portfolios should be compensated for their risk by high expected returns. That they are not is an example of a breakdown in an otherwise efficient stock market. Do you agree or disagree?

21. In your own words, describe the capital market line.
22. What advantages are there to investing in a risk-free asset and a portfolio of common stocks?
23. The point of tangency between the capital market line and the efficient set (of common stocks) is called the market portfolio. Is this portfolio really the market portfolio, or is it misnamed? Briefly discuss this question.
24. There are many stock market indices, including the Dow Jones Industrial Average (DJIA) and the Standard & Poor's 500. Would you expect the risk and return of these indices to vary significantly from one another? Why or why not?
25. Would you expect the risk and return of the market portfolio (M) on the capital market line to be significantly different from those of the S&P 500 index? Why or why not?
26. Using the logic of the capital market line, should stock portfolio managers occasionally have a portion of their portfolio in Treasury bills (or money market funds)? Why or why not?
27. Consider the following two investors:

    Investor 1: Yale Cabot Lodge III, most of whose wealth is in the family business, Gigantic Industries, Inc.

    Investor 2: Ace Ventura, the former pet detective, who is now a stock speculator. Ace's secret: Find the best stock, borrow from your friends, and buy as much of the stock as you can.

    Neither has a diversified portfolio. Can you justify this lack of diversification?
28. A Japanese investor, seeking to diversify his stock portfolio, would probably be better off investing in (choose one) (a) Malaysia; (b) the United States; (c) Canada. Why?
29. From the following list of stocks, pick a portfolio of three stocks that is most likely to minimize portfolio risk. (Ignore the risk of the individual stocks.)

IBM	Toshiba (Japanese computer manufacturer)
Intel	Sumitomo Bank (Japan)
Boeing	Nomura Securities (Japan)
Microsoft	

30. Each of these three common stock mutual funds invest in a diversified portfolio of stocks. Based on the information provided here, which of these three mutual funds probably has the least risk?

    Fund A: 100 U.S. stocks, 50 foreign stocks, total 150 stocks
    Fund B: 300 U.S. stocks
    Fund C: 500 U.S. stocks

31. (True or False) All portfolios of three or more stocks lie on the efficient set.
32. (True or False) If a small investor cannot afford to invest in at least 10 stocks, she would do just as well by investing in a single stock.
33. (True or False) Market risk can be virtually eliminated by holding a portfolio of stocks from many countries.
34. (True or False) An investor who spends time searching for a U.S. stock that is negatively correlated to the U.S. market is probably wasting her time.
35. (True or False) The expected return on a diversified stock portfolio is the weighted average of individual stock returns.

36. (True or False) The expected return on an undiversified stock portfolio is the weighted average of individual stock returns.
37. (True or False) The standard deviation of a diversified stock portfolio is the weighted average of individual stock standard deviations.
38. All else being equal, which portfolio has the greater risk?
    i. A portfolio containing two negatively correlated stocks
    ii. A portfolio containing two positively correlated stocks
39. In adding stocks to a portfolio to reduce risk, greater risk reduction occurs by adding
    i. A third stock to a 2-stock portfolio
    ii. A sixteenth stock to a 15-stock portfolio
40. Given the importance of correlation in reducing portfolio risk, investors should do extensive research to find low correlation stocks to add to their portfolios. Do you agree or disagree? Why?
41. Which of the following best describes the correlation coefficients between stocks in the U.S. stock market?
    a. +1
    b. Between 0 and 1
    c. 0
    d. Between −1 and 0
    e. −1
42. A diversified portfolio of U.S. stocks should have
    Market risk only
    Unique risk only
    Both market and unique risk
    No risk
43. Following are the risks and returns for six stock portfolios.

	A	B	C	D	E	F
$E(r_P)$	13%	8%	18%	11%	13%	20%
SD_P	6%	5%	11%	4%	8%	10%

    Assuming that these are the only portfolios available to us, which are on the efficient set?
44. Undiversified portfolios contain unique as well as market risk. Therefore, in a competitive market, undiversified portfolios should have higher returns, all else being equal. Do you agree or disagree with this statement? Briefly explain.
45. If you or your parents own a mutual fund or participate in a pension plan:
    a. Do you know which securities constitute the largest holdings of your mutual fund or pension plan?
    b. After reading this chapter, will you try to find out?
46. In a national recession not all industries and companies suffer equally.
    a. Can you think of some industries or products that are somewhat "recession proof"?
    b. Is this an example of unique or market risk?

47. From the following pairs of stock returns, identify which one is:
  a. perfectly positively correlated
  b. not perfectly positively correlated
  c. not perfectly negatively correlated
  d. perfectly negatively correlated

	PERCENT RETURNS							
YEAR	A	B	C	D	E	F	G	H
1	3	11	5	11	5	5	3	14
2	4	12	6	9	6	8	4	13
3	8	13	7	7	7	11	8	6
4	6	14	8	5	8	14	6	5

48. A U.S. investor is considering one of two international stock portfolios. Portfolio A invests in Germany, Canada, and Japan. Portfolio B invests in Britain, Argentina, and Malaysia. Which of these two portfolios is likely to offer the greater diversification (lowest correlations between countries)? Why?
49. The capital market line combines a ________ asset with a common stock portfolio.
50. How might a common-stock investor benefit by also investing in a risk-free asset (or a money market fund)?

DEMONSTRATION PROBLEMS

Standard Deviations of Two-Stock Portfolios

1. **a.** A stock portfolio consists entirely of two stocks, Bach Corp. and Beethoven, Inc. Using the following data, calculate the standard deviation of the portfolio.

$$CORR_{BB} = 0.6$$

BACH		BEETHOVEN
\$700	Amount invested	\$300
0.11	Standard deviation	0.23

b. If you wanted to increase the risk of your portfolio, what would you do?
c. Make the changes to part (b) and recalculate the portfolio standard deviation.

SOLUTION

a. This is most easily solved using a spreadsheet. However, it may also be solved using Equations (7.4) and (7.5). First, calculate covariance using Equation (7.4).

$$COV_{BB} = (SD_B)(SD_B)(CORR_{BB}) = (0.11)(0.23)(0.6) = 0.015$$

Using Equation (7.5), we are now able to calculate portfolio standard deviation:

$$SD_P = \sqrt{(0.7)^2(0.11)^2 + (0.3)^2(0.23)^2 + 2(0.7)(0.3)(0.15)} = 0.130$$

b. Increase the weighting of Beethoven because it has the higher standard deviation.

c. Any increase in the proportion of Beethoven will increase portfolio risk. In this example, we increase the proportion of Beethoven to 0.7 by investing $700 in it. The covariance remains the same. Recalculating portfolio standard deviation gives

$$SD_P = \sqrt{(0.3)^2(0.11)^2 + (0.7)^2(0.23)^2 + 2(0.7)(0.3)(0.015)} = 0.183$$

Risk and Return of Two-Stock Portfolios

2. For two stocks $r_A = 0.13$, $r_B = 0.22$, $\text{corr}_{AB} = 0.7$, $SD_A = 0.3$, and $SD_B = 0.5$.

a. What are the expected returns and standard deviations of portfolios consisting entirely of A and entirely of B?

b. Now vary the proportions of A and B as follows:

PROPORTION A	PROPORTION B
0.2	0.8
0.4	0.6
0.6	0.4
0.8	0.2

Calculate the portfolio standard deviation and expected return for these different proportions.

c. Using a graph as in Figure 7.6, plot the portfolio risk and return points for parts (a) and (b), and connect your points. You may use either graph paper or the graphing function of a spreadsheet program.

SOLUTION

a. For a portfolio consisting entirely of stock A, $r_P = 0.13$ and $SD_P = 0.3$. For a portfolio consisting entirely of stock B, $r_P = 0.22$ and $SD_P = 0.5$.

b. To avoid tedious calculations, use a spreadsheet to calculate portfolio standard deviations. First, calculate covariance using Equation (7.4).

$$COV_{AB} = (SD_A)(SD_B)(CORR_{AB}) = (0.3)(0.5)(0.7) = 0.105$$

Weighted average portfolio returns and portfolio standard deviations are as follows.

PORTFOLIO A	PORTFOLIO B	RETURN	STANDARD DEVIATION
0	1	0.22	0.50
0.2	0.8	0.20	0.44
0.4	0.6	0.18	0.39
0.6	0.4	0.17	0.35
0.8	0.2	0.15	0.32
1	0	0.13	0.30

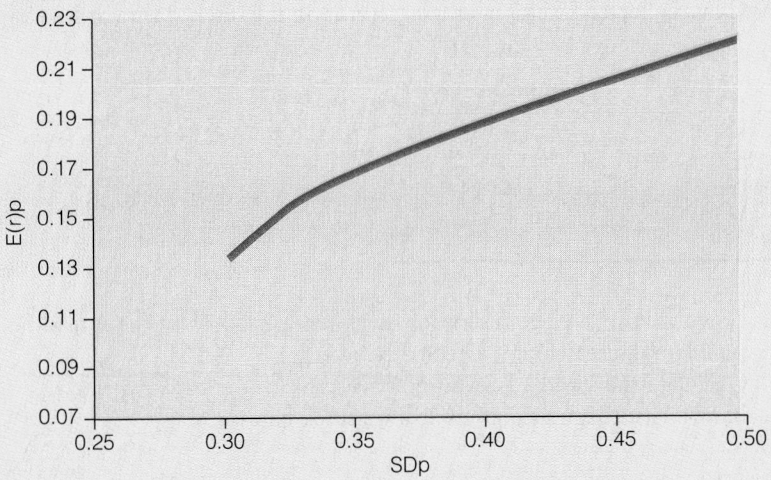

FIGURE 7.12

c. The plot of portfolio returns and standard deviations will be a slightly curved line, reflecting the correlation of 0.7. See Figure 7.12.

PROBLEMS

1. Serendipity Corporation's stock price on December 31, 1991, was $34.50. One year later, December 31, 1992, it was $31.00. During 1992, Serendipity paid $4.50 in dividends to its shareholders. What was the rate of return on this stock during 1992?

Annual Rate of Return on Common Stock
1. 2.90%

2. Serendipity Corporation's stock price on December 31, 1992 was $31.00. One year later, December 31, 1993, it was $28.50. During 1993, Serendipity paid a $2.00 dividend. What was the rate of return on this stock during 1993.

Annual Rate of Return on Common Stock
2. −1.61%

3. We have collected 5 years of annual returns on the stock of Pierson, Inc.

	ANNUAL RETURN
1990	8%
1991	17
1992	4
1993	1
1994	7

Average Returns and Standard Deviation of Returns
3. a. 7.27%
b. 5.39%

a. Calculate the average return for the 5-year period. (Use the spreadsheet template that calculates a geometric average.)
b. Calculate the standard deviation of returns for the 5-year period.
c. How might this information about a stock be used?

4. We have collected 5 years of annual returns on the stock of Ezra Stiles Corp.

	ANNUAL RETURN
1990	32%
1991	17
1992	4
1993	26
1994	11

Average Returns and Standard Deviation of Returns
4. a. 17.57%
b. 10.07%

a. Calculate the average return for the 5-year period. (Use the spreadsheet template that calculates a geometric average.)
b. Calculate the standard deviation of returns for the 5-year period.
c. How might this information about a stock be used?

Interpreting Returns and Standard Deviations

5. Which of the stocks in Problems 3 and 4 would you rather own? (Be careful, this is a trick question.)

6. a. A stock portfolio consists entirely of two stocks, Bonnie Corp. and Clyde, Inc. Using the following data, calculate the standard deviation of the portfolio.

Standard Deviations of Two-Stock Portfolios
6. a. 19.78%

$$CORR_{BC} = 0.74$$

BONNIE		CLYDE
$700	Amount invested	$300
0.19	Standard deviation	0.26

b. If you wanted to increase the risk of your portfolio, what would you do?
c. Make the changes in part (b) and recalculate the portfolio standard deviation.
d. Why might you want to increase the risk of your portfolio?

7. a. A stock portfolio consists entirely of two stocks, Calhoun Corp. and Davenport, Inc. Using the following data, calculate the standard deviation of the portfolio.

Standard Deviations of Two-Stock Portfolios
7. a. 16.11%
b. 18.00% (CORR = 1); 12.76% (CORR = 0)

$$CORR_{CD} = 0.6$$

CALHOUN		DAVENPORT
$600	Amount invested	$400
0.16	Standard deviation	0.21

b. Recalculate the portfolio standard deviation assuming correlations of 0 and 1, respectively.
c. Using your answers in parts (a) and (b), what can you conclude about the effect of correlation on portfolio standard deviation?

d. Suppose you wanted the greatest possible portfolio risk (and, presumably, return). What proportions of each stock would you have in your portfolio?

8. A portfolio consists only of the common stocks of Saybrook, Inc., and Silliman Corp.

SAYBROOK		SILLIMAN
0.35	Portfolio weighting	0.65
0.27	Standard deviation	0.14

The Effect of Correlation on Portfolio Standard Deviation
8. a. 18.55%
b. 18.55% (CORR = 1); 16.07% (CORR = 0.5); 13.12% (CORR = 0)

a. Calculate the weighted average portfolio standard deviation using the data supplied. (Do not use the equation for the standard deviation of a portfolio.)
b. Calculate portfolio standard deviations for correlations of 0, 0.5 and 1.
c. What can you conclude about the effect of correlation on portfolio standard deviation?

9. A stock portfolio consists entirely of two stocks, Branford Corp. and Berkeley, Inc. The correlation between their returns is −0.4 (negative correlation). The standard deviation of Branford's returns is 0.19, and that for Berkeley's returns is 0.13.
a. By changing the proportion of each stock in the portfolio, find the proportions that minimize portfolio risk. Use trial and error, and remember that the proportions must add up to 1.
b. Repeat part (a) assuming a correlation of +0.4 (positive correlation).
c. What can you conclude from your answers in parts (a) and (b)?

Constructing a Minimum-Risk Portfolio
9. a. 13.00% (Branford = 0); 19.00% (Branford = 1)

10. For two stocks $r_A = 0.1$, $r_B = 0.2$, $CORR_{AB} = 0.4$, $SD_A = 0.3$, and $SD_B = 0.8$.
a. What are the expected returns and standard deviations of portfolios consisting entirely of A and entirely of B?
b. Now vary the proportions of A and B as follows:

Risk and return of Two-Stock Portfolios
10. a. SD = 80.0%, $E(r)$ = 20% (A = 0); SD = 30.0%, $E(r)$ = 10% (A = 1)

A	B
0.2	0.8
0.4	0.6
0.6	0.4
0.8	0.2

Calculate portfolio standard deviation and expected return for these different proportions.
c. Using a graph as in Figure 7.5, plot the portfolio risk and return points for parts (a) and (b), and connect your points. You may use either graph paper or the graphing function of a spreadsheet program.

Risk and Return of Two-Stock Portfolios
11. a. SD = 80.0%, $E(r)$ = 20% (A = 0); SD = 30.0%, $E(r)$ = 10% (A = 1)

11. Repeat Problem 10, but assume that the returns on stocks A and B are perfectly correlated: $\text{CORR}_{AB} = 1$.

The Effect of Correlation on Portfolio Risk

12. **a.** For each set of portfolios in Problems 10 and 11, identify the efficient set.
b. Which set of portfolios would you rather have, those in Problem 10 or Problem 11? Why?
c. Why are the shapes of the portfolio sets different?

Risk and Return of Two-Stock Portfolios
13. a. SD = 18.0%, $E(r)$ = 17% (A = 0); SD = 14.0%, $E(r)$ = 12% (A = 1)

13. For two stocks $r_A = 0.12$, $r_B = 0.17$, $\text{CORR}_{AB} = -0.4$ (negative correlation), $\text{SD}_A = 0.14$, and $\text{SD}_B = 0.18$.
a. Calculate the expected return and standard deviation of portfolios consisting entirely of A and entirely of B.
b. Now vary the proportions of A and B as follows:

A	B
0.2	0.8
0.4	0.6
0.6	0.4
0.8	0.2

Recalculate the portfolio standard deviation and expected return for these different proportions.
c. Using a graph as in Figure 7.5, plot the portfolio risk and return points for parts a and b, and connect your points. You may use either graph paper or the graphing function of a spreadsheet program.

Risk and Return of Two-Stock Portfolios
14. a. SD = 18.0%, $E(r)$ = 17% (A = 0); SD = 14.0%, $E(r)$ = 12% (A = 1)

14. Repeat Problem 13 but assume that the returns on stocks A and B are perfectly correlated: $\text{CORR}_{AB} = 1$.

The Effect of Correlation on Portfolio Risk

15. **a.** For each set of portfolios in Problems 13 and 14, identify the efficient set.
b. Which set of portfolios would you rather have, those in Problem 13 or Problem 14? Why?
c. Why are the shapes of the portfolio sets different?

Standard Deviations of Two-Stock Portfolios
16. 23.10%

16. Calculate the standard deviation of a portfolio consisting of 70% stock A and 30% stock B.

$$\text{SD}_A = 0.28$$

$$\text{SD}_B = 0.14$$

$$\text{CORR}_{AB} = 0.8$$

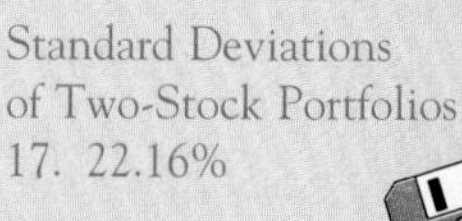

Standard Deviations of Two-Stock Portfolios
17. 22.16%

17. Calculate the standard deviation of a portfolio consisting of 70% stock A and 30% stock B.

$$SD_A = 0.29$$

$$SD_B = 0.19$$

$$CORR_{AB} = 0.2$$

18. What conclusions can you draw from your answers in Problems 16 and 17?

Standard Deviations of Two-Stock Portfolios

19. A portfolio consists of the following four stocks:

STOCK	AVERAGE RETURN	STANDARD DEVIATION OF RETURNS
A	6%	14%
B	14	11
C	10	18
D	11	27

Assume that the portfolio consists of equal values of the four stocks.

a. Calculate portfolio return.
b. Calculate the weighted average of the stocks' standard deviations.
c. In part (b), have you calculated portfolio standard deviation? Why or why not?

Returns and Standard Deviations of Portfolios of More Than Two Stocks
19. a. 10.25%
b. 17.50%

20. In Problem 19

a. What additional information would you need to find the portfolio standard deviation?
b. Which of the following is the only possible portfolio standard deviation?
i. 18% **ii.** 16% **iii.** 20%

Returns and Standard Deviations of Portfolios of More Than Two Stocks
20. b. 16%.

21. A portfolio consists of the following four stocks:

STOCK	AVERAGE RETURN	STANDARD DEVIATION OF RETURNS
A	9%	7%
B	13	12
C	17	19
D	11	10

Assume that the portfolio consists of equal values of the four stocks.

a. Calculate portfolio return.
b. Calculate the weighted average of the stocks' standard deviations.
c. In part (b), have you calculated portfolio standard deviation? Why or why not?

Returns and Standard Deviations of Portfolios of More Than Two Stocks
21. a. 12.5%
b. 12.0%

22. In Problem 21

a. What additional information would you need to find the portfolio standard deviation?
b. Which of the following is the only possible portfolio standard deviation?
i. 15% **ii.** 13% **iii.** 10%

Returns and Standard Deviations of Portfolios of More Than Two Stocks
22. b. 10%.

Calculating Covariance

An alternative method of calculating covariance is shown here. This method does not rely on prior calculations of standard deviation and correlation. Covariance is the mean of the product of the deviations of annual returns from their means. Covariance of Union Camp and the S&P 500 is calculated.

COVARIANCE CALCULATION UNION CAMP AND THE S&P 500

	(1) RETURN UNION CAMP	(2) RETURN S&P 500	(3) RETURN—MEAN UNION CAMP	(4) RETURN—MEAN S&P 500	(5) COL. (3) TIMES COL. (4)
			ruc − xuc	rsp − xsp	(ruc − xuc)(rsp − xsp)
1979	−0.071	0.184	−0.198	0.016	−0.003
1980	0.256	0.324	0.129	0.156	0.020
1981	0.033	−0.049	−0.094	−0.217	0.020
1982	0.263	0.214	0.137	0.046	0.006
1983	0.409	0.225	0.282	0.057	0.016
1984	−0.112	0.063	−0.239	−0.105	0.025
1985	0.158	0.322	0.032	0.153	0.005
1986	0.313	0.185	0.186	0.017	0.003
1987	0.090	0.052	−0.037	−0.116	0.004
1988	−0.028	0.168	−0.155	0.000	0.000
1989	0.101	0.315	−0.026	0.147	−0.004
1990	−0.003	−0.032	−0.130	−0.200	0.026
1991	0.419	0.306	0.293	0.137	0.040
1992	−0.053	0.077	−0.180	−0.091	0.016
mean = x	0.127	0.168			0.013

Covariance is .013.

APPENDIX 7B

Using Matrices to Calculate Portfolio Standard Deviation

Matrices simply provide an orderly way of arraying data. They allow complex calculations to be broken down into several simpler calculations. In calculating standard deviations of portfolios containing many stocks, an algebraic solution, such as Equation (7.5), becomes unwieldy. Exhibits 7A1 and 7A2 show 2 by 2 or 4 cell matrices for Black and Decker and Stone Container.

w_B = weighting Black & Decker

w_S = weighting Stone Container

SD_B = standard deviation Black & Decker

SD_S = standard deviation Stone Container

The cell values are the products of the weights and standard deviations for each stock. Notice in Exhibit 7A.1 that the top left cell contains values for Black & Decker, and the bottom right cell contains values for Stone Container. The other two cells combine both stocks. In these cells, the standard deviations are multiplied in a special way. ($SD_B \times SD_S$) yields $(SD_B)(SD_S)(CORR_{BS})$, which equals COV_{BS}.

Exhibit 7A.2 is a variance-covariance matrix. The variance terms are at the top left and bottom right. Notice also that the two covariance cells are identical because the Black-Stone covariance equals the Stone-Black covariance, or $COV_{BS} = COV_{SB}$.

We use the variance-covariance matrix to calculate portfolio standard deviation by first calculating the cell values and then summing those values to obtain portfolio variance.[27] The square root of variance is standard deviation.

[27]The summed cells yield variance because we are multiplying standard deviations in each cell. Recall that $SD \times SD = SD^2$ = variance.

EXHIBIT 7A.1

PRODUCT MATRIX INCLUDING CORRELATION

	w_B SD_B	w_S SD_S
w_B SD_B	$(w^2_B)(SD^2_B)$	$(w_B)(w_S)(SD_B)(SD_S)(CORR_{BS})$
w_S SD_S	$(w_B)(w_S)(SD_B)(SD_S)(CORR_{BS})$	$(w^2_S)(SD^2_S)$

EXHIBIT 7A.2

THE VARIANCE-COVARIANCE PRODUCT MATRIX

	w_B SD_B	w_S SD_S
w_B SD_B	$(w^2_B)(SD^2_B)$	$(w_B)(w_S)(COV_{BS})$
w_S SD_S	$(w_B)(w_S)(COV_{BS})$	$(w^2_S)(SD^2_S)$

For Black and Stone, the matrix is

	Black	Stone
Black	$(0.5)^2(0.335)^2 = 0.028$	$(0.5)(0.5)(0.148) = 0.037$
Stone	$(0.5)(0.5)(0.148) = 0.037$	$(0.5)^2(0.532)^2 = 0.071$

Summing the values produces portfolio variance.

$$0.028 + 0.037 + 0.037 + 0.071 = 0.173$$

Portfolio standard deviation is

$$\sqrt{0.173} = 0.416$$

This is exactly the same result obtained using Equation (7.5).

When we add a third stock to our portfolio, the matrix contains nine cells—three rows and three columns. To illustrate a three-stock portfolio, we will add Cincinnati Milacron to our portfolio. This new portfolio contains equal proportions of Black & Decker, Stone Container, and Cincinnati Milacron.

	Black	Stone	Cincinnati
Black	$(w_B^2)(SD_B^2)$	$(w_B)(w_S)(COV_{BS})$	$(w_B)(w_C)(COV_{BC})$
Stone	$(w_B)(w_S)(COV_{BS})$	$(w_S^2)SD_S^2)$	$(w_S)(w_C)(COV_{SC})$
Cincinnati	$(w_B)(w_C)(COV_{BC})$	$(w_S)(w_C)(COV_{SC})$	$(w_C^2)(SD_C^2)$

As with the two-stock matrix, portfolio standard deviation is the square root of the sum of the cells. The added information needed to accommodate the new stock is

$$SD_C = 0.338$$

$$CORR_{BC} = 0.394$$

$$CORR_{SC} = 0.433$$

$$w_B = \tfrac{1}{3}$$

$$w_S = \tfrac{1}{3}$$

$$w_C = \tfrac{1}{3}$$

$$\text{COV}_{BC} = (0.335)(0.338)(0.394) = 0.045$$

$$\text{COV}_{SC} = (0.532)(0.338)(0.433) = 0.078$$

	Black	Stone	Cincinnati
Black	$(\frac{1}{3})^2(0.335)^2$	$(\frac{1}{3})(\frac{1}{3})(0.148)$	$(\frac{1}{3})(\frac{1}{3})(0.045)$
Stone	$(\frac{1}{3})(\frac{1}{3})(0.148)$	$(\frac{1}{3})^2(0.532)^2$	$(\frac{1}{3})(\frac{1}{3})(0.078)$
Cincinnati	$(\frac{1}{3})(\frac{1}{3})(0.045)$	$(\frac{1}{3})(\frac{1}{3})(0.078)$	$(\frac{1}{3})^2(0.338)^2$

This matrix contains three variance cells on the diagonal from top left to bottom right and six covariance cells. Summing these cell values produces a portfolio variance of 0.117. Portfolio standard deviation is the square root of the variance:

$$\sqrt{0.117} = 0.342$$

CHAPTER 8

Required Rates of Return in the Capital Market

Why invest with these places when I'm getting 100 percent on my investments . . . guaranteed!

The loan shark is able to earn exorbitant rates of return with little risk of loss by using unconventional (and illegal) collection techniques. Most people, however, invest in competitive (and legal) capital markets, where high expected returns are obtained only by making high risk investments.

n this chapter, we build upon the discussion of portfolios in Chapter 7 to determine the required return on individual securities. The conclusions reached in this chapter may be generalized to all securities; however, we continue to focus on the stock market. First, we develop a measure of the market risk of stocks. This risk measure is called beta, and it is the centerpiece of a simple, but elegant, risk-return model, called the capital asset pricing model. We then use this model to produce estimates of the required returns for common stocks. Later in the chapter, we demonstrate several applications of the capital asset pricing model.

THE RISKINESS OF INDIVIDUAL STOCKS

The relevant risk of a stock held in a diversified portfolio is the amount of risk the stock contributes to the portfolio.

In Chapter 7, we concluded that well-diversified portfolios contain only market risk. Individual stocks contain both unique and market risk, but diversified portfolios effectively cancel stocks' unique risk. Therefore, investors are concerned only with stocks' market risk. As we suggested in Chapter 7, stocks contain different amounts of market risk. For example, home builders are more affected than most companies by changes in market rates of interest. Companies producing staples, such as food, are probably less affected by recession than those producing household appliances. The market risk of a portfolio is the average of the market risks of its component stocks. Each stock, therefore, contributes to overall portfolio market risk. In this chapter, we develop a measure of the risk that each stock contributes to the portfolio.

This is not a strict equality; however, point out that the major stock market indexes move together. Have students watch the nightly news or check the daily newspaper for daily changes in the DJIA, S&P 500, NASDAQ, and the NYSE composite index.

In Chapter 7 we saw that the returns of the sample portfolio of common stocks, and virtually all diversified stock portfolios, are highly correlated with those of the S&P 500. The S&P 500, in turn, is considered to be representative of the stock market as a whole.[1] With this in mind, we may propose a rough identity with regard to portfolio risk and return.

$$\textbf{stock market} \approx \textbf{S\&P 500} \approx \textbf{a typical diversified stock portfolio}$$

Using this identity, we will take the S&P 500 as our typical portfolio in determining how stocks affect portfolio risk.

ESTIMATING THE MARKET RISK OF AN INDIVIDUAL STOCK

Estimating a Stock's Market Risk—Method 1

Beta may be estimated by Equation (8.1) or by constructing a characteristic line.

In Chapter 7, we pointed out that calculating standard deviations for portfolios containing many stocks is unwieldy because of the many covariance calculations required. Constructing a portfolio from a population of 1,000 stocks requires

[1]We should point out that the S&P 500 is more representative of stocks of large rather than small companies. These so-called small-cap stocks, *cap* meaning capitalization, generally have greater risk and return than large company stocks.

nearly a half million calculations, and including all traded stocks in the U.S. requires about 35 million calculations.

In the 1960s, economist William F. Sharpe and others developed a process for simplifying these calculations. In doing so, they transported portfolio theory from academe to Wall Street and transformed modern finance.[2]

Suppose our portfolio is the S&P 500. To determine how much risk a particular stock contributes to the portfolio, we must calculate the covariances between the returns of that stock and all 499 other stocks in the S&P 500. Sharpe reasoned that we could accomplish the same thing by simply calculating the covariance between returns of the individual stock and the S&P 500 index itself. Thus, he was able to substitute one calculation for hundreds.

By dividing the covariance of the stock with the S&P 500 by the variance of the S&P 500, Sharpe produced a standardized measure, or index, of a stock's risk. This index number is called **beta**. To find beta (*B*) for stock (S),

$$B_S = \frac{COV_{S,S\&P500}}{VAR_{SP500}} \tag{8.1}$$

Beta measures the sensitivity of a stock's returns to overall market returns, using the S&P 500 as a proxy, or substitute, for the market. As we pointed out in Chapter 7, market returns reflect general economic and social conditions. High-beta securities are those that are very sensitive to these general conditions. Stocks that are less affected have lower betas.

Beta has two important attributes. First, it is easy to calculate using available data on stock and S&P 500 returns. Secondly, it is a standardized risk measure, meaning that the beta for any stock may be compared to the beta of any other stock.[3]

It is important to calculate beta as accurately as possible. Therefore, it is common to collect returns data for the stock and the S&P 500 for the most recent 60 months.[4] Exhibit 8.1 shows monthly returns for the 5 years ending in 1992 for United Technologies and the S&P 500. These data yield the following statistics:

$$SD_{United} = 0.0631$$

$$SD_{SP500} = 0.0386$$

$$CORR_{United,SP500} = 0.7375$$

The covariance is calculated using Equation (7.4).[5]

$$COV_{United,SP500} = 0.0018$$

[2]Sharpe drew upon the earlier work of Harry Markowitz, who developed portfolio theory. For their work they shared the Nobel Prize in Economic Science in 1990. This work is chronicled in a most interesting way in Peter L. Bernstein, *Capital Ideas: The Improbable Origins of Modern Wall Street*, (New York: Free Press, 1992).

[3]What makes it standardized is that each stock's covariance is divided by a common denominator, the variance of the S&P 500.

[4]Returns include price changes and dividends.

[5]$COV_{(United,SP500)} = CORR_{(United,SP500)} SD_{United} SD_{SP500}$.

EXHIBIT 8.1

CALCULATING BETA FOR UNITED TECHNOLOGIES

Estimate the beta for United Technologies.

	MONTHLY RETURNS			MONTHLY RETURNS	
	UNITED	S&P 500		UNITED	S&P 500
Jan. 88	0.133	0.043	Sep. 90	−0.125	−0.049
Feb. 88	0.071	0.047	Oct. 90	0.056	−0.004
Mar. 88	−0.043	−0.030	Nov. 90	−0.001	0.064
Apr. 88	−0.003	0.011	Dec. 90	0.073	0.027
May 88	−0.025	0.008	Jan. 91	−0.008	0.044
Jun. 88	0.027	0.046	Feb. 91	0.057	0.072
Jul. 88	−0.026	−0.004	Mar. 91	−0.025	0.024
Aug. 88	−0.009	−0.033	Apr. 91	−0.052	0.003
Sep. 88	0.085	0.042	May 91	0.029	0.043
Oct. 88	0.044	0.027	Jun. 91	−0.051	−0.046
Nov. 88	−0.026	−0.014	Jul. 91	0.048	0.047
Dec. 88	0.025	0.018	Aug. 91	0.036	0.024
Jan. 89	0.073	0.072	Sep. 91	−0.060	−0.016
Feb. 89	0.001	−0.025	Oct. 91	0.081	0.013
Mar. 89	0.040	0.024	Nov. 91	−0.011	−0.040
Apr. 89	0.143	0.052	Dec. 91	0.139	0.114
May 89	−0.004	0.040	Jan. 92	−0.065	−0.019
Jun. 89	−0.022	−0.005	Feb. 92	0.003	0.013
Jul. 89	0.092	0.090	Mar. 92	0.032	−0.020
Aug. 89	0.023	0.019	Apr. 92	0.038	0.029
Sep. 89	−0.002	−0.004	May 92	−0.019	0.005
Oct. 89	−0.040	−0.023	Jun. 92	−0.005	−0.015
Nov. 89	−0.023	0.021	Jul. 92	0.091	0.040
Dec. 89	0.048	0.024	Aug. 92	−0.027	−0.020
Jan. 90	−0.081	−0.067	Sep. 92	−0.109	0.012
Feb. 90	0.034	0.013	Oct. 92	−0.066	0.004
Mar. 90	0.120	0.026	Nov. 92	−0.009	0.034
Apr. 90	−0.039	−0.025	Dec. 92	0.072	0.013
May 90	0.074	0.098			
Jun. 90	−0.023	−0.007		COV	.0018
Jul. 90	0.035	−0.003		CORR	.7375
Aug. 90	−0.168	−0.090		Calc. beta	1.19

Using Equation (8.1), beta = 0.0018/0.0015 = 1.19. The denominator (0.0015) is the square of SD_{SP500}.

With a little effort, nearly anyone can calculate betas for a large number of stocks. The calculation itself is relatively simple, using familiar Chapter 7 concepts; monthly returns of virtually all traded stocks and the S&P 500 are available in print and on computer data bases.[6]

Estimating a Stock's Market Risk—Method 2

Beta may also be estimated using regression analysis, which is a common technique for determining the relationship between two variables. In this case, the variables are stock returns and S&P 500 returns.

[6]Standard & Poor's Daily Price Records from the New York and American Stock Exchanges, and from NASDAQ provide data in print. Market data is available in the Ibbotson Associates yearbooks cited in chapter 7. Popular on-line computer services, such as Compuserve provide access to stock and market data, for a price.

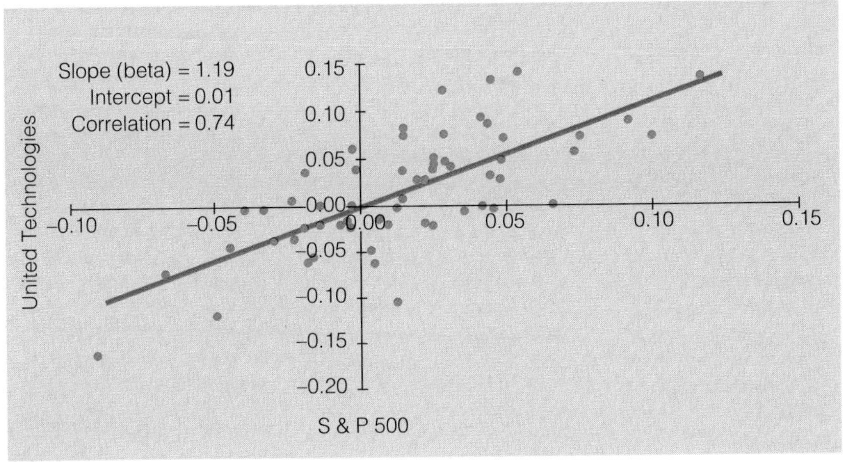

FIGURE 8.1

PLOTTING MONTHLY STOCK RETURNS: UNITED TECHNOLOGIES VERSUS THE S&P 500

Transparency Available

Figure 8.1 shows a graph in which monthly returns of United Technologies stock appear on the vertical axis and the corresponding monthly returns of the S&P 500 appear on the horizontal axis.

The slope of the regression line is beta. The beta of 1.19 indicates that the return on United Technologies stocks is 1.19 times the return on the S&P 500.

The regression line relating stock returns to market returns is called the **characteristic line**. Beta is the slope of the characteristic line.[7] The slope of the line in Figure 8.1 is 1.19, which is identical to the beta calculated using Equation (8.1). This value indicates that every 1% return for the S&P 500 would, on average, result in a 1.19% return for United Technologies stock. For example, if the return on the S&P 500 were 10%, then we would expect that the return for United Technologies would be 11%, in other words, 1.19 times the market's return.

If the returns on the S&P 500 and United Technologies were perfectly correlated, all plots would be on the characteristic line. The scatter plot indicates that the market is not the sole determinant of stock returns.

The relationship between returns on the stock and the S&P 500 is imperfect. If United Technologies' returns were perfectly linked to the S&P 500 returns, then all the points would fall on the regression line. If this were the case, United Technologies would contain only market risk, and we would be certain of the relationship. However, because United Technologies has some nonmarket risk associated with its returns, the regression line is not a perfect fit.

Exhibit 8.2 shows beta calculations for our 20 sample stocks, along with betas calculated by Standard & Poors. Standard & Poors, Merrill Lynch, and many other financial services companies produce estimates of beta for thousands of common stocks. These companies calculate beta much as we have; however, they may use proprietary methods of analyzing the returns data. Nonetheless, the resulting betas tend to be similar, as seen in Exhibit 8.2.

Although betas are calculated from historical data, it is really the future that is of interest to investors. When we use historical betas to evaluate stocks' riskiness, we are assuming that these betas will not change very much in the future. However, betas do change over time because of corporate restructuring as well as changes in products, markets, and technologies.

[7]The slope of the regression line is

$$\frac{\text{vertical movement}}{\text{horizontal movement}}$$

EXHIBIT 8.2

THERE IS MORE THAN ONE ESTIMATED BETA

	CALCULATED BETA	REPORTED BETA[1]
Black & Decker	1.7	1.6
Boeing	1.1	1.2
Brown & Sharpe	0.8	1.0
Capital Holding	1.6	1.3
Cincinnati Milacron	1.7	1.6
Citicorp	1.0	1.1
Enron	0.3	0.7
Fleet Financial	1.6	1.2
Fleming Co.	0.7	0.9
Gannett Co.	1.3	1.2
Golden West	2.1	2.1
Melville Corp.	1.1	1.2
Pennzoil	0.4	0.4
Polaroid	1.0	1.1
Quaker Oats	0.5	0.6
Stone Container	1.8	1.8
Tandy Corp	1.5	1.3
Union Camp	1.0	1.0
United Technologies	1.2	1.2
Warner-Lambert	1.0	1.1
Average[2]	1.1	1.1
S&P 500	1.0	1.0

[1]*S&P Corporate Reports* (January 1993).

[2]Betas shown are rounded.

Interpreting Beta

The beta of a diversified portfolio is approximately 1. Stocks with betas greater than 1 increase portfolio risk.

Beta's virtue is that it measures the amount of market risk an individual stock contributes to a portfolio. The higher the beta, the greater the risk. However, to find out whether a particular stock will increase or decrease the risk of a diversified portfolio, we must know the risk of the portfolio, as measured by beta. The S&P 500's beta may be determined using Equation 8.1.

$$B_{SP500} = \frac{COV_{SP500,SP500}}{VAR_{SP500}}$$

$$COV_{SP500,SP500} = CORR_{SP500,SP500}SD_{SP500}SD_{SP500}$$

$$CORR_{SP500,SP500} = 1, \text{ and } SD_{SP500}SD_{SP500} = VAR_{SP500}$$

So Equation (8.1) reduces to $B_{SP500} = VAR_{SP500}/VAR_{SP500} = 1$.[8]

As you can see, the beta of the S&P 500 is 1. The beta of United Technologies stock is 1.19, which means that if it were added to such a portfolio, it would slightly increase the portfolio's risk. We saw earlier that a 1% increase in return of the S&P 500 is associated with a 1.19% increase in return of United Technologies. This relationship also works in the negative, so that a market loss would be accompanied by an even larger stock loss, thus increasing the risk. Similarly, stock betas of less than 1 would decrease the risk of an average portfolio.

[8]Using regression produces the same result. The slope of the line regressing returns on the S&P 500 against itself is 1.

Beta is the second measure of stock risk that we have encountered. The first is the variance, or standard deviation, of stock returns, which measures a stock's total risk. By contrast, beta measures only market risk. The difference between the two is unique risk.

total risk = market risk + unique risk

Total risk, measured by standard deviation, is the risk of a stock that is not part of a diversified portfolio. *Market risk*, measured by beta, is the risk of a stock in a diversified portfolio. *Unique risk* is eliminated from a diversified portfolio.

The standard deviation measures total risk, which is appropriate for a stock not held in a diversified portfolio. The beta measure of market risk is the appropriate risk measure for stocks held in a diversified portfolio.

Stocks with high total risk do not necessarily have high betas, and vice versa. The oil industry provides an example of this. Most would agree that oil exploration is a risky business. Yet this does not mean that betas in this industry are high. This result is because the probability of striking oil is independent of inflation, recession, and other forces that drive the national economy and the stock market. By contrast, oil refining and distribution companies, such as Exxon and Texaco, have much less total risk; however, their stock returns are tied to the demand for petroleum products, which, in turn, is tied to economic conditions in the United States and around the world. Betas for these companies may very well be higher than those for the exploration and drilling companies.

Stocks, whose returns are very volatile (high total risk), do not necessarily have high betas (high market risk).

Portfolio Betas

Although the beta of the average diversified stock portfolio is 1, this isn't true for all portfolios. A good example is a mutual fund that specializes in stocks of a particular industry, such as health care or banking. These are called **sector funds**, and their betas reflect the average betas for these industries rather than the market as a whole.[9]

The precise beta of a particular portfolio may be calculated by taking the weighted average of the betas of the stocks in the portfolio. The formula is

$$B_P = w_1B_1 + w_2B_2 + w_3B_3 + \cdots + w_NB_N \tag{8.2}$$

Portfolio betas may vary greatly from 1 if its stocks are not diversified across industries or if stocks are held in proportions that over represent some industries and under represent others.

where N is the total number of stocks in the portfolio, $w_1, w_2, w_3, \ldots, w_N$ are the proportions of total funds invested in each of the N stocks, and $B_1, B_2, B_3, \ldots, B_N$ are the betas.

The beta of the 20-stock sample portfolio shown in Exhibit 8.2, 1.1, is the average of all the stocks' betas. In this case, we assumed an equal investment in each stock and found the portfolio beta by multiplying each stock's beta by $\frac{1}{20}$ and adding. By changing the proportions of stocks, we are able to create portfolios of varying risk. For instance, high-risk portfolios would have greater proportions of stocks such as Golden West Financial (beta = 2.1) and Stone Container (beta = 1.8), whereas low-risk portfolios would have greater proportions of stocks such as Pennzoil (beta = 0.4) and Quaker Oats (beta = 0.5). These portfolios may still be diversified, but their betas will no longer be close to 1 because we have purposely changed their risk.

[9]These funds also contain unique risk because they are not well diversified.

With the risk-return relationship that exists in the capital markets, low betas are associated with low returns and high betas, with high returns. Investors can use this knowledge to tailor their portfolios to match their individual risk-return preferences. For example, common-stock investors may choose to load their portfolios with either high-beta or low-beta stocks. Mutual funds provide a good example of portfolio risk management. Most common-stock mutual funds hold diversified portfolios, which means that they virtually eliminate unique risk. However, even diversified funds may pursue very different risk-return objectives, ranging from high-risk aggressive growth funds to low-risk income funds emphasizing dividends.

RISK AND RETURN OF INDIVIDUAL SECURITIES

The Security Market Line

In this section we combine the beta measure of risk with our understanding of the risk-return trade-off in the capital markets to produce a risk-return function for individual securities. Once again, we confine our discussion to common stocks.

Risk is defined as standard deviation on the CML and beta on the SML. Beta is also the slope of the characteristic line.

Figure 8.2 is a graph of a risk-return function, called the *security market line* (SML). At first glance, it appears similar to the capital market line (CML) in Chapter 7 (Figure 7.11). Indeed, both have a positive slope, indicating that investors require higher returns for greater risk, and both intersect the vertical axis at the risk-free return. However, the CML deals with portfolios whose risk is measured by standard deviation, whereas the SML deals with individual securities whose risk is measured by beta.

The security market line for a prior period is easily constructed from market data. In this case, we used a 60-month average rate of return on U.S. treasury bills as the risk-free return.[10] For the period 1988–1992, this rate was 6.3%. For

FIGURE 8.2

THE SECURITY MARKET LINE

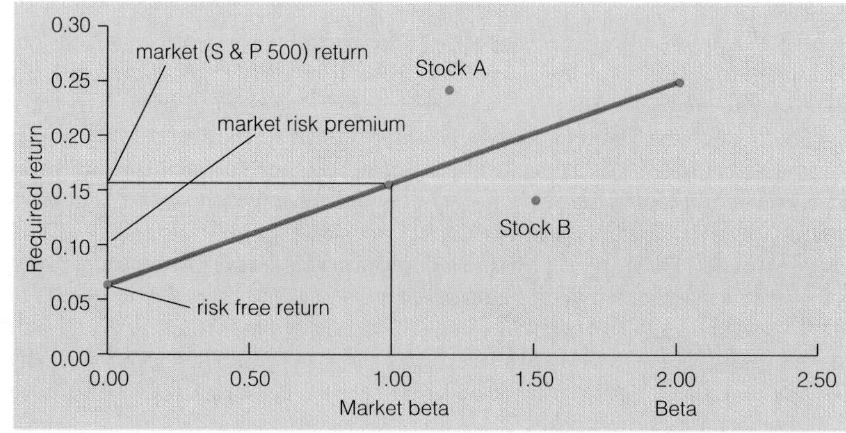

Transparency Available

[10]Some analysts prefer to use rates of return on long-term treasury bonds, reasoning that maturities on these bonds more closely match those of stocks. Others feel that there may be some risk attached to long-term Treasuries and therefore prefer short-term Treasury bills.

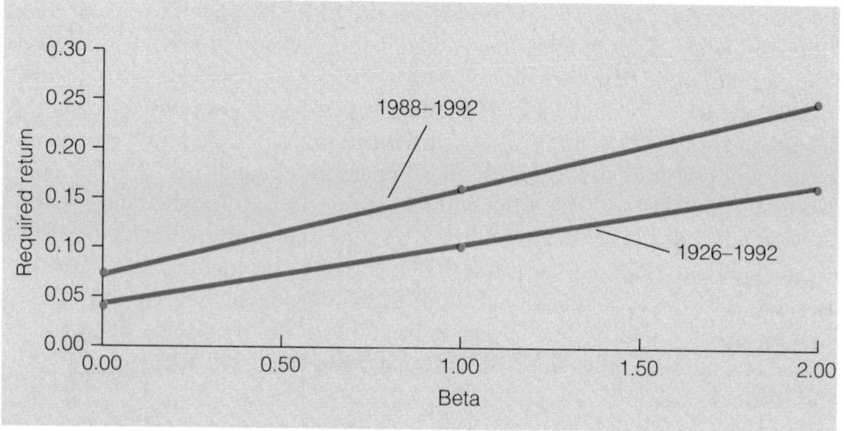

FIGURE 8.3

SECURITY MARKET LINES FOR TWO HISTORICAL PERIODS

this same period, the average rate of return on the S&P 500 was 15.9%.[11] Treasury bills are presumed to have no risk, so their beta is 0, whereas the beta for the S&P 500 is 1. With these two rates and their betas, we can construct the SML shown in Figure 8.2.[12]

The difference between the rate of return on the S&P 500 of 15.9% and the return on Treasury bills of 6.3% is called the **market risk premium**. The concept of a **risk premium** is used frequently in finance. Think of it as the added return necessary to compensate investors for taking risk. The market risk premium (15.9% − 6.3% = 9.6%) is an average risk premium for all stocks. Later, we will learn about risk premiums for individual stocks.

Explain the concept of a risk premium as the added return required for taking added risk.

Market risk premiums and risk-free rates change over time, affecting the slope and the position of the SML. For example, for the long period 1926–1992, stocks returned an average of 10.3% and Treasury bills returned an average of only 3.7%, creating a market risk premium of 6.6%.[13] Figure 8.3 shows the security market lines for 1926–1992 and 1988–1992. The risk-free return for 1988–1992 is higher, and the slope of the line is steeper. A steeper slope indicates a higher market risk premium, whereas a higher risk-free rate indicates higher short-term interest rates. Therefore, during 1988 through 92, the market risk premium and interest rates were higher than their long-term averages.

Attraction of Securities to the SML

The security market line specifies a relationship between risk, represented by beta, and the required return on securities. If return were determined entirely by beta, then the actual returns of all securities would lie on the SML. For instance, using the SML in Figure 8.2, a stock with a beta of 1 should be priced to have a rate of return of about 16%. To understand why, let's consider two stocks that, for some reason, are mispriced and lie off the SML. These are stocks A and B in Figure 8.2. Stock A's beta is slightly greater than 1, meaning that its return should

[11]Both rates are from *Stocks, Bonds, Bills and Inflation, 1993 Yearbook*, (Chicago: Ibbotson Associates, 1993).

[12]We have found two points and have, therefore, defined a straight line.

[13]*Stocks, Bonds, 1993 Yearbook.*

be slightly greater than 16%, if it were on the SML. However, its actual return is much higher. Such a stock offers a windfall opportunity to the alert investor. She can earn more than the required return while enduring no more than average risk. However, in an efficient market, many investors will soon discover stock A. These investors will bid for this stock, driving its price up. As a result, its expected return will fall until it is equal to all other stocks of equal risk. At that point, bidding will cease, and the stock will lie on the SML. In finance jargon, stock A was undervalued because its price was too low (its return too high) for its risk.

Stock B is overvalued, meaning that its price is too high and its return too low. Once investors conclude that the stock is overvalued, they will want to sell. However, there will be few buyers at this high price. Thus, the price will be forced down, raising the expected return, and this stock will approach the SML, just as stock A did.

The SML is a magnet, attracting stocks to the line. The strength of the magnet is determined by the market's competitiveness and efficiency. Because the market is not perfect, not all stocks lie on the line.

It may be useful to think of the SML as a magnet, tending to pull errant stocks back onto the line. The magnet is energized by an efficient stock market, and the market is kept efficient by the flow of information. Economists explain such a market as one tending toward equilibrium, with equilibrium occurring when all stocks lie on the SML. In Chapter 2 we explained that efficient, competitive markets provide little opportunity to investors seeking extraordinary returns. However, they provide ample opportunity to earn "fair" rates of return that adequately compensate investors for risk.

Usefulness of the SML

Although we have described the SML using only stocks, it applies to all securities that trade in relatively efficient markets and are at least partial substitutes for stocks. This includes most well-known securities, such as corporate bonds and options. Most corporate bonds have less risk and return than stocks and would lie on the SML to the left of stocks. Stock options are more risky than stocks and would lie on the SML to the right of stocks.[14]

The security market line provides a snapshot of risk and return relationships in the capital markets at a moment in time. In fact, the markets are dynamic, continually reacting to new information and adjusting estimates of risk and required rates of return. As a result, the SML itself adjusts; and these adjustments are reflected in changing market risk premiums and risk-free returns.

The "magnetic" attraction of the SML does not ensure that all securities lie on the SML all the time. The attraction of the SML is only as strong as the capital markets are efficient and competitive. Because these markets are not perfectly competitive or completely efficient, there are occasional opportunities for alert investors to discover undervalued stocks, such as stock A in Figure 8.2. However, to draw an historical analogy to the gold rushes in California and the Yukon, the potential rewards are great, but such opportunities are quickly identified and exploited. Only a very few of the tens of thousands of gold prospectors struck it rich. Some made a modest living and others went broke. So it is in the stock market for those who attempt to pick mispriced stocks hoping for an extraordinary return.

---

[14]Options are more risky because the investment required to buy an option is only a small fraction of the value of the stock itself. It has the same effect as if the investor were borrowing, or using leverage, to acquire stocks. Options were introduced in Chapter 3.

THE CAPITAL ASSET PRICING MODEL

Deriving the CAPM from the SML

Next, we derive an equation for the security market line. Because the SML is a straight line, only simple algebra is required. Once we have specified the equation, we will see that it is a handy tool for understanding the relationship between risk and return in the capital markets.

In Figure 8.4 we have redrawn the SML and converted names in Figure 8.2 to notation. This process makes it easier to write an equation. We have designated the market risk premium as $E(r_m) - r_f$ and have designated the required return on stock S, $R(r_s)$.

FIGURE 8.2	FIGURE 8.4
Required return on stock S(y axis)	$R(r_s)$
Beta (x axis)	B_s
Expected return on the market portfolio	$E(r_m)$
Return on the risk-free asset	r_f

Because the return on the market portfolio is risky, this is an *expected* return. The return on the risk-free asset is certain. We begin with a generic equation of a straight line, $y = a + bx$, where a is the y intercept and b is the slope. Substituting our own notation produces the following equation:

$$y = a + (b)x$$

$$R(r_s) = r_f + [E(r_m) - r_f]B_s \tag{8.3}$$

$$R(r_s) = r_f + B_s[E(r_m) - r_f]$$

Notice that points along the x axis on the SML are betas (B_s). This fact is often confusing to students who are used to thinking of beta as the slope of the regression line, as in Figure 8.1. Because B_s is the x value, then its coefficient must

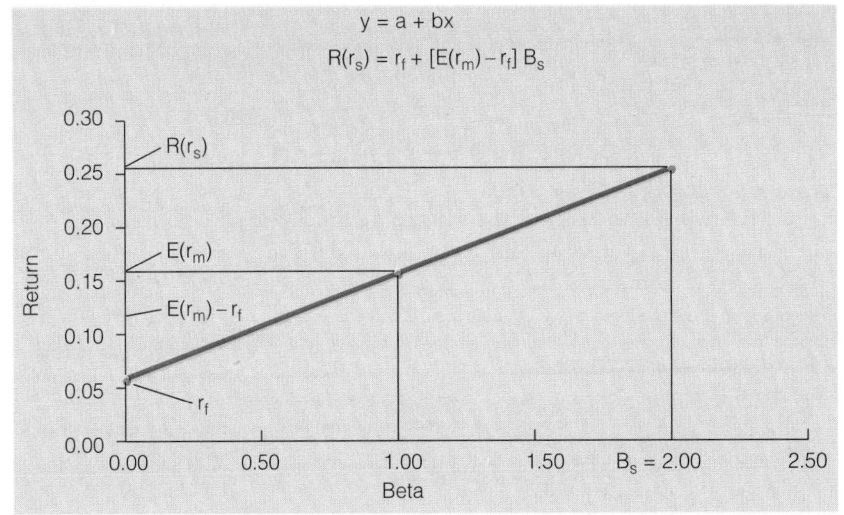

FIGURE 8.4
THE CAPITAL ASSET PRICING MODEL

Transparency Available

be the slope of the SML. Thus the slope is the market risk premium $E(r_m) - r_f$.[15] Earlier in the chapter, we discussed how a change in the market risk premium changes the slope of the SML.

Equation (8.3) is known as the **capital asset pricing model** (CAPM).[16] It is probably the most familiar equation in finance. Its primary attribute is that it expresses, very simply, the required return on a particular common stock as a function of the stock's market risk. Let's dissect the CAPM.

Transparency Available

$$\begin{array}{c} \text{required return} \\ \text{on common stock} \end{array} = \text{risk-free return} + \text{common-stock risk premium}$$

$$R(r_s) = r_f + B_s[E(r_m) - r_f]$$

The required return on common stock equals the risk-free return plus a **common-stock risk premium**. This is the most basic statement of the relationship between return and risk. Now, let's take a closer look at the risk premium.

Transparency Available

$$\text{common stock risk premium} = \text{beta} \times \text{market risk premium}$$

$$B_s[E(r_m) - r_f] = B_s \times [E(r_m) - r_f]$$

The common stock risk premium equals the market risk premium times the stock's beta, which is the factor relating the risk of the stock to the risk of the market.

Using CAPM to Calculate Required Returns on Common Stock

Now we will put the CAPM to work. To use the CAPM, we must have three pieces of information: the risk-free return, the market risk premium (or, alternatively, the expected market return), and the beta for our particular stock. The SML in Figures 8.2 and 8.4 was drawn with $r_f = 6.3\%$ and $E(r_m) - r_f = 9.6\%$. In Figure 8.4, we have identified a stock with a beta of 2 and a required return of slightly more than 25%. We can calculate its required return more precisely using the CAPM.

$$\begin{aligned} R(r_s) &= 0.063 + 2(0.096) \\ &= 0.255 = 25.5\% \end{aligned}$$

Of course, the required return for a stock with a beta of 1 would be equal to the expected market return.

$$\begin{aligned} R(r_s) &= 0.063 + 1(0.096) \\ &= 0.159 = 15.9\% \end{aligned}$$

Thus, for any beta, we can easily calculate the stock's required return.

Figure 8.5 shows the same security market line for the 20 stocks in our sample

---

[15]Because we know two points on our line, r_f and $E(r_m)$, we can find the change in y and the change in x and solve for the slope. $E(r_m) - r_f$ is the change in y. The change in x is 1 (market beta) − 0 (risk-free beta). Therefore,

$$\frac{\text{change in } y}{\text{change in } x} = \frac{E(r_m) - r_f}{1 - 0} = E(r_m) - r_f$$

[16]Notice that the CAPM calculates a required return, even though it is called a pricing model. Price, in turn, depends on required return.

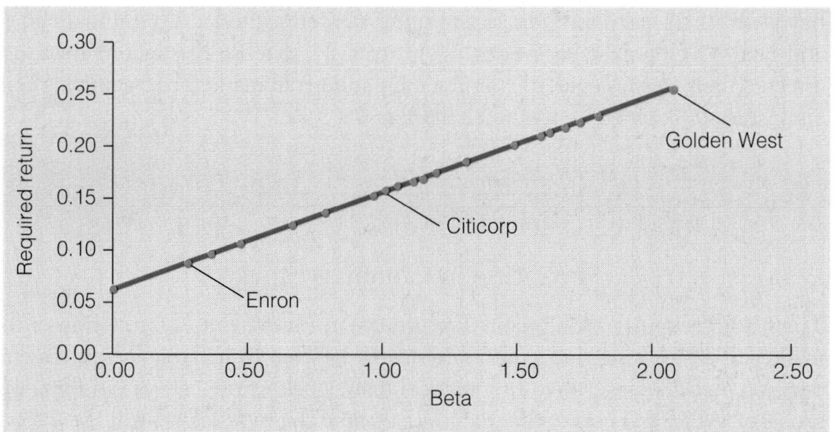

FIGURE 8.5

THE SECURITY MARKET LINE FOR 20 STOCKS

portfolio. We have identified three of these stocks on the graph. Enron, a gas pipeline company, has a low beta. Golden West Financial, a savings and loan, has a high beta, and Citicorp, the largest commercial bank in the United States, has a beta of 1. The calculations are

$$R(r_{\text{Enron}}) = 0.063 + 0.28(0.096) = 0.090$$

$$R(r_{\text{Citicorp}}) = 0.063 + 1(0.096) = 0.159$$

$$R(r_{\text{Golden}}) = 0.063 + 2.06(0.096) = 0.261$$

Improving on the CAPM

If stocks contained only market risk, then beta would be the complete measure of risk. If this were true, then all data points in Figure 8.1 would be plotted on the characteristic line, and all stocks would be plotted on the SML. However, a quick look at Figure 8.1 tells a different story. The characteristic line is a line of best fit but not one of perfect fit. We may interpret this to mean that stocks contain some nonmarket risk, such as unique risk, even though they are part of diversified portfolios. Another possibility is that there are common factors, other than the market, that affect stock returns.

Pursuing this line of reasoning, researchers have attempted to develop multiple-factor models to replace the CAPM. However, identifying specific factors that improve on the CAPM has proved elusive. The search has centered on macroeconomic factors such as inflation, GNP, and industrial production indices. One alternative model is the **arbitrage pricing model**. The new model would take the general form of Equation 8.4:

$$R(r_s) = r_f + b_1(E(f_1)) + b_2(E(f_2)) + b_3(E(f_3)) + \cdots + b_n(E(f_n)) \quad \textbf{(8.4)}$$

f_1, f_2, f_3, f_n are risk factors, such as inflation and GNP, and $b_1, b_2, b_3, \ldots, b_n$ are coefficients relating these factors to the required return on stock, $R(r_s)$.

Even if beta did capture all risk, betas would change over time as the companies themselves changed. There are many examples of companies "reinventing" themselves. W. R. Grace transformed itself from a shipping company into a multidivisional medical care, packaging and chemical company. Western railroads have used their vast land holdings to enter the forest products, mining, energy, and land-development businesses. More recently, defense contractors have redirected their technologies to consumer and industrial markets and adapted their companies to compete in a market economy.

USING CAPM IN INVESTMENT DECISIONS

Investing in Common Stock

The CAPM expresses the required return on an investment as a function of its market risk. Knowing this required return is essential to making an investment decision. Let's consider investing in a common stock whose beta is 1.1. First, we use the CAPM and our market data to calculate the required return:

Using the CAPM to estimate a stock's required return allows an analyst to compare this to the estimated expected return using the dividend growth model, or to use the dividend growth model to estimate a stock's value.

$$\begin{aligned} \text{beta} &= 1.1 \\ r_f &= 6.3\% \\ E(r_m) &= 15.9\% \\ R(r) &= 0.063 + 1.1(0.096) = 0.169 = 16.9\% \end{aligned}$$

The investor must now determine whether the stock is expected to provide a return equal to or greater than 16.9%, given its current market price. Here, the dividend growth model from Chapter 6 can be used. Suppose we have the following information on our stock:

$$\begin{aligned} \text{dividend:} \quad & D_1 = \$2 \\ \text{growth rate:} \quad & g_n = 0.05 \\ \text{stock price:} \quad & P_0 = \$15 \end{aligned}$$

$$E(r) = \frac{D_1}{P_0} + g_n \qquad (8.5)$$

$$= \tfrac{\$2}{\$15} + 0.05 = 0.183 = 18.3\%$$

At its current price of \$15, the stock appears to be a good investment because its expected return of 18.3% is greater than the required return of 16.9%, or $E(r) > R(r)$.

There is another way to approach this decision, by solving for stock value rather than return.

$$V = \frac{D_1}{R(r) - g_n} \qquad (8.6)$$

$$= \frac{\$2}{(0.169 - 0.05)} = \frac{\$2}{0.119} = \$16.81$$

This result tells us that the stock would provide our 16.9% required return at a price of \$16.81. However, the stock currently carries a bargain price of \$15 and, therefore, appears to be a good investment. Notice that both approaches indicate that we should buy the stock. They would also agree if the stock were overpriced. For example, if the stock price were \$20, the expected return would be 15%, which is below our required return of 16.9%. In this case $E(r) < R(r)$, so we would not buy the stock.

In the example of an undervalued stock, the market price is $15, with an expected return of 18.3%, which puts it above the SML. This is similar to stock A in Figure 8.2. If the stock were on the SML, it would have a price of $16.81 and an expected return of 16.9%. In an efficient and competitive stock market, we expect stocks to lie on the SML. In other words, expected returns should equal required returns, or $E(r) = R(r)$, making the stock in our example something of an aberration. This aberration would be quickly removed as demand for the stock raises its price and lowers its return.

Investing in Corporate Assets

The CAPM may also be used to evaluate corporate investments in real assets. In these product markets, less competition and less efficiency can yield investment opportunities where expected returns are greater than required returns, or $E(r) > R(r)$.

Investors provide capital to a corporation, not to particular corporate investment projects, and it is ultimately the responsibility of the corporation's management to provide its investors with their required return. This required return is, of course, a function of corporate risk. However, a corporation is, in a sense, a portfolio of investment projects. Each of these projects carries its own risk, demanding its own unique risk-adjusted required rate of return. Because it is a risk-return model, the CAPM may be used for estimating these required returns.

As with stocks, corporate investment decisions may be approached in two ways. We may calculate a project's required return, which is then compared to its expected return. The expected return on a project is known as its internal rate of return (IRR). We may also calculate the project's present value, which is compared to its cost, a technique known as finding the project's net present value (NPV). Both methods require estimating a project's required return, which is generally done using the CAPM. The procedures for using the CAPM to find project required returns, and employing these returns in the corporate investment decision process are covered in Chapter 10.

SUMMARY

In Chapter 7, we concluded that stocks held in diversified portfolios are subject to market risk only, the unique risk having been eliminated by diversification. In Chapter 8, we developed beta, which is the measure of a stock's market risk. We then used beta to construct the security market line, which describes the relationship between beta and the required returns on stocks. Because securities are held in diversified portfolios, the security market line describes the approximate relationship between their market risk and required return. The capital asset pricing model is the algebraic expression of the security market line and allows us to calculate, for many different types of assets, their required returns as a function of their market risk.

What is ahead of us? We must spend some time more fully developing the criteria and process for selecting the firm's investment projects. Finding the required returns of assets such as delivery trucks, lathes and advertising campaigns is more difficult than finding the required returns for stocks and bonds, although the logic is the same. Nevertheless, to value these left-hand-side investments, we must estimate their required returns in order to compare the values of the investment projects to their costs. Making the correct left-hand-side decisions is crucial to corporate success and is the topic of Chapters 9, 10, and 11.

KEY TERMS

beta
characteristic line
sector funds
market risk premium
risk premium
capital asset pricing model
common-stock risk premium
arbitrage pricing model

KEY FORMULAS

Common stock beta

$$B_S = \frac{COV_{S,SP500}}{VAR_{SP500}}$$

Weighted average portfolio beta

$$B_P = w_1B_1 + w_2B_2 + w_3B_3 + \cdots + w_NB_N$$

Capital asset pricing model

$$R(r_s) = r_f + B_s[E(r_m) - r_f]$$

QUESTIONS

1. What is a risk premium? Give an example.
2. A stock's risk may be measured by the standard deviation of its returns. Yet this risk measure is inappropriate if the stock is part of a diversified portfolio? Why?
3. If a portfolio consists of 20 financial services stocks (banks, S&Ls, and insurance companies), is beta the appropriate risk measure for these stocks?
4. On the accompanying SML, label
   a. Risk-free return
   b. Expected return on the market
   c. Market risk premium

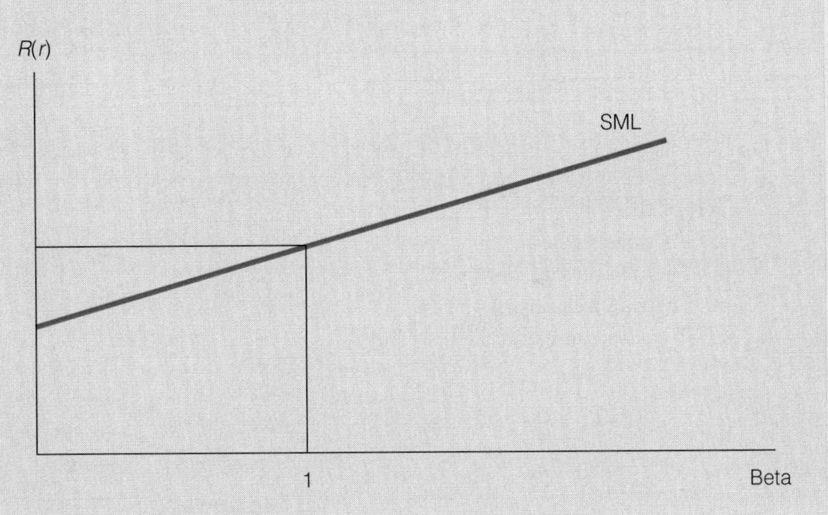

5. The risk measure for a stock held in a diversified portfolio must have two attributes:
   a. It must measure the ________ risk of the stock.
   b. It must measure the stock's contribution to the risk of the ________ .
6. a. On the Question 4 graph, plot and identify an undervalued and an overvalued stock.
   b. On the same graph, show the relative placement of the following securities:
      i. Corporate A rated bonds
      ii. Stock of average risk
      iii. U.S. Treasury bonds
      iv. Corporate AAA rated bonds
      v. A stock of slightly higher than average risk
      vi. Stock options
7. a. If the SML rotates as shown in the accompanying figure, would that affect each of the following?
      i. The market beta
      ii. The market risk premium
      iii. The risk-free return
   b. What would cause the SML to rotate?

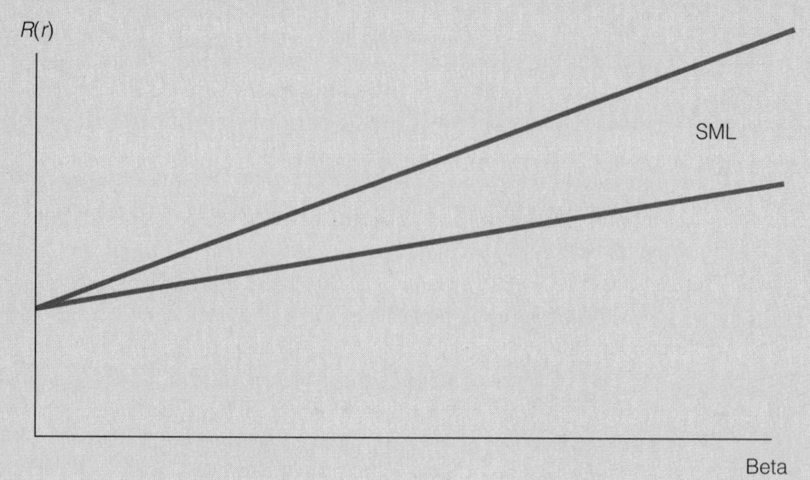

8. a. If the SML shifts as shown in the accompanying figure, would that affect each of the following?
   i. The market beta
   ii. The market risk premium
   iii. The risk-free return
   b. What would cause the SML to shift?

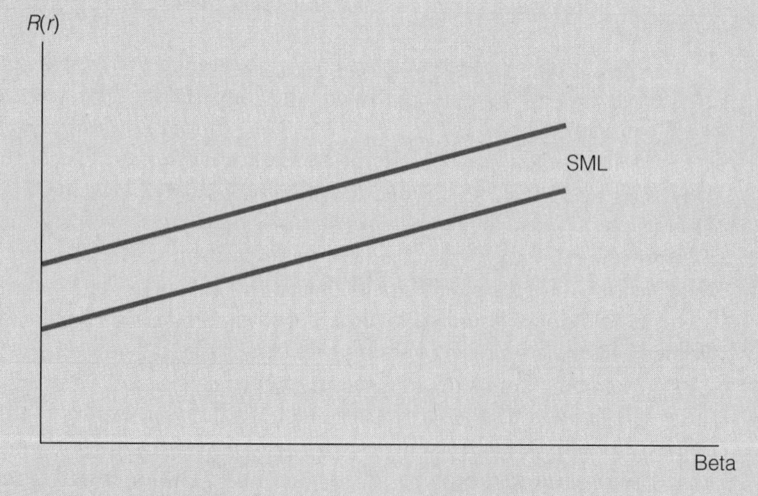

9. Does a high beta necessarily mean that a stock's total risk is also high? Explain the difference between beta and total risk.
10. a. What would you expect the portfolio betas to be for the following?
   i. A diversified 20-stock portfolio
   ii. A diversified 100-stock portfolio
   iii. A diversified 2,000-stock portfolio
   b. For which portfolio would you be more confident in your estimate's accuracy?

11. Many investment advisors claim to have found undervalued stocks. For a fee, they will divulge the names of these stocks.
    a. What is an undervalued stock? If you found one, should you buy or sell the stock?
    b. Why should you be skeptical of such claims?
12. a. Write the equation for the security market line (SML) and label its parts.
    b. Identify the market risk premium.
    c. Identify the risk premium for the stock.
13. a. If a single-product company diversifies into several unrelated product lines, perhaps by acquiring other companies, would you expect its beta to change? Why?
    b. If this same company became a conglomerate, with hundreds of products in dozens of industries, what value would you predict for its beta?
14. a. Explain the difference between the expected return and the required return on common stock.
    b. If the stock market were perfectly efficient and competitive, would you expect any difference between a stock's expected and required return? Why?
15. A financial advisor tells you that because the stock prices of gold producers are highly variable, you should not add any of these stocks to your portfolio. Is this good advice? Explain.
16. Why might automobile manufacturers have higher betas than grocery food chains?
17. (True or false) A security with a beta of zero offers a zero return.
18. (True or false) Beta is the slope of the characteristic line.
19. (True or false) Beta is the slope of the SML.
20. What is the difference between the risk premium of the market and the risk premium of a stock?
21. If the market risk premium were greater than a stock risk premium, what would you know about the stock's beta?
22. If the interest rate on U.S. Treasury bills falls, how would that affect the SML?
23. If the market risk premium rose, how would that affect the SML?
24. American Barrick Resources is a U.S. and Canadian gold producer. Its stock price is tied closely to the price of gold. General Electric is a diversified consumer products, industrial products, and broadcasting company.
    a. Which of these two stocks has more total risk?
    b. Does the high-risk stock (part a) necessarily have greater market risk? Explain.
    c. Would you consider including the high-risk stock (part a) in a diversified stock portfolio? Why or why not?
25. Suppose your stock portfolio consisted only of electronics industry stocks.
    a. Would beta be the appropriate risk measure for your stocks? Why or why not?
    b. Would you expect your portfolio beta to be approximately 1? Why or why not?
26. If it became fairly easy to find undervalued and overvalued stocks, what would that suggest about the stock market's competitiveness and efficiency?
27. You are considering investing in one of the following three common stock mutual funds. The portfolio betas for the funds are

fund X	0.6
fund Y	1.1
fund Z	1.7

a. Based on these betas, does it appear that all three funds have well diversified stock holdings? Why or why not?

b. What possible explanations can there be for the betas of funds X and Z?

28. You have a portfolio of 30 stocks representing a number of diverse industries, yet your average portfolio beta is 1.5. How would you explain this apparent contradiction?

29. Here is a question that will test your understanding of finance. Suppose it became fairly easy to find undervalued and overvalued securities in the capital markets. How might that affect the objectives and functioning of corporations?

30. Pogo Inc.'s stock is overpriced, meaning that its market price is greater than its SML price. Investors would tend to ______ (buy/sell) this stock, driving its price ______ (up/down).

31. Pogo Inc.'s stock is underpriced, meaning that its market price is less than its SML price. Investors would tend to ______ (buy/sell) this stock, driving its price ______ (up/down).

32. If you have data on returns for the market (S&P 500) and the common stock of Pogo, Inc., explain how you can determine Pogo's beta graphically.

DEMONSTRATION PROBLEMS

Calculating Beta

1. Calculate the beta for Emmett Corp.'s stock using the following information:

$$SD_{Emmett} = 0.08$$

$$SD_{SP500} = 0.065$$

$$CORR_{Emmett,SP500} = 0.85$$

SOLUTION

Using Equation (8.1), solve for beta:

$$B_S = \frac{COV_{s,sp500}}{VAR_{SP500}}$$

$$= \frac{(0.85)(0.08)(0.065)}{(0.065)^2} = 1.11$$

Required Return and Stock Value

2. We have the following information on the stock of Pogo, Inc., and the market (S&P 500).

$$beta_{Pogo} = 1.3$$

$$\text{risk-free rate} = 4\%$$

$$\text{expected return on the S\&P 500} = 10\%$$

a. What is the required rate of return on Pogo, Inc., stock?
b. What is the market risk premium?
c. Pogo, Inc., is expected to pay a $2.50 dividend next year. The dividend is expected to grow at a sustainable rate of 4% per year. Calculate the price of Pogo's stock.

SOLUTION

a. The required return on the stock can be found using the CAPM:

$$R(r_s) = r_f + B_s[E(r_m) - r_f]$$
$$= 0.04 + 1.3[0.10 - 0.04] = 0.118 = 11.8\%$$

b. The market risk premium equals $E(r_m) - r_f = 0.10 - 0.04 = 0.06$.
c. Stock value is calculated using Equation (8.6).

$$V = \frac{D_1}{R(r) - g_n}$$
$$= \frac{\$2.50}{0.118 - 0.04} = \$32.05$$

PROBLEMS

1. Calculate the beta for Kelly Corp.'s stock using the following information:

Calculating Beta
1. 1.25

$$SD_{Kelly} = 0.11$$
$$SD_{SP500} = 0.04$$
$$CORR_{Kelly,SP500} = 0.45$$

2. Suppose Kelly Corp.'s stock (Problem 1) had a beta of 0.75. How would this change Kelly's beta?

Calculating Beta
2. 2.06

3. If Kelly Corp.'s stock (Problem 1) became more volatile, so that its standard deviation rose to 0.183, how would this change Kelly's beta?

Calculating Beta
3. 2.06

4. Referring to Problem 1, if the S&P 500 index became less volatile, so that its standard deviation dropped to 0.024, how would this change Kelly's beta?

Calculating Beta
4. 2.05

5. What do your answers in Problems 1–4 reveal about the effect of changes in correlation and standard deviations on beta?

The Effects of Correlation and Standard Deviation on Beta

6. Comparing returns on the common stock of JME, Inc., to the S&P 500 yields the following statistics:

Calculating and Interpreting Beta
6. a. 0.96
c. 0.96

$$SD_{JME} = 0.15$$
$$SD_{SP500} = 0.07$$
$$CORR_{JME,SP500} = 0.45$$

a. Calculate the beta for JME, Inc.
b. All else equal, would you expect JME, Inc., to increase or decrease the risk of a diversified portfolio of stocks?
c. Using returns data for JME, Inc. and the S&P 500, we can construct a regression line. What would the slope of that line be?

Portfolio Beta
7. 1.2

7. Calculate the weighted average beta of the following portfolio.

COMPANY	WEIGHTING	BETA
A	0.10	0.7
B	0.25	0.9
C	0.05	2.1
D	0.20	1.1
E	0.30	1.4
F	0.10	1.6

Portfolio Beta
8. 1.3

8. If the portfolio in Problem 7 contained equal amounts of each stock, what would the portfolio beta be?

Portfolio Beta

9. Reassign the proportional weightings in Problem 7 to reduce portfolio beta; then recalculate the beta.

Portfolio Beta
10. a. 1.14

10. A diversified stock portfolio contains equal amounts of the following stocks:

STOCK	BETA
MTV	0.6
GM	1.4
ITT	1.7
AT&T	0.9
GE	1.1

a. What is the portfolio beta?
b. If we wished to increase the riskiness of our portfolio, what might we do?
c. Why might we want to increase the risk of our portfolio (part b)? Are we crazy?

Using CAPM to Calculate Required Returns
11. MTV: 0.082; GE: 0.117

11. Given the following information, use the capital asset pricing model (CAPM) to find required rates of return on the five stocks in Problem 10.

The risk-free return is 4%.

The market risk premium is 7%.

Required Versus Expected Returns
12. $R(r) = 15.1\%$

12. The risk-free rate is 6%, and the market risk premium is 7%. If a stock with a beta of 1.3 had an expected return of 17%, would you be more likely to buy or sell this stock? Explain.

13. If the stock in Problem 12 had an expected return of 15%, would you be more likely to buy or sell this stock? Explain.

Required Versus Expected Returns

14. The risk-free rate is 4%, and the expected return on the market is 11%. Key West Industries' stock has a beta of 0.85. It expects to pay a $2.40 dividend, and the dividend is expected to grow at a rate of 4% annually.
   a. What is the required return on this stock?
   b. What should the market price of the stock be in a perfect market?

Required Returns and Stock Values
14. a. 10.0%
b. $40

15. The risk-free rate is 4%, and the expected return on the market is 11%. Key West Industries' stock has a beta of 0.85. It expects to pay a $2.40 dividend, and the dividend is expected to grow at a rate of 4% annually.
   a. If the current stock price were $30, what would be its expected return?
   b. Would you be likely to buy or sell this stock at a price of $30? $40? $50? Answer for each of these prices.

Required Returns and Stock Values
15. a. 12%
b. 10% ($40); 8.8% ($50)

16. ABC (American Brewing Company) stock has a current price of $42 and a beta of 1.3. The stock is expected to pay a $2 dividend this coming year. This dividend should grow by 4% each year forever. Checking market data, we find that the risk-free return is 3% and the average return on the S&P 500 is 8%.
   a. What is the required return on ABC's stock?
   b. What is the expected return on ABC's stock?
   c. What is the value of ABC's stock?
   d. Based on these calculations, would you buy or sell this stock? Why?
   e. Would ABC stock lie above, on, or below the SML?

Required Returns, Expected Returns, and Stock Values
16. a. 9.5%
b. 8.8%
c. $36.36

17. **a.** The stock of ACME, Inc., has a beta of 1.25. If the expected return on the market portfolio is 14% and the risk-free return is 6%, what is ACME's required rate of return?
   b. If you expected ACME to return 22% next period, would you buy or sell? Explain. What would your action (and the action of investors like you) do to ACME's expected return?

Required Versus Expected Returns
17. a. 16%

18. We have the following information on returns of the common stock of Pogo, Inc. and the S&P 500 market index.

Beta and Market Risk
18. a. 0.79
b. 7.9%

$$CORR_{Pogo,SP500} = 0.5$$
$$SD_{Pogo} = 11\%$$
$$SD_{SP500} = 7\%$$

   a. Calculate the beta for Pogo.
   b. If you expected the market return to rise by 10%, would you predict the return on Pogo to rise or fall? By how much?
   c. Is Pogo's stock more or less risky than the market?

Portfolio Beta
19. a. 1.125

19. Your portfolio consists of four stocks.

	BETA
A	1.4
B	0.8
C	1.6
D	0.7

a. If you have equal proportions of each stock, what is your portfolio beta?
b. Is your portfolio more or less risky than the market as a whole? Why?
c. To make your porfolio risk equal to the risk of the market, you would have to sell ______ (which stocks) and buy ______ (which stocks). (No calculation is required.)

Analyzing the Security Market Line

20. On the graph (below) of the security market line
a. Label the axes.
b. Label the expected return on the market.
c. Label the risk-free rate.
d. Show the market risk premium.
e. Show where a high-risk (higher than market) stock would lie on the SML.

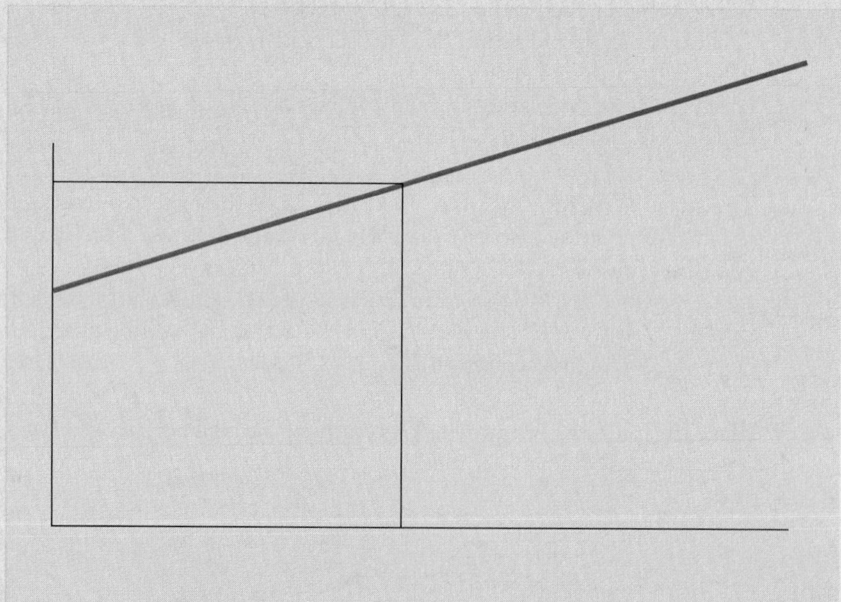

Required Return and Stock Value
21. a. 11.8%
b. 6%
c. $32.05

21. We have the following information on the stock of Pogo, Inc., and the market (S&P 500).

$$\text{Beta}_{\text{Pogo}} = 1.3$$

$$\text{risk-free rate} = 4\%$$

$$\text{expected return on the S\&P 500} = 10\%$$

a. What is the required rate of return on Pogo, Inc. stock?
b. What is the market risk premium?
c. Pogo, Inc., is expected to pay a $2.50 dividend next year. The dividend is expected to grow at a sustainable rate of 4% per year. Calculate the price of Pogo's stock.
d. If Pogo's stock were currently selling at $40 in the market, would you be inclined to buy or sell the stock? Why?

The CAPM and Market Risk
22. a. 9%
b. 6.75%

22. The risk-free rate is 7%, and the expected return on the market is 16%.
a. What is the market risk premium?
b. The stock's beta is 0.75. What is the stock's risk premium?
c. If the risk-free rate fell to 4%, what would the expected return on the market have to be to maintain the same risk premium?

CHAPTER 9

Corporate Investments

Sure it was a gamble, but we were really searching for a market where the competition wasn't quite so intense.

Companies often look for markets where competition is low as they search for highly profitable investment projects. However, having few competitors doesn't guarantee that a project is a good one: There may be reasons for the lack of competitors in a market!

ith Chapter 8, we have completed discussion of the various components of the valuation model. In Chapters 9–11, we apply the valuation model to the corporate investing decision, focusing our attention on the left-hand side (LHS) of the financial balance sheet.

In this and the next two chapters, we discuss investing strategies, valuing risky investments and corporate capital budgets. In this chapter we address the fundamentals of corporate investing. First, we discuss product market opportunities created by imperfect competition. Next, we develop some guidelines for identifying and selecting investment opportunities. We then examine the investment decision itself, paying special attention to decision criteria and discounted cash flows. Finally, we discuss options that are intrinsic to many corporate investments.

LINKING CORPORATE INVESTMENT TO VALUE CREATION

Investing Principles

Four factors important to corporate investing are cash flow, timing, required rate of return, and risk.

The purpose of corporate investing is to create value for the company and its shareholders. Successful investing requires the corporation to identify and capitalize on promising investment opportunities to create value. There are several important ideas that we will draw upon in our discussion of corporate investing:

- It is cash flows, not income or earnings, that measure the success of a business or investment.
- The value of a cash flow depends on when it is paid or received; in other words, timing—as well as the dollar amount—determines the value of money.
- The effect of time on the value of future cash flows is determined by the discount rate.
- The appropriate discount rate is the investor's required rate of return.
- This required rate of return is a function of risk.

"Sounds as easy as oatmeal," Louis Lowenstein.

Investors buy bonds and stocks that represent claims against future corporate cash flows. Corporate investments must, therefore, generate at least enough cash flow to provide all investors with their required returns. If they generate less, the value of the corporate securities—and, therefore, the value of the corporation—will decline.

Investments that generate just enough cash flow to provide investors with their required returns neither add value to the corporation nor increase the wealth of its shareholders. A wealth-creating investment must provide cash flows of greater value than its cost. As we have seen in earlier chapters, the value of cash flows depends on their timing and risks as well as their dollar amount, so any investment must be judged on these attributes.

Investing in Fixed Assets

In October 1990 United Airlines placed purchase orders and options for 128 new aircraft from Boeing, with deliveries scheduled to begin in 1995. About half of the planes were purchased. On the rest, United bought call options that gave it the right but not the obligation to buy the additional planes at a specified price.[1] The total value of the planes purchased and optioned was $22 billion, making it the largest order ever placed for commercial aircraft. The aircraft included advanced-technology Boeing 777 aircraft, positioning United as an industry leader, and long-range 747-400 aircraft to serve United's recently expanded overseas routes. The order committed United to make progress and option payments on aircraft that would not produce revenues for many years. This was quite a risky investment, considering the volatile nature of the airline industry.

The United Airlines example is continued through Chapter 11.

Business risk is an integral part of every corporate investment. A primary source of risk for United and other established airlines was industry deregulation, which allowed the entry of low-cost carriers. Fare wars ensued, cutting operating margins; a number of airlines, notably Eastern, Braniff, and Pan American, went out of business. In this perilous environment, United used call options to hedge its risk. This historic investment underscores a basic attribute of capital investing: Investments often require committing large amounts of capital for long time periods in a risky product market.

Depending on the industry, much corporate investment is in long-term, or **fixed, assets**. Traditional capital-intensive "smokestack" industries invest in factories that manufacture durable goods, such as metals, chemicals, transportation equipment, and machinery. However, virtually all companies, not just manufacturers, have fixed assets. Retailers either own or lease stores. R&D firms have laboratories and patents. Book and music publishers have copyrights and, perhaps, long-term contracts with writers and musicians. Sports teams have long-term contracts with players and coaches.[2] One of the best-known assets is the secret formula for Coca-Cola.

Investments include any spending that is intended to enhance corporate value, such as employee training, reorganization, research, patents, and copyrights.

Fixed assets are often classified as tangible (machinery, real estate) or intangible (copyrights, patents, contracts). In the 1980s and 1990s, companies began to restructure themselves to adapt to global competition and new technologies. Financial resources were used to create new organization structures, train employees, and invest in research. Although much of this investment is intangible and does not appear on the accounting balance sheet, it may be essential to the long-run viability of these corporations.

Product Market Opportunities

The financial model of the corporation is based on the premise that product markets provide valuable investment opportunities for firms. Firms that identify and capitalize on these opportunities create value because they do what their shareholders individually cannot do. Identifying and evaluating potential opportunities is the first step in the investment process. The search for investment opportunities occurs within the overall mission and strategic plan of the corporation. For example, United Airlines' $22 billion aircraft order underscored its

[1]Options are introduced in Chapter 3.

[2]Long-term contracts are both assets and liabilities. They are assets because they obligate the performer to the company. They are liabilities because they obligate the company to the performer.

intention to compete vigorously in a number of domestic and international markets.

Investment opportunities are often short-lived because successful investments attract competitors. The success of Starbuck's coffee spawned many purveyors of specialty coffees and espresso. The presence of competition requires firms to remain alert for new opportunities, and to protect their existing markets from their competitors. Even the most protected markets may be vulnerable. Before Japanese autos entered the market, the United States was the nearly exclusive turf of the big-three U.S. automakers. The deregulation of U.S. airlines introduced competition that caused Pan American, once the world's premier airline, to go out of business.

Challenge the class to provide other examples of competition eroding investment returns and companies erecting barriers to competitors.

Firms have a number of weapons with which to fend off competitors. Patents and copyrights protect, for a time, valuable intellectual property such as inventions, publications, and computer software. Sometimes protecting a competitive position requires investment. For example, McDonald's preempted their competitors by being the first to buy choice restaurant locations. Investing in a more modern plant may give companies a competitive advantage by lowering production costs or increasing product quality. Similarly, investing in corporate restructuring may lower overhead costs.

Seeking out and successfully pursuing valuable investments place great demands on companies. There are many potential pitfalls. Managers may fail to recognize opportunities, or they may chase opportunities that do not exist. High profits in a particular market don't necessarily present an opportunity to outsiders. The cost of overcoming capital, technological, or regulatory barriers may be too great.

When an apparent investment opportunity reveals itself, managers should ask two initial questions:

1. If this is a genuine opportunity, why is there not greater competition in this market? Is it possible that it is more competitive than it appears? Are there costly barriers to entry?
2. Is the current competitive posture likely to remain over the long haul? Are market forces already at work to increase competition? Perhaps other companies have already spotted the opportunity.

Taking reasonable precautions should actually encourage investments by making poor investments less likely. Companies that have a record of successful investing may be more aggressive in searching for new opportunities than those that do not.

PROJECT SELECTION

Each firm must develop a competitive strategy for capitalizing on market opportunities. Such strategies usually take the form of cost leadership or differentiation.[3] A low-cost producer can undercut its competitor's prices. Discount retailers such as K-Mart and WalMart have successfully used this strategy. A differenti-

[3]This discussion borrows from Michael E. Porter's book, *Competitive Advantage* (New York: The Free Press, 1985).

Select an industry of interest either to yourself or your students. Look for examples of cost leadership and differentiation.

ation strategy may take many forms. A company may offer higher quality, a functionally distinct product, or better service. Among clothing retailers, there are Nordstrom and Niemann Marcus (quality and service) and L. L. Bean (functionally distinct). United Airlines' aircraft order was a manifestation of a differentiation strategy. United sought to be the first airline to fly an advanced technology aircraft and to establish its preeminence in the trans-Pacific market. A firm's competitive strategy determines where it looks for market opportunities. For example, WalMart would not be likely to focus on product quality and service if that jeopardized its position as a cost leader.

Analyzing potential investments requires identifying relevant cash flows, discounting the cash flows at a required rate of return, and applying appropriate decision rules.[4] However, before these analytical tools can be applied, we must identify a set of potential projects. To do this requires the following steps:

- Identify potential projects, following a corporate strategic plan or mission.
- Classify projects by size and purpose so that management resources can be directed to the more important projects.
- Eliminate or integrate dependent projects.

Each of these steps is treated in turn.

Identifying Potential Projects

Ideally, a company's search for investment opportunities would transcend its traditional products and markets. For example, a company doing business in the United States would consider overseas markets. A bank might consider entering the computer services business. A manufacturer of industrial equipment might consider making consumer products. Each opportunity would be thoroughly evaluated, and all investments adding value to the company would be taken. In practice, however, companies generally limit the scope of their search. Thus, United Airlines, by ordering its fleet of new aircraft, avoided the cost leadership strategy adopted by the no-frills carriers, such as Southwest Airlines.

Some companies that departed from traditional lines found that diversification is not necessarily the road to riches. Before deregulation, some airlines (including United), with large and secure cash flows broadened their mission to include associated tourist and travel businesses. They bought hotels, resorts, charter fleets, food-service companies, and travel agencies. When the crunch of deregulation came, they were no longer able to support these ventures with cash flows from their scheduled air service, and most quickly abandoned these subordinate lines of business.

A company's size, product line, and geographic reach reflect its strategic plan. More is not always better. Coors struggled when it attempted to distribute its beer nationally. Small, single-product entrepreneurial companies are often able to outmaneuver large competitors. IBM was forced to divide itself into smaller entrepreneurial units to compete with specialized computer manufacturers. By contrast, there is General Electric, which has achieved success by being large, diverse, and global. The search for projects should reflect the particular abilities

[4]Each of these topics is covered in previous chapters: cash flows in Chapter 3, discounting and decision rules in Chapter 5, and risk in Chapters 3, 7, and 8.

of the company. Companies must balance between being too expansive and too narrow in their search. This need for balance underscores the importance of having a corporate identity and mission.

Classifying Projects

Companies often find it useful to categorize potential projects by their size and the company experience with such projects. Large projects with which the company has little experience require careful scrutiny. An example of such a project would be investing large sums in research to develop a new compound, fiber, drug, or computer chip. On the other hand, replacing a worn-out machine with one that is similar requires much less management attention. Management resources are finite. By confining the search to projects that fit the company's mission and then classifying them, management attention can be directed to a relatively few crucial projects.

Following is a representative scheme for classifying projects according to the amount of management attention required.

Replacement projects update or upgrade existing capacity, such as replacing worn-out or obsolete machinery and equipment. These are relatively routine investments and may be handled by divisions or operating entities rather than by senior management.[5]

Expansion projects are used to expand existing capacity, such as adding new machinery or equipment to increase output. Airlines buy more aircraft to handle increased demand. Retailers add space at existing locations. Because capacity expansion is a response to increased demand, or anticipated demand, it entails only moderate management scrutiny.

Dispersion (geographical extension) is distinguished from diversification (new products).

Diversification, *or* ***dispersion, projects*** add new products or new regions to a company's operations. Demands on management may vary greatly, depending on how related the new products or regions are to existing ones. The initial overseas expansion of a domestic corporation may require more management attention than a multinational corporation adding Czech Republic and Poland to its Western European operations. Investing in freight cars to lease to private carriers is closely related to a railroad's primary business. However, investing in land development and resource management takes a railroad into relatively uncharted territory.[6] Projects that may seem risky and deserving of great management scrutiny must be judged in the context of existing company operations. For example, mining and integrated oil companies are equipped for the risky business of mineral exploration, and the perilous task of developing new drugs and bringing them to market is the core business of biotechnology companies.

There are two other investment categories that don't fit neatly into a risk classification. One is investment mandated by law, such as pollution control and

---

[5]Project termination is the flip side of project replacement. The decision not to continue an investment is one of the more difficult and overlooked left-hand-side decisions managers must face. Yet all projects must be abandoned at some point. This decision is treated in the options section later in this chapter.

[6]Western railroads did enter these businesses, but most chose to spin off their development and resource businesses into independent companies. In this way, they protected their core railroad business from the risks of these new ventures.

plant improvements to conform to occupational safety and health codes. The other is buying other companies. Mergers always carry some risk because they combine corporate cultures. Most mergers expand existing capacity, diversify product lines, or expand operations into new regions. They are covered in Chapter 16.

Eliminating Project Dependencies

When we first identify potential investments, we may include projects that are either complementary or mutually exclusive. Suppose a multinational company is contemplating construction of a factory in Nigeria. Company managers know that if they build the plant, they will have to invest in motor transport to haul materials and finished goods between the factory and the port of Lagos. These two investments—the factory and the trucks—are **complementary projects**, and should be subsumed into a single investment, called the factory/truck project.

Mutually exclusive projects are substitutes for each other, requiring either-or decisions. The Nigerian factory may include constructing a metal fabrication shop. As an alternative, the company may elect to expand its existing metal fabrication facility in Ireland. It must choose between building the shop in Nigeria and adding capacity in Ireland. It may be that there is yet a third option. However many there are, the company must identify each set of mutually exclusive projects and eliminate all but one in each set.

It is important, from an analytical standpoint, to identify independent projects.

Once the company's financial analysts have combined complementary projects and chosen among mutually exclusive projects, those that are left are **independent projects**. By identifying independent projects, each one attains equal status; that is, the company may invest in all, or none, or any combination of projects, knowing that each investment decision does not affect the others.[7] This greatly simplifies the analysis and allows management to focus on the process of creating wealth.

ESTIMATING PROJECT CASH FLOWS

Once a company's financial analysts have identified an array of independent projects, they must evaluate each as a potential investment. First, they must identify cash flows that are associated with the project. These include the initial investment, operating income and expenses spread over the life of the project, and, finally, cash flows associated with project termination. Expected future cash flows from the project are discounted to their present value and then compared to the initial investment. If the present value of the future cash flows is greater than the initial investment, the investment has a positive **net present value**. A positive net present value indicates that the investment will add value to the company.

Net present value is defined.

net present value = present value of future cash flows − initial investment

[7]In reality life is not quite this simple. We introduce one complication, credit rationing, in Chapter 11.

In order to calculate net present value, we must estimate the amount and timing of the investment's cash flows. In this section, we provide some ground rules for estimating cash flows and then show how they are used in a discounted cash flow model.

Consider Only Incremental Cash Flows

Incremental cash flows are the change in corporate cash flows attributable to the project.

The most difficult part of project analysis is identifying and quantifying the cash flows related to the project. Here, the guiding principle is to include only **incremental cash flows**, defined as the change in corporate cash flows attributable to the project. The relevant question is, How will this project affect the cash flow of the company? This question seems simple enough, but these cash flows can be elusive. Even the cost of some projects may be impossible to pin down. Consider how difficult it is to estimate the completed cost of an office building or plant that may take years to complete. Some cash flows may escape attention altogether, such as the effect of one project on another project's cash flows. Following are a few guidelines to assist in identifying incremental cash flows.

- *Beware of* **allocated costs**, *such as corporate overhead.* These costs do not usually change as a result of taking on projects. For example, a new project may make use of existing idle capacity in the corporate computing department. Assuming that there is no alternative use for the computers and support staff, the cost of computer services is not an incremental cost. On the other hand, if the project's demand for computer services forces the company to add capacity or deprives other corporate units of computing services, those costs would be incremental and should be included in the cost of the project.

These concepts are best taught by using examples.

- *Consider the* **opportunity costs** *of currently owned resources.* In the computer example, if the company did not invest in new computers but instead took computing resources from some other unit in the corporation, the project

EXHIBIT 9.1

CLASSIFYING PROJECT CASH FLOWS

Initial Investment	
Project cost	[Outflow]
Investment tax credit	[Inflow]
Change in net working capital	[Outflow/inflow]
Sale of asset	[Inflow]
Tax effect of sale	[Outflow/inflow]
Operating Cash Flows (Incremental)	
Cash revenues [S]	[Inflow]
Cash expenses [E]	[Outflow]
Depreciation [dep]	(noncash expense)
Earnings before tax (EBT = S − E − dep)	
Tax = EBT * tax rate	[Outflow]
Earnings after tax (EAT = EBT − tax)	
Add back depreciation (EAT + dep)	
Project Termination Cash Flows	
Income from sale	[Inflow]
Tax effect of sale	[Outflow/inflow]
Recovering net working capital	[Outflow/inflow]

Transparency Available

should be charged for the costs incurred by denying services to the other unit. Perhaps this other unit is not as productive as a result. Perhaps the computer resources could have been used to improve corporate management systems. The foregone value of these improved systems is chargeable to the project.

Another example of an opportunity cost is a plant built on land owned by the company. The land entails no out-of-pocket costs; however, it is not a free resource because it has alternative uses. The analyst must consider, as the cost of the land, the income that could be produced from its next-best use. Perhaps it could become a parking lot, be sold, or be used for growing tomatoes.

- *Ignore* **sunk costs**. Sunk costs are monies that have already been spent. Sometimes it is difficult to ignore homilies such as, "Don't throw good money after bad." However, the "bad money" is a sunk cost and is irrelevant. It is not easy to abandon projects on which a great deal of money has been spent. Abandonment has its own costs, and sometimes finishing a project that may have been unwise to begin with is the only way to recover at least some of its costs. The analyst must consider the incremental costs and revenues of completing a project.[8]
- *Consider* **incidental effects** *of the project*. A new product may reduce sales of other company products. For instance, when instant Jell-O was introduced, sales of regular Jell-O fell. A decision by McDonald's to install pizza ovens in its stores must take into account lost sandwich sales. If a retailer opens a second location in the same town, it may draw customers from the original store. There may be positive incidental effects as well. In the 1930s, Averill Harriman developed Sun Valley, Idaho, to create demand for passenger service on his Union Pacific Railroad.[9] Small feeder airlines are subsidized by the large carriers to deliver passengers to and from their hub airports. For the Sun Valley resort and the feeder airlines, these incidental benefits make them viable. Including all incidental effects of a project is easier said than done. Often, as in the Jell-O project, they are not evident. Projects that depend on incidental effects, such as the Sun Valley resort, may be very risky; for instance, suppose skiers come to Sun Valley by another mode of transportation.

Cash Flow Categories

Project cash flows are normally broken down into three categories—the initial investment, annual operating cash flows for the life of the project, and project-termination cash flows. Each category includes cash flows from different sources. We will treat each category in turn, starting with the initial investment.

---

[8]There are many such examples. In the early 1980s the infamous Washington Public Power Supply System had partially completed several nuclear electric-generating plants before realizing that there was little demand for their electricity. After defaulting on its bonds, WPPSS finished construction of one plant even though it would not be profitable. In this case, the incremental cost of finishing the plant produced a positive NPV investment.

[9]Many of the great resort hotels in U.S. and Canadian national parks were built by railroads for the same reason.

Investment can occur over several years.

Initial Investment

- *Project cost* (cash outflow): Project cost may include transportation, insurance, setup, employee training, maintenance, and warranties. For some projects, it may also include infrastructure costs, such as roads and utilities. It also may include planning and design costs, such as architectural fees. For simple projects, the outflow occurs at the present time ($t = 0$). However, large projects, such as plant construction, may take several years to complete.
- *Investment tax credits* (cash inflow): A tax credit reduces taxes paid in some proportion to the project cost. From time to time, governments provide tax credits for certain kinds of investments. Currently, there is no general ITC in the United States, but there are ITCs in other countries.
- *Change in net working capital* (ITC—a cash outflow or inflow): Expansion, diversification, and dispersion projects may require additions to net working capital. Increased inventories, receivables, and perhaps cash may be needed to support increased production. These current assets are tied to the investment and are, therefore, incremental costs. Generally, we assume that this increased working capital is reduced to its prior level upon termination of the project, resulting in a decrease, or **recovery of net working capital**. Some investments may actually reduce the need for net working capital. For example, a new production facility may use just-in-time inventory control, reducing the need for inventory stocks.
- *Sale of existing asset* (cash inflow): Generally, a sale of an existing asset occurs only for replacement projects.
- *Tax effect of asset sale* (cash inflow or outflow): If the sale price of the asset is greater than its depreciated book value, the company will owe tax on the difference. If the sale price is less than the book value, the loss reduces the company's taxable income.

Operating Income and Expense

Operating income and expense are annual revenues and expenses occurring during the operating life of the project and are the most difficult to identify. The analyst must remember that only incremental cash flows should be included.

- *Cash revenues* include sales and other incidental income. These cash flows are usually not an annuity because unit sales and prices will not be constant from year to year.

Operating expenses do not include interest or other capital costs.

- *Cash expenses* include inventory, labor, fuel or power, maintenance, rents, contract services, and any number of other incremental costs. As with sales, they normally vary from period to period. These are operating expenses and *do not include interest or other capital costs*. Costs of capital are included in the discount rate. Replacement projects often reduce expenses, which produces cash savings.
- *Depreciation* of fixed assets is a noncash, tax-deductible expense. Depreciation actually reduces cash outflow because it is a noncash expense that provides a tax deduction for the company. For a replacement project, only the change in depreciation between the new and old projects is relevant.

Project Termination

- *Income from sale of the project* (cash inflow): Projects often have economic value that lasts beyond their term of service to the company. They may be sold intact, sold in parts, or perhaps sold for scrap. Companies often plan to resell projects or assets after a specified period. The resale or terminal value of a project may add significantly to its investment value.
- *Tax effect of a project sale* (cash inflow or outflow): The tax effect of this future sale is treated in same way as that on the sale of the existing asset.
- *Recovery of net working capital* (cash inflow or outflow): With termination of a project, the initial change in net working capital is reversed in order to return to the original net working capital position.

Cash Flow Calculations

In this section, we look at two types of project cash flows that require specific calculations.

The Tax Effect of Asset Sales

If an asset has a depreciated book value of $2,500 and is sold for $3,000, the $500 gain increases corporate tax by $500 times the marginal corporate tax rate.[10] If the tax rate were 34%, the added tax would equal $500 × 0.34 = $170. If the asset were sold for $2,000, the $500 loss would decrease taxes by $170. Some or all of the gain on an asset sale actually represents the recapture of depreciation and not a capital gain.[11] Currently, the tax rate on capital gains and losses is the same as the tax rate on income, so the source of the gain is immaterial. However, there have been periods when the capital gain tax rate is less than that on ordinary income.

To illustrate the tax effect on initial investment and termination cash flows, consider a project in which existing equipment is to be replaced by new equipment costing $10,000. The existing equipment may be sold for $3,000, but it has a depreciated book value of $2,500, creating a $500 taxable gain on the sale. The tax rate is 34%. Cash flows are starred (*):

*project cost	($10,000)	
*sale price of existing asset	$ 3,000	
book value of existing asset	$ 2,500	
gain (loss)	$ 500	
*tax effect of sale	$ (170)	(500 × 0.34)

[10]The marginal tax rate is the effective incremental rate for that project. Corporate income tax rates are not as graduated as personal tax rates, meaning that over a large range of earnings, the rate is flat.

[11]An asset that originally cost $5,000 has been depreciated to a book value of $3,000. The $2,000 depreciation is a tax-deductible expense. If the asset is sold for $3,500, the actual depreciation should be $1,500 rather than $2,000. Therefore, the company is obliged to pay back the taxes saved on the difference ($500 = $2,000 − $1,500).

initial cash flow = project cost + sale price + tax effect
= (10,000) + 3,000 + (170) = ($7,170)

Operating Cash Flows

The estimates of annual operating income and expenses must be converted to operating cash flows. This is done using the net income approach to calculating cash flows introduced in Chapter 4. The first step is to subtract depreciation and operating expenses from cash revenues to produce earnings before tax (EBT). Corporate income tax (tax) is the product of EBT and the marginal corporate tax rate. Tax is subtracted from EBT to produce earnings after tax (EAT). Finally, depreciation, which is a noncash expense, is added to EAT to produce operating cash flow. Project cash flows and the calculation of operating cash flow are summarized in Exhibit 9.1.

The Challenge of Estimating Project Cash Flows

These guidelines for estimating project cash flows do not capture the difficulty of actually gathering information and producing estimates. A single independent project may include building a plant, installing production equipment, buying trucks, and training workers. Such a project involves gathering and sifting large quantities of information. Incomplete or inaccurate information may lead to an incorrect decision. The large amounts of capital required by many projects make the costs of incorrect decisions that much greater.

Some cash flows are easier to estimate than others because they are determined by contract (buying equipment) or by law (taxes). Estimating these cash flows is relatively straightforward. Future cash flows that are dependent on the success of the project require more sophisticated and time-consuming estimates. In Exhibit 9.2, project cash flows are divided into two categories: those that are fairly easy to estimate and those that are more difficult. Keep in mind that these categories are guidelines only and not absolutes. For example, project cost is very difficult to estimate if the project is a multimillion-dollar factory.

For complex projects, initial investment and termination cash flows may occur over several years. For example, it may take years to plan, build, and equip a new plant. Similarly, closing a major facility may also take several years.

EXHIBIT 9.2
ESTIMATING PROJECT CASH FLOWS

	LESS DIFFICULT TO ESTIMATE	MORE DIFFICULT TO ESTIMATE
Initial Investment	Project cost Investment tax credit Sale of existing asset Tax effect of asset sale	Change in net working capital
Operating Cash Flows	Depreciation	Cash revenues Expenses
Project Termination		Income from sale of project Tax effect of project sale Recovery of net working capital

To illustrate how the timing of cash flows might differ, consider the following two projects:

LESS COMPLEX PROJECT	
	YEARS
Initial investment	0
Operating cash flows	1–6
Project termination	6
MORE COMPLEX PROJECT	
	YEARS
Initial investment	0–4
Operating cash flows	5–23
Project termination	23–25

Notice that for both projects, operating cash flows may occur concurrently with termination cash flows. The less complex project may continue to operate until the day it is sold. The more complex project's production may be phased out over several years.

ANALYZING THE JACKLINE HARDWARE PROJECT

Project Cash Flows

Pogo Offshore Ltd. (POL) is a supplier of high-quality hardware and gear for offshore cruising and racing sailboats. The company was started 7 years ago by a young engineer named Jack Elihu. POL has developed a superior method for rigging jacklines on off-shore boats.[12] Rigging these lines requires several custom deck hardware items, and POL is considering producing these items and selling them as a package with lines and safety harnesses. To produce the hardware

EXHIBIT 9.3

POGO OFFSHORE LTD., JACKLINE HARDWARE PROJECT: CALCULATING THE TAX EFFECTS OF ASSET SALES

Transparency Available

CORPORATE TAX RATE = 34%	
Sale of Existing Asset (year 0)	
Book value (book)	$ 0
Sale price (sale)	$13,500
Tax effect of sale	
[(sale − book) * tax rate]	$ 4,590
Sale of Jackline Hardware Assets (year 6)	
Purchase price	$133,000
Book value (book)	$ 0
Sale price (sale)	$ 29,000
Tax effect of sale	
[(sale − book) * tax rate]	$ 9,860

[12]Jacklines run fore and aft along the deck and are securely attached to the boat. Crew members attach safety harnesses to the lines to avoid being swept overboard from a boat pitching and rolling in high seas.

EXHIBIT 9.4

POGO OFFSHORE LTD., JACKLINE HARDWARE PROJECT: CASH FLOWS

	YEAR						
	0	1	2	3	4	5	6
Initial Investment							
Project cost	($133,000)						
ITC	$0						
Added net working capital	($ 29,260)						
Sale of asset	$ 13,500						
Tax effect of sale	($ 4,590)						
	($153,350)						
Operating Cash Flows (incremental)							
Cash revenues [S]		$61,818	$66,145	$70,775	$77,145	$84,088	$96,702
Expenses [E]		$27,200	$26,458	$28,310	$28,544	$29,431	$33,846
Depreciation [dep]		$26,600	$42,560	$25,536	$15,322	$15,322	$ 7,661
Earnings before tax (EBT = S − E − dep)		$ 8,018	($ 2,873)	$16,929	$33,280	$39,336	$55,195
tax (rate = .34) [(EBT)(tax rate)]		$ 2,726	$0	$ 5,756	$11,315	$13,374	18,766
Earnings after tax [EAT = EBT − tax]		$ 5,292	($ 2,873)	$11,173	$21,965	$25,962	$36,429
Add back depreciation [EAT + dep]		$31,892	$39,687	$36,709	$37,286	$41,283	$44,090
Project Termination Cash Flows							
Income from sale							$29,000
Tax effect of sale							($ 9,860)
Recovering net working capital							$29,260
							$48,400
Annual depreciation rate		20.00%	32.00%	19.20%	11.52%	11.52%	5.76%

Use the Exhibit 9.4 transparency to explain how project cash flows are derived and displayed.
Transparency Available

requires an investment of $133,000 in tools to make blocks and fasteners. This will allow POL to retire some existing tools used for making hardware for old-style jacklines. POL expects to produce this hardware for 6 years. In 6 years, Elihu figures that demand will have grown to the point where he will either have to make a major investment in the product to increase production or license the product to a larger firm. Either way, POL will no longer need the existing tools. Tools of this type are depreciated using a 5-year accelerated cost recovery schedule.[13] The projected cash flows for this project are shown in Exhibits 9.3 and 9.4.

Exhibit 9.3 presents data on the sale of the existing asset and the sale in year 6 of the assets of the jackline hardware project. Exhibit 9.4 presents the cash flows for the project.

Calculating the Net Present Value and Internal Rate of Return for the Jackline Hardware Project

The net present value (NPV) of an investment is the present value of the future cash flows minus the initial investment (NPV = PV − II).[14] Present value (PV)

[13]Tax depreciation schedules are presented in Appendix 9A.

[14]Remember that the initial investment is always a cash outflow. In many of the exhibits in this chapter, we express the initial investment as a negative number.

is the summation of the discounted operating cash flows (OCF) plus the discounted terminal cash flows (TCF). Net present value measures the dollar value added to the firm by the investment. The formula for calculating NPV is

Relate Equation (9.1) to Exhibit 9.5.

$$\text{NPV} = -\text{II} + \sum_{t=1}^{n} \frac{\text{OCF}_t}{(1 + R(r))^t} + \frac{\text{TCF}_n}{(1 + R(r))^n} \tag{9.1}$$

where

II = initial investment
OCF_t = operating cash flows in year t
TCF = terminal cash flows
t = year
n = life span (in years) of the project
$R(r)$ = project required rate of return

For this project, we will use a 10% required rate of return. In Chapter 10, we will show how to estimate the required rate of return for a project. Using Equation (9.1), the NPV for the jackline hardware project is

$$\begin{aligned}\text{NPV} &= -153{,}350 + \frac{\$31{,}892}{1.1} + \frac{\$39{,}687}{1.1^2} + \frac{\$36{,}709}{1.1^3} \\ &\quad + \frac{\$37{,}286}{1.1^4} + \frac{\$41{,}283}{1.1^5} + \frac{\$44{,}090}{1.1^6} + \frac{\$48{,}400}{1.1^6} \\ &= \$39{,}331\end{aligned}$$

Exhibit 9.5 summarizes the project cash flows and calculation of NPV. The NPV indicates that if our cash flow estimates are correct and if 10% is the appropriate required rate of return, the jackline hardware project will add $39,331 in value to the company.

Transparency Available

EXHIBIT 9.5

POGO OFFSHORE LTD., JACKLINE HARDWARE PROJECT: CASH FLOW SUMMARY AND NET PRESENT VALUE

	YEAR						
	0	1	2	3	4	5	6
Initial investment	($153,350)						
Operating cash flows		$31,892	$39,687	$36,709	$37,286	$41,283	$44,090
Termination cash flows							$48,400
Cash flows	($153,350)	$31,892	$39,687	$36,709	$37,286	$41,283	$92,490
Present value	($153,350)	$28,993	$32,799	$27,580	$25,467	$25,634	$52,208
Net present value	$ 39,331						
Required rate of return	10.00%						
IRR	17.13%						

A project's **internal rate of return** (IRR) is its expected rate of return.[15] IRR discounts future project cash flows at this expected rate of return, producing a net present value of zero. The IRR is calculated by solving for the discount rate that satisfies the condition NPV = 0 (PV = II). Solving for a project's IRR is equivalent to solving for a bond's yield-to-maturity (YTM). IRR and YTM were introduced in Chapter 6.

For a single future cash flow or a multiple-period annuity cash flow, IRR can be solved algebraically.[16] However, as we pointed out earlier in the chapter, cash flows for a project are seldom annuities. For nonannuities, we must find the discount rate that satisfies the condition NPV = 0 through trial and error.[17] This is a tedious process without the assistance of a calculator or computer.

The formula for IRR is

$$\text{II} = \sum_{t=1}^{n} \frac{\text{OCF}_t}{(1 + \text{IRR})^t} + \frac{\text{TCF}_n}{(1 + \text{IRR})^n} \tag{9.2}$$

$$\$153{,}350 = \frac{\$31{,}892}{1 + \text{IRR}} + \frac{\$39{,}687}{1 + \text{IRR}^2} + \frac{\$36{,}709}{1 + \text{IRR}^3} + \frac{\$37{,}286}{1 + \text{IRR}^4}$$
$$+ \frac{\$41{,}283}{1 + \text{IRR}^5} + \frac{\$44{,}090}{1 + \text{IRR}^6} + \frac{\$48{,}400}{1 + \text{IRR}^6}$$

For the jackline hardware project, the IRR is 17.13%.

Comparing NPV and IRR Results

If we discount future project cash flows at 17.13%, their present value equals the initial investment, which means that NPV = 0. This tells us that 17.13% is the project's IRR. Notice that the IRR for this project is much greater than the required rate of return (17.13% > 10%). This relationship is true for every project that has a positive net present value. If the NPV of the jackline hardware were negative (less than 0), the IRR would be less than the required rate of return of 10%. Symbolically, the relationship between NPV and IRR may be stated as follows:

If NPV > 0, then IRR > (*R*)*r*.
If NPV = 0, then IRR = (*R*)*r*.
If NPV < 0, then IRR < (*R*)*r*.

To help in understanding the relationship between NPV and IRR, it may be useful to calculate NPV at various discount rates, including 17.13%, which is the project's IRR. Exhibit 9.6 shows the jackline project net present values at various discount rates.

---

[15]Our discussion of IRR assumes that the project has a typical cash flow pattern, which is an initial cash outflow followed by cash inflows in future years. If there is a cash outflow in any of the future years, the IRR solution and interpretation is ambiguous.

[16]See Chapter 5.

[17]Financial calculators and computer spreadsheet programs use a process of iteration for finding IRR.

DISCOUNT RATE	NPV
0%	$125,998
2%	$104,621
4%	$ 85,543
6%	$ 68,465
8%	$ 53,133
10%	$ 39,331
12%	$ 26,872
14%	$ 15,596
16%	$ 5,365
17.13%	$ 0
18%	($ 3,940)
20%	($ 12,422)

EXHIBIT 9.6

POGO OFFSHORE LTD., JACKLINE HARDWARE PROJECT: NET PRESENT VALUE IS A FUNCTION OF THE DISCOUNT RATE

The discount rate and NPV are inversely related.

Figure 9.1 is a plot of the Exhibit 9.6 values. The IRR of 17.13% is the point at which NPV = 0. (This value is where the line crosses the x axis.)

Note that at discount rates less than 17.13%, NPV is positive, whereas rates above 17.13% yield negative NPVs.

Decision Criteria

An independent project should be taken if its NPV is positive (NPV > 0). NPV measures the project's contribution to firm wealth. In our example, the jackline hardware project adds $39,331 to the value of Pogo Offshore Ltd. Stated another way, if Pogo Offshore does not take on the project, it will have missed an opportunity to increase firm value by that amount. Following this argument, even projects that have small NPVs should be taken. Any positive NPV project is expected to produce a cash flow in excess of that needed to provide required rates of return to the company's investors. A project whose NPV is 0 is expected to produce just enough cash flows to provide these required rates of return. However, such a project would produce no residual cash flows to increase shareholder wealth. Therefore, shareholders would be indifferent toward the project.

Although IRR does not directly measure the project's contribution to firm

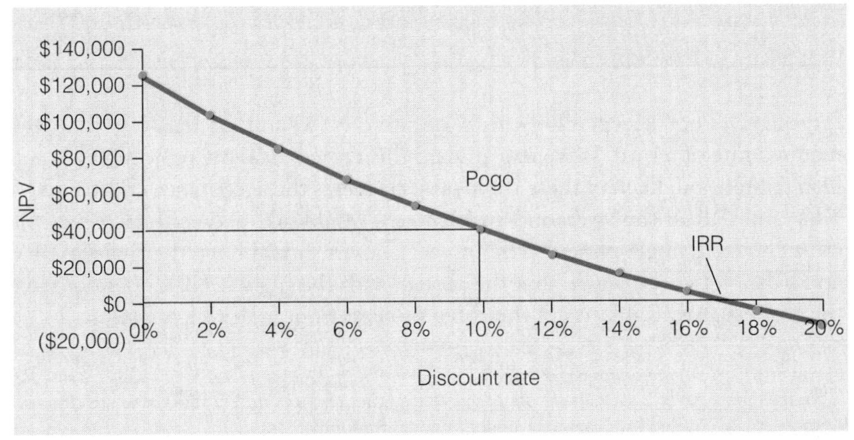

FIGURE 9.1

POGO OFFSHORE LTD., JACKLINE HARDWARE PROJECT

NPV IS A FUNCTION OF THE DISCOUNT RATE.

Transparency Available

wealth, any project whose IRR is greater than $R(r)$ should be accepted and any project whose IRR is less than $R(r)$ should not. This idea leads to an important point.

NPV and IRR cause us to accept and reject the same independent projects.

For independent projects such as the jackline hardware project (assuming no other restrictions), both NPV and IRR analyses will cause us to accept and reject the same projects. Therefore, it does not matter which method of analysis we choose. Both use discounted cash flows and the required rate of return in the investment decision. Net present value uses the required rate of return as a discount rate and produces a dollar value for the project; IRR uses the required return as a **hurdle rate**, or reference point against which to compare the project's internal rate of return.

CHOOSING BETWEEN NET PRESENT VALUE AND INTERNAL RATE OF RETURN

Why We Must Choose

In the last section, we showed that, for independent projects with no other restrictions, net present value and internal rate of return agree on which projects are acceptable and which are not.[18] However, NPV and IRR may not agree on the acceptability of projects when we must choose between projects that are not independent.

Recall that dependent projects may be either complementary or mutually exclusive. Complementary dependencies are easily removed by combining these projects into a single independent project. Mutually exclusive projects, however, require us to choose between competing projects, all of which are acceptable using our NPV/IRR criteria. We illustrate with an example.

Projects A through D are mutually exclusive. The first step in the analysis is to calculate each project's NPV and IRR, shown below. The required rate of return $R(r)$, equals 10%.

Choosing between acceptable mutually exclusive projects requires ranking the projects by NPV or IRR. These rankings may differ, forcing a choice between NPV and IRR.

PROJECT	NPV	IRR
A	$1453	15.3%
B	$1849	14.6%
C	−$1596	3.7%
D	$1468	19.4%

Project C is not acceptable, with a negative NPV and an IRR less than the required rate of return, so we may discard this project, leaving projects A, B, and D in contention. Each of these three projects meets the acceptance criteria under NPV and IRR. If they were independent, we would take them all. However, we must choose a single project. The project chosen should have the highest NPV and IRR. Notice, however, that the project with the highest NPV does not have the highest IRR. Rankings of the three projects from high to low are:

[18] We have been pretty cagey about identifying these other restrictions. For those who are curious, restrictions are covered in Chapter 11 under "Capital Rationing."

PROJECT NPV	PROJECT IRR
B	D
D	A
A	B

The choice of project depends on the method chosen. NPV favors project B and IRR favors project D. Neither selects project A. In the next section, we explain why this conflict occurs.

The Timing of Project Cash Flows

When conflicts in ranking, such as in projects A–D, occur, there are two possible explanations: (1) The timing of the future cash flows between projects may be considerably different, or (2) the initial investments in the projects may be considerably different.

Exhibit 9.7 shows the cash flows, NPVs, and IRRs for projects A–D. Because project C is not acceptable, we are interested only in the remaining three projects. An examination of their cash flows reveals that they differ with respect to their timing over the 6 year period. Project A is an annuity; project B's cash flows occur mostly in the later years; and project D's cash flows occur mostly in the early years. Project B, whose cash flows occur late, has the highest NPV; project D, whose cash flows occur early, has the highest IRR.

The timing of cash flows produces different rankings because of the different discount rates used by the two methods. IRR discounts cash flows at the IRR, whereas NPV discounts at the required rate of return, $R(r)$. Because each of these projects is acceptable, IRR is greater than $R(r)$ [IRR $>$ $R(r)$].

NPV assumes that project cash flows are reinvested at $R(r)$, whereas IRR assumes that they are reinvested at the IRR. The reinvestment rate affects projects with early cash flows more than those with later cash flows, because early cash flow returns are compounded over more periods.

In analyzing investments that generate cash flows over several years, we must make some assumption about the rate at which those cash flows are reinvested. Companies seldom leave money idle. In Chapter 5, we showed that discounting and compounding are two sides of the same coin.[19] In other words, project cash

EXHIBIT 9.7

MUTUALLY EXCLUSIVE PROJECTS WITH DIFFERENT TIMING OF CASH FLOWS

	YEAR								
PROJECT	0	1	2	3	4	5	6	NPV (10%)	IRR
A	−9,000	2,400	2,400	2,400	2,400	2,400	2,400	$1,453	15.3%
B	−9,000	500	500	2,000	2,000	6,000	6,000	$1,849	14.6%
C	−9,000	1,700	1,700	1,700	1,700	1,700	1,700	($1,596)	3.7%
D	−9,000	5,000	5,000	1,000	1,000	300	300	$1,468	19.4%

[19]Recall from Chapter 5 that the rate (r) is both a compound rate of return and a discount rate. If $r = 10\%$, compounding cash flows at that rate yields their future value. Discounting future cash flows at that rate yields their present value.

flows are reinvested to earn a compound rate of return that is equal to the discount rate. When NPV is used, we assume that project cash flows are reinvested at $R(r)$. When IRR is used, we assume that the cash flows are reinvested at the IRR which is greater than $R(r)$.

This difference in **reinvestment rate** affects project D more than the other two. This is because project D's cash flows occur early in the 6 year period. A year 1 cash flow is reinvested, at a compound rate of return, for the next five years. By contrast, a year 5 cash flow is reinvested for only a single year. Thus, the higher reinvestment rate under IRR makes those early cash flows in project D more valuable. By the same token, project B's value is less affected because its cash flows occur relatively late in the project's life. Notice that project B has the lowest IRR of the 3 acceptable projects. In general, projects whose cash flows occur mostly in the early years have an advantage under IRR, and those whose cash flows occur more in the later years are at a disadvantage. This condition holds whenever IRR is greater than $R(r)$.

Differences in Initial Investment

Exhibit 9.8 illustrates four projects, E–H, that vary in their initial investment. Ranking these four projects, starting with the highest, produces the following:

PROJECT NPV	PROJECT IRR
H	E
G	F
F	G
E	H

In these four projects, we see the tendency for projects with large initial investments to have high NPVs but low IRRs. Large projects should produce greater dollar values. However, there is a tendency for such projects to have lower rates of return (IRR) because of their large initial investment. This is the case with projects E–H.

Resolving the Conflict: Choosing NPV Over IRR

Conflict in project ranking arises only when we must choose from among acceptable, but mutually exclusive, projects. This potential conflict should cause analysts to examine carefully their estimates of cash flows and required rates of return.[20]

[20]Admittedly, to illustrate the potential for such conflicts, we have created sets of competing projects with cash flow timing and size differences that are uncommon in real life. Size and timing differences will always be present; however, mutually exclusive projects are bound by a common purpose, so in most cases these differences will be less than those illustrated.

EXHIBIT 9.8

MUTUALLY EXCLUSIVE PROJECTS WITH DIFFERENT INITIAL INVESTMENTS

	YEAR								
PROJECT	0	1	2	3	4	5	6	NPV (10%)	IRR
E	−5,000	1,800	1,800	1,800	1,800	1,800	1,800	$2,839	27.7%
F	−10,000	3,300	3,300	3,300	3,300	3,300	3,300	$4,372	23.9%
G	−15,000	4,500	4,500	4,500	4,500	4,500	4,500	$4,599	19.9%
H	−20,000	5,700	5,700	5,700	5,700	5,700	5,700	$4,825	17.9%

When we are faced with conflicting rankings between NPV and IRR, which do we use? There are three reasons for choosing NPV.[21]

When NPV and IRR rankings differ, there are three reasons for choosing NPV.

Reason 1: The Reinvestment Rate

NPV assumes that project cash flows are reinvested at the required rate of return, whereas IRR for an acceptable project assumes that cash flows are reinvested at a higher rate [IRR > $R(r)$]. Consider project D in Exhibit 9.7 with its IRR of 19.4%. This project generates a $5,000 cash flow in year 1, yet the project's life is 6 years. The IRR method implicitly assumes that this $5,000 is reinvested for the remaining 5 years in some other investment, which yields 19.4% per year. The NPV method, on the other hand, assumes that the $5,000 is reinvested at 10%, which is the required return. Which of these reinvestment assumptions is more realistic? Unless the company can continue to find projects that yield 19.4%, it is more prudent to assume that project cash flows will be reinvested at the lower rate. This assumption gives the edge to NPV.

Reason 2: Value Creation

By calculating NPV for independent projects, we are able to sum these NPV dollar amounts to determine how much value the investment program is adding to the firm. We have seen that for mutually exclusive projects the IRR method may not favor those that actually add the most value. Certainly NPV is a more direct measure of value.

Reason 3: Multiple IRRs

The cash flows for all investments follow the same basic pattern: An initial investment (cash outflow) is followed by cash inflows, usually over a number of years. Sometimes the initial investment may last for several years before the cash inflows begin. For most projects, once the cash inflows begin, they continue

[21]While there are compelling arguments for choosing NPV, IRR is often preferred in practice. One reason is that a rate of return is intuitively more meaningful to decision makers than a dollar NPV measure. For example, an IRR may be directly compared to a corporate cost of capital, current interest rates or some other benchmark.

until the project is terminated. However, there are cases where a project may require a midlife reinvestment. A planned upgrade of a plant or a piece of equipment would be an example. The cash flow pattern of such an investment would look like this:

YEAR	CASH FLOW (+/−)
0	−
1	+
2	+
3	+
4	−
5	+
6	+

With this or any cash flow pattern involving more than one sign change, there is more than one discount rate that renders NPV = 0. Therefore, the project has more than one IRR. For such projects, the calculated IRR is unreliable, and IRR should be abandoned in favor of NPV.

PAYBACK AS AN ALTERNATIVE TO NPV AND IRR

Several decades ago, **payback** was the predominant means of evaluating a project. Payback is simply a measure of how many years it takes a project to recoup its initial investment. Consider a $10,000 investment that returns the following cash flows:

YEAR	CASH INFLOW	CUMULATIVE CASH INFLOW
1	$3,000	$ 3,000
2	4,000	7,000
3	6,000	13,000
4	5,000	
5	3,000	
6	2,000	

The payback period for this project is $2\frac{1}{2}$ years. This value is calculated by summing the cash inflows, starting with year 1, until the sum equals the initial investment. The number of years required to recoup the investment is the payback period. In this case, we can see that the payback is between 2 and 3 years. A more exact answer requires interpolation. The year 3 cash flow is $6000, but only half of that, $3000/$6000, is needed to recover the initial investment of $10,000. The payback period is 2 years plus half of year 3, or $2\frac{1}{2}$ years.

Payback has several serious shortcomings.

Payback has some serious shortcomings. First, we have not discounted future cash flows, so the time value of money is ignored. This flaw could be overcome by calculating a payback period using discounted annual cash flows. However, discounting cannot overcome payback's other flaws.

Payback also disregards cash flows occurring after the payback period. For this project, these cash flows occur in the second half of year 3 and in years 4 through

6. To see that this problem is serious, disregard the cash flows in years 4–6 in the preceding project. The payback period remains the same, but there can be no doubt that the project's value changes.

The final shortcoming of payback is that it provides no rational decision criterion. Both NPV and IRR use the required rate of return, either as a discount rate or a hurdle rate, and both provide generally agreed-upon and defensible decision criteria. By contrast, there are no guidelines for determining an acceptable payback period. Short of designating an arbitrary time period, there is no way of knowing whether a $2\frac{1}{2}$-year payback period is acceptable. If it is acceptable, why? If not, why not?

In spite of its shortcomings, payback may be used by companies facing serious illiquidity, meaning that the company has trouble raising cash to meet its obligations. Illiquidity may signal impending failure. Companies in such a state will probably curtail investing and may adopt a liquidity criterion for those remaining essential investments. Therefore, projects that return cash flows quickly would be taken in preference to those whose cash flows were spread over a longer period of time.

In the case of illiquidity, payback may approximate a wealth-maximizing approach to valuing investments. Illiquidity is an extreme form of risk, raising the required rate of return on investments. The high discount rate severely penalizes more distant cash flows and, therefore, longer-lived projects. The possibility that payback may choose the same projects as NPV does not justify the use of payback in preference to NPV.

OPTIONS IN CAPITAL PROJECTS

Learning to Recognize Options

One of the most important innovations in corporate finance has been the recognition and valuation of options, or **contingent claims**. In this section we provide a nonmathematical introduction to options and option valuation, particularly options associated with investments in real assets. Although this will not prepare you to place a dollar value on an option contract, it will provide an intuitive understanding of what options are, how they can affect the firm's investment decisions, and what determines an option's value.

Here is a definition of a basic option contract: An option gives the holder or owner of the option the *right* to complete a *transaction* for a *specific asset* at a *prespecified price* within a *set time period*. Let's look at the various parts of this definition separately. The owner has the right to complete a transaction but has no obligation to do so. The owner has the option of completing the transaction if she feels it is beneficial for her to do so. The transaction may be either a purchase or a sale. As options are applied to more situations, *transaction* must be more broadly defined to include a range of activities. For example, having the option to open or close a silver mine, depending on silver prices, does not involve buying or selling but is nonetheless an option. Options to buy assets are called **call options**, whereas options to sell are called **put options**.[22] Options can involve

[22]*Exercising a call option* means calling the asset away from someone, and *exercising a put option* means putting the asset to someone.

a variety of assets, such as shares of stock, futures contracts, parcels of land, or airplanes. The asset upon which an option is based is called the **underlying asset**. The option contract specifies the price, called the **exercise price**, at which the transaction will occur if the owner opts to complete the transaction. Finally, options expire; that is, options must be exercised (or the transaction must be completed) on or before some preestablished **expiration date**.

Shopping coupons often do not state a price but instead state the amount that the price will be reduced. In this case, the exercise price is the retail price less the coupon amount.

The definition of an option may appear to be complicated, but you have almost certainly dealt with options at some time. For example, suppose your student newspaper has a coupon that lets you buy a pizza for $9.99. The coupon lets you complete a transaction (buy a pizza) for a specific asset (one Super Large Kitchen Sink pizza) at a prespecified price ($9.99) within a set time period (on or before November 15). This is an option.

Pie in the Sky Pizza
Coupon
Only $9.99 for a Super Large Kitchen Sink Pizza
The pizza with absolutely everything, even the kitchen sink!
Normally $13.99
Coupon expires November 15

Thus, the pizza coupon satisfies the attributes of a call option contract.

Underlying asset: The pizza is the asset to be traded and so determines the option's value.
Call option: The coupon gives the holder the right to buy the underlying asset.
Expiration date: November 15 is the last day the option can be exercised.
Exercise price: $9.99 will be the transaction price if the option is exercised.

Here is an example of another option. You find an item in a shop that you like and ask the salesperson to put it aside for you until tomorrow, by which time you will have decided whether or not you really want to buy it. This agreement includes the key attributes of an option contract. The agreement is for a limited time period, the purchase price has been established, and there is no obligation to buy the item; you may choose to complete or not to complete the transaction at your discretion without penalty.

In the two examples of options just described, no one paid for the options, but the options had value nonetheless. The store gives away the set-aside option to provide service to customers. The price of that service is included in the price of the items the shop sells. The pizza coupon draws customers from other pizza parlors, so it introduces new customers to Pie in the Sky pizzas. Their repeat business will eventually pay for the value of the coupon. Do not think that because you did not explicitly pay for an option that it has no value. All options with a chance of being exercised have value, and you will certainly pay for the option in some way.

When the value of an option is not included in the price of other items or captured through repeat transactions, the option is purchased, much as a friend might buy the pizza coupon from you. At the beginning of this chapter we gave an example of a purchased option. When United Airlines bought options for Boeing 747 airliners, it paid for those options. When a real estate developer obtains an option to buy a parcel of land, he must pay the owner for that option. In the next section we discuss several factors that determine the price of options.

Factors that Affect the Value of an Option

Although pizza coupons are free, they still have a value. In this section we discuss the factors that determine the value of simple option contracts. We begin by considering when the pizza coupon would be used; that is, what conditions must hold for a person to use the coupon rather than buy the pizza at its regular price? We then examine several factors that affect the value of the coupon prior to its being used.

When Would You Exercise the Option?

We **exercise a call option** (an option to buy an asset) if the current market price exceeds the exercise price.[23] That is, we buy the asset using the cheapest means available. If the market price exceeds the option's exercise price, then using the option saves us money. If the market price is below the exercise price, then we pay less by ignoring the option and buying the asset at its market price. For example, you would use the coupon to buy a pizza (assuming you want a pizza) only if the price without the coupon were more than $9.99.[24] If the price without the coupon were only $9.50, possibly because of another sale, then you would rather pay $9.50 than use the coupon and pay $9.99. If pizza prices remain at $9.50 through November 15, you would let the option expire unexercised. The coupon is worthless because exercising it would cost more than simply buying the pizza for $9.50.

The pizza example isn't perfect. You would exercise the pizza coupon only if you wanted to eat pizza. With stock options you exercise the option whenever it is profitable to do so, whether or not you want to own the stock.

Having determined when we would exercise an option, we now discuss the

[23]We exercise a put option (an option to sell an asset) if the exercise price exceeds the current market price. This allows us to go to the market, buy the asset, and immediately resell it at the exercise price for a profit.

[24]This situation points out a difference between options on some real assets (e.g., pizzas, machines, or land) and options on financial assets. Often, options on real assets are exercised only if the holder wants the asset. In the pizza example, you would have to want to eat a pizza. But options on financial assets—commodities or shares of stocks—are always exercised if the appropriate relationship of market price to exercise price holds because the asset can easily be sold to realize a profit. Because liquid secondary markets do not exist for all real assets (Where do you sell a preowned pizza?), the exercise rule may not always apply.

factors that determine an option's value before it is exercised. Like the prices of many assets, the value of options fluctuate through time. The following guidelines provide some insight to the factors that cause the value of options to rise or fall.

Suppose you have one of only a few pizza coupons that were printed. A friend who likes pizza might offer to buy the coupon from you so that she can save money on her next pizza purchase. What might influence how much your friend pays you for the coupon? The regular price of Super Large Kitchen Sink pizzas is $13.99. Suppose that there are two coupons available with different exercise prices: Coupon A lets the bearer buy the pizza for $9.99, and coupon B lets the bearer buy the pizza for $7.50. Would your friend pay more for coupon A (with its savings of $4.00 = $13.99 minus $9.99) or coupon B (with its savings of $6.49 = $13.99 minus $7.50)? The savings from coupon B are much greater, so your friend would pay more for the coupon with the lower exercise price. Thus, the exercise price of the option plays a major role in the value of the option. For call options, the lower the exercise price, the more valuable the option, all else equal.[25] Notice too that the exercise price sets a limit on how much a person will pay for an option. In the pizza example, no one will pay more than $4.00 for the $9.99 coupon, because doing so means paying more than $13.99 for the pizza ($9.99 plus more than $4.00 for the coupon).

All else equal, as an option's exercise price goes down, the value of a call option increases.

If the exercise price of the option is fixed, say at $9.99, then the value of a call option increases as the price of the underlying asset increases. As the price of the underlying asset rises (i.e., the price of the pizza increases), the value of the option to buy the asset for the fixed price of $9.99 also increases. With increasing asset prices, the option to purchase at a fixed price implies greater and greater savings and, thus, a more valuable call option.[26] As the market price of the underlying asset fluctuates, the value of options based on that asset also fluctuate.

All else equal, the higher the price of the underlying asset, the higher the value of a call option.

Ask students if they would prefer (i.e., value more highly) a 1 hour or a 3 day extension on a term-paper deadline. More time is better.

If today is September 1 and the coupon expires on November 15, there will almost certainly be an occasion during the next $2\frac{1}{2}$ months when someone you know will want pizza. If today is November 14 and the coupon expires tomorrow, there is a much smaller chance anyone will use it. Therefore, the value of the

---

[25]Because several factors affect the value of an option, we must hold other factors constant, or hold all else equal, while we talk about the effect of any single factor. In economics this is referred to as ceteris paribus (Latin: other things being equal).

[26]For put options—that is, options to sell at a fixed exercise price—the value of the option rises as prices go down. As the market price falls below the exercise price (i.e., the selling price), there is greater profit potential. If the market price of an asset is $70 and an investor has a put option to sell an asset for $100, then she can go to the market, buy the asset for $70, and immediately sell it for $100, making $30. If the market price continues to fall, she can buy the asset for an even lower price and make greater profits.

coupon depends on the likelihood it will be used, which in turn depends on the length of time remaining before it expires, all else held equal. With a longer time to expiration, the coupon has relatively high value because it will almost certainly be used.

All else equal, as the time to expiration increases, the value of a call option increases.

If pizza prices change a great deal, then the value of the coupon increases. Suppose pizzas vary in price from one week to the next. One week the price is $13.99, the next it is $12.00, and the following it is $14.75. If your friend is concerned that he may have a serious craving for pizza when prices are high, then the value of the coupon (i.e., the value of the option) increases further. The more volatile pizza prices are, the larger the potential savings and the higher the value of the coupon.

One approach to demonstrating the effect of volatility is to use two sine waves (representing asset price) on a single axis, one with large amplitude and the other with lower amplitude. A line above and parallel to the axis can represent the exercise price. The diagram should show that with high amplitude there is more chance of the option having value—i.e., the sine wave exceeding the exercise price line.

More price variability means a wider range of possible future prices. All else equal, a wider range of possible prices implies a higher probability that the future market price of the underlying asset will exceed the exercise price, making the option worth exercising. To make money with call options, the price of the underlying asset must exceed the exercise price plus the amount you paid for the option, and the price must do this prior to the expiration date. Therefore, the more variable an asset's price, the more likely the option will be profitable within the expiration period. So investors are willing to pay more for options on assets with high price variability than for those with low variability. Figure 9.2 shows how the probability of exercising an option increases as the variability of a stock's price increases. As the distribution of possible stock prices gets wider (i.e., variability increases), a larger area of the distribution exceeds the exercise price. Recall from statistics that area is synonymous with probability, so greater area indicates higher probability.[27]

All else equal, the more volatile the price of the underlying asset, the more valuable is the option.

Interest rates are a final factor that affect the value of most options. Consider two strategies for purchasing an asset that is selling for $1,000 today. We could go out and buy it today for $1,000, or we could buy an option (say for $4.00) with an exercise price of $1,000. The option lets us defer the large outlay for the asset (the exercise price). If we think of options as allowing us to postpone the purchase of an asset, then options allow us to keep our money (the exercise price) in the bank from today until the option's expiration date. If interest rates are high, keeping our money in the bank may more than offset the price we paid for the option—i.e., the interest earned exceeds the price we paid for the option.

---

[27]You may wonder why the increased chance of a low price is not a concern. Remember that at expiration an option has no value if the asset's price is below the option's exercise price. In terms of the option's value, all prices below the exercise price look the same. It is the distribution of prices above the exercise price that matters. The greater the probability of the asset's price exceeding the exercise price and the greater the range of these profitable outcomes, the greater the value of the option.

FIGURE 9.2

VARIABILITY OF STOCK PRICE AND THE PROBABILITY OF PROFITABLE EXERCISE OF A CALL OPTION

Transparency Available

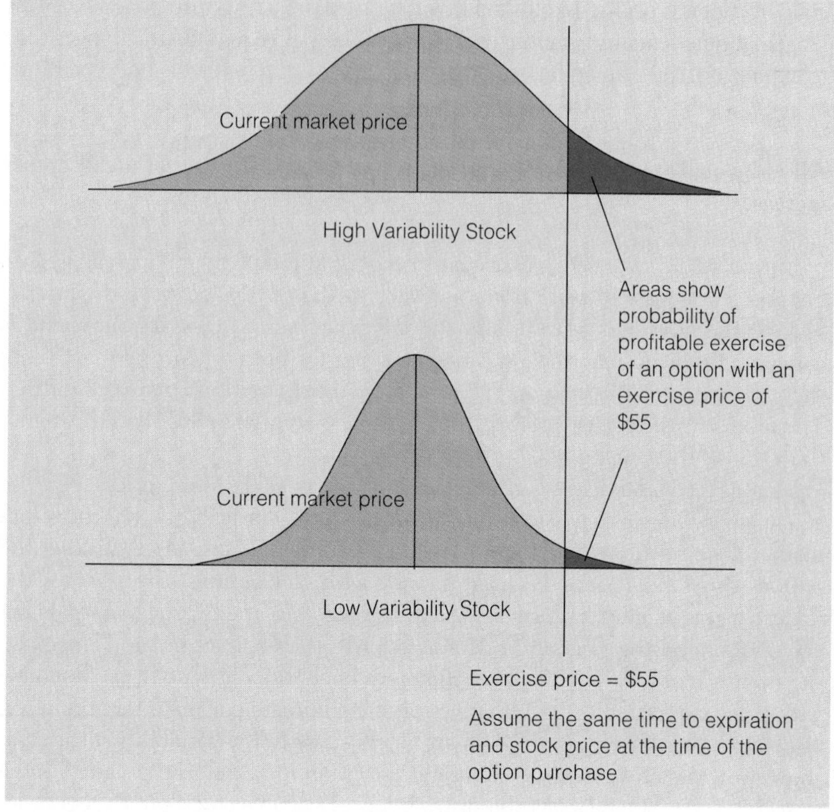

Alternatively, we can look at the opportunity costs involved. If we buy the asset outright for $1,000, we give up the opportunity to earn interest on our money. The higher the interest rate, the greater the value of this lost or foregone opportunity, making the option more attractive. As interest rates rise, so do the opportunity costs associated with spending money today. With high interest rates, we want to keep our money in the bank as long as possible. Because options give us a means for delaying withdrawing our money from the bank, the value of options increases as interest rates rise.

All else equal, as interest rates rise, the value of option contracts also increase.

Transparency Available

The following table summarizes the factors that affect the value of options.

FACTORS AFFECTING THE VALUE OF OPTIONS

- As an option's *exercise price* goes down, the value of a call option increases.
- The higher the *price of the underlying asset*, the higher the value of a call option.
- As the *time to expiration* increases, the value of a call option increases.
- Higher *volatility of the price of the underlying asset* increases the value of the option.
- As *interest rates* rise, the value of option contracts also increases.

Examples of Options in Capital Investments

Options as a Strategic Investment

Returning to the Boeing–United Airlines example, United bought an option for 68 Boeing 747s in addition to placing an order for 60 planes. Delivery dates for these planes stretched from 1995 through 2000, depending on how many options UAL exercised. Why would UAL buy options for so many planes? Instead, why not wait to see how business—flier-miles—grows and buy planes appropriate for that growth? Boeing can build only a limited number of planes per period. If UAL found that its business was booming, it could exercise the options, take delivery, and realize the profits from that growth. If flier-miles do not increase, UAL does not want to be saddled with a fleet of expensive new planes that it cannot pay for. So options are an ideal vehicle for preparing for an uncertain future. If things go well, UAL can exercise its options. But if growth is slow, they can let the options expire without being exercised. Buying the options allows UAL to pursue a high-growth strategy if industry economics warrant such a strategy. Suppose that other airlines bought options from Boeing but UAL did not. If the industry expands, UAL's competitors will increase their fleets and capture the growth. At that time, UAL may not be able to increase its fleet because no new planes are available or the price is too high to make expansion profitable. Thus, United will not share in the industry's growth. UAL's options on airliners allow the company to reduce the effect of risk or uncertainty. Having options prepares the company for a variety of future industry conditions and so reduces its vulnerability to an uncertain future. For this reason, options are often thought of as tools for reducing or eliminating risk.

Toyota provides another example of an investment in a strategic option. In a plant built in 1990, Toyota paid an extra $3 million in equipment, design and manufacturing costs to have an assembly line that could manufacture a broad range of automobile models with short changeover times between models. By building the *option* to switch manufacturing from one model to another, Toyota prepared for unforeseen changes in demand. This is another example of using options to reduce risk. Toyota could have invested less in a plant designed to manufacture just one or two models of cars. Had demand for those models decreased, the plant would require extensive (and expensive) retrofitting. By building in the option to manufacture a variety of models, Toyota reduced the risk of unforeseen changes in demand.

Options to Close Down and Start Up

The option to close down a facility temporarily and then reopen it can have value. For example, a mine can be closed when mineral prices fall below variable costs of production. Closing the mine, with the option of reopening it when mineral prices rise, can help the mining company prevent losses from operating at low prices. The exercise price of this option includes the cost of severance pay for employees, the costs of preparing for the closure, and the cost of any required maintenance while the mine is closed. If these costs are less than the losses that the company would suffer by continuing operations at the low mineral price, then exercising the **closure option** benefits shareholders.

The option to abandon, temporarily close, or postpone starting a project allows a company to make investment decisions when additional information is available.

The Option to Abandon a Project

In NPV analysis, we estimate the life of the project which is usually the economic life of the project's assets. However, in almost all cases a project can be abandoned prior to the end of its economic life, but most NPV analyses ignore this abandonment option. The abandonment option works like this: At any time in a project's life, the current salvage value can be compared to the present value of the project's remaining cash flows. If the salvage value exceeds the present value of the remaining cash flows, then immediate abandonment increases shareholder wealth.

We demonstrate the analysis of the **abandonment option** using data from a printing press project. The project involves a single asset, a printing press with an initial cost of $60,000, which will be used to print a regional weekly business newspaper. Revenues from the project come from both advertising income and subscription payments. The project's after-tax cash flows follow a typical life cycle pattern. They rise as sales build and then flatten and decline as the project matures and competitors enter the field. Because the press has many alternative uses, its salvage value initially declines slowly, reflecting wear and tear rather than obsolescence. At a discount rate of 12%, the appropriate rate for this project, the project has a positive NPV of $14,410, so the project is accepted.

CASH FLOWS FROM PRINTING PRESS PROJECT

	YEAR					
	1	2	3	4	5	6
Cash flow (000s)	12	16	18	18	14	10
Salvage value (000s)	56	52	48	44	34	27

Early termination of a project is beneficial to the company if it earns more from selling the asset than it can from continuing to operate the asset. To determine the optimal termination date, we must compute the NPVs for each year if we abandon the project in that year. Thus, abandonment after 1 year implies earning a cash flow of $12,000 and selling the machine for $56,000. Discounting at 12% results in an NPV(abandon after year 1) of $714.29

$$\text{NPV(year 1)} = \frac{12{,}000 + 56{,}000}{1.12} - 60{,}000 = \$714.29$$

Using this approach, the NPV of abandonment at years 2 through 5 are

$$\text{NPV(year 2)} = \frac{12{,}000}{1.12} + \frac{16{,}000 + 52{,}000}{1.12^2} - 60{,}000 = \$4{,}923.47$$

$$\text{NPV(year 3)} = \frac{12{,}000}{1.12} + \frac{16{,}000}{1.12^2} + \frac{18{,}000 + 48{,}000}{1.12^3} - 60{,}000$$
$$= \$10{,}446.90$$

$$\text{NPV(year 4)} = \frac{12{,}000}{1.12} + \frac{16{,}000}{1.12^2} + \frac{18{,}000}{1.12^3} + \frac{18{,}000 + 44{,}000}{1.12^4} - 60{,}000$$
$$= \$15{,}683.60$$

$$\text{NPV(year 5)} = \frac{12{,}000}{1.12} + \frac{16{,}000}{1.12^2} + \frac{18{,}000}{1.12^3} + \frac{18{,}000}{1.12^4} + \frac{14{,}000 + 34{,}000}{1.12^5} - 60{,}000 = \$14{,}957.20$$

As these values show, the highest NPV occurs when the project ends after year 4. Beyond year 4, the present value of the additional cash inflows does not compensate for the loss in the asset's salvage value. In other words, the cost of continuing—the loss in the value of the asset—exceeds the benefits of continuing—the cash inflows. Being able to abandon the project early, in year 4, earns shareholders an additional \$1,273.50. If the company had to buy the option to terminate the project before year 6, it could pay up to this amount and shareholders would still benefit. Thus, the abandonment option is worth \$1,273.50.

The value of the abandonment option depends on the relation through time between the asset's salvage value and the project's remaining cash flows. The higher the salvage value, the higher the value of the abandonment option. Determining the qualities associated with a relatively higher salvage value provides clues about how to increase the value of the abandonment option. Salvage value is higher when demand for used assets is high. Demand depends in part on the variety of uses an asset has. The more specialized an asset is, the fewer alternative uses, and the lower the salvage value. Although a specialized asset, e.g., a machine designed to make only size-nine ski boots, has lower per-unit production costs, it also has a low salvage value; for instance, there are only a few ski boot manufacturers, and none may use the boot design built into the machine. The more potential buyers, the higher the price, all else equal. When considering an asset, it pays to consider investing in a slightly more generic model rather than a highly specialized model to increase the value of the abandonment option.

The Option to Postpone Investment

Having the **option to delay** an investment can have great value. Postponement means having more information with which to make a decision, and having more information invariably leads to a better decision. Moreover, that additional information may suggest ways that the project can be configured to increase its NPV. The Clean Air Act of 1990 provides an interesting example of the option to postpone investment. The act imposes standards for the emission of sulfur dioxide (SO_2), a chief contributor to acid rain. The first standard went into effect in 1993, with a much more stringent standard to be imposed in the year 2000. Each year, coal-fired electric power plants are given a certain number of **pollution rights**. Each right allows the company to emit one ton of SO_2. The number of rights declines over time in accordance with the act's pollution standards in that year. Power companies have several choices. Companies may pollute up to the limit of the rights received, companies may purchase extra rights from power companies with surplus rights (they emit less SO_2 than their assigned rights allow), or companies may invest in equipment so their emissions and rights comply with the law. Several companies have chosen a strategy of buying rights, thinking that the cost of pollution-control equipment will drop in the near future, making the investment less expensive than it would be now. These companies apparently think that the option to delay (and thereby purchase technologically superior equipment in the year 2000) is worth at least as much as the cost of the pollution rights they must buy.

Adjusting NPV for the Option Effect

For a negative NPV project, the option analysis must determine if the project becomes acceptable if the company makes the additional investment required to obtain the option. For positive NPV projects the analysis must determine if the benefits of obtaining the option more than offset the additional investment; in other words, is the option investment itself a positive NPV investment?

Computing a precise value for options associated with investment decisions is quite difficult. In some analyses there is no need to expend effort on determining the value of the imbedded options. For example, suppose that a project has a positive NPV before consideration of the abandonment option. Because the option will only add value to the project, the NPV will be larger but still positive. When the value of the options associated with a project will not change the investment decision, no matter what the value of the option, then the option does not need to be valued. This implies that in many situations we need determine only the direction that an option will shift the computed NPV rather than the actual value of the option. If the option makes a good project better or a bad project worse, the original analysis is adequate to make the final investment decision.

When a project has a slightly negative NPV before consideration of potentially value-enhancing options, then we need an estimate of the option's value. A sufficiently valuable option could cause us to accept a project that would have otherwise been rejected. We can compute a rough estimate of an option's value by understanding the factors that affect that value. More precise valuation must be postponed for advanced classes in financial economics.

When valuing options included in investment decisions, we must first try to determine if the option will ever be used. An option that will never be exercised has no value. For example, if we know we will continue a project through its entire economic life, then the abandonment option has no value and no further consideration is needed.

If a possibility of exercising the option exists, then some estimates about the option's value must be made. As an example, we discuss some of the items that financial analysts at United Airlines might have considered when deciding to buy options on Boeing's new 777 jets. First, UAL managers must have some uncertainty about what the future holds in terms of demand for airline transport. If they knew what air traffic patterns would be in the future, they could decide today whether or not the planes are needed. Therefore, buying the options implies that they think there is some *chance* that those planes would be needed, but it is also possible they will not be needed.

Other types of uncertainty could be underlying the decision to buy the options on new jet airliners. For example, suppose UAL managers are concerned that in response to several airline accidents, Federal Aviation Agency safety regulations might change, requiring companies to replace planes at an earlier age. The options UAL bought prepare the company for a slightly faster replacement of their fleet. The options allow UAL to continue at current activity levels if changes in the Federal Aviation Agency safety restrictions dictate earlier retirement of passenger jets.

These two scenarios point out how options help managers prepare for an uncertain future. By postponing major decisions until more information is available, options allow managers to make better decisions. In the long run, more informed decisions will increase cash flows available to shareholders and thereby increase shareholder wealth.

But does the potential increase in cash flows justify the price paid for options today? This is a difficult question, but here are some rules of thumb.

1. We are willing to pay more for options as the probability of their being profitably exercised increases. For example, people in Florida would pay more for hurricane insurance than people in Arizona because the probability of needing that type of insurance is much greater in Florida than in Arizona. In the UAL example the probability of increased air traffic could be estimated by looking at changes in air traffic in the past. If air traffic varies so much that it is difficult to predict, then the probability of profitable exercise increases; that is, the more variable the value of the underlying asset, the more valuable the option on that asset.
2. We pay more for options as the potential profit from their being exercised increases. For example, suppose two investments have a 50-50 chance of being successful. One is a coffee stand in Seattle, Washington, and the other is a movie starring Arnold Schwartznegger and Whoopi Goldberg. You can buy options that for an exercise price of $100 will give you 1% of the profits from either of these business ventures. Which option would you pay more for? Because the movie could earn millions of dollars, the 1% interest is much more valuable than a 1% interest in a coffee stand in Seattle. Therefore, we would pay much more for the movie option than the coffee stand option. In the UAL example, profit potential might be affected by growth in the airline industry as well as changes in the price of the Boeing planes. Locking in a price today generates savings if prices increase.
3. We pay more for options the higher interest rates are. An option is like a deferred purchase. We postpone paying the complete price for an asset until we exercise the option. The value of delaying cash expenditures increases with higher interest rates because we can invest the money and earn those high rates. You probably recognize this as an *opportunity cost* argument.
4. We pay more for options the lower their exercise price. Lower exercise prices provide higher profits. If you were a UAL manager, would you pay more for an option to buy a Boeing 777 for $1.5 million or $1.75 million? You could pay up to $250,000 more for the option with the $1.5 million dollar exercise price and still come out ahead. Thus, the lower the exercise price, all else equal, the more valuable the option.
5. We pay more for options as the time to expiration increases. More time to expiration increases the probability that the option can be profitably exercised. More time corresponds to more information and less uncertainty, both of which are valuable. So UAL would pay more for options that could be exercised anytime before 2002 than for those that had to be exercised by 1997.

The more of these five factors that affect an option, the higher the option's value. So options will sell for a higher price the longer the time until expiration, the lower the exercise price, and the more volatile the price of the underlying asset.[28] Thus, a project with a slightly negative NPV before the consideration of options could be profitable if the assets underlying the options have highly variable prices and the options' exercise prices are low.

Ignoring the options that are attached to investment projects means ignoring some of the project's potential value. Ignoring such options as abandonment, delayed investment, or closure and reopening implies that some profitable projects will be rejected. Although we cannot give a simple formula for computing the precise value of such options, we introduce the valuation of options by identifying five factors that influence their value. When evaluating potential investment projects, creative managers can use these five factors to make an educated guess about the value of the options attached to those projects. Considering these options, even in this rough way, helps managers identify profitable investments. However, a final word of caution is necessary. Care must be exercised when modifying rigorous analyses with educated guesses. It is possible for a manager to use such seat-of-the-pants analysis to make any project look profitable. If a project is accepted because of the value of its attached options, then those options and the source of their value must be carefully articulated. Recognizing and attaching value to the options associated with investments in real assets is an important managerial tool, but like all such tools, if misused it can be harmful to the company and its shareholders.[29]

---

[28]A mathematical formula called the Black-Scholes option-pricing model combines all these factors so call options can be valued precisely. If you continue on in finance you will certainly be introduced to this important pricing equation.

[29]For more discussion of options in capital budgeting, see Nalin Kulatilaka and Alan Marcus, "Project Valuation under Uncertainty: When Does DCF Fail?" *Journal of Applied Corporate Finance* 5, no. 3 (Fall 1992): 92–100. This article also contains references to more technical works that provide formulas for estimating option values.

SUMMARY

The decision to invest in long-term assets is crucial to the long-run success of a corporation. This investment represents the implementation of the corporate mission and goals. If the company does not have a clear sense of where it is going, it may invest its resources in inappropriate product markets. In this chapter, we outlined a process for translating a corporate strategic plan into identification of specific projects. We suggested a method of classifying projects according to the amount of management attention required. For example, senior management is unlikely to be involved in replacement project decisions, except in an oversight capacity.

We then showed how to distill dependent projects down to an array of independent projects, which can be evaluated using either NPV or IRR. We showed that NPV and IRR methods of analysis are entirely consistent with each other for independent projects but may give conflicting accept/reject signals when used to choose from among mutually exclusive projects. If such conflicts arise, we should opt to select projects on the basis of NPV rather than IRR. In the final analysis, NPV gives us a direct measure of the value added to the company by an investment project.

Finally, we showed that many investment projects also contain call options on future investment opportunities and put options on projects that may be terminated. Although these options may be difficult to value explicitly, they may nonetheless be valuable enough to influence the investment decision.

In the next chapter, we continue our presentation of corporate investing. First, we discuss risk, especially project-specific risk, that may cause us to raise or lower our required rate of return for a project. We also show how to compute a discount rate that includes the required rate of return to both debt and equity investors.

Because projects may last for many years, the value of their cash flows will most likely be affected by inflation during that period. In Chapter 11, we show how to incorporate inflation into the discounted cash flow model. In this chapter we assumed that companies were free to accept or reject independent projects without budget constraints. However, it often happens that not all acceptable projects can be taken because of spending limits. This forces companies to choose from among acceptable, independent projects, and this requirement affects the decision process. Finally, we end our discussion of corporate investing by explaining the benefits and risks of international investing.

KEY TERMS

fixed assets
replacement projects
expansion projects
diversification projects
dispersion projects
complementary projects
mutually exclusive projects
independent projects
net present value
incremental cash flows
allocated costs
opportunity costs
sunk costs
incidental effects
recovery of net working capital
internal rate of return

hurdle rate
reinvestment rate
payback
contingent claims
call option
put option
underlying asset
exercise price
expiration date
exercise a call option
closure option
abandonment option
option to delay
pollution rights

KEY FORMULAS

Net Present Value

$$NPV = -II + \sum_{t=1}^{n} \frac{OCF_t}{(1 + R(r))^t} + \frac{TCF_n}{(1 + R(r))^n}$$

Internal Rate of Return

$$II = \sum_{t=1}^{n} \frac{OCF_t}{(1 + IRR)^t} + \frac{TCF_n}{(1 + IRR)^n}$$

QUESTIONS

1. Individuals and families, as well as corporations, have long-term investments. Can you think of two investments that most families have?
2. There are companies, such as Motorola, that spend millions of dollars each year on employee training. The cost of this training is treated as an accounting expense, but we have suggested in the chapter that it may really be an investment. Help us defend our policy. Why might training be an investment?
3. In the late 1970s IBM decided to develop and market a personal computer—the IBM PC. It turned out to be a phenomenally successful investment for IBM. Yet, by the late 1980s IBM's profits from its PC business had deteriorated. What market opportunities in the late 1970s probably prompted IBM to enter the PC business, and why did these opportunities apparently disappear a decade later?
4. When IBM decided to build its PC (see Question 3), IBM dominated the worldwide market for mainframe computers. In contrast to the mainframe market, the fledgling PC market was tiny. IBM created a separate subsidiary company in Florida (company headquarters are in New York) to develop and build the PC. The subsidiary was financed by IBM but had virtually no other contact with the home office. Why do you think IBM treated its subsidiary in this manner? In retrospect, did IBM make a mistake?
5. Before deregulation in the late 1970s, airlines invested heavily in new airplanes, even though the old airplanes were still very serviceable. Since deregulation, airlines are flying their airplanes much longer, and the average age of their fleet has lengthened considerably. Why do you think the airlines have reduced their investment in new airplanes?
6. Computer software development, especially for PCs, has traditionally been a *cottage industry*, in which individuals wrote program code in their homes.

Now we have Microsoft, which dominates the software industry. If you wanted to form a small software development company by investing in a few computers and leasing some office space, what entry barriers would you be facing now? Consider what difficulties you would have that Bill Gates and his contemporaries 20 years ago did not have.

7. In the chapter, we have suggested two competitive strategies for capitalizing on market opportunities:

   Differentiation
   Cost leadership

   We have provided some examples of each in the chapter. Can you provide some other examples of each strategy?
8. We stated in the chapter that ideally companies would search for investment opportunities without regard to geography, industry, or cost. In fact, companies do limit their searches with regard to these three factors. Why do you think companies limit their searches? Consider each of the three factors individually.
9. Many years ago, W. R. Grace was a shipping company. Now it is a multidivisional medical care, packaging and chemical company. Did W. R. Grace lose its way? That is, did it lose focus on its corporate mission?
10. What is the minimum rate of return that an investment should provide in order to be acceptable to the corporation?
11. Is an investment more or less valuable if the resulting product can be patented? Briefly explain.
12. An airline redefines its corporate mission and becomes a transportation company. Later, it broadens its corporate mission to be in the customer-service and people business. Are there dangers in making the corporate mission too broad? Explain.
13. A company develops a brand-new product, captures the market, and sees sales and profits grow rapidly. Can the company realistically count on making large profits on its product over the long run? Briefly explain.
14. In most cases, does economic regulation, such as occurred with the airlines and occurs today with banking, tend to increase or decrease firm profits? Briefly explain.
15. Two U.S. companies are competing for rights to build a manufacturing plant in Brazil. One is a multinational company. The other is a purely domestic company. Is this investment in Brazil equally risky for both companies? Briefly explain.
16. Classify the following projects using the given categories:

    Replacement project
    Expansion project
    Diversification project
    Dispersion project
    Mandated (by law) project

    a. A computer maker opens retail electronics stores.
    b. A computer chip manufacturer installs new electrical fixtures in its plant to adhere to the fire code.
    c. A wholesaler upgrades its fleet of delivery vans.
    d. General Motors buys Hughes Aircraft Company.

e. An East Coast distributor expands its operations to the Midwest.
f. Nike, which sells athletic shoes in the United States, builds a factory and sells shoes in China.
g. A company fires its security guards and installs a high-tech electronic security system.

17. Consider the following projects for a large auto manufacturer who is considering entering the minivan market. The company will build only one assembly plant, and will either build a plant to produce parts or purchase parts from independent suppliers. Eliminate complementary projects by combining projects. Are the remaining projects independent? Explain.
a. A minivan assembly plant in the United States
b. Ships to transport minivans into the United States
c. A minivan assembly plant in Korea
d. A plant to produce minivan parts in Taiwan
e. A plant to produce minivan parts in Malaysia
f. A distribution network for minivans in the United States—rail cars, warehouses, etc.

18. For a project to build a large distribution warehouse, which of these are incremental cash flows? The year is 19X4.
a. Fees paid to a plant location consultant in 19X3
b. The sale of existing smaller warehouses in the same region
c. The land on which the new warehouse will sit has been owned by the company for 8 years (It has recently had the land value appraised.)
d. The allocation of corporate overhead to warehouses based on their volume of sales.
e. The cost of building the plant
f. The cost of constructing access roads, which were completed 18 months ago, into the plant
g. Training of new employees to work in the warehouse

19. We have the following information for a project:

DISCOUNT RATE	NPV
8%	$1700
9%	$1100
10%	$ 300
11%	−$ 150

Based on this information, what is the approximate internal rate of return for this project?

20. We have the following information for these mutually exclusive projects. All have equal required rates of return.

	NPV	IRR
A	$3800	11%
B	$1250	14%
C	−$ 560	7%
D	$2500	12%
E	$ 0	9%

a. What is the required rate of return on these projects?
b. Rank acceptable projects using NPV.
c. Rank acceptable projects using IRR.

21. For Question 20, if all projects required the same initial investment, what is the probable explanation for the differences in ranking between IRR and NPV?
22. Which of the following projects would you *expect* to have the highest NPV? Obviously, we do not have enough information to know for certain.

	INITIAL INVESTMENT
A	$16,000
B	$34,000
C	$64,000

23. A project has an NPV of $18,200 and an IRR of 14%. The required rate of return on this project is 9%. For this project, IRR assumes that project cash flows are reinvested at ________ (rate), and NPV assumes that project cash flows are reinvested at ________ (rate).
24. In principle, we prefer NPV to IRR when they produce different project rankings. Why do we prefer NPV? (Cite at least two reasons.)
25. Cite one reason why payback is generally inferior to NPV and IRR for evaluating projects.
26. Explain the options in the following investments. In your explanations, include
    i. What does the option allow the company to do?
    ii. Why is the option valuable, e.g., why bother with the option at all?
    a. A new manufacturing plant is configured for an easy changeover from one product to another.
    b. A bank designs its own branches so that they can be converted to pizza parlors. (Pizza ovens can be installed in the bank vault, etc.)
    c. United Airlines takes options on, rather than ordering, new airplanes from Boeing.
27. Calculating the value of an option attached to an investment can be difficult. For which of the following investments should we attempt to value the option?
    a. A new factory, designed for quick product changeover, has a slightly negative NPV.
    b. An agribusiness company buys a large lettuce farm. The investment has a positive NPV. The farm has potential value as a site for a future industrial park.
    c. A positive NPV investment has been designed so that it may be terminated at low cost before its planned life of 15 years.
    d. An agribusiness company buys a large lettuce farm. The investment has a negative NPV. The farm has potential value as a site for a future industrial park.
28. Consider airlines placing orders for new aircraft. Categorize each of these orders as

Replacement
Expansion
Diversification/dispersion
Mandated (law)

- **a.** A domestic airline orders Boeing 747s to serve newly acquired trans-Pacific routes.
- **b.** An airline buys new Boeing 737s because its old 737s are too expensive to maintain.
- **c.** An airline buys new 300-seat aircraft from Airbus Industries to serve routes now flown by 150-seat Boeing 737 aircraft.
- **d.** An airline replaces 20-year-old 150-seat Boeing 727 aircraft with new 300-seat aircraft from Airbus Industries.
- **e.** An airline buys small commuter aircraft for its new subsidiary, which will feed passengers from smaller airports to its Midwest hub airport.
- **f.** An airline reequips its airplanes with new, fuel-efficient jet engines.
- **g.** An airline reequips its airplanes with new, quieter engines to meet noise abatement standards at certain airports.
- **h.** An airline retrofits its airplanes with advanced avionics equipment designed to avert midair collisions.

29. List the five factors that influence the value of an option.
30. Fill in the blanks: A call option gives the owner of the option the ______ to ______ the underlying asset at a prespecified price on or before the option's ______ date. The prespecified price is known as the ______ price. Owning a call option creates ______ obligation to buy the underlying asset.
31. Explain which option you would pay more for and why.
    - **a.** An option that expires in 1 month, or an otherwise identical option that expires in 3 months.
    - **b.** A call option with an exercise price of $50, or an otherwise identical option with an exercise price of $45.
    - **c.** A call option when interest rates are high, or an otherwise identical option when interest rates are lower.
32. Federal law now requires that banks gives borrowers a 72-hour period to think over whether or not they really want to take out a loan. The 72-hour period begins when you actually sign the loan papers and have set an interest rate and repayment schedule. At any time in the 72-hour (or 3-day) period, the borrower may tell the loan officer that she has changed her mind and does not want the loan.
    - **a.** What optionlike features does this cool-off period contain?
    - **b.** If this is an option, what is the underlying asset?
    - **c.** In terms of interest rates, when would a borrower decide to call off the loan agreement (i.e., if rates go up or down during the 72-hour period)?
    - **d.** Who gains from having this option, the bank or the borrower?
33. The owner of a commercial bakery regularly contracts to buy flour at a prespecified price for future delivery. Is this an option agreement as described in this chapter? Why or why not?
34. Many airlines offer frequent-flier programs. These programs allow travelers

to accumulate miles toward future free travel. United Airlines has the Mileage Plus© program, which gives participants a free airline ticket within the United States for every 25,000 miles of paid travel they do on United. International travel requires more miles, as does first-class travel. The *tickets* expire 3 years from the date of issuance. We use Mileage Plus© tickets if air fares are high but prefer to pay for tickets when prices are low. What optionlike attributes do these frequent-flier tickets have? What is the underlying asset? What is the exercise price? If the exercise price is zero, does that mean that travel with frequent-flier tickets is truly free? (For an in-depth analysis of frequent-flier programs see Jeff Blyskal, "The Frequent Flier Fallacy," Worth 3, no. 4 (May 1994): 60–68.)

35. Owning a call option gives the owner the right to buy an asset but does not create an obligation to do so. If you give or sell someone an option, what rights and obligations have you incurred? For example, suppose you sell someone an option to buy a piece of land. You receive $2,500 for the option, and the buyer has three months to decide whether or not he wants to buy the land at some agreed-upon price. How are you, as the seller of the option, obligated or restricted? If the optionholder decides to exercise the option, what does that imply about changes in the value of the land? Who gains and who loses?
36. Use the discussion of options in this chapter to describe the optionlike features, including what the option is and who owns it, of the following items:
    a. A ski area sells, for $52, a 3-day pass that must be used on three consecutive days. For $57 you can buy a 3-day pass that may be used anytime during the ski season.
    b. A supermarket coupon saves you 50¢ on a quart of Ben & Jerry's ice cream. The coupon expires this coming July 4.
    c. A friend is thinking about selling a mountain bicycle. You ask if she will notify you first if she decides to actually sell the bike. In other words, you have right of first refusal.
    d. You have graduated, found a job, and just found a condominium you would like to buy. Demand for housing in your city is high. You give the owner $500 of *earnest money* to start the purchase process. If you decide not to go through with the deal, the owner keeps the money. If, through no fault of your own, you cannot get financing, the $500 is returned to you. You and the seller agree that you will give a definitive yes or no within 30 days.

DEMONSTRATION PROBLEMS

Calculating Cash Flows and NPV

1. Morris Corp. is planning to invest in some equipment. It will cost Morris $34,000 to buy the equipment, which is expected to last for 5 years. Annual cash revenues are expected to be $17,500, and annual project related expenses are expected to be $6500. The equipment will depreciate on a straight line

basis over the 5 years. The equipment should be sold in 5 years for $4,500. The required rate of return on this investment is 12%. The tax rate is 30%.

a. What are the cash flows for $t = 0$ and $t = 1–5$?

b. Calculate the project NPV.

SOLUTION

The following table shows the cash flows and NPV for the project. Annual depreciation is $34,000/5. Tax is 30% × EBT. Cash flow is EAT + depreciation. The tax effect of the project sale is 30% × $4,500. NPV is the sum of the discounted cash flows.

		1	2	3	4	5	5
Project cost	(34,000)						
Sale price	—						4,500
Book value	—						—
Gain	—						4,500
Tax effect	—						(1,530)
S − E		11,000	11,000	11,000	11,000	11,000	
Depreciation		6,800	6,800	6,800	6,800	6,800	
EBT		4,200	4,200	4,200	4,200	4,200	
Tax		1,260	1,260	1,260	1,260	1,260	
EAT		2,940	2,940	2,940	2,940	2,940	
Cash flow	(34,000)	9,740	9,740	9,740	9,740	9,740	2,970
Discounted CF	(34,000)	8,696	7,765	6,933	6,190	5,527	1,685
NPV	2,796						

Evaluating Mutually Exclusive Projects

2. The Glacier Co. has two mutually exclusive projects under consideration. The required investment for each is $28,000. The required return on each is 7%. The cash flows are as follows:

YEAR	PROJECT A	PROJECT B
1	$ 3,000	$16,000
2	6,000	11,000
3	10,000	8,000
4	14,000	6,000
5	18,000	2,000
IRR	18.0%	22.8%

a. Calculate the NPV for each project.

b. Which project would be selected using the NPV criterion? Which would be selected using IRR?

c. Why do NPV and IRR select different projects?

SOLUTION

a. The following table shows the calculation of NPV for each project. NPV is the sum of the discounted cash flows.

PROJECT A	0	1	2	3	4	5
Cash flow		$ 3,000	$ 6,000	$10,000	$14,000	$18,000
Discounted CF	$(28,000)	$ 2,804	$ 5,241	$ 8,163	$10,681	$12,834
NPV	$11,722					
IRR	18.0%					

PROJECT B	0	1	2	3	4	5
Cash flow		$16,000	$11,000	$ 8,000	$ 6,000	$ 2,000
Discounted CF	$(28,000)	$14,953	$ 9,608	$ 6,530	$ 4,577	$ 1,426
NPV	$ 9,095					
IRR	22.8%					

b. Project A has the greatest NPV, and project B has the highest IRR. NPV would select project A, and IRR would select project B.

c. IRR and NPV select different projects because the timing of project cash flows is very different. Project A's cash flows occur for the most part in the later years, whereas most of project B's cash flows occur early. Because of differences in the reinvestment rates between IRR and NPV, IRR tends to favor projects whose cash flows occur more in the early years, and NPV tends to favor those whose cash flows occur more in the later years.

PROBLEMS

Problems 1–3 deal with the Hinckley Corp.

1. Hinckley Corp. is planning to invest in some equipment. It will cost Hinckley $15,000 to buy the equipment, which is expected to last for 5 years. Annual cash revenues are expected to be $7500, and annual project related expenses are expected to be $3500. The equipment will depreciate on a straight-line basis over the 5 years. The equipment should be sold in 5 years for $2,000. The required rate of return on this investment is 12%. There are no taxes. What are the cash flows for $t = 0$ and $t = 1–5$?

Project Cash Flows
1. Year 0, −$15,000; years 1–4, $4,000; year 5, $6,000

2. **a.** Calculate the NPV in Problem 1.
   b. Calculate the NPV in Problem 1 using a discount rate of 14%.

Calculating NPV Under Various Required Rates of Return
2. a. $553.96
   b. −$228.94

3. Given your answers in Problem 2, what is the approximate internal rate of return? No calculation is necessary.

Estimating a Project's Internal Rate of Return
3. IRR between 12% and 14%

4. A project costs $172,000 and generates a cash flow of $42,000 per year for 5 years.
   a. Over 5 years, this project generates $210,000 in positive cash flows ($42,000 × 5). This provides a project NPV of $38,000 ($210,000 − $172,000). Based on this evidence, would you take on this project?
   b. What required rate of return is implied in part (a)?
   c. What is the project NPV at a required rate of return of 10%?

The Effect of the Required Rate of Return on Project Value
4. a. yes
   b. 0%
   c. −$12,787

Relating Internal Rate of Return and Required Rate of Return

5. a. $163
   b. Close to 7%
   c. Yes
   d. No

5. A project costs $152,774 and generates a cash flow of $37,300 per year for 5 years.
   a. What is the project NPV at a required rate of return of 7%?
   b. What is the approximate IRR of this project (no calculation)?
   c. If the required rate of return on this project were 5%, would you accept the project (no calculation)?
   d. If the required rate of return on this project were 9%, would you accept the project (no calculation)?
   e. Using your answers in parts (c) and (d), what would be a sensible investment decision rule for those using IRR to evaluate projects?

Project Cash Flows and NPV

6. a. Year 0, −$34,000; years 1–8, $6,106; year 9, $9,506
   b. −$240
   c. no

6. The South Seas Navigation Company is considering buying new sextants for its celestial navigation school. The sextants cost $34,000 and are expected to generate annuity operating cash flows of $7,500 per year for 9 years. The sextants will be depreciated using straight-line depreciation for 10 years; however they will be sold in 9 years for $3,400. The corporate tax rate is 34%. The required rate of return for this project is 12%.
   a. Calculate the annual cash flows.
   b. Calculate the project's net present value.
   c. Would you make this investment?

Project Cash Flows and NPV

7. a. Year 0, −34,000; years 1–8, $6,106; year 9, $11,222
   b. $379
   c. yes

7. The South Seas Navigation Company is considering buying new sextants for its celestial navigation school. The sextants cost $34,000 and are expected to generate annuity operating cash flows of $7,500 per year for 9 years. The sextants will be depreciated using straight-line depreciation for 10 years; however they will be sold in 9 years for $6,000. The corporate tax rate is 34%. The required rate of return for this project is 12%. If South Seas decides to buy the new sextants, it will sell its old sextants, which have a book value of $4,000, for $8,000.
   a. Calculate the annual cash flows.
   b. Calculate the project's net present value.
   c. Would you make this investment?

Evaluating Mutually Exclusive Projects

8. a. A: $4,245; B: $2830
   b. NPV, proj. A; IRR, proj. B
   c. Timing of cash flows
   d. A

8. Voyageur Ltd. has two mutually exclusive projects under consideration. The required investment for each is $15,000. The required return on each is 6%. The cash flows are as follows:

YEAR	PROJECT A	PROJECT B
1	$ 2,000	$8,000
2	4,000	6,000
3	7,000	4,000
4	10,000	2,000
IRR	15.2%	16.1%

   a. Calculate the NPV for each project.
   b. Which project would be selected using the NPV criterion? Which would be selected using IRR?

c. Why do NPV and IRR select different projects?
d. Which project would you select? Why?

9. Cape Horn Ltd. has two mutually exclusive projects under consideration. The required return on each is 8%. The cash flows are as follows:

Evaluating Mutually Exclusive Projects
9. a. A: $9,746; B: $7,497
b. A: 22%; B: 25%
c. NPV, proj. A; IRR, proj. B
d. Size
e. A

YEAR	PROJECT A	PROJECT B
0	−$30,000	−$19,000
1	12,000	8,000
2	12,000	8,000
3	12,000	8,000
4	12,000	8,000

a. Calculate the NPV for each project.
b. Calculate the IRR for each project.
c. Which project would be selected using the NPV criterion? Which would be selected using IRR?
d. Why do NPV and IRR select different projects?
e. Which project would you select? Why?

10. Two projects each cost $12,000 and produce the following cash flows:

Payback versus NPV
10. a. 1. 3 yr.; 2. 2 yr.
b. 1: $2,513; 2: $2,054
c. 1
d. 2

YEAR	PROJECT 1 CASH FLOWS	PROJECT 2 CASH FLOWS
1	$8,500	$8,500
2	$2,500	$3,500
3	$1,000	$3,500
4	$8,000	$3,000

a. Calculate the payback period for each project.
b. Using a required rate of return of 15%, calculate the NPV of each project.
c. Using the NPV criterion, which of these projects is preferred.
d. Using the payback period, which of these projects is preferred?

Problems 11 through 17 deal with the basic project described here. A 6-year capital project, code name Jackal, costs $27,695 (year 0). It is expected to produce the following operating cash flows (revenues minus expenses).

YEAR	OPERATING CFs
1	$6,250
2	6,688
3	7,156
4	7,657
5	8,192
6	8,766

Project NPV and IRR (Straight-Line Depreciation)
11. a. $1,036
b. 10.2%
c. Yes
d. NPV = $2,008; IRR = 11.3%

11. The Jackal project will be straight-line depreciated over its 6-year life. The corporate tax rate is 34%, and the required rate of return on the project is 9%.
   a. What is the project's NPV?
   b. What is the project's IRR?
   c. Would you recommend taking on this project?
   d. How would a reduction in the corporate tax rate to 26% change your answers in parts (a) and (b)?

Project NPV and IRR (ACRS Depreciation)
12. a. $830
b. 10%
c. Yes
d. NPV = $1,851, IRR = 11.2%

12. The Jackal project will be depreciated using 5-year ACRS. The corporate tax rate is 34%, and the required rate of return on the project is 9%.
   a. What is the project's NPV?
   b. What is the project's IRR?
   c. Would you recommend taking on this project?
   d. How would a reduction in the corporate tax rate to 26% change your answers in parts (a) and (b)?

Project NPV (Sale of Existing Asset)
13. a. $24,705
b. $4,026
c. $4,706
d. (b) $5,118; (c) $5,638

13. The Jackal project will be straight-line depreciated over its 6-year life. The corporate tax rate is 34%, and the required rate of return on the project is 9%. The Jackal project will replace an existing project (code name Condor) that has a book value of $2,000. The Condor project will be sold for $3,500.
   a. Calculate the initial-investment (year 0) cash flows for this project.
   b. What is the project's NPV?
   c. If the Condor project had a book value of $4,000, how would that change the NPV of the Jackal project?
   d. How would a reduction in the corporate tax rate to 26% change your answers in parts (b) and (c)?

Project NPV (Project-Termination Cash Flows)
14. a. $3,036
b. $2,846

14. The Jackal project will be straight-line depreciated over its 6-year life. At the end of 6 years, the company expects to sell the Jackal project for $4,600. The corporate tax rate is 34%, and the required rate of return on the project is 9%.
   a. Calculate the project termination cash flows for this project.
   b. What is the project's NPV?

Project NPV (Project-Termination Cash Flows)
15. a. $6,803
b. $2,276
c. $3,263
d. (b) $3,602; (c) $4,357

15. Assume that the Jackal project is straight-line depreciated over 10 years, meaning that it has a book value at the end of its 6-year life. At the end of 6 years, the company expects to sell the Jackal project for $4,600. The corporate tax rate is 34%, and the required rate of return on the project is 9%.
   a. Calculate the project-termination cash flows for this project.
   b. What is the project's NPV?
   c. Suppose that instead of using 10-year straight-line depreciation, we had used 5-year ACRS. How would that change the project's NPV?
   d. How would a reduction in the corporate tax rate to 26% change your answers in parts (b) and (c)?

16. The Jackal project will be straight-line depreciated over its 6-year life. The corporate tax rate is 34%, and the required rate of return on the project is 12%.
    a. What is the project's NPV?
    b. What is the project's IRR?
    c. Answer part (a) for required rates of return of 6% and 8%.
    d. Why might a project's required rate of return change?

Project NPV and IRR under Various Required Rates of Return

16. a. −$1,468
    b. 10.2%
    c. (6%) $3,929; (8%) $1,953

17. The Jackal project will be depreciated using 5-year ACRS. The corporate tax rate is 28%.
    a. Starting with a required return (discount rate) of 0%, calculate the NPV for the project at rates of 2%, 4%, 6%, 8%, 10%, 12%, 14%, 16%.
    b. Using a graph similar to Figure 9.1, plot NPV versus discount rate. Identify the IRR on the graph.
    c. Calculate the IRR for Jackal, and compare to the IRR from part (b). Are they the same? Would you expect them to be the same?

Project NPV and IRR Under Various Required Rates of Return

17. a. (0%) $11,641; (16%) −$3,708
    c. 10.9%

Problems 18 through 21 deal with Paradise Sail Charters. Paradise Sail Charters (PSC) has just been formed to enter the sailboat-chartering business in the Caribbean. The company plans to lease 21 slips in a marina on the island of St. Croix, U.S.V.I., and buy three used sailboats to start its chartering service. It plans to offer boats in the 30-foot to 39-foot range for bareboat charters (without a paid crew), and boats in the 40-foot to 49-foot range for crewed charters. Initially, it will start with two bareboats and one crewed boat. PSC is a closely held corporation. Except for a revolving credit line from a Florida bank, PSC is entirely equity-financed. The stockholders have agreed that their minimum required rate of return is 12%.

18. PSC has contacted several Florida yacht brokers about used sailboats and has narrowed the search to the following list. Group these seven boats into independent projects.

Identifying Independent Projects

MANUFACTURER AND LENGTH (FEET)	AGE IN YEARS
Hunter 33	4
Catalina 34	3
Beneteau 38	2
Island Packet 35	4
Cabo Rico 34	6
Hunter 42	2
Beneteau 44	3

19. Each of the sailboats listed in Problem 18, will have a 4-year life. Net operating cash flows are from charter revenues. At the end of 4 years, the boats will be sold. Operating data for two of the boats are presented in the following table. Some tax incentives from the government of the U.S.V.I. have lowered PSC's effective tax rate to 26%. Five-year straight-line depreciation is used for all boats.

Calculating Project Cash Flows

19. Hunter 33:
    Year 0, −$42,000
    Year 1, $10,028
    Year 2, $10,404
    Year 3, $10,798
    Year 4, $31,544

HUNTER 33

	YEAR				
	0	1	2	3	4
COST	$42,000				
Cash revenues		$12,800	$13,440	$14,112	$14,394
Cash expenses		$ 2,200	$ 2,332	$ 2,472	$ 2,670
Depreciation		$ 8,400	$ 8,400	$ 8,400	$ 8,400
Income from sale					$25,000

BENETEAU 38

	YEAR				
	0	1	2	3	4
COST	$74,000				
Cash revenues		$19,800	$20,790	$21,830	$22,266
Cash expenses		$ 2,800	$ 2,968	$ 3,146	$ 3,398
Depreciation		$14,800	$14,800	$14,800	$14,800
Income from sale					$50,000

Calculate the annual cash flows for each of these boats.

Calculating Project NPV
20. Hunter 33, $2,980; Beneteau 44, $28,859

20. Following are the expected cash flows for the boats being considered by PSC. For each, calculate the NPV using the required rate of return of 12%.

	YEAR				
	0	1	2	3	4
Hunter 33					
Cost	$ 42,000				
Operating cash flows		$10,028	$10,404	$10,798	$10,860
Terminal cash flow					$20,684
Catalina 34					
Cost	$ 58,000				
Operating cash flows		$11,900	$12,733	$13,370	$14,306
Terminal cash flow					$34,500
Beneteau 38					
Cost	$ 74,000				
Operating cash flows		$16,428	$17,036	$17,674	$17,811
Terminal cash flow					$40,848
Island Packet 35					
Cost	$ 68,000				
Operating cash flows		$15,800	$16,432	$17,418	$18,115
Terminal cash flow					$35,000
Cabo Rico 34					
Cost	$ 52,500				
Operating cash flows		$10,300	$11,021	$11,792	$12,618
Terminal cash flow					$36,500
Hunter 42					
Cost	$140,000				
Operating cash flows		$29,900	$32,890	$37,495	$40,494
Terminal cash flow					$102,000

	YEAR				
	0	1	2	3	4
Beneteau 44					
Cost	$133,000				
Operating cash flows		$34,200	$34,542	$34,887	$35,236
Terminal cash flow					$89,000

Choosing Among Mutually Exclusive Projects

21. Following are the IRRs for the seven sailboats. Given this information and the NPVs calculated in Problem 20, rank, by NPV and IRR, the five smaller boats (30 feet to 39 feet) and the two larger boats (40 feet plus). What conflicts between NPV and IRR rankings do you see? Explain why these conflicts occur.

	IRR
Hunter 33	14.7%
Catalina 34	14.1
Beneteau 38	14.1
Island Packet 35	15.0
Cabo Rico 34	15.4
Hunter 42	19.5
Beneteau 44	19.9

APPENDIX 9A

Accelerated Cost Recovery Tax Depreciation Schedules

	RECOVERY CLASS PERIOD					
YEARS	3-YEAR	5-YEAR	7-YEAR	10-YEAR	15-YEAR	20-YEAR
1	33.33	20.00	14.29	10.00	5.00	3.75
2	44.45	32.00	24.49	18.00	9.50	7.22
3	14.81	19.20	17.49	14.40	8.55	6.68
4	7.41	11.52	12.49	11.52	7.70	6.18
5		11.52	8.93	9.22	6.93	5.71
6		5.76	8.93	7.37	6.23	5.28
7			8.93	6.55	5.90	4.89
8			4.45	6.55	5.90	4.52
9				6.55	5.90	4.46
10				6.55	5.90	4.46
11				3.29	5.90	4.46
12					5.90	4.46
13					5.90	4.46
14					5.90	4.46
15					5.90	4.46
16					2.99	4.46
17						4.46
18						4.46
19						4.46
20						4.46
21						2.25

CHAPTER 10

Estimating the Discount Rate for Use in Capital Budgeting

Estimating the "right discount rate" for use in net present value calculations is the topic of Chapter 10. By the way, Dogbert is correct: Pulling numbers out of the hat is no better than mumbo jumbo.

hapter 9 described the various capital budgeting techniques employed by corporate managers. Among the techniques, NPV (net present value) emerges as the best measure of a project's contribution to shareholder wealth. In NPV analysis, the present value of a project's expected future cash flows is compared to the initial investment, and the project is accepted if the present value exceeds the initial investment. In this chapter you will learn how to estimate the discount rate used in the capital budgeting process for finding the present value of expected cash flows.

ESTIMATING THE DISCOUNT RATE

In Chapter 9, we assumed that the appropriate discount rate for computing the present value of the future cash flows is known. In fact, we must estimate this discount rate. The NPV of Pogo Ltd.'s jackline project ($39,331) discussed in Chapter 9 was found by discounting its after-tax cash flows at a 10% required return. The project's internal rate of return (17.1%) is compared to this same rate, 10%, which serves as the hurdle rate. The 10% rate is critical to the analysis. Had the required return been 20%, for example, the project would have been rejected using either criterion.

This rate, 10%, was not pulled out of a hat. Rather, it represents the required return of investors who would supply the capital for funding the project. Recall that the cost of the Jackline project was $153,350, meaning that Jack Elihu must raise that amount in order to fund the firm's LHS investment in machinery and working capital. Let's say Elihu has decided to fund future projects using the same proportional mix of debt, preferred stock, and common equity as the firm's existing overall financing. Pogo targets a capital mix of 39.1% debt financing and 19.6% preferred financing, with the remaining financing (41.3%) coming from common stock.[1] Pogo will, therefore, raise $60,000 by selling bonds and $30,000 by selling preferred stock and will retain $63,350 of residual cash flow (representing that part of the project's funding supplied by common stockholders). If the jackline project produces cash inflows as expected, they will flow to these claimants in order of the priority of their claims: first to bondholders, then to preferred stockholders, and finally to common stockholders. Figure 10.1 illustrates the flow of capital and cash flows we just outlined.

Transparency Available

The costs of capital for regulated utilities are set by public utilities commissions. If the allowed rate is too low, the value of investors' stakes in the utility will decline. A rate that is too high will result in stock price increases, but consumers will suffer.

Pogo is able to raise capital by selling these securities to investors because they expect to receive a return on their investment. The benefit of owning a security is the return that flows to its holder. Any investor purchasing Pogo's securities must expect that the returns will be equal to or greater than her required return for an investment having the same risk as the jackline project. (Chapters 7 and 8 developed the relationship between risk and return requirements.) If, for example, expected returns were lower than required, investors would look elsewhere for investment opportunities or would offer to pay a lower price for Pogo's securities (paying less would effectively increase investors' expected returns). Thus, Elihu must be confident that the discount rate he uses to value the project will provide the required return to each class of investors from whom Pogo receives

[1]Pogo arrived at this targeted capital mix after Elihu and members of the board of directors read Chapter 12 on capital structure.

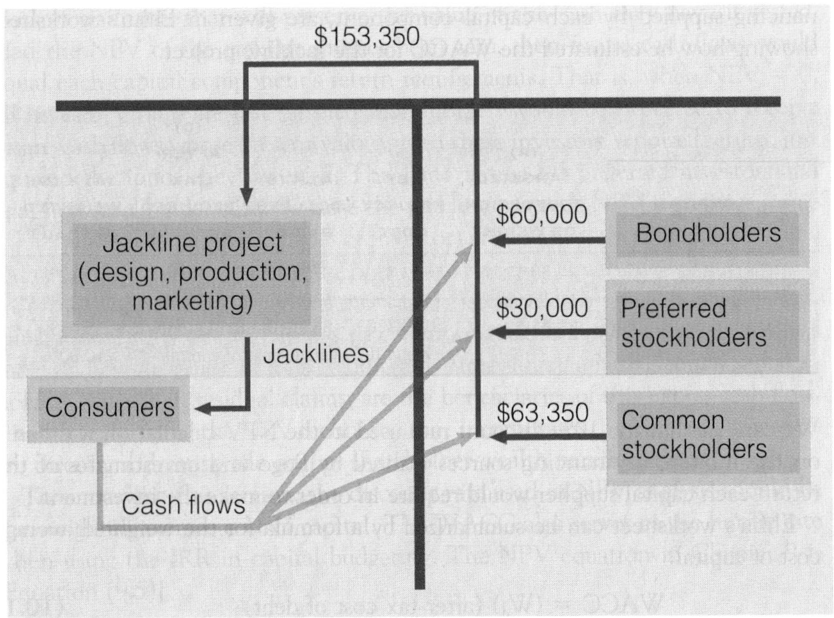

FIGURE 10.1

THE FINANCING MIX AND CASH FLOWS FOR POGO'S JACKLINE PROJECT

capital. This discount rate is known as the **cost of capital** for the project because the returns investors require are the "cost," like rent, which must be paid for the use of the capital.

THE WEIGHTED AVERAGE COST OF CAPITAL

Calculating the Weighted Average Cost of Capital

The cost of capital is a *weighted average* of the required returns for each capital source. Thus, for the Jackline project, the **weighted average cost of capital** (WACC) will be a mixture of the after-tax[2] required return for the bonds being sold, the required return for preferred stock sold, and the required return of the common stockholders whose cash is being retained. The weightings in the WACC are the proportions contributed by each group of investors. Of the $153,350 being raised, $60,000 (39.1%) is contributed by the bondholders, $30,000 (19.6%) is contributed by the preferred stockholders, and $63,350 (41.3%) is contributed by the common stockholders in the form of retained earnings.

It may help students to grasp the cost of capital concept to point out that it is also called the cost of money.

We will soon explain how to estimate the after-tax required return on debt (or **cost of debt**), the required return for preferred (or **cost of preferred**) and the required return for equity (or **cost of equity**). First, though, we will assume that Elihu has already made these estimates for us. The after-tax required returns for the types of capital being raised, along with the proportion of total project fi-

[2]When we stress the *after-tax* required return, we mean the returns after corporate taxation. Returns are generated by cash flows to investors. These cash flows are either tax-deductible interest payments or are distributed after corporate taxes are paid. Thus, they are after-tax returns.

For bonds,

$$K_D^{new} = \text{YTM*} \qquad \text{YTM* calculated using } P_{net} \text{ for bonds} \tag{10.12}$$

$$P_{net} \text{ for bonds} = \$1{,}214 - \$50 = \$1{,}164$$

$$\$1{,}164 = \frac{\$55}{(1 + \text{YTM*})^1} + \frac{\$55}{(1 + \text{YTM*})^2} + \cdots + \frac{\$1{,}055}{(1 + \text{YTM*})^{30}}$$

$$\text{YTM*} = 4.47\% \text{ semiannually}$$

$$K_d^{new} = 8.94\% \text{ annually}$$

$$K_d^{new}(1 - t) = (8.94\%)(0.66) = 5.90\%$$

For preferred,

$$P_{net} = \$39.93 - 0.80 = \$39.13$$

$$K_{pfd}^{new} = \frac{D}{P_{net}} = \frac{\$4.50}{\$39.13} = 11.50\% \tag{10.13}$$

Note that equity comes in the form of retained earnings. This is *internally* rather than *externally* raised capital. Therefore, there are no transaction costs involved in this financing. Pogo's K_e of 13.2% needs no adjustment. However, practitioners often differentiate between the cost of internal equity and the cost of new, external equity by using the terms **cost of retained earnings** ($K_{ret.earn.}$) and **cost of new stock** ($K_{new\ stock}$), respectively. The cost of new stock is calculated using the discounted cash flow approach and the net price of the common stock being sold.

$$K_{new\ stock} = \frac{D_1}{P_{net}} + g_n \tag{10.14}$$

where

$$P_{Net} = P - \text{flotation costs}$$

Again, the jackline project's equity financing is being done with retained earnings, so Elihu's analysis was correct in its original form.

$$K_{ret\ earn} = 13.2\%$$

Note that the after-tax cost of debt, 5.90%, the cost of preferred, 11.50%, and the cost of equity, 13.2%, are the same component costs Elihu used in his WACC worksheet shown at the beginning of the chapter. You should now understand how the component's costs are estimated and combined to form the WACC. At least one mystery remains: How did Pogo decide on the capital mix (the dollar amounts raised using each capital source) to finance the project? We give you a simple answer in the next section, but determining the capital mix used to finance a firm is a complex issue we cover in detail in Chapter 12.

The Financing Mix and Weights in the WACC

The weights in the WACC formula could reflect any financing mix the corporation targets. If the firm decides it will always use internal equity as its sole source of capital, then the weight of equity would be 1: $W_e = 1.00$. More precisely, the weight of retained earnings should be 1 because internal equity implies no new stock would be sold. The WACC would equal the cost of retained earnings because internal equity is its only capital source. Another firm might choose a 50-50 mix of debt and equity. This firm's WACC weights would be 0.50 and 0.50 for W_d and W_e, respectively.

Here, we assume that Pogo is financing the Jackline project using the same mix of capital as used in its existing projects. We expect firms that are satisifed with their current capital mix to maintain that mix.

The existing mix of capital of a firm can be determined by examining the RHS of the financial balance sheet. Recall that the financial balance sheet reflects market values, in contrast to the accounting balance sheet's book values. These values are used because current market values are relevant to determining the capital component's costs, whereas the historical security prices and rates in accounting statements may bear no resemblance to today's values and required returns. Bonds that sold at par, $1,000, in 1982 probably had coupon rates of 12%, but in 1992 such bonds were probably selling for over $1,000, because required returns had fallen to well below 10%. For example, suppose, in 1992, this bond had a market value of $1,200. The 1992 value of this bondholder's capital contribution to the company was not $1,000, as reflected in the accounting statement, but rather $1,200, reflecting the current price of the bond. To see this, imagine that the firm wished to replace this bondholder's capital with equity capital. The company must raise $1,200 in equity (not $1,000) in order to repurchase the bond from the bondholder.

Elihu determined the current financing mix by constructing the RHS of Pogo's financial balance sheet. Knowing he must find the market values of each of Pogo's capital sources, he first found the current prices for the company's bonds and preferred and common stock. Next, he found how many bonds were outstanding and the number of shares of each type of stock. Multiplying the price per security times the number of securities, he found the total market value of each capital component. Summing these yielded the total market value of Pogo's capital.

CAPITAL COMPONENT	PRICE PER BOND OR SHARE	NUMBER OUTSTANDING	TOTAL MARKET VALUE OF COMPONENT
Debt (bonds)	$1,214/bond	2,000 bonds	$2,428,000
Preferred stock	$39.93/share	30,481 shares	$1,217,105
Common stock	$11.75/share	218,265 shares	$2,564,614
		Total market value of capital	$6,209,719

Transparency Available

Next, he found the proportion of financing supplied by each component.

$$\text{equity's proportion of financing} = \frac{\$2,564,614}{\$6,209,719} = 0.413$$

Transparency Available

$$\text{preferred's proportion of financing} = \frac{\$1{,}217{,}105}{\$6{,}209{,}719} = 0.196$$

$$\text{debt's proportion of financing} = \frac{\$2{,}428{,}000}{\$6{,}209{,}719} = 0.391$$

Here we see the proportion of capital sought from each source for the jackline project. These are, again, numbers reflected on Elihu's worksheet early in this chapter.

For the Jackline project, the weighted average cost of capital was 10%. Let's look once more at the WACC formula and where that 10% discount rate came from.

Transparency Available

$$\begin{aligned} \text{WACC} &= (W_d)(K_d^{\text{new}})(1 - t) + (W_{\text{pfd}})(K_{\text{pfd}}^{\text{new}}) \\ &\quad + (W_{\text{ret earn}})(K_{\text{ret earn}}) \\ &= (0.391)(8.94)(1 - 0.34) + (0.196)(11.50) \\ &\quad + (0.413)(13.20) \\ &= 2.30\% + 2.25\% + 5.45\% \\ &= 10\% \end{aligned} \tag{10.15}$$

Glancing at Equation (10.15), you may wonder why Elihu doesn't finance the entire project's cost using borrowed funds. After all, the after-tax cost of debt is only (8.94%)(1 − 0.34) = 5.90%. Using 5.9% rather than 10% as the cost of capital would certainly raise the Jackline project's NPV. But if debt is used this year, then equity might be used next year in order for Pogo to achieve its targeted capital mix. If Pogo financed the next project with equity and used the cost of equity, 13.2%, as the project's discount rate, the firm might erroneously reject a promising project. The correct treatment is to use the firm's target capital mix consistently to calculate WACC, regardless of whether the project under consideration is to be financed using the exact targeted mix or solely using debt or solely using equity. This approach is correct because future projects will be funded in such a way that the targeted mix is eventually achieved. Such a method ensures that the firm's investment activities will not be biased in favor of projects considered during years when low-cost debt is being raised and biased against projects being considered during periods when higher-cost equity is used for financing investment. In short, the capital budgeting decision should be separated from the decision regarding what financing source will be utilized.

ESTIMATING THE DISCOUNT RATE FOR INDIVIDUAL PROJECTS

Carrying out an NPV analysis requires having after-tax cash flows and an appropriate discount rate. In many project analyses the firm's overall (or weighted average) cost of capital can be used as a discount rate. *Using the WACC requires that the project being examined has the same risk as the entire firm.*

Elihu believes the new jackline project has the same risk as Pogo's existing business. Elihu reasons that Pogo's existing business of producing specialized sailing gear, including old-style jacklines, is so similar to the new jackline project that the risks are nearly identical. He believes there are new uncertainties, to be sure, in producing a new model of jackline hardware, but existing jackline equipment is exposed to the risk that another manufacturer will produce an improved model, making Pogo's existing product obsolete. Overall, he feels that the new risk inherent in bringing improved equipment to the market is about the same as the risk of old equipment becoming obsolete. He feels Pogo is simply substituting one risk for another, leaving total risk about the same. Elihu also realizes that the risks that are relevant for estimating return requirements are the marketwide, or nondiversifiable, risks of the business (he apparently read Chapters 7 and 8). The new jackline hardware is probably about as sensitive to marketwide forces as is the old hardware. Both are equally sensitive to economic recession (in which case sales of discretionary products will decline), unemployment, changes in the tax law, etc. Thus, he reasons that return requirements for the new project will be the same as those for Pogo's existing projects.

Why a Project's Risk May Differ from the Company's Overall Risk

For many projects this condition will not hold. In such cases we must estimate a discount rate that reflects the project's risk. This section describes why differences in risk might arise and how discount rates for individual projects might be estimated. Consider Campbell Soup. The company has a dominant position in its industry and produces a product for which there is fairly constant demand. Thus, we would expect that Campbell Soup has average or slightly below average risk. Now suppose that two projects are being proposed by Campbell Soup's managers. The first is a tomato soup with a spicy Mexican taste. Suppose this soup follows the successful introduction of a spicy Italian tomato soup in 1992. The second proposal is to start a chain of small soup cafes—tentatively called "17 Flavors Soup Cafes." The cafes would feature 17 flavors (thereby the name) of Campbell's soups ready for immediate serving.

These two proposals probably do not have the same risk. The spicy Mexican soup proposal is a standard Campbell's product. They have enormous experience evaluating, producing, marketing, and distributing such products. The successful introduction of a similar soup—the spicy Italian tomato soup—gives them insight into how to proceed with this product. Consider the other project. A chain of fast-food restaurants differs dramatically from any of Campbell's other businesses. The fast-food industry is very competitive, with several dominant chains vying for market share. Campbell's managers may have limited experience operating in such a competitive industry. The two projects differ dramatically in how their sales might respond to economywide risk factors. In a recession, for example, individuals are likely to conserve cash, eating out less but perhaps consuming more canned soup at home.

The risk of the soup cafe project will be quite different from that of the soup proposal or the risk of Campbell's as a whole. Thus, although it is not appropriate to use the company's existing weighted average cost of capital to evaluate the soup cafe proposal, it is appropriate for the spicy Mexican tomato soup proposal. The WACC can be used if the project being evaluated has risk identical to that of the entire company. If the project diverges from the company's primary activities, then a discount rate that reflects the project's risk must be used in NPV analysis.

Estimating a Risk-Adjusted Discount Rate for NPV Analysis

Chapters 7 and 8 introduced the capital asset pricing model (CAPM) and the idea that the capital markets price only market risk—that is, only the risk that cannot be diversified away matters for investors holding well-diversified portfolios. We use the same concept of market risk when determining a project's discount rate: A project's discount rate should reflect the market or nondiversifiable risk of that project. Using the CAPM, the required rate of return on any project will be

$$\text{required rate (project A)} = \text{risk-free rate} + (\text{beta}_A)(\text{market return} - \text{risk-free rate}) \quad \textbf{(10.16)}$$

You should recognize all the terms in this expression, except possibly beta_A. Beta_A is the **asset beta,** or measure of market risk, for the project being evaluated. In the next section we discuss how to estimate a project's beta.

Estimating a Project's Beta

Recall from Chapter 8 that beta measures an asset's systematic risk, or the extent to which the returns to an asset (real or financial) move with changes in the returns to a market portfolio, such as the S&P 500. One cannot directly calculate the beta for a new and different project, such as Campbell's 17 Flavors Soup Cafes. Instead, the analyst must wear the hat of a detective and look for clues as to the project's risk. One widely used technique for estimating a project's cost of capital is the **pure-play** method. A pure-play is a publicly traded firm that engages primarily in the same line of business as the project being considered. The beta of this pure-play's equity may then be found and used as a proxy, or stand-in, for the project's beta.[3] By incorporating the pure-play's beta into the search for the project's beta, a cost of capital is found that has been adjusted for the project's expected riskiness. This new cost of capital is therefore called a **risk-adjusted discount rate** (RADR).[4]

A good pure-play has several important characteristics. First, as we've mentioned, it should be in the same line of business as the project being analyzed. For Campbell's soup cafes, a good pure-play would be another small chain of fast-food, niche-type restaurants or eating establishments. Another chain of soup cafes would be ideal, but none probably exists. Wendy's would likely be a better proxy than McDonald's because of size. Perhaps Baskin-Robbins would be better yet: It's in food service, it's not too large, it has a specialized menu, and ice cream is somewhat seasonal (like soup). A good manager would continue this line of search until several publicly traded firms are identified that seem to be reasonable proxies given their products and markets.

A second characteristic of an ideal pure-play is the capital mix of the proxy

---

[3]Here we are assuming that the pure-play engages in the same business *and* uses the same mixture of debt and equity in its financing.

[4]To be precise, all discount rates should be RADR's, including, for example, the WACC used in the jackline project. Because the jackline project is expected to have the same risk as Pogo's existing projects, no adjustment is necessary.

firm. The best choice is a firm that is solely equity-financed (with no or very little debt). If a pure-play can be found with no debt, the project's required return can be estimated directly using the CAPM. The project required return can then be used as a discount rate in NPV analysis or as a hurdle rate when using the IRR criteria. Suppose, for example, a chain of soup cafes existed whose capital mix included only common stock whose beta was 1.3. The RADR of Campbell's cafe project could be estimated directly using the pure-play's beta. We will assume $r_f = 4\%$ and $E(r_m) = 10.3\%$.

$$\begin{aligned} \text{RADR} &= \text{required return}_{\text{project A}} = r_f + B_A(E(r_m) - r_f) \\ &= 4\% + 1.3(10.3\% - 4\%) = 12.19\% \end{aligned}$$

At times, the pure-play located has a capital mix that includes debt. To estimate the asset beta for such a firm, one must use the **Hamada equation.**[5]

$$B_{\text{assets}} = \frac{B_{\text{equity}}}{1 + (1 - t)(D/E)} \qquad (10.17)$$

Here B_{equity} is the beta of the pure-play's common stock. The pure-play's tax rate is t, and D/E is the ratio of the market value of the firm's debt to its equity's market value. If we find a pure-play with debt of $1 million and equity worth $2 million, a tax rate of 30%, and B_{equity} equal to 1.5, we can estimate its assets' beta as follows.

$$B_{\text{assets}} = \frac{1.5}{1 + (1 - 0.30)(\frac{1}{2})} = 1.154$$

This beta can then be used to estimate the project's appropriate discount rate.

$$\text{RADR} = 4\% + 1.154(10.3\% - 4\%) = 11.27\%$$

Of course, for many projects a pure-play cannot be found. The methods for estimating the RADR under such circumstances range from ad hoc techniques (such as adding or subtracting a few percentage points to the firm's existing WACC) to developing betas based on accounting information. The ad hoc technique requires good judgment on the part of the analyst. For projects of different risks, different adjustments must be made to the discount rate. Should Campbell's, for example, add 2% to its current WACC to reflect the risk of the cafes vis-à-vis its core business? Or, perhaps, should it add 5%? Other new projects may be perceived as less risky than existing lines of business, so a few percentage points would be subtracted from the current WACC. The difficulties encountered using this method are obvious, but at times there is no choice. Accounting betas are found by measuring the comovement of an accounting-based standard of performance of a firm in a similar line of business with an average of a broad sample of firms' accounting results. This technique is beyond the scope of this text, but it is useful when a pure-play is identified but is closely held (it has no stock being traded, so calculating a traditional beta is impossible). Such firms' accounting reports are sometimes available, however, and then an accounting beta may be estimated.

---

[5]See Robert Hamada, "The Effect of the Firm's Capital Structure on the Systematic Risk of Common Stock," *Journal of Finance* (May 1972): 435–52.

SUMMARY

Choosing the correct rate at which to discount project cash flows is critically important to valuing a capital project. The discount rate is the weighted average of the required rates of return for each class of investor. The principal investor classes are the bondholders, preferred stockholders, and common stockholders. Each of these investor classes contributes capital to the firm as a whole, rather than to individual projects, and each is compensated for the risk that it incurs by investing in the firm. The discount rate that provides each investor class with its required rate of return is the weighted average cost of capital (WACC).

The WACC is the appropriate discount rate for a project whose risk is equal to that of the firm as a whole. However, the cash flows of projects that increase firm risk—and, therefore, the risk of its investors—should be discounted at a rate greater than the WACC. In the same way, cash flows of projects that reduce firm risk should be discounted at a rate less than the WACC. The rate that reflects project-specific risk is the risk adjusted discount rate (RADR).

KEY TERMS

cost of capital
weighted average cost of capital
cost of debt
cost of preferred
cost of equity
cost of retained earnings
cost of new stock
flotation costs
pure-play
risk-adjusted discount rate (RADR)
asset beta
hamada equation

KEY FORMULAS

cost of debt

$$K_d = \text{Yield to Maturity}$$

$$\text{after tax} = K_d(1 - t)$$

cost of preferred

$$K_{pfd} = \text{dividend/price}$$

cost of equity

CAPM method $K_e = r_f + B(E(r_m) - r_f)$

discounted cash flow $K_e = D_1/Po + g_n$

equity-debt risk premium $K_e = K_d + RP$

formulas for new external financing

$$P_{net} = P - (\text{flotation costs})$$

$$K_d^{new} = YTM^*$$

$$K^{new}{}_{pfd} = \text{dividend}/P_{net}$$

$$K_{new\ stock} = D_1/P_{net} + g_n$$

weight of debt

$$w_d = (\text{market value of debt})/(\text{total market value})$$

weight of preferred

$$w_{pfd} = (\text{market value of preferred})/(\text{total market value})$$

weight of equity

$$w_e = (\text{market value of equity})/(\text{total market value})$$

weighted average cost of capital

$$\text{WACC} = (w_d)(K_d)(1 - t) + (w_{pfd})(K_{pfd}) + (w_e)(K_e)$$

Hamada equation

$$B_{asset} = (B_{equity})/\{1 + (1 - t)(D/E)\}$$

QUESTIONS

1. A fellow student comments that if a project has an NPV equal to zero, then the project will generate no cash flows for the common stockholders. You argue that it *will* produce such cash flows. What is your argument? (By the way, you are correct. It will produce cash for the common stockholders.)
2. Accounting balance sheets reflect the book values of claims, based on the historical contributions of capital suppliers. Suppose a firm raised its initial capital 10 years ago, and its accounting statements currently reflect a capital mix of half debt and half equity. No more debt has been issued since the original bonds were sold. Interest rates have not changed, but the firm has been exceptionally successful.
   a. Do you think common stockholders would be willing to sell their stock today for its book value?
   b. Interest rates have not changed, but the firm's bonds are selling at a premium, above their book values. Why?
   c. If the firm has been wildly successful, and given your answers to parts (a) and (b), what do you think has happened to the total market value of the firm? Is it above or below its total book value?
   d. How do you think the firm's capital mix, based on market values, compares to the 50-50 mix reflected on the accounting balance sheet?
3. Explain why $(1 - t)$ does not appear in the cost of preferred and the cost of common equity formulas.
4. Suppose a firm uses all equity financing, but half that financing is internal equity and half is external equity.
   a. Name the capital components for the firm.
   b. What will be the weights for each component?
   c. Write the firm's WACC formula.
5. Which of the following hypothetical projects would appropriately use the firm's current WACC as the discount rate in capital budgeting, and which do you feel require some risk adjustment?
   a. Boeing is considering producing a new version of the 767 aircraft, altered for use as a cargo plane. It will be called the 767C.

b. Pogo Offshore, discussed in this chapter, is analyzing the market for producing windsurfing equipment.
c. AT&T is considering the production of fax machines.
d. McDonald's is analyzing the addition of a new menu item, onion rings.

6. (True or False) A project with a NPV < 0 generates enough cash to provide the minimum required returns to bondholders and stockholders.
7. (True or False) A project with a NPV = 0 generates just enough cash to provide the minimum required returns to bondholders and stockholders.
8. (True or False) A project with a NPV > 0 generates just enough cash to provide the minimum required returns to bondholders and stockholders.
9. Consider a project for which NPV = $18,000. Which set of claimants has a claim on this net present value amount?
10. There are three methods of estimating the cost of corporate equity. Name or briefly describe two of these methods.
11. Flotation costs ______ (raise/lower) the corporate cost of capital.
12. The corporate weighted average cost of capital is the appropriate required rate of return for which of the following?
    a. All corporate projects
    b. Projects whose risk is about equal to overall corporate risk
    c. Projects whose risk is generally less than overall corporate risk
    d. Projects whose risk is generally greater than overall corporate risk
    e. None of the above
13. (True or false) A project beta provides a way to estimate the required return to reflect project risk.

DEMONSTRATION PROBLEM: STAN & OLLIE'S WACC

1. Stan and Ollie's Popcorn is considering a new fat-free product for distribution in movie theaters. The firm's management believes the new product has about the same risk as the firm's current product line. Management therefore believes the firm's current WACC is the appropriate discount rate for finding the project's NPV. The RHS of the firm's financial balance sheet is shown here and reflects the market value of each capital component.

CAPITAL SOURCE	MARKET VALUE
Bonds, 100,000 outstanding; 8% annual coupon rate; payable semiannually; mature in 15 years	$ 64,636,183
Preferred stock, $5 annual dividend, 2,000,000 shares outstanding	$ 71,420,000
Common stock, 13,000,000 shares outstanding	$312,000,000
Total	$448,056,183

The common stock just paid a dividend of $2.25 per share. Dividends are expected to grow at 6% annually. Find Stan and Ollie's WACC if the tax rate is 34%.

SOLUTION

$$WACC = W_dK_d(1 - t) + W_{pfd}K_{pfd} + W_eK_e$$

STEP 1

Find the weights of each capital source.

$$W_d = \frac{\text{value debt}}{\text{total value}} = \frac{\$64{,}636{,}183}{\$448{,}056{,}183} = 0.1443$$

$$W_{pfd} = \frac{\text{value preferred}}{\text{total value}} = \frac{\$71{,}420{,}000}{\$448{,}056{,}183} = 0.1594$$

$$W_e = \frac{\text{value equity}}{\text{total value}} = \frac{\$312{,}000{,}000}{\$448{,}056{,}183} = 0.6963$$

Check:

$$W_d + W_{pfd} + W_e \stackrel{?}{=} 1.0000$$

$$0.1443 + 0.1594 + 0.6963 \stackrel{?}{=} 1.0000$$

$$1.0000 = 1.0000$$

Now, we know

$$WACC = (0.1443)K_d(1 - t) + (0.1594)K_{pfd} + (0.6963)K_e$$

STEP 2

Find the costs.

a. K_D = YTM on bonds. The price of each bond is \$64,636,183 divided by the total number of bonds outstanding, 100,000: \$64,636,183 ÷ 100,000 = \$646.

$$\$646 = \frac{\$40}{(1 + \text{YTM})^1} + \frac{\$40}{(1 + \text{YTM})^2} + \cdots + \frac{\$40}{(1 + \text{YTM})^{30}} + \frac{\$1{,}000}{(1 + \text{YTM})^{30}}$$

Because the annual coupon rate is 8%, the annual coupon payment is \$80, but payments are made semiannually and therefore equal \$40 each. Because there are 15 years to maturity, there will be 30 semiannual periods until the bond matures. In absence of a stated maturity or par value, $1,000 is assumed. Solving for YTM results in

$$\text{YTM} = 6.79\% \text{ semiannually or}$$

$$\text{YTM} = 13.58\% \text{ per year}$$

$$K_D = 13.58\%$$

b.

$$K_{\text{pfd}} = \frac{\text{coup}}{\text{price}} = \frac{\$5}{\text{price}}$$

The price per share of the preferred can be found by dividing the total market value by the number of preferred shares outstanding,

$$\text{price per share} = \frac{\$71{,}420{,}000}{2{,}000{,}000}$$

$$= \$35{,}71$$

$$K_{\text{pfd}} = \frac{\$5}{\$35.71}$$

$$= 0.14 = 14\%$$

c.

$$K_E = \frac{D_1}{P} + g_n$$

$$g_n = 6\% = 0.06$$

$$D_1 = D_0(1 + g_n) = \$2.25(1.06) = \$2.385$$

$$P = \frac{\$312{,}000{,}000}{13{,}000{,}000} = \$24$$

$$K_E = \frac{\$2.385}{\$24} + 0.06 = 0.1594 = 15.94\%$$

STEP 3

Insert the costs and tax rate, and solve.

$$\begin{aligned} \text{WACC} &= (0.1443)(0.1358)(1 - 0.34) + (0.1594)(0.14) \\ &\quad + (0.6963)(0.1594) \\ &= 0.01293 + 0.02232 + 0.11099 \\ &= 0.14624 \\ &= 14.624\% \end{aligned}$$

PROBLEMS

Cost of Debt

1. 6.67%

1. Three years ago, Ron's Rubbish Service issued 30-year bonds at par with an annual coupon rate of 8%, payable semiannually. Today, these bonds are selling for $875 each. What is Ron's after-tax cost of debt if the company is in the 28% tax bracket?

2. Dr. Watson's Frosty Mornin' Spring Water, Inc., has an equity beta of 1.5. Assuming Treasury bills are yielding 7% annually and the market risk premium is 5%, what is Watson's cost of equity?
3. Telebrations is a rapidly growing business. Its niche is allowing virtual parties by providing a closed-circuit video linkup for people all across the country. Thus, grandparents in New Jersey can "attend" Tommy's first birthday in Arizona. Telebrations' dividends have been growing at an 8% rate annually. The last dividend paid was $1.15 and the stock is selling for $9.50 per share.
   a. What is Telebrations' cost of retained earnings?
   b. If flotation costs are 30¢ per share, what is Telebrations' cost of new stock?
4. If Telebrations' (see Problem 3) bonds yield 13%, what would be a reasonable range, in your estimation for the firm's cost of equity?
5. What is a firm's cost of preferred if it pays an annual dividend of $3 a share and is selling for $18 per share?
6. A corporation's capital structure consists of bonds and common stock. There are $8 million in corporate bonds outstanding, selling at par value. Book value of the common equity is $6 million. There are 1 million shares of common stock outstanding. Currently, the market price per share is $18.
   a. What are the proportions of debt and equity using book values?
   b. What are the proportions of debt and equity using market values?
   c. Which is preferred for calculating WACC, book or market values?
7. A company has a capital structure as reflected on the following accounting balance sheet.

Bonds ($1000 par) 500 outstanding	$ 500,000
Preferred stock ($3 coupon) (100,000 shares outstanding)	$ 800,000
Common stock (100,000 shares outstanding)	$1,000,000

   a. What are the firm's capital structure proportions based on book values?
   b. The bonds pay interest semiannually, have an 8% annual coupon rate, and mature in 10 years. Currently, investors require a 6% annual return from these bonds. What is the current price of each bond? What is the total current value of these bonds?
   c. The required return for the preferred stock is 8%. What is the current price per share of the preferred and what is preferred's total value?
   d. Common stock is expected to pay a $1.10 dividend next year. Dividends are expected to grow at an 8% rate for the foreseeable future. Investors require a 10% return from their investment in securities that have the same risk as this stock. What is the stock's current price and total value?
   e. Now, construct the RHS of this corporation's financial balance sheet. Then find the weights, based on market values, that would be used in finding this firm's WACC.
8. Mainsail Corporation is financed by the following proportions of capital:

long-term debt	30%
preferred stock	5%
common equity (retained cash)	65%

Cost of Equity (CAPM)
2. 14.5%
Cost of Equity
3. a. 21.07%
Cost of New Stock Discounted Cash Flow Approach
b. 21.50%
Cost of Equity
4. 16% to 19%
Cost of Preferred
5. 16.7%
Finding Weights
6. a. $w_d = 0.57$; $w_e = 0.43$
b. $w_d = 0.31$; $w_e = 0.69$
Finding Weights
7. a. $w_d = 0.22$; $w_{pfd} = 0.35$; $w_e = 0.43$
b. $1,148.77; $574,387
c. $37.50; $3,750,000
d. $55; $5,500,000
e. $w_d = 0.06$; $w_{pfd} = 0.38$; $w_e = 0.43$

WACC
8. a. 6.3%
b. 13%
c. 16.45%
d. 13.23%
e. 13.23%

Mainsail's corporate tax rate is 30%.

a. The yield to maturity on long-term debt is 9%. What is the after-tax cost of this debt to Mainsail?

b. The preferred stock dividend is $6.50 per share. The price of the preferred stock is $50. What is the cost of preferred stock to Mainsail?

c. The risk-free interest rate is 8%. The market risk premium is 6.5%. The company's beta is 1.3. What is the cost of common equity to Mainsail?

d. Calculate the weighted average cost of capital for Mainsail.

e. If the project is financed solely by debt, what is the required rate of return for the project, assuming its risk is the same as that of the overall company and the firm will maintain its current capital structure as its long-term target?

Comprehensive WACC
9. a. Loan, bonds, new stock
b. $w_L = 0.048$; $w_B = 0.178$; $w_{\text{new stock}} = 0.774$
c. Loan = $96,000; bonds = $356,000; stock = −$548,000
d. 10.18%
e. 375 bonds
f. 73,715 shares
g. 11%, 7.26%
h. 9%, 5.94%
i. 15.38%
j. Yes
k. 13.48%

9. Santa Fe Industries manufactures frozen tamales, which are distributed throughout the Southwest. The corporation is considering a geographic expansion into New England. The project requires additional processing capacity in the Santa Fe factory. Total initial investment will be $2,000,000. You have been hired by Santa Fe to estimate the cost of capital for the project. The firm wishes to maintain its current capital mix and considers the project to have risk equal to its existing business. Santa Fe's management has provided the following details of its existing capital from its accounting balance sheet.

Long-term debt	
Bank loan[1]	$ 1,500,000
Bonds (originally sold at par)[2]	$ 6,000,000
Equity	
Common stock, $1 per share par	$ 1,000,000
Additional paid in capital	$ 9,000,000
Retained earnings	$13,000,000

[1]The bank loan floats at the prime rate.

[2]Bonds are $1,000 par value, mature 12 years from today, and pay coupons annually at a 9% rate.

You have done some research on your own. The following notes reflect the pertinent information.

Bonds: Santa Fe's bonds are selling for $920. Investment bankers charge $50 per bond to sell a new issue.

Bank loan: The bank is willing to extend a long-term loan to Santa Fe at 9% current APR, with interest paid monthly. The bank will waive any loan-origination fees.

Equity: Santa Fe has no internal cash flow available for investment in the project. Common stock is selling for $24 per share. Dividends were $1.20 last year and were $0.50 per share 10 years ago. Investment bankers will charge $3 per share to market a new issue of stock.

a. What are the components of capital for Santa Fe?

b. What are the weights of each component?

c. Of the $2,000,000, how many dollars must be raised from each capital source?

d. For the new bonds to be sold at par value ($1,000 each), what annual coupon rate should they carry?
e. How many bonds must Santa Fe sell? (Round up to the next bond if your answer is not a whole number.)
f. How many shares of stock must be sold to raise the needed capital? (Round up if you have a fractional answer.)
g. What is the cost of bond debt? What is the after-tax cost of bond debt if Santa Fe is in the 34% marginal tax bracket?
h. What is the cost of bank debt? What is the after-tax cost of bank debt?
i. What is the cost of equity?
j. Does the cost of equity you calculated in part (i) fall within the range found using the equity-debt risk premium?
k. What is the WACC?

RADR, Pure Play, and Hamada Equation
10. a. 1.385
b. 14%
c. No

10. Santa Fe (Problem 9) is also considering starting a new chain of fast-food restaurants called the Santa Fe Cafe. These will be funded using 100% equity, all of it internally generated cash. To calculate the risk-adjusted discount cost of capital for this project, you have found the betas of two pure-plays:

Tijuana Tacos	beta = 1.6
The Big Burrito	beta = 1.4

You note that Tijuana Tacos' capital mix is 20% debt and 80% equity, whereas The Big Burrito uses no debt in its capital structure. Tijuana Taco's tax rate is 33%.
a. Estimate Santa Fe Cafe's beta.
b. The market risk premium has historically been close to 6%, and Treasury bills are yielding 5.7%. What is the cost of equity for the cafe project?
c. Will the WACC for the project differ from the cost of equity in this case?

NPV, IRR
11. NPV = −$78,902;
IRR = 12.73%

11. If the Santa Fe Cafe project (Problem 10) requires an initial investment of $1,500,000 and is expected to generate cash flows of $180,000 in year 1, $250,000 in year 2, and $300,000 for the next 8 years, what is the project's NPV? What is its IRR? Would you recommend that the project be pursued? Why or why not?

Pure Play, Hamada Equation
12. 1.07

12. Suppose that Campbell's finds a comparable firm with which it can estimate the beta of the 17 Flavors Soup Cafe project (see the text for a complete description). The pure-play firm is called Chicago Soup Kitchens. Chicago's equity beta is 1.30, its tax rate is 35%, and its debt-equity ratio based on market values is $\frac{1}{3}$. What is your estimate of the 17 Flavors' asset beta?

WACC
13. 14.31%

13. Barnstorm Aircraft, Inc., has a target capital structure of 45% debt and 55% equity. Its cost of equity is 19%, its tax rate is 34%, and its cost of debt is 13%. What is Barnstorm's WACC?

Weights
14. $w_d = 0.07$; $w_{pfd} = 0.39$;
$w_e = 0.54$

14. The management of Blue Thumb Tools believes the firm's current capital structure is optimal and intends to maintain it in the future. Blue Thumb's bonds are selling for $950 each. Its common stock is selling for $37 a share and its preferred stock is selling for $88 per share. There are 50,000 bonds outstanding, 10,000,000 shares of stock, and 3,000,000 shares of preferred stock outstanding, respectively. What are the current weights of Blue Thumb's capital sources?

WACC
15. 11.08%
NPV
16. NPV = $177,366

15. Blue Thumb's (see Problem 14) stock has a beta of 1.2. The current Treasury bill yield is 5.5%, and the expected return on the market portfolio is 11.5%. The company's preferred stock pays a dividend of $8.50 per share each year. The yield-to-maturity of Blue Thumb's bonds is currently 9.2%. If Blue Thumb is in the 29% tax bracket, what is the company's WACC?

16. Suppose Blue Thumb Tools is considering the introduction of a new, heavier hammer to be used for driving spikes. The new hammer is called the Black Thumb. Use the WACC you found in Problem 15 to find the NPV of the Black Thumb project. The project's projected cost and cash flows are as follows.

cost = $459,000

YEAR	CASH FLOW
1	$178,000
2	$239,000
3	$225,000
4	$180,000

CHAPTER 11

Risk, Inflation, and the Corporate Capital Budget

"I've called the family together to announce that, because of inflation, I'm going to have to let two of you go."

Inflation drives up costs. Unless income rises to keep pace with pace with inflation, company investors (and families) experience reduced purchasing power. Companies sometimes react to inflation by reducing their work force, an option not readily available to families!

hapters 9 and 10 have provided the framework for analyzing corporate investments. In these chapters, we covered the processes of estimating cash flows and the required rate of return. We also showed how these estimates were incorporated into the discounted cash flow model to evaluate projects. In this chapter, we discuss two topics that may affect our estimates of cash flows and required rate of return. The first is handling risk in estimates of future cash flows. The second is handling expected inflation in the discounted cash flow model.

To wrap up our coverage of corporate investing, we switch from individual-project analysis to considerations of the corporate capital budget as a whole. First, we show that, in principle, the value of a corporation is the aggregate value of its investments, past and present. Next we cover two investment issues that confront corporate managers. One is whether corporations should diversify projects much as securities investors diversify their portfolios. The other is the practice of limiting the number of dollars spent on projects, irrespective of investment opportunities. Finally, we discuss the special opportunities and challenges facing companies that invest internationally.

"It is a far, far better thing to have a firm anchor in nonsense than to put out on the troubled seas of thought,"
J. K. Galbraith

HANDLING RISK IN PROJECT CASH FLOW ESTIMATES

Understanding Sources of Risk in Estimated Future Cash Flows

In Chapter 10, we showed how to adjust the discount rate in the NPV model for project risk. The risk-adjusted discount rate raises the required rate of return for high-risk projects, which makes it less likely that the company would accept these projects. However, as we saw in Chapter 10, the risk adjustment is somewhat arbitrary, and the process of determining the discount rate provides little insight into the nature or the sources of risk in those future cash flows.

We may begin to understand the sources of risk by referring to the project classifications introduced in Chapter 9. The classification scheme is based on project size and similarity to existing company projects. The categories are

Replacement projects
Expansion projects
Diversification or dispersion projects

Generally, risk, which is the uncertainty of future outcomes, is lowest for replacement projects, and greatest for diversification and dispersion projects.

Replacement projects are meant primarily to save operating costs, such as maintenance, energy, or labor. Modern airliners, such as Boeing's 777, are more fuel efficient and require smaller flight crews than older planes. However, the 777 uses new and untested jet engines. What is the chance that these engines will not deliver their promised fuel economy? The most modern airliners have been certified for operation with only two, rather than the customary three, people on the flight deck. The Boeing 777 was designed to be the first such twin-engine airliner to be certified for over-water flights. Bad luck or a design flaw could force airlines to add more crew or confine the 777 to domestic routes.

Expansion projects increase productive capacity and therefore depend on increased demand for the company's product. New airliners, besides offering greater operating efficiency, have greater capacity. Airlines replace 150-seat airplanes with 250-seat airplanes because they expect greater demand for air travel or increased market share. Fare wars, the entry of low-cost competitors, and the ever-present possibility of recession are possible sources of risk for the airlines.

Diversification or dispersion projects are risky because they take the company into relatively uncharted waters. Estimates of future cash flows are based more on assumptions than experience. United Airlines bought expensive Boeing 747-400 aircraft to serve its newly acquired trans-Pacific routes. However, United, primarily a domestic airline, had little experience with long overseas flights or with Asian markets. In these situations, identifying specific sources of risk is difficult.

Risk assessment entails costs and may not be appropriate for small or routine projects. For larger projects, especially those related to diversification and dispersion, risk analysis may be difficult and costly, but also vital.

Using Sensitivity Analysis to Analyze Risk in Replacement and Expansion Projects

We indicated in the last section that we may be able to identify sources of risk for replacement and expansion projects. If so, we can use **sensitivity analysis** to identify possible conditions, sometimes called states of nature, and their effects on project value. We illustrate with the case of TopFlight Airlines. The airline is considering a 20-year investment in larger airplanes in anticipation of increased demand. TopFlight recognizes that the demand for seats depends on three factors:

- The general state of the economy over the 20-year period will affect overall demand (passenger miles) for air travel.
- Fare wars among existing competitors would affect revenue per passenger mile.
- The entry of low-cost airlines would increase price competition, triggering further fare wars and perhaps reducing TopFlight's market share.

TopFlight Airlines is considering buying 15 new 250-seat planes for $80 million each. They expect that these airplanes will have an economic life of 20 years, at which time they will be worthless. The markets that TopFlight serves are expected to generate 7 billion passenger miles per year (market = 7 billion). TopFlight expects to have 30% of these markets (share = 30%). Revenues per seat mile and variable costs are expected to be 16¢ and 9¢, respectively (price = $0.16, cost = $0.09). From the information given, expected revenues and variable costs can be calculated.

$$\text{revenues} = (\text{market})(\text{share})(\text{price}) \tag{11.1}$$

$$\text{revenues (\$000)} = (7{,}000{,}000)(0.3)(\$0.16) = \$336{,}000$$

$$\text{variable costs} = (\text{market})(\text{share})(\text{cost}) \tag{11.2}$$

$$\text{variable costs (\$000)} = (7{,}000{,}000)(0.3)(\$0.09) = \$189{,}000$$

The planes will be depreciated using straight-line depreciation for 15 years.[1] TopFlight's required rate of return is 6%. The data are summarized in Exhibit 11.1. The annual cash flows are shown in Exhibit 11.2.

The NPV of this investment is $317,012.[2] This represents TopFlight's best

[1] The airplanes are fully depreciated before their economic life ends, which is usually the case with airplanes.

[2] The NPV calculation is shown in the appendix exhibit 11A.2.

EXHIBIT 11.1

TOPFLIGHT AIRLINES INVESTMENT IN 250-SEAT AIRPLANES

Investment (000)	$1,200,000
No. of planes	15
Cost per plane (000)	$ 80,000
Passenger miles (000)	7,000,000
Market share	30%
Revenues per seat mile (price)	$ 0.16
Variable costs per seat-mile	$ 0.09
Annual depreciation (000)	$ 80,000
Required rate of return	6%
Tax rate	22%
Project life	20 years

estimates of economic conditions, fare wars, and competition from low-cost airlines. However, TopFlight must consider the effects of unexpected occurrences, both good and bad. Exhibit 11.3 presents TopFlight's estimates of possible outcomes for each of the three factors. The *below-normal* economic condition means more years of economic recession. With regard to fare wars and the entry of low-cost airlines, TopFlight is expecting some effects on its passenger-mile revenues and market share. However, the actual outcomes could be either better or worse than expected.

Transparency Available

The spreadsheets for this example are presented in Appendix 11A.

The outcomes in Exhibit 11.3 result from a spreadsheet analysis of the effects of economic and market conditions on NPV. The analysis is presented in Appendix 11A. The NPVs suggest that TopFlight can survive most economic cycles but would be most threatened by the entry of low-cost airlines. In general, it appears that fare wars, whether from existing carriers or low-cost carriers, are potentially damaging. Sensitivity analysis identifies the most important risk factors, in this case the entry of low-cost airlines and fare wars, so that management can develop strategies to counteract this risk.

This example shows how sensitivity analysis may be used. In real life, we would identify more possible outcomes and would consider the timing of events such as the entry of low-cost carriers, rather than looking at 20-year averages. Of course, the quality of the analysis depends on the quality of our estimates of future events and their effect on future cash flows. Although the analytical technique may be relatively simple, gathering reliable estimates is not.

EXHIBIT 11.2

TOPFLIGHT AIRLINES ANNUAL CASH FLOWS

	YEAR	
	0	1–20
Initial Investment	($1,200,000)	
Operating Cash Flows		
Revenues (*R*)		$336,000
Variable costs (*E*)		$189,000
Depreciation (dep)		$ 80,000
Earnings before tax (EBT = *R* − *E* − dep)		$ 67,000
Tax (tax)		$ 14,740
Earnings after tax (EAT = EBT − tax)		$ 52,260
Cash flow (cash) (cash = EAT + dep)		$132,260

ECONOMIC CONDITIONS	AVERAGE PASSENGER MILES	NPV
Normal	7,000,000	$317,012
Below normal	5,500,000	$ 35,196
Above normal	8,500,000	$598,828

FARE WARS AMONG EXISTING AIRLINES	REVENUE PER PASSENGER MILE	NPV
Normal fare wars	$0.16	$317,012
Worse than normal	$0.13	($246,620)
Better than normal	$0.18	$692,766

ENTRY OF LOW-COST AIRLINES	REVENUE PER PASSENGER MILE	MARKET SHARE	NPV
1 carrier	$0.16	30%	$317,012
0 carrier	$0.17	35%	$755,392
2 carriers	$0.14	25%	($215,307)
3 carriers	$0.13	20%	($557,684)

EXHIBIT 11.3

TOPFLIGHT AIRLINES SENSITIVITY ANALYSIS

Transparency Available

Using Simulations to Analyze Risk in Diversification and Dispersion Projects

Diversification and dispersion projects are generally ground-breaking undertakings for the company. With virtually no experience with such projects, gathering data on expected outcomes and their effects on future cash flows would be difficult indeed. Without such information, we cannot use sensitivity analysis.

There is an alternative technique for analyzing risk called **simulation analysis**. Simulations do not require us to estimate cash flows directly. In simulation analysis we must still identify the primary factors that affect future cash flows, such as the effects of market demand, market share, and price on sales. However, rather than having to estimate specific values for each of these factors, we estimate a distribution of possible outcomes. Assuming that the distribution is normal, we need estimate only its mean and standard deviation.[3] Let's see how this would work with TopFlight Airlines.

From the discussion of sensitivity analysis, we see that passenger miles (market), TopFlight's market share (share), revenue per seat-mile (price), and variable cost per seat-mile (cost) are the key factors in estimating future cash flows. However, to use simulation, we need merely to specify an expected value and a standard deviation of possible values for each factor. For TopFlight, we estimate the following values:

	MEAN (EXPECTED VALUE)	STANDARD DEVIATION
Market	7,000,000	1,500,000
Share	30%	5%
Price	$0.16	$0.025
Cost	$0.09	$0.015

[3]You may recall from statistics that a normal distribution is symmetric, with the mean, median, and mode having the same value. In such a distribution, we can use the mean and standard deviation to calculate the probability of occurrence for any value within the distribution.

EXHIBIT 11.5

COMPUTER PROJECT: PROJECT NPV, EXCLUDING INFLATION

	YEAR						
	0	1	2	3	4	5	6
Initial Investment	($15,000)						
Operating Cash Flows							
Savings (S)		$7,500	$7,500	$7,500	$7,500	$7,500	$7,500
Expenses (E)		$2,000	$2,000	$2,000	$2,000	$2,000	$2,000
Depreciation (dep)		$ 0	$ 0	$ 0	$ 0	$ 0	$ 0
Earnings before tax (EBT = S − E − dep)		$5,500	$5,500	$5,500	$5,500	$5,500	$5,500
tax (rate = .34) [EBT * tax rate]		$1,870	$1,870	$1,870	$1,870	$1,870	$1,870
Earnings after tax (EAT = EBT − tax)		$3,630	$3,630	$3.630	$3,630	$3,630	$3,630
Add back depreciation (EAT + dep)		$3,630	$3,630	$3,630	$3,630	$3,630	$3,630
Ending Cash Flows							
Income from sale							$6,000
NPV at 4.76% $8,105	($15,000)	$3,630	$3,630	$3,630	$3,630	$3,630	$9,630

Transparencies available for Exhibits 11.5 and 11.6

When inflation is treated inconsistently, project value is affected.

With these estimates, we may calculate the NPV of the computer project using cash flows and required returns that incorporate the 5% inflation (Exhibit 11.4), or we may make the same calculation with inflation removed from cash flows and required returns (Exhibit 11.5). In these examples that we have eliminated the effects of depreciation to simplify the analysis.

Notice that in both cases project NPV equals $8105. The NPVs are equal because we were consistent in our handling of inflation with respect to cash flows and required returns. Exhibit 11.6 shows the results of an inconsistent handling of inflation. In this case, inflation is included in the required returns, but not in the cash flow estimates. The NPV in Exhibit 11.6 is $4196, considerably below our original estimates. This low estimate occurs because the cash flows, without

EXHIBIT 11.6

COMPUTER PROJECT: PROJECT NPV WITH INCONSISTENT TREATMENT OF INFLATION

	YEAR						
	0	1	2	3	4	5	6
Initial Investment	($15,000)						
Operating Cash Flows							
Savings (S)		$7,500	$7,500	$7,500	$7,500	$7,500	$7,500
Expenses (E)		$2,000	$2,000	$2,000	$2,000	$2,000	$2,000
Depreciation (dep)		$ 0	$ 0	$ 0	$ 0	$ 0	$ 0
Earnings before tax (EBT = S − E − dep)		$5,500	$5,500	$5,500	$5,500	$5,500	$5,500
tax (rate = .34) [(EBT)(tax rate)]		$1,870	$1,870	$1,870	$1,870	$1,870	$1,870
Earnings after tax (EAT = EBT − tax)		$3,630	$3,630	$3,630	$3,630	$3,630	$3,630
Add back depreciation (EAT + dep)		$3,630	$3,630	$3,630	$3,630	$3,630	$3,630
Ending Cash Flows							
Income from sale							$6,000
NPV at 10% $4,196	($15,000)	$3,630	$3,630	$3,630	$3,630	$3,630	$9,630

inflation, are too low for the discount rate which includes inflation. To correct this inconsistency, we should either increase our cash flows to include inflation or decrease the discount rate from 10% to 4.76%.

This example illustrates two important points to keep in mind when dealing with inflation:

- We must be consistent in treating inflation in the cash flow estimate and the required rate of return (discount rate).
- If we assume that inflation affects cash flow estimates and the required rate of return equally, inflation has no effect on project NPV. The corollary is that unequal inflation effects do change the NPV.[7]

In the following section, we see how unequal inflation rates affect project NPVs.

The Effect of Unequal Inflation Rates on Project NPV

Inflation affects companies differently, depending on their market power.

The primary problem with inflation is that not all costs and prices inflate at the same rate. Market competition and regulation determine the extent to which market prices rise in response to inflationary pressures. Producers in markets in which there is little competition may be able to raise prices at or above the inflation rate. Producers in more competitive markets may be unable to raise prices to keep up with inflation.

Suppose a refrigerator manufacturer is considering buying some new equipment to produce environmental-friendly refrigerators. These refrigerators will use a new coolant that the manufacturer will have to purchase from an outside supplier. If the refrigerator market is very competitive, the company may be unable to raise its prices to offset the effect of inflation. On the other hand, if the coolant market is not very competitive, the coolant supplier may be able to raise prices, placing

Transparency Available

EXHIBIT 11.7

COMPUTER PROJECT: THE EFFECT OF UNEQUAL INFLATION RATES ON PROJECT VALUE

	YEAR						
	0	1	2	3	4	5	6
Initial Investment	($15,000)						
Operating Cash Flows							
Savings (S)		$7,875	$8,269	$8,682	$9,116	$9,572	$10,051
Expenses (E)		$2,140	$2,290	$2,450	$2,622	$2,805	$ 3,001
Depreciation (dep)		$ 0	$ 0	$ 0	$ 0	$ 0	$ 0
Earnings before tax (EBT = S − E − dep)		$5,735	$5,979	$6,232	$6,495	$6,767	$ 7,049
tax (rate = .34) [EBT * tax rate]		$1,950	$2,033	$2,119	$2,208	$2,301	$ 2,397
Earnings after tax (EAT = EBT − tax)		$3,785	$3,946	$4,113	$4,287	$4,466	$ 4,653
Add back depreciation (EAT + dep)		$3,785	$3,946	$4,113	$4,287	$4,466	$ 4,653
Ending Cash Flows							
Income from sale							$ 8,041
NPV at 10% $7,658	($15,000)	$3,785	$3,946	$4,113	$4,287	$4,466	$12,693

[7]Depreciation would change NPV slightly, depending on our treatment of inflation. This result occurs because depreciation affects cash flows but not the discount rate.

Transparency Available

These are some common-sense tips on dealing with inflation.

the refrigerator company in a price-cost squeeze. This unfavorable inflation effect reduces the value of the equipment project. Of course, this can work in reverse—i.e., if coolant suppliers were unable to raise prices but the refrigerator manufaturer could, the manufacturer could actually benefit from inflation.

Exhibit 11.7 illustrates the effect of unequal inflation rates on the computer project. Cash savings rise at a 5% rate, as before, but expenses rise at a 7% rate. The capital market discount rate remains at 10%, reflecting expected inflation of 5%. The result is a decrease in the project value to $7,658.

In summary, we offer a few guidelines for handling inflation in capital project decisions:

- Do not ignore inflation. Inflation is probably imbedded in your project's required rate of return but may not be in your cash flow estimates.
- Recognize that inflation seldom affects all prices and costs equally. Thus, if you are too casual in your handling of inflation, the quality of your estimates and the quality of your analysis will suffer.
- The time to worry most about inflation is when it is high or variable. Variable inflation rates increase the chance of forecast error and also make it more difficult for producers in some markets to respond by changing prices.

THE CORPORATE CAPITAL BUDGET

Aggregating Independent Projects

To this point in our discussion of corporate investing, we have concentrated on evaluating and selecting individual projects. However, in the final analysis it is the combination of investments, rather than individual projects, that is most important to corporations. The portfolio of corporate investments consists of human resources, organization, management, working capital and intangibles as well as capital projects. The total amount a corporation spends on these investments in a given time period (usually a year) is called the **capital budget**.

Finding the best porfolio of corporate assets is much more difficult than an investor finding the best portfolio of securities. Competitive and efficient capital markets defeat most active portfolio strategies. However, the unique opportunities presented in the varied product markets invite active and innovative investment strategies.

By emphasizing the importance of portfolios, we are treating corporate investments much as we did securities investments in Chapter 7 where the emphasis was also on portfolios. However, there are important differences between securities and corporate investments. The efficiency and competitiveness of securities markets place limits on the returns that investors can earn. These market-imposed limits cause most investors to adopt fairly simple investment strategies, such as diversifying their securities portfolios.

By contrast, investment opportunities available in the product markets require that corporations invest in the "right" mix of projects to capitalize on those opportunities. For example, an addition to production capacity may be worthless if the corporation does not simultaneously increase its sales force and advertising to sell this expanded output. The expanded marketing effort may be part of a larger corporate strategy, and not tied to a specific expansion project. However, the expansion project may be successful in every way, except that the marketing effort does not generate additional sales. As a result of these lost sales, expected cash flows from increased production do not materialize.

Suppose an investment by an airline in new aircraft includes the expectation that new terminal facilities will be built at a particular hub. Shortly after the aircraft are delivered to the airline and the terminal is built, the changing economics of air transportation force the airline to abandon the hub system. This leaves the airline with misallocated terminal capacity and, possibly, airplanes that are not suited to their new roles. These examples illustrate two important points regarding corporate investment portfolios.

- Generalized rules for forming investment portfolios in the securities markets do not apply in diverse and specialized product markets.
- Relationships between investments can be quite complex. It is difficult to identify all incidental effects for each project. Adding to this complexity is the fact that portfolios of corporate investments are not very liquid, so new investments are added to existing investments. For any but the simplest replacement projects, it is difficult for managers to understand all the effects that any one investment may have on other investments, both old and new.

All investments should add value to the corporation. New projects must have positive NPVs. Existing investments are monitored to determine if the value of the option to terminate is greater than the value of continuing the investment. Referring to the LHS of the financial balance sheet, the value of the corporation is the sum of the value of these individual investments. This **value additivity rule** follows from two established principles. The first is that each investment is independent; therefore, the value of one does not affect the value of any other investment. The second is that the LHS investments are the only sources of value for the corporation. As with virtually all principles or assumptions, there are exceptions. For instance, as we discussed before, we can never be certain that projects are completely independent. We also know that value-creating opportunities sometimes occur in the capital markets, such as the opportunity to obtain government-subsidized loans. However, as a general rule, value additivity presents a useful way of viewing the corporation because it causes us to focus on corporate investing in product markets as the most reliable means of creating value.

The Question of Corporate Investment Diversification

In Chapter 7 we saw how important it is for securities investors to diversify their holdings to reduce portfolio risk. At first glance, it would seem that corporations would similarly benefit by diversifying their investment portfolios between industries, product lines, regions, and countries.

It is true that diversifying investments may reduce the variability of corporate operating cash flows. However, for corporations the price of diversification may be unacceptably high and may not produce any payoff in increased shareholder wealth. To understand this idea, let's consider the process of investment diversification in both the securities and product markets. In the securities markets, diversification is relatively easy. Stocks and bonds are traded in active markets with low transactions costs. This means that, for a given number of dollars to invest, there is little added cost to building a diversified portfolio as opposed to one that is not diversified.[8]

Although diversifying investments may reduce the variability of corporate operating cash flows, the price of diversification may be unacceptably high and may not produce any payoff in increased shareholder wealth.

By contrast, investment diversification for corporations is much more costly and time consuming and may carry added risks. In Chapter 9 we made the point

[8]The added costs may be in paying somewhat higher brokerage fees and in the costs of gathering information on more securities.

that diversification and dispersion projects generally carry added risks because the company has no prior experience in estimating future cash flows. These projects may divert management's attention from other pressing business and divert limited capital resources from other deserving projects. They may also force costly reorganization to enable the company to manage multiple product lines or geographically distant operations. In short, corporate diversification is usually costly and may produce unintended effects. In the 1980s imprudent foreign loans brought down several large and otherwise successful U.S. banks. The primary reason for the huge foreign loan losses was the relative inexperience of U.S. bankers in overseas lending.[9]

Business periodicals often contain stories of failed diversification attempts by companies. For more than 30 years, since the first Surgeon General's report on smoking and health, U.S. tobacco companies have channeled their operating cash flows away from cigarettes and into other industries, anticipating a decline in cigarette sales. Many of these diversification attempts failed or were pursued at great cost. In contrast to these attempts to diversify, officers of many well-known companies speak of concentrating on "core" businesses and divesting other tertiary lines.

Because it is relatively easy and inexpensive for securities investors to diversify but not so easy and inexpensive for corporations to diversify, it follows that diversification activities are probably best left to the investors. An undiversified shareholder of American Tobacco Co. in 1964 may have concluded, after publication of the Surgeon General's report, that she should diversify her portfolio. This could have been accomplished with a phone call to her stock broker. American Tobacco's attempt to diversify was not so easy.

Why do some companies persist in following a diversification strategy? In some cases, this may be a manifestation of an agency problem in the company. For instance, it is possible that a cigarette producer, contemplating a declining market, may ultimately liquidate its corporate assets, pay off its investors, and close its doors. In other words, the option to terminate corporate operations may be more valuable than continuing in business. This action would be in the best interest of the shareholders but not in the best interest of the managers and employees of the corporation. Managers may therefore adopt strategies to increase their chance of survival but not necessarily the wealth of their shareholders.

It would be unfair to suggest that all diversified companies have pursued a strategy that is detrimental to their shareholders. There are many examples of successful, diversified companies. General Electric, which is both diversified and global, is one. Companies may become diversified merely by searching out and pursuing valuable investment opportunities. If they find and successfully capitalize on opportunities that represent departures from their existing business lines, they are pursuing a wealth-maximizing strategy. We must distinguish between these companies and those that seemingly substitute the goal of diversification for wealth maximization. Given the great differences between companies in terms of organization, management style, experience, financial strength, etc., it is not surprising that some are better able to diversify than others.

---

[9]The most famous of these was BankAmerica Corp., which was, at the time, the largest U.S. bank. See Gary Hector, *Breaking the Bank: The Decline of BankAmerica* (Boston: Little Brown, 1988).

Summary

Because future cash flows from a project are uncertain, it is important to consider their riskiness as well as their expected value. Sensitivity analysis is useful for assessing the effect of risk for replacement and expansion projects. For diversification and dispersion projects, estimates of cash flows are more tentative. Simulation analysis is probably a better choice for assessing risk affects of these projects because it does not require specific estimates of future outcomes.

Inflation can affect the value of project cash flows. Inflation estimates must be explicit and applied consistently to the required rate of return and estimated cash flows. Inflation seldom affects all economic sectors and markets equally. Different inflation rates in product, factor, and capital markets may significantly affect project value, particularly if they are large.

In the final analysis, the success of corporate investing depends on the entire array of investments, past and present. In examining their array of investments, corporations should guard against substituting a diversification strategy for wealth maximization. Risks of diversification and the ease with which investors can diversify among many stocks suggest that a diversification strategy may not be in the interest of shareholders.

In any given period, a corporation should take on all independent positive NPV projects. However, many companies ration capital, which limits the dollars of investment in a single period. Rationing causes the firm to turn down valuable projects, resulting in a loss of value. A firm that is subject to rationing should select the combination of projects, within the budget limit, that adds the most value to the firm.

More companies are expanding their scope of investing to include projects in foreign countries. International investing introduces exchange rate, political and foreign financial risk. However, it also provides access to new markets and resources. Global investing may also reduce risk by reducing the variability of operating cash flows.

Key Terms

sensitivity analysis
simulation analysis
capital budget
value additivity rule
rationing capital
profitability index
multinational corporations
political risk
joint venture
licensing agreements

Key Formulas

Real rate of return

$$\text{real rate} = \frac{1 + \text{nominal rate}}{1 + \text{inflation rate}} - 1$$

Profitability index

$$PI = \frac{\text{PV of future cash flows}}{\text{Investment}}$$

QUESTIONS

1. Monte Carlo simulation depends on the values of critical decision factors being normally distributed.
   a. Describe a normal distribution.
   b. In what ways might a distribution of factors not be normal?
   c. To the analyst, what is the advantage in assuming that distributions are normal?
2. Given the insight into sources of risk provided by sensitivity analysis and simulations, we should use at least one of these techniques to analyze virtually all capital projects. Do you agree or disagree? Why?
3. Ace Trucking Company is considering buying a fleet of new, fuel-efficient trucks. A consulting engineer has calculated that these trucks will save $200,000 per year in fuel costs over their 10-year life. Inflation is not included in this estimate. Ace's financial vice president estimates the company's cost of capital to be 12%. To calculate the present value of this annuity cash flow, should you discount the $200,000 annuity at 12%? Why or why not?
4. Referring to Question 3, you gather some information on expected inflation over the next 10 years. You learn that the consumer price index (CPI) is expected to rise at a 3% rate, and the cost of diesel fuel is expected to rise at a rate of 5%. Which inflation rate is most appropriate for your investment? Why?
5. Ace Drummond Enterprises is a distributor of several popular brands of U.S. beer. The beer market is highly competitive, forcing all the distributors to offer frequent promotional price reductions. The primary cost of distribution is the salaries of the delivery truck drivers. These drivers are organized through the Teamsters Union. Do you think that Ace Drummond Enterprises would gain or lose from a rise in inflation?
6. Ace Drummond (Question 5) has changed his beer distribution business. Now he sells only a few premium foreign beers and ales. These brands sell at premium prices, and demand is not price elastic. Ace now uses only a few nonunion drivers. Do you think that the new Ace Drummond Enterprises would gain or lose from a rise in inflation?
7. Asset diversification reduces the variability of cash inflows from investing. This makes asset diversification a desirable strategy, both for securities investors and corporate investors in plant, machinery and equipment. Comment on this statement.
8. It is clear that a company that has widely diversified product lines and geographically dispersed businesses did not get there by accident. By that, I mean that the company must have had the *intent* to diversify and, therefore,

did not act in the best interests of its stockholders. Comment on this statement.

9. Capital rationing by corporate management is irrational because it reduces the value of the company. Comment on this statement.
10. It seems absurd, on the face of it, to argue that companies are justified in pursuing a strategy of foreign investing but that such a dispersion strategy within the United States may be counterproductive. It's absurd, when one considers all the risk inherent in foreign investments. Comment on this statement.
11. The French franc is currently depressed relative to the U.S. dollar. However, over the next few years, the franc is expected to rise in value relative to the dollar. Does this suggest that France may offer an attractive investment opportunity? Why or why not?
12. Briefly state the purpose of using sensitivity analysis to evaluate project cash flows.
13. Future cash flows from ______ (replacement/diversification) projects are subject to greater uncertainty than cash flows from ______ (replacement/diversification) projects.
14. If future project cash flows include expected inflation, they should be discounted at a ______ (real/nominal) rate.
15. If future project cash flows do not include expected inflation, they should be discounted at a ______ (real/nomimal) rate.
16. Project revenues and expenses may not inflate at the same rate. Briefly, why?
17. An analyst tells you that a project should generate revenues of $4,000 per year for 8 years. Is it likely that this estimate includes inflation?
18. It is as important for industrial corporations to diversify their investments as it is for individuals to diversify securities investments. Do you agree or disagree? Why?
19. Corporate investments are ______ (more/less) liquid than securities investments.
20. Is asset portfolio diversification more easily handled by individual investors or industrial corporations?
21. All else being equal, would it be better for a U.S. company to invest in a country whose currency was expected to fall or rise in value?
22. These questions are about the Wayfarer Industries case at the end of the chapter.
    - **a.** If the project has a positive NPV, would you make the investment? Why?
    - **b.** If the project has a negative NPV, would you make the investment? Why?
    - **c.** What may Wayfarer do to reduce the risk of this investment?

DEMONSTRATION PROBLEMS

The Effect of Inflation on Project Value

1. Nautica Publishing is planning to spend $42,000 on a color scanner. The scanner is expected to produce added operating cash flows for 5 years. Management estimates that the before-tax cash flow will be $12,000 the first year

and will grow by 4% per year thereafter as business builds. Nautica's required rate of return is 8%, and the tax rate is 30%.

a. Based on the nominal rate of 8% and an expected inflation rate of 3%, what is the real rate of interest?
b. What is the NPV of the scanner?

SOLUTION

a. Use Equation (11.3) to solve for the real rate of interest:

$$\text{real rate} = \frac{1 + \text{nominal rate}}{1 + \text{inflation rate}} - 1$$

$$= \frac{1.08}{1.03} - 1 = 4.85\%$$

b. Cash flows grow at 4% per year, starting with $12,000 in year 1. Because we are discounting at the real required rate of return, we do not apply an inflation rate to these cash flows. After-tax cash flows are the real cash flows × (1 − 0.30). The discount rate is 4.85%. At a cost of $42,000, the NPV of the scanner is −$2,592. Therefore, we would not make the investment.

	YEAR				
	1	2	3	4	5
Real cash flow	12,000	12,480	12,979	13,498	14,038
After tax	8,400	8,736	9,085	9,449	9,827
Discounted	8,011	7,946	7,881	7,817	7,753
NPV	(2,592)				

Capital Rationing

2. A company has the following investment opportunities:

PROJECT	COST	PV OF FUTURE CASH FLOWS	NPV
A	$ 7,000	$ 9,000	$ 2,000
B	$21,000	$25,500	$ 4,500
C	$15,000	$17,500	$ 2,500
D	$42,000	$53,000	$11,000
E	$23,000	$30,500	$ 7,500

a. If there is no capital rationing, how much will the company spend on investments? What is the total value added from these investments (NPV)?
b. Rank projects by NPV and PI.
c. If the company rations capital by establishing a budget limit of $75,000, which projects would it accept under each ranking criterion?
d. By restricting the budget to $75,000, what is the cost to the company in lost NPV under each criterion?

SOLUTION

The data needed to solve this problem are presented in the following table.

PROJECT	INVESTMENT	NPV	RANK	PI	RANK
A	$ 7,000	$ 2,000	5	1.286	2
B	$ 21,000	$ 4,500	3	1.214	4
C	$ 15,000	$ 2,500	4	1.167	5
D	$ 42,000	$11,000	1	1.262	3
E	$ 23,000	$ 7,500	2	1.326	1
Total	$108,000	$27,500			

a. In the absence of rationing, the capital budget is $108,000 and total NPV is $27,500.

b. Rankings for NPV and PI are shown in the table.

c. The following table shows that NPV ranking invests a total of $65,000, yielding an NPV of $18,500. PI invests $72,000 yielding an NPV of $20,500.

NPV	CUM. INVESTMENT	CUM. NPV	PI	CUM. INVESTMENT	CUM. NPV
D	$42,000	$11,000	E	$23,000	$ 7,500
E	$65,000	$18,500	A	$30,000	$ 9,500
			D	$72,000	$20,500

d. NPV ranking sacrifices an NPV of $9,000 = $27,500 − $18,500. PI ranking sacrifices an NPV of $7,000 = $27,500 − $20,500.

PROBLEMS

Real Versus Nominal Rates of Return
1. a. 8.74%
b. 4.67%

1. **a.** A company has a required return on a project of 12%. If the inflation rate is expected to be 3%, what is the real required rate of return?
   b. Company management feels that they cannot accept a real rate of return on a project of less than 7%. With a nominal (actual) required return of 12%, how much inflation can they tolerate?

Real Versus Nominal Rates of Return
2. a. 6.86%
b. 1.87%

2. **a.** A company has a required return on a project of 9%. If the inflation rate is expected to be 2%, what is the real required rate of return?
   b. Company management feels that they cannot accept a real rate of return on a project of less than 7%. With a nominal (actual) required return of 9%, how much inflation can they tolerate?

The Effect of Inflation on Project Value
3. b. $198,633

3. Refer to the Ace Trucking Company project in Questions 3 and 4. Assume that the trucks will have no value in 10 years. The corporate tax rate is 30%. The project's initial investment is $800,000. Ignore depreciation.
   a. Calculate the annual after-tax fuel-cost savings, *including* the appropriate inflation rate.

b. Calculate the NPV of this truck project using the appropriate discount rate.

The Effect of Inflation on Project Value
4. b. $198,633

4. Refer to the Ace Trucking Company project in Questions 3 and 4. Assume that the trucks will have no value in 10 years. The corporate tax rate is 30%. The project's initial investment is $800,000. Ignore depreciation.
   a. Calculate the annual after-tax fuel-cost savings, *excluding* inflation.
   b. Calculate the NPV of this truck project using the appropriate discount rate.

The Effect of Inflation on Project Value
5. b. $334,238

5. Refer to the Ace Trucking Company project in Questions 3 and 4. Assume that the trucks will have no value in 10 years. The corporate tax rate is 30%. The project's initial investment is $800,000. The trucks are depreciated using straight-line depreciation for 10 years, with no ending value.
   a. Calculate the annual after-tax fuel-cost savings, *including* the appropriate inflation rate.
   b. Calculate the NPV of this truck project using the appropriate discount rate.

The Effect of Inflation on Project Value
6. b. $369,827

6. Refer to the Ace Trucking Company project in Questions 3 and 4. Assume that the trucks will have no value in 10 years. The corporate tax rate is 30%. The project's initial investment is $800,000. The trucks are depreciated using straight-line depreciation for 10 years, with no ending value.
   a. Calculate the annual after-tax fuel-cost-savings, *excluding* inflation.
   b. Calculate the NPV of this truck project using the appropriate discount rate.

The Effect of Depreciation on Project Value

7. Compare your answers in Problems 3 and 4 with those in Problems 5 and 6. How has depreciation changed the effect of inflation on project value?

Inconsistent Treatment of Inflation
8. a. −$13,454
   b. −$5,303

8. Dirty Harry's Key West Bar and Grill is planning to spend $82,000 to upgrade its interior decor. The decor is expected to produce added operating cash flows for 7 years. Harry figures that the added cash flow will be $20,000 the first year and will grow by 5% per year thereafter as business builds. Harry's required rate of return is 12%, and the tax rate is 34%.
   a. What is the NPV of the decor upgrade?
   b. Harry's friend Ernest reminds him that these projected cash flows do not include an expected 3% annual inflation rate. How will inflation affect the NPV of the decor upgrade? (*Hint:* Remember that you are dealing with two growth rates, 5% and 3%.)

Inconsistent Treatment of Inflation
9. a. 8.74%
   c. $6,701
   d. No

9. Dirty Harry's Key West Bar and Grill is planning to spend $82,000 to upgrade its interior decor. The decor is expected to produce added operating cash flows for 7 years. Harry figures that the added cash flow will be $20,000 the first year and will grow by 5% per year thereafter as business builds. Harry's required rate of return is 12%, and the tax rate is 34%.

a. Harry's friend Pilar, recognizing that Harry knows nothing about inflation, decides to calculate a real rate of interest based on the nominal rate of 12% and an expected inflation rate of 3%. What is the real rate of interest?
b. Harry recognizes that he must inflate these cash flows by 3% per year. What are annual cash flows? (*Hint:* Remember that you are dealing with two growth rates, 5% and 3%.)
c. Harry now decides to calculate the NPV of the decor upgrade by discounting his part (b) cash flows by Pilar's discount rate calculated in part (a) What is the NPV of the decor upgrade?
d. Is the NPV in part (c) correct? Explain.

The Effect of Inflation on Project Value
10. a. 8.74%
b. −$5,303

10. a. Dirty Harry's Key West Bar and Grill is planning to spend $82,000 to upgrade its interior decor. The decor is expected to produce added operating cash flows for 7 years. Harry figures that the added cash flow will be $20,000 the first year and will grow by 5% per year thereafter as business builds. Harry's required rate of return is 12%, and the tax rate is 34%.
a. Harry's friend Ernest, recognizing that Harry knows nothing about inflation, decides to calculate a real rate of interest based on the nominal rate of 12% and an expected inflation rate of 3%. What is the real rate of interest?
b. What is the NPV of the decor upgrade?

The Effect of Inflation on Project Value
11. $21,496

11. Dirty Harry's Key West Bar and Grill is planning to spend $104,000 to buy a portrait of Harry Sr.'s friend and frequent bar patron, Ernest Hemingway. The portrait is expected to produce added operating cash flows for 7 years. Harry figures that the added cash flow will be $20,000 the first year and will grow by 5% per year thereafter as business builds. Harry's cash flow estimates do not include inflation. Harry's required rate of return is 12% (nominal) and 9% (real), and the tax rate is 34%. The cost of the decor upgrade will be straight-line depreciated for 5 years. What is the NPV of the Hemingway portrait?

The Effect of Inflation on Project Value
12. b. $20,190

12. Dirty Harry's Key West Bar and Grill is planning to spend $104,000 to buy a portrait of Harry Sr.'s friend and frequent bar patron, Ernest Hemingway. The portrait is expected to produce added operating cash flows for 7 years. Harry figures that the added cash flow will be $20,000 the first year and will grow by 5% per year thereafter as business builds. Harry's cash flow estimates do not include inflation. Harry's required rate of return is 12% (nominal) and 9% (real), and the tax rate is 34%. The cost of the decor upgrade will be straight-line depreciated for 5 years.
a. Harry decides to add a 3% inflation rate to his cash flow projections. What are annual cash flows? (*Hint:* Remember that you are dealing with two growth rates, 5% and 3%.)
b. What is the NPV of the Hemingway portrait?

Capital Rationing
13. Projects C, B, G (NPV)
Projects D, B, F, C (PI)

13. HushRush, Inc., is considering the following investment projects.

INVESTMENT PROJECT	PV OF FUTURE CASH FLOWS	INITIAL INVESTMENT
A	$13,500	$13,000
B	$27,000	$21,000
C	$53,500	$46,000
D	$12,000	$ 8,500
E	$18,200	$17,500
F	$13,500	$11,000
G	$33,000	$29,000

a. Calculate the NPV and profitability index for each project. Rank each project according to its NPV and profitability index (PI).

b. If there is no capital rationing, what will be HushRush's capital budget? How much total value will these investments add to the company?

c. HushRush's management has imposed a limit of $100,000 on the capital budget. Which projects will be taken using NPV as the ranking criterion? Which projects will be taken using PI as the ranking criterion?

Capital Rationing
14. a. $19,500 (PI); $17,500 (NPV)
b. $5200 (PI)

14. You must solve Problem 13 before answering this problem.

a. Based upon your answer in Problem 13, which ranking criterion yields the greatest total NPV under rationing?

b. Using the better of the ranking criteria (NPV or PI) from part (a), how much value is being sacrificed by rationing?

c. Because neither NPV nor PI spend the entire budget of $100,000, what projects would you add under each to spend the total? What process did you use to select these added projects?

Capital Rationing
15. a. NPV = $25,500
b. Projects E, D, B, A, C
c. $6,000
d. Projects E, D, B, C
e. $1500

15. A company has the following investment opportunities:

PROJECT	COST	NPV
A	$10,000	$ 1,500
B	$18,000	$ 3,000
C	$ 5,000	$ 500
D	$20,000	$ 3,500
E	$80,000	$16,000

a. If there is no capital rationing, how much will the company spend on investments? What is the total value added from these investments (NPV)?

b. If the company rations capital by establishing a budget limit of $100,000, which projects should it accept?

c. By restricting the budget to $100,000, what is the cost to the company in lost NPV?

d. If the company rations capital by establishing a budget limit of $125,000, which projects should it accept?

e. By restricting the budget to $125,000, what is the cost to the company in lost NPV?

16. A company has the following investment opportunities:

PROJECT	COST	NPV
A	$ 90,000	$13,000
B	$108,000	$18,000
C	$ 45,000	$ 4,000
D	$ 60,000	$ 7,500
E	$180,000	$33,000

Capital Rationing
16. a. $483,000
b. Projects E, B
c. $24,500
d. Projects E, B, A
e. $11,500

a. If there is no capital rationing, how much will the company spend on investments?
b. If the company rations capital by establishing a budget limit of $300,000, which projects should it accept?
c. By restricting the budget to $300,000, what is the cost to the company in lost NPV?
d. If the company rations capital by establishing a budget limit of $400,000, which projects should it accept?
e. By restricting the budget to $400,000, what is the cost to the company in lost NPV?

17. Naples Pizza has experienced a recent surge in demand from local college students. The owner, Karen Adams, is contemplating building an addition to the restaurant that will cost $85,000. Karen believes that she can project cash flows from the addition for only 5 years. She estimates that the addition will enable her to sell 10,000 more pizzas per year. The average price of a pizza is $6.50, and the average cost of labor and ingredients is $3.75. Karen is able to fully depreciate the addition over 5 years, straight-line. Her required rate of return on the addition is 11%, and Naples has a tax rate of 28%.

Sensitivity Analysis
17. a. $5,771
b. $9,819
c. $856

a. Calculate the NPV of the addition.
b. Karen thinks that she may be able to raise prices, and therefore revenues, by 3% per year. She also recognizes that her labor and ingredients costs will probably rise at the same rate. How does this inflation rate affect the NPV of the addition?
c. Karen is worried about rising interest rates and thinks that she may need to make 15% return on the addition. What effect would this have on the NPV of the addition? Assume the 3% inflation rate remains.

18. Naples Pizza has experienced a recent surge in demand from local college students. The owner, Karen Adams, is contemplating building an addition to the restaurant that will cost $85,000. Karen believes that she can project cash flows from the addition for only 5 years. She estimates that the addition will enable her to sell 10,000 more pizzas per year. The average price of a pizza is $6.50, and the average cost of labor and ingredients is $3.75. Karen thinks that she may be able to raise prices, and therefore revenues, by 3% per year. She also recognizes that her labor and ingredients costs will prob-

Sensitivity Analysis
18. b. −$4,321
c. −$5,626
d. −$8,434

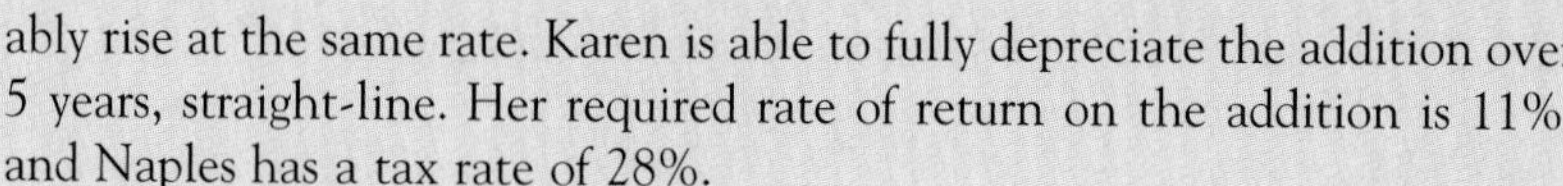
ably rise at the same rate. Karen is able to fully depreciate the addition over 5 years, straight-line. Her required rate of return on the addition is 11%, and Naples has a tax rate of 28%.

a. Calculate the NPV of the addition. (If you answered part b of Problem 15, disregard this part.) In parts (b), (c) and (d), return to the part (a) solution, then make the change called for in the question.

b. Karen's business is profitable, partly because she is able to keep costs down by hiring part-time workers. She wonders how the value of the addition would be affected if her costs rose by 10%.

c. Karen is also worried about competition. There are two possible effects of competition. One would be to reduce demand for pizzas, perhaps to 8,000 per year. How would this affect the value of the addition?

d. The other effect of competition is to force Karen to reduce the price of pizzas by 10%. How would this affect the value of the addition?

Sensitivity Analysis
19. b. $9,949
c. $26,286; −$22,724
d. Network $8328; system −$7077

19. The Freedom95 Design Company is considering upgrading its computer system. The system will consist of 60 workstations costing $2,500 each, tied together by a network costing $7,500. The system will be straight-line depreciated over its expected life of 5 years. The required rate of return on this investment is 9%, and the corporate tax rate is 30%.

The system should produce operating savings, mostly in reduced labor costs, of $800 per year per workstation. However, management has identified two potential risks. The first is that the network, which is generally unproven, may not function as planned. At best, it could operate so well that savings could actually increase. The other risk is that the system may become technologically obsolete in 3 years, necessitating an upgrade. It is possible that only the network would have to be upgraded at a cost of $3,000, or the entire system would be upgraded at a cost of $27,000. These risks are summarized here:

RISK	EFFECT
Network worse than planned	Annual savings $600
Network better than planned	Annual savings $900
Network upgrade	Cost $3,000, year 3
System upgrade	Cost $27,000, year 3

a. Calculate the annual cash flows, using annual savings of $800 and no upgrades. The initial investment occurs in year 0, and the operating cash flows occur in years 1–5. (*Hint:* Operating cash flows are an annuity.)

b. Calculate the NPV of the project. Would you take this project?

c. What will be the effect on the cash flows and NPV if the network is worse or better than planned?

d. What will be the effect on the cash flows and NPV if either upgrade is needed?

e. Based on your analysis, what would you advise management about risk?

Sensitivity Analysis

20. The Freedom95 Design Company is considering upgrading their computer system. The system will consist of 60 workstations costing $3,000 each, tied

Restricting Investment Dollars

In Chapter 9 we pointed out that companies should take on all independent investments that add value. The selection criterion that best accomplishes this is NPV. In concept, the task is straightforward: We should take on *all* positive NPV projects, regardless of their cost.

In adopting such a strategy we are using signals sent by the capital markets to tell us how much money to invest in projects. The capital markets fund these investments either directly with securities issues or indirectly through reinvested residual cash flows belonging to the shareholders. If, for instance, we were considering a particularly risky investment, the risk-adjusted required rate of return would rise to compensate those who have contributed capital, lowering the project's NPV and making it less likely that the investment would be made. Unconventional investments sometimes require unconventional and expensive financing.[10] In spite of all this, if investors are willing to fund a project at a cost that yields a positive NPV, a company that declines the investment is foregoing an opportunity to enrich its shareholders.

However, there is evidence that companies often impose limits on their capital budgets. If this causes a company to forego valuable investment opportunities, then the company is **rationing capital**. In spite of incurring the cost of foregone investment opportunities, companies may ration capital for several reasons:[11]

Rationing capital reduces the value of the firm by leaving value enhancing projects unfunded. Rationing forces companies to select from among an array of acceptable projects, requiring them to rank projects.

- Rationing may be used by corporate management to control the activities of subsidiaries or semi-autonomous divisions.
- Rationing aids the planning process because it sets a limit on the amount of capital that the company will have to raise from internal and external sources.
- Rationing may reflect particularly high risk aversion by management. It may mean that management wants to commit capital only to "sure things," or the best investments, even though it leaves other attractive investments on the table.
- Rationing may reflect a lack of faith in the company's ability to analyze projects. Sometimes this lack of faith is caused by project proponents "*cooking*" the numbers to favor the project.

Capital rationing poses an analytical problem. Without rationing, a company does not have to choose between acceptable independent projects. Rationing, however, requires selecting from among acceptable projects. You may recall in Chapter 9 that we faced a similar problem with mutually exclusive projects.

---

[10]Sometimes investment bankers, acting as surrogates for the capital market, advise companies that the market is not likely to fund a particularly large or risky investment. This forces the company, if it still wishes to pursue the project, to use less conventional and often expensive financing. Such was the case in the 1970s with Standard Oil of Ohio, a relatively small oil company, which suddenly found itself trying to raise capital to fund the trans-Alaskan oil pipeline. The project size was larger than the total company net worth. See Paul D. Phillips, John C. Groth, and R. Malcolm Richards, "Financing the Alaskan Project: The Experience of Sohio," *Financial Management* 8, no. 3 (1979): 7–16.

[11]Most rationing is imposed by management. However, there are instances when rationing is imposed by a court against a company in bankruptcy or by creditors to a company that has defaulted on debt.

There is always a question of an appropriate risk premium for foreign investments. Inexperienced U.S. companies may assign a higher risk premium to such investments than more experienced MNCs. However, companies should not overlook the potential for foreign investments to reduce corporate risk by increasing international diversification. Investments in even a few countries reduces political, financial, and exchange rate risk from any one country or currency. To provide some sense of the considerations intrinsic to foreign investing, we present the case of Wayfarer Industries in the next section.

Wayfarer Industries: Evaluating a Foreign Investment

Students are asked to provide a subjective evaluation of the proposed investment in Question 22 at the end of the chapter.

Wayfarer Industries is a U.S. manufacturer and distributor of hiking and walking shoes. For many years, Wayfarer has exported its shoes to Europe, where it has gained an increasing share of a growing market. However, its shoes are subject to high tariffs in European countries. Wayfarer has been considering building a manufacturing facility in Europe. The European common market means that shoes manufactured in any European country may be shipped duty free to any other country in the European community. By locating in Europe, Wayfarer hopes to stimulate more sales and reduce its labor costs. Its U.S. workers are unionized.

Wayfarer has been in contact with the Spanish government about buying a former shoe factory in the city of Pamplona in northern Spain, near the French border. This region is poor, and the government has offered tax incentives to Wayfarer to locate in Pamplona. Unemployment is high, and there are no labor unions to contend with. A factory in Spain would give Wayfarer access to local markets for shoes and would place it near the source of the fine Spanish leather prized by shoe manufacturers. Wayfarer feels that a base in Spain would give it access to new markets in central Europe, the former Soviet states, and the eastern Mediterranean.

Wayfarer has several concerns about this investment. First, it has no overseas experience, except for exporting, which has always been handled by a U.S. export-management company. Second, there has been political unrest in this region of Spain that has, on occasion, been violent. Finally, Wayfarer is concerned about the foreign exchange risks of making a long-term investment in Spain. Historically, the peseta has been unstable relative to the dollar.

This relatively simple case illustrates some of the complexity of foreign investing. Wayfarer was driven to consider the investment in Spain because of high tariffs. However, it also found an opportunity to export high-wage U.S. jobs, buy locally supplied leather, and perhaps gain access to new markets. The Spanish government is offering incentives to locate in a poor and politically unstable region in northern Spain. With the unstable peseta, Wayfarer must balance its opportunities against both political and financial risk.

together by a network costing $10,000. The system will be straight-line depreciated over its expected life of 5 years. The required rate of return on this investment is 8%, and the corporate tax rate is 30%.

The system should produce operating savings, mostly in reduced labor costs, of $1,100 per year per workstation. However, management has identified two potential risks. The first is that the network, which is generally unproven, may not function as planned. At best, it could operate so well that savings could actually increase. The other risk is that the system may become technologically obsolete in 3 years, necessitating an upgrade. It is possible that only the network would have to be upgraded at a cost of $9,000, or the entire system would be upgraded at a cost of $33,000. These risks are summarized here:

20. b. $39,980
c. $73,519; −$27,097
d. Network $34,979; system $20,452

RISK	EFFECT
Network worse than planned	Annual savings $700
Network better than planned	Annual savings $1,300
Network upgrade	Cost $9,000, year 3
System upgrade	Cost $33,000, year 3

a. Calculate the annual cash flows, using annual savings of $1,100 and no upgrades. The initial investment occurs in year 0, and the operating cash flows occur in years 1–5. (*Hint:* Operating cash flows are an annuity.)
b. Calculate the NPV of the project. Would you take this project?
c. What will be the effect on the cash flows and NPV if the network is worse or better than planned?
d. What will be the effect on the cash flows and NPV if either upgrade is needed?
e. Based on your analysis, what would you advise management about risk?

APPENDIX 11A

Sensitivity Analysis Using a Spreadsheet: Topflight Airlines

This appendix presents details of the TopFlight Airlines example in this chapter. The sensitivity analysis was performed on a single spreadsheet using Microsoft Excel. The investment is 15 airplanes. Exhibit 11A.1 contains three sections. The top section (operating data) is discussed in the chapter. A critical estimate is the number of passenger miles. This is the airlines' equivalent of unit sales. The middle section (estimating passenger miles) derives this estimate in two ways. The micro approach applies a load factor, which takes into account empty seats, to a capacity calculation. The macro approach estimates the total market and then applies a market share. The bottom section shows details of the income and cash flow calculations.

Exhibit 11.3 presents the assumptions for each factor that form the basis for the sensitivity analysis. Exhibit 11A.2 is the spreadsheet printout for the calculation of the NPV of $317,012 under the basic assumptions. Exhibit 11A.3 shows the changes in the spreadsheet, assuming above normal economic conditions. Average passenger-miles rise from 7,000,000 to 8,500,000. This raises both revenues and variable costs.

$$\begin{aligned} \text{revenues} &= \text{demand} \times \text{market share} \times \text{revenues per seat-mile} \\ &= 8{,}500{,}000 \times 30\% \times \$0.16 = \$408{,}000 \\ \text{variable costs} &= \text{demand} \times \text{market share} \times \text{variable cost per seat-mile} \\ &= 8{,}500{,}000 \times 30\% \times \$0.9 = \$229{,}500 \end{aligned}$$

The result is that NPV rises to $598,828.

Exhibit A11.4 shows the results of the entry of three low-cost airlines into the market. This reduces revenue per mile from $0.16 to $0.13 because of fare wars. It also reduces TopFlight's market share from 30% to 20%. The effect on revenues and variable costs are

$$\text{revenues} = 7{,}000{,}000 \times 20\% \times \$0.13 = \$182{,}000$$

$$\text{variable costs} = 7{,}000{,}000 \times 20\% \times \$0.09 = \$126{,}000$$

The result is a project NPV of ($557,684).

EXHIBIT 11A.1
TOPFLIGHT AIRLINES

Operating Data	
Cost per plane	$ 80,000
No. of planes	15
Initial Investment (invest)	$1,200,000
Total passenger miles (market)	7,000,000
Market share (share)	30%
Revenues per seat-mile (price)	$ 0.16
Variable costs per seat-mile (cost)	$ 0.09
Depreciation (dep)	$ 80,000
Required rate of return	6%
Tax rate	22%
Estimating Passenger Miles for TopFlight	
Seats per plane (seats)	250
No. of planes (planes)	15
Miles per day (miles)	2300
No. of days per year (days)	310
Total seat-miles available (000) (= seats × planes × miles × days)	2,673,750
Passenger load factor (load)	80%
Passenger-miles for TopFlight-1st estimate (= total seat miles × load)	2,139,000
Total passenger-miles (market)	7,000,000
Market share (share)	30%
Passenger-miles for TopFlight-2nd estimate (= market × share)	2,100,000
Earnings and Cash Flow Calculations	
revenues (R)	R = market × share × price
variable costs (E)	E = market × share × cost
depreciation (dep)	dep = invest/15
earnings before tax	EBT = $R - E$ − dep
tax (tax)	tax = EBT × tax rate
earnings after tax	EAT = EBT − tax
cash flow (cash)	cash = EAT + dep

EXHIBIT 11A.2

TopFlight Airlines: NPV Calculation Under Basic Assumptions

	YEAR									
	0	1	2	3	4	5	6	7	8	9
Invest	$(1,200,000)									
Operating cash flows										
Revenues (*R*)		$336,000	$336,000	$336,000	$336,000	$336,000	$336,000	$336,000	$336,000	$336,000
Variable costs (*E*)		$189,000	$189,000	$189,000	$189,000	$189,000	$189,000	$189,000	$189,000	$189,000
Depreciation (dep)		$ 80,000	$ 80,000	$ 80,000	$ 80,000	$ 80,000	$ 80,000	$ 80,000	$ 80,000	$ 80,000
Earnings before tax		$ 67,000	$ 67,000	$ 67,000	$ 67,000	$ 67,000	$ 67,000	$ 67,000	$ 67,000	$ 67,000
Tax (tax)		$ 14,740	$ 14,740	$ 14,740	$ 14,740	$ 14,740	$ 14,740	$ 14,740	$ 14,740	$ 14,740
Earnings after tax		$ 52,260	$ 52,260	$ 52,260	$ 52,260	$ 52,260	$ 52,260	$ 52,260	$ 52,260	$ 52,260
Cash flow (cash)		$132,260	$132,260	$132,260	$132,260	$132,260	$132,260	$132,260	$132,260	$132,260
Discounted cash flow		$124,774	$117,711	$111,048	$104,762	$ 98,832	$ 93,238	$ 87,960	$ 82,982	$ 78,284

	YEAR										
	10	11	12	13	14	15	16	17	18	19	20
Revenues (*R*)	$336,000	$336,000	$336,000	$336,000	$336,000	$336,000	$336,000	$336,000	$336,000	$336,000	$336,000
Variable costs (*E*)	$189,000	$189,000	$189,000	$189,000	$189,000	$189,000	$189,000	$189,000	$189,000	$189,000	$189,000
Depreciation (dep)	$ 80,000	$ 80,000	$ 80,000	$ 80,000	$ 80,000	$ 80,000	$ 80,000	$ 80,000	$ 80,000	$ 80,000	$ 80,000
Earnings before tax	$ 67,000	$ 67,000	$ 67,000	$ 67,000	$ 67,000	$ 67,000	$ 67,000	$ 67,000	$ 67,000	$ 67,000	$ 67,000
Tax (tax)	$ 14,740	$ 14,740	$ 14,740	$ 14,740	$ 14,740	$ 14,740	$ 14,740	$ 14,740	$ 14,740	$ 14,740	$ 14,740
Earnings after tax	$ 52,260	$ 52,260	$ 52,260	$ 52,260	$ 52,260	$ 52,260	$ 52,260	$ 52,260	$ 52,260	$ 52,260	$ 52,260
Cash flow (cash)	$132,260	$132,260	$132,260	$132,260	$132,260	$132,260	$132,260	$132,260	$132,260	$132,260	$132,260
Discounted cash flow	$ 73,853	$ 69,673	$ 65,729	$ 62,009	$ 58,499	$ 55,187	$ 52,064	$ 49,117	$ 46,336	$ 43,714	$ 41,239
NPV	$317,012										

CHAPTER 12

Capital Structure: Right-Hand-Side Decisions and the Value of the Firm

In Chapter 12 we demonstrate that financial leverage has its "upside," but one must watch out for its "downside" as well!

Chapters 9, 10, and 11 discussed how the investment decisions, reflected on the left-hand side of the financial balance sheet, affect shareholders' wealth. Investing in positive NPV projects adds to the wealth of shareholders, whereas investing in negative NPV projects detracts from it. In this chapter we examine the choice of financing utilized by a corporation to raise needed capital. As we turn our attention to the decisions reflected on the right-hand side of the balance sheet, we assume that capital budgeting decisions have been made. Our concern is choosing the mix of debt and equity used to fund the firm's investment projects and whether this **capital structure** choice can affect shareholders' wealth.

Why do utility companies usually have relatively high levels of debt in their capital structures and computer firms have relatively little? Why did some firms in the 1980s decide to increase their use of debt to the extent that 80% or 90% of their capital came from borrowing? Why do some firms use no debt financing? The general answer is that in each case managers believe they are choosing a capital structure that maximizes their firm's worth. How each of these decisions can be optimal yet so different is explained in this chapter as we explore the link between capital structure and firm value.

When a firm's value is calculated, its expected cash flows are discounted using the firm's cost of capital. In order for capital structure decisions to impact shareholder wealth, therefore, the capital structure must affect either the level of expected cash flows ($E(CF_t)$) or the cost of capital (r). The formula used to calculate value is

$$V = \sum_{t=1}^{\infty} \frac{E(CF_t)}{(1 + r)^t}$$

What financial managers seek is a capital structure that maximizes value by maximizing expected cash flows, by minimizing required returns, or both. Such a debt-equity mix is known as the firm's *optimal capital structure.*

PERFECT CAPITAL MARKETS AND IRRELEVANCE OF CAPITAL STRUCTURE

Perfect Capital Markets

You can point out that physics formulas, such as the acceleration due to gravity, are often correct only in a frictionless world.

Our discussion of the debt-equity mix begins by assuming that capital markets are perfect. It will be apparent that perfect capital markets are an ideal and do not reflect reality. Nevertheless, perfect markets are very useful for developing an understanding of capital structure's impact on share value and also in understanding dividend policy in Chapter 13. We will see that capital structure has no impact on value when markets are perfect. We will show that right-hand-side decisions are irrelevant to shareholders under perfect market conditions. **Irrelevance of capital structure** in a perfect market setting will serve as a foundation upon which we can build a useful understanding of capital structure, as we relax the perfect market conditions to better reflect reality. **Perfect capital markets** may be characterized as

1. being *strong-form efficient*;
2. having *no information asymmetry*;

3. having *no leakages* as cash flows move between left and right sides of the financial balance sheet.

Strong-form efficiency defines a market in which security prices reflect all pertinent information. Prices in such markets are unbiased estimates of value, fully reflecting the cash flows and risk expected to accrue to securityholders. In strong-form-efficient markets, securities offering the same cash flows with equal risk will be equally priced.

As strong-form efficiency suggests, the information reflected in prices includes both insider and outsider information. This result is a natural outcome of the second characteristic of perfect markets, their lack of **information asymmetry**. Because everyone has the same information, no distinction between insiders and outsiders is necessary in perfect capital markets. Furthermore, there is no agency problem in these markets. If, for example, managers were lazy or granting themselves excessive perquisites, these actions would be observed by their employers, the shareholders. Shareholders, in turn, would correct such inappropriate behavior—possibly firing managers. Because managers can foresee this, they would not act inappropriately in the first place.

The last characteristic is that no *leakages* occur as cash flows move between the firm and capital suppliers. **Leakages** refer to payments of operating cash flows to parties other than financial claimants.[1] Leakages would, for example, include

Transparency Available

FIGURE 12.1

THE FINANCIAL BALANCE SHEET, ILLUSTRATING SOME LEAKAGES

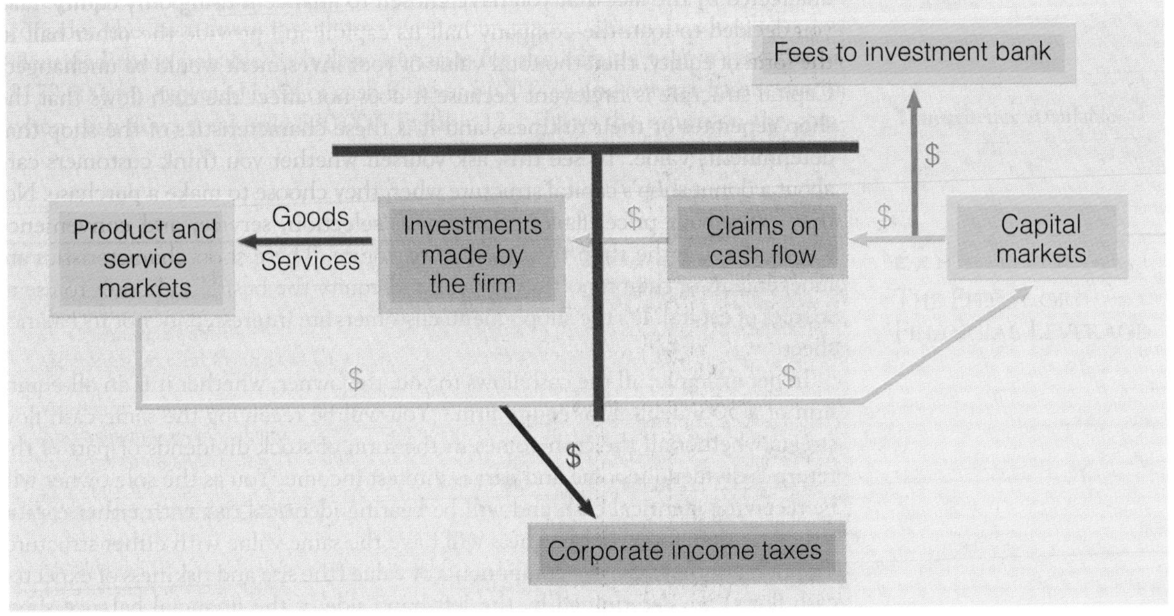

[1]Operating cash flows would be the financial counterpart to accounting's EBIT (earnings before interest and taxes). The main difference is that noncash expenses (e.g., depreciation) have been deducted when we calculate EBIT. When we calculate operating cash flows, we ignore depreciation.

accepting such a gift. In a bankruptcy, such an asset would have a very high transfer cost. A delivery truck used in business can be more easily sold, because it can be used in a variety of ways. Such a vehicle's use is not highly specific, a characteristic that enhances its marketability.

To summarize, bankruptcy's impact on leverage depends upon the likelihood of its occurrence and the costs associated with the procedure should it occur. Evaluation of these considerations involves analysis of the firm's future cash flow–generating capacity and of the nature of the assets underlying the business. It is no wonder that lenders look at two factors when considering the debt capacity of a borrower: the **primary source of repayment** (cash flow) and the **collateral** (the assets backing the loan), which can be sold as a **secondary source of repayment**. Firms (or individuals) with high and steady cash flows who hold assets easily marketed for their full value can borrow more than those without these characteristics. By borrowing more, they are able to take greater advantage of debt's tax-shielding benefit.

Agency Problems

Companies whose cash flows are high and yet are in a mature stage, with few positive NPV projects in which to invest, find themselves with excess cash on hand. They are flush with **free cash flow** (cash not needed to fund promising projects). In such firms the potential for wasted money and time is greater than in firms in their formative stages. Managers of large companies with **widely dispersed ownership** are less likely to be held closely accountable for their actions, because no single stockholder owns enough stock to present a threat to incumbent management. When combined, free cash flow and widely dispersed ownership are ingredients fostering wasted resources. These firms may benefit from the discipline of debt. By leveraging upward, more pressure is put on management to perform effectively and efficiently. More free cash flow is guaranteed to be paid out as fixed claims increase, reducing the potential for discretionary expenditures like excessive perquisites. In such cases, added leverage can increase to firm value.

Signaling

The final consideration is the use of leverage as a credible signal to outside shareholders and analysts. If, for example, managers are confident that the firm's performance is improving, then a strong signal would be to borrow funds and use the proceeds to repurchase some shares. More debt signals the ability to produce the cash necessary to meet a higher level of fixed claims in order to avoid default. Additionally, insiders would direct the firm to repurchase shares when the shares' price is below their value.

Summary

Debt acts like a lever. When the firm is doing well, financial leverage increases the return to stockholders. When times are tough, it magnifies the negative effect on shareholders' returns. The more leverage, the greater the magnifying effect. Thus, although leverage can increase expected returns, it also increases variability or risk. In perfect capital markets, these two effects just offset one another, leaving value unchanged.

In reality, market imperfections exist that make the capital structure choice similar to a balancing act between the benefits of debt and its effects that harm value. Debt may increase cash flows to claimants by avoiding corporate taxes, by limiting agency problems, and by sending a positive signal to outsiders. On the other hand, added leverage increases the likelihood of a costly bankruptcy.

Although there is no precise method for finding the optimal capital structure of a firm, certain characteristics of corporations help to guide managers toward an appropriate target structure. First, firms with high taxable income operating in areas with high corporate tax rates should consider higher leverage than unprofitable firms. Next, corporations with widely dispersed ownership and excess free cash flow may find that leverage lowers potentially wasteful cash expenditures. Leverage may also be used as a signal of the increased debt capacity of the borrower.

These benefits of leverage must be balanced against the corporation's potential bankruptcy costs. Firms with more volatile cash flows are in greater jeopardy of experiencing financial distress than firms with stable cash flows. Therefore, businesses should consider the stability of their income when targeting their debt levels. Should a firm have financial difficulty, those with highly liquid or marketable assets should experience lower bankruptcy costs than those whose assets are unique or specific to their current use. Firms with illiquid, highly specific assets have higher potential bankruptcy costs and must carefully consider their levels of debt.

Key Terms

capital structure
irrelevance of capital structure
perfect capital markets
leakages
information asymmetry
strong-form efficiency
friction
financial leverage
imperfections in capital markets
trade-offs
tax shield of debt
bankruptcy costs
default
direct bankruptcy costs
indirect bankruptcy costs
financial distress
discipline of debt
signal
operating leverage
fixed operating costs
variable operating costs
tangible assets
intangible assets
liquidity
nearness to cash
asset specificity

primary source of repayment
secondary source of repayment
collateral
free cash flow
widely dispersed ownership
inelastic demand
cyclical business
total leverage (question 12-16)
margin (problem 12-4)

QUESTIONS

1. **a.** Explain why there is no agency problem when there is no information asymmetry.
   b. Why does the Securities and Exchange Commission require firms with traded securities to have their financial statements audited by an outside accounting firm according to generally accepted accounting principles? (*Hint:* Think of information asymmetry).
   c. Is the cost of having the firm's financial statements audited an agency cost? Why or why not?
2. Name four examples of frictions, or cash flow leakages, that exist in imperfect capital markets.
3. The "law of one price" states that things with the same characteristics (perfect substitutes) should sell for the same price. In a perfect capital market, the law of one price holds and was used in our discussion of capital structure irrelevance. Explain where in the chapter we relied on the law of one price to demonstrate irrelevance.
4. In perfect capital markets, the formula (from Chapter 10) for the weighted average cost of capital becomes

$$\text{WACC} = W_d K_d + W_e K_e$$

   a. Why is the factor $(1 - t)$ missing from the WACC formula in perfect capital markets?
   b. In perfect capital markets, leverage does not affect firm value. If this is true, does leverage affect the WACC?
5. **a.** If fixed claimants (e.g., bondholders) supply half of a corporation's capital and residual claimants (stockholders) supply the other half of the capital, then will these two classes of claimants each be exposed to half the firm's total risk? Why not?
   b. Will each class of claimants receive half of the firm's cash flows? Explain why not using your answer to part (a) and what you know about the risk and return relationship.
6. Suppose a savings and loan must foreclose on an individual's house because the homeowner is unable to meet the mortgage payments. What costs will potentially lower the value of the house to the savings and loan? Can you think of both direct and indirect costs in this example of financial distress?
7. Do you think a corporation must actually declare bankruptcy to incur costs associated with financial distress? Could rumors of financial problems lead to costs? How would these costs lower firm value? Explain your answers.
8. Which of the following hotels could potentially carry a greater proportion

of debt in its capital structure and why? Both Hotel A and Hotel B have the same cost and the same expected cash flows, their cash flows are equally risky, and they are located across the street from one another, but Hotel A is built so that it could be easily converted to a nursing home and Hotel B is built so that its conversion to another use is impractical.

9. Suppose two countries have identical economic environments, but Country X allows interest payments to be deductible for corporate income tax purposes and Country Y allows only half of a firm's interest expense to be deducted. Would you expect to see, on average, greater use of leverage by Country X's or Country Y's corporations?
10. Bioearth, Inc., is a new corporation developing a promising technology. They should produce a product in about 4 years that will remove toxic waste from sewage by the use of genetically engineered salmon that thrive on raw sewage and produce low-grade caviar as a by-product. How would potential bankruptcy costs influence Bioearth's capital structure decision?
11. Suppose that firms experiencing financial distress often cut maintenance in an effort to conserve cash and avoid bankruptcy. Customers, reading of a firm's financial difficulties, anticipate that maintenance may be deferred at such businesses. If customers have a high level of concern, they may take their business elsewhere.
    - **a.** Would you be more concerned about deferred maintenance at an auto parts store, a motel, or an airline?
    - **b.** How would firm value be impacted if customers stayed away from a business?
    - **c.** Which of the three industries described would be most concerned with the adverse effects of financial distress? What effect will such concern have on the capital structure of companies in that industry?
12. Affiliated Industries Incorporated (AII) is a corporate giant. It is highly profitable, producing cash flows far beyond those required to fund its new positive net present value projects because it is in a mature industry with few growth opportunities. Yet AII has traditionally retained much of this residual cash rather than paying it out as dividends. Would you, as a stockholder, be pleased or displeased if AII announced an increase in leverage by using its cash to repurchase a large proportion of its stock? Explain using an agency-related rationale.
13. Acme, Inc., has lost money for several years and has a large tax-loss carryforward. However, the firm has made a rich discovery of gold that should ensure profitability for decades to come. Acme's tax-loss carry-forward will shelter Acme's expected income from taxes for 3 years. As the chief financial officer (CFO) of Acme, you have been asked your opinion of what the firm's capital structure strategy should be for the next 5 years. What would you recommend?
14. The use of leverage is often found to be similar among firms in the same industry. Explain this using the considerations discussed in this chapter.
15. The Smith twins are each shopping for a loan. They both have good payment records on their other debts and have impeccable characters. They both earn, on the average, $40,000 each year. Sam Smith is a registered nurse and Linda Smith is a carpenter. Which twin do you think has the greater debt capacity, and why?

16. *Total leverage* describes a firm's degree of operating leverage plus its degree of financial leverage. Consider two utility companies, each with 50% debt in their capital structure. Washington State Electric generates hydroelectric power at its dam across the Rapid River in the Pacific Northwest. Smokey Mesa Power is located in Arizona and generates its power at the coal-burning Black Cloud Power Plant. What are the raw materials for each electric-generation process? Which utility is exposed to more price uncertainty regarding its cost of these raw materials? Which utility has more operating leverage? More total leverage?
17. Managers naturally want to protect their jobs. For them, the chance of a firm's bankruptcy is more threatening than for the firm's shareholders. Given this, do you think managers are biased against certain potential investment projects that have high risk? Assuming they are, is this bias in the best interest of shareholders? What if the risky project has a positive NPV? Could this bias affect firm value, and, if so, will its effect get stronger as the firm takes on more debt? Is this type of agency cost a pro-leverage or anti-leverage argument?
18. A home mortgage is a loan made to an individual for the purpose of purchasing a house. Mortgage lenders usually have guidelines that a borrower must meet in order to qualify for a loan. These guidelines usually include a maximum *loan to value ratio* of 80%, for example. This means the amount of the loan cannot exceed 80% of the home's appraised value. Lenders also generally have a guideline that says that monthly loan payments cannot exceed, for instance, one-third of the borrower's gross income. What is the primary source of repayment for a home mortgage? What is the secondary source of repayment? Which guidelines address which repayment source?

DEMONSTRATION PROBLEMS: LEVERAGE'S EFFECT ON RETURN AND RISK

1. Suppose you have $10,000 to invest. You may choose to invest the $10,000 in a project that will pay one of two equally likely amounts in 1 year, either $15,000 or $8,000. As an alternative, you could borrow an additional $10,000 at 10% interest and invest a total of $20,000 in the project, which would then have equally likely payoffs of either $30,000 or $16,000. Find the expected return for both alternative investment strategies and then comment on the relative returns and risk of the leveraged versus the unlevered approach.

SOLUTION

	UNLEVERED INVESTMENT TOTALING $10,000	LEVERAGED INVESTMENT TOTALING $20,000
A. Amount borrowed	$ 0	$10,000
B. Equity	$10,000	$10,000

2. Repeat Demonstration Problem 1, this time assuming that the interest rate is 18%. Comment.

	UNLEVERED INVESTMENT TOTALING $10,000		LEVERAGED INVESTMENT TOTALING $20,000	
C. Gross cash flow	$15,000	$8,000	$30,000	$16,000
D. Loan payoff	0	0	11,000	11,000
E. Cash to equity	$15,000	$8,000	$19,000	$ 5,000
F. Return on equity	50%	−20%	90%	−50%
G. Expected return	(0.5)(50%) + (0.5)(−20%) = 15%		(0.5)(90%) + (0.5)(−50%) = 20%	

Leverage increases the expected return on your $10,000 by 5%, but the risk also increases, because with leverage you could lose up to $5,000 rather than a maximum loss of $2,000 with the unlevered investment.

SOLUTION

	UNLEVERED INVESTMENT TOTALING $10,000		LEVERAGED INVESTMENT TOTALING $20,000	
A. Amount borrowed	$ 0		$10,000	
B. Equity	$10,000		$10,000	
C. Gross cash flow	$15,000	$8,000	$30,000	$16,000
D. Loan payoff	0	0	11,800	11,800
E. Cash to equity	$15,000	$8,000	$18,200	$ 4,200
F. Return on equity	50%	−20%	82%	−58%
G. Expected return	(0.5)(50%) + (0.5)(−20%) = 15%		(0.5)(82%) + (0.5)(−58%) = 12%	

In this case the use of leverage actually reduces the expected return from 15% to 12%. The reason for this reduction is that the investment's expected return of 15% is below the borrowing rate of interest, 18%.

PROBLEMS

Operating Leverage

1. Firm A has a high degree of operating leverage. All its operating expenses are fixed at $12,500 a month. Firm B utilizes no operating leverage. Its operating expenses are all tied to sales, equaling 60% of total revenues. Suppose both Firm A and Firm B have sales of $20,833 in June, $30,000 in July, and $15,000 in August. Find the operating cash flows for each firm for each of the 3 months. Which has the more variable operating cash flows? Which firm could take on more financial leverage?

1. Firm	*June*	*July*	*Aug.*
A	$8,333	$17,500	$2,500
B	$8,333	$12,000	$6,000

Tax Shields and Bankruptcy Costs

2. **a.** Suppose there is a one-third probability that a firm will have operating cash flow of $100,000 next year. There is a one-third chance that the firm will have operating cash flow of $150,000, and a one-third chance of having operating cash flow of $200,000. You may purchase all of the stock in the firm (50,000 shares) if you wish. The corporate income tax rate is 40%. What will be next year's total cash flow on the potential stock purchase under each of the three outcomes?
   b. Now, suppose the firm leverages itself. You can still purchase all the firm's securities ($1,200,000 of bonds paying 10% interest and 10,000 shares of

2. a. $60,000; $90,000; $120,000
   b. $100,000; $138,000; $168,000
   c. With bankruptcy, $132,000; without, $135,333

stock). Corporate income tax rates are still 40%. What will be your total cash flow for these investments next year under each outcome for the leveraged firm?

c. Should operating cash flows fall below the level required to make interest payments, the firm will be forced to file bankruptcy papers, which will cost the firm $10,000, paid before distributions to claimants. How does this potential bankruptcy cost affect the total expected cash flows on your claim? (*Hint*: Recall that $E(\text{CF}) = P_1(\text{CF}_1) + P_2(\text{CF}_2) + P_3(\text{CF}_3)$, where P_1, P_2, and P_3 denote probabilities that CF_1, CF_2, and CF_3 will occur, respectively). How does the expected cash flow for part (c) compare with the expected cash flow calculated using the answers to part (b) of this problem?

Financial Leverage
3. a. −10%; −28%
b. 2%; −4%
c. 10%; 12%

3. Suppose you buy some vacant land as an investment. You can invest $50,000 of your own money. The land is selling for $5,000 an acre. You can buy either a 10-acre parcel or a 20-acre parcel. If you buy the smaller parcel, you will invest only your own funds. If you decide on the larger parcel, you will borrow $50,000 at an 8% interest rate and fund the balance of the purchase price with your money. Ignore taxes in this problem. If you hold the land 1 year, what is the percentage return on your $50,000 out-of-pocket investment for both strategies in each of the following cases?
   a. You sell the land for $4,500 per acre.
   b. You sell the land for $5,100 per acre.
   c. You sell the land for $5,500 per acre.
   d. Why didn't using leverage raise your return in part (b)? After all, the value of the land increased?

Margin
4. a. J: 26%, 32%
b. J: −20%, −34%, −48%
c. J: 8%, 8%, 8%

4. Buying stock on *margin* occurs when an investor borrows funds from the brokerage firm in order to buy shares of stock. In effect, margin buying is the use of leverage by individual investors.
   a. Complete the following table.

A. Individual's funds	$10,000	$10,000	$10,000
B. Borrowed funds	$ 0	$ 5,000	$10,000
C. Total investment (A + B)	$10,000	$15,000	$20,000
D. Purchase price per share	$ 10	$ 10	$ 10
E. Shares purchased (C ÷ D)	1,000	1,500	______
F. Selling price per share	$ 12	$ 12	$ 12
G. Total revenue from sale	$12,000	______	$24,000
H. Interest expense (8% of B)	0	______	______
I. Net profit (G − H − C)	$ 2,000	______	______
J. Return on equity investment (I ÷ A)	20%	______	______

   b. Reproduce this table, assuming the stock selling price declined to $8 per share (line F).
   c. Reproduce this table, assuming the stock selling price (F) increased to $10.80.
   d. Comment on the results in parts (a), (b) and (c).

Tax Shield
5. $150,000; $157,500

5. The Whole Donut is expected to produce operating cash flows of $200,000 a year in perpetuity. If the firm was financed using 100% equity, then cal-

culate the total annual dividends paid by the firm assuming the Whole Donut pays all its after-tax cash flows out to individuals.

operating cash flows

− taxes (25%)

= after-tax cash flows

= total dividends paid

Now, suppose the firm is financed with $500,000 of 6% debt, and the balance is financed by equity. Again, no operating cash is retained. What will be the Whole Donut's total cash flows to claimants?

operating cash flow

− interest payments

= cash flow before taxes

−taxes (25%)

= after-tax cash flows

= total dividends

+ interest payments

= total cash flows to claimants

6. All Lowrisk Corporation's expenses, excluding taxes, vary directly with sales, amounting to 80% of sales. All Hiyield, Inc.'s, expenses are fixed at $50,000 per year. Consider the following possible sales levels for each firm. Then complete the table. Whose before-tax cash flows are more variable? Which firm could probably carry a higher level of debt?

Operating Leverage
6. Low risk can carry more debt.

	SALES		
	$50,000	**$75,000**	**$100,000**
Lowrisk's expenses	_______	_______	_______
Lowrisk's before-tax cash flow	_______	_______	_______
Hiyield's expenses	_______	_______	_______
Hiyield's before-taxes cash flow	_______	_______	_______
	_______	_______	_______

7. In the following table are listed the total dollar values for long-term debt and equity utilized in 1989 for four different industries according to *value line*. Calculate the debt/equity ratio for each industry and comment on why the industries exhibit the differing uses of leverage that they do.

Business Risk
7. Apparel, 0.76; utility, 1.00; software, 0.24; auto 0.76

	LONG-TERM DEBT (MILLIONS)	EQUITY (MILLIONS)
Apparel	$ 2,895	$ 3,826
Utilities (Eastern U.S.)	$175,500	$175,500
Computer software	$ 1,297	$ 5,409
Automobiles	$ 50,934	$ 67,078

Tax Shield
8. $306,000

8. Frank Baez hates to pay taxes and decides to change the capital structure of the firm he manages in order to avoid paying some corporate tax. The firm currently has earnings before tax of $3,000,000 and is in the 34% tax bracket. All the firm's present financing is in the form of equity. Frank intends to issue $10,000,000 worth of 9% bonds and trade each bond with shareholders for some of their stock. The interest payments on the bonds are tax deductible. If the company pays out all its after-tax earnings as dividends, how much more cash will stockholders, as a group, receive with Frank's plan? (*Hint*: Find the tax savings with the leveraged capital structure).

Asset Liquidity
9. Firm 1

9. Two firms have assets with identical total book value, each equal to $10,000,000. The composition of each firm's assets is given below.

	FIRM 1	FIRM 2
Cash	$ 500,000	$ 500,000
Accounts receivable[1]	$ 500,000[1]	$4,000,000[a]
Inventory[2]	$ 500,000[2]	$3,000,000[b]
Land[3]	$8,500,000[3]	$2,500,000[c]

[1]All accounts are current.

[2]Inventory is finished goods.

[3]Land is a 5,000-acre ranch near Boulder, Colorado, acquired in 1954.

[a]All accounts are current except for $2,000,000 which is 125 days past due.

[b]Inventory is half finished goods and half work-in-progress.

[c]Land is a recently acquired papaya farm in Columbia, S. America.

Which firm has the less liquid assets? Which do you think has the greater borrowing capacity and which has the largest potential bankruptcy costs?

Asset Liquidity
10. Firm 1, $28,980,000; firm 2, $4,060,000

10. Imagine that you have a job as a loan officer at the Deep Pockets Bank. It is the bank's policy to value, for lending purposes, finished goods inventory at 70¢ per dollar of book value and to value work-in-progress inventory at 25¢ on the dollar. Cash is valued one-to-one, and current receivables are appraised at 75¢ per dollar. Receivables' value declines to 50¢ per dollar at 60 days past due, and any receivables over 100 days past due are valued at 20¢ per dollar. Certified appraisals from an outside source are required for real estate. The bank then sets its lending limit at 80% of total appraised value. Suppose that the appraisals for the land owned by Firm 1 and Firm 2 come in at $35,000,000 and $1,250,000, respectively. What are your estimates for the maximum loan size that Deep Pockets Bank would establish for the two firms based on their asset's values?

CHAPTER 13

Dividend Policy: Distributions to Shareholders

©1988 Tribune Media Services, Inc.
All Rights Reserved

"Dear shareholder: In an effort to reduce an overstocked inventory, you will be receiving under separate cover a number of the company's household products of equal or greater value than your regular quarterly dividend."

Do you think the decision to send products in lieu of cash dividends will cause the stock's price to increase or decrease? Chapter 13 examines how the dividend decision can affect stockholders' wealth.

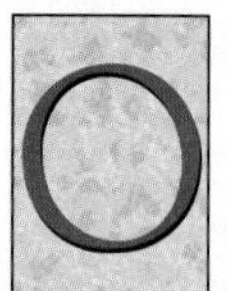

Our study of the capital budgeting process in Chapters 9, 10, and 11 covered the appropriate technique for identifying projects that are expected to increase the wealth of corporate shareholders—the NPV criterion. Chapter 12 analyzed the considerations that should be made when selecting the mix of debt and equity utilized to finance these investment projects. Again, this analysis was presented within the framework of maximizing shareholders' wealth. In this chapter we discuss **dividend policy**, the distribution of residual cash to shareholders, an act upon which shareholders' wealth ultimately depends. See Figure 13.1.

To understand the importance of dividends, let's return to the fundamental equation for value, first presented in Chapter 3.

$$\text{value} = \sum_{t=1}^{\infty} \frac{CF_t}{(1 + r)^t} \tag{13.1}$$

This equation expresses value as the sum of future cash flows, discounted at a risk-adjusted required return. As we saw in Chapter 6, this formula may be applied to stocks by recognizing that the cash flows distributed to shareholders come in the form of dividends.

$$\text{value} = \sum_{t=1}^{\infty} \frac{D_t}{(1 + r)^t} \tag{13.2}$$

Transparency Available

Now, suppose a fictitious stock had in its corporate charter an ironclad, irrevocable promise never to pay a dividend of any kind. What would be the value of a share of this stock? According to Equation (13.2), the value would be zero.

FIGURE 13.1

THE FINANCIAL BALANCE SHEET, ILLUSTRATING THE DIVIDEND DECISION

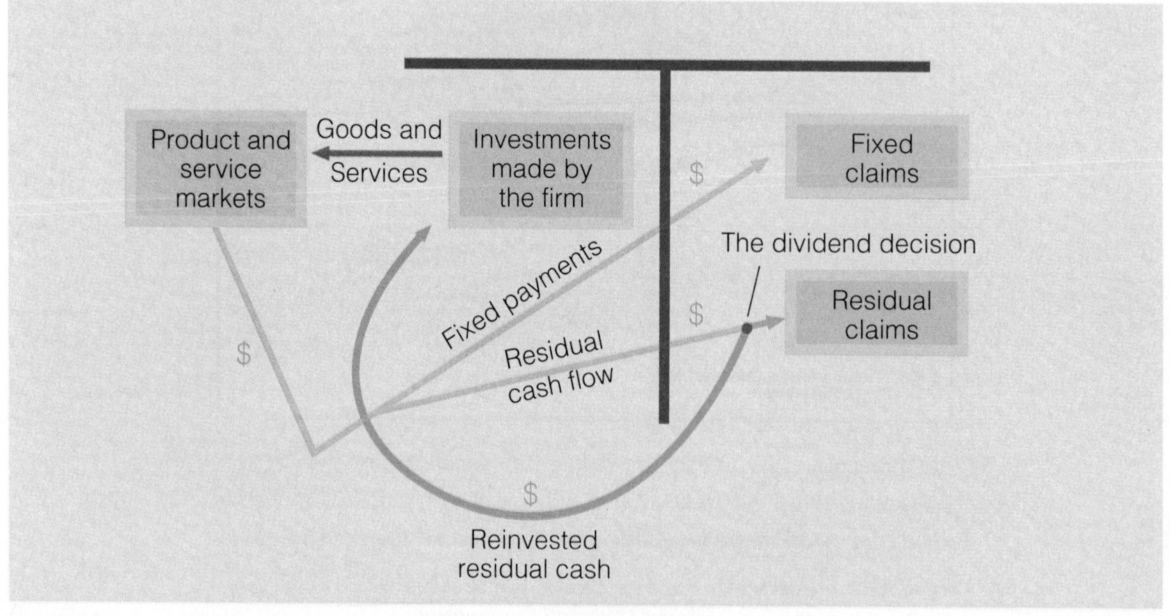

Although the firm might be quite profitable, it would by its own charter be forced to retain all residual cash flows and never distribute any funds to its shareholders. Because the present value of an infinite stream of zeros is zero, such a firm would be worthless to shareholders. For those of you who argue that you would buy the stock because you could make money via price appreciation, consider who would be willing to purchase this stock from you (especially at a higher price). Such an investment strategy is known as the "next-bigger-fool" strategy. It will, sooner or later, break down when there are no more fools available, and the last fool will be left holding a worthless security.

Yet, you may be aware of firms that pay no dividends and sell for relatively high prices. At one time in the 1980s, Digital Equipment Corporation (DEC) sold for more than $100 per share but paid no dividends. The explanation for such valuation rests in future dividend-paying capacity. Although DEC paid no dividends, there was the expectation that it might (at any time) initiate a dividend. Because DEC was a profitable, large[1] firm, its dividend, when initiated, could be very large. A second possibility for DEC was that the firm's equity might be bought out in a corporate takeover, in which case a single **liquidating dividend** could be paid, which would be high indeed. Since neither DEC nor any other corporation has an ironclad no dividend rule, the potential for future dividends supported its value.[2]

This discussion points out two important facts about dividend policy: First, dividends are essential to stock value, and second, large future dividends may occur even if current dividends are small or nonexistent.

DIVIDEND POLICY IN PERFECT CAPITAL MARKETS

To formalize the discussion of dividend policy, we will assume that the firm has identified its investment projects and established its mix of debt and equity financing. Thus, capital budgeting is done, capital structure has been targeted, and we may isolate the dividend decision. Because we know our target capital structure, we also know how much equity financing is needed to fund the firm's promising investment projects. Following the format used to analyze capital structure, we begin the analysis of dividend policy within an economic environment where capital markets are perfect.

Like capital structure, dividend policy is also irrelevant to shareholders in perfect capital markets. A firm is equally valuable whether it pays all its residual cash to shareholders (a 100% **payout**) or if it retains all its cash flow (a 100% **retention**, or **plowback**, **rate**). Under either dividend policy and all policies between these extremes, shareholders' wealth is unchanged.

Perfect market assumptions underlie the logic of dividend policy irrelevance. Recall that in perfect markets there are no frictions, so corporations may raise new capital without incurring transaction costs. Individuals may also buy (or sell) securities without commissions or tax ramifications. Additionally, perfect markets

[1]Here we mean the firm is large relative to the number of shares of stock outstanding. Thus, each share has a claim on a relatively large amount of cash flow or assets.

[2]It is interesting that DEC's stock price subsequently fell precipitously as the outlook for its computer sales fell, reducing the prospect for high future dividends.

Summary

Identifying a firm's optimal dividend policy, like the capital structure decision, is a challenging task. No formula exists that provides the answer, nor is there general agreement on the wisdom of a particular strategy. However, by careful and farsighted forecasting with the intention of minimizing transaction costs, limiting potential agency problems, and attempting to meet the expectations of investors, managers can feel some comfort in that they are not straying too far afield. Most firms, in fact, follow a pattern of slow but steady dividend growth, supplemented by an occasional special dividend.

Key Terms

dividend policy
liquidating dividend
retention, or plowback, rate
payout
internal equity
retained and reinvested cash
external equity
homemade dividends
income stocks
growth companies
dividend clientele
residual dividend policy
tax-deferred
regular dividends
special dividends
quasi-fixed cost
the signaling effect
payout of free cash flow
payout ratio
smooth-stream dividend strategy
date of record
dividend payment date
ex-dividend date
settle (a stock transaction)
stock repurchase
open market purchases
tender offer
bid price
bid premium
oversubscribed
treasury stock
stock dividend
stock split
reverse split
dividend yield (see study question #1)
bird in the hand theory (see study question #1)
trading range (see question #11 and problem #6)
dividend reinvestment plans (see question #7)

Questions

1. Recall from Chapter 6 that an investor's return from a stock investment comes from two sources, price appreciation and dividend yield. For a stock with constant dividend growth, the return formula is

$$r = \frac{D_1}{P_0} + g_n$$

where D_1/P_0 is the return from dividend payments, also known as the *dividend yield,* and g_n is the rate of dividend growth, which also equals price appreciation. It has been argued that dividend payments are less risky and therefore more valuable than price appreciation, because dividend payments tend to fluctuate less than stock prices. This is known as the *bird-in-the-hand* theory. Identify the fallacy in this argument. [*Hint:* One way of lowering the riskiness of one's stock portfolio is to sell some shares and put the cash in Treasury bills or some other nearly riskless investment. In order words, by "cashing out" of a stock investment, one can lower risk and, in efficient markets, also lower returns. Now consider what an investor in a high-dividend-yield security is going to do with the cash received from dividend payments. If the investor does not reinvest the dividends in the stock (or another security of similar risk), what will happen to the return on his portfolio?]

2. Investors and stock analysts are *forward-looking.* They are concerned with expected future dividends when estimating value. There are occasions when these analysts see a firm's problems even before management faces up to the difficulties. Explain why a stock's price might increase when the firm announces it is lowering its dividend and will use the retained cash to retool an inefficient factory.
3. Suppose Bioenergy, Inc., has a market value of $50,000,000 and is 100% equity financed. Its market value per share is $25, because there are 2,000,000 shares outstanding. The firm pays no dividend. At the last shareholders' meeting there were complaints about the no-dividend policy. As a director of Bioenergy, what factors should you consider as you contemplate initiating a dividend? [*Hint:* Discuss why you should analyze (a) the current and expected level of cash flows, (b) the cash needed to fund expected positive NPV investment opportunities, (c) the variability of expected cash flows, (d) other means of financing investment projects and the costs associated with using other sources of capital, and (e) if there have been some wasted funds expended in the firm in the past.]
4. On Thursday, May 3, the board of directors of ACME, Inc., declares a $1.50 per share dividend, payable on Thursday, May 31, to the shareholders of record on Thursday, May 17. When is the ex-dividend date? Do you think it is a good idea to buy the stock on May 8 and then sell it on May 15? Why or why not?
5. Look in recent *Wall Street Journals* for several stocks that went ex-dividend on the day of trading reported. Compare the price change with the level of quarterly dividend reported (*Note:* The dividend reported is an annual dividend rate and probably needs to be divided by four to translate it into a quarterly dividend, which is the frequency of most firms' payments).
6. In your opinion, is there any economic difference between a two-for-one stock split and a 100% stock dividend?
7. *Dividend Reinvestment Plans* (DRPs) are in place at many large corporations. DRPs allow stockholders to have their dividends automatically reinvested in the company's stock. Stockholders avoid brokerage commissions by participating in DRPs, and at times the firm sells the stock to plan participants at a light (3% to 5%) discount from the current market price. What clientele might find this feature attractive?

8. Why might a firm repurchase its own stock rather than distributing excess cash via a special dividend?
9. Why might an investor prefer capital gains to dividend income?
10. What kind of dividend policy would you expect growth companies to have? Why?
11. One motive for stock splits is the *trading range hypothesis*. The argument says that stocks with high prices tend not to be bought by many small investors. Thus, lowering the price per share by way of a stock split makes the stock more attractive to the low-price clientele. More demand for the stock should increase equity's value. Do you think this is true? Why or why not?

DEMONSTRATION PROBLEMS

Solving for dividends per share

1. Blue Gene's Jazz Cafe has net income of $500,000. The firm has 125,000 shares of stock outstanding and has a 40% retention rate. What is Blue Gene's dividend per share? What is the payout rate? What total amount of cash will Blue Gene's pay in dividends?

SOLUTION

First, find Blue Gene's payout ratio, which is (1 − retention rate) = 1 − 0.40 = 0.60. Next, multiply total earnings by the payout ratio to find total dividend payments:

$$(\$500{,}000)(0.60) = \$300{,}000$$

Last, divide total dividends by the number of shares outstanding: $300,000 ÷ 125,000 = $2.40 per share.

Planning dividend policy

2. Blue Gene's management is trying to plan future dividend policy. The firm forecasts residual cash flows of $700,000, $1,300,000, and $850,000 for the next 3 years, respectively. The company also forecasts reinvestment needs of $100,000, $120,000, and $300,000 in each of the years.
   a. What is the projected cash available for dividends each of the next 3 years?
   b. Devise a dividend policy that would ensure that the firm did not need to needlessly incur transaction costs and would be sustainable, not necessitating a lowered dividend in any year.

SOLUTION

a.

	YEAR 1	YEAR 2	YEAR 3
Residual cash flow	$700,000	$1,300,000	$850,000
Reinvestment needs	$100,000	$ 120,000	$300,000
Cash available for dividends	$600,000	$1,180,000	$550,000

b.

Dividend	$600,000	$830,000	$900,000
Cash carry over to next year	$ 0	$350,000	$ 0

PROBLEMS

Payout and Retention Ratios

1. a. $1,500,000
   b. $1,500,000
   c. 50%
   d. 50%

1. Groundhog Excavation, Inc., has net income of $3,000,000. There are 6,000,000 shares of common Groundhog stock outstanding. The firm's board has just announced a 25¢ annual dividend.
   a. What is the total amount of cash that the firm will pay as dividends?
   b. What will be Groundhog's retained earnings for this year?
   c. What is Groundhog's plowback rate?
   d. What is the firm's payout ratio for this year?

Planning Dividend

2. a. $0.60; $4.33; $0.33; $1.67
   b. $0.63; $1.37; $2.11; $2.85; 65%
   c. $0.63; $0.87; $1.20; $1.67; $7.79 million

2. A firm has expected cash flows after payment of fixed claims of $4,000,000, $15,000,000, $3,000,000, and $7,000,000 for the next 4 years. There are 3,000,000 shares of common stock outstanding. The firm's management foresees promising investment opportunities that will require equity investments of $2,000,000 a year in each of the next 4 years. The firm's management also has a policy of keeping a reserve balance of cash equal to $200,000 on hand for unexpected contingencies, and the cash balance is currently only $100,000.

	YEAR 1	YEAR 2	YEAR 3	YEAR 4
Total residual cash flows available	$4,000,000	$15,000,000	$3,000,000	$7,000,000
Less investment needs	−2,000,000	−2,000,000	−2,000,000	−2,000,000
Less cash needed for contingencies	− 100,000	0	0	0
Cash available for dividends	$1,900,000	$13,000,000	$1,000,000	$5,000,000

   a. Following a strict residual dividend policy, what would be the firm's expected dividend per share for each year?
   b. Following the smooth-stream dividend strategy, what would be each year's dividend per share? What would be the growth rate of dividends over this period? [To find the dividend growth rate, solve for r in the single cash flow formula, $FV_4 = PV_1(1 + r)^{-t}$ where PV_1 = dividend in year 1, FV_4 = dividend in year 4, and $t = 3$.] What will be the level of free cash flow in years 1, 2, 3, and 4? Could this be a problem?
   c. In order to minimize the free cash flow problems identified in 2(b), design a smooth-stream *regular* dividend policy with one *special dividend*. What will be your special dividend amount per share, and when will you pay it?

Dividend Yield

3. 11.6%; 3.6%; 8%

Dividend Payout and Growth

4. Colgate: div. growth = 3.3%, EPS growth = 8.4%; Home Depot: div. growth = inf.; EPS growth = 40.9%.

3. A share of stock is selling for $30. Its dividends are expected to grow at an 8% rate for the foreseeable future. The stock just paid a $1.00 per share dividend. What return should an investor expect from purchasing this stock? Decompose this return into dividend yield and price appreciation components. (*Hint:* Review Question 1.)
4. The following table lists the earnings per share (EPS) and dividends per share (DPS) for three firms from 1983 through 1988. Calculate the payout ratio and the retention rate for each firm. Then calculate the growth rate of

dividends and earnings for each company over the 6-year period. Now, research each company and determine whether you would classify it as a mature firm or a growth firm. Look at the variability of each firm's earnings per share and compare them. Comment.

	RYLAND GROUP		COLGATE PALMOLIVE		HOME DEPOT	
	EPS	*DPS*	*EPS*	*DPS*	*EPS*	*DPS*
1988	$3.10	$0.53	$3.42	$1.48	$1.00	$0.07
1987	$2.46	$0.40	$2.97	$1.39	$0.75	$0.05
1986	$2.02	$0.38	$2.52	$1.36	$0.40	0
1985	$1.27	$0.33	$2.13	$1.32	$0.13	0
1984	$0.76	$0.30	$1.85	$1.28	$0.25	0
1983	$1.26	$0.25	$2.28	$1.26	$0.18	0

Stock Split
5. $60; $1.00; 9 million

5. Suppose Altamont Productions declares a three-for-one stock split. Prior to the split, Altamont's shares were selling for $180 each and its dividend was expected to be $3 per share. No other news affecting Altamont was announced around the day the split went into effect. What do you think Altamont's new expected dividend will be after the split? What about its price? If Altamont had 3,000,000 shares outstanding prior to the split, then how many shares are outstanding after the split? Will the split impact shareholder wealth, in your opinion?

Stock Split
6. a. Dividend $0.89
b. Disagree
c. >$60

6. Consider your answer to Problem 5.
   a. How would your answers change if the costs of paperwork and legal fees involved with the split total $1,000,000?
   b. The directors of Altamont have argued that the split is necessary, because the old price per share of $180 was prohibitively high for small investors to include in their portfolios. By splitting and lowering the price, they argue, the stock will be in a better *trading range*, increasing demand for the stock. These directors reason that price will increase with an increase in demand. Do you agree or disagree with this rationale?
   c. Considering your answers to Problem 5, if the new dividend per share after the split was actually $2, would this be above or below your expectations? What do you think the new price will be given this new information?

Payout, Growth
7. $D_1 = \$3.78$; $EPS_6 = \$19.04$; $D_6 = \$5.55$

7. Suppose a firm's earnings per share are expected to grow at 8% per year for the next 6 years. The most recent dividend paid was $3.50 and the most recent EPS figure was $12. If the firm expects to maintain a constant payout ratio, then what will be next year's dividend? What will be the firm's EPS and dividend in 6 years?

After-tax Yield
8. 6.5% 9.1%

8. Firm A has declared a $3 per share dividend. Its current share price is $33. What will be the after-tax dividend yield on this stock for an investor in the 28% personal income tax bracket? What will be the after-tax dividend yield for an investor in the zero tax bracket?

Stock Dividend
9. a. $1.60 $1.33
b. 120 shares, same
c. no change

9. A firm has $50,000,000 in net income and 12,500,000 shares outstanding. The company now declares a 20% stock dividend. The firm's payout ratio before and after the stock dividend is 40%.

a. What is the firm's cash dividend per share before and after the stock dividend (assuming earnings don't change)?

b. If you owned 100 shares prior to the stock dividend, how many shares will you own after the dividend? What will be your cash dividend income (assuming earnings don't change) before and after the stock dividend?

c. Considering your answer to part b, do you think the total value of your stock ownership in this firm has changed because of the stock dividend?

Reverse Split
10. $3.60, $6.00, $72

10. A corporation announces a one-for-three reverse split. Prior to the split, the dividend per share is $1.20, the earnings per share total $2, and the price of the stock is $24 per share. What do you expect these values will be after the split?

Share Repurchase
11. 100,000 shares, 25% premium

11. Suppose a company has $1,000,000 of free cash flow available and chooses to repurchase some shares of its own stock. The stock is selling for $8 per share and the firm's management has decided to make a tender offer of $10 per share. Given this bid price, how many shares can the firm repurchase and what is the bid premium expressed as a percentage?

Share Repurchase
12. $3.16

12. Referring to Problem 11, if prior to the repurchase the firm had 2,000,000 shares outstanding and paid a dividend of $3 per share, then what will be the new dividend per share after the repurchase assuming no change in total income?

Tax Clientele
13. Hiyield

13. Suppose you could purchase $5,000 worth of stock. You're trying to choose between the stock of two firms: Higrowth and Hiyield. Higrowth's stock pays no dividend, but its price is expected to appreciate 12% annually. Hiyield's shares cost $50 each and pay a $6.50 per share dividend at the end of each year. Hiyield's share price is expected to stay at $50 forever. You are in the 20% tax bracket, and taxes are paid each year on the dividends received, whereas taxes are paid on capital gains only when the stock is sold. Given this information, which stock would be the better investment if your expected holding period is 3 years?

Growth, Payout
14. $3.62

14. Suppose that Bioclean, Inc., pays no dividend. Current earnings per share are $3, and earnings are supposed to grow at a 22% rate for the next 7 years. At the end of 7 years Bioclean plans to initiate a dividend, planning for a 30% payout rate. What will be Bioclean's first dividend?

CHAPTER 14

Managing Corporate Liquidity

I'm sorry sir, but effective this evening, the management requires that payment of all goods and services be made in cash.

Selling on credit may increase the sales and income of a business but these benefits must be balanced against the losses from uncollected accounts receivable.

Never ask of money spent
Where the spender thinks it
went.
Nobody was ever meant
To remember or invent
What he did with every cent.
—Robert Frost

Cash circulates through the firm in a continual but somewhat erratic stream.

From the beginning, we have emphasized the importance of cash to the firm. In Chapter 4 we referred to cash as the lifeblood of a business and pointed out that companies that run out of cash and exhaust their sources of cash will most certainly fail.

This chapter concerns the management of cash flows through the company. In discussing cash management, we depart from our strategic, or long-term, view of the firm and concentrate on short-term events. In cash management, the relevant time frame is days rather than years because cash circulates through the firm in what may be described as a continual but somewhat erratic stream. Cash balances, therefore, are constantly changing, meaning that the firm could possibly be awash in cash one day and broke the next. The challenge of cash management is to ensure that the firm has enough—but not too much—cash. To accomplish this, managers must carefully plan their cash needs and monitor the flow of cash through the firm.

THE CASH CYCLE AND CORPORATE LIQUIDITY

In Chapter 4 we showed how cash flows through the firm.[1] Routine cash receipts and payments occur in conjunction with the operating cycle. The operating cycle begins with the purchase of inventory; then, after labor and other components are added, the product becomes a finished good and is sold.[2]

The firm's cash cycle is related to the operating cycle but differs in an important way. The operating cycle deals with buying inventories and making sales. The cash cycle recognizes that payment often lags behind the receipt of inventory, and cash receipts often lag behind sales. The cash cycle therefore focuses on the timing of disbursements and receipts of cash rather than the timing of purchases and sales.

A firm's operating cash flow, which is receipts minus operating disbursements, should be sufficient to pay taxes, interest on debt, and dividends on stock. Most companies also rely on internally generated cash to fund some of their long-term investments. Aside from operating cash flows, companies have other sources of cash. These other sources include selling securities, selling assets and borrowing from banks and other short-term lenders.

The timing of cash receipts and disbursements can never be precisely coordinated. At any given time, a company may have either more than enough or not enough cash to pay its suppliers, employees, investors, taxes, etc. Thus, at one time a company may have to find uses for excess cash; and at another, it may have to raise cash to pay bills. Such activity is not necessarily indicative of poor management. It simply reflects the uneven timing of cash flows in most companies.

Firms that manufacture seasonal products routinely experience uneven cash flows. Sales of outdoor recreational equipment, such as bicycles, canoes, and skis, are seasonal. However, manufacturing is generally more efficient if production

[1]You may want to glance at Figures 4.1 and 4.2 to refresh your memory.

[2]Most examples of the operating cycle are for manufacturers that convert raw materials into finished goods. Retailers, wholesalers, and other service firms also have operating cycles. Instead of physically transforming inventories, these firms may add value by marketing, distributing, or storing inventories.

occurs at a more or less constant rate throughout the year. For example, a canoe manufacturer may produce at a steady rate all year. However, its sales are highly seasonal, occurring in just a few summer months. By the end of the summer, the company will have a cash surplus; however, it must draw on that cash to pay its production costs during the rest of the year. It is possible that, in the month or two before it begins to collect on its summer sales, the company will have to borrow to pay its bills. Managing uneven cash flows requires anticipating the amount and timing of receipts and disbursements, developing strategies for making the best use of excess cash, and arranging to borrow when necessary.

A company is considered liquid if it has cash balances or timely access to cash to meet its cash needs. For instance, a company with little cash on hand and no cash flow is technically not illiquid if it has no payments to make. A company that must make payments that exceed its cash balance is still liquid if it has access to sufficient cash. For example, a company that expects to collect receivables, or will be able to borrow in time to meet its cash needs, is liquid even though it has a small cash balance. In this chapter we discuss the relationship between liquidity and corporate value. We also present techniques for managing liquidity, including cash planning, managing receivables, payables, and inventories, and short-term borrowing.

A company is considered liquid if it has cash balances or timely access to cash, to meet its cash needs.

LIQUIDITY AND CORPORATE VALUE

Does Liquidity Management Really Matter?

With perfect capital markets, managing a firm's **liquidity** is as irrelevant as managing its dividend payout (see Chapter 13). Perfect markets are efficient, with no information asymmetry, no agency problems, no leakages, and no transactions costs. A firm uses its liquidity to make payments to suppliers, employees, creditors, and others and to invest in the product markets. Excess liquidity is distributed to the shareholders as dividends. **Insolvency**, the inability to make payments as they come due, would not occur in this ideal world because valuable investment opportunities would attract sufficient quantities of cash.[3] If investment opportunities did not exist, the firm would sell assets to meet its current obligations. In the extreme case, a firm with no investment opportunities would liquidate all its assets and go out of business.

Because of imperfections in the financial markets, companies do not have instant or costless means of finding the best use for excess cash or acquiring cash.

With perfect markets, the firm is able to instantly and costlessly adjust its liquidity to reflect its current needs. However, in reality, adjustments cannot be made instantaneously. Transactions costs associated with continuous adjustments, such as paying dividends or borrowing, would be prohibitive. If a firm is insolvent even for a few days because of an unexpected cash shortage, it faces the prospect of having to cease operations.[4] In liquidity management, timing is everything.

---

[3]There is another meaning of insolvency, sometimes called theoretical insolvency, which means that a company has a negative net worth. [George W. Gallenger, and P. Basil Healey, *Liquidity Analysis and Management* (Reading, Mass.: Addison-Wesley, 1987, pp. 6–7.)]

[4]The unexpected shortage may be due to information asymmetry between the firm and its creditors or its customers. For example, a firm may expect to have access to credit or may expect to collect on sales, but its potential creditors and customers know that it will not.

FIGURE 14.3

JOURNEY OF A CHECK

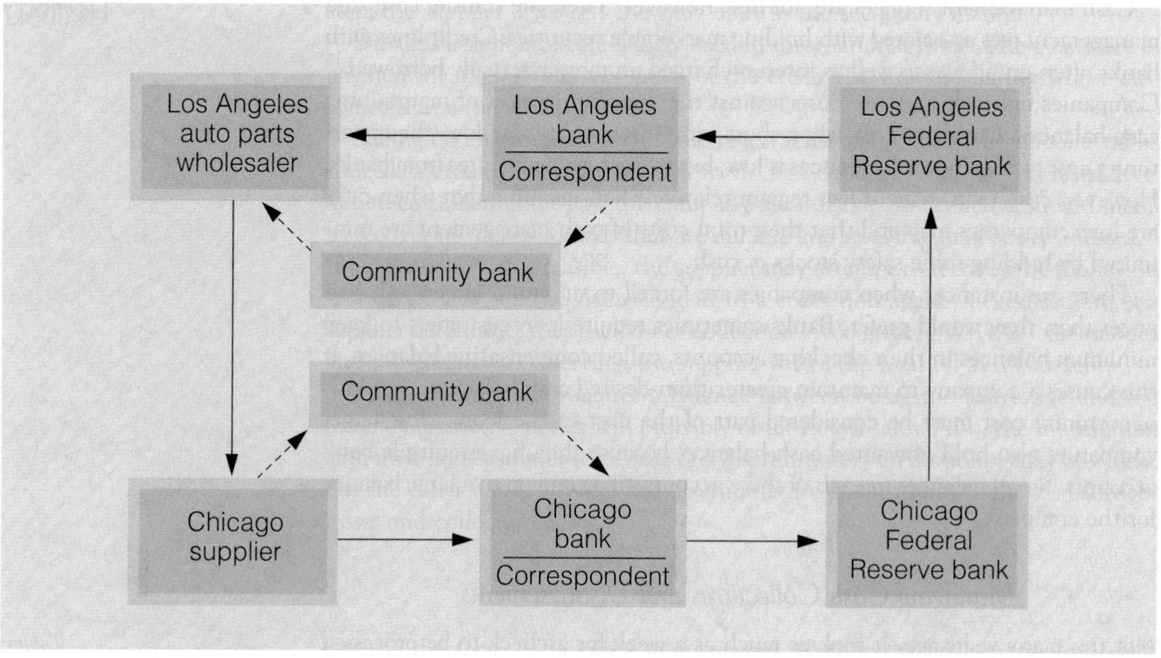

Transparency Available

As we suggested in the auto parts example, float occurs because of the mails, in-house processing by companies, and the bank-clearing process. In our example the banks in Chicago and Los Angeles and the Federal Reserve System all handled the check. If either the payer or the recipient of the check had his account at a small community bank, this bank would have forwarded the check to a larger bank in its region for processing, producing more float. In this case, the larger bank is acting as **correspondent bank** on behalf of the smaller bank. These community banks are also included in Figure 14.3. In contrast to the auto parts example, clearing checks locally is relatively quick and easy. Larger cities process checks through a local **clearinghouse**.[17]

Several methods for reducing float have been in place for many years. The most common of these is the use of **lockboxes** by recipients of checks. In our auto parts example, much of the float occurred because of the distance between Los Angeles and Chicago. This float can be reduced by having the supplier's

[17]Before optical scanners and microcomputers, city clearinghouses were places where bags of checks were physically delivered from one bank to another. The following example describes the clearinghouse in Los Angeles in the 1960s. At the end of the business day, couriers in cars and trucks descended on a warehouselike structure downtown, hauling heavy canvas sacks of checks, each sack destined for a different bank. Once all the sacks had been delivered, the bank couriers hauled them out to their cars or trucks and sped away, bound for their banks' processing centers. Employees at the processing centers worked through the night, so that by morning, the checks were sorted and ready to be delivered to the branches.

customers in Southern California mail their payments to a local post office box (lockbox). A local bank collects checks, processes them, and deposits them in the supplier's Los Angeles bank account.

Lockboxes are often used in conjunction with concentration banking. The lockbox speeds the process for crediting the supplier's bank account, but that account resides in Los Angeles. A large company may have lockboxes and bank accounts in dozens of cities. Funds from many locations may be transferred to **concentration banks** in one or several central locations, where they can be more effectively managed. At these banks, the funds are under the direct control of the corporate cash manager.

For many years, there has been talk of a checkless society, in which virtually all payments would be made electronically. The electronic payment system has been slow in coming, but electronic fund transfers are becoming more commonplace, especially between companies and banks.

The check-clearing process provides an opportunity to discuss the banking system, the Federal Reserve, and electronic funds transfer.

Interbank check processing has been a large part of float. In the auto parts example, the Federal Reserve System handled the movement of the check from Chicago to Los Angeles. Now, this process can be accelerated by the Fedwire wire transfer service operated by the Federal Reserve System. Similarly, many clearinghouse activities are handled electronically through CHIPS (Clearing-House Interbank Payments System).[18]

Increasing emphasis on liquidity management has prompted efforts to reduce float. The result has been a great reduction in float in recent years. Consumers are, themselves, contributing to this reduction by making greater use of bank cash machines and credit and debit cards. The checkless society is not yet here, and neither is zero float. However, the opportunity for payers to use float to their advantage is considerably less than it once was.

SHORT-TERM CREDIT

With the high cost of holding cash balances, short-term borrowing has become an important source of liquidity. Those companies that are large enough to sell marketable securities have many borrowing options. Even smaller companies may have access to several credit sources. In this section we examine a number of sources of short-term credit, beginning with marketable securities.

Marketable Securities

Marketable securities are short-term IOUs, maturing in 1 year or less. A security is considered liquid if it can be converted to cash at any time, at low cost, with little or no loss of value. Transactions costs are generally low, because the markets in which these securities are traded are efficient and compeitive.[19]

As opposed to capital market securities, short-term marketable securities carry little credit and interest rate risk.

Loss of value may result from interest rate risk and credit risk. Interest rate risk

[18]Wire transfers eliminate mail float but are expensive. Electronic transfers and clearinghouses such as CHIPS are more complete and efficient systems, but they require a large initial investment in computers and software. CHIPS is used for international as well as domestic funds transfers.

[19]In most cases, paper securities do not change hands. Transactions are handled electronically through linked computers.

SUMMARY

The flow of cash through a business, from receipts to disbursements, is uneven. This means that, at any given time, a firm may have excess cash or must temporarily augment its cash by borrowing or drawing upon its marketable securities. A company is liquid if it has access to cash when needed.

If capital markets were perfect, companies would not have to manage liquidity. Investors would provide cash to the company when needed, and excess cash would be used to fund investment opportunities. However, in reality, information is neither costless nor complete, and transactions costs impede the free flow of cash. This means that companies must devote resources to managing liquidity.

Managers must continually strike a balance between having too much and too little liquidity. Too much liquidity wastes scarce resources. Too little liquidity risks financial distress and insolvency. Gradually rising interest rates have raised the cost of liquidity as well as the cost of holding receivables and inventories. This has led firms to seek ways to reduce their investment in cash, marketable securities, receivables and inventories.

The essential planning tool for liquidity is the cash budget. A well-prepared cash budget warns the firm when and how much added cash will be needed. The firm may then begin to store liquidity, reduce the period of its cash cycle or arrange for credit. The cash budget also forecasts when the firm will have excess cash to invest.

KEY TERMS

liquidity
insolvency
economic order quantity
just-in-time
trade credit
discriminant analysis
trade discount
sight draft
time draft
banker's acceptance
compensating balances
float
correspondent bank
clearinghouse
lockboxes
concentration banks
commercial paper
negotiable certificates of deposit
Yankee CDs
repurchase agreements
money market mutual funds
Eurodollars
LIBOR
money market preferred stock
commercial bank
credit lines
revolving credit agreement
commitment fee
prime rate
factor
trust receipts
warehouse receipts
term loans
discounting
cash budget

KEY FORMULAS

Annualized rate of return on a marketable security

$$\text{return} = \left(\left[1 + \left(\frac{V_e - V_b}{V_b}\right)\right]^{365/\text{days}}\right) - 1$$

Approximate annualized cost of forgoing a trade discount

$$\text{cost} = \frac{\text{discount\%}}{100\% - \text{discount\%}} \times \frac{365}{\text{additional period (days)}}$$

Effective annualized loan rate

$$\text{effective rate} = \left(1 + \frac{\text{interest dollars}}{\text{net loan proceeds}}\right)^{365/\text{days}} - 1$$

Approximate rate on a compensating balance loan

$$\text{approximate rate} = \left(\frac{\text{interest percent}}{100\% - \text{compensating balance percent}}\right)$$

Approximate rate on a discounted loan

$$\text{approximate rate} = \left(\frac{\text{interest percent}}{100\% - \text{interest percent}}\right)$$

QUESTIONS

1. A well-managed company is one in which monthly cash inflows always equal or exceed monthly cash disbursements. Do you agree or disagree? Why?
2. Using short-term borrowing or drawing upon its reserves of marketable securities to meet cash shortfalls indicates that the company is illiquid. Do you agree or disagree? Why?
3. Comment on this statement: Liquidity is cash in the bank.
4. We have indicated that liquidity also includes access to short-term borrowing. How, then, would you respond to the following statement? A business cannot count on short-term borrowing because when you need it the most, it may not be available.
5. You can never have too much liquidity. Do you agree or disagree? Why?
6. Cash is a nonearning asset. Therefore, it is unwise to maintain cash balances. Comment on this statement.
7. Some companies maintain large balances of cash and marketable securities because they don't want to run the risk of illiquidity. Are they being illogical? Comment on this statement.
8. Too much or too little liquidity reduces the value of the firm. Explain the connection between liquidity and value. Give an example of how illiquidity and excess liquidity may lead to a loss of value.
9. Your company manufactures ski apparel and accessories. You maintain a constant manufacturing rate all year. Most of your sales occur in August through November. In what month(s) would you expect the company's cash

balance to be at its highest? In what month(s) would you expect the lowest cash balance? All company sales are for cash.

10. How would your answer to Question 9 change if the company sold all products on credit, and it took an average of 60 days to collect receivables?
11. Which of these two companies is the least liquid? Neither company has marketable securities or access to short term debt.
    Company A has a zero cash balance. It expects no cash flow nor disbursements for the next 30 days.
    Company B has a cash balance of $20,000, and expects cash inflows over the next 30 days to total $30,000. During this 30 day period, the company must make cash disbursements of $65,000.
12. What is the opportunity cost of excess liquidity?
13. Even in the early stages of becoming illiquid (before insolvency), a company incurs costs associated with illiquidity. What are some of these costs?
14. Comment on this statement: The central question in inventory management is not whether inventories should be held, but who holds them.
15. What are the benefits and costs to a company employing just-in-time (JIT) inventory management?
16. What are the costs and benefits of having loose and restrictive credit policies? These policies refer to whether or not to extend credit to customers.
17. Explain the difference between a time draft and a banker's acceptance.
18. How may a supplier, who has received a banker's acceptance, receive early payment for his shipment?
19. Given the proliferation of credit losses (customers who do not pay), it would seem that all credit customers should be thoroughly screened. Do you agree or disagree? Why?
20. Why are compensating balances sometimes costly to the firm?
21. Define and give an example of float.
22. Whom does float benefit, those making or those receiving payment?
23. What are the principal causes of float, and what is being done to reduce float in the payments system?

24. Provide a brief description of the following marketable securities. In your description, include the following:
    Who issues the security?
    Is the security sold at a discount to par?
    What is its range of maturities?
    a. Treasury bills
    b. Commercial paper
    c. Negotiable CDs
    d. Repurchase agreements
    e. Money market mutual funds
    f. Banker's acceptances
    g. Eurodollars
    h. Money market preferred stock
25. Why are accounts payable and accruals considered to be spontaneous financing sources?
26. Comment on this statement: Companies who routinely take trade discounts are getting their supplies and inventories at bargain prices.

27. Comment on this statement: Suppliers will probably discontinue credit to firms who routinely pay late (after the net period).
28. What are the primary distinctions between a credit line and a revolving credit agreement?
29. Comment on this statement: When banks charged interest on the amount actually borrowed, with no fees, firms negotiated the largest credit line they could get, even if they had no intention of borrowing that money. Now that banks charge fees, based on the amount of the credit line, firms ask only for the amount of credit they think they will need.
30. Because the interest rates on commercial paper are lower than on bank loans, most companies would be better off selling commercial paper rather than borrowing from banks. Do you agree or disagree? Why?
31. Both receivables and inventories may serve as collateral for short-term loans. Briefly explain the typical financing arrangements involving receivables and inventories.
32. Two $10,000 Treasury bills are sold at auction for $9,900. One matures in 91 days, the other in 181 days. Which has the highest annual rate of return? No calculation is necessary.
33. $10,000 Treasury bills, maturing in 91 days, are sold at auction for $9,925. A month later, 91 day treasury bills are sold at auction for $9,980. Have interest rates risen or fallen over that month? No calculation is necessary.

DEMONSTRATION PROBLEMS

Rate of Return on Marketable Securities

1. A 6-month (182-day) $100,000 negotiable CD is sold at par and will be redeemed for $103,400. Calculate its annual rate of return.

SOLUTION

The return on a marketable security can be calculated using Equation (14.1).

$$\text{return} = \left(\left[1 + \left(\frac{V_e - V_b}{V_b}\right)\right]^{365/\text{days}}\right) - 1$$

$$= \left(\left[1 + \left(\frac{103{,}400 - 100{,}000}{100{,}000}\right)\right]^{365/182}\right) - 1$$

$$= 6.94\%$$

Cash Budget

2. Sam's Barbeque and Chinese Restaurant is located on the island of Maui, Hawaii. Most of its business is in the winter, during the tourist season. Collections on receivables are based on prior months' sales. Inventory purchases are based on future sales, and payments are made in the months following purchases. Using Exhibits 14.4 and 14.5, prepare a 12-month cash budget for Sam's Barbeque and Chinese Restaurant.

SOLUTION

The worksheet and cash budget are shown in Exhibits 14.6 and 14.7.

EXHIBIT 14.4

SAM'S BARBEQUE AND CHINESE RESTAURANT: CASH BUDGET WORKSHEET

	19X5 Nov	Dec	19X6 Jan	Feb	Mar	Apr	May	Jun	Jul	Aug	Sep	Oct	Nov	Dec
Sales	$142,800	$174,700	$172,900	$167,300	$149,100	$147,500	$121,500	$117,100	$97,700	$74,400	$96,900	$117,300	$140,500	$173,600
Collections on sales														
20% 1st month														
80% 2nd month														
Total sales receipts														
Inventory purchases														
33% current mo. sales														
Payments														
70% 1st month														
30% 2nd month														
Total payments														

EXHIBIT 14.5

SAM'S BARBEQUE AND CHINESE RESTAURANT: CASH BUDGET

	19X6 Jan	Feb	Mar	Apr	May	Jun	Jul	Aug	Sep	Oct	Nov	Dec
Sales receipts												
Inventory payments												
Wages (54% sales)												
Other cash expenses	$15,500	$15,500	$15,500	$15,500	$15,500	$15,500	$15,500	$15,500	$15,500	$15,500	$15,500	$15,500
Net operating cash flow												
Taxes	$ 9,500			$ 9,500			$ 9,500			$ 9,500		
Net cash flow												
Beginning cash	$14,400											
Ending cash												

EXHIBIT 14.6

SAM'S BARBEQUE AND CHINESE RESTAURANT: CASH BUDGET WORKSHEET

	19X5 Nov	Dec	19X6 Jan	Feb	Mar	Apr	May	Jun	Jul	Aug	Sep	Oct	Nov	Dec
Sales	$142,800	$174,700	$172,900	$167,300	$149,100	$147,500	$121,500	$117,100	$ 97,700	$ 74,400	$96,900	$117,300	$140,500	$173,600
Collections on sales														
20% 1st month			$ 34,940	$ 84,580	$ 33,460	$ 29,820	$ 29,500	$ 24,300	$ 23,420	$ 19,540	$14,880	$ 19,380	$ 23,460	$ 28,100
80% 2nd month			$114,240	$139,760	$138,320	$133,840	$119,280	$118,000	$ 97,200	$ 93,680	$78,160	$ 59,520	$ 77,520	$ 93,840
Total sales receipts			$149,180	$174,300	$171,780	$163,660	$148,780	$142,300	$120,620	$113,220	$93,040	$ 78,900	$100,980	$121,940
Inventory purchases														
33% current-mo. sales	$ 47,124	$ 57,651	$ 57,057	$ 55,209	$ 49,203	$ 48,675	$ 40,095	$ 38,643	$ 32,241	$ 24,552	$31,977	$ 38,709	$ 46,365	$ 57,288
Payments														
70% 1st month			$ 40,356	$ 39,940	$ 38,646	$ 34,442	$ 34,073	$ 28,067	$ 27,050	$ 22,569	$17,186	$ 22,384	$ 27,096	$ 32,456
30% 2nd month			$ 14,137	$ 17,295	$ 17,117	$ 16,563	$ 14,761	$ 14,603	$ 12,029	$ 11,593	$ 9,672	$ 7,366	$ 9,593	$ 11,613
Total payments			$ 54,493	$ 57,235	$ 55,763	$ 51,005	$ 48,833	$ 42,669	$ 39,079	$ 34,162	$26,859	$ 29,750	$ 36,689	$ 44,068

EXHIBIT 14.7

SAM'S BARBEQUE AND CHINESE RESTAURANT: CASH BUDGET

	19X6 Jan	Feb	Mar	Apr	May	Jun	Jul	Aug	Sep	Oct	Nov	Dec
Sales receipts	$149,180	$174,340	$171,780	$163,660	$148,780	$142,300	$120,620	$113,220	$93,040	$78,900	$100,980	$121,940
Inventory payments	$ 54,493	$ 57,235	$ 55,763	$ 51,005	$ 48,833	$ 42,669	$ 39,079	$ 34,162	$26,859	$29,750	$ 36,689	$ 44,068
Wages (54% sales)	$ 93,366	$ 90,342	$ 80,514	$ 79,650	$ 65,610	$ 63,234	$ 52,758	$ 40,176	$52,326	$63,342	$ 75,870	$ 93,744
Other cash expenses	$ 15,500	$ 15,500	$ 15,500	$ 15,500	$ 15,500	$ 15,500	$ 15,500	$ 15,500	$15,500	$15,500	$ 15,500	$ 15,500
Net operating cash flow	($ 14,179)	$ 11,263	$ 20,003	$ 17,505	$ 18,837	$ 20,897	$ 13,283	$ 23,382	($ 1,645)	($29,692)	($ 27,079)	($ 31,372)
Taxes	$ 9,500			$ 9,500			$ 9,500			$ 9,500		
Net cash flow	($ 23,679)	$ 11,263	$ 20,003	$ 8,005	$ 18,837	$ 20,897	$ 3,783	$ 23,382	($ 1,645)	($39,192)	($ 27,079)	($ 31,372)
Beginning cash	$ 14,400	($ 9,279)	$ 1,984	$ 21,987	$ 29,992	$ 48,828	$ 69,725	$ 73,509	$96,891	$95,246	$ 56,055	$ 28,976
Ending cash	($ 9,279)	$ 1,984	$ 21,987	$ 29,992	$ 48,828	$ 69,725	$ 73,509	$ 96,891	$95,246	$56,055	$ 28,976	($ 2,397)

PROBLEMS

Rate of Return on Marketable Securities
1. 2.03%

1. A 91-day (10,000 par) Treasury bill is sold at auction for $9,950. Calculate its annual rate of return.

Rate of Return on Marketable Securities
2. 2.46%

2. A 181-day (10,000 par) Treasury bill is sold at auction for $9,880. Calculate its annual rate of return.

Rate of Return on Marketable Securities
3. 11.71%

3. A 3-month (91-day) $100,000 negotiable CD is sold at par and will be redeemed for $102,800. Calculate its annual rate of return.

Rate of Return on Marketable Securities
4. 6.85%

4. A $1 million commercial paper issue is sold at a discounted price of $982,000. It matures in 100 days. Calculate its annual rate of return.

Redemption Value of Marketable Securities
5. $101,343

5. A 3-month (91-day) $100,000 negotiable CD is sold at par and will provide an annual rate of return of 5.5%. What is its redemption value? This problem requires trial and error. Do not attempt to solve it without a calculator or spreadsheet.

Cost of Forgoing a Trade Discount
6. 24.83%

6. A firm is offered trade credit terms of 2/15, net 45. What is the annualized cost of forgoing the discount?

Cost of Forgoing a Trade Discount
7. 10.53%

7. A firm is offered trade credit terms of 1/10, net 45. If the firm could borrow short-term at a 15% rate of interest, should it take the trade discount?

Cost of Forgoing a Trade Discount
8. 14.75%

8. Assume that you could borrow short-term at a 15% rate of interest and your supplier offered you a choice of credit terms:

1/5 net 30

net 30

Which would you take?

Cash Budget
9. Ending cash (Dec.) = $1,560

9. Alaska Refrigerator Company is a refrigerator retailer. Most of its sales are in the winter, when people use their refrigerators to keep their food warm. Collections on receivables are based on prior months' sales. Inventory purchases are based on future sales, and payments are made in the months following purchases.
   a. Using Exhibits 14.8 and 14.9, prepare a 12-month cash budget for Alaska Refrigerator.
   b. Based on this 12-month cash budget, is Alaska Refrigerator Company likely to have cash balances that are either too large or too small? If so, should the company take any corrective action, such as investing surplus cash or borrowing?

EXHIBIT 14.8

ALASKA REFRIGERATOR COMPANY: CASH BUDGET WORKSHEET

	19X5		19X6												19X7	
	Nov	*Dec*	*Jan*	*Feb*	*Mar*	*Apr*	*May*	*Jun*	*Jul*	*Aug*	*Sep*	*Oct*	*Nov*	*Dec*	*Jan*	*Feb*
Sales	$39,800	$42,700	$43,300	$41,600	$39,200	$33,200	$21,500	$20,100	$17,700	$17,400	$26,900	$38,300	$40,500	$43,600	$44,200	$42,400
Collections on sales																
40% 1st month																
60% 2nd month																
Total sales receipts																
Inventory purchases																
40% 2nd-mo. sales																
Payments																
50% 1st month																
50% 2nd month																
Total payments																

EXHIBIT 14.9

ALASKA REFRIGERATOR COMPANY: CASH BUDGET

	19X6											
	Jan	*Feb*	*Mar*	*Apr*	*May*	*Jun*	*Jul*	*Aug*	*Sep*	*Oct*	*Nov*	*Dec*
Sales receipts												
Inventory payments												
Wages (40% sales)												
Other cash expenses	$5,500	$5,500	$5,500	$5,500	$5,500	$5,500	$5,500	$5,500	$5,500	$5,500	$5,500	$5,500
Net operating cash flow												
Taxes	$2,500			$2,500			$2,500			$2,500		
Net cash flow												
Beginning cash	$2,400											
Ending cash												

Cash Budget
10. Ending cash (Dec.) = −$17,773

10. Alaska Refrigerator Company is a refrigerator retailer. Most of its sales are in the winter, when people use their refrigerators to keep their food warm. Collections on receivables are based on prior months' sales. Inventory purchases are based on future sales, and payments are made in the months following purchases.
    a. Using Exhibits 14.10 and 14.11, prepare a 12-month cash budget for Alaska Refrigerator.
    b. Based on this 12-month cash budget, is Alaska Refrigerator Company likely to have cash balances that are either too large or too small? If so, should the company take any corrective action, such as investing surplus cash or borrowing?

Cash Budget
11. Ending cash (Dec.) = −$17,628

11. Alaska Refrigerator Company is a refrigerator retailer. Most of its sales are in the winter, when people use their refrigerators to keep their food warm. Collections on receivables are based on prior months' sales. Inventory purchases are based on future sales, and payments are made in the months following purchases.
    a. Using Exhibits 14.12 and 14.13, prepare a 12-month cash budget for Alaska Refrigerator.
    b. Based on this 12-month cash budget, is Alaska Refrigerator Company likely to have cash balances that are either too large or too small? If so, should the company take any corrective action, such as investing surplus cash or borrowing?

The Effect of Changing Cash Flow Estimates on Cash Balances
12. Prob. 10, scheduling of receipts/payments
Prob. 11, inventory 45% of sales

12. Each of the worksheets for Problems 9, 10, and 11 represents different estimates of collections, payments, and inventory and labor costs for the Alaska Refrigerator Company.
    a. Using the Problem 9 estimates as a baseline, what changes are represented in Problems 10 and 11? In other words, how do the estimates in Problem 10 differ from those in Problem 9 and those in Problem 11 differ from those in Problem 9?
    b. If you have the solutions to Problems 9–11, analyze how these estimated changes affect the company's cash flows and cash balances. If you do not have the solutions, how do you *think* the changing estimates would affect cash flows and balances?

Cash Budget
13. Ending cash (Dec.) = $135,150

13. Endless Tread Shoe Company faces steadily declining sales. Collections on receivables are based on prior months' sales,. Inventory purchases are based on future sales, and payments are made in the months following purchases.
    a. Using Exhibits 14.14 and 14.15, prepare a 12-month cash budget for Endless Tread.
    b. Based on this 12-month cash budget, is Endless Tread Shoe Company likely to have cash balances that are either too large or too small? If so, should the company take any corrective action, such as investing surplus cash or borrowing?

EXHIBIT 14.10

ALASKA REFRIGERATOR COMPANY: CASH BUDGET WORKSHEET

	19X5 Nov	Dec	19X6 Jan	Feb	Mar	Apr	May	Jun	Jul	Aug	Sep	Oct	Nov	Dec	19X7 Jan	Feb
Sales	$39,800	$42,700	$43,300	$41,600	$39,200	$33,200	$21,500	$20,100	$17,700	$17,400	$26,900	$38,300	$40,500	$43,600	$44,200	$42,400
Collections on sales																
20% 1st month																
75% 2nd month																
Total sales receipts																
Inventory purchases																
40% 2nd-mo. sales																
Payments																
80% 1st month																
20% 2nd month																
Total payments																

EXHIBIT 14.11

ALASKA REFRIGERATOR COMPANY: CASH BUDGET

	19X6 Jan	Feb	Mar	Apr	May	Jun	Jul	Aug	Sep	Oct	Nov	Dec
Sales receipts												
Inventory payments												
Wages (40% sales)												
Other cash expenses	$5,500	$5,500	$5,500	$5,500	$5,500	$5,500	$5,500	$5,500	$5,500	$5,500	$5,500	$5,500
Net operating cash flow												
Taxes	$2,500			$2,500			$2,500			$2,500		
Net cash flow												
Beginning cash	$2,400											
Ending cash												

EXHIBIT 14.12

Alaska Refrigerator Company: Cash Budget Worksheet

	19X5 Nov	Dec	19X6 Jan	Feb	Mar	Apr	May	Jun	Jul	Aug	Sep	Oct	Nov	Dec	19X7 Jan	Feb
Sales	$39,800	$42,700	$43,300	$41,600	$39,200	$33,200	$21,500	$20,100	$17,700	$17,400	$26,900	$38,300	$40,500	$43,600	$44,200	$42,400
Collections on sales																
40% 1st month																
60% 2nd month																
Total sales receipts																
Inventory purchases																
45% 2nd-mo. sales																
Payments																
50% 1st month																
50% 2nd month																
Total payments																

EXHIBIT 14.13

Alaska Refrigerator Company: Cash Budget

	19X6 Jan	Feb	Mar	Apr	May	Jun	Jul	Aug	Sep	Oct	Nov	Dec
Sales receipts												
Inventory payments												
Wages (40% sales)												
Other cash expenses	$5,500	$5,500	$5,500	$5,500	$5,500	$5,500	$5,500	$5,500	$5,500	$5,500	$5,500	$5,500
Net operating cash flow												
Taxes	$2,500			$2,500			$2,500			$2,500		
Net cash flow												
Beginning cash	$2,400											
Ending cash												

EXHIBIT 14.14

ENDLESS TREAD SHOE COMPANY: CASH BUDGET WORKSHEET

	19X5		19X6												19X7	
	Nov	*Dec*	*Jan*	*Feb*	*Mar*	*Apr*	*May*	*Jun*	*Jul*	*Aug*	*Sep*	*Oct*	*Nov*	*Dec*	*Jan*	*Feb*
Sales	$409,000	$404,910	$400,861	$396,852	$392,884	$388,955	$385,065	$381,215	$377,403	$373,629	$369,892	$366,193	$362,531	$358,906	$355,317	$351,764
Collections on sales																
35% 1st month																
65% 2nd month																
Total sales receipts																
Inventory purchases																
40% 2nd-mo. sales																
Payments																
70% 1st month																
30% 2nd month																
Total payments																

EXHIBIT 14.15

ENDLESS TREAD SHOE COMPANY: CASH BUDGET WORKSHEET

	19X6											
	Jan	*Feb*	*Mar*	*Apr*	*May*	*Jun*	*Jul*	*Aug*	*Sep*	*Oct*	*Nov*	*Dec*
Sales receipts												
Inventory payments												
Wages (42% sales)												
Other cash expenses	$65,000	$65,000	$65,000	$65,000	$65,000	$65,000	$65,000	$65,000	$65,000	$65,000	$65,000	$65,000
Net operating cash flow												
Taxes	$11,900			$11,900			$11,900			$11,900		
Net cash flow												
Beginning cash	$54,000											
Ending cash												

Cash Budget
14. Ending cash (Dec.) = −$113,193

14. Endless Tread Shoe Company faces steadily declining sales. Collections on receivables are based on prior months' sales. Inventory purchases are based on future sales, and payments are made in the months following purchases.
    a. Using Exhibits 14.16 and 14.17, prepare a 12-month cash budget for Endless Tread.
    b. Based on this 12-month cash budget, is Endless Tread Shoe Company likely to have cash balances that are either too large or too small? If so, should the company take any corrective action, such as investing surplus cash or borrowing?

Cash Budget
15. Ending cash (Dec.) = −$89,995

15. Endless Tread Shoe Company faces steadily declining sales. Collections on receivables are based on prior months' sales. Inventory purchases are based on future sales, and payments are made in the months following purchases.
    a. Using Exhibits 14.18 and 14.19, prepare a 12-month cash budget for Endless Tread.
    b. Based on this 12-month cash budget, is Endless Tread Shoe Company likely to have cash balances that are either too large or too small? If so, should the company take any corrective action, such as investing surplus cash or borrowing?

The Effect of Changing Cash Flow Estimates on Cash Balances
16. Prob. 14, labor 42% of sales
Prob. 15, inventory 42% of sales scheduling of receipts/payments

16. Each of the worksheets for Problems 13, 14, and 15 represents different estimates of collections, payments, beginning cash balances, and inventory and labor costs for the Endless Tread Shoe Company.
    a. Using the Problem 13 estimates as a baseline, what changes are represented in Problems 14 and 15? In other words, how do the estimates in Problem 14 differ from those in Problem 13 and those in Problem 15 differ from those in Problem 13?
    b. If you have the solutions to Problems 13–15, analyze how these estimated changes affect the company's cash flows and cash balances. If you do not have the solutions, how do you *think* the changing estimates would affect cash flows and balances?

Rate of Return on Marketable Securities

17. Using Equation (14.1) and the information provided for the negotiable securities in the section entitled "The Rate of Return on Marketable Securities," verify the annual returns provided for the following securities:

6-month Treasury bill	commercial paper
6-month negotiable CD	3-month Euro CD

Effective Cost of Bank Loans
18. a. $227,273
b. 10.23%

18. A company needs to borrow $200,000 for 1 year. A bank has agreed to lend the required amount at an interest rate of 9%. However, the bank requires a compensating balance of 12%. Ordinarily, the company would keep a zero balance in its checking account.
    a. How much must the company borrow to realize loan proceeds of $200,000?
    b. What is the effective cost of the loan?

EXHIBIT 14.16

ENDLESS TREAD SHOE COMPANY: CASH BUDGET WORKSHEET

	19X5 Nov	Dec	19X6 Jan	Feb	Mar	Apr	May	Jun	Jul	Aug	Sep	Oct	Nov	Dec	19X7 Jan	Feb
Sales	$409,000	$404,910	$400,861	$396,852	$392,884	$388,955	$385,065	$381,215	$377,403	$373,629	$369,892	$366,193	$362,531	$358,906	$355,317	$351,764
Collections on sales																
35% 1st month																
60% 2nd month																
Total sales receipts																
Inventory purchases																
40% 2nd-mo. sales																
Payments																
70% 1st month																
30% 2nd month																
Total payments																

EXHIBIT 14.17

ENDLESS TREAD SHOE COMPANY: CASH BUDGET WORKSHEET

	19X6 Jan	Feb	Mar	Apr	May	Jun	Jul	Aug	Sep	Oct	Nov	Dec
Sales receipts												
Inventory payments												
Wages (42% sales)												
Other cash expenses	$65,000	$65,000	$65,000	$65,000	$65,000	$65,000	$65,000	$65,000	$65,000	$65,000	$65,000	$65,000
Net operating cash flow												
Taxes	$11,900			$11,900			$11,900			$11,900		
Net cash flow												
Beginning cash	$38,000											
Ending cash												

EXHIBIT 14.18

Endless Tread Shoe Company: Cash Budget Worksheet

	19X5 Nov	Dec	19X6 Jan	Feb	Mar	Apr	May	Jun	Jul	Aug	Sep	Oct	Nov	Dec	19X7 Jan	Feb
Sales	$409,000	$404,910	$400,861	$396,852	$392,884	$388,955	$385,065	$381,215	$377,403	$373,629	$369,892	$366,193	$362,531	$358,906	$355,317	$351,764
Collections on sales																
25% 1st month																
70% 2nd month																
Total sales receipts																
Inventory purchases																
42% 2nd-mo. sales																
Payments																
80% 1st month																
20% 2nd month																
Total payments																

EXHIBIT 14.19

Endless Tread Shoe Company: Cash Budget Worksheet

	19X6 Jan	Feb	Mar	Apr	May	Jun	Jul	Aug	Sep	Oct	Nov	Dec
Sales receipts												
Inventory payments												
Wages (40% sales)												
Other cash expenses	$65,000	$65,000	$65,000	$65,000	$65,000	$65,000	$65,000	$65,000	$65,000	$65,000	$65,000	$65,000
Net operating cash flow												
Taxes	$11,900			$11,900			$11,900			$11,900		
Net cash flow												
Beginning cash	$54,000											
Ending cash												

19. A bank has agreed to lend $100,000 for 3 months (91 days) at an interest rate of 9%. However, the bank requires a compensating balance of 12%. Ordinarily, the company would keep a zero balance in its checking account.
    a. How much must the company borrow to realize loan proceeds of $100,000?
    b. What is the effective cost of the loan?

Effective Cost of Bank Loans
19. a. $113,636
b. 10.23% (Eq. 14.4)

20. A company needs to borrow $100,000 for 1 year. The bank has agreed to lend the required amount at 9%. However, the interest will be discounted from the principal amount of the loan.
    a. How much must the company borrow to realize loan proceeds of $100,000?
    b. What is the effective cost of the loan?

Effective Cost of Bank Loans
20. a. $109.890
b. 9.89%

21. A company needs to borrow $100,000 for 6 months (182 days). The bank has agreed to lend the required amount at a 5% discount for 6 months.
    a. How much must the company borrow to realize loan proceeds of $100,000?
    b. What is the effective cost of the loan?

Effective Cost of Bank Loans
21. a. $105,263
b. 11.11% (Eq. 14.5)

APPENDIX 14A

Economic Order Quantity

To calculate economic order quantity (EOQ), we must settle on a relevant time period. In this example, the time period is 1 month.

rate = the usage rate of inventory (units per month)

cost = fixed cost per order

carry = cost of carrying a unit of inventory (per month)

The simple EOQ model is

$$\text{EOQ} = \left[\frac{2(\text{rate})(\text{cost})}{\text{carry}}\right]^{1/2}$$

To see how this model is used, consider the following example:

rate = 80 units per month

cost = $4.50 per order

carry = $16.00 per month

$$\text{EOQ} = \left[\frac{2(80)(4.50)}{16.00}\right]^{1/2}$$

$$= 6.7, \text{ or } 7 \text{ units per order}$$

Because they use 80 units per month, they should order $\frac{80}{7}$ = 11 times per month, approximately. The EOQ requires a fairly constant usage rate, in this case, 80 units per month.

CHAPTER 15

Financial Analysis: Evaluation of Corporate Performance

"Well, shoot. I just can't figure it out. I'm movin' over 500 doughnuts a day, but I'm still just barely squeakin' by."

ccounting courses usually cover the calculation and interpretation of financial ratios such as the current ratio, return on equity (ROE), inventory turnover, and so on. In part, this chapter represents a review of ratio analysis, but the chapter moves well beyond these techniques. You will also become familiar with other methods for evaluating corporate performance, gain an appreciation for the complexities that confront a financial analyst, and, we hope, also gain a sense of the importance that judgment and logic play in evaluating a firm's results. Good financial analysis is like good detective work on a complex case: Seldom does a solution appear in boldface. Rather, the case is solved by evaluating pieces of evidence for clues which, through logical interpretation, eventually lead to a clear picture of what has transpired. Furthermore, understanding what *has happened* at a business can help you understand what is likely *to happen* in the future. Good analysis provides a useful tool for evaluating past performance and for planning for the future as well.

EVALUATING CORPORATE PERFORMANCE: WHO? WHY? HOW?

Is the corporation doing well? This is a difficult question. What is meant by doing well? Who is asking the question? If stockholders pose the query, then doing well probably refers to the stock's price performance. Bondholders, bankers, and other fixed claimants are more interested in the likelihood of bankruptcy. Managers are interested in keeping their jobs, improving their salaries, and enhancing their reputations. Thus, managers will judge doing well based on the incentive system upon which their performance will be rewarded.

Corporate performance is therefore defined differently depending upon who is doing the evaluation. Fixed claimants, residual claimants, and employees all have different agendas: Fixed claimants want to be paid as promised. Residual claimants want high returns in comparison to their risk exposure. Employees, such as managers, want job security and remuneration. Corporate performance for each of these groups would be defined differently, and the analysis used by each group would vary depending upon the group's agenda. How one does the analysis ultimately depends on why the analysis is being done. Why, in turn, depends upon who is asking the question, Is the corporation doing well?

In addition to financial claimants, other groups of interested parties have their own agendas. Consumers, for example, may judge a manufacturer's performance based on product reliability. A community in which a business is located may be concerned with the environmental impact of the factory's waste emissions. Such groups are referred to as **stakeholders**, because each has a stake, or interest, in some aspect of corporate performance. We will largely confine our attention to the financial stakeholders (the financial claimants)[1] and, therefore, will focus on the analysis of corporate[2] financial performance.

---

[1]Because financial claims are valued according to investors' perceptions about the firm's future prospects, all activities that can have an impact on future cash flows are of interest to the analyst. For example, unethical behavior may eventually tarnish a firm's reputation and adversely affect a company's business. *Ethics*, therefore, are an important dimension of business decision making. Ethics and its link to finance are discussed in Appendix 15A.

INFORMATION SOURCES AND THEIR CHARACTERISTICS

Like a detective, an analyst must know where to look for evidence before the clues may be evaluated. This section presents the most important sources of information generally available to the analyst.

Accounting Statements

All publicly traded firms and many privately held firms have financial statements prepared on a regular basis by an external accountant. Detailed financial data are included in the company's **annual report**, which includes the firm's **balance sheet** as of the end of its fiscal year, its **income statement**, **statement of cash flows**, and written statements by management and notes to the statement written by the firm's accountant. Large publicly traded firms also complete **10-K** reports, which are filed with the **Securities and Exchange Commission** (the **SEC**). 10-K's provide even more detailed financial data, often broken down by divisions or subsidiaries.

Firms whose statements are externally **audited** and compiled according to **generally accepted accounting principles (GAAP)** are providing independently verified information to interested parties. GAAP ensures that, to the greatest degree possible, standard methods of accounting have been consistently applied, enabling one firm's numbers to be compared to another firm's and allowing this year's results to be compared to last year's. Because of these reporting standards, accounting statements have traditionally been the foundation upon which financial analysis is built. Moreover, the auditors' statement appearing at the end of an annual report is considered to be of paramount importance to the analyst. This statement, known as an **unqualified opinion**, provides the analyst with confidence that the information is representative of the firm's activities for the period. Failure to gain an unqualified opinion (getting a **qualified opinion**) is a red flag for the analyst, signaling that something odd may be going on. What follows is an example of an unqualified auditor's opinion.

We have examined the consolidated balance sheets of the Company and Subsidiaries as of December 31, 19XX, and the related consolidated statements of income, stockholders' equity, and changes in financial position for the period. Our examinations were made in accordance with generally accepted auditing standards and, accordingly, included such tests of the accounting records and such other auditing procedures as we considered necessary in the circumstances.

In our opinion, these financial statements present fairly the consolidated financial position of the Company and Subsidiaries as of December 31, 19XX,

[2]Note that, although we focus on corporations, most of what follows applies to any business. A sole proprietorship, for example, may be thought of as a corporation with only one share of stock outstanding. Thus, much of what is said about a corporation may be said of a sole proprietorship as well.

and the consolidated results of their operations and changes in their financial position for the period in conformity with generally accepted accounting principles applied on a consistent basis.

The Accountant

There are a variety of reasons why a firm's auditor will render a qualified opinion. For example, inadequate disclosure of information leads to a qualified opinion:

The Company declined to present a statement of cash flows for the years ended December 31, 19X2 and 19X1. Presentation of such statement summarizing the Company's operating, investing, and financing activities is required by generally accepted accounting principles.

An unjustified change in accounting procedures leads to the following qualified opinion.

As disclosed in Note X to the financial statements, the Company adopted, in 19X2, the first-in, first-out method of accounting for its inventories, whereas it previously used the last-in, first-out method. Although use of the first-in, first-out method is in conformity with generally accepted accounting principles, in our opinion the Company has not provided reasonable justification for making this change, as required by generally accepted accounting principles.

Any qualified opinion is a warning sign and should make the analyst search for the cause.

Small businesses often have accounting statements prepared on an unaudited basis. **Unaudited** financial statements are compiled based on the numbers supplied to the accountant by management. Thus, if management says the firm holds a $100,000 receivable from a customer, that number is simply reported on the balance sheet without the accountant ever actually confirming that the customer owes the amount reported. Data on unaudited statements have not been independently verified. Needless to say, analysts put less faith in unaudited than audited statements.

Although reliability and comparability of audited financial statements are their strength, they do have several weaknesses. First, there is some latitude allowed by GAAP as to what method may be used in compiling data. For example, firms may choose the type of depreciation method they use for certain assets, or they may choose different methods for valuing inventory [last-in, first out (LIFO) versus first-in, first-out, (FIFO)]. Two firms, identical in all other respects, could report dramatically different results if one switched accounting methods vis-à-vis its identical twin. In Exhibit 15.1 note the radically different operating incomes; yet the cash flows from the two firms are identical.

Management also has some latitude in the timing of its expense and revenue recognition and in ordering inventory. For example, near the end of the fiscal year, management could choose to let inventory stocks run low. Doing so lowers the inventory account balance on the year-end balance sheet, inflating the in-

EXHIBIT 15.1

LIFO VERSUS FIFO

DATE	ACTIVITY	CASH FLOW
Oct. 1	Purchase 100 widgets @ $2 each	$200 outflow
Dec. 1	Purchase 100 widgets @ $3 each	$300 outflow
Dec 30	Sell 100 widgest at $6 each	$600 inflow

	FIRM A LIFO	FIRM B FIFO
Sales	$600	$600
Cost of goods sold	−300	−200
Operating income	$300	$400
Cash inflow	$600	$600
Cash outflow	−500	−500
Cash flow	$100	$100

ventory turnover ratio.[3] This strategy could cosmetically alter ratios, making them look more favorable than they actually are. The practice of manipulating accounts so they appear more favorable is known as **window dressing** by management.

A third shortcoming of accounting data is its focus on profit (and not cash flow) and on book values (and not market values). These problems have been discussed earlier in the text. In Chapter 1 we highlighted the difference between the financial balance sheet and the accounting balance sheet, and in Chapter 4 we covered the importance of cash and how accounting profits may be restated as cash flows. It is important to have a good grasp of that earlier material as you attempt to analyze financial data.

A fourth weakness is that accounting results are purely historical in nature. In many cases, good historic results do not necessarily translate into good future results. For example, large profits by a firm often invite entry into the firm's market by competitors. For planning purposes, it would be foolish to count on extraordinary profits continuing simply because they have been consistently achieved in the past. Likewise, dismal past performance does not always mean the future will also be dismal.

The last weakness of accounting data is that it reports results in a single dimension: profitability. A firm that maximizes profits (or even cash flows) without regard to risk may be unwittingly lowering shareholder's wealth. For example, a firm that chooses a strategy that will double profits may see its share price decline if the high-profit strategy actually triples investors' required returns because of the risk involved in the new venture. In terms of the value of the firm's stock, higher dividends could be offset by a higher discount rate. Thus, higher profits (better accounting-based results) do not necessarily translate into a higher stock price, which should be management's ultimate goal. Exhibit 15.2 lists accounting statements' strengths and weaknesses.

The strengths of accounting statements are their availability and conformance with rigorous standards of reporting. It is important to note that **financial analysis of foreign firms** is often confounded because many countries lack GAAP-type

[3]Inventory turnover equals sales for the year divided by the inventory balance. Lowering inventory makes the turnover ratio higher. Generally, higher turnover is preferred by analysts.

EXHIBIT 15.2

STRENGTHS AND WEAKNESSES OF ACCOUNTING STATEMENTS

Strengths

- Independently audited GAAP statements provide some assurance of reliability and comparability. Information asymmetry is lowered.
- Statements are widely available.

Weaknesses

- Differences in accounting methods may lower the comparability of results.
- Window dressing may lower the reliability of the data reported.
- Accounting statements do not focus on cash flows, nor do they report market values.
- They are purely historical in nature.
- No consideration is given to risk when accounting performance is reported.

standards of reporting. In many emerging markets, e.g., those in former communist countries, the lack of reliable and comparable accounting statements makes investment, planning, and control of operations very difficult. Thus, reliable accounting statements are critical for good analysis despite their shortcomings.

Market Data

The second important information source is market data. As its name implies, market data are those data generated in a market place. We will discuss two types: stock market performance (measured by stock returns) and product market performance (measured by market share). Because it is generated by millions of market participants, market-based data are less subject to manipulation (window dressing) by management than are accounting data. Managers have a difficult time misleading millions of investors in the stock market or millions of consumers in product markets.

Stock Returns

Early on, shareholder-wealth maximization was identified as the corporation's ultimate objective. This goal leads us directly to the necessity of evaluating share price changes or stock returns. Stock returns measure changes in shareholder wealth. Returns are available in many formats. The Center for Research in Security Prices' (CRSP) tapes offer users a data set of daily security returns decades long covering thousands of publicly traded firms. Returns may also be calculated by gathering share price and dividend information from newspapers such as the ***Wall Street Journal***. Recall that prices and dividends for any period may be converted to a periodic return using the following formula:

$$\text{periodic return} = \frac{\text{Price}_{\text{end}} - \text{Price}_{\text{begin}} + \text{Dividends paid}}{\text{Price}_{\text{begin}}}$$

Stock prices and returns are also useful to the analyst because they are forward-looking and they implicitly consider risk. Recall that two shortcomings of accounting statements are their historical nature and the fact that they don't incorporate risk. To see that stock prices (and therefore returns) do not suffer from these faults, examine the formula for stock valuation first presented in Chapter 6:

$$\text{price}_{t=0} = \sum_{t=1}^{\infty} \frac{D_t}{(1 + r)^t} = \frac{\text{dividend}_{t=1}}{r - g_n}$$

Stock prices are forward-looking because they include the present value of *future* expected dividends. Investors' required return, r, depends upon the riskiness of the firm's future cash flows, as discussed in Chapters 7 and 8. Therefore, when today's price changes, it's responding to changes in expected return requirements (which can be caused by a perceived change in risk) and to changes in expected dividends.

Stock returns have a shortcoming as well. We may observe a decline in share price, signaling poor performance, but it's impossible to know why the price declined without more information. Did price decline because the overall market declined? If so, this is outside the firm's ability to control. Or was the decline a signal of lower expected dividends and/or higher risk? Fortunately, there is a method for helping to separate the portion of a stock's return caused by a marketwide movement from the part of a stock's return with a firm-specific cause. The method is to simply subtract the market's return from the stock's return. What is left is known as the stock's **abnormal return** (AR), or **market-adjusted return**, for the period. The AR is the firm-specific part of the period's return, which has been isolated from that part of the return attributed to the general market trend. For example, let's say XYZ, Inc., had a good year last year according to its C.E.O. Its stock increased in value by 15%. Yet, you probe a bit more and find that the overall stock market[4] had a 20% return last year. XYZ's market-adjusted[5] return last year was −5% [AR = 15% − 20% = −5%]. Thus, the firm underperformed the market, and its firm-specific return was negative. Now, let's suppose the negative AR is caused by lower expected dividends. The analyst must still determine the reasons dividends are expected to decrease. Searching out these causes requires analysis of other information, including accounting-based data. Did sales decline? Did costs increase? Was there a lawsuit?

You can see, at this point, that in analysis no single source of information will provide you with all the pieces to the puzzle, yet each makes a contribution toward understanding the total picture.

Market Share

The financial balance sheet model of the corporation identifies two markets critical to the success of a business. Financial markets are the source of the external capital the corporation needs in order to fund its investment projects. Stock returns measure the success of the firm in financial markets. Product and service markets are the arenas in which the firm's products compete, and these markets provide the cash which flows back to claimants. Ultimately, the risks and returns to which claimants are exposed are determined by the success or failure of the firm's output in the product market. One method of gauging this success is through the calculation of a product's **market share**. Here the demand for the

---

[4]Of course, you will be using a proxy (such as S&P 500) for the true market, just as was done in Chapter 10.

[5]For the precision-oriented, there are also **industry-adjusted returns** and **risk-adjusted returns**. These techniques are developed in the problem set (Problem 5).

product is reflected, and product-pricing strategies, product differentiation, quality, reliability, service, delivery, brand-name recognition, and other attributes are collectively judged by consumers in comparison to competing products of other firms.

Market share is calculated by dividing the firm's product sales by the total sale of products perceived to be similar and competing for the same consumer purchases. A declining market share indicates that competitors are taking business away from the firm. Lower profits may result if sales decline, if prices are lowered in order to recapture market share, or if marketing expenses increase to promote greater demand.

Hand in hand with market share information is the size of the market. If, over time, total industry sales within a market are flat or trending downward, the company must implement a strategy that addresses the problem. Similarly a growing market calls for a plan to meet potentially high growth. Firms in shrinking markets are challenged to gain a greater share in a smaller market. Such firms may attempt to develop new products that capitalize on company strengths to replace current products that may be headed toward obsolescence. A good example is horse-drawn carriage manufacturers at the turn of the century who, seeing demand for carriages decline, entered automobile body manufacturing. In the 1990s defense contractors saw military spending severely cut back, and many sought new opportunities in other high-tech markets in which their technological expertise could be advantageously applied. Firms in growing markets tend to pay no dividends, opting instead to reinvest all their cash flows to meet consumer demand for their products.

Market size and share information are available from several sources. Government and industry publications are widely available, as are information services such as Compustat and Standard & Poor's. The potential size of a market, for example, may be determined using the *Census of Manufacturers*, published by the U.S. Department of Commerce, or a private source such as the "Survey of Buying Power," published in *Sales and Marketing Management.*

Opinions of Other Analysts

Many large firms are closely followed by securities analysts. In fact, an industry exists whose product is the publication of analysts' opinions and forecasts of firm performance. The best known of these are **Moody's**, **Standard & Poor's**, and **Value Line**. Almost any library carries one or more of these companies' publications. Another source is brokerage firms, who often make the reports of their analysts available to investors.

Moody's and Standard & Poor's are best known as bond-rating agencies. Ratings are based on the agency's opinion of the likelihood that a bond will default and on the protection afforded the claimant by the bond contract in the event that default does occur. Exhibit 15.3 shows the major rating categories used by

Transparency Available

EXHIBIT 15.3
Bond Ratings

	VERY HIGH QUALITY	HIGH QUALITY	SPECULATIVE	VERY POOR
Standard & Poor's	AAA AA	A BBB	BB B	CCC D
Moody's	Aaa Aa	A Baa	Ba B	Caa C

Transparency Available

EXHIBIT 5.4

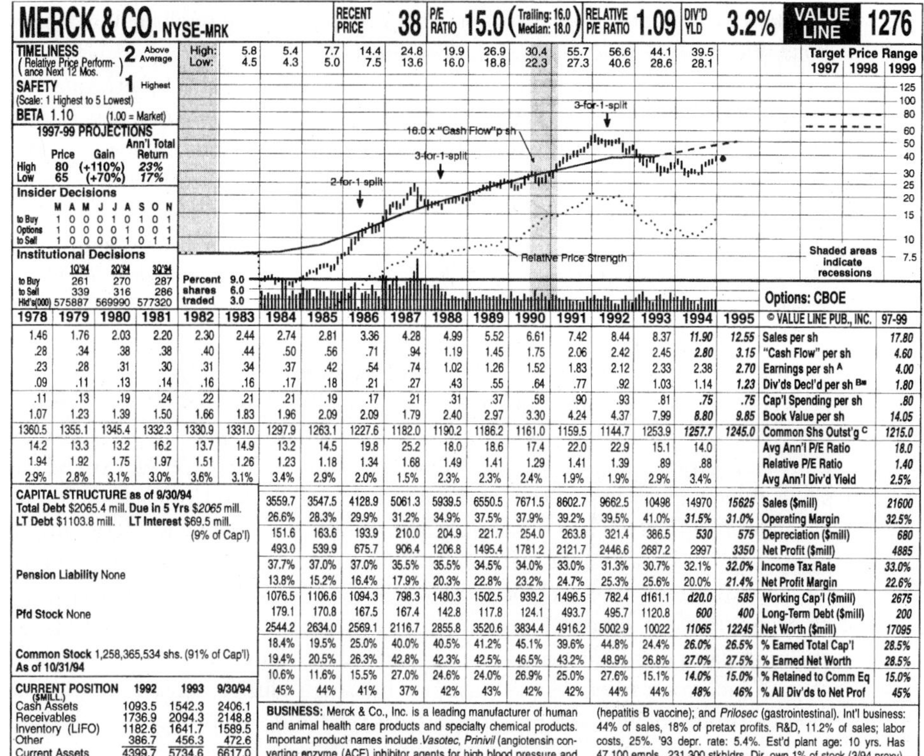

MERCK & CO. NYSE-MRK | RECENT PRICE 38 | P/E RATIO 15.0 (Trailing: 16.0 Median: 18.0) | RELATIVE P/E RATIO 1.09 | DIV'D YLD 3.2% | VALUE LINE 1276

TIMELINESS 2 Above Average (Relative Price Performance Next 12 Mos.)
SAFETY 1 Highest (Scale: 1 Highest to 5 Lowest)
BETA 1.10 (1.00 = Market)

High:	5.8	5.4	7.7	14.4	24.8	19.9	26.9	30.4	55.7	56.6	44.1	39.5
Low:	4.5	4.3	5.0	7.5	13.6	16.0	18.8	22.3	27.3	40.6	28.6	28.1

Target Price Range 1997 1998 1999

1997-99 PROJECTIONS

	Price	Gain	Ann'l Total Return
High	80	(+110%)	23%
Low	65	(+70%)	17%

Insider Decisions

	M	A	M	J	J	A	S	O	N
to Buy	1	0	0	0	1	0	1	0	1
Options	1	0	0	0	0	1	0	0	1
to Sell	1	0	0	0	0	1	0	1	1

Institutional Decisions

	1Q'94	2Q'94	3Q'94
to Buy	261	270	287
to Sell	339	316	286
Hld's(000)	575887	569990	577320

1978	1979	1980	1981	1982	1983	1984	1985	1986	1987	1988	1989	1990	1991	1992	1993	1994	1995	© VALUE LINE PUB., INC.	97-99
1.46	1.76	2.03	2.20	2.30	2.44	2.74	2.81	3.36	4.28	4.99	5.52	6.61	7.42	8.44	8.37	11.90	12.55	Sales per sh	17.80
.28	.34	.38	.38	.40	.44	.50	.56	.71	.94	1.19	1.45	1.75	2.06	2.42	2.45	2.80	3.15	"Cash Flow" per sh	4.60
.23	.28	.31	.30	.31	.34	.37	.42	.54	.74	1.02	1.26	1.52	1.83	2.12	2.33	2.38	2.70	Earnings per sh A	4.00
.09	.11	.13	.14	.16	.16	.17	.18	.21	.27	.43	.55	.64	.77	.92	1.03	1.14	1.23	Div'ds Decl'd per sh B■	1.80
.11	.13	.19	.24	.22	.21	.21	.19	.17	.21	.31	.37	.58	.90	.93	.81	.75	.75	Cap'l Spending per sh	.80
1.07	1.23	1.39	1.50	1.66	1.83	1.96	2.09	2.09	1.79	2.40	2.97	3.30	4.24	4.37	7.99	8.80	9.85	Book Value per sh	14.05
1360.5	1355.1	1345.4	1332.3	1330.9	1331.0	1297.9	1263.1	1227.6	1182.0	1190.2	1186.2	1161.0	1159.5	1144.7	1253.9	1257.7	1245.0	Common Shs Outst'g C	1215.0
14.2	13.3	13.2	16.2	13.7	14.9	13.2	14.5	19.8	25.2	18.0	18.6	17.4	22.0	22.9	15.1	14.0		Avg Ann'l P/E Ratio	18.0
1.94	1.92	1.75	1.97	1.51	1.26	1.23	1.18	1.34	1.68	1.49	1.41	1.29	1.41	1.39	.89	.88		Relative P/E Ratio	1.40
2.9%	2.8%	3.1%	3.0%	3.6%	3.1%	3.4%	2.9%	2.0%	1.5%	2.3%	2.3%	2.4%	1.9%	1.9%	2.9%	3.4%		Avg Ann'l Div'd Yield	2.5%
						3559.7	3547.5	4128.9	5061.3	5939.5	6550.5	7671.5	8602.7	9662.5	10498	14970	15625	Sales ($mill)	21600
						26.6%	28.3%	29.9%	31.2%	34.9%	37.5%	37.9%	39.2%	39.5%	41.0%	31.5%	31.0%	Operating Margin	32.5%
						151.6	163.6	193.9	210.0	204.9	221.7	254.0	263.8	321.4	386.5	530	575	Depreciation ($mill)	680
						493.0	539.9	675.7	906.4	1206.8	1495.4	1781.2	2121.7	2446.6	2687.2	2997	3350	Net Profit ($mill)	4885
						37.7%	37.0%	37.0%	35.5%	35.5%	34.5%	34.0%	33.0%	31.3%	30.7%	32.1%	32.0%	Income Tax Rate	33.0%
						13.8%	15.2%	16.4%	17.9%	20.3%	22.8%	23.2%	24.7%	25.3%	25.6%	20.0%	21.4%	Net Profit Margin	22.6%
						1076.5	1106.6	1094.3	798.3	1480.3	1502.5	939.2	1496.5	782.4	d161.1	d20.0	585	Working Cap'l ($mill)	2675
						179.1	170.8	167.5	167.4	142.8	117.8	124.1	493.7	495.7	1120.8	600	400	Long-Term Debt ($mill)	200
						2544.2	2634.0	2569.1	2116.7	2855.8	3520.6	3834.4	4916.2	5002.9	10022	11065	12245	Net Worth ($mill)	17095
						18.4%	19.5%	25.0%	40.0%	40.5%	41.2%	45.1%	39.6%	44.8%	24.4%	26.0%	26.5%	% Earned Total Cap'l	28.5%
						19.4%	20.5%	26.3%	42.8%	42.3%	42.5%	46.5%	43.2%	48.9%	26.8%	27.0%	27.5%	% Earned Net Worth	28.5%
						10.6%	11.6%	15.5%	27.0%	24.6%	24.0%	26.9%	25.0%	27.6%	15.1%	14.0%	15.0%	% Retained to Comm Eq	15.0%
						45%	44%	41%	37%	42%	43%	42%	42%	44%	44%	48%	46%	% All Div'ds to Net Prof	45%

CAPITAL STRUCTURE as of 9/30/94
Total Debt $2065.4 mill. **Due in 5 Yrs** $2065 mill.
LT Debt $1103.8 mill. **LT Interest** $69.5 mill.
(9% of Cap'l)

Pension Liability None

Pfd Stock None

Common Stock 1,258,365,534 shs. (91% of Cap'l)
As of 10/31/94

CURRENT POSITION ($MILL.)	1992	1993	9/30/94
Cash Assets	1093.5	1542.3	2406.1
Receivables	1736.9	2094.3	2148.8
Inventory (LIFO)	1182.6	1641.7	1589.5
Other	386.7	456.3	472.6
Current Assets	4399.7	5734.6	6617.0
Accts Payable	1461.9	2378.3	2485.0
Debt Due	825.2	1736.0	961.6
Other	1330.2	1781.4	2173.9
Current Liab.	3617.3	5895.7	5620.5

ANNUAL RATES of change (per sh)	Past 10 Yrs.	Past 5 Yrs.	Est'd '91-'93 to '97-'99
Sales	13.5%	14.0%	15.0%
"Cash Flow"	19.0%	19.5%	12.0%
Earnings	21.0%	22.5%	11.5%
Dividends	19.5%	24.5%	12.0%
Book Value	13.0%	21.5%	18.0%

Calendar	QUARTERLY SALES ($ mill.) Mar.31	Jun.30	Sep.30	Dec.31	Full Year
1991	2048	2124	2117	2313	8602.7
1992	2223	2374	2464	2601	9662.5
1993	2379	2575	2544	3000	10498
1994	3514	3792	3792	3872	14970
1995	3700	3925	3950	4050	15625

Calendar	EARNINGS PER SHARE A Mar.31	Jun.30	Sep.30	Dec.31	Full Year
1991	.42	.48	.48	.45	1.83
1992	.48	.56	.55	.53	2.12
1993	.54	.61	.62	.56	2.33
1994	.54	.61	.62	.61	2.38
1995	.62	.68	.70	.70	2.70

Calendar	QUARTERLY DIVIDENDS PAID B■ Mar.31	Jun.30	Sep.30	Dec.31	Full Year
1991	.187	.187	.187	.21	.77
1992	.21	.23	.23	.25	.92
1993	.25	.25	.25	.28	1.03
1994	.28	.28	.28	.30	1.14
1995	.30				

BUSINESS: Merck & Co., Inc. is a leading manufacturer of human and animal health care products and specialty chemical products. Important product names include *Vasotec*, *Prinivil* (angiotensin converting enzyme (ACE) inhibitor agents for high blood pressure and angina); *Mevacor*, *Zocor* (cholesterol-lowering agents); *Primaxin*, *Mefoxin* (antibiotics); *Pepcid* (anti-ulcer agent); *Recombivax HB* (hepatitis B vaccine); and *Prilosec* (gastrointestinal). Int'l business: 44% of sales, 18% of pretax profits. R&D, 11.2% of sales; labor costs, 25%. '93 depr. rate: 5.4%. Est'd plant age: 10 yrs. Has 47,100 empls., 231,300 stkhldrs. Dir. own 1% of stock (3/94 proxy). Chairman & C.E.O.: P.R. Vagelos. Inc.: NJ. Address.: P.O. Box 100, Whitehouse Station, NJ 08889-0100. Tel. 908-423-1000.

Merck has an impressive product portfolio. Its biggest selling drug, with sales of $2.2 billion in 1994 (up 6%), is *Vasotec*, which is also the world's leading cardiovascular medicine. The company's two other billion-dollar sellers—*Mevacor* and *Zocor*—are cholesterol-lowering agents. Their combined top-line contribution rose 18% last year (to $2.6 billion), with sales of the latter increasing a robust 39% (to $1.3 billion); we expect *Zocor* sales to remain on a steep uptrend, augmented by recent data that revealed its efficacy in reducing mortality in both cardiac and noncardiac patients. A fourth key product is *Prilosec*, which had 1994 revenues of $900 million (up 54%). Due to a November agreement with Astra, it will no longer be included in Merck's revenues, but its bottom-line significance should continue to surge, given likely new indications. Importantly, too, most of the aforementioned revenue gains are coming from volume increases—with an assist from Medco.

Merck has several drugs that could become significant contributors in the near future. Its best prospects are *Cozaar* (a new antihypertensive) and *Fosamax* (an osteoporosis medicine). The former is awaiting marketing approval from the FDA, and an application for the latter will be filed very shortly. In addition, an over-the-counter version of *Pepcid* is likely sometime this year.

We look for Merck to generate double-digit percentage share profit gains going forward. Using its ample cash flow and proceeds from recent asset sales, the drugmaker has paid off all the Medco purchase-related short- and long-term debt. As such, interest costs should be lower henceforth. Factoring in continued cost cutting, additional benefits from Medco, and an active stock buyback program, we look for share net to rise 13%, to $2.70, in 1995. Our initial estimate for '96 is $3.10 a share. (Merck recently initiated a $2 billion stock repurchase program.)

We like this top quality issue. It has good price momentum, and we look for earnings comparisons, which turned positive in 1994's final period, to remain favorable for the foreseeable future. The stock is timely for the year ahead, and we think it will also perform well out to 1997-99.

George I.H. Rho *February 3, 1995*

(A) Based on average shares outstanding. Excludes a 40¢/share charge in '92 for the adoption of three accounting changes. Excludes a nonrecurring loss in '93, 46¢. Next earnings report due late Apr. (B) Next dividend meeting about Feb. 25. Goes ex about Mar. 2. Dividend payment dates: January 2, April 2, July 2, October 1. ■ Dividend reinvestment plan available. (C) In millions, adjusted for stock splits.

Company's Financial Strength	A++
Stock's Price Stability	80
Price Growth Persistence	80
Earnings Predictability	95

Factual material is obtained from sources believed to be reliable, but the publisher is not responsible for any errors or omissions contained herein. For the confidential use of subscribers. Reprinting, copying, and distribution by permission only. Copyright 1995 by Value Line Publishing, Inc. ® Reg. TM—Value Line, Inc.

To subscribe call 1-800-833-0046.

these two agencies, along with their meanings. Naturally, the higher the rating, the lower will be investors' required return on the bonds and the lower will be the cost of debt for the company. AAA or Aaa bonds, for example, will have lower yields to maturity than BB or Ba bonds. Ratings are published in *Moody's Bond Guide* and *Standard & Poor's Bond Guide*.

Value Line Investment Survey analyzes more than 1,500 stocks. Equities are rated for future price appreciation potential (timeliness) and relative riskiness (safety), and Value Line provides explicit estimates of future dividends, dividend growth, sales, and earnings, among other forecasts. Stocks are categorized by industry, and the publication includes some discussion of each firm's prospects and challenges as well as brief industry analysis. Value Line also provides some historical data and calculates several ratios. Exhibit 15.4 is Value Line's analysis of Merck, a major pharmaceutical manufacturer.

We must keep in mind that if markets are efficient, the information included in reports, such as Moody's or Value Line's, is already included in the market price of the firm's bonds and stock. Additionally, these ratings and opinions represent those of only one or of a small handful of analysts. However, when one is analyzing the financial performance of a firm, these sources provide useful data about the company in question and the industry of interest. Moreover, opinions of other analysts serve as a benchmark with which your own conclusions may be compared. To be sure, management of companies whose securities are followed by Moody's, Standard & Poor's, or Value Line pay attention to these widely read opinions of their companies. Finally, there are other rating agencies that specialize in particular industries. For example, A. M. Best ranks the financial safety of insurance companies. Major brokerage houses produce company and industry reports, which include analysts' forecasts and recommendations.

Comparative Data

Suppose your employer's sales increased 10% last year. Is this unexpectedly high or disappointing? To answer that question you must compare the result to (1) historical results, (2) the results of your competitors, and (3) your firm's targeted sales. Historical results are readily available by looking at prior years' annual reports. In fact, annual reports include data from several years for just this purpose. If, in the last 5 years, sales had increased by a minimum of 15% per year, then a 10% increase for this year could be disappointing. On the other hand, if 10% were the largest increase in a decade, then it might indicate outstanding performance. The historical record provides the analyst with a clue.

Look for comparable firms that are competitors in the same product market. Ideally, comparables would be about the same size and have the same product mix as the firm you're analyzing. If comparable firms had increases that averaged 20%, your firm's 10% increase might look rather dismal. Of course, if comparables showed no sales growth, then your firm looks like a superstar.

You may have difficulty locating comparables. Diversified firms may not fit neatly into an industry classification. You may think, for example, that Coca Cola and Pepsi Cola are natural comparables; yet, if you investigate, you will find that Pepsi owns Pizza Hut, Frito Lay, Kentucky Fried Chicken, and Taco Bell. In fact only one-third of Pepsico's sales are from soft drinks, compared to Coke's

87% (1993 data). Thus, they are not as comparable as common knowledge suggests.

For firms that do fit into an industry classification, there are publications that produce industry average ratios[6] for comparison purposes. Among the most widely available industry averages are those published by **Dun & Bradstreet**, **Robert Morris**, and the annual surveys appearing in **Forbes** and **Business Week**. Value Line, as previously mentioned, classifies firms by industry and can be another useful source for comparables' data.

The Press

When analyzing quantitative data like ratios and growth rates, there is the danger that performance will be evaluated, understood, and explained using numbers alone. This level of analysis is not "understanding," nor is it "explaining" performance. For instance, a conclusion that share price declined because earnings were lower is not very useful information. If we take the quantitative analysis a step further and discover that earnings were lower because sales were down, then we've added to our knowledge but have not really reached the level of understanding that is useful for decision making. What a manager or a claimant needs to know is why sales were down. Did the company lose market share because a competitor introduced a superior product? Did competitors lowered their prices? Were sales down because the overall market shrank? Perhaps there was a recession last year, causing consumers to cut back their overall purchases. Maybe adverse press surrounded the product, causing the decline. Sales can decline because of internal problems at the company. A strike may have hurt production, or perhaps a key salesperson retired. There are a myriad of possibilities, and it is the analyst's job to find the correct one. Ratios are useful because they raise red flags in certain areas, allowing analysts to focus their attention in the correct places.

The point is that an analyst must look beyond the numbers. We have already mentioned two sources of information that are not quantitative in nature: the discussions included in annual reports and those published in analysts opinions such as Value Line. The press offers a wealth of similar information. The *Wall Street Journal*, *Barrons'*, *Business Week*, *Forbes*, and *Fortune* are just a few of the outlets of information devoted to business and economics. Most libraries carry the ***Reader's Guide to Business Periodicals*** as well as the ***Wall Street Journal Index*** and ***Barron's Index*** in their reference sections. Here an analyst can refer to articles about the company, about the industry, or discussing economic trends that may help in truly understanding and explaining a firm's performance. On-line information services, such as the Dow-Jones News Retrieval System, are becoming widely available and are closely scrutinized by professional analysts.

---

[6]A problem with published ratios is that there is no standard method for calculating them. For example, the debt ratio is sometimes found by dividing total debt by total assets. The same ratio is calculated by others as long-term debt divided by total long-term capital. These will yield different answers, so it is important that your calculations conform to those in the publication you're using to find industry norms.

FINANCIAL STATEMENT ANALYSIS

Exhibit 15.5 shows 1992, 1993, and 1994 income statements for Shingard, Inc., a manufacturer of plastic shin guards used primarily by soccer players. Exhibit 15.6 shows the firm's balance sheet for the same years. These two exhibits provide the information we will use to demonstrate techniques used to analyze financial statements.

Trend Statements

Trend statements are used to uncover evidence of patterns in the data. They are constructed by taking a beginning year's account balance as the "benchmark" year. Each account for all subsequent years is then divided by the benchmark year's balance. Thus, all accounts are reexpressed in a trend statement as a multiple of the beginning year's balance. Following are the balances of the revenue and cost of goods sold (COGS) accounts for Shingard and their trend statement values.

DOLLAR VALUES	1992	1993	1994
Revenue	52,846	50,280	57,394
Calculating the trend values	$\frac{52,846}{52,846}$	$\frac{50,280}{52,846}$	$\frac{57,394}{52,846}$
Trend values	1.000	0.951	1.086

DOLLAR VALUES	1992	1993	1994
COGS	$23,781	$23,632	$29,271
Calculating trend values	$\frac{23,781}{23,781}$	$\frac{23,632}{23,781}$	$\frac{29,271}{23,781}$
Trend values	1.000	0.994	1.231

Transparency Available

Exhibit 15.7 shows abbreviated trend income and balance sheets for Shingard. The most striking features of the trend statements for Shingard are as follows:

EXHIBIT 15.5

SHINGARD, INC.
INCOME STATEMENTS
1992–1994 (IN 000S)

	1992	1993	1994
Revenue	$52,846	$50,280	$57,394
Cost of goods sold (COGS)	−23,781	−23,632	−29,271
Selling, general, & administrative expense (SG&A)	−15,569	−14,050	−13,035
Depreciation	−3,250	−3,250	−3,250
Earnings before interest and taxes (EBIT)	$10,246	$ 9,348	$11,838
Interest expense	−1,830	−1,642	−1,701
Earnings before taxes (EBT)	$ 8,416	$ 7,706	$10,137
Taxes (34%)	−2,861	−2,620	−3,447
Net income (N.I.)	$ 5,555	$ 5,086	$ 6,690
Dividends	$ 2,000	$ 2,000	$ 2,500
Retained earnings	$ 3,555	$ 3,086	$ 4,190

EXHIBIT 15.6

SHINGARD, INC.
BALANCE SHEETS
DECEMBER 31: 1992, 1993, AND 1994
(IN 000S)

Assets	1992	1993	1994
Cash	$ 270	$ 148	$ 172
Marketable securities (Mkt. Sec.)	30	30	30
Accounts receivable (A/R)	2,490	2,723	2,909
Inventory (INV)	11,743	17,357	16,800
Total current assets (C.A.)	$14,533	$20,258	$19,911
Equipment and buildings	27,400	27,400	27,400
Less accumulated depreciation	− 8,310	−11,560	−14,810
Net equipment and buildings	$19,090	$15,840	$12,590
Land	259	259	259
Total fixed assets (F.A.)	$19,349	$16,099	$12,849
Total assets (T.A.)	$33,882	$36,357	$32,760
Liabilities and owner's equity	1992	1993	1994
Accounts payable (A/P)	$ 984	$ 1,112	$ 1,092
Wages payable (W/P)	229	250	273
Notes payable (N/P)	1,500	1,740	1,350
Total current liabilities (C.L.)	$ 2,713	$ 3,102	$ 2,715
Long-term debt (L.T.D.)	$18,000	$17,000	$ 9,600
Common stock (par value $0.10)	20	20	20
Paid-in surplus of par	1,000	1,000	1,000
Retained earnings	12,149	15,235	19,425
Total equity (T.E.)	$13,169	$16,255	$20,445
Total liabilities and owner's equity	$33,882	$36,357	$32,760

Transparency Available

(1) Net income was down in 1993 and made a dramatic recovery in 1994; (2) total assets were actually smaller at the end of 1994 than they were at the end of 1992; and (3) total equity was more than 50% higher in 1994 than 1992. Closer investigation of the trend statements and the underlying accounting statements reveals that net income was down in 1993 because of lower sales. 1994's recovery was driven by higher sales and control of SG&A expenses. The latter factor was vital, beacuse it offset higher COGS in the same year. Total assets declined slightly as depreciation expense outstripped the increase in current asset accounts. And the total equity increase was fueled by 1994's outstanding earnings, which led to a large increase in retained earnings. This internal capital replaced external long-term debt in the firm's capital structure.

EXHIBIT 15.7

SHINGARD, INC.
TREND INCOME STATEMENT AND BALANCE SHEET
SELECTED ACCOUNTS: 1992–1994

Trend Income Statement	1992	1993	1994
Revenue	1.000	.951	1.086
Cost of goods sold	1.000	.994	1.231
Selling, general, and administrative	1.000	.902	.837
Net income	1.000	.916	1.204
Trend Balance Sheet	1992	1993	1994
Inventory	1.000	1.478	1.431
Current assets	1.000	1.394	1.370
Net equipment and buildings	1.000	.830	.660
Total assets	1.000	1.073	.967
Current liabilities	1.000	1.143	1.001
Long-term debt	1.000	.944	.533
Total equity	1.000	1.234	1.553

Transparency Available

It is apparent from the trend statements that something unusual took place in 1994. Sales and profits were up dramatically. Remember that numbers do not explain things; they simply provide clues. If we were to investigate further by carefully reading 1994's annual report or perhaps some industry literature for that year, we would discover that the World Cup for Soccer was held in the United States in 1994. It is natural that the interest created in the sport might be a factor stimulating the soccer equipment market. Here we've come closer to explaining 1994's outstanding results, but keep in mind it was the trend statement that highlighted that year's dramatic turnaround, putting us on the correct investigative path.

Common Size Statements

Common size statements allow the analyst to compare the relative composition of the company's accounts over time. Each year's common size income statement is found by dividing each account by that year's revenue. Common size balance sheets are constructed by dividing each account by that year's total assets. For example, the common size COGS account for 1993 is $23,632 ÷ $50,280 = 0.470, and the common size INV account for 1993 is 0.477. Exhibit 15.8 shows abbreviated common size income and balance sheet statements.

Focusing our attention on the contrast between the common size statements of 1992 and 1994, there are two glaring changes. First, COGS sharply increased as a proportion of revenue, whereas selling, general, and administrative expense (SG&A) decreased. To explain this we would need to decompose COGS: Was the increase due to labor costs or raw materials? If labor caused the increase, was the rise due to a renegotiated union contract? Or, perhaps was management paying overtime to meet 1994's increased demand (rather than hiring more employees)? Again, as analysts we need to look beyond the numbers. The decrease in selling, general, and administrative expense may be an intentional cost-cutting act on management's part as a response to the increased COGS. Perhaps management canceled an advertising campaign, cut the excess expenses in the central office, or began to pay salespeople on salary rather than by commission. We would

Transparency Available

EXHIBIT 15.8

SHINGARD, INC.
COMMON SIZE INCOME STATEMENT AND BALANCE SHEET SELECTED ACCOUNTS: 1992–1994 (IN 000S)

Common Size Income Statement	1992	1993	1994
Revenue	1.000	1.000	1.000
COGS	0.450	0.470	0.510
SG&A	0.295	0.279	0.227
EBIT	0.194	0.186	0.206
EBT	0.159	0.153	0.177
NI	0.105	0.101	0.117
Common Size Balance Sheet	**1992**	**1993**	**1994**
Total Assets	1.000	1.000	1.000
INV	0.347	0.477	0.513
C.A.	0.429	0.557	0.608
F.A.	0.571	0.443	0.392
C.L.	0.080	0.085	0.083
L.T.D.	0.531	0.468	0.293
T.E.	0.389	0.447	0.624

need to look beyond the accounting numbers to find how and why SG&A declined.

The second dramatic change takes place in the common size balance sheet long-term debt and total equity accounts. Clearly, retained earnings have been used to pay down debt balances. Thus, Shingard is using less financial leverage. However, there is a troubling aspect to this use of retained earnings: Recall that, from the trend balance sheet, total assets were shrinking over the period. Thus, management has apparently chosen to pay off debt rather than reinvest in new equipment or other assets. This policy could lead to trouble in the future if the equipment begins to break down. A second concern is the signaling content of lower leverage (recall Chapter 12). Perhaps shareholders will believe that management is concerned that the firm's future cash flows cannot support the previous level of debt. If you, for example, served on Shingard's board of directors, you would require some explanation convincing you that paying off debt is wise policy.

Ratio Analysis

Exhibit 15.10, beginning on p. 506, shows the most common **financial ratios** calculated from Shingard's 1994 accounting statements. We will not burden you with in-depth coverage of ratios' mechanics. Like the skilled detective who leaves the DNA testing to the crime lab, we will leave the calculation of ratios to the calculator. You should, however, carefully review Exhibit 15.10, paying particular attention to each ratio's calculation and how the calculation relates to the ratio's use.

What we are most interested in is understanding what clues to look for, where to look for them, and how to interpret them once they're found. Forgive us for one more analogy: A school for detectives cannot cover all possible crimes, nor can it review all potential pieces of evidence. Rather, the detective's school tries to cover some major types of crime in the hope that the ability to analyze one case will carry over to other new and different cases. In that spirit, we present some events that commonly occur in business and analyze how these events are manifested in the firm's ratios.

Case A: Increasing Leverage and ROE

Suppose a corporation decides to raise capital by borrowing. Will its decision to "lever-up" have a positive or a negative impact on the firm's ROE? The answer is that it depends on the interest charged by the lender and the firm's earning power (EP = EBIT/total assets). If the firm's earning power is less than the interest rate, then ROE will fall, and vice versa.

If EP > *i*, ROE increases with leverage.
If EP < *i*, ROE decreases with leverage.

This is the result first presented in Chapter 12, now expressed using ratios. Exhibit 15.9 shows two firms of equal size, with equal debt ratios, being charged the same interest rate, but with drastically different earning power. Note what happens to their respective ROE's as their debt ratios change.

EXHIBIT 15.9

ILLUSTRATION OF EARNING POWER, LEVERAGE, AND ROE

Transparency Available

	FIRM A FAVORABLE FINANCIAL LEVERAGE		FIRM B UNFAVORABLE FINANCIAL LEVERAGE	
	Before	*After*	*Before*	*After*
Debt	500	1,000	500	1,000
Equity	500	500	500	500
Total assets	1,000	1,500	1,000	1,500
Debt/total assets	0.50	0.67	0.50	0.67
EP%	20%	20%	9%	9%
EBIT	200	300	90	135
INT (10%)	−50	−100	−50	−100
EBT	150	200	40	35
Tax (40%)	−60	−80	−16	−14
NI	90	120	24	21
ROE%	18%	24%	4.8%	4.2%

Case B: Increasing Competition at Apple Computer

On June 1, 1993, Apple Computer's stock closed at $57 per share. By the end of that month, Apple's stock was down by nearly 33%. In July the stock had fallen to just over $27 per share as the firm posted its first quarterly loss in 2 years. Why? The answer is competition.

The PC price wars of the early 1990s affected not only IBM, but also Apple as the bargain-priced IBM clones attracted business away from the premium-priced Apple machines. To fight losing market share to low-priced competition, Apple cut the prices on its Macintosh computers. Unfortunately, the company could not find cost-cutting measures to counteract the financial effect of lower sales prices. Consequently, the firm's gross margin declined, leading to a lower bottom line.

Astute shareholders had the opportunity to avoid the negative returns by anticipating Apple's precipitous drop. On Apple's March 26, 1993, quarterly report (which was public information by the beginning of May), the firm's gross margin was showing signs of trouble.

The tumble in gross profit margin, coupled with industry information one could easily gather, led toward the conclusion that PC price wars would take a big bite from Apple profits.[7]

APPLE COMPUTER (IN MILLIONS)

	QUARTER ENDED	
	March 26, 1993	*March 27, 1992*
Net sales	$1,974	$1,716
COGS	1,213	960.5
Gross profit	$ 761	$ 755.5
Gross profit margin	$\frac{\$761}{\$1,974} = 0.386$	$\frac{\$755.5}{\$1,716} = 0.440$

[7]What does this suggest about market efficiency? Be careful as you consider this question, because there is a chance that Apple could have responded more successfully to price wars. Remember that we are viewing this after the fact, and hindsight is perfect!

Gross margins are a good indicator of corporate health. Competition, as in Apple's case, can force a firm to cut its product's sales price. Only cutting expenses or higher volume can make up for lower sales prices. The problem is that expenses can't arbitrarily be lowered. Another factor that might impact margins is the firm's product mix. A restaurant that introduces a very low margin, but popular, menu item may find sales going up, gross margins going down, and profits declining, if it cuts into sales of other items.

Case C: Bad Product Decisions at Merry-Go-Round Enterprises

In the spring of 1993, Merry-Go-Round Enterprises' stock was selling for $17 per share. The clothing store chain, which catered to younger customers, had just announced its acquisition of Chess King, a clothing rival. Analysts on Wall Street liked the merger and had just raised earnings estimates. Within 1 year, however, Merry-Go-Round was in bankruptcy and the stock was trading at $3 per share. All this was foreshadowed in the firm's accounting statements. The January 30, 1993, balance sheet showed inventories had increased 37% from 12 months earlier, whereas sales had grown by only 15%. By the next quarter, the inventory problem was acute. Inventory had now increased by 48%, but sales were up only 8.5%. A trend of widening gap between the growth rate of inventory and the growth rate of sales was indicating the retailer's goods were simply not selling. Unpopular inventory can be sold, but it may require a drastic reduction in sales price, which could lead, once again, to lower margins and earnings.

Case D: Just-in-Time Inventory

Just-in-time inventory systems are meant to deliver inventory directly to the assembly line as needed rather than being stockpiled in a warehouse, as is traditional. Thus, materials are delivered just in time for their use in the manufacturing process. This is a very efficient system. Less capital is invested in inventory, freeing the cash for other projects or uses. Furthermore, less warehouse space is needed to stockpile inventory, and less labor is required to store the inventory and retrieve it when it is needed. Considering these characteristics of just-in-time, let's see what efficiency ratios would be impacted if a manufacturer successfully initiates such an inventory system. **Inventory turnover** would certainly increase, because less inventory would need to be kept on hand. Asset turnover increases as total assets decline, because of lower inventory and lower warehouse requirements.

If just-in-time inventory would improve these efficiency ratios, why don't all manufacturers adopt the system? The answers in financial analysis don't all come from the accounting numbers. The downside of a just-in-time system is its risk. The manufacturing firm becomes ultradependent on its supplier and on its own ability to correctly gauge and time demand for the finished product. It may be that for some firms the risks associated with the just-in-time system outweigh the benefits.

Now let's consider a firm that has difficulties with its new just-in-time system. If the supplier cannot meet delivery schedules or if the manufacturer has difficulty gauging its own material requirements, then it is likely that production schedules

EXHIBIT 15.10

FINANCIAL RATIOS FOR SHINGARD, INC. 1994

(a) *Debt ratios* measure the firm's ability to meet principal and interest payments over the long term.

RATIO / FORMULA	USE
1. Debt ratio $= \dfrac{\text{long-term debt}}{\text{total long-term capital}} = \dfrac{9{,}600}{30{,}045} = 0.32$	Measures the proportion of capital supplied by creditors.
2. Leverage ratio (LEV) $= \dfrac{\text{total assets}}{\text{total equity}} = \dfrac{32{,}760}{20{,}445} = 1.60$	Measures how many dollars of assets the firm utilizes for each dollar of contributed equity.
3. Times interest earned ratio $= \dfrac{\text{EBIT}}{\text{interest (dollars)}} = \dfrac{11{,}838}{1{,}701} = 6.96$	Measures the ability to make interest payments.

(b) *Liquidity ratios* measure the firm's ability to meet its maturing obligations and unexpected cash needs over the short term.

RATIO / FORMULA	USE
1. Current ratio $= \dfrac{\text{current assets}}{\text{current liabilities}} = \dfrac{19{,}911}{2{,}715} = 7.33$	Measures short-term debt-paying capacity.
2. Quick ratio (acid test) $= \dfrac{\text{current assets} - \text{inventory}}{\text{current liabilities}} = \dfrac{3{,}111}{2{,}715} = 1.15$	Measures immediate short-term liquidity.

(c) *Profitability ratios* measure the income or operating success of the entreprise.

RATIO / FORMULA	USE
1. Net profit margin $= \dfrac{\text{net income}}{\text{revenue}} = \dfrac{6{,}690}{57{,}394} = 0.117$	Measures earnings generated per dollar of sales.
2. Return on assets (ROA) $= \dfrac{\text{net income}}{\text{total assets}} = \dfrac{6{,}690}{32{,}760} = 0.204$	Measures the profitability of the use to which assets are being put.
3. Return on equity (ROE) $= \dfrac{\text{net income}}{\text{total equity}} = \dfrac{6{,}690}{20{,}445} = 0.327$	Measures the profits accruing to shareholders per dollar of contributed equity.
4. Gross profit margin $= \dfrac{\text{revenue} - \text{COGS}}{\text{revenue}} = \dfrac{28{,}123}{57{,}394} = 0.490$	Measures product pricing in comparison with its basic cost.
5. Earning power $= \dfrac{\text{EBIT}}{\text{total assets}} = \dfrac{11{,}838}{32{,}760} = 0.361$	Measures the profitability of the firm's assets independent of leverage and tax effects.

(d) *Efficiency ratios* measure the effectiveness and intensity of the firm's management of its resources.

RATIO / FORMULA	USE
1. Inventory turnover $= \dfrac{\text{cost of goods sold}}{\text{inventory}} = \dfrac{29{,}271}{16{,}800} = 1.742$	Measures the liquidity and control of inventory.
2. Days sales outstanding $= \dfrac{\text{receivables}}{\text{annual revenue/360}} = \dfrac{2{,}909}{159.43} = 18.25$ days	Measures the liquidity and control of receivables.
3. Asset turnover $= \dfrac{\text{revenues}}{\text{total assets}} = \dfrac{57{,}394}{32{,}760} = 1.752$	Measures sales generated per dollar of assets.

(e) *Per-share measures* express key financial variables on a per-share-of-stock basis.

RATIO / FORMULA	USE
1. Earnings per share (EPS) $= \dfrac{\text{net income}}{\text{no. of shares}^{1}} = \dfrac{\$6{,}690{,}000}{200{,}000} = \$33.45$	Expresses profits on a per-share basis.
2. Book value per share (BVPS) $= \dfrac{\text{total equity}}{\text{no. of shares}} = \dfrac{\$12{,}849{,}000}{200{,}000} = \$64.25$	Expresses the capital contributed by shareholders on a per-share basis.[2]
3. Dividend per share (DPS) $= \dfrac{\text{total dividends}}{\text{no. of shares}} = \dfrac{2{,}500{,}000}{200{,}000} = \$12.50$	Measures amount paid as dividends to each share of stock.

(f) *Measures of relative value*

RATIO	FORMULA	USE
1. Price-earnings ratio (P/E)	$= \frac{\text{price per share}^3}{\text{EPS}} = \frac{\$234.15}{\$33.45} = 7$	Expresses stock value as multiple of last year's earnings.
2. Price-to-book (P/B)	$= \frac{\text{price per share}}{\text{book value share}} = \frac{\$234.15}{\$64.25} = 3.64$	Expresses stock price as a multiple of equity holders' historical contributions to capital.

[1]Number of shares is found by dividing the common stock account by the par value per share, less any repurchased treasury stock. Because Shingard has no treasury stock, its shares outstanding are $20,000/$0.10 = 200,000 shares.

[2]Keep in mind that retained earnings represents capital contributed by shareholders (rather than being paid out as dividends)

[3]Current market price is found in the stock quotes in the newspaper. For Shingard, we'll assume the price per share was $234.15 on the date of these calculations.

cannot be met. Chances are that sales will be lost and some raw materials will need to be rushed to the assembly line at a high cost in order to meet promised delivery dates. So, although the inventory turnover ratio may be improved, it is also likely that sales will decline and profit margins will shrink.

Transparency Available

These brief cases are meant to illustrate how the actions of a business may manifest themselves in financial statements and ratios. As was pointed out earlier, there are endless possibilities, making an exhaustive study of ratio analysis impossible. However, it is a good habit when reading the business news to imagine some of the possible financial ramifications of the newsworthy event. Doing so will aide you in becoming an astute and sophisticated analyst.

SUMMARY

Financial analysis is one of the most important tools available to a firm's managers, potential investors, bankers considering lending the corporation funds, suppliers who may offer the firm trade credit, new graduates interviewing with a corporation, sales personnel identifying their target market, and a number of others who have some interest in a firm's financial performance. This chapter has introduced several sources of information useful to the financial analyst and has provided an overview of the mechanics of financial statement analysis. Most importantly, the chapter has illustrated how analysis can help lead the analyst toward the issues that may explain a company's performance and are key to the firm's future success.

Thus far in the book, consideration has been given to how firms make decisions about what projects they should pursue in order to increase the wealth of owners. Similar consideration was given to the factors that should influence a firm's choice of financing alternatives and dividend payment policy. To aid in making these decisions, concepts such as market risk and the time value of money have been introduced, along with tools such as the mathematics of discounting. Some theories, such as the CAPM, were also discussed. Chapter 15 covered information sources and techniques that will be useful in evaluating how effectively the firm is utilizing the tools, theories, and concepts discussed earlier in the book. The next chapter covers a specific type of decision, restructuring, which involves a dramatic change in the entire company. It is a good example of how financial decision makers can bring together much of the material covered in this course as they make strategic choices.

KEY TERMS

stakeholders
annual report
10-K
Securities and Exchange Commission (SEC)
balance sheet
income statement
statement of cash flows
audited
unaudited
generally accepted accounting principles (GAAP)
unqualified opinion
qualified opinion
window dressing
financial analysis of foreign firms
abnormal return
market adjusted return
industry-adjusted return
risk-adjusted return
market share
Moody's
Standard & Poor's
Value Line
A.M. Best
Dun & Bradstreet
Robert Morris
Wall Street Journal
Forbes
Business Week
Reader's Guide to Business Periodicals
Wall Street Journal Index
Barrons' Index
trend statement
common size statement
financial ratios
just-in-time inventory
debt ratio

leverge ratio
times interest earned
quick ratio
acid test
current ratio
net profit margin
return on assets
return on equity
gross profit margin
earning power
inventory turnover
days sales outstanding
earnings per share
book value per share
dividend per share
price earnings ratio
price-to-book
ethics

QUESTIONS

1. We classified inventory turnover as an efficiency ratio. In what other classification category do you think it could belong? Why?
2. Under what condition will financial leverage increase ROE?
3. Under what circumstances do you think the current ratio and quick ratio would give opposite signals of the liquidity of a firm?
4. Industry averages are often used as benchmarks in ratio analysis. Justify this practice.
5. Why is interest expense for a bank similar to cost of goods sold for a manufacturer?
6. How do you think the average leverage ratio in the banking industry would compare to the average leverage ratio among computer manufacturers?
7. Go to the library and copy the pages for banking and computer makers from an industry averges source book (e.g., Robert Morris). How do these averages compare to your intuitive answer for Question 6?
8. Find an accounting book or another finance text that covers ratio analysis. Identify a ratio that is calculated differently in our book than it is in the other book. Discuss the difference in the formulas.
9. Identify the three ratios from Exhibit 15.10 that you feel are most important for
   a. Performance analysis by stockholders
   b. Performance analysis by bondholders
   Justify your choices.
10. **a.** If a box of chocolates made by Firm A costs $30 and a box made by Firm B costs $10, then which chocolates are most expensive? Now, consider that firm A's box holds 5 pounds of chocolates and firm B's box holds 1 pound of chocolates. Whose chocolates are most expensive given this new information? Why would consumers pay more per pound for B's chocolates?
    b. Let's say that one share of Acme's stock is selling for $250 and one share of Zeta's stock is selling for $15. Whose stock is more expensive? Consider that EPS for Acme was $100 last year and EPS for Zeta was $1. What are the P/E for Acme and the P/E for Zeta? Now which stock do you think is more expensive? Why do you think Zeta may have a higher P/E than Acme?
    c. Is there some similarity between the story of the relative price of chocolates and the relative price of the stock? Explain.

11. Suppose your father owns a stock that he feels has done very well. "In fact," he says, "it went up 18% last year!" Do you think that 18% was good performance? How would you go about deciding whether 18% was good, bad, or mediocre for the past 12 months?
12. A corporation has decided to change its depreciation method to write off assets over a longer term. Thus, each year depreciation expense will be significantly lower, although nothing else about the business will be materially different. What do you think will happen to the firm's financial results because of this change? (*Hint:* Consider changes in depreciation expense, net income, net profit margin, ROE, ROA, and any others you wish to comment on.) What happens to cash flow because of this change?
13. Artistic Designs, Inc., has a current ratio of 3.0. What will be the impact on the current ratio if the company
    a. Uses cash to pay off some current debt
    b. Uses cash to repurchase some outstanding shares of stock
    c. Uses cash to pay a dividend
    d. Borrows cash from a local bank to purchase a company-owned automobile (The loan is short-term, due in 6 months.)
    e. Borrows short term and uses the funds to increase inventory.
14. Adelle Jones, the treasurer at Acme Industries, notices that the firm keeps several million dollars in marketable securities invested in very short term treasury securities. Maturities are from 1 week to 3 weeks. Adelle notices that by investing in longer-term government securities, the company can earn, on average, one full percentage point more income on the marketable securities account balance. Let's assume that Adelle implements her strategy and invests in government bonds with 10-year maturities.
    a. Consider what would happen if market interest rates suddenly rise (remember the teeter-totter of bond values from Chapter 6).
    b. Let's say that interest rates don't rise immediately, and the long-term bonds do raise income. What impact will Adelle's decision have on ROE?
    c. What impact will Adelle's decision have on the riskiness of the firm?
    d. If stockholders knew of Adelle's action, what impact do you think it would have on their valuation of the firm?
15. Honest John's Used Cars began an advertising campaign stating, "We'll sell you a car. We'll finance it. And we won't check your credit." John's car lot went crazy with business. John knew he was taking some big risks lending money to anybody, but he reasoned that he could increase his sales prices to improve his margins and pay for the inevitable bad debt losses. Explain what you think will happen to Honest John's asset turnover, inventory turnover, and days sales outstanding. Explain your reasoning. What do you think will happen to Honest John's net income?
16. Borrowers pay thousands of dollars to have their bond issue rated by Standard & Poors or Moody's. Why would borrowers pay so much for these analysts' opinions and their publication? (*Hint:* Why might investing in having your bonds rated be a positive NPV project?)
17. Some businesspeople have advocated gaining market share as a good indicator of firm performance. What's your opinion of this idea? (*Hint:* How could a company easily increase its market share, perhaps to 100? Would this tactic be good business?)

18. Care must be taken to ensure that the beginning year used as a benchmark for constructing a trend statement is a representative year. If, for example, the benchmark year had unusually good sales and profits, what will be the impact on subsequent years in the trend statement?

DEMONSTRATION PROBLEMS

For Demonstration Problems 1, 2, and 3, refer to the following financial statements.

EVERGREEN TIMBER, INC. INCOME STATEMENT

Sales	$3,000,000
COGS	750,000
Gross p.	$2,250,000
SG&A exp.	1,000,000
Depreciation	250,000
EBIT	$1,000,000
Interest	360,000
EBT	$ 640,000
Tax (20%)	128,000
Net inc.	$ 512,000

12/31/XX BALANCE SHEET

Cash	$ 150,000
A/R	200,000
Inventory	100,000
Tot. C assets	$ 450,000
Net F assets	13,200,000
Total assets	$13,650,000
C liabilities	$ 600,000
Debt (12%)	3,000,000
Equity	10,050,000
Total L & E	$13,650,000

shares outstanding: 1,000,000

current price per share: $21.50

1. Calculate the following ratios for Evergreen Timber:

Earning power	Gross profit margin
Inventory turnover	Return on assets
Quick ratio	Current ratio
EPS	Days sales outstanding
P/E ratio	Price-to-book

SOLUTION

earning power = 7.3%	gross profit margin = 0.75
inventory turn = 7.5	return on assets = 3.75%
quick ratio = 0.583	current ratio = 0.75
EPS = $0.51	days sales out = 24 days
P/E ratio = 42	price-to-book = 2.14

2. Evergreen offers purchasers of its timber products terms of net 30, meaning the buyers have 30 days to pay the net amount of the bill. Does Evergreen seem to be having any difficulty collecting its receivables?

SOLUTION

There appears to be no problem with bad debts, because the days sales outstanding ratio of 24 days is less than the firm's 30-day payment policy.

3. Does the use of leverage appear to be enhancing Evergreen's return to its stockholders (review Chapter 12)?

SOLUTION

Recall that leverage will magnify return on equity if the interest rate is less than the firm's earning power. Evergreen's earning power is 7.3%, which is less than the interest rate on the firm's debt, 12%. Thus, for Evergreen, leverage is currently lowering ROE.

PROBLEMS

1. 1994 trend sales = 1.41; 1994 common size NI = 0.04

1. Compute common size and trend statements for the following income statements.

	(IN $000,000S)			
	1991	*1992*	*1993*	*1994*
Sales	393.9	431.2	458.1	556.0
COGS	336.7	365.6	390.1	483.3
Interest	4.1	4.3	3.0	2.7
NI	17.2	19.1	21.3	24.7

2. Lower interest expense

2. In Problem 1, what was the most important factor in the improvement in profit margins from 1991 to 1994?

3. NPM = 2.7%, 2.6%; ROA = 7.7%, 3.6%; ATO = 2.83X, 1.37X

3. Following are abbreviated financial statements for Flour Corporation. Given this information, compute the financial ratios given in Exhibit 15.10 for Flour for 1980 and 1981. Analyze Flour's profitability.

	(IN $000,000S) 1980	1981
Revenues	4,826	6,073
COGS	−4,557	−5,698
SG&A	−45	−42
INT	20	−44
Taxes	−112	−130
NI	132	159
EPS	2.73	2.83
Cash	217	187
A/R	242	497
INV	466	672
Other CA	32	64
Total CA	956	1,420

	1980	1981
Net fixed assets	601	2,504
Other fixed assets	148	503
Total assets	1,705	4,427
CL	775	1,255
LTD	378	1,484
TE	552	1,688
	1,705	4,427

4. In the library look up Flour in the 1980 and 1981 *Wall Street Journal Index* or *Reader's Guide to Business Periodicals*. What happened between 1980 and 1981?

4. A major acquisition

5. **a.** Let's say that Public Service of Colorado stock was up 12% last year. The S&P 500 was up 15% last year. What was Public Service's firm-specific return after adjustment for marketwide movements?

   b. Another way to isolate firm-specific stock returns is to adjust for overall industry performance. If, for example, an index of utility company stocks was up 10%, then did Public Service outperform, underperform, or just stay even with the industry?

   c. The most sophisticated way to isolate firm-specific stock performance is via risk-adjusted returns. This method explicitly accounts for the firm's risk by incorporating beta in the analysis. Recall that beta measures the stock's sensitivity to market movements, thus measuring the firm's systematic or market risk. If Public Service's beta was 0.80, then we would expect its stock to return 80% of the market return. Given Public Service's beta of 0.8 and the S&P 500's return of 15%, what return would you expect for Public Service? Because Public Service's actual return was 12%, did the company have a positive risk-adjusted return, a negative risk-adjusted return, or a risk-adjusted return equal to zero?

   d. Considering market-adjusted performance described in part (a), do you think Public Services' CEO deserves a bonus? Considering industry-

5. a. −3%
b. Outperformed by 2%
c. 0%
d. No; yes; no
e. Bad; −4%

adjusted performance described in part (b), do you think the CEO should get a bonus? How about a bonus based on part (c), the risk-adjusted return? Which method do you think is the most meaningful way of isolating firm performance? Why?

e. After doing this problem, return to Question 11 and answer it again, assuming your father's stock had a beta of 1.6 and the S&P return was 14%.

6. $345,200

6. A firm has sales of $3 million per year, all of which are credit sales. Its average collection period is 42 days. What is the average balance in accounts receivable?

7. 18.8

7. Total interest expense at a business was $30,000 per year. Sales were $4,000,000 and profit margin was 8%. If the business' tax rate was 40%, then what was the firm's times interest earned ratio?

8. 13.2%

8. A firm's net profit margin is 12% and its asset turnover is 1.1. What is the firm's ROA?

9. 7.5%

9. Half a firm's capital, based on book values, comes from equity. This firm's ROE is 15%. What is its ROA?

10. 2.0

10. A firm's inventory equals its total current liabilities. The company's quick ratio equals 1. What does its current ratio equal?

11. 4.65, down from 7.33

11. Suppose in 1995 Shingard's current assets increased by $2,000,000 from 1994's level. Current liabilities also increased by $2,000,000. What is Shingard's 1995 current ratio if all other accounts were unchanged? Did the current ratio increase, decrease, or stay the same compared to the prior year? (Refer to Exhibit 15.6)

12. CA = 1.51; CL = 1.74

12. Referring to Problem 11 and the trend statement from Exhibit 15.6, calculate the 1995 trend values for Shingard's current asset and current liability accounts. Why was the change so much more dramatic for the current liability account's trend compared to the change in current assets?

13. a. $37.50
b. 17.1 times

13. A firm's sales were $25,000,000. Its net profit margin was 7%, and there are 800,000 shares of common stock outstanding. The company's leverage ratio is 2.0. Its assets total $20,000,000. The company's price-to-book is 3.

a. What is the price per share of the corporation's stock?

b. What is its P/E multiple?

For Problems 14 through 18, refer to the financial statements given in the demonstration problems for this chapter and reproduced here.

EVERGREEN TIMBER, INC. INCOME STATEMENT

Sales	$3,000,000
COGS	750,000
Gross p.	$2,250,000
SG&A exp.	1,000,000
Depreciation	250,000
EBIT	$1,000,000
Interest	360,000
EBT	$ 640,000
Tax (20%)	128,000
Net inc.	$ 512,000

12/31/XX BALANCE SHEET

Cash	$ 150,000
A/R	200,000
Inventory	100,000
Tot. C assets	$ 450,000
Net F assets	13,200,000
Total assets	$13,650,000
C liabilities	$ 600,000
Debt (12%)	3,000,000
Equity	10,050,000
Total L & E	$13,650,000

share outstanding: 1,000,000

current price per share: $21.50

14. Calculate the following ratios for Evergreen. (Evergreen's financial statements are given here and are the same as those used in the demonstration problem.)

Net profit margin	Leverage ratio
Return on equity	Asset turnover
Times interest earned	

14. NPM = 0.171; ROE = 0.051; ATO = 0.220; LEV = 1.35

15. Multiply together the leverage ratio, net profit margin, and asset turnover ratio found in Problem 14 and compare the product to ROE.

15. same as ROE

16. Prove, using algebra and the definitions of the ratios, that the result found in Problem 15 is always the case.

16. (TA/E)(NI/S)(S/TA) = (NI/E) = ROE

17. Following are the industry average ratios for Evergreen (the fine hardwood timber plantations).

17. Low ATO, low ROE

net profit margin = 15%

ROE = 16%

times interest earned = 8 times

leverage = 1.55

current ratio = 1.7

quick ratio = .52

asset turnover = .70

Compare these ratios with those found for Evergreen in Problem 15 and in Demonstration Problem 1. Comment. Do you think that Evergreen is well managed based on what you can observe in this brief analysis?

18. Now, suppose you have just learned that the bulk of Evergreen's assets are growing hardwood trees. Evergreen's trees are, on average, the optimal growing age, adding about 23% to their marketable board feet each year. Does that change what you said in Problem 17? Why or why not?

18. Growing trees offer better return.

APPENDIX 15A

Ethics and Firm Value

The financial balance sheet lists the values of tangible corporate assets such as land, cash, factories, and equipment, and it values intangible assets such as brand name recognition and the firm's reputation. A reputation for ethical behavior can be one of the most valuable intangible assets of a business enterprise. Ethical behavior is doing what's "good", or "the right thing," according to one's value system.

Ethical behavior can add to corporate value in several ways. First, a firm whose word can be relied upon can operate at a lower cost than firms whose integrity is in question. This is because it's much less expensive to do business based on an *implicit contract* (on one's word) than on an *explicit contract* (a formal contract). To see this, imagine you're purchasing an expensive pedigree dog. Doing business with a breeder you trust may simply involve the breeder's promise to stand behind the dog, and the deal is sealed with a handshake. On the other hand, dealing with a breeder with whom you are unfamiliar may involve the expense of having a vet check to certify the puppy's health and perhaps a written agreement regarding the purchaser's rights should a genetic defect be discovered at a later date. The cost of the vet check and the contract will lower the profit to the breeder (even if the customer pays for the vet, this cost will lower the price they would otherwise be willing to pay for the dog).

A second way in which ethics can enhance value is via increased revenue. Again, in the breeder example, if a kennel has a bad ethical reputation, it is doubtful that customers will patronize the breeder even *with* an explicit contract. Firms also attempt to distinguish their ethics in an effort to appeal to a market segment that prefers to do business with companies whose values match their own. Ben & Jerry's Ice Cream has been successful by doing the right thing according to a social mission. Note that their ice cream may be judged just equal to, say, Baskin-Robbins' by some consumers, but a certain clientele will prefer to purchase Ben & Jerry's product because this market segment gains satisfaction from supporting the social mission of the firm. Ben & Jerry's sales will be enhanced if the clientele attracted by the prospect of supporting the firm's mission outweighs those potential customers who are lost because they disagree with the firm's social objectives.

Questions

1. Why do companies advertise that they have "been in business since 1958" (for a long time)?
2. Look up Ben & Jerry's social mission. Then research the social causes of the Coors family (of beer fame). Do you think these two businesses are likely to share values as to what is the "right thing" in all cases? How could each one's comformance to its values enhance company value? How could they detract from value?
3. At the library or in Value Line find the price of Manville's stock in 1968 and the price in 1988. What happened?

CHAPTER 16

Corporate Restructuring: An Application of Financial Tools

"Have a seat, chief—While you were out the company was restructured."

Sometimes shareholder wealth maximization requires restructuring the entire corporation—i.e., making major changes in the company's organization, the businesses it pursues, and even who controls the company's assets. This chapter discusses such corporate **restructuring**. Corporate restructuring refers to mergers, takeovers, divestitures, and going-private transactions, all of which involve a change in who controls a company's assets.[1] In a takeover, a new management team acquires control of the target company's assets. When a corporation sells, or divests, a subsidiary, it relinquishes control of those assets. Thus, another way of thinking about corporate restructurings is as a market for the control of corporate assets. Many financial economists refer to restructurings as being the outcome of activity in the **market for corporate control**. We will use both of these terms, *corporate restructuring* and the *market for corporate control*, when referring to merger, acquisition, and divestiture transactions.

We play to the greed, power, pride, wealth, changing fortunes, and cunning of some of these transactions.

As preparation ask students to look through the *Wall Street Journal* for restructuring examples and the associated stock price changes.

We examine restructurings because of their magnitude and impact on corporations as well as to demonstrate how corporations actually use the various financial tools and concepts introduced in earlier chapters. We also see how corporations evolve to exploit emerging opportunities or solve existing problems. For example, takeovers and divestitures help shift corporate assets from industries and markets in decline to those on the rise and from inefficient to more efficient managers. Thus, corporate restructurings play an important role in assuring that our economy remains competitive and that assets are put to their most highly valued use.

Stress that mergers are generally friendly, but tender offer acquisitions can be quite hostile. At times the hostility may simply be a bluff to get a higher price.

Corporate restructurings include the merger of two corporations, the acquisition of one company by another, the sale or purchase of business units, and changes in the organizational form of business enterprises. Examples of restructurings abound. During just 3 days in July 1994, Eli Lilly acquired PCS Health Systems for $4 billion; the shareholders of UAL (the parent of United Airlines) approved an employee buyout of the firm in exchange for wage and benefit concessions; CBS (Columbia Broadcasting System) and QVC (a home shopping network) agreed to merge, but the deal fell apart when Comcast bid for QVC; AT&T neared completion of its purchase of McCaw Cellular for $12.6 billion; Parker & Parsley Petroleum won a bidding war for Australia's Bridge Oil Limited; and Great Southern Corporation, Britain's largest provider of funeral and cemetery services, announced it would fight a takeover bid from Service Corporation International, a large U.S. funeral home company. These were just some of the transactions reported over a fairly typical 3-day period.

In fact, most transactions are the friendly sale or purchase of relatively small business units or subsidiaries. These transactions receive very little press.

Restructuring transactions involve enormous amounts of money; $1 billion deals are commonplace. Exhibit 16.1 shows the number of merger and acquisition transactions (limited to transactions of more than $5 million involving at least one U.S. company), the aggregate value of those transactions, the average value of transactions, and the number of transactions valued at more than $1 billion.

[1]As with many terms in business, restructuring sometimes is used in contexts other than mergers, acquisitions, and changes in organizational form. For example, negotiating modifications in the terms of a company's loans is often referred to as *debt restructuring*, and layoffs and plant closings are sometimes considered to be part of a company's restructuring efforts. Here we apply the term narrowly to mergers, takeovers, acquisitions, divestitures, and changes in organizational form, which have traditionally been of interest to corporate finance specialists.

EXHIBIT 16.1

U.S. MERGER AND ACQUISITION ACTIVITY FROM 1984–93, INCLUDING MERGERS, ACQUISITIONS, DIVESTITURES, AND GOING-PRIVATE TRANSACTIONS VALUED AT $5 MILLION OR MORE AND INVOLVING AT LEAST ONE U.S. COMPANY

YEAR	NUMBER OF TRANSACTIONS	AGGREGATE VALUE IN BILLIONS OF DOLLARS	AVERAGE VALUE IN MILLIONS OF DOLLARS	NUMBER OF TRANSACTIONS OVER $1 BILLION
1984	2255	152.3	67.5	19
1985	1728	148.4	85.9	26
1986	2521	220.1	87.3	34
1987	2513	194.8	77.5	30
1988	3008	271.5	90.3	42
1989	3798	311.0	81.9	33
1990	4287	200.4	46.7	32
1991	3513	138.3	39.4	19
1992	3678	124.8	33.9	17
1993	3930	168.7	42.9	17

SOURCE: *Mergers and Acquisitions* (May/June 1994)

15 LARGE RESTRUCTURING TRANSACTIONS FROM THE LAST DECADE

BUYER	ACQUISITION	TYPE OF TRANSACTION AND YEAR	AMOUNT (BILLIONS OF DOLLARS)
Kohlberg, Kravis & Roberts	RJR Nabisco Inc.	MBO, 1989	$30.6
Time Inc.	Warner Communications Inc.	Acquisition, 1990	14.1
Phillip Morris Inc.	Kraft Inc.	Acquisition, 1988	13.4
Chevron	Gulf Oil	Merger, 1984	13.3
Texaco	Getty Oil	Merger, 1984	12.1
Bristol-Myers Co.	Squibb Corp.	Merger, 1989	10.1
AT&T Co.	NCR Corp.	Acquisition, 1991	7.9
General Electric	RCA	Merger, 1986	6.4
Management Group	Beatrice Foods	LBO, 1986	6.2
Merck & Co.	Medco Containment Svcs.	Acquisition, 1993	6.1
BankAmerica Corp.	Security Pacific Corp.	Acquisition, 1992	4.3
General Electric	Montgomery Ward	Divestiture, 1988	2.8

SOURCE: Various business publications, various years.

Some of the largest transactions involving U.S. companies are also listed. In 1993 there were almost 16 transactions per working day (based on about 250 trading days on the NYSE).

More important than the number of dollars involved, however, is the impact these transactions have on the future of the participating companies and their shareholders, employees, customers, and competitors. When AT&T finally acquires McCaw, its entry into cellular phones will make it a much different company than it was in 1993. The CBS and QVC merger would have given CBS a new CEO, Barry Diller, and the UAL employee buyout will change the cost structure of United Airlines flights as well as the incentives of the company's employees. Even failed transactions can affect companies. Service Corporation's

EXHIBIT 16.2

A LEXICON OF TAKEOVER DEFENSES

- **Antitakeover Charter Amendments:** A variety of amendments to the corporate charters can help fend off unwanted takeovers. Changing the corporate charter requires shareholder approval. A few examples of antitakeover amendments include:
  1. **Supermajority voting:** Requires more than the usual 50% of votes to approve a takeover. Supermajorities have been set at 65%, 70%, and even 90%. If managers hold much stock, a high supermajority level can make it impossible for a bidder to gain approval of a takeover without the managers' approval.
  2. **Staggered board elections:** Boards are divided into classes and one class is elected each year. Usually companies have three classes, so even with all the votes, a bidder must wait 2 years before gaining control of the board.
  3. **Fair price provisions:** Assure that all shareholders receive the same price for their shares in a takeover. This provision arose to combat two-tiered tender offers in which the first 51% of shares received a high price and the remaining shares a below market value price. The two-tiered bid strategy played on the fear of shareholders, forcing them to tender their shares quickly or risk receiving the lower price.
- **Crown Jewels:** These are particularly attractive assets of a takeover target that are sold to make the company less attractive, thereby reducing the likelihood of being acquired. Without its most outstanding assets the resulting firm may also be much less valuable to shareholders. The crown jewel defense becomes particularly problematic if the assets sell for a low price in order to facilitate a quick transaction. In such cases, managers save their jobs, but shareholders experience a reduction in their wealth. Such actions by managers completely contradict their fiduciary responsibility as agents of shareholders.
- **Golden Parachutes:** Some corporate executives have very generous severance packages that apply only if the executive loses his or her position due to a takeover. An executive of a target company fired during the acquisition makes a very soft landing due to the severance pay, thereby the name golden parachute. Although sometimes thought to be a takeover defense, golden parachutes reduce the incentives of managers to fight takeovers, because the ramifications of job loss are reduced when a golden parachute is in place.
- **Greenmail (targeted repurchase transactions):** Greenmail transactions occur when a hostile takeover threatens the ouster of incumbent managers. The company purchases the block of stock held by the potential acquirers and usually receives a *standstill* agreement that prevents the investors from attempting another takeover in the next few years. The repurchase price of the block is at a premium to share price (or the purchase price the acquiring group paid), so it results in a significant profit for the bidding investors. No other shareholders are allowed to participate in the repurchase, thereby the name targeted repurchase. An example of such a transaction occurred when the board of directors of Walt Disney Productions offered the takeover group headed by Saul Steinberg \$300 million, which was \$32 million more than the group paid for the stock a short time before, for the group's block of 11% of the outstanding Disney shares.* Disney also paid Steinberg's group \$28 million for "out-of-pocket" costs. When investors learned that the takeover would not occur, Disney's stock price immediately dropped. In Disney's case, this event spurred management to make some drastic changes that eventually returned the company to profitability. One suspects that without the takeover attempt those changes might never have occurred.

profits go directly to shareholders (called *unitholders* in MLPs), where investors pay tax on the profits received. Managers operate a set of existing assets but rarely retain funds to invest in growth. Often MLPs contain natural-resource assets such as a paper company's forest lands or an oil company's petroleum reserves. MLPs also hold specific assets or activities of some companies. For example, a number of research-and-development MLPs exist. Companies want to separate the risk

- **Leveraged Recapitalizations and Leveraged Cash-outs:** Sometimes a company's high cash reserves and/or low debt attracts bidders. The bidder can use the cash or the debt capacity to reduce the cost of the takeover; that is, the target firm's assets help pay for the takeover. Low-debt/high-cash firms reduce the likelihood of being targeted by increasing debt levels and paying shareholders a huge cash dividend. Sometimes companies use the proceeds from the debt issue to repurchase shares at a premium of current share price. Unlike most takeover defenses, leveraged recapitalizations and leveraged cash-outs result in an increase in shareholder wealth. The company distributes cash and makes better use of a resource—cash or debt capacity.
- **Pac-Man Defense:** An early video game had a character that swallowed nearly everything it came into contact with. The Pac-Man takeover defense involves a targeted company making a bid for the bidder. The most famous Pac-Man defense occurred in 1982 when Bendix and Martin Marietta made offers for one another. In the end, a weakened Bendix was acquired by Allied Corporation.
- **Poison Pills (Shareholder Rights Plan):** Many types of poison pills exist. They are new securities issued by the company and distributed in the form of *rights* (thereby the name shareholder rights plans) to existing shareholders. The characteristic common to all these securities is that when a bidder accumulates a predetermined percentage of the target's stock (the trigger level), something happens that will make completing the takeover very expensive for the bidder. To proceed with the takeover means swallowing the poison pill or financial suicide for the bidder. Most often triggering the right requires the company to repurchase the right from shareholders at a very high price. Poison pills always include an escape clause, so managers could, in theory, allow a takeover to proceed without the right being triggered.
- **Scorched Earth:** This maneuver involves changing the company to make it an unattractive takeover target. Adding large amounts of debt to the company's capital structure, selling profitable assets, and buying unprofitable assets are all approaches that managers have taken to stave off takeovers. Sadly, these machinations often result in a much weaker and less profitable company, so shareholders' wealth falls while managers protect their jobs.
- **Shark Repellents:** Shark repellents refer to any efforts by a target firm to defend against a hostile takeover attempt.
- **White Knights:** Managers of some targeted firms feel so strongly that they do not want to be acquired by a particular investor or investment group that they find an alternative acquirer; that is, they identify a bidder by whom they would prefer to be acquired and approach them about making a bid. One of the earliest white knights was Chevron. In 1984, T. Boone Pickens and his investment group tried to buy Gulf Oil. The managers of Gulf were adamant about not allowing Pickens to own the company, so they convinced Chevron to "rescue" them from the Pickens investment group.

*For a more in-depth look at Disney during this period, see *Storming the Magic Kingdom* by John Taylor (New York: Ballantine Books, 1987).

of their research efforts from the rest of the company and use the MLP for this separation. These transactions occur only occasionally, but they point out how corporate managers and their financial advisors constantly look for better ways to organize a company's activities.[4]

[4]For a more in depth discussion of MLPs and royalty trusts see "Royalty Trusts, Master Partnerships and Other Organizational Means of 'Unfirming' the Firm" by John Kensinger and John Martin, *Midland Corporate Finance Journal* (Summer 1986) and their companion piece "An Economic Analysis of R&D Limited Partnerships," *Midland Corporate Finance Journal* (Winter 1986).

Lessons from the History of the Market for Corporate Control

Restructurings often represent a major change in a company's direction and prospects, so they often arise from significant forces for change. Restructuring's historical record shows that as market forces, investor concerns, laws, and tax codes change, the dominant type of restructuring transaction also changes. We cannot view restructurings as an event unique to a specific company, somehow separate from larger economic and technological trends. Rather, we should recognize restructurings as a response to changing markets, the changing perceptions of investors, and changing opportunities. The recent history of corporate restructurings provides some insights into how corporations have responded to changes in market forces and may suggest how they will respond to future changes. Moreover, examining distinct periods in the evolution of the market for corporate control demonstrates some of the many reasons that companies have chosen to restructure. As we progress through our historical overview, we will discuss the reasons underlying the type and magnitude of restructuring events in each era.

The 1960s: Synergistic Mergers

Recent events provide a narrow set of economic circumstances from which to draw examples. History shows how agents react to a variety of different economic conditions.

Restructurings have been occurring for hundreds of years. In the United States some of our largest companies, such as Exxon and USX (U.S. Steel), arose from the acquisition and consolidation of many smaller firms. We will not go back that far to begin our overview of the market for corporate control. We begin in the 1960s, when most of the significant restructuring events were friendly mergers. Members of one company's board negotiated with the directors of the other company. When the two teams of directors reached a satisfactory agreement, they would recommend that their respective shareholders approve the transaction. In the 1960s shareholders were generally passive in corporate matters, so they only rarely challenged the recommendation of the board.

Value Line lists the many product lines of diversified firms. It may be useful for students to look up a company's Value Line sheet and find this information.

During the late 1960s and 1970s a wave of mergers and acquisitions occurred that created a number of **diversified conglomerates**. These corporations, such as Textron, Dial Corporation, TRW, United Technologies, and ITT, entered a wide range of industries by acquiring existing companies in those industries.[5] For example, Textron manufactures helicopters, aircraft and automobile parts, turbine engines, and various consumer products and is active in consumer lending and insurance. During this period the stock market loved conglomerates. Investors recognized that firms participating in an array of markets or holding a diversified portfolio of businesses would have relatively stable earnings, because poor earnings in one market were offset by higher earnings in another. Moreover, economies of scale from centralizing routine organizational tasks, such as payroll, accounting, and cash management, generated savings that translated into profits.

[5]In a number of cases companies diversified in order to reduce dependence on their core business area. Thus, we see many conglomerates emerge from the inherently uncertain defense industry or from industries tied to exhaustible resources such as petroleum or forest products.

The search for *synergistic mergers*, combinations in which the value of the whole exceeded the value of the sum of the parts, became the restructuring rage.[6] Business parodies joked that mergers would end only when a single, enormous corporation owned everything.

Synergistic gains motivated many transactions during the era of friendly mergers. **Synergy** implies that the combination of firms itself creates value. Gains from synergy can arise from a variety of sources. One of the most commonly stated reasons for mergers and acquisitions in the 1960s was that synergistic gains arose from the risk reduction produced by diversification. Recall that as risk decreases, the discount rate investors apply to future cash flows also decreases. A lower discount rate implies a higher present value, all else equal, so diversifying mergers created gains through risk reduction. Many companies used this rationale to explain their acquisition activities. But investors quickly realized that by buying and selling stock, they could diversify their portfolios much more thoroughly and at lower cost than a company could via acquisitions. Moreover, owning shares in a diversified company forced investors to own the company's mix of industry exposure, which may not fit the risk preferences of all—or even most—investors. Gains from pure diversifying mergers were illusory at best.[7]

A rationale for mergers that we do not discuss is the P/E effect.

If diversification does not explain mergers, why did so many smart executives spend time and money on these transactions? Very likely, the successful mergers and acquisitions of the 1960s relied on other sources of synergy to generate benefits. A few of the possible sources of gains include the following.

Increasing Market Power

Early mergers often saw companies in similar business lines join forces. Economists label such combinations *horizontal* mergers. Antitrust legislation prevents such combinations from resulting in monopolistic **market power** that creates the ability to raise prices indiscriminately. Nonetheless, larger firms may obtain some gains from their improved ability to negotiate with suppliers.

Growth for growth's sake is never a sufficient reason for a merger or acquisition. Nonetheless, there have almost certainly been acquisitions completed solely for this reason. Managers have incentives to run larger companies. CEO compensation plans often relate salary to the size or growth rate of the company. The pride and prestige of managing a larger company may also affect some acquisition decisions. Managers who increase firm size to realize personal gains almost always harm shareholders. When expansion increases shareholder wealth, those gains probably arise from economies of scope and scale, which we discuss next, rather than sheer size.

---

[6]Synergy refers to combinations that produce some type of extra benefits; i.e., synergies exist when combining two companies creates a single company with a higher value than the sum of the values of the two companies when operated separately.

[7]Academic research is accumulating showing that diversified firms actually sell for less than an identical set of companies operated individually. Evidence of this result, as well as a discussion of its causes, is presented in "Diversification's Effect on Firm Value," by Philip G. Berger and Eli Ofek, *Journal of Financial Economics* Vol. 37, No. 1, January 1995, pp. 39–65.

Economies of Scale

When companies merge, eliminating duplicated business functions can produce cost savings. If the total cost of performing a task increases more slowly than changes in volume, then the production cost per unit falls. Economists call this condition decreasing average costs, or **economies of scale**. The costs of many business tasks, such as almost any computer-related task, behave this way. For example, suppose a grocery store chain in the Midwest has 4,000 employees. If it acquires a grocery food chain in the Southeast with 3,000 employees, it might consolidate all payroll, insurance, and benefits programs at a single office. It does not cost much more to print 7,000 paychecks a week than the original 4,000. Once a computer system is up and running, the marginal cost of printing an additional paycheck is very low. The major cost is setting up the system initially. Economies of scale most often exist when a large investment is required to initiate an activity. The more units over which the initial investment can be spread, the lower the per unit cost. Economies of scale explain some of the benefits associated with diversifying mergers.

Exploiting an Expertise (Economies of Scope)

Some mergers and acquisitions arise from **economies of scope**. Economies of scope arise when a company applies the same skill to a variety of products. For example, suppose that a company has a special skill in distributing items to drug stores. Currently the company manufactures and distributes only vitamins and diet supplements. The company might consider adding to the lines of goods it distributes to further exploit its distribution expertise. Adding product lines adds very little to the company's cost structure but increases its sales and profit potential. Thus, the firm might search for an acquisition candidate that would allow it to make fuller use of its distribution channels. Firms that can identify and exploit their special skills can earn profits that increase shareholders' wealth.

Vertical Integration

Vertically integrated companies own several links in the entire production and sales chain. An example of **vertical integration** is an oil refining company that invests in oil reserves (the input to production) and gas stations (the retail distribution channel). Vertical integration assures a supply of inputs or outlets and can help protect a company's proprietary information.[8]

Surprisingly, little evidence exists supporting the value of vertical integration. Possibly the costs of vertical integration offset any gains from risk reduction. Integration requires companies to enter markets or industries in which managers may have little expertise. By integrating the production and sales activities, a company may miss important signals from suppliers or customers. For example,

[8]In some instances specifying the type of inputs needed from suppliers requires that a company divulge information it would prefer to keep secret. Also, simple information about quantities ordered and preferred dates of arrival can be valuable to competitors. Keeping such information in house eliminates concerns about information leakage.

suppose an automobile manufacturer acquires a car-rental company to assure an outlet for a portion of its production.[9] If consumers dislike a particular car model, sales figures may not show their displeasure because a certain level of sales are guaranteed. Rather than quickly responding to consumer preferences, the company may continue producing the car with its undesirable features because sales have not fallen sufficiently to alert them to the problem.

Vertically integrated companies may lose the benefits of economies of scale. If the division that supplies a company's inputs is not large enough to produce at the lowest cost volume, the cost of inputs produced internally may be higher than those purchased from optimally sized independent producers. The value of following a strategy of vertical integration depends on the frequency and cost of input shortages or the lack of outlets, and these benefits must be large enough to offset the various costs of integration.

During the 1960s and early 1970s many companies restructured to exploit economies of scale or scope. Such investments increased profits by decreasing costs or increasing revenues. Most restructurings were friendly, with corporate boards agreeing on the nature of the merger before announcing the proposal to shareholders. Although diversification was offered as the rationale for many combinations, in retrospect it probably contributed very little of benefit to these transactions.

The Late 1970s and 1980s: Competition, Hostile Takeovers, and Junk Bonds

Times and management theories change. In the late 1970s and 1980s several coincidental events brought about a dramatic change in managers' and investors' attitudes about the organization of corporations and, thereby, the type of restructuring transactions that would increase shareholder wealth. Global competition increasingly affected U.S. corporations during this period. Increased competition requires companies to become more efficient. Some firms respond to this call for increased efficiency by shedding subsidiaries and focusing on business areas in which they have substantial expertise. Others simply continue with business as usual.

During the 1980s, investors and the managers of competing companies quickly identified corporations that were not responding to this new level of competition. As the stock price of a noncompetitive company fell, it became an ideal target for acquisition. The incumbent managers of these unresponsive companies rarely agreed to a friendly merger, recognizing that there was little room for them in the successor firm. For a time the rules of civilized conduct applied, and spurned suitors left the targeted companies in peace. Eventually, however, the desire to acquire and reorganize inefficiently managed companies (and the potential profits from doing so successfully) overcame these conventional rules of business behavior. When the boards of the bidding and target companies could not negotiate a merger or when the target company's managers simply refused to consider any type of combination, bidders began to make offers directly to shareholders. *Tender*

[9]Presumably Ford invested in Hertz for this reason.

offers always include a premium over the target company's pre-offer stock price, and payment could be in cash, stock, or a combination of cash and securities. Tender offers give shareholders the opportunity to decide whether or not they want incumbent managers to continue running the company. Tender offers also show shareholders the value other, presumably highly informed, investors place on the company. These transactions differ from typically friendly mergers and are usually distinguished from mergers by denoting them as *hostile takeovers*, or *hostile tender offers*.

The emergence of hostile tender offers as a restructuring tool changed the U.S. business landscape. Suddenly inefficiently operated midsized and small corporations became the takeover targets of larger, acquisitive, bidders. To managers of targeted firms, the threat of being taken over was serious. Almost certainly inefficient managers would be replaced.[10] Besides losing their salary and perquisites, the fired managers might have a difficult time finding a comparable job, having already been identified as inefficient managers in one company. Some managers responded by trying to improve their companies' performance. Others looked to lawyers and investment bankers to design takeover defenses for them. Some managers did both.

The 1980s were an extraordinary era in U.S. financial history.[11] As the pace of restructuring quickened, multibillion dollar takeovers regularly appeared as front-page news. Potential targets, with expensive legal help, designed takeover defenses, which, whether effective or not, brought a new vocabulary to corporate finance—poison pills, crown jewels, scorched earth, the Pac-Man defense, shark repellents, greenmail, golden parachutes, and white knights.[12] In some cases the defensive maneuvers of potential targets required taking steps that increased corporate performance and, thereby, shareholder wealth; the threat of takeover was sufficient to cause managers to make decisions that increased shareholder wealth.

One of the most common strategies for improving performance was the sale of underperforming divisions. Such divestitures undid some of the diversifying mergers of the 1960s and 1970s. But this corrective mechanism affected only a subset of corporations. Very large companies and those in which managers owned a significant stake of stock (usually a 25% to 30% block gave effective control) felt little threat from hostile takeovers. The inability of another corporation or an investor group to raise enough money to finance a tender offer made large corporations immune. A large manager-owner stockholding meant a bidder would have a very difficult (or expensive) time acquiring a controlling interest

[10]Interesting evidence on poor managers losing their positions and good managers surviving is provided by Albert A. Cannella, Jr., Donald R. Fraser, and D. Scott Lee, "Firm Failure and Managerial Labor Markets: Evidence from Texas Banking," *Journal of Financial Economics* Vol. 38, No. 2, June 1995, pp. 185–210.

[11]Michael Jensen suggests that this period represents a new industrial revolution. Technological change has been so dramatic and competition has increased so much that fundamental changes were required in U.S. industry. A number of industries had excess capacity and so needed to contract. Takeovers, particularly hostile takeovers, helped industries shrink when internal incentives to contract failed. For his entire argument, see "The Modern Industrial Revolution, Exit, and the Failure of Internal Control Systems," *Journal of Applied Corporate Finance* (Winter 1994).

[12]These takeover defenses are described in Exhibit 16.2.

in the firm. As the 1980s progressed, changes in financial markets would solve the problem of finding sufficient funds to acquire very large companies.

Michael Milken, of the investment banking firm Drexel Burnham Lambert, introduced and oversaw the development of the multibillion dollar market in high-yield debt, pejoratively known as **junk bonds**.[13] Besides financing growth in midsized and smaller firms, Milken used high-yield debt to create investment pools of hundreds of millions of dollars. These war chests of money allowed takeover artists, known as *corporate raiders*, and managers of smaller corporations to attempt takeovers of much larger firms. With junk-bond financing, raiders could target all but the very largest corporations. Suddenly supersized corporations such as Gulf Oil and Boeing Aircraft began to feel threatened by the market for corporate control.

Michael Milken and junk bonds were catalysts of the tremendous takeover activity of the 1980s. He changed history and had an incredible rise and fall.

Besides the financial innovations developed in the 1980s, investment bankers also introduced new restructuring vehicles. The most popular innovation was the leveraged buyout (LBO) or management buyout (MBO). Buyouts are also known as going-private transactions, because once the transaction is completed the company's stock no longer trades publicly. In a buyout, a small investment group, which usually includes some of the company's managers, purchases all a company's outstanding stock using a small equity stake, supplemented by an enormous amount of debt. Debt-to-equity ratios of 10:1 or 15:1 were not uncommon in buyouts. Much of the debt, which comes from banks as well as junk bonds, is secured by the company's assets, and some debt has provisions that allows the company to postpone interest and principal payments.[14] These high debt levels, with their very real threat of bankruptcy, help focus managers' attention. Because managers often own a substantial portion of the company, usually from 10% to 25%, they have powerful incentives to make the company profitable. Moreover, other members of the buyout group have seats on the board, so they can carefully monitor the management team's efforts. Often the buyout group's first action is to sell some of the company's assets and use the proceeds to pay down the debt. Selling assets not only makes the debt burden easier to endure, but it also helps the company focus on those activities at which it has a competitive advantage. With their high leverage and changes in ownership and corporate governance structures, buyout transactions almost always result in improved corporate performance.

[13]Milken's insight about high-yield debt came from work he did as a finance student on "fallen angels," bonds originally issued with a high-quality rating that eventually were severely downgraded. He determined than when fallen angels were combined into portfolios the risk they added was much less than that implied by their low prices; i.e., the return on fallen angels was high relative to the risk contribution they made to a bond portfolio. Two excellent books on Michael Milken and Drexel Burnham are *The Predators' Ball* by Connie Bruck (New York: Simon Schuster, 1988) and *April Fools* by Dan Stone (New York: Donald I. Fine, 1990).

[14]*PIK*, or *payment in kind, debt* allows the borrower to pay interest or issue additional bonds with a value equal to the interest payments. PIKs gave managers of highly leveraged companies some breathing room. Another innovative debt instrument used in buyouts is the *reset note*, which is originally issued with a comparatively low coupon rate. At some future date the company resets the coupon so the bond sells at par. For a few companies the price was at such a deep discount that the reset coupon rate exceeded 25%.

Digital Equipment, American Express, and Westinghouse. Active investors, particularly the employee pension funds of large states or cities, helped fill the vacuum created by the fall of Drexel. **Institutional investor activism**, although not a form of restructuring, disciplines inefficient managers much as hostile takeovers did in the 1980s, though in a much less disruptive manner.

As we reach the mid-1990s takeover activity is once again increasing, though the nature of the transactions differs significantly from those of the 1980s. Rather than raiders identifying and acquiring inefficiently operated companies, takeovers now seem to be motivated by strategic concerns. Companies try to keep up with shifts in markets by identifying acquisition targets that will allow them to quickly follow those market changes. Companies can more quickly make these shifts by buying an existing company rather than trying to develop a subsidiary from scratch. The merger of telephone and cellular telephone companies is an example of the conventional telephone companies acquiring access to a new, very promising, technology. Eli Lilly's purchase of PCS Health Systems was a strategic response to changes in the way health-care delivery operates. Eli Lilly manufactures pharmaceutical drugs. Increasingly insurance companies rely on *prescription-benefit managers* to determine which drugs the insurers approve for payment for certain health problems. Buying PCS, the largest prescription-benefit manager in the United States, helps assure that Lilly's products will be on lists of preferred drugs for insurance reimbursement.

IBM's acquisition of Lotus Development gives IBM a head start on Microsoft in the development of groupware (software that allows a group to work on a single document or project).

Other examples of strategic restructurings include UAL's employee buyout in exchange for wage and benefit concessions, which allowed United Airlines to develop a no-frills, short-route carrier to compete with profitable Southwest Airlines, and AT&T's purchase of McCaw Cellular, which gives it entry into the high-growth cellular telephone industry. These are strategic restructurings. They are designed to move the company into new markets or increase the company's competitiveness in its existing markets and have none of the disciplinary overtones of the takeovers of the 1980s.

The prevalence of strategic restructurings in the 1990s reflects the need to maintain competitiveness as markets and technologies change. During the 1980s many inefficient companies were absorbed or dissolved. In the 1990s increased competition and stronger internal control systems reduced the need for disciplinary restructurings. The earlier restructuring transactions moved corporations to a reasonable level of efficiency; today's restructurings try to maintain that competitiveness and prepare companies to be competitive in the future.

NUMERICAL ANALYSES OF TWO RESTRUCTURINGS

Ideally, managers restructure only if the transaction enhances the wealth of shareholders. Applying the net present value (NPV) technique presented in Chapter 9 indicates whether or not a restructuring transaction benefits shareholders. The acceptance rule is identical to that for other types of investments: Companies should complete restructuring transactions with positive NPVs—i.e., make the investment if the present value of future after-tax cash flows discounted at the appropriate risk-adjusted rate exceeds the cost of the investment. In this section we use discounted cash flows to analyze two hypothetical restructuring transactions, an acquisition and an MBO.

Example 1: A Synergistic Acquisition

ACME Office Supply and Southern Office Products both distribute office supplies to retailers. ACME operates in the midwestern United States and Southern's business is spread throughout the southeastern United States. For simplicity's sake, assume both companies are the same size, have the same sales, profit margins, tax rates, etc., that neither company has any debt outstanding, and no overlap exists in their markets. The directors of ACME are meeting to discuss making a bid for Southern. The directors foresee two sources of cost savings resulting from the acquisition: reduced cost of goods sold due to buying in larger quantities from manufacturers and administrative savings from the consolidation of billing, payroll, and some accounting and planning functions. Sales, however, would not change. How might the ACME directors arrive at a reasonable bid price to offer for Southern?

We begin by looking at the companies' income statements in Exhibit 16.3. In this example we focus just on the income statements, assuming there are no synergies that affect the balance sheets. The market value of both firms is calculated using a 10% discount rate and assuming that their cash flows are perpetuities. From Chapter 5, we know that the present value of a perpetuity is just the annual amount divided by the discount rate, or

Students may need some help to understand these numerical examples.

$$\text{present value of perpetuity} = \frac{\text{annual cash flow}}{\text{discount rate}}$$

For ACME the \$8 perpetual cash flow (net income of \$3 plus depreciation of \$5) represents a present value of \$80, computed as follows:

$$\text{ACME value} = \frac{\$8}{10\%} = \$80$$

We use the same procedure to calculate the values of Southern and the combination of the two companies. Dividing the value of the firm by the number of shares gives the share price.

If no synergies exist, then ACME's income statement after the acquisition is

	ACME	SOUTHERN	POSTACQUISITION WITHOUT SYNERGIES	POSTACQUISITION WITH SYNERGIES
Sales	$100	$100	$200	$200
COGS	70	70	140	136
Gross Margin	30	30	60	64
GA&S Expense	20	20	40	34
Depreciation	5	5	10	10
Taxable Income	5	5	10	20
Taxes	2	2	4	8
Net Income	3	3	6	12
Perpetual cash flow	8	8	16	22
Discount rate	10%	10%	10%	10%
Value of firm	$80	$80	$160	$220
Shares out	10	10	20	20
Share price	$8	$8	$8	$11

EXHIBIT 16.3

INCOME STATEMENTS BEFORE AND AFTER ACME'S ACQUISITION OF SOUTHERN WITH PRO FORMA INCOME STATEMENTS FOR THE POSTACQUISITION FIRM WITHOUT AND WITH THE EFFECT OF SYNERGIES SHOWN simply the sum of the two companies' separate income statements. However, if synergies exist, then the combined income statement will show increased profits compared to the sum of the two separate income statements. The rightmost column of Exhibit 16.3 shows how synergies (in this case from economies of scale) would affect the postacquisition company. Savings in cost of goods sold total $4 and general, administrative and sales expense (GA&S expense) savings are $6. The annual perpetual cash flow increases from $16 when no synergies exist to $22 when these cost savings apply (net income of $12 plus depreciation of $10). The higher cash flow of $22 results in a total value of the firm of $220 and a share price of $11 (we assume that 20 shares are outstanding after the acquisition). The present value of the gains from synergies is $60, the increase in the market value of the merged firm above the values of the two companies if operated separately.

Exhibit 16.4 shows the effect on ACME's shareholders at various tender offer prices for Southern. The change in ACME's shareholders' wealth compares the original (preacquisition) value of $80 to the value based on a total value of $160 less the purchase price of Southern. In the without-synergies case, the most ACME can pay for Southern is $80, and this does not include the attorney and investment banker fees for arranging the deal.[16] If they offer more than $80, they reduce the wealth of ACME shareholders. Of course, an offer of $80, or $8 per share, simply matches the current market value of the stock. Without being offered a premium over current stock price, Southern shareholders have no incentive to tender their shares. At bid prices that offer a premium, ACME shareholders suffer a wealth reduction. The tender offer premium transfers some of their wealth to the Southern shareholders. Without synergies, there can be no transaction that produces gains for ACME's shareholders and at the same time attracts Southern shareholders to tender their shares; that is, without synergies (or some other type of economic benefits) the transaction makes no sense.

Exhibit 16.5 shows various bid prices and their affect on ACME's shareholders when synergies exist. In the with-synergies case, ACME can pay up to $140 for Southern. Typically, the tender offer price includes a 20% to 30% premium over the current share price. A 25% premium would result in a bid of $10 per share,

EXHIBIT 16.4

THE IMPLIED VALUE OF ACME AND THE GAIN ACCRUING TO ACME SHAREHOLDERS AT VARIOUS TENDER OFFER PRICES FOR SOUTHERN WITH NO SYNERGIES

	A	B	C	D
ACME's value with Southern (no synergies)	$160	$160	$160	$160
Purchase price for Southern	70	80	90	100
Implied value of ACME	90	80	70	60
Change in ACME's shareholders' wealth	10	0	−10	−20
Premium paid to Southern shareholders	−10	0	10	20

[16]Fees associated with restructurings can be quite high. It is not uncommon for investment bankers to earn several percent of the purchase price in fees. Other out-of-pocket costs can add several million more dollars to the total bill of an average-size ($250 to $500 million) acquisition of a publicly traded company.

	A	B	C	D	E
Value with Southern (with synergies)	$220	$220	$220	$220	$220
Purchase price for Southern	80	100	110	140	160
Implied value of ACME	140	120	110	80	60
Change in ACME shareholders' wealth	60	40	30	0	−20
Premium paid to Southern shareholders	0	20	30	60	80

EXHIBIT 16.5

THE IMPLIED VALUE OF ACME AND THE GAIN ACCRUING TO ACME SHAREHOLDERS AT VARIOUS TENDER OFFER PRICES FOR SOUTHERN WITH SYNERGIES ENHANCING TOTAL FIRM VALUE

or $100 for all Southern's outstanding shares. Exhibit 16.5 shows that a $100 bid for Southern produces a $40 gain for ACME's existing shareholders and a premium of $20 for Southern's shareholders.

ACME's directors represent the interests of ACME shareholders, so they want to capture as much of the synergistic gains as possible for ACME's stockholders. Tender offer bids between $80 and $110 for Southern give the majority of the gains to ACME stockholders. At bid prices between $110 and $140, the wealth of ACME's stockholders increases, but they receive less of the total gain than Southern's shareholders. ACME's directors might initially bid between $100 and $110 and try to secure more of the total gain for the shareholders whom they represent. ACME's directors want to make the bid high enough so that many of Southern's shareholders will tender but not so high that they give too large a portion of the total gain away.

This situation is a bilateral bidding situation in which Southern's directors want the highest price and can defend against the merger until that price is reached.

In practice, bidders often increase their bids until they receive only a relatively small portion of the total gain. Evidence from hundreds of takeovers shows that targeted firms usually capture the bulk of the gain. How the bidder and target share the total gain depends on whether other bidders appear, thereby creating a competitive auction, and how the target estimates the value of the acquisition to the bidder. Additional bidders will force the bid price up, so more gains go to the target. If the target company computes a gain similar to that computed by the bidder, then the target will reject bids that give the bidder a significant portion of the gain. In fact, the target company's directors could continue forcing up the bid price until almost the entire gain goes to the shareholders of the target firm. In our example, ACME continues to bid at prices of $135 and even $138, because a small gain still accrues to ACME's shareholders.

In this example we applied the standard NPV (net present value) discounted cash flow technique to an acquisition investment. The NPV analysis gave us the range of tender offer bid prices that would increase the wealth of the bidder's shareholders. The economic rationale for the acquisition was that synergies or economies of scale would be realized by combining the operations of the two companies. We also discussed how these gains—the value increase from combining the two companies—might be shared between the bidder and the target. Evidence suggests that target companies capture the majority of the gain.

Example 2: An MBO (Management Buyout) Transaction

This example will require some interpretation by the instructor. It is complicated.

Argonaut Metals Incorporated consists of two divisions. The metals division produces high-purity, rare-metal ingots for use in aerospace applications and accounts for about 75% of total sales and assets. The fastener division manufactures a variety of standard-dimension titanium fasteners. The company has no debt and earns stable profits, despite being slow to respond to shifts in demand. For instance, although competitors developed and brought to market titanium screws and nails for orthopedic surgery, Argonaut never considered entering that market. Instead, Argonaut chose to rest on the success of its metals division. Argonaut has several long-term contracts with suppliers of rare-metal ores. These contracts allow Argonaut to buy a fixed amount of metal at a price established in 1991, well below the price competitors must pay today. Having a portion of its supply at this low price assures Argonaut of a healthy profit margin, so Argonaut managers have little incentive to develop new products or enter new markets. Of the ten top managers, six plan on retiring in the next 2 to 4 years. They enjoy working at Argonaut and receive a generous selection of perquisites and benefits. The other four managers joined the executive ranks within the past 5 years and are eager to have an impact on the company.

Over time the quality of LBO candidates, in terms of stable cash flows and debt coverage, deteriorated. See "The Evolution of Buyout Pricing and Financial Structure (or What Went Wrong) in the 1980s," by Steve Kaplan and Jeremy Stein, *Journal of Applied Corporate Finance* 6 (Spring 1993): 72–88.

An investment banker has approached the group of younger managers about trying to take Argonaut private with a leveraged management buyout. Given Argonaut's stable cash flows, the banker believes the company could support the debt necessary to complete the buyout. The young managers know that cost savings could be realized by reducing executive perquisites and excess benefits, instituting more efficient production techniques, and decreasing administrative expenses. After preliminary discussions, the banker brings the following analysis to the buyout group. The analysis assumes the following:

1. The buyout group offers $500 (or $10 per share) for the company, a 25% premium over current share price.
2. The management group and the investment bank contribute $50. The four managers use nearly all the money at their disposal to make the investment.
3. The company borrows the remaining $450 from a syndicate of banks. The debt comes in three pieces: $200 at 8%, $150 at 10% and $100 at 13%.
4. The buyout group sells the fastener division for $120 as soon as the buyout transaction is complete to a client the investment banker has located. Managers will use proceeds from the sale to pay down a portion of the debt.
5. Managers reduce cost of goods sold and general, administrative, and sales expense.
6. At least 80% of all cash flow is used to reduce debt until total long-term debt reaches $150, the target permanent debt level for the company.
7. To simplify the analysis we assume the company holds no inventory, sells only on a cash basis (so has no accounts receivables), and uses no trade credit, and all cash is used to repay debt or purchase assets or is distributed as dividends (no cash is held in reserve). In other words, there are no current assets or liabilities to worry about.

Exhibit 16.6 presents Argonaut's most recent income statement and balance sheet as well as some market information. Argonaut stock currently sells for $8, which represents a total market value of $400. This share price reflects investors' beliefs that Argonaut will continue to earn steady profits but that cash flows will not grow in the future.

We estimate cash flow by adding depreciation to net income. The discount rate of 10% is the company's weighted average cost of capital and is appropriate

INCOME STATEMENT		BALANCE SHEET	
Sales		**Assets**	
Metals division	$375	Fixed assets	400
Fasteners	125	Total assets	400
Total sales	500		
Cost of goods sold	350	**Liabilities and Equity**	
Gross margin	150	Debt	0
GA&S	100	Common stock	400
Depreciation	25	Total liabilities and equity	400
Interest expense	0		
Taxable income	25		
Tax (40%)	10		
Net income	15		
Cash flow	40		
Discount rate	10%		
Firm value	$400		
Shares out	50		
Share price	$8/Share		

EXHIBIT 16.6

ARGONAUT METALS: PREBUYOUT FINANCIAL STATEMENTS

for both divisions. We assume that the cash flow of $40 per year will continue into perpetuity, so we calculate the market value of the company and share price as

$$\text{present value of a perpetuity} = \frac{\text{perpetual cash flow}}{\text{discount rate}} = \frac{\$40}{10\%} = \$400$$

$$\text{share price} = \frac{\text{firm value}}{\text{no. of shares outstanding}} = \frac{\$400}{50} = \$8/\text{share}$$

The initial MBO transaction involves several steps: buying the company with borrowed funds and selling the fastener division. Exhibit 16.7 shows how the company's balance sheet changes at each of these steps. The MBO group borrows $450 and invests $50 of their own money (a debt-to-equity ratio of 9:1). The

	BEFORE THE MBO TRANSACTION OCCURS	THE MOMENT THE MBO IS COMPLETED	AFTER FASTENER DIVISION SOLD (DAY 1 OF MBO)
Assets			
Plant, property, and equipment	400	500	380
Total assets	400	500	380
Liabilities and Equity			
Debt 8%	0	200	200
Debt 10%	0	150	130
Debt 13%	0	100	0
Common stock	400	50	50
Total liabilities and equity	400	500	380

EXHIBIT 16.7

ARGONAUT METALS: PRO FORMA BALANCE SHEETS AS MBO TRANSACTION IS COMPLETED

To compute the share price premium, divide the net present value of the savings by the number of shares outstanding.

$$\text{maximum premium per share} = \frac{\$6{,}300{,}000}{5{,}000{,}000} = \$1.26 \text{ per share}$$

To compute the percentage price premium, divide the premium by the current stock price.

$$\text{tender offer premium} = \frac{\$1.26}{\$9.50} = 0.1326 = 13.26\% \text{ of current stock price}$$

Comment: Southeast should offer no more than a \$1.26 per share premium. This premium is within the 10% to 15% premium that has been seen historically in tender offer bids, so it should be an acceptable offer to Hart Brothers shareholders.

PROBLEMS

$4,700,000, or $47 per share

1. Western Distributors and Arizona Wholesaling both supply western wear and equipment stores with a variety of supplies. Western has annual sales of $10 million and generates after-tax cash flow of $1.0 million. Arizona Wholesaling is smaller, having sales of $3 million per year, which produce an annual after-tax cash flow of $300,000. Western is considering making a tender offer bid for Arizona Wholesaling. Given the following assumptions, determine the maximum amount that Western should bid for Arizona Wholesaling:
   1. The companies have no overlapping sales territories, so no change in sales is expected.
   2. The current discount rate for both companies is 10%, and that will be the appropriate rate after the takeover.
   3. Western's financial analysts believe that savings from consolidation of some business functions will increase after-tax cash flows $200,000 per year.
   4. The analyst has been advised to treat the cash flows as perpetuities.
   5. Arizona Wholesaling has 100,000 shares of stock outstanding, and the stock currently sells for $30 per share.
   6. Attorney and investment banker fees are expected to total $300,000.

   Compute either the highest price Western can pay for all Arizona Wholesaling's stock in aggregate or the highest share price that Western can offer.

NPV = $40.1 million; maximum bid price = $36.60; IRR = 18% at $25 bid

2. You are a financial analyst for a medium-sized investment firm located in Chicago. Your firm has been putting together a management buyout deal with an investment group and some of the managers of Lakeshore Garment Company, a small publicly traded manufacturer of men's suits and formal wear. The preliminary analysis has been completed and you have been asked to put the numbers together into a rough estimate for the maximum bid price. Use the following data to generate a first estimate of the bid price.
   1. Currently Lakeshore stock is selling for $18.00 per share, with 3,450,000 shares outstanding.

2. Estimated after-tax cash flows to equityholders for the next 7 years are shown in the table. It is expected that after year 6, cash flows will be constant at the year 7 levels indefinitely into the future.

Year	1	2	3	4	5	6	7
After-Tax Cash Flow (millions of dollars)	$0	$0	$8	$15	$21	$25	$28

3. The required rate of return for equity based on Year 7 leverage ratios is 11%. The following table shows the appropriate required rates of return for equityholders for each year from 1 through 7 based on changing leverage ratios. If the management group buys all the outstanding stock for $25 per share, what is the NPV of this transaction? What is the internal rate of return?

Year	1	2	3	4	5	6	7
Equity Required Rate of Return	20%	19%	17%	15%	13.5%	12%	11%

CHAPTER 17

The Journey Through Corporate Finance

. . . and that concludes our course on corporate finance.

"It begins in delight and ends in wisdom," according to Robert Frost.

In this final chapter, we present two fictional cases, Northwood Publishing Co. and Bowditch Chart Company. Together, they illustrate how some of the important ideas of finance are actually applied in a business. An analysis of the Northwood case is provided so that you may see what decisions were made, why they were made, and what resulted. The Bowditch case is not complete. We end the case with questions for you to answer. In other words, you must decide what course of action to take.

Neither case presents much quantitative data to analyze. This is done in order not to obscure the primary ideas illustrated in the cases. In more realistic situations, financial decisions depend on gathering and analyzing often large quantities of accounting, engineering, production, marketing, economic, and financial data. In these two cases, most of this work is done for you.

Both cases demonstrate that much of what we have taught in this book may be applied to actual business situations. For a field of study so concerned with value, it would not be appropriate to teach ideas that were themselves without practical value.

Following the Bowditch case, we discuss a few themes common to many business decisions that transcend finance. Finally, we add some thoughts on finance—past, present, and future—that seek to place in perspective what you have studied in this book.

CASE 1
NORTHWOOD PUBLISHING CO.: AN APOCRYPHAL TALE OF FINANCE[1]

How Northwood Got into Trouble

Northwood Publishing Co. is a regional publisher located in Coeur d'Alene, Idaho. It has three divisions. One division publishes a daily and several weekly newspapers. Another publishes books by regional authors, featuring Northwest history and the natural environment. The third division operates a newsprint plant, supplying Northwood's newspapers as well as a number of weekly papers in the inland Northwest.

About 20% of the stock is held by members of the Bunyan family. The grandfather, Paul, a large man who traveled in company with an ox, started as a lumberjack, became a partner and then sole owner of a sawmill, and built the region's first newsprint plant. His children began the publishing business in the 1960s. From 1963, through early 1993, the board chairman and CEO was Paul Bunyan, Jr.

This case is an extreme example of an agency problem. Ask students to identify the problem. Ask if the management breakdown is an agency problem.

Northwood's stock is traded over the counter. There are about 700 stockholders, most of whom reside in the Northwest. Aside from Paul, Jr., five other Bunyans, representing two generations, have held management positions. In the past, they have drawn large salaries, and some have been notably absent from work. Starting in the late 1970s, Northwood invested in a number of recreational properties, including a lodge overlooking lake Coeur d'Alene, several ski chalets, and condominiums in Puerto Vallerta, Mexico, and on the island of Kauai. At various

[1]*Apocryphal* is an adjective meaning of questionable authenticity.

times, Northwood has been the owner of an executive twin-engine turbo-prop airplane and a 47-foot sailing yacht. During the 1980s, profitability of Northwood eroded, especially in its newsprint and newspaper divisions. One cause was a prolonged strike at the newsprint plant, resulting in a long shutdown, lost contracts, and poor employee morale. A second cause was that Northwood had become a high-cost operation, relative to its competitors. For example a plant, which employed the latest in cost-saving technology, had been built by a rival newspaper in nearby Spokane, Washington. Also, Northwood continued to use old printing presses, whereas other printers in the region used the latest in computer-controlled presses. Finally, it appeared that some of Northwood's weekly newspapers were not profitable, but they lacked the financial data to be certain.

The Turnaround

Northwood's stock began trading over the counter in 1971, at about $4 per share. In 1978, the average price was $14. However, 10 years later, in 1988, the price had fallen to $6. In 1992, the stock was trading at about $5. In early 1993, fearing an attempted takeover by the Spokane newspaper, Northwood took several actions to boost the price of its stock. First, it reconstituted its board of directors. Paul Bunyan, Jr., resigned, his sister Pauline became board chairman, and the board began to search for a new CEO. Also, the board was expanded with outside members, so that the Bunyan family no longer had control. Second, Northwood reduced the salaries of its executives and authorized, through the board, an executive stock option plan. This tied part of their compensation to the company's stock price. Third, the board formed an investment committee, with review authority over all capital investments. Finally, the board authorized a $0.15 quarterly divided ($0.60 per year) on its common stock, beginning with the third quarter of 1993. This change was the first in the dividend since the stock began public trading in 1971. At that time, the dividend was set at $0.10 per quarter, or $0.40 per year.

Actions taken by the board:

1. Remove the senior Bunyan as chairman and CEO.
2. Add outside directors, removing control from the Bunyan family.
3. Tie executive compensation to stock options.
4. Form an investment committee to preempt frivolous spending.

In late 1993, Northwood hired a new CEO, Harry Luce, who had extensive experience in the New York publishing business. Luce became an ex-officio member of the corporate board, and Pauline Bunyan remained as chairman. Luce immediately began divesting nonessential real estate assets, including the lodge, chalets, and condos. He also presented to the board a business plan that included investing in new printing presses and modern equipment for the newsprint plant. Luce also began setting up a computer-based information system that would allow management to collect detailed financial data on their various operations. By the end of 1993, Northwood's stock was trading at $8.75, and the volume of trading was at an historic high. Investors were reacting to the increased dividend and were anticipating a turnaround for Northwood.

Actions taken by the new CEO:

1. Divest nonessential assets.
2. Prepare a plan to invest in modern printing presses and equipment for the newsprint plant.
3. Install a modern information system.
4. Hire a new chief financial officer.

It was now up to Luce to implement his plan for recovery. First, he replaced the chief financial officer (CFO), Paul Bunyan III, with Nancy Welch, an experienced financial manager from Seattle. Luce and Welch recognized that selling the corporate real estate would not begin to pay for the new newsprint and printing equipment. Also, Northwood's cash balances were low, reflecting the past excesses of the Bunyan family and the cost of the company's new computer equipment. This meant that money would have to be raised from outside, through the sale of securities.

Ask students' opinions of actions taken by the board and the CEO. Too little? Too much?

Evaluating the Investment Projects

Welch established an ad hoc committee to evaluate the latest in computer-controlled newsprint machinery and printing presses. Welch chaired the committee, which included the manager of the newsprint plant, the business manager of the daily newspaper, and a financial analyst from Welch's staff. In addition, Welch hired a consulting engineer who was technically expert with such equipment and made him a consultant to the committee. The committee had a difficult time understanding and choosing from among competing systems and technologies. Also, friction developed between the newsprint manager and the newspaper business manager over the allocation of dollars between the two projects. The consulting engineer pressed for equipment incorporating the latest technology, but Welch balked at the cost. The financial analyst was kept busy analyzing the cash flows for the several competing newsprint systems and presses. His cash flow estimates were challenged repeatedly by the engineer and the two managers. However, the committee gradually settled on the specific machinery and equipment for each project.

Reinforce the problems that arose during this process: cost vs. technology, limited investment dollars, interdivisional conflict and the viability of the newsprint plant.

Throughout the process, there were questions raised about the viability of the newsprint operation. The plant was operating below current capacity. The new machinery would make the plant more cost-efficient and would also increase its capacity. About 60% of its current production was used to supply the in-house newspapers. At normal capacity, this proportion would drop to 50%. With the new machinery, operating at normal capacity, that value would drop to 40%. This division was having trouble developing its outside market. It had lost much of its market during and after the plant closure and was facing strong competition from the newsprint plant in Spokane. This led Welch to suggest that the risk premium for the newsprint investment should be greater than that for the newspaper.

Required Returns on Investments

Northwood maintained credit lines for short-term financing with banks in Coeur d'Alene and Spokane. It carried no long-term debt. The cost of capital for Northwood, therefore, was the cost of equity, the market value of which was determined in the regional over-the-counter market.

By mid 1994, Northwood's stock was trading at $9. Using the dividend valuation model, where the required return equals the dividend yield plus a growth rate, Welch calculated a required return on Northwood's stock of 10.7% (0.107 = 0.60/9 + 0.04). This assumed a sustainable growth rate of 4%. Welch felt that 4% was, if anything, optimistic. However, she also intuitively thought that the required return of 10.7% was too low, primarily because the stock price of $9 was too high. She thought that the stock price might reflect unrealistic expectations about Northwood's recovery. She knew that the market for Northwood's stock was relatively inactive, trading only three or four times a month, and she questioned whether such a market was sufficiently competitive and efficient to establish a price that reflected the stock's intrinsic value. Welch found that by arbitrarily lowering the stock price to $7, the required return rose to 12.6% (0.126 = 0.60/7 + 0.04).

The decision of the CFO to adjust the stock's market price may be debated among the students. This is an opportunity to discuss market efficiency and competitiveness in a thinly traded regional OTC market.

Using the CAPM, Welch calculated a required return on equity of 11.7%.

She estimated the market risk premium at 7%. In mid-1994, the yield on 3-month Treasury bills was 4%. Welch also estimated Northwood's beta to be 1.1, based on betas for comparable firms. [The calculation was 11.7 = 0.04 + 1.1(0.07).] This confirmed her intuition that the stock was probably overpriced. She settled on a cost of equity for Northwood of 12%.

Divisional Rates of Return

Determining the cost of equity was only the first step. The next was to determine the amount of the additional risk premium to apply to the newsprint equipment. Welch could find no pure-play company that produced only newsprint. She was convinced that the newsprint division carried the highest risk and that the newspaper division carried the lowest risk. There was little competition in the local newspaper markets, and the markets themselves were growing, reflecting population growth in the Pacific Northwest. Even though some of the weeklies were what she termed marginal operations, she felt that they could be made more efficient by combining some editorial staffs and employing the latest in printing technology. The book-publishing division was profitable; however, with relatively few books in print at any one time, sales and income were variable. The book division contributed only 20% of corporate revenues and earnings. The newspaper division contributed half of the corporate revenues and, currently, more than half of the earnings. The newsprint division contributed 30% of revenues and proportionately less earnings. Welch assigned the following divisional betas:

	BOOK	NEWSPRINT	NEWSPAPER
Proportion (weight)	0.2	0.3	0.5
Beta	1.1	1.35	0.95

The weighted average of these betas equaled the corporate beta of 1.1. This meant that the newsprint equipment had a required rate of return of 13.5% [(0.135 = 0.04 + 1.35(.07)], and the newspaper presses had a required return of 10.7% [0.107 = 0.04 + 0.95(0.07)].

Project Financing

There were several issues related to project financing. One was, of course, financing costs. Another was control of the company. Additional equity capital would have to be raised through a public stock offering, diminishing the Bunyan family's ownership share. Also, there remained the question of whether Northwood had access to the market for long-term debt. Could it sell bonds? Could it find an institutional lender, such as an insurance company? In the fall of 1994, Luce and Welch met with a regional investment banker in Seattle to discuss both equity and debt issues. The investment banker told them that her company could place bonds through a regional broker/dealer network and that the bonds would probably carry a risk rating of BBB or BBB- (Standard & Poor's). These bonds normally carried a risk premium of 3% over treasury bonds of the same maturity. At the time, 20-year Treasuries were yielding about 6.25%, meaning

The debt/equity decision may be debated. The control issue creates a conundrum for the board. Debt preserves control and may reduce the cost of capital but is risky and may carry a substantial risk premium.

that Northwood's bonds would probably have a coupon of 9.25%. Because of the small issue size and the cost of selling through a broker/dealer network, flotation costs would be 8% of the par value of the bonds, meaning that the effective cost to Northwood would be 0.0925/0.92 = 10%. Northwood's effective corporate tax rate was 34%, making the after-tax cost of bonds 6.6%. The investment banker warned that the bond issue would have to be large enough to cover some fixed issuing costs. In her opinion, given the amount of money to be raised, it would be unwise to split project financing between debt and equity. If the entire amount were financed by bonds, the debt proportion of Northwood's capital structure would rise from 0 to more than 30%.

The investment banker also told Luce and Welch that, assuming a market price of $9, common stock could be sold to net Northwood about $7.75 per share. This discount from the market price included underpricing and flotation costs. The cost of new equity would then be 0.60/7.75 + 0.04 = 11.7%. If the market price fell to $8, the net to Northwood would be $7, making the cost of equity 12.6%.

In November 1994 the Northwood board met and decided that, in view of its business uncertainty, it would finance its new investments through a common stock issue. This was agreed to by the Bunyan family, who would see their proportional ownership fall from 20% to 9% if both projects were undertaken.

The Investment Decision

In early January 1995, Welch and her financial analyst presented their report on the two projects to the investment committee of the board. The internal rate of return (IRR) of the newsprint equipment project was 10%, and the net present value (NPV) at a risk-adjusted discount rate of 13.5% was negative. Welch recommended against the investment. The IRR of the printing presses was 14%, with a positive NPV at a discount rate of 10.7%. Welch recommended that the company proceed with that investment. The investment committee agreed, and in April the board authorized a new common stock issue, which netted Northwood $7 per share. With only the printing presses to finance, the proportional ownership of the Bunyan family fell to 13%, rather than the 9% they had anticipated. The new presses were ordered in late spring and delivered in the fall.

Epilogue

By mid-1996, it became clear that the newsprint operation was not viable. In the first half of that year, production dropped to 60% of capacity. The new computer-based information system indicated that the division was producing a negative cash flow. In the early fall, the board met to consider a recommendation from Luce and Welch that Northwood divest the newsprint plant and use the cash to invest elsewhere. Luce was directed by the board to present a plan for reinvesting the money from the sale of the newsprint plant. And so the final act in the transformation of Northwood was about to be played. The newsprint business started by Paul Bunyan, the large man with the ox, was put up for sale. At the end of the second quarter of 1996, Northwood's stock was trading at $9.50, and late that summer, the board authorized a quarterly dividend increase to $0.18.

A Note on Northwood Publishing Co.

In this fictional case, we have woven in many of the financial issues that face companies. You will note that Northwood is not a Fortune 500 company. Corporate finance applies to companies of all sizes.

In the first part of the case we have an extreme example of an agency problem, as the Bunyan family uses their de facto control of Northwood for their own purposes. However, the resulting decline in stock value makes Northwood a takeover candidate, arousing board action. The board attempts to reduce the agency problem by establishing performance incentives and reconstituting the board. The crisis also draws attention to the company's dividend policy.

Later, management grapples with the difficulties of evaluating competing investment proposals. In this case, divisions are competing for investment dollars. Early concerns about the newsprint plant are manifested in the higher-risk-adjusted discount rate. Estimating the company's cost of equity is complicated by management's distrust of the stock's current market price. This distrust stems from the fact that the stock is thinly traded in a regional over-the-counter market.

Reaffirm the connection between the agency problem and the investment decision.

Financing choices for smaller companies are constrained by access to capital, high flotation costs, corporate control, and the ability of the company to absorb financial risk. In this case, risk aversion won over corporate control.

In the end, NPV-IRR analysis of the two projects confirmed earlier intuitions about the newsprint investment, and only the printing presses were purchased. Without the investment, the decline of the newsprint division accelerated, and it became a candidate for divestiture. Northwood then began to consider ways to reinvest monies from the sale of the newsprint division.

CASE 2
BOWDITCH CHART COMPANY: AN INTERNATIONAL INTRIGUE

Background and Organization

Bowditch Chart Company is the oldest producer and distributor of marine charts and navigation equipment in the United States. The company was started in 1745 by George Wilson Bowditch to provide coastal charts of New England to American and English sailors. Company headquarters remain at the site of its founding in Old Saybrook, Connecticut. Today, Bowditch is a multiproduct, multinational company. It is organized into three operating divisions.

Bowditch is an importer and exporter. Its primary products are marine charts, books, sextants, and electronic navigation systems.

Hydrographics, Charts, and Publishing Division (HCP)

Bowditch remains the world's largest private producer of marine charts. It competes with a number of government chart producers, including the National Oceanic and Atmospheric Administration and the British Admiralty. Bowditch competes by updating its charts more frequently and producing charts targeted to certain markets, such as recreational sailors. This division also publishes a number of specialized books on marine navigation, weather, and seamanship.

Navigational Instruments Division (NI)

This division got its start in the late 1700s, when Franklin Bowditch, the founder's son, began producing sextants and nautical almanacs. However, by the early twentieth century, Bowditch found that it could not compete with German sextant producers, so it began importing and distributing high-quality German sextants in the United States. Today, Bowditch is the largest distributor of sextants in the United States, most of which come from Shanghai, China. The instruments division also distributes high-quality plotting tools produced in the United States and abroad.

Electronic Products Division (EP)

Bowditch has also entered the electronic age. It produces integrated electronic navigation systems, which link GPS (global positioning satellites) and microcomputers to provide graphic displays of positions set on the background of an electronic chart. Bowditch produces the software, the electronic charts, and the "black box" that allows data from GPS receivers to be fed into a computer. These systems are sold complete, with GPS receivers, all the necessary hardware (except the computer), and software. The division also distributes several brands of GPS receivers as well as hand-held navigational computers.

All Bowditch products are retailed worldwide through a mail-order distribution center in West Hartford, Connecticut, and company products are sold in marine chandleries around the world. Bowditch also buys a number of foreign-made products for resale. The company is particularly adept at finding foreign producers of high-quality, innovative products. Imports currently come from Western and Central Europe, South America, and Asia. Charts and books are printed at a company plant in Lagos, Portugal. Bowditch has field offices in Tampa, San Francisco, Shanghai, Brisbane, Sao Paulo, Genoa, and Rotterdam. These offices support regional distributors, retailers, and suppliers.

Ownership and Control

Bowditch's common stock is publicly traded on the over-the-counter market. There are 1,648,000 shares outstanding, about a third of which remain in the hands of the Bowditch family. Camilla Pierson Dexter, a linear descendent of George Wilson Bowditch, is board chair and owns 21% of the company's stock. Another 13% is owned by several cousins. One of the cousins, Branford Pierson, owns 6% of the stock and is on the corporate board. The balance of the seven-person board comprises Alex Cutter, President and CEO; Linda Serra, Vice President—Finance; Victor Craft, Vice President—Administration and Corporate Counsel; Thomas D'Alesandro, President of Old Saybrook National Bank; and Ivana Olsen, President of Marine Supplies, Inc., a major distributor to chandleries along the Atlantic and Gulf coasts. In total, the officers and employees of Bowditch own 14% of the corporate stock. The balance, about 52%, is publicly held, with no single person owning more than 0.5% (one half of one percent). There are about 1,600 shareholders of record.

Competing objectives can exist among members of a corporate board. In this case the competition is between wealth maximization and maintenance of the company tradition.

Bowditch's common stock is currently trading at about $14 per share. Because its trading volume is low, the stock price changes slowly. However, over the past

8 years, the stock price has declined more or less steadily from a high of $19 in 1988. Bowditch's price-earnings ratio (P/E) is currently about 6. This price decline has caused an unusual amount of contention at some board meetings. Curiously, much of it has been between Camilla Dexter and Branford Pierson, representing the cousins. The cousins, who are not otherwise wealthy, have seen much of their net worth dissipated and have been pressuring the board to more aggressively grow the business. Camilla Dexter married into a wealthy family and sees her role as preserving the traditions of Bowditch, which she considers a national treasure.

Performance

In 1995 Bowditch celebrated its 250th anniversary, making it one of the few companies in the United States to continue its corporate identity from colonial times. Bowditch has traded on its tradition and reputation for quality, while adapting to changing markets and technologies. The tradition/technology conundrum is evident in its product line, which ranges from satellite receivers to sextants, a centuries-old technology. Bowditch has also been a business pioneer. It became an international company in the early twentieth century, when it began to import German sextants, and it was one of the first successful specialty mail-order retailers.

Bowditch has always turned a profit. However, in the past 7 years, 1990 through 1996, net income as a percent of sales has declined, a trend that troubles management and the board of directors. The weakest performer has been the HCP (hydrographics, charts, and publishing) division, whose net income has actually declined in the past 7 years. This is particularly distressing to some of the traditionalists at Bowditch, because this division represents direct ties to the company's original business of producing navigation charts.

	1996 REVENUES AND NET INCOME (THOUSANDS OF DOLLARS)			
	HCP	*NI*	*EP*	*Total*
Revenues	$9,365,404	$6,130,228	$16,427,362	$31,922,994
Net income	$1,123,848	$1,042,139	$ 1,478,463	$ 3,644,450
	PERCENT GROWTH RATE (1990–1996)			
	HCP	*NI*	*EP*	*Total*
Revenues	2.03%	3.11%	4.38%	3.41%
Net income	−1.13%	2.14%	3.45%	1.53%

The Shanghai Instrument Company

Since the late 1980s, Bowditch has been importing sextants from the Shanghai Instrument Company. They are sold under the brand name *Sealest* in the United States. These sextants are optically and mechanically equal to the best from Germany and retail for about half the price. Sealest sextants have been largely responsible for a resurgence in interest in celestial navigation in the United States. The number of navigation schools has increased, most using Sealest sextants. For 20 years prior to the introduction of the Sealest, sales of the NI (navigational instruments) division had fallen, and the viability of the division was in doubt.

In the past few years, Shanghai Instrument has had difficulty meeting demand for its sextants. Other importers are buying the sextants, and some, especially in Europe, are experiencing growth in demand similar to Bowditch. Shanghai Instrument has raised prices, but Bowditch has cautioned them that significant price increases may cause a loss of market share to the Germans. So far, Bowditch, which takes about 70% of Shanghai Instrument's production, has prevailed. However, low prices have prevented Shanghai Instrument, which has little capital, from expanding its plant. There are also increasing indications that Shanghai Instrument is finding even modest growth difficult to manage. Managers from Bowditch have visited the company several times and report antiquated facilities, inefficient production processes, and few financial controls. The sextants are assembled by hand from parts machined either at the plant or at nearby small machine shops. The optics come from Nanjing, about 300 kilometers from Shanghai.

Shanghai Instrument is owned and operated by the Kee family, who have been making precision optical instruments for many generations. Prior to World War II the Kees exported sextants and theodolites to Europe and the United States. Over the past year, Bowditch has been talking informally to the Kees about forming a joint venture with Bowditch to expand and upgrade the plant. Bowditch's contribution would be capital, management training, and technical assistance. Recently, the Kees have expressed interest in selling a majority interest in Shanghai Instrument to Bowditch. The Kees would retain a minority interest to facilitate approval of the acquisition with the provincial and national governments.

In the spring of 1997, a team from Bowditch spent a month in Shanghai evaluating the business. The team consisted of Linda Serra, Victor Craft, a production engineer, and the head of information systems for Bowditch. They retained a legal firm in Shanghai with ties to the provincial government to provide advice on doing business in China. The team reported its findings to the board in May. Its basic conclusions were

These statements are conclusions of the Bowditch team sent to evaluate Shanghai Instrument.

- In spite of political instability elsewhere in China, political risk is minimal in Shanghai, the most Western of all Chinese cities. Many U.S., Japanese, and European companies do business there with little government interference.
- Because of labor-intensive assembly and inspection of the sextants, few economies of scale would be possible. However, plant improvements, worker training, and modern equipment could lower the unit cost of production without sacrificing quality.
- A modern information system would reduce inventory costs and improve financial controls.

To give students some feel for the issues attending an international investment, each of the visiting team's findings could be discussed in class.

- By reconfiguring the existing plant, building a small addition, and adding equipment, production capacity could be increased to meet anticipated demand. Bowditch would take about 80% of the expanded plant's production.
- The cost of expanding and upgrading the plant, training workers, and installing new management systems would be about $8 million.

- The Kees are asking $6 million in U.S. dollars for selling an 80% share in Shanghai Instrument. In return, they would help Bowditch through the transition.
- There is an active foreign exchange market in Shanghai. Dollars and renminbi (the Chinese currency) are freely exchanged. However, the renminbi is not generally traded in the world currency markets. The exchange rate is relatively stable. Currently there are few restrictions on repatriation of earnings, although the Chinese government offers incentives for reinvesting in China.

Linda Serra provided the board with her financial projections for Shanghai Instrument. Revenue in 1996 was $6.54 million, and net income was $960 thousand. Estimated revenues and net income for 1997 are $6.8 million and $1.02 million, respectively. Plant expansion should increase revenues to $8.5 million in 1998. She estimates that revenues should grow at a 5% rate through 2005 and 3% thereafter until 2012. Improvement in efficiency and management should increase net income as a percent of revenues from the current 15% to about 28% in 2002. With these projections, Serra estimates that Bowditch's 80% share will provide the following net present values.

DISCOUNT RATE	NPV
8%	$19,600,000
10%	$17,100,000
12%	$15,000,000
15%	$12,500,000

Some of these discount rates are higher than Bowditch's cost of capital; however, Serra believes that this project is particularly risky and may deserve a higher discount rate.

Financing the Shanghai Instrument Project

Serra knew that a decision on the Shanghai Instrument project, as it was now called, was in part dependent on financing costs. She realized that raising $14 million would force Bowditch to make some tough choices. Immediately after the May board meeting, she began to gather needed financing information.

Aside from some short-term debt, Bowditch has financed its investments with cash generated through its operations. Abstaining from long-term borrowing has been a tradition at Bowditch, reflecting its conservative heritage. Although this has contributed to Bowditch's financial stability over the years, it has restricted the company's growth. In recent years, the company has not had enough operating cash flows to finance some desirable investments. Bowditch's last major capital project was construction, 8 years ago, of its product-distribution center in West Hartford. This project drew down much of Bowditch's cash reserves.

Over the past 5 years, Bowditch has generated between $3 and $4 million in cash annually before paying common dividends. About half of that cash has been used to pay dividends. Much of the rest has been used to finance a number of small capital projects, most of which were for replacement and modernization of existing plant and equipment. This has left Bowditch with about $2.5 million in cash balances and marketable securities.

Serra expects Bowditch to produce about $2 million in cash, after dividends, in 1997. Of the $2 million, about half is earmarked for ongoing or high-priority projects. Serra also is reluctant to lower cash reserves below $2 million. By taking $1 million from its current cash flow, and drawing down $0.5 million in cash balances, Bowditch is able to provide $1.5 million toward the $14 million needed to finance the Shanghai Instrument project.

Financing the project will require Bowditch to seek external financing for the first time. In spite of the company's aversion to debt, Serra felt that she should present the board with information needed to make an informed choice between debt and equity.

Equity Financing

In 1996, Bowditch earned $2.21 per share. With its traditional 50% payout ratio, dividends per share were $1.11. A stock price of $14 gave Bowditch a dividend yield of about 8%. In recent years, dividends have grown, along with earnings, at about 1.5% per year. Using the dividend growth model, with a growth rate of 2%, Serra estimates Bowditch's cost of retained earnings equity to be 10%.

Serra estimates that if new common stock is sold at $14 per share, 992,000 shares would have to be issued to raise $12.5 million and cover flotation costs. With flotation costs, the cost of equity would be 10.8%. If this new stock were sold to the public, the proportion owned by the Bowditch family would fall from 34% currently to 21%, and Camilla Dexter's proportion would fall from 21% to 13%. Public ownership of Bowditch would increase from 52% to 70%.

Long-Term-Debt Financing

The financing issue is similar to the one faced by Northwood Publishing Co.: loss of control versus risk.

Serra has been told by an investment banker that Bowditch would be able to sell 10-year bonds carrying an 8.6% coupon. At a tax rate of 34%, Bowditch's after-tax cost would be 6%, including flotation costs. Bowditch would have to borrow $13,150,000 to raise $12.5 million and cover flotation costs. Debt would lower Bowditch's cost of capital to 8.5%. However, debt as a proportion of total capital would rise from 0 to 36%, substantially altering the company's capital structure.

Summer 1997

Several times throughout the summer, informal meetings between board members and management were held to discuss the Shanghai Instrument project. Attending these meetings were Camilla Dexter, Branford Pierson, Alex Cutter, Linda Serra, and Victor Craft. By late summer, the sessions grew more intense, because the Kee family was pressuring Bowditch for a decision. An early summer visit to Old Saybrook by Chun Fat Kee, the head of Shanghai Instrument, had gone well, but Mr. Kee had made it clear that his $6 million asking price was not negotiable. He implied that he had another potential buyer from Sweden. He did, in fact, fly from the United States to Sweden before returning to China.

Aside from questions about the viability of the Shanghai Instrument project, there were concerns about the financing alternatives. Three issues were clearly influencing the deliberations. First was the lackluster financial performance of Bowditch in recent years, which had left the company with cash reserves inadequate to finance the project. Second was a skepticism about the long-term future for the sextant business. Would satellites and electronics soon overwhelm this three-century-old technology? Finally, there was concern that Camilla Dexter, the largest single shareholder, board chair, and a person of considerable wealth, would be influenced more by tradition and inate conservatism than by purely financial and economic arguments.

Epilogue

A summary of the important issues and questions raised in the case is presented.

This is the end of the case. Notice that we have not presented you with a lot of numbers and calculations to make. All the required quantitative information is included in the case.

You will have to decide whether to take on the Shanghai Instrument project. Before you do, however, consider the financing options and the background information provided. First, the ability to find a satisfactory means of financing the project will greatly affect the investment decision. Second, the investment must be weighed in the context of the company, which is rich in tradition but, in recent years, short on performance.

The investment decision is complicated by the fact that it is in China, a country that remains an enigma to the United States. One factor to consider is whether Bowditch has the experience to manage a production facility in China. Another factor to consider is that the product—the sextant—which is seeing renewed popularity but competes with GPS technology. On the other hand, consider that if Bowditch does not buy Shanghai Instrument, its supply of these popular and well-made sextants may be cut off. Currently, the Sealest sextant has no competition in its price range. Finally, you must decide whether this project deserves a risk premium. If so, how much?

There are any number of lesser issues, including the potential conflict between Camilla Dexter and the other stockholders, particularly those represented by Branford Pierson. There is also the question of foreign exchange. Even though the renminbi may be exchanged for dollars in Shanghai, the renminbi is not traded in the world markets, meaning that Bowditch may be dependent on the Shanghai foreign exchange market. Also, why is the Kee family insisting on being paid in dollars? Are they driven primarily by a desire to liquidate their Chinese assets? A related question is why they are pressuring Bowditch for a quick decision. Such questions of trust and understanding often impinge on foreign business transactions.

Financing of the project may be the toughest issue to deal with. First, the investment requires outside financing. Secondly, equity financing reduces the Bowditch family's stake in the company. On the other hand, debt financing greatly increases financial leverage and risk. A potentially important advantage of debt is the reduction in the corporate cost of capital. To avoid further complication, assume that Bowditch cannot mix debt and equity financing. That is, external financing must be entirely equity or debt. This may indeed be the case, because flotation costs can be prohibitively high for small securities issues.

After considering all of these factors, you must do what Bowditch's board must

CONTINUING EDUCATION IN FINANCE

Aside from the popular business periodicals, such as the *Wall Street Journal*, *Forbes*, *Business Week*, and *Fortune*, *The Economist*, a weekly magazine, published in London, covers world news and business from the British perspective. As its name implies, it has a distinct economics and finance orientation. *Euromoney*, a British monthly magazine, covers the world's financial markets.

There are several journals whose contributors and readers are academics and practitioners. These include *Financial Analysts Journal* (investments), *Financial Management* (business finance) and the more applied *Financial Practice and Education*. The latter two are publications of the Financial Management Association, the largest national association of finance scholars and practitioners. The Association also sponsors a series of books on applied business finance, called the Survey and Synthesis Series.

Several of the leading business schools publish journals that include nontechnical articles on finance. The best known of these is *The Harvard Business Review*. Others include *Business Horizons* (Indiana University), the *Sloan Management Review* (MIT), and the *California Management Review* (The University of California).

Finally, there are some excellent journals written primarily for practitioners but read also by academics. These include *The Journal of Applied Corporate Finance*, published by Stern, Stewart Management Services, Inc., and *The Journal of Portfolio Management*, published by Institutional Investor, Inc. This latter journal is oriented toward investments; however, it features articles on applications of capital market theory, covered in Chapters 7 and 8 of this book.

Acquaint your students with the possibilities of supplementing magazines and journals with on-line services, the internet, and worldwide web.

This is far from an exhaustive list of resources for keeping abreast of developments in finance. However, the periodicals mentioned here are particularly notable for their lucid explanations of the ideas of modern finance and for showing how these ideas are applied in the working world of finance.

A FINAL THOUGHT

We set out to write the perfect text. Then we scaled back our goal merely to writing the best finance text. Now, at the end, we might settle for just a good text. There were times, with deadlines near, when any text would suffice. We sincerely hope that we have provided you with a solid foundation in finance. For many, this will be your only finance course. We would like to hear from you in about two years to find out how many of these basic ideas you still retain. If you still remember the most important ones, we will have succeeded. If you don't, we will have to do better. In the preface, we invited your comments. You can help us do better. Let us know how.

I am always ready to learn, but I do not always like being taught.
—Winston Churchill

For now, the teaching of finance is over. Now you can follow Churchill's dictum and begin to learn.

REFERENCE MATERIALS

APPENDIX A.1

Future Value Interest Factor (FVIF) ($1 at *r*% for *n* years); $FV_n = PV_0(FVIF_{r,n})$

PERIOD, *n*	1%	2%	3%	4%	5%	6%	7%	8%	9%	10%	11%	12%	13%
0	1.000	1.000	1.000	1.000	1.000	1.000	1.000	1.000	1.000	1.000	1.000	1.000	1.000
1	1.010	1.020	1.030	1.040	1.050	1.060	1.070	1.080	1.090	1.100	1.110	1.120	1.130
2	1.020	1.040	1.061	1.082	1.102	1.124	1.145	1.166	1.188	1.210	1.232	1.254	1.277
3	1.030	1.061	1.093	1.125	1.158	1.191	1.225	1.260	1.295	1.331	1.368	1.405	1.443
4	1.041	1.082	1.126	1.170	1.216	1.262	1.311	1.360	1.412	1.464	1.518	1.574	1.630
5	1.051	1.104	1.159	1.217	1.276	1.338	1.403	1.469	1.539	1.611	1.685	1.762	1.842
6	1.062	1.126	1.194	1.265	1.340	1.419	1.501	1.587	1.677	1.772	1.870	1.974	2.082
7	1.072	1.149	1.230	1.316	1.407	1.504	1.606	1.714	1.828	1.949	2.076	2.211	2.353
8	1.083	1.172	1.267	1.369	1.477	1.594	1.718	1.851	1.993	2.144	2.305	2.476	2.658
9	1.094	1.195	1.305	1.423	1.551	1.689	1.838	1.999	2.172	2.358	2.558	2.773	3.004
10	1.105	1.219	1.344	1.480	1.629	1.791	1.967	2.159	2.367	2.594	2.839	3.106	3.395
11	1.116	1.243	1.384	1.539	1.710	1.898	2.105	2.332	2.580	2.853	3.152	3.479	3.836
12	1.127	1.268	1.426	1.601	1.796	2.012	2.252	2.518	2.813	3.138	3.498	3.896	4.335
13	1.138	1.294	1.469	1.665	1.886	2.133	2.410	2.720	3.066	3.452	3.883	4.363	4.898
14	1.149	1.319	1.513	1.732	1.980	2.261	2.579	2.937	3.342	3.797	4.310	4.887	5.535
15	1.161	1.346	1.558	1.801	2.079	2.397	2.759	3.172	3.642	4.177	4.785	5.474	6.254
16	1.173	1.373	1.605	1.873	2.183	2.540	2.952	3.426	3.970	4.595	5.311	6.130	7.067
17	1.184	1.400	1.653	1.948	2.292	2.693	3.159	3.700	4.328	5.054	5.895	6.866	7.986
18	1.196	1.428	1.702	2.026	2.407	2.854	3.380	3.996	4.717	5.560	6.544	7.690	9.024
19	1.208	1.457	1.754	2.107	2.527	3.026	3.617	4.316	5.142	6.116	7.263	8.613	10.197
20	1.220	1.486	1.806	2.191	2.653	3.207	3.870	4.661	5.604	6.728	8.062	9.646	11.523
24	1.270	1.608	2.033	2.563	3.225	4.049	5.072	6.341	7.911	9.850	12.239	15.179	18.790
25	1.282	1.641	2.094	2.666	3.386	4.292	5.427	6.848	8.623	10.835	13.585	17.000	21.231
30	1.348	1.811	2.427	3.243	4.322	5.743	7.612	10.063	13.268	17.449	22.892	29.960	39.116
40	1.489	2.208	3.262	4.801	7.040	10.286	14.974	21.725	31.409	45.259	65.001	93.051	132.782
50	1.645	2.692	4.384	7.107	11.467	18.420	29.457	46.902	74.358	117.391	184.565	289.002	450.736
60	1.817	3.281	5.892	10.520	18.679	32.988	57.946	101.257	176.031	304.482	524.057	897.597	1,530.05

Appendix A.1 *continued*

PERIOD, *n*	14%	15%	16%	17%	18%	19%	20%	24%	28%	32%	36%	40%
0	1.000	1.000	1.000	1.000	1.000	1.000	1.000	1.000	1.000	1.000	1.000	1.000
1	1.140	1.150	1.160	1.170	1.180	1.190	1.200	1.240	1.280	1.320	1.360	1.400
2	1.300	1.322	1.346	1.369	1.392	1.416	1.440	1.538	1.638	1.742	1.850	1.960
3	1.482	1.521	1.561	1.602	1.643	1.685	1.728	1.907	2.067	2.300	2.515	2.744
4	1.689	1.749	1.811	1.874	1.939	2.005	2.074	2.364	2.684	3.036	3.421	3.842
5	1.925	2.011	2.100	2.192	2.288	2.386	2.488	2.932	3.436	4.007	4.653	5.378
6	2.195	2.313	2.436	2.565	2.700	2.840	2.986	3.635	4.398	5.290	6.328	7.530
7	2.502	2.660	2.826	3.001	3.185	3.379	3.583	4.508	5.629	6.983	8.605	10.541
8	2.853	3.059	3.278	3.511	3.759	4.021	4.300	5.590	7.206	9.217	11.703	14.758
9	3.252	3.518	3.803	4.108	4.435	4.785	5.160	6.931	9.223	12.166	15.917	20.661
10	3.707	4.046	4.411	4.807	5.234	5.695	6.192	8.594	11.806	16.060	21.647	28.925
11	4.226	4.652	5.117	5.624	6.176	6.777	7.430	10.657	15.112	21.199	29.439	40.496
12	4.818	5.350	5.926	6.580	7.288	8.064	8.916	13.215	19.343	27.983	40.037	56.694
13	5.492	6.153	6.886	7.699	8.599	9.596	10.699	16.386	24.759	36.937	54.451	79.372
14	6.261	7.076	7.988	9.007	10.147	11.420	12.839	20.319	31.961	48.757	74.053	111.120
15	7.138	8.137	9.266	10.539	11.974	13.590	15.407	25.196	40.565	64.359	100.712	155.568
16	8.137	9.358	10.748	12.330	14.129	16.172	18.488	31.243	51.923	84.954	136.969	217.795
17	9.276	10.761	12.468	14.426	16.672	19.244	22.186	38.741	66.461	112.139	186.278	304.914
18	10.575	12.375	14.463	16.879	19.673	22.901	26.623	48.039	85.071	148.023	253.338	426.879
19	12.056	14.232	16.777	19.748	23.214	27.252	31.948	59.568	108.890	195.391	344.540	597.630
20	13.743	16.367	19.461	23.106	27.393	32.429	38.338	73.864	139.380	257.916	468.574	836.683
24	23.212	28.625	35.236	43.297	53.109	65.032	79.497	174.631	374.144	783.023	1,603.00	3,214.20
25	26.462	32.919	40.874	50.658	62.669	77.388	95.396	216.542	478.905	1,033.59	2,180.08	4.499.88
30	50.950	66.212	85.850	111.065	143.371	184.675	237.376	634.820	1,645.50	4,142.07	10,143.0	24,201.4
40	188.884	267.864	378.721	533.869	750.378	1,051.67	1,469.77	5,455.91	19,426.7	66,520.8	219,562	700,038
50	700.233	1,083.66	1,670.70	2,566.22	3,927.36	5,988.91	9,100.44	46,890.4	229,350	*	*	*
60	2,595.92	4,384.00	7,370.20	12,335.4	20,555.1	34,105.0	56,347.5	402,996	*	*	*	*

*These interest factors exceed 1,000,000

APPENDIX A.3

Present Value of an Annuity Interest Factor (PVIFA) (\$1 per year at r% for n years); PV_0= (CF) ($PVIFA_{n,r}$)

PERIOD, n	1%	2%	3%	4%	5%	6%	7%	8%	9%	10%	11%	12%	13%
1	0.990	0.980	0.971	0.962	0.952	0.943	0.935	0.926	0.917	0.909	0.901	0.893	0.885
2	1.970	1.942	1.913	1.886	1.859	1.833	1.808	1.783	1.759	1.736	1.713	1.690	1.668
3	2.941	2.884	2.829	2.775	2.723	2.673	2.624	2.577	2.531	2.487	2.444	2.402	2.361
4	3.902	3.808	3.717	3.630	3.546	3.465	3.387	3.312	3.240	3.170	3.102	3.037	2.974
5	4.853	4.713	4.580	4.452	4.329	4.212	4.100	3.993	3.890	3.791	3.696	3.605	3.517
6	5.795	5.601	5.417	5.242	5.076	4.917	4.766	4.623	4.486	4.355	4.231	4.111	3.998
7	6.728	6.472	6.230	6.002	5.786	5.582	5.389	5.206	5.033	4.868	4.712	4.564	4.423
8	7.652	7.325	7.020	6.733	6.463	6.210	5.971	5.747	5.535	5.335	5.146	4.968	4.799
9	8.566	8.162	7.786	7.435	7.108	6.802	6.515	6.247	5.995	5.759	5.537	5.328	5.132
10	9.471	8.983	8.530	8.111	7.722	7.360	7.024	6.710	6.418	6.145	5.889	5.650	5.426
11	10.368	9.787	9.253	8.760	8.306	7.887	7.499	7.139	6.805	6.495	6.207	5.938	5.687
12	11.255	10.575	9.954	9.385	8.863	8.384	7.943	7.536	7.161	6.814	6.492	6.194	5.918
13	12.134	11.348	10.635	9.986	9.394	8.853	8.358	7.904	7.487	7.103	6.750	6.424	6.122
14	13.004	12.106	11.296	10.563	9.899	9.295	8.745	8.244	7.786	7.367	6.982	6.628	6.302
15	13.865	12.849	11.938	11.118	10.380	9.712	9.108	8.559	8.061	7.606	7.191	6.811	6.462
16	14.718	13.578	12.561	11.652	10.838	10.106	9.447	8.851	8.312	7.824	7.379	6.974	6.604
17	15.562	14.292	13.166	12.166	11.274	10.477	9.763	9.122	8.544	8.022	7.549	7.120	6.729
18	16.398	14.992	13.754	12.659	11.690	10.828	10.059	9.372	8.756	8.201	7.702	7.250	6.840
19	17.226	15.678	14.324	13.134	12.085	11.158	10.336	9.604	8.950	8.365	7.839	7.366	6.938
20	18.046	16.351	14.877	13.590	12.462	11.470	10.594	9.818	9.128	8.514	7.963	7.469	7.025
24	21.243	18.914	16.936	15.247	13.799	12.550	11.469	10.529	9.707	8.985	8.348	7.784	7.283
25	22.023	19.523	17.413	15.622	14.094	12.783	11.654	10.675	9.823	9.077	8.422	7.843	7.330
30	25.808	22.397	19.600	17.292	15.373	13.765	12.409	11.258	10.274	9.427	8.694	8.055	7.496
40	32.835	27.355	23.115	19.793	17.159	15.046	13.332	11.925	10.757	9.779	8.951	8.244	7.634
50	39.196	31.424	25.730	21.482	18.256	15.762	13.801	12.233	10.962	9.915	9.042	8.304	7.675
60	44.955	34.761	27.676	22.623	18.929	16.161	14.039	12.377	11.048	9.967	9.074	8.324	7.687

Appendix A.3 *continued*

PERIOD, *n*	14%	15%	16%	17%	18%	19%	20%	24%	28%	32%	36%	40%
1	0.877	0.870	0.862	0.855	0.847	0.840	0.833	0.806	0.781	0.758	0.735	0.714
2	1.647	1.626	1.605	1.585	1.566	1.547	1.528	1.457	1.392	1.332	1.276	1.224
3	2.322	2.283	2.246	2.210	2.174	2.140	2.106	1.981	1.868	1.766	1.674	1.589
4	2.914	2.855	2.798	2.743	2.690	2.639	2.589	2.404	2.241	2.096	1.966	1.849
5	3.433	3.352	3.274	3.199	3.127	3.058	2.991	2.745	2.532	2.345	2.181	2.035
6	3.889	3.784	3.685	3.589	3.498	3.410	3.326	3.020	2.759	2.534	2.399	2.168
7	4.288	4.160	4.039	3.922	3.812	3.706	3.605	3.242	2.937	2.678	2.455	2.263
8	4.639	4.487	4.344	4.207	4.078	3.954	3.837	3.421	3.076	2.786	2.540	2.331
9	4.946	4.772	4.607	4.451	4.303	4.163	4.031	3.566	3.184	2.868	2.603	2.379
10	5.216	5.019	4.833	4.659	4.494	4.339	4.193	3.682	3.269	2.930	2.650	2.414
11	5.453	5.234	5.029	4.836	4.656	4.486	4.327	3.776	3.335	2.978	2.683	2.438
12	5.660	5.421	5.197	4.988	4.793	4.611	4.439	3.851	3.387	3.013	2.708	2.456
13	5.842	5.583	5.342	5.118	4.910	4.715	4.533	3.912	3.427	3.040	2.727	2.469
14	6.002	5.724	5.468	5.229	5.008	4.802	4.611	3.962	3.459	3.061	2.740	2.478
15	6.142	5.847	5.575	5.324	5.092	4.876	4.675	4.001	3.483	3.076	2.750	2.484
16	6.265	5.954	5.669	5.405	5.162	4.938	4.730	4.033	3.503	3.088	2.758	2.489
17	6.373	6.047	5.749	5.475	5.222	4.990	4.775	4.059	3.518	3.097	2.763	2.492
18	6.467	6.128	5.818	5.534	5.273	5.033	4.812	4.080	3.529	3.104	2.767	2.494
19	6.550	6.198	5.877	5.584	5.316	5.070	4.844	4.097	3.539	3.109	2.770	2.496
20	6.623	6.259	5.929	5.628	5.353	5.101	4.870	4.110	3.546	3.113	2.772	2.497
24	6.835	6.434	6.073	5.746	5.451	5.182	4.937	4.143	3.562	3.121	2.776	2.499
25	6.873	6.464	6.097	5.766	5.467	5.195	4.948	4.147	3.564	3.122	2.776	2.499
30	7.003	6.566	6.177	5.829	5.517	5.235	4.979	4.160	3.569	3.124	2.778	2.500
40	7.105	6.642	6.233	5.871	5.548	5.258	4.997	4.166	3.571	3.125	2.778	2.500
50	7.133	6.661	6.246	5.880	5.554	5.262	4.999	4.167	3.571	3.125	2.778	2.500
60	7.140	6.665	6.249	5.882	5.555	5.263	5.000	4.167	3.571	3.125	2.778	2.500

CHAPTER 8

1. 1.25
3. 2.06
7. 1.2
11. MTV: .082
    GE: .117
15. a. 12%
    b. 10% ($40); 8.8% ($50)
17. a. 16%
19. a. 1.125
21. a. 11.8%
    b. 6%
    c. $32.05

CHAPTER 9

1. Year 0, −$15,000; years 1–4, $4,000; year 5, $6,000
3. IRR between 12% and 14%
5. a. $163
   b. Close to 7%
   c. Yes
   d. No
7. a. Year 0, −34,000; years 1–8, $6,106; year 9, $11,222
   b. $379
   c. yes
9. a. A: $9,746; B: $7,497
   b. A: 22%; B: 25%
   c. NPV, proj. A; IRR, proj. B
   d. Size
   e. A
11. a. $1,036
    b. 10.2%
    c. Yes
    d. NPV = $2,008; IRR = 11.3%
13. a. $24,705
    b. $4,026
    c. $4,706
    d. (b) $5,118;
       (c) $5,638
15. a. $6,803
    b. $2,276
    c. $3,263
    d. (b) $3,602;
       (c) $4,357
17. a. (0%) $11,641; (16%) −$3,708
    c. 10.9%
19. Hunter 33:
    Year 0, −$42,000
    Year 1, $10,028
    Year 2, $10,404
    Year 3, $10,798
    Year 4, $31,544

CHAPTER 10

1. 6.67%
3. a. 21.07%
   b. 21.50%
5. 16.7%
7. a. $w_D = 0.22$; $w_{PFD} = 0.35$;
      $w_E = 0.43$
   b. $1,148.77; $574,387
   c. $37.50; $3,750,000
   d. $55; $5,500,000
   e. $w_D = 0.06$; $w_{PFD} = 0.38$;
      $w_e = 0.43$
9. a. Loan, bonds, new stock
   b. $w_L = 0.048$; $w_B = 0.178$;
      $w_{\text{new stock}} = 0.774$
   c. Loan = $96,000;
      bonds = $356,000;
      stock = $548,000
   d. 10.18%
   e. 375 bonds
   f. 73,715 shares
   g. 11%, 7.26%
   h. 9%, 5.94%
   i. 15.38%
   j. Yes
   k. 13.48%
11. NPV = −$78,902; IRR = 12.73%
13. 14.31%
15. 11.08%

CHAPTER 11

1. a. 8.74%
   b. 4.67%
3. b. $198,633
5. b. $334,238
9. a. 8.74%
   c. $6,701
   d. No
11. $21,496
13. Projects C, B, G (NPV)
    Projects D, B, F, C (PI)
15. a. NPV = $25,500
    b. Projects E, D, B, A, C
    c. $6,000
    d. Projects E, D, B, C
    e. $1500
17. a. $5,771
    b. $9,819
    c. $856
19. b. $9,949
    c. $26,286; −$22,724
    d. Network $8328; system −$7077

CHAPTER 12

1.

Firm	*June*	*July*	*Aug.*
A	$8,333	$17,500	$2,500
B	$8,333	$12,000	$6,000

3. a. −10%; −28%
   b. 2%; −4%
   c. 10%; 12%
5. $150,000; $157,500
7. Apparel, 0.76; utility, 1.00; software, 0.24; auto 0.76
9. Firm 1

CHAPTER 13

1. a. $1,500,000
   b. $1,500,000
   c. 50%
   d. 50%
3. 11.6%; 3.6%; 8%
5. $60; $1.00; 9 million
7. D_1 = $3.78; EPS_6 = $19.04;
   D_6 = $5.55
9. a. $1.60 $1.33
   b. 120 shares, same
   c. no change
11. 100,000 shares, 25% premium
13. Hiyield

CHAPTER 14

1. 2.03%
3. 11.71%
5. $101,343
7. 10.53%
9. Ending cash (Dec.) = $1,560
11. Ending cash (Dec.) = −$17,628
13. Ending cash (Dec.) = $135,150
15. Ending cash (Dec.) = −$89,995
19. a. $113,636
    b. 10.23% (Eq. 14.4)
21. a. $105,263
    b. 11.11% (Eq. 14.5)

CHAPTER 15

1. 1994 trend sales = 1.41;
   1994 common size NI = 0.04
3. NPM = 2.7%, 2.6%; ROA = 7.7%, 3.6%; ATO = 2.83X, 1.37X
5. a. −3%
   b. Outperformed by 2%
   c. 0%
   d. No; yes; no
   e. Bad; −4%
7. 18.8
9. 7.5%
11. 4.65, down from 7.33
13. a. $37.50
    b. 17.1 times
15. same as ROE
17. Low ATO, low ROE

CHAPTER 16

1. $4,700,000, or $47 per share

GLOSSARY

abandonment option The option to terminate or sell a project before the end of its functional life.

accounts payable days Number of days the company takes to pay its suppliers.

acquisition The purchase of a company or business unit.

after-tax cost of a tax-deductible expense Net cost after tax savings = Cost (1 − tax rate).

agency cost reduction A motive for restructurings aimed at reducing managerial inefficiency.

agency costs The reduction of value that results from the separation of the ownership of assets from control over these assets. When managers act as owners' agents, they make decisions like granting themselves excessive perquisites that are costly to the owners. Large corporations with many widely-dispersed stockholders are most susceptible to agency costs.

allocated costs Costs, such as overhead costs, that do not necessarily change as a result of taking on a project.

allocative efficiency Economic efficiency based on allocating inputs to their most highly valued uses.

amortized loan A loan that is paid-off in equal periodic payments. Automobile loans and home mortgages are often amortized loans.

annual percentage rate (APR) The annualized cost of borrowing based on simple interest.

annualized return Returns adjusted to a one year holding period to allow comparability of investments.

annuities A finite stream of cash flows of a fixed amount, equally-spaced in time. Ordinary annuities make payments at the end of each period whereas annuities due make payments at the beginning of each period.

anti-takeover defenses A variety of mechanisms or strategies used by target firms to avoid being acquired or to increase the bid price.

arbitrage pricing model Attempts to relate required returns on securities to multiple factors such as inflation, GNP and industrial production indices. It is an alternative to the CAPM.

ask price The price at which a dealer will sell, the price being asked.

asset beta Refers to the systematic or market risk of an investment asset.

asymmetric information A situation in which one party has more information than another, so can extract extra value fom a transaction.

balance sheet Snapshot of a company's financial position at a moment in time. The left-hand side lists assets and the right-hand side lists liabilities and owners' equity.

banker's acceptance A bank signs a time draft, promising to pay a supplier on a future date. Based on the bank's credit, the acceptance can be sold by the supplier in a secondary market.

bears More pessimistic or conservative investors who expect prices to fall.

before-tax expense The cash outlay for an item or service before considering tax consequences.

beta A standardized measure, or index, of a stock's market risk.

bid-ask spread The difference between the Ask price and the Bid price.

bid price The price a dealer is willing to pay for an asset.

board of directors As the elected panel of stockholder representatives, the board directs the corporation's strategic activities, and hires, fires, and compensates mangers, and ratifies major corporate decisions.

bonds The security that represents the issuers' promise to pay a predetermined amount of interest over a fixed term and to re-pay the principal on the security's maturity date.

book value of an asset The historic cost less accumulated deprecia-

tion. Book Value may differ from market value.

bulls aggressive or optimistic investors who expect prices to rise.

call option The right, but not the obligation, to buy an asset at a specified price within a specified time period.

capital asset pricing model (CAPM) Specifies that the required return on an asset equals the risk free rate plus a risk premium. The risk premium is the asset's beta times the market risk premium. The CAPM is the equation of the security market line.

capital budget The total amount a corporation spends on investments in a given time period (usually a year).

capital gain Gain from the price appreciation of an asset.

capital gains or price appreciation The return to investors from price changes.

capital market line Indicates the total risk and return of portfolios consisting of combinations of the market portfolio and the risk free asset. Some segments of the line represent leveraged positions in which investors have borrowed at the risk free rate to invest in the market portfolio.

capital markets Financial markets trading intermediate and long-term securities.

cash budget Forecasts future company cash flows. Its purpose is to predict shortages and surpluses of cash.

cash cycle The sequence of activities associated with cash moving through the company.

cash flow The amount of money that passes through a corporation. Residual cash flow, for example, refers to the amount of money that stockholders have a claim on after all other claims have been paid.

certificates of deposit (CDs) Interest bearing investments often offered by banks and savings & loans companies.

characteristic line The regression line relating stock returns to market returns. Beta is the slope of the characteristic line.

clearinghouse An association that handles the exchange of checks between banks.

closely-held corporation A corporation whose stock is not publicly traded and with relatively few shareholders.

closure option The option to temporarily close-down a facility.

commercial bank A bank whose primary business has traditionally been commercial lending. Deregulation and competition have caused many commercial banks to develop other business lines. Commercial banks include Citicorp, Chase Manhattan and BankAmerica.

commercial paper Unsecured promissory notes, sold by large and creditworthy corporations, with maturities ranging from a few weeks to 9 months.

commitment fee Fee charged by banks for making credit lines available to businesses.

common stock risk premium Equals the market risk premium times the stock's beta.

compensating balances Customer deposit balances required by banks as partial compensation for lending.

complementary projects Investment projects that are related such that all or none must be taken.

compound interest Earning interest on previously earned interest.

concentration bank A bank in one or several central locations where corporate funds from many locations are transferred. At these banks, the funds are under the direct control of the corporate cash manager.

constant growth formula A present value formula applied to stock valuation where dividends are modeled as a growing perpetuity.

consumers price index (CPI) Shows relative price over time of a standard basket of goods and services used by consumers, so acts as a measure of inflation.

contingent claims A claim against an asset, the value of which is dependent on the value of the asset.

correlation Indicates whether two variables are related, and measures the direction and strength of that relationship. Correlation values range from $[-1]$ to $[+1]$, with a value of 0 indicating no relationship.

correspondent bank A bank that provides services, such as check clearing, to other banks.

cost of capital The rate of return that must be earned in order to satisfy investors.

cost of debt The required return of investors in the company's bonds. Usually, the cost of debt is measured by finding the yield to maturity of outstanding bonds.

cost of equity The required return of investors in the corporation's stock.

cost-of-living-adjustments (Cola) Adjustments to maintain purchasing power often based on changes in the CPI.

coupon payments The fixed amount of interest paid (usually semi-annually) by a bond issuer to bond holders. Coupon payments = (coupon rate) (par value).

coupon rate The fixed interest paid by a bond, stated as a percentage of par value.

covariance Measures both degree and magnitude of co-movement of two variables. Covariance is the product of the correlation between two variables and their standard deviations.

credit line Allows the firm to overdraw its checking account. Credit lines are intended to finance very short term credit needs.

current yield The annual coupon payment made by a bond divided by the bond's current price.

the days model Model for determining a company's financing gap (Financing Gap in days = A/R days + Inventory days − A/P days).

default The act of making a scheduled payment when due. Default can lead to bankruptcy.

depreciation An accounting expense designed to reflect the wear-and-tear or use of an long-lived asset.

discount, premium and par Bonds are said to be selling at a discount, a premium or at par if the sales price is less than, greater than, or equal to par value, respectively.

discount rate The interest rate used to find the present value of a future payment or series of payments. For many investments, investors' required return is the discount rate used to find the present value.

discounted loan Deducting interest on a loan in advance, reducing the amount actually received by the borrower.

discriminant analysis A credit scoring technique which identifies certain key attributes that differentiate payers from non-payers.

dispersion projects Investments that add new geographic regions, including other countries, to a company's operations.

diversification projects Investments that add new products or product lines to a company's operations.

diversified conglomerates Companies producing goods and services in a variety of industries.

divestitures The sale of a subsidiary or business unit. Often completed so a company can better focus on a single or few leins of business.

dividend yield The return due to dividends received equals the annual dividend divided by share price.

dividends Payments made to stockholders by the corporation. Cash dividends are payments of money. Regular cash dividends are often made quarterly. Stock dividends are additional shares of stock issued to existing shareholders.

dominated portfolio A portfolio whose expected return is less than, and its standard deviation is greater than, that of another portfolio. A portfolio is also dominated if either its expected return or its standard deviation are equal to that of another portfolio as long as the other condition (greater standard deviation or lower expected return) is met.

Dow-Jones Industrial Average (DJIA) A stock price index of 30 large U.S. industrial companies. It is the most widely followed indicator of stock market activity.

e 2.714, the base of natural logs used in continuous compounding.

economic order quantity Each time inventory is ordered, the economic order quantity is the number of units per order that minimizes total inventory costs.

economies of scale Cost savings per unit of production generated by higher production levels.

economies of scope The cost savings from increased asset utilization or reduced redundancy when many different products are produced by one company rather than several.

effective annual percentage rate (EAR) The annualized compound rate of interest.

efficient financial markets Markets that quickly and accurately impound information into prices so prices represent the market consensus fair value of an asset.

efficient markets hypothesis The theory that argues that financial markets are efficient.

efficient set Contains all portfolios that are not dominated by other risky portfolios. In theory, investors choose from among these portfolios depending on their risk-return preferences.

equilibrium conditions A set of prices across goods such that there is no imbalance in supply and demand.

eurodollars Dollar denominated deposits in foreign banks and foreign branches of U.S. banks.

ex ante return The anticipated return from an investment.

ex post return The historical or after-the-fact return from owning a security which may differ from its *ex ante* or expected return.

exchange rates The rate at which one currency is exchanged or translated into another currency.

exercise a call option The purchase of an asset under the terms of an option contract.

exercise price Price at which an asset may be bought or sold by the owner of an option.

expansion projects Investments that expand existing capacity, such as adding new machinery or equipment to increase output.

expected cash flow The future cash flow from an investment computed by assigning probabilities to various outcomes.

expected return The probability weighted return, computed by assigning a probability of occurrence to the various possible future returns.

expected value The probability weighted value of an investment, computed by assigning a probability of occurrence to the various possible future values.

expiration date The date that an

option to buy or sell an asset lapses.

externalities Unwanted by-products of production like pollution, the costs of which are not borne by the producers but by society.

face amount or par value The amount a bond will repay to the bondholder when it matures. Corporate bonds often have a face amount of $1000.

factor A financial institution that buys a company's accounts receivable at a discount from face value, and assumes the risk and incurs the cost of collecting the debt.

financial balance sheet Finance's conceptual counter-part to accounting's balance sheet. The financial balance sheet is used throughout this text to help illustrate corporate financial decisions and activities.

financial markets Markets for all types of financial securities.

financing gap The days or dollars that a company must finance with reserves before cash from sales flow into the company.

Fisher equation An equation that links nominal interest rates to real rates and inflation.

fixed assets Long term investments. They may be tangible, such as machinery and equipment, or intangible, such as patents and employee training.

fixed claims Suppliers of corporate financing hold fixed claims if they are for a set amount of money. Bonds, notes, mortgages, and payables are examples of fixed claims.

float The time it takes for a check to make its way through the payments system. Float occurs because of the mails, in-house processing by companies and the bank clearing process.

flotation costs The transaction costs incurred when raising capital externally, for example, when selling newly issued stock or bonds.

fundamental analysis Investment analysis which examines economic, financial political, and other information fundamental to the success of a company and its industry.

future value. A cash flow, or stream of cash flows, re-expressed as an equivalent amount at some future date.

generally accepted accounting principles (GAAP) The accounting rules that define how companies construct their financial reports. Designed to provide as accurate as possible a picture of a company's operational activities and financial position.

geometric series A series of mathematical terms where each successive term is a fixed factor times its predecessor. The technique used to sum a geometric series is covered in the appendix to chapter 5 and is used to derive perpetuity, annuity and growing perpetuity valuation formulas.

going private transactions The purchase of all of the stock of a public company by a small investor group who then delist the company making it a private, rather than a public, company.

growing perpetuity An infinite cash flow stream that makes payments at regular intervals (e.g., monthly, annually, etc.), with each payment equaling its predecessor times a fixed growth factor.

holding period return The return for the period a security is actually held.

hubris Excessive confidence in one's ability. In restructurings hubris occurs when managers believe they can successfully manage companies in any industry of any size.

hurdle rate A required rate of return, or reference point, against which to compare a project's internal rate of return.

imperfectly competitive Markets where entry and imitation has been blocked to some degree, so offer opportunities for creating shareholder wealth.

incidental effects Indirect effects of an investment. Costs or revenues not normally associated with the investment.

income statement A record for a period of a company's operational activities. Sometimes referred to as a P/L or Profit/Loss statement because the bottom line of the report provides profit or loss income information.

incremental cash flows The change in corporate cash flows attributable to a project.

indenture A contract specifying repayment dates, interest payment schedules, and conditions which must be satisfied to keep the bond out of default.

independent projects The decision to invest in any project has no impact on the decision to invest in any other project.

inflation Changes in overall price levels.

information asymmetry Refers to the difference between the information that insiders, such as managers, have regarding a firm and the information that outsiders, like stockholders, have.

informational efficiency Efficiency based on information being quickly and accurately impounded into asset prices.

initial public offering (IPO) The offering of a security to the market for the first time, usually IPOs refer to first-time stock offerings by emerging companies.

insider trading Trading by managers in the stock of the company for which they work. Sometimes

illegal since managers presumably know much more than other investors about the company.

insolvency The inability of a company to make payments as they come due.

institutional investor activism The monitoring of corporate managers by representatives of large pension and mutual funds.

interest rate The amount of money paid by a borrower to a lender for the use of the borrowed principal. The rate is expressed as a percentage of the principal owed.

internal rate of return (IRR) The discount rate that equates the present value of an investment's future cash flows with the investment's cost.

inventory turnover days The number of days, on average, that finished goods stay in inventory before being sold.

joint venture A partnership between two companies, or between a company and a government, to engage in business activities. Joint ventures are often used in international business.

junk bonds High-risk, high-yield debt often associated with Michael Milken.

just-in-time Approach to inventory management in which a continuous supply of raw materials arrives at the production facility hours before the materials are placed in production.

law of one price An economic rule that states that the same item may not appear in the same market at two or more different prices. In well-functioning markets profit opportunities will quickly drive prices to a single market-wide price.

LBOs (leveraged buyouts) Going private transactions financed primarily with debt.

LIBOR–London Interbank offered rate The interest rate at which large international banks often lend to each other.

licensing agreement A company in the first country produces goods whose production rights are held by a company in the second country. The company in the second country may provide technical and management support, and perhaps capital to the project. In return this company earns royalties from the sale of the product.

limited liability There is an upper limit to the amount of loss when one has limited liability. Corporations and limited partnerships offer their investors limited liability.

liquidity The ability of a company to meet its cash needs either from cash balances or timely access to cash. Also refers to the ease with which an asset or security can be turned into cash.

liquidity preference A theory of interest rate term structures that assumes that investors prefer shorter maturities, so must be paid a premium to hold long maturity instruments.

lockbox A local post office box from which a bank collects checks, processes and deposits them in a company's local bank account.

marginal tax rate The rate at which each additional dollar of income is taxed.

market for corporate control Restructurings are the result of bidding by competing management teams to control corporate assets.

market power Having sufficient market share to control price to some extent.

market risk The risk common to all securities and portfolios. It cannot be eliminated by diversifying securities portfolios.

market risk premium The difference between the rate of return on the market (e.g., S&P 500) and the risk-free return (e.g., treasury bills).

market segmentation A theory of interest rate term structures that argues that the yield curve reflects the supply and demand for different maturity debt instruments.

market value of an asset The price for which an asset can be sold. This price may differ from book value.

the matching principle The accounting rule that matches expenses for a period to the number of units sold during the period. Designed to help users of financial statements determine whether a firm can earn profits.

maturity date The date at which a debt instrument must repay the original principal amount.

maximizing shareholder wealth The financial goal of a corporation and the primary objective of corporate management. Shareholder wealth is increased by investing in positive net present value projects.

MBOs (management buyouts) Going private transactions in which part of the management team joins the investment group to buy all of a company's outstanding shares, often using very high leverage.

merger The friendly combination of two companies.

money markets Markets in which short-term securities are traded.

money market mutual fund A mutual fund that invests in short term, liquid securities such as commercial paper, negotiable CDs and treasury bills.

money market preferred stock Preferred stock whose dividend adjusts every 49 days at auction.

more highly valued uses The economic efficiency rationale for some takeovers.

multinational corporation A corporation with investments in at

least two and often a large number of countries.

mutually exclusive projects Investment projects that are related such that only one can be taken.

NASDAQ The National Association of Securities Dealers Automated Quote system that is the electronic network of over-the-counter stock trading in the U.S.

negative cash flow Cash outflows exceed cash inflows. Even profitable companies may experience negative cash flow on occasion.

negotiable certificate of deposit A deposit liability of a bank, sold as a negotiable security with a minimum denomination of $100,000.

net present value (NPV) The present value of future cash flows minus the initial investment. NPV is the present value of all cash flows connected to an investment.

nominal rate The stated rate or yield which reflects expectations about inflation.

NYSE The New York Stock Exchange, the largest, in terms of dollar volume, stock exchange in the U.S.

opportunity cost The amount of the highest valued forgone alternative.

option to delay The option to postpone an investment until more information is available.

options Future alternatives that may be costlessly ignored. Options occur as securities as well as part of many investments in real assets.

over-the-counter market A computer network of dealers trading the shares of thousands of companies including most of the smaller publicly traded companies in the U.S.

par value See face amount.

pareto optimality A situation where no one can be made better off without injuring at least one other person.

partnerships When two or more individuals join to pursue a business venture.

payback A measure of how many years it takes to recoup the initial investment in a project.

perfectly competitive Markets in which entry and exit are easy and consumers consider price alone when making their purchase decisions. Commodity markets can be nearly perfectly competitive.

perpetuity An infinite stream of equal cash flows, each equally spaced in time.

perquisites Benefits of employment beyond direct monetary compensation. Perquisites, also called perks, commonly include health insurance, vacation, company cars, and day care. Excessive perks are those which don't contribute to corporate value by motivating employees or other means.

political risk The risk of doing business in a foreign country in which governments are unstable or hostile. These countries are often socially volatile as well.

pollution rights Rights, issued by government, allowing companies to emit a specified amount of pollution. Rights may be traded between companies for a price.

portfolio A group of securities held by an investor.

portfolio effect The reduction in risk (standard deviation) that occurs through the blending of stocks into a portfolio.

present value A future cash flow, or stream of cash flows, re-expressed as an equivalent current amount of money.

price of risk The premium above the risk-free rate that investors demand for holding a risky asset.

primary markets Markets in which companies raise funds by selling securities to investors.

prime rate The rate at which banks offer short term loans to their largest and most credit worthy customers. The prime rate is set by banks, and acts as a bellwether rate for bank commercial loans.

principal The amount of money borrowed.

pro forma (or projected) income statements Income statements for future periods constructed based on historic financial ratios and assumptions about how the firm will perform in the future. They are useful tools for analyzing many types of corporate decisions.

producers price index (PPI) Shows relative price over time of a standard basket of goods and services used by producers, so acts as a measure of inflation for corporations.

product differentiation Efforts by companies to reduce the substitution of competitors' products for their products, thereby reducing competitiveness and enhancing opportunities to earn abnormal profits.

product markets Markets in which goods and services are sold.

profitability index Divides PV of future cash flows by the dollar investment. It is an index of present value per dollar invested for an investment project. [Chap. 11]

proxy A form that shareholders sign to allow a designee to vote in their place at the company's annual meeting.

pure play An actively-traded firm whose sole product is similar to an investment project being analyzed. By finding the required return for the pure play, the appropriate return requirement for the investment project can be estimated.

put option The right, but not the obligation, to sell an asset at a specified price within a specified time period.

rational self-interest An economic model of human behavior that as-

sumes people make decisions that are logical and in their own interest.

rationing capital Limits imposed by the company or the capital markets on the amount of money the company may commit to investments in a single period.

real rates Interest rates with no adjustment for inflation, historically between 2% and 4%. A nominal rate lest the inflation rate equals the real rate.

realized returns The actual return received from an asset which may differ from its expected return.

receivables days The number of days, on average, that it takes the company to collect cash for its credit sales.

recovery of net working capital The reduction in net working capital associated with the termination of an investment.

reinvestment rate The rate of return on reinvested cash flows from an investment.

replacement projects Investments that update or upgrade existing capacity; such as replacing worn out or obsolete machinery and equipment.

repurchase agreement Very short term security sold by government securities dealers and banks, in which the seller transfers title to government securities to the buyer, but agrees to repurchase the securities at a specified time. These agreements usually last from a single day to a week.

required rate of return The minimum return investors must expect in order to be interested in investing in an asset.

residual claims Investors hold residual claims if they have a claim on the cash flows left over after all fixed claims are paid. Residual claimants include common stockholders.

restructurings Significant corporate changes of assets and/or ownership.

retained earnings Profits retained within the firm to help fund expansion or repay debt.

revenue recognition Accounting rules that explain when a company may recognize a transaction as a sale. Companies with aggressive accounting strategies recognize revenue as early as possible, while more conservative companies delay until they are certain of the amount to be collected.

revolving credit agreement A lending agreement between a bank and a firm that is more formal than a credit line. It generally obligates the bank to extend credit to a firm for several years.

risk-adjusted discount rate (RADR) A rate of return that has been adjusted to reflect the risk in a new investment project vis-a-vis the risk of the firm's existing projects.

risk aversion A behavioral trait in which people focus more on losses than on equivalent gains. Risk aversion implies that investors must be paid to bear risk.

risk premium The added return necessary to compensate investors for taking added risk.

the risk-return trade-off The requirement that increased risk must be offset by increased expected returns.

seasoned security issue The sale of a security which already is traded so a market price and other information are available to value it.

secondary markets Markets in which investors trade securities between themselves with no direct impact on the funds available to corporations.

sector fund A mutual fund that invests in stocks of particular industry groups.

securities Documents representing claims on the firm's cash flows and assets. Stocks and bonds are both securities.

semi-strong form efficiency A level of informational efficiency in which all publicly available information is quickly and accurately impounded into security prices.

sensitivity analysis An analytic technique that examines variations in assumptions to determine how sensitive results are to uncertainties about the future.

sight draft A demand by a supplier for immediate payment from a customer.

simulation analysis Uses estimates of the probability distributions of primary factors, such as market demand, market share, price, etc. to calculate a probability distribution of project values.

sole proprietorship A business whose owner and manager are one individual.

specialist A trader charged by the stock exchange with maintaining a fair and orderly market in a set of assigned stocks.

spontaneously-generated financing Refers to corporate funding that is automatically provided as part of normal business activity. For example, accounts payable represents a financing source that is spontaneously supplied when the firm orders new inventory.

Standard & Poor's 500 Index (S&P 500) A price index of 500 stocks representing a broad cross section of industries often used to represent the entire stock market's activity.

statement of cash flows An accounting statement that shows cash from operating, investing, and financing activities.

stock Represents an ownership interest in a corporation, entitling its owner to vote in the board of director's election, and grants the holder a residual claim on the firm's cash flows.

strong form efficiency A level of informational efficiency in which all information, public and private, is quickly and accurately impounded into security prices.

sunk costs A cost that has already been incurred. The cost is irretrievable. Sunk costs are not relevant in decision making.

suppliers' credit terms The length of time until payment is due and early payment discounts offered by suppliers. Also called terms of trade.

synergy An extra benefit arising from combining two companies, sometimes stated as two plus two equaling five.

tangible and intangible assets Recorded on the left-hand-side of the financial balance sheet, tangible and intangible assets represent corporate investment projects. Tangibles include land, cash, inventory, factory and equipment investments. Intangible investments include brand name recognition, human resources, and the firm's reputation.

tender offer An acquisition bid made directly to shareholders and not needing the approval of the target company's management.

term loans Loans, with a maturity of 1 to 10 years, made by banks to commercial customers.

thinly-traded Securities that trade infrequently, making them less liquid than frequently traded securities.

time draft A demand by a supplier for payment from a customer at a specified future date.

time preference of money A preference among investors for early rather than late cash flows which leads to the discounting of future cash flows to compute an asset's present value.

trade credit Credit extended by one firm to another in the normal course of buying/selling inventory.

trade discount A discount offered by a supplier to a customer who makes early payment on trade credit.

transaction costs The costs incurred in buying or selling assets. Sometimes, these costs can be sufficiently large to offset an asset's price appreciation.

transferability The ability to sell, or transfer ownership, of an asset. Without transferability it is difficult to realize increases in an asset's value.

trust receipt Pledges specific inventory to the lender, and guarantees that revenues from the sale of the inventory belong to the lender until the loan is repaid.

U.S. treasury bills (t-bills) Short-term debt obligations of the Federal government often used as a measure of risk-free interest rates.

unbiased expectations A theory of interest rate term structures that argues that the yield curve reflects the unbiased expectations, or consensus beliefs, about future interest rates.

underlying asset The asset upon which an option is based.

unique risk Affects primarily one company or industry. Unique risk may be mitigated by diversifying one's portfolio.

unjustified growth Growth motivated more by managerial pride than economic logic.

unseasoned issues Issues of securities that are brand new to the market so no market price information is available for them, making initial pricing more difficult.

value additivity rule Referring to the left hand side of the financial balance sheet, the value of the corporation is the sum of the values of its individual investments.

vertical integration Several steps of the production process being completed by a single company. For example, exploring for, producing, and refining oil.

warehouse receipt Pledges inventories, that are normally stored for long aging periods, to lenders.

weak form efficiency A level of informational efficiency in which all historical price information is quickly and accurately impounded into security prices.

weighted average cost of capital The discount rate that may be found by incorporating the required returns (costs) for each capital source used to finance the firm.

widely-held corporation A corporation with publicly-traded stock held by a large number of geographically-dispersed owners.

Yankee CD Certificate of deposit sold by foreign banks in the U.S.

yield curve A curve relating a government debt instrument's yield to its maturity.

yield-to-maturity The yield of a debt security computed by considering its price and the timing of all cash flows, identical to an IRR (internal rate of return).

INDEX

A

B

D

E

F

J

L

M

N

S

Cartoon Credits

1 Doug Blackwell; **27** Ron Welch; **61** Ron Welch; **103** Ron Welch; **149** Gary Larson; **189** Ron Welch; **211** John Monks; **253** Ron Welch; **279** Ron Welch; **331** Scott Adams' Dogbert; **357** Drawing by Joseph Farris; © 1974 The New Yorker Magazine, Inc.; **395** Ron Welch; **421** Tribune Media Services; **443** Ron Welch; **489** Universal Press Syndicate; **519** Bob Mankoff, The Cartoon Bank; **551** Ron Welch

CHECK ANSWERS TO ODD-NUMBERED PROBLEMS

CHAPTER 3

1. \$30.50
3. Total return = 20%; capital gain = 15.56%; dividend yield = 4.44%
5. 10%
7. No
9. No, less than \$1 million
11. EV = 0, so would not accept
13. EVs are long-run averages.
15. High inflation during the 1978–86 period

CHAPTER 4

1. \$335,000
3. 1995 (revised): \$7,863
5. \$468
7. Unrealistic projections
9. See Instructor's Manual.

	10% Lower	10% Higher
Month 1	674	866
Month 2	880	1,100
Month 3	998	1,262
Month 4	1,116	1,424
Month 5	1,116	1,424
Month 6	1,116	1,424
	20% Lower	20% Higher
Month 1	578	962
Month 2	770	1,210
Month 3	866	1,394
Month 4	962	1,578
Month 5	962	1,578
Month 6	962	1,578

11.

Year	Cash flow
1	−5.0
2	123.3
3	269.5
4	374.0
5	258.0
6	258.0
7	258.0
8	88.6
9	33.0
10	−54.0

Assumes losses in years 1 and 10 can be used against other income.

13.

1995 cash flow from operations:	\$216,381
1995 cash flow from investing:	−149,083
1995 cash flow from financing:	−70,000
Change in cash position:	−2,702

15. Financing gap = 48 days or \$88,110
17. Earns an extra 0.445% of interest income on every sales dollar.
19.

Bangkok	\$100.20
Tokyo	\$205.89
Toronto	\$124.88

21.

	Principal	Interest
Pounds	250,000	24,688
Dollars	379,500	37,476
Francs	2,077,500	205,153
Marks	617,500	60,978

CHAPTER 5

1. a. \$909.09
   b. \$905.21
   c. \$904.84
3. a. \$1,120.00
   b. \$1,126.83
   c. \$1,127.50
5. a. \$4,375.72
   b. \$4,000.00
   c. \$4,578.15
7. a. 9.31%
   b. 9.5%
   c. 9.2%
9. 9.05%
11. 9.5 y
13. 26 y
15. \$17,669.72
17. \$88,385.82
19. \$29,617.83
21. \$5,825.01
23. 22.74%
25. \$44,090.58
27. a. \$353.05/month
    b. Interest paid month 6: \$60.82
29. a. \$9,167.97
    b. \$8,655.16
    c. \$12,207.65
31. No rebate: \$343.71; with rebate \$313.38
33. \$2.06
35. 5.94%
37. \$1,359.02
39. Enter draft: \$11,253,494; stay in school: \$12,250,590

CHAPTER 6

1. \$213.80
3. \$85.71
5. \$21.00
7. \$21.40
9. a. X: \$864.10; Y: \$1,000.00; Z: \$802.07
   b. X: discount; Y: par; Z: discount
   c. X: \$750.76; Y: \$875.38; Z: \$656.82
   d. YTM = 4.73%/y
11. YTM = 10.66%; coupon = 8.5%/year
13. a. D_1 = \$2.16
       D_2 = \$2.33
       D_3 = \$2.52
    b. \$54.00
    c. \$58.25
    d. 12%
15. 10%
17. a. D_1 = \$1.50; D_2 = \$1.80
    b. D_3 = \$1.92
    c. P_2 = \$18.29
    d. D_1 = \$1.28; D_2 = \$1.32; P_2 = \$13.36
    e. P_0 = \$15.96
19. \$93.44
21. YTM = 13%; r = 15%
23. a. \$182.70
    b. \$204.62
    c. 12%
25. a. \$182.70
    b. \$141.33
    c. −22.64%

CHAPTER 7

1. 2.90%
3. a. 7.27%
   b. 5.39%
7. a. 16.11%
   b. 18.00% (CORR = 1); 12.76% (CORR = 0)
9. a. 13.00% (Branford = 0); 19.00% (Branford = 1)
11. a. SD = 80.0%, $E(r)$ = 20% (A = 0); SD = 30.0%, $E(r)$ = 10% (A = 1)
13. a. SD = 18.0%, $E(r)$ = 17% (A = 0); SD = 14.0%, $E(r)$ = 12% (A = 1)
17. 22.16%
19. a. 10.25%
    b. 17.50%
21. a. 12.5%
    b. 12.0%